1 3
17.2.06

Em

Se

University of
Chester

Library

This book is to be returned on or before the last date stamped
below. Overdue charges will be incurred by the late return of
books.

Emmins on Sentencing

Fourth Edition

Martin Wasik, LLB, MA

of Gray's Inn, Barrister
Professor of Criminal Justice, Keele University

OXFORD
UNIVERSITY PRESS

OXFORD
UNIVERSITY PRESS

Great Clarendon Street, Oxford OX2 6DP

Oxford University Press is a department of the University of Oxford.
It furthers the University's objective of excellence in research, scholarship,
and education by publishing worldwide in

Oxford New York

Auckland Bangkok Buenos Aires Cape Town Chennai
Dar es Salaam Delhi Hong Kong Istanbul Karachi Kolkata
Kuala Lumpur Madrid Melbourne Mexico City Mumbai Nairobi
São Paulo Shanghai Taipei Tokyo Toronto

Oxford is a registered trade mark of Oxford University Press
in the UK and in certain other countries

Published in the United States
by Oxford University Press Inc., New York

A Blackstone Press Book

British Library Cataloguing in Publications Data

A record for this book is available from the British Library

Library of Congress Cataloguing in Publications Data

Data applied for

ISBN 1-84174-245-7

5 7 9 10 8 6 4

Typset by Style Photosetting Limited, Mayfield, East Sussex
Printed in Great Britain
on acid-free paper by
Biddles Ltd, King's Lynn

Contents

Preface

Only three years have passed since the last edition of this book, but there have been many changes to the law of sentencing. Much of this has been driven by legislation. In 1998 the project for consolidation of sentencing legislation was just under way. It is now the Powers of Criminal Courts (Sentencing) Act 2000. That Act provided a valuable service by bringing the great bulk of sentencing provisions together in one place. Inevitably, however, given the high political profile of 'law and order' issues, there have since been numerous amendments to that consolidated scheme, brought about by the Criminal Justice and Court Services Act 2000. Some of those changes are not yet in force, but the consolidation Act is already unreliable as a complete guide to the modern law. A summary of the main statutory changes is given at the end of Chapter 1, but one of the most important provisions in the CJCSA is not yet in force. Section 61 will change the age of eligibility for imprisonment from 21 to 18, by abolishing the sentences of detention in a young offender institution and custody for life. It will also, by implication, extend the use of suspended sentences to those aged 18, 19 or 20. At the time of writing no date had been set for implementing this change.

In 1999 the author was appointed as the first chairman of the Sentencing Advisory Panel, set up under the Crime and Disorder Act 1998 to advise and assist the Court of Appeal in framing and revising sentencing guidelines. This work is now bearing fruit, with the Court of Appeal having adopted proposals from the Panel in three areas so far — importation of opium, racially aggravated offences, and handling stolen goods.

The volume of appellate sentencing cases continues unabated. Among the most important recent decisions discussed in this edition are *Offen and Others* [2001] 1 WLR 253 (on automatic life sentences — not to be confused with the first appeal in *Offen* [2000] 1 Cr App R (S) 565), *Saunders* [2000] 2 Cr App R (S) 71 and *Kelly* [2001] Crim LR 411 (guidelines on racially aggravated offences), *Perks* [2001] 1 Cr App R (S) 66 (on victim impact evidence) and *Morris* [2001] 1 Cr App R (S) 297 (on analysis of drug purity).

In line with the approach originally taken by Christopher Emmins, I have tried to describe and explain the law on sentencing as fully and clearly as possible. As always, I am grateful to the publishers for their efficiency, encouragement and, above all their patience.

Preface to the First Edition

The sentencing of offenders is a subject which may be considered from many different points of view. There is the high philosophical approach, which seeks to explain and provide a moral justification for the infliction of punishment by society upon offenders. There is the criminological and sociological approach, which describes what the various forms of sentence entail as far as the person undergoing the sentence is concerned, and may also suggest what sentences are the most effective in deterring and/or reforming criminals. There is the approach which concentrates upon the decisions of the Court of Appeal, seeking to extract from those decisions an approved sentencing pattern for common types of crime. All these approaches are, of course, of great value, and the third especially is of considerable relevance to this book. However, my aim in writing is not encapsulated within any of the aforementioned approaches to sentencing. My aim is to describe, from a practical point of view, how offenders are sentenced in the Crown Court, magistrates' courts and juvenile courts; what procedures are gone through after conviction and before sentence is pronounced; what possible avenues of appeal are open to an offender who considers himself harshly treated; what powers of sentence are available to the courts and how they are likely, in practice, to exercise those powers. As Parliament has placed an ever more varied and complicated array of sentencing powers at the disposal of sentencers, so the need for a straightforward exposition of those powers has increased. It is my hope that this book will provide such an exposition, and will be of interest and value to students, to practitioners (especially the young ones who have not yet had time to learn by experience anything that these pages may be able to teach) and even, perhaps, to some sentencers.

Now is a particularly apt time to bring out a work on sentencing. Parliament has been especially active in the field in recent years, completely re-shaping the structure of sentences for young offenders; introducing a new form of sentence (part-suspended imprisonment) for offenders over 21, and making a host of other less important, but still significant, changes. In addition, the Court of Appeal has sought to influence sentencing at first instance more directly and forcefully than had hitherto been its practice. It has, for example, recommended a general reduction in the lengths of prison sentences for certain categories of crime, while for other offences (e.g. causing death by reckless driving and importing drugs) it has established sentencing brackets within which the penalty should normally fall. These developments are fully explained in the text. It was, in fact, written in the summer of 1984, and seeks to state the law as it then was, although I have been able to incorporate developments occurring up until late autumn.

My thanks are due, and gladly given, to a large number of people who have helped in the writing of what follows. Especially, I would like to thank those involved in various ways with sentencing who have answered my many questions on sentencing matters, and given much valuable background information. Particular mention must be made of the magistrates' court clerks, studying for their Bar Finals at the Inns of Court School of Law, who spared time from their revision to talk with me about sentencing practice in the courts where they work. My thanks as well to my publishers for their hard work and friendliness, and to all others involved in the production of the book. Finally, my thanks to my father for bearing patiently with the incessant clatter of typewriter keys, for making innumerable cups of tea, and for enabling me to concentrate all my energies upon writing.

Table of Cases

Table of Statutes

Table of Statutory Instruments

Table of Home Office Circulars

List of Abbreviations

A-G's Ref	Attorney-General's Reference
BA	Bail Act
CA	Courts Act
CAA	Criminal Appeal Act
CDA	Crime and Disorder Act
CJA	Criminal Justice Act
CJCSA	Criminal Justice and Court Services Act
CJPOA	Criminal Justice and Public Order Act
CLA	Criminal Law Act
CPIA	Criminal Procedure and Investigations Act
CPO	Community Punishment Order
CPRO	Community Punishment and Rehabilitation Order
CPS	Crown Prosecution Service
CRO	Community Rehabilitation Order
C(S)A	Crime (Sentences) Act
CSP	*Current Sentencing Practice*
CYPA	Children and Young Persons Act
DPP	Director of Public Prosecutions
DSS	Department of Social Security
DTA	Drug Trafficking Act
DVLA	Driver and Vehicle Licensing Authority
DTTO	Drug Treatment and Testing Order
ECHR	European Convention on Human Rights
FSA	Football Spectators Act
HMSO	Her Majesty's Stationery Office
IA	Immigration Act
MCA	Magistrates' Courts Act
MDA	Misuse of Drugs Act
MHA	Mental Health Act
MHRT	mental health review tribunal
OAPA	Offences against the Person Act
PACE	Police and Criminal Evidence Act
PCA	Proceeds of Crime Act
PCC(S)A	Powers of Criminal Courts (Sentencing) Act
POA	Prosecution of Offences Act
PSD	petty sessional division
RMO	responsible medical officer

ROA	Rehabilitation of Offenders Act
RTA	Road Traffic Act
RTOA	Road Traffic Offenders Act
SCA	Supreme Court Act
SOA	Sexual Offences Act
SO(A)A	Sexual Offences (Amendment) Act

1   Introduction

Any attempt to describe the current body of sentencing law and sentencing principles must begin by acknowledging that the bulk and complexity of this topic have increased dramatically in recent years. The most important statutory developments in this area began with the passing of the Criminal Justice Act 1991, which for the first time provided a general framework for sentence decision-making. The basic principle of that legislation was that the severity of the sentence imposed should reflect primarily the seriousness of the offence committed. The 1991 Act has been much amended since, but the key principle remains, albeit with a number of important exceptions. Last year, in response to many complaints that sentencing law was complex and unwieldy, Parliament passed the Powers of Criminal Courts (Sentencing) Act 2000. This has not changed the law, but is an important consolidating measure. It brings together the 1991 Act provisions with other sentencing legislation, so that the great bulk of sentencing law can now be found in one place — the PCC(S)A 2000. Most statutory references in the rest of this book will, inevitably, be to the PCC(S)A 2000, although occasionally it will be necessary to refer to principles founded in 'the 1991 Act'. The aims of this chapter are as follows:

(a)   To outline the current sentencing arrangements in England and Wales, describing those courts which, and those individuals who, are given the power to pass sentence upon persons convicted of criminal offences.

(b)   To consider the range of aims which are traditionally associated with sentencing. A detailed discussion of sentencing philosophy lies outside the scope of this book, but without some explanation of that important debate modern developments in sentencing law and practice cannot fully be understood.

(c)   To consider the existing legal framework for sentencing. This is an amalgam of statutory provision, appellate decisions and administrative and practical arrangements. The CJA 1991 represented a watershed in this context, and all the sentencing law and sentencing principles set out in this book must be seen against that background.

A reader wishing to gain an overview of the sentencing system should begin here. Someone already familiar with that system, or someone investigating a specific sentencing issue such as the powers available to the courts to pass a community punishment order, may prefer to start at the relevant section of the book. But, in the end, it is suggested, the detailed information can only be fully understood in the context of the material in this chapter.

Sentencing is closely connected with matters of criminal procedure. A general discussion of criminal procedure lies outside the scope of this book, although an outline of procedure as it directly affects sentencing is given in the following paragraphs. Readers seeking more detailed coverage are referred to *Emmins on Criminal Procedure* 8th ed, 2000, by John Sprack.

1.1   AN OUTLINE OF PROCEDURE RELEVANT TO SENTENCING

Sentencing is about the way courts deal with a person *after* he or she has pleaded guilty or has been found guilty — in other words, it is about what happens from the moment when a person charged with an offence ceases to be merely 'the accused' and becomes 'the offender'.

1.1.1   Two methods of trial

Criminal trials in England and Wales take one of two forms — they are either summary trials or trials on indictment.

Summary trial takes place in a magistrates' court. Most judges in this court are lay (i.e. unpaid) magistrates. Magistrates are also known as justices of the peace (JPs). They are not lawyers, but are people drawn from the local community. They receive training in various aspects of their work, including sentencing. A much smaller number of judges in the magistrates' courts are professional lawyers, paid a salary to work full time in the courts. Formerly known as stipendiary magistrates, following the Access to Justice Act 1999 they are now referred to as district judges or, more precisely, district judges (magistrates' courts), to distinguish them from district judges sitting in the county courts. Lay magistrates cannot sit alone. In fact a lay bench normally comprises three magistrates, although two is sufficient. District judges generally sit alone, although in the youth court they often sit with lay colleagues. Magistrates and district judges are assisted in their work in court by a court clerk. Clerks are qualified either as barristers or solicitors, or are in the latter stages of their training, or hold a diploma in magisterial law. The clerk advises the magistrates or district judge on the law when it is appropriate to do so, but does not otherwise interfere in their decisions.

A summary trial commences with the charge or *information* being put to the accused by the clerk. For this reason summary trial is also known as 'trial on information'. Where it is alleged that two or more persons acted together to commit an offence they may be jointly charged in one information, and will normally be tried together. This applies whether they were joint principal offenders or aiders and abettors or a combination thereof. An information must allege only one offence, but two or more informations may be tried together if *either* the accused (or all the accused where there is more than one) consent *or* the magistrates or district judge think that the informations are linked together so that the interests of justice are best served by a single trial. If the accused pleads guilty to the information, there is no need for evidence about the offence to be called, and the magistrates or district judge commence the procedures leading up to sentence being pronounced. If the accused pleads not guilty, the prosecution makes a short opening speech; the prosecution witnesses are called, each witness being first questioned 'in chief' by the prosecution legal representative and then cross-examined by the defence; the defence may, if they so wish, submit that there is no prima facie case against the accused, and if the magistrates or district judge agree they acquit forthwith; if no such submission is made or if one is made unsuccessfully, the defence may (but need not) call witnesses who may (but need not) include the accused; after the defence evidence (if any) the defence legal representative makes a closing speech and then the magistrates or district judge announce their verdict.

Trial on indictment takes place in the Crown Court. In legal theory the Crown Court is a single court, but in fact it sits in over 90 different locations scattered throughout the country, the status of the locations depending on whether High Court judges sit there and whether there are facilities for civil as well as criminal work. The trial on indictment is nearly always preceded by *committal proceedings* which take place in a magistrates' court. The magistrates (who for these purposes are referred to as 'examining justices') receive the evidence the prosecution wish to put forward against the accused, and decide whether it discloses a prima facie case against that person in respect of any indictable offence, not necessarily the charge which was originally brought (see **1.2.3** for the meaning of 'indictable offence'). If there is no case to answer, the examining justices discharge the accused; if there is a case, they commit (i.e. send) the accused to the Crown Court to be tried. The committal may be in custody or on bail, at the examining justices' discretion. Committal proceedings for offences which are triable only on indictment (see **1.2.3** below) were abolished from January 1999, the accused being sent straight to Crown Court for trial.

Once the accused has been committed for trial an *indictment* is drawn up. This is done by a representative of the Crown Prosecution Service (CPS). An indictment contains one or more *counts*, each count charging the accused with a single indictable offence. The person drafting the indictment reads through the committal statements and includes counts for those offences which are disclosed by the evidence in the statements. The indictment is not restricted to counts for offences with which the accused was charged at the police station or in respect of which the examining justices found there was a case to answer. In general, an indictment should contain sufficient counts to represent fairly the criminal conduct alleged against the accused — it is not good practice, in a case where one piece of criminal conduct could be said to amount in law to several offences of roughly equivalent gravity, to include counts for all the offences. Ultimately, though, it is for the person drafting the indictment to decide whether an extra count would genuinely add something to the prosecution case or would merely overload the indictment.

A single count may allege that two or more persons committed an offence jointly, and there is no need to distinguish between principal offenders and aiders or abettors. Two or more counts against one accused may be put into one indictment provided the relevant offences are either founded on the same facts or comprise or form part of a series of offences of the same or a similar character. 'Founded on the same facts' covers cases where several offences are committed in a continuous piece of conduct (for example, if the accused opened a locked car door by use of a piece of wire, drove the car off without the owner's consent and, when spotted by a police car, drove at 60 mph on the wrong side of the road, one indictment could include counts for going equipped for theft, taking a motor vehicle without lawful authority and dangerous driving). In the example given the prosecution would seek convictions on all three counts, but two or more counts are also appropriate in cases where the prosecution are not sure which of several offences the accused is guilty of and merely seek a conviction on one count. Thus, if the prosecution case is that the accused pushed a glass into the victim's face causing a cut to the cheek which required 10 stitches, the evidence prima facie might justify a conviction either for the more serious offence of wounding with intent to cause grievous bodily harm contrary to s. 18 of the Offences against the Person Act 1861 or for the less serious offence of unlawful wounding contrary to s. 20 of the 1861 Act. The indictment may include counts for both offences so that the jury can decide on which, if either, count to convict. Counts for assault occasioning actual bodily harm and common assault would not be justified because they would add nothing to the count for unlawful wounding, even though the prosecution evidence suggests that the accused is guilty of both offences (see the preceding paragraph on not overloading the indictment).

The second limb of the rule, that counts may be included in one indictment if the offences are/form part of a series of offences of the same or a similar character, has been generously interpreted by the courts. To be similar within the meaning of the rule, offences must be similar both legally and factually. Yet counts may be legally similar even though they allege contravention of different statutory provisions (see *Ludlow* v *Metropolitan Police Commissioner* [1971] AC 29 where the House of Lords approved joinder of counts for robbery and attempted theft on the basis that both offences involved the element of theft). As to factual similarity, *Ludlow* shows that even a tenuous link in the time, place, mode of commission etc. of the offences will satisfy the rule. Finally, it should be noted that even when the joinder of counts and/or defendants in a single indictment is legally justified the trial judge has a discretion to sever the indictment and order separate trials if a single trial would prejudice or embarrass the defence.

A trial on indictment begins with the clerk of the court putting the counts in the indictment to the accused. If the plea is guilty to all counts, the court embarks upon the procedures leading up to the pronouncement of sentence. By pleading guilty the accused does not necessarily concede that the allegations against him are entirely correct. A count merely sets out the bare essentials of the prosecution case, giving the name of the offence (e.g. 'Theft contrary to s. 1(1) of the Theft Act 1968') and particulars of the offence (e.g. 'John Brown, on the 24th day of December 2000, stole a turkey belonging to Spencer and Marks Ltd'). The count says nothing about the *way* the offence was committed. Thus, if the committal statements indicate that John Brown stole the turkey by a sophisticated method suggesting that he is a 'professional' shoplifter, it is nevertheless open to the defence to argue that he stole on the spur of the moment, in a blatant and amateurish way. The issue would probably be relevant to the sentence he might receive.

If the accused pleads not guilty to all the counts in the indictment a jury is sworn in to try the case. A jury consists of 12 men and women, drawn largely at random from a wide (but not complete) cross-section of the adult population aged between 18 and 70. Generally jurors are summoned to attend at the Crown Court for a fortnight's jury service, and that may well be their only experience of the criminal courts. Their function is to bring in, at the end of the case, verdicts of guilty, not guilty or (sometimes) guilty of a lesser offence. They bring in a separate verdict in respect of each count in the indictment and each accused charged in a count. Of course, it is open to them to acquit on one count and convict on another, or they may acquit one accused and convict the other. Where the indictment charges an accused with offences of differing degrees of gravity arising out of one incident, the fact that the jury convict only on the less serious alternative has a considerable bearing on the appropriate sentence. The course of the trial is controlled by a professional Crown Court judge. The judge decides all questions of law and procedure which may arise (e.g. whether evidence is admissible and whether the indictment should be amended). The sequence of events is essentially the same as at a summary trial, save that the prosecution have a closing as well as an opening speech and the defence also sometimes have two speeches. After closing speeches and before the jury retire to consider their verdict, the judge sums up the case to the jury, telling them what the relevant law is and reminding them of the evidence they have heard. It will be apparent that a judge can have a considerable influence on the outcome of a case, but the fact remains that only the jury — not the judge — can find an accused guilty. It follows that if the jury convict an accused of only one offence out of several on the indictment the judge must sentence on the basis that the offence of which the accused has been convicted is the only offence the offender has committed, even if the judge thinks that the jury's verdict was perverse and the offender quite obviously committed all the offences alleged against him. As implied above, sentences in the Crown Court are determined by a Crown Court judge. The jury's active role finishes the moment they have pronounced their verdict.

If the accused pleads guilty to some, but not all, of the counts on the indictment the prosecution have a choice. They can either agree not to proceed on the counts denied by the accused, arguing that the accused can properly and fairly be sentenced on the basis of the admitted offences, or they can insist that a jury be sworn in to try the not guilty pleas, in which case the guilty pleas still stand and the accused may be sentenced for those matters whatever the outcome of the jury trial. If the accused is considering pleading guilty to part of the indictment, defence counsel usually mentions the possibility to prosecuting counsel, who will indicate whether the proposed pleas are acceptable to the prosecution or not. If they are not, the accused might well decide to plead not guilty to the whole indictment. If they are, it is the general practice to ask the judge in private whether the proposed course is a suitable way of dealing with the case. Should the judge disapprove of the proposal the prosecution would almost certainly proceed on the whole indictment.

A final option sometimes open to the accused on trial in the Crown Court is to plead not guilty to the offence alleged in a count but guilty of some other (lesser) indictable offence which is expressly or impliedly included in the wording of the count (see Criminal Law Act 1967, s. 6, as explained in *MPC* v *Wilson* [1984] AC 242). It is clear, for example, that an accused may plead not guilty of murder but guilty of manslaughter; not guilty of robbery but guilty of theft; not guilty of rape but guilty of indecent assault, or not guilty of burglary by entering as a trespasser and stealing but guilty of theft. If the accused does tender such a plea the prosecution may reject it and insist that the accused be tried for the offence alleged in the count — the plea of guilty to a lesser offence is then impliedly withdrawn and a not guilty plea entered on behalf of the accused. Even if the prosecution are willing to accept a plea to a lesser offence the judge may refuse to allow it if it is considered that the evidence in the committal statements shows the accused to be guilty as charged. In all cases where the accused offered or could have offered a plea to a lesser offence the jury, on a not guilty plea, may find the accused not guilty as charged but guilty of the lesser offence (e.g. not guilty of murder, but guilty of manslaughter etc.).

Three simple points relevant to sentencing emerge from the above brief description of trial procedures. First, an offender is often sentenced on one occasion for several offences. This follows from the fact that the rules governing joinder of counts in one indictment and joint trial of several informations in the magistrates' courts frequently result in a single jury or a single bench of magistrates convicting an accused of a number of offences. Second, if the accused pleads not guilty, the sentencer (the Crown Court judge presiding over a trial on indictment or the bench of magistrates or district judge trying a case summarily) will hear evidence about the facts of the offence during the trial of the not guilty plea, whereas, if the accused pleads guilty, very limited information will be available at this stage about the offence. Third, the court has no control over the charges laid against the accused since it is the prosecution who are responsible for the laying of informations and the drafting of indictments. The judge's role in this context is essentially negative. The judge can prevent the prosecution dropping their case on the indictment as originally drafted in exchange for a plea of guilty to a lesser offence or a plea of guilty to some but not all the counts, but the judge cannot force the prosecution to put extra or more serious counts into the indictment even if as drafted it seems to under-represent the extent of the accused's criminal conduct.

1.2 AN OVERVIEW OF SENTENCING

1.2.1 What is a sentence?

There is no statutory or case law definition of 'sentence' which is of general application. It is not, for example, a term defined in the Interpretation Act 1978. Certainly it must include the punishment, such as a fine or a custodial sentence, which the court imposes upon an offender for the offence. It should also include orders imposed upon the offender on conviction which cannot properly be described as punishments: a hospital order is a good example. Most lawyers would say that it should also include other orders which the court may make at the same time as imposing the punishment. These 'ancillary orders' are made against the offender to benefit individuals who have suffered loss or have been put to expense by reason of the offence. Examples are compensation orders and orders to pay costs. In this book the term 'sentence' is to be understood in the broad sense indicated here. Such a meaning is consistent with s. 50 of the Criminal Appeal Act 1968 (CAA 1968). Section 50 provides that, for the purposes of the CAA 1968 (which deals *inter alia* with the right to appeal to the Court of Appeal against sentence) 'sentence . . . includes any order made by a court when dealing with an offender including a hospital order . . . and a recommendation for deportation'. Thus s. 50 defines sentence to include punishments, orders in lieu of punishment and ancillary orders.

Wide though this definition is, there are a number of orders which a court may make against an offender which do not come within it. First, when a murderer is sentenced to life imprisonment, the judge may recommend that he serve a minimum term in prison before being considered for early release. It has been held that such a recommendation is not a sentence for the purposes of an appeal against sentence because it is not binding on the Parole Board, and so is not an order of the court (*Aitken* [1966] 1 WLR 1076). This stands in contrast with the power which a sentencer has to recommend the minimum period to be served by a discretionary life sentence prisoner, under C(S)A 1997, s. 28, which can be the subject of an appeal. Second, when a court orders that a legally aided offender pays a contribution to the costs incurred by the legal aid fund in providing him with representation, that is not part of the sentence because even an acquitted defendant may be ordered to make such a contribution (see *Raeburn* (1982) 74 Cr App R 21).

TABLE 1 MAXIMUM TERMS OF IMPRISONMENT

The primary purpose of this table is to indicate the maximum terms of imprisonment available for the most commonly encountered imprisonable offences. In addition the table shows whether the offences listed in it are triable only on indictment, triable either way, or triable only summarily. If there is an entry in column 3 but not in column 4 the offence is triable only on indictment; if there are entries in both columns 3 and 4 the offence is triable either way, and if there is an entry only in column 4 the offence is triable only summarily. Only a few summary offences appear in the table because the great majority of summary offences are non-imprisonable.

Offence	Statutory provision creating the offence[1]	Maximum prison term on indictment	Maximum prison term on summary conviction	Statutory provisions fixing maximum prison term[2]
HOMICIDE				
1. Manslaughter[3]	Common law	Life	—	OAPA 1861, s. 5
2. Infanticide	Infanticide Act 1938, s. 1	Life	—	Infanticide Act 1938, s. 1
3. Child destruction	Infant Life (Preservation) Act 1929, s. 1(1)	Life	—	Infant Life (Preservation) Act, s. 1(1)
4. Causing death by dangerous driving	Road Traffic Act 1988, s. 1	10 years	—	RTOA 1988, sch. 2
5. Causing death by careless driving while under the influence of drink or drugs	Road Traffic Act 1988, s. 3A	10 years	—	RTOA 1988, sch. 2
OFFENCES OF VIOLENCE				
6. Causing grievous bodily harm/wounding with intent	OAPA 1861, s. 18	Life	—	OAPA 1861, s. 18
7. Administering poison with intent to endanger life	OAPA 1861, s. 23	10 years	—	OAPA 1861, s. 23
8. Administering poison with intent to injure	OAPA 1861, s. 24	5 years	—	OAPA 1861, s. 24
9. Unlawful wounding[4]	OAPA 1861, s. 20	5 years	6 months	OAPA 1861, s. 20 and MCA 1980, s. 17
10. Assault occasioning actual bodily[5] harm	OAPA 1861, s. 47	5 years	6 months	OAPA 1861, s. 47 and MCA 1980, s. 17
11. Assault with intent to resist arrest	OAPA 1861, s. 38	2 years	6 months	OAPA 1861, s. 38 and MCA 1980, s. 17

Offence	Statutory provision creating the offence[1]	Maximum prison term on indictment	Maximum prison term on summary conviction	Statutory provisions fixing maximum prison term[2]
12. Common assault and battery[6]	CJA 1988, s. 39	—	6 months	CJA 1988, s. 39
13. Assault on P.C. in execution of his duty	Police Act 1996, s. 89	—	6 months	Police Act 1996, s. 89
SEXUAL OFFENCES				
14. Rape	SOA 1956, s. 1	Life	—	SOA 1956, s. 37 and sch. 2
15. Sexual intercourse with a girl under 13	SOA 1956, s. 5	Life	—	SOA 1956, s. 37 and sch. 2
16. Sexual intercourse with a girl under 16	SOA 1956, s. 6	2 years	6 months	SOA 1956, s. 37 and sch. 2
17. Incest	SOA 1956, ss. 10 and 11	7 years[7]	—	SOA 1956, s. 37 and sch. 2
18. Indecent assault on a woman	SOA 1956, s. 14	10 years	6 months	SOA 1956, s. 37 and sch. 2 and MCA 1980, s. 17
19. Buggery with an animal	SOA 1956, s. 12	Life	—	SOA 1956, s. 37 and sch. 2; SO(A)A 2000
20. Buggery by a person aged 21 or over of a person aged under 16	SOA 1956, s. 12	5 years	—	SOA 1967, s. 3; SO(A)A 2000
21. Buggery[8]	SOA 1956, s. 12	2 years	—	SOA 1967, s. 3; SO(A)A 2000
22. Gross indecency between men[8]	SOA 1956, s. 13	2 years[9]	6 months	SOA 1956, s. 37 and sch. 2 and MCA 1980, s. 17
23. Indecent assault on a man	SOA 1956, s. 15	10 years	6 months	SOA 1956, s. 37 and sch. 2
24. Indecency with a child under 16	Indecency with Children Act 1960, s. 1	10 years	6 months	Indecency with Children Act 1960, s. 1; Crime (Sentences) Act 1997, s. 52
25. Taking, distributing, publishing etc. indecent photographs of children	Protection of Children Act 1978, s. 1	10 years	6 months	Protection of Children Act 1978, s. 6; CJCSA 2000, s. 41
25A. Possessing indecent photograph of a child	CJA 1988, s. 160	5 years	6 months	CJA 1988, s. 160; CJCSA 2000, s. 41
26. Living on earnings of prostitution	SOA 1956, s. 30	7 years	6 months	SOA 1956, s. 37 and sch. 2
OFFENCES OF DISHONESTY				
27. Robbery	Theft Act 1968, s. 8(1)	Life	—	Theft Act 1968, s. 8(2)

No.	Offence	Statute	Maximum on indictment	Summary	Statute
28.	Assault with intent to rob	Theft Act 1968, s. 8(2)	Life	—	Theft Act 1968, s. 8(2)
29.	Blackmail	Theft Act 1968, s. 21(1)	14 years	—	Theft Act 1968, s. 21(3)
30.	Aggravated burglary	Theft Act 1968, s. 10(1)	Life	—	Theft Act 1968, s. 10(2)
31.	Burglary of a dwelling[10]	Theft Act 1968, s. 9(1)	14 years	6 months	Theft Act 1968, s. 9(3) and MCA 1980, s. 17
32.	Burglary of a building other than a dwelling	Theft Act 1968, s. 9(1)	10 years	6 months	Theft Act 1968, s. 9(3) and MCA 1980, s. 17
33.	Handling stolen goods	Theft Act 1968, s. 22(1)	14 years	6 months	Theft Act 1968, s. 22(2) and MCA 1980, s. 17
34.	Theft	Theft Act 1968, s. 1	7 years	6 months	Theft Act 1968, s. 7 and MCA 1980, s. 17
35.	Obtaining property by deception	Theft Act 1968, s. 15(1)	10 years	6 months	Theft Act 1968, s. 15(1) and MCA 1980, s. 17
36.	Obtaining services by deception	Theft Act 1978, s. 1	5 years	6 months	Theft Act 1978, s. 4
37.	Evasion of liability by deception	Theft Act 1978, s. 2	5 years	6 months	Theft Act 1978, s. 4
38.	Making off without payment	Theft Act 1978, s. 3	2 years	6 months	Theft Act 1978, s. 4
39.	Forgery and using a forged instrument	Forgery and Counterfeiting Act 1981, ss. 1 and 3	10 years	6 months	Forgery and Counterfeiting Act 1981, s. 6
40.	Possession of certain specified forged instruments[11]	Forgery and Counterfeiting Act 1981, s. 5(2)	2 years	6 months	Forgery and Counterfeiting Act 1981, s. 6
41.	Counterfeiting currency notes or protected coins and passing or tendering such notes or coin[12]	Forgery and Counterfeiting Act 1981, ss. 14(1) and 15(1)	10 years	6 months	Forgery and Counterfeiting Act 1981, s. 22
42.	Taking a motor vehicle without the owner's consent	Theft Act 1968, s. 12(1)	—	6 months	Theft Act 1968, s. 12(2)
43.	Aggravated vehicle taking[13]	Theft Act 1968, s. 12A	2 years (but 5 years if death results)	6 months	Theft Act 1968, s. 12A

Offence	Statutory provision creating the offence[1]	Maximum prison term on indictment	Maximum prison term on summary conviction	Statutory provisions fixing maximum prison term[2]
44. Interfering with a motor vehicle	Criminal Attempts Act 1981, s. 9(1)	—	3 months	Criminal Attempts Act 1981, s. 9(3)
45. Going equipped for burglary, theft or cheat	Theft Act 1968, s. 25(1)	3 years	6 months	Theft Act 1968, s. 25(2) and MCA 1980, s. 17

OFFENCES OF DAMAGE TO PROPERTY

Offence	Statutory provision creating the offence[1]	Maximum prison term on indictment	Maximum prison term on summary conviction	Statutory provisions fixing maximum prison term[2]
46. Destroying/damaging property where damage is more than £5,000[14]	Criminal Damage Act 1971, s. 1(1)	10 years	6 months	Criminal Damage Act 1971, s. 4(2) and MCA 1980, s. 17
47. Destroying/damaging property where damage is not more than £5,000[15]	Criminal Damage Act 1971, s. 1(1)	—	3 months	Criminal Damage Act 1971, s. 4(2) and MCA 1980, s. 22 and sch. 2
48. Arson[16]	Criminal Damage Act 1971, s. 1(3)	Life	6 months	Criminal Damage Act 1971, s. 4(1) and MCA 1980, s. 17
49. Destroying/damaging property with intent etc. to endanger life	Criminal Damage Act 1971, s. 1(2)	Life	—	Criminal Damage Act 1971, s. 4(2)

OFFENCES AGAINST PUBLIC ORDER

Offence	Statutory provision creating the offence[1]	Maximum prison term on indictment	Maximum prison term on summary conviction	Statutory provisions fixing maximum prison term[2]
50. Riot	Public Order Act 1986, s. 1	10 years	—	Public Order Act 1986, s. 1(6)
51. Violent disorder	Public Order Act 1986, s. 2	5 years	6 months	Public Order Act 1986, s. 2(5)
52. Affray	Public Order Act 1986, s. 3	3 years	6 months	Public Order Act 1986, s. 3(7)
53. Fear or provocation of violence[17]	Public Order Act 1986, s. 4	—	6 months	Public Order Act 1986, s. 4(4)
54. Intentionally causing harassment, alarm or distress[18]	Public Order Act 1986, s. 4A	—	6 months	Public Order Act 1986, s. 4A
55. Harassment, putting person in fear of violence (stalking)[19]	Protection from Harassment Act 1997, s. 4	5 years	6 months	Protection from Harassment Act 1997, s. 4

No.	Offence	Statute	Indictment	Summary	Statute
56.	Harassment (stalking)[20]	Protection from Harassment Act 1997, s. 2	—	6 months	Protection from Harassment Act 1997, s. 2
57.	Bomb hoax	Criminal Law Act 1977, s. 51(1)	7 years	6 months	Criminal Law Act 1977, s. 51(4)
58.	Contamination of goods	Public Order Act 1986, s. 38(1)	10 years	6 months	Public Order Act 1986, s. 38(4)
59.	Stirring up racial hatred	Public Order Act 1986, s. 18	2 years	6 months	Public Order Act 1986, s. 27(3)

OFFENCES AGAINST ADMINISTRATION OF JUSTICE

No.	Offence	Statute	Indictment	Summary	Statute
60.	Perverting the course of justice	Common law	Life	—	Common law
61.	Intimidation of witness, juror etc.	Criminal Justice and Public Order Act 1994, s. 51	5 years	6 months	Criminal Justice and Public Order Act 1994, s. 51
62.	Perjury	Perjury Act 1911, s. 1(1)	7 years	—	Perjury Act 1911, s. 1(1)
63.	Wasting police time	Criminal Law Act 1967, s. 5(2)	—	6 months	Criminal Law Act 1967, s. 5(2)
64.	Escape from legal custody	Common law	Life	—	Common law
65.	Assisting offenders[21]	Criminal Law Act 1967, s. 4(1)	3–10 years depending on the offence committed by the offender assisted	6 months	Criminal Law Act 1967, s. 4(3) and MCA 1980, s. 17

DRUGS OFFENCES

No.	Offence	Statute	Indictment	Summary	Statute
66.	Possessing a controlled drug in:	MDA 1971, s. 5(2)			
	Class A		7 years	6 months	MDA 1971, sch. 4
	Class B		5 years	3 months	
	Class C		2 years	3 months	
67.	Supplying/offering to supply a controlled drug and being in possession with intent to supply:	MDA 1971, ss. 4(3) and 5(3)			
	Class A		Life	6 months	MDA 1971, sch. 4
	Class B		14 years	6 months	
	Class C		5 years	3 months	

DRIVING OFFENCES

	Offence	Statutory provision creating the offence[1]	Maximum prison term on indictment	Maximum prison term on summary conviction	Statutory provisions fixing maximum prison term[2]
68.	Dangerous driving	Road Traffic Act 1988, s. 2	2 years	6 months	RTOA 1988, sch. 2
69.	Driving while disqualified	Road Traffic Act 1988, s. 103	—	6 months	RTOA 1988, sch. 2
70.	Driving while unfit through drink or drugs	Road Traffic Act 1988, s. 4(1)	—	6 months	RTOA 1988, sch. 2
71.	Being in charge of a motor vehicle when unfit through drink or drugs	Road Traffic Act 1988, s. 4(2)	—	3 months	RTOA 1988, sch. 2
72.	Driving with excess alcohol in breath, blood or urine	Road Traffic Act 1988, s. 5(1)(a)	—	6 months	RTOA 1988, sch. 2
73.	Being in charge of a motor vehicle with excess alcohol in breath, blood or urine	Road Traffic Act 1988, s. 5(1)(b)	—	3 months	RTOA 1988, sch. 2
74.	Failing to provide specimen for analysis	Road Traffic Act 1988, s. 7	—	6 months[22]	RTOA 1988, sch. 2

OFFENCES CONCERNING WEAPONS

	Offence	Statutory provision creating the offence[1]	Maximum prison term on indictment	Maximum prison term on summary conviction	Statutory provisions fixing maximum prison term[2]
75.	Possession of firearm with intent to endanger life	Firearms Act 1968, s. 16	Life	—	Firearms Act 1968, sch. 6
76.	Use of firearm to resist arrest	Firearms Act 1968, s. 17(1)	Life	—	Firearms Act 1968, sch. 6
77.	Carrying firearm with intent to commit indictable offence	Firearms Act 1968, s. 18(1)	Life	—	Firearms Act 1968, sch. 6
78.	Carrying loaded firearm in a public place	Firearms Act 1968, s. 19	7 years	6 months	Firearms Act 1968, sch. 6
79.	Shortening a shotgun	Firearms Act 1968, s. 4(1)	7 years	6 months	Firearms Act 1968, sch. 6
80.	Possessing a firearm without holding a firearm certificate	Firearms Act 1968, s. 1(1)	5 years[23]	6 months	Firearms Act 1968, sch. 6
81.	Having an offensive weapon in a public place	Prevention of Crime Act 1953, s. 1	4 years	6 months	Prevention of Crime Act 1953, s. 1
82.	Having article with blade or point in public place	CJA 1988, s. 139	2 years	6 months	CJA 1988, s. 139

MISCELLANEOUS

83. Bigamy	OAPA 1861, s. 57	7 years	6 months	OAPA 1861, s. 57 and MCA 1980, s. 17
84. Communicating etc. information useful to an enemy	Official Secrets Act 1911, s. 1	14 years	—	Official Secrets Act 1911, s. 8(1)
85. Disclosure of security information entrusted in confidence	Official Secrets Act 1989, s. 1	2 years	6 months	Official Secrets Act 1989, s. 10(1)
86. Prison mutiny	Prison Security Act 1992, s. 1	10 years	—	Prison Security Act 1992, s. 1
87. Obstructing a police officer in the execution of his duty	Police Act 1996, s. 89	—	1 month	Police Act 1996, s. 89
88. Attempt to commit an indictable offence	Criminal Attempts Act 1981, s. 1	The maximum is the maximum which can be imposed for the offence attempted[24]	The maximum is the maximum which can be imposed upon summary conviction for the offence attempted	Criminal Attempts Act 1981, s. 4(1)
89. Conspiracy to commit an offence	Criminal Law Act 1977, s. 1	The maximum is the maximum which may be imposed for the offence to which the conspiracy related	—	CLA 1977, s. 3
90. Conspiracy to defraud	Common law	10 years	—	CJA 1987, s. 12
91. Aiding and abetting an offence	Common law	The maximum is the maximum which may be imposed upon the principal offender	The maximum is the maximum which may be imposed upon the principal offender upon summary conviction	Accessories and Abettors Act 1861, s. 8; MCA 1980, s. 44(1)

Where a statute creates an indictable offence and states that it is punishable with imprisonment but does not specify a maximum term, an offender may be sentenced to up to 2 years' imprisonment following conviction on indictment (PCC(S)A 2000, s. 77).

Notes

1. Where the offence is not created by statute but is an offence at common law the words 'Common law' are entered in column 2. Similarly if the maximum sentence is, by reason of common law, one of life imprisonment, the words 'Common law' are entered in column 5.

2. A reference to 'MCA 1980, s. 17' indicates that the offence is triable either way by reason of being listed in sch. 1 to MCA 1980. The maximum term imposable on summary conviction will therefore be 6 months' imprisonment, as provided in MCA 1980, s. 32.

3. The sentence for murder is not included in this table because the table lists maximum terms of imprisonment which may be imposed, and the sentence for murder (life imprisonment if the offender is over 21) is a mandatory one in respect of which the sentencer has no discretion.

4. Where the offence is racially aggravated the maximum on indictment is 7 years (CDA 1998, s. 29).

5. Where the offence is racially aggravated the maximum on indictment is 7 years (CDA 1998, s. 29).

6. Where the offence is racially aggravated, it becomes triable on indictment with a maximum of 2 years (CDA 1998, s. 29).

7. If the incest was with a girl under 13, and the offence is so charged in the indictment, life imprisonment may be imposed.

8. Of course, no offence is committed if the homosexual acts are between consenting parties aged 16 or over and in private. (See SOA 1967, s. 1.)

9. If the offender is aged 21 or over and the other party is under 16 imprisonment for up to 5 years may be imposed.

10. If the burglary comprises the commission of, or an intention to commit, an offence which is triable only on indictment, then the burglary is also triable only on indictment. If the burglary is in a dwelling, and any person in the dwelling was subjected to violence or the threat of violence, the offence is triable only on indictment (MCA 1980, sch. 1, para. 28). There is a minimum custodial sentence of three years for the third domestic burglary committed by the offender after 30 November 1999 (PCC(S)A 2000, s. 111).

11. The offence under the Forgery and Counterfeiting Act 1981, s. 5(3) of having equipment to make the forged instruments which it is an offence under s. 5(2) to possess is punishable with up to 10 years' imprisonment following conviction on indictment, and up to 6 months summarily.

12. The lesser offence under the Forgery and Counterfeiting Act 1981, s. 14(2) of making counterfeit notes or coins without lawful authority is punishable with up to 2 years' imprisonment following conviction on indictment, and up to 6 months summarily.

13. The maximum penalty on indictment is increased to 5 years where it is proved that the accident caused the death of the person concerned.

14. Where the offence is racially aggravated, the maximum on indictment is 14 years (CDA 1998, s. 30).

15. This provision is not applicable to cases of arson. Where the offence is racially aggravated it becomes triable on indictment with a maximum of 14 years (CDA 1998, s. 30).

16. Aggravated arson, contrary to the Criminal Damage Act 1971, s. 1(2) and s. 1(3) is triable only on indictment.

17. Where the offence is racially aggravated, it becomes triable on indictment with a maximum of 2 years (CDA 1998, s. 31).

18. Where the offence is racially aggravated, it becomes triable on indictment with a maximum of 2 years (CDA 1998, s. 31).

19. Where the offence is racially aggravated, the maximum on indictment is 7 years (CDA 1998, s. 32).

20. Where the offence is racially aggravated, it becomes triable on indictment with a maximum of 2 years (CDA 1998, s. 32).

21. This offence is triable either way where the offence to which the assisting relates is triable either way.

22. Where the offender was required to provide a specimen to ascertain the proportion of alcohol in his breath, blood or urine at a time when he was in charge of a motor vehicle (but not driving or attempting to drive it), the maximum term of imprisonment which may be imposed is 3 months.

23. Or, where the firearm was a shortened shotgun, 7 years.

24. SOA 1956, sch. 2 makes the maximum penalty for attempts to commit certain offences under the Act lower than the maximum for the completed offence.

TABLE 2 A SUMMARY OF MAIN SENTENCING POWERS

Nature of punishment	Offences for which imposable	Age groups for which imposable	Procedural requirements	Maximum and minimum terms	Sanctions for failure to comply with order	Statutory Authorities
1 IMPRISONMENT Detention in prison for a period specified by the court when passing sentence. Imprisonment may be for a determinate period, or for life. The actual period which is served by the offender is crucially affected by the rules as to early release.	All common law offences are imprisonable; statutory offences are imprisonable if the statute creating the offence so provides in the section dealing with punishment for the offence. 'Imprisonable offence', therefore, means an offence which is punishable with imprisonment in the case of an adult. The offence of murder has a penalty which is 'fixed by law' as life imprisonment.	21 is the minimum age for a sentence of imprisonment; there is no maximum age. The minimum age will change to 18 when the CJCSA 2000, s. 61 is brought into force	(a) The offender must be given the opportunity of legal representation before sentence (unless he has already served a sentence of imprisonment). (b) A pre-sentence report is required, unless the court is of the view that it is 'unecessary' to obtain one. (c) A custodial sentence cannot be imposed unless either (i) the offence, or the combination of the offence and one or more offences associated with it, was so serious that only such a sentence can be justified, or (ii) the offence is a violent or sexual offence and only such a sentence would be adequate to protect the public from serious harm, or (iii) the offender is unwilling to comply with requirements in a community order which by law require his agreement. (d) The length of a custodial sentence (apart from one the length of which is fixed by law), or which falls within the presumptive sentence provisions of the PCC(S)A 2000, ss. 109–111, shall be either (i) for such term as is commensurate with the seriousness of the offence and other offences associated with it, or (ii) where the offence is a violent or sexual offence, for such longer term as in the opinion of the court is necessary to protect the public from serious harm. (e) Reasons must be given in open court for imposing the sentence.	Common law offences are punishable with imprisonment for life. If a statutory offence is punishable with imprisonment the statute creating the offence specifies the maximum term imposable. Magistrates' courts are limited to a maximum of six months for any offence, or the statutory maximum for the offence, whichever is the less. The minimum prison sentence in a magistrates' court is five days	Breach of prison rules may result in loss of privileges or the addition of extra time to the sentence length. After early release the offender may be returned to prison on commission of a further offence	(a) PCC(S)A 2000, s. 83(1) (legal representation); (b) PCC(S)A 2000, s. 81 (pre-sentence report); (c) PCC(S)A 2000, s. 79(1), (2) and (3) (justification for custody); (d) PCC(S)A 2000, s. 80 (custodial sentence length); (e) PCC(S)A 2000, s. 79(4) (giving reasons). (f) PCC(S)A 2000, s. 116 (return to custody)

2 SUSPENDED PRISON SENTENCE

Nature of punishment	*Offences for which imposable*	*Age groups for which imposable*	*Procedural requirements*	*Maximum and minimum terms*	*Sanctions for failure to comply with order*	*Statutory Authorities*
A sentence of imprisonment which will not be served unless during a period fixed by the court (the operational period) the offender commits a further imprisonable offence.	All imprisonable offences except those for which the sentence is fixed by law.	As for 1.	(a) A suspended sentence may not be passed unless a sentence of immediate imprisonment would otherwise have been appropriate, and where suspension of the sentence can be justified by the exceptional circumstances of the case. (b) A pre-sentence report is required, unless the court is of the view that it is 'unecessary' to obtain one. (c) Procedural requirements (c), (d) and (e) in relation to immediate imprisonment also apply to suspended sentences. (d) Whenever a court passes a suspended sentence, it must consider whether also to impose a fine or an order for compensation.	The term suspended must not exceed two years. The operational period must be not less than one and not more than two years.	If the offender is convicted of an imprisonable offence committed during the operational period of a suspended sentence, the normal consequence is that the suspended sentence is brought into effect for its full term in addition to any penalty for the later offence.	PCC(S)A 2000, ss. 118–125.

3 DETENTION IN A YOUNG OFFENDER INSTITUTION [to be abolished when CJCSA 2000, s. 61 comes into force]

Nature of punishment	*Offences for which imposable*	*Age groups for which imposable*	*Procedural requirements*	*Maximum and minimum terms*	*Sanctions for failure to comply with order*	*Statutory Authorities*
Detention in a young offender institution may be for a determinate period specified by the court when passing sentence, or it may be custody for life. The actual period which is served by the offender is crucially affected by the rules as to early release.	All imprisonable offences. In the case of custody for life, any offence which carries life imprisonment as the maximum penalty for an adult, or where the sentence is fixed by law.	Offenders aged between 18 and 20 inclusive.	(a) Procedural requirements (a) to (e) in relation to imprisonment also apply here, but (a) is not subject to the restriction given there. (b) A sentence of detention in a young offender institution cannot be suspended.	(a) The maximum is the same as the maximum sentence of imprisonment available in the case of an adult. (b) The minimum sentence is 21 days.	Breach of young offender institution rules may result in loss of privileges or the addition of extra time to sentence length. (After early release the offender may be returned to detention on commission of a further offence.)	(a) PCC(S)A 2000, ss 96 and 97 (maximum and minimum terms); (b) PCC(S)A 2000, s. 83(2) (legal representation); (c) PCC(S)A 2000, s. 81 (pre-sentence report); (d) PCC(S)A 2000, s. 79 (imposition of custody);

					(e) PCC(S)A 2000, s. 80 (custodial sentence length); (f) PCC(S)A 2000, s. 79(4), (reasons); (g) PCC(S)A 2000, s. 94 (custody for life). (h) PCC(S)A 2000, s. 116 (return to custody).
4 DETENTION AND TRAINING ORDER A detention and training order may be passed for one of the determinate periods specified in PCC(S)A 2000, s. 101(1). The sentence is served in such secure accommodation as may be determined by the Secretary of State. The first half of the term is served in custody, the second half under supervision.	All imprisonable offences. Offenders aged between 12 and 17 inclusive.	(a) Procedural requirements (a) to (e) in relation to imprisonment also apply here, but (a) is not subject to the restriction given there. (b) A detention and training order cannot be suspended.	(a) The maximum term is 24 months. The minimum term is 4 months.	Commission of further offence during the second part of the order may result in the offender being ordered to return to custody for the remainder of the original term.	(a) PCC(S)A 2000, s. 101(1) (specified terms of the order); (b) PCC(S)A 2000, s. 83(2) (legal representation); (c) PCC(S)A 2000, s. 81 (pre-sentence report); (d) PCC(S)A 2000, s. 79 (imposition of custody); (e) PCC(S)A 2000, s. 80 (custodial sentence length); (f) PCC(S)A 2000, s. 79(4) (reasons); (g) PCC(S)A 2000, s. 105 (return to custody).

5 DETENTION UNDER PCC(S)A 2000, s. 91

Nature of punishment	Offences for which imposable	Age groups for which imposable	Procedural requirements	Maximum and minimum terms	Sanctions for failure to comply with order	Statutory Authorities
Detention in accordance with the Home Secretary's directions (e.g. in local authority secure accommodation, young offender institution or prison). The actual period served by the offender is crucially affected by the rules as to early release.	Offences which are punishable with 14 years' imprisonment or more, excluding murder but including indecent assault and (where the offender is 14 or more) causing death by dangerous driving or causing death by careless driving while under the influence of drink or drugs. An offender convicted of murder who was under 18 when he committed the offence must be sentenced to be detained at Her Majesty's pleasure, under PCCS(A) 2000, s. 90.	Offenders aged between 10 and 17.	(a) Powers under s. 91 are limited to conviction on indictment. (b) Procedural requirements (a) to (e) in relation to imprisonment also apply here, but (a) is not subject to the restriction given there. (c) Detention under s. 91 may be ordered only if all the other methods of dealing with the offender are unsuitable.	The maximum term is the maximum term of imprisonment to which the offender could be sentenced were he eligible for that sentence.	After early release the offender may be returned to detention on commission of a further offence.	(a) PCC(S)A 2000, s. 91 (general powers); (b) PCC(S)A 2000, s. 83 (legal representation); (c) PPC(S)A 2000, s. 81 (pre-sentence report); (d) PCC(S)A 2000, s. 79 (imposition of custody); (e) PCC(S)A 2000, s. 80 (custodial sentence length); (f) PCC(S)A 2000, s. 79(4) (reasons). (g) PCC(S)A 2000, s. 116 (return to custody).

6 COMMUNITY REHABILITATION ORDER (formerly probation order)

An order placing the offender under the supervision of a probation officer for a period of time specified by the court. Various requirements may be written into the order (such as a requirement of residence or a requirement of treatment for a mental condition).	Any offence except those where the sentence is fixed by law or falls to be imposed under PCC(S)A 2000, ss. 109–111.	The minimum age is 16. There is no maximum age.	(a) A CRO is a community order and the offence must be serious enough to warrant the use of a community order. (b) The order should (i) be the most suitable for the offender in all the circumstances and (ii) have restrictions upon liberty contained within it which are commensurate to the seriousness of the offence. (c) A CRO must be desirable in the interests of (i) securing the rehabilitation of the offender, or (ii) protecting the public from serious harm or preventing the commission of further offences. (d) The offender must express a willingness to comply with any requirement of treatment for his mental condition or for his dependency on drugs or alcohol. (e) A pre-sentence report is desirable in all cases and is required before additional requirements are added to the order, unless the court is of the view that it is 'unnecessary' to obtain a report. (f) The court must explain the order to the offender in open court and in ordinary language.	The court fixes the period of the CRO. The minimum period is 6 months; the maximum is 3 years.	An offender who is in breach of a CRO (by failure to comply with any one of its requirements) may *inter alia* be fined up to £1,000, be made subject to a CPO or be made subject to an attendance centre order; alternatively the CRO may be revoked and the offender re-sentenced. An offender subject to a CRO who commits a further offence may be dealt with by revocation of the order and re-sentencing.	(a) PCC(S)A 2000, s. 35 (community orders); (b) PCC(S)A 2000, s. 41 (general powers); (c) PCC(S)A 2000, sch. 3 (enforcement of community orders); (d) PCC(S)A 2000, sch. 2 (requirements in CROs).

Nature of punishment	Offences for which imposable	Age groups for which imposable	Procedural requirements	Maximum and minimum terms	Sanctions for failure to comply with order	Statutory Authorities
7 COMMUNITY PUNISHMENT ORDER (formerly community service order)						
Performance of unpaid work in what would otherwise be the offender's spare time.	All imprisonable offences except those for which the sentence is fixed by law or falls to be imposed under PCC(S)A 2000, ss. 109–111.	The minimum age is 16. There is no maximum age.	(a) Procedural requirements (a), (b) and (f) in relation to CROs also apply here. (b) A pre-sentence report is required before the order is made, unless the court is of the view that it is 'unnecessary' to obtain one. (c) The necessary local arrangements need to be made for the work to be carried out and the offender must be suitable.	The minimum number of hours the court may order is 40; the maximum 240. Normally the order must be completed within 12 months.	An offender who is in breach of a CPO (by failure to carry out the work as specified) may be fined up to £1,000 or made subject to a further CPO; alternatively the CPO may be revoked and the offender re-sentenced. A person under a CPO who commits a further offence may be dealt with (in addition to the sentence for the new offence) by revocation of the order and re-sentencing.	(a) PCC(S)A 2000, s. 35 (community orders); (b) PCC(S)A 2000, s. 46 (general powers); (c) PCC(S)A 2000, sch. 3 (enforcement of community orders).

8 COMMUNITY PUNISHMENT AND REHABILITATION ORDER (formerly combination order)

An order which places the offender under the supervision of a probation officer *and* requires the offender to perform unpaid work in what otherwise would be the offender's spare time.	All imprisonable offences except those for which the sentence is fixed by law or falls to be imposed under the PCC(S)A 2000, ss. 109–111.	The minimum age is 16. There is no maximum age.	(a) Procedural requirements (a)–(d) and (f) in relation to CROs also apply here. (b) A pre-sentence report is required before the order is made, unless the court is of the view that it is 'unnecessary' to obtain one. (c) The necessary local arrangements need to be made for the work to be carried out under the CPO part of the CPRO, and the offender must be suitable.	The court fixes the period of CRO, which must be between 12 months and 3 years. The minimum number of hours' CPO the court may order is 40; the maximum 100.	An offender who is in breach of a CPRO may be fined up to £1,000 or made subject to a CPO; alternatively the CPRO may be revoked and the offender re-sentenced. A person under a CPRO who commits a further offence may be dealt with (in addition to the sentence for the new offence) by revocation of the order and re-sentencing.	(a) PCC(S)A 2000, s. 35 (community orders); (b) PCC(S)A 2000, s. 51 (general powers); (c) PCC(S)A 2000, sch. 3 (enforcement of community orders).

Nature of punishment	*Offences for which imposable*	*Age groups for which imposable*	*Procedural requirements*	*Maximum and minimum terms*	*Sanctions for failure to comply with order*	*Statutory Authorities*
9 CURFEW ORDER						
An order which requires an offender to remain at a place specified in the order (such as the offender's home) for specified periods of time.	Any offence except those for which the sentence is fixed by law or falls to be imposed under the PCC(S)A 2000, ss. 109–111.	All ages.	(a) Procedural requirements (a), (b), and (f) in relation to CROs are also applicable here. (b) A pre sentence report is not required, but is desirable since the court must obtain information about the place to be specified in the order and the attitude of other persons likely to be affected. (c) Curfew orders may be enforced by electronic monitoring of the offender.	The court may require the offender to remain at the place (or places) specified in the order for specified periods of between 2 and 12 hours per day for a period of up to six months or, in the case of an offender aged 10 to 15, up to three months.	An offender who is in breach of a curfew order may be fined up to £1,000 or made subject to a CPO or, if the offender is under the age of 16, an attendance centre order; alternatively the curfew order may be revoked and the offender re-sentenced. A person under a curfew order who commits a further offence may be dealt with (in addition to the sentence for the new offence) by revocation of the order and re-sentencing.	(a) PCC(S)A 2000, s. 35 (community orders); (b) PCC(S)A 2000, s. 37 (general powers); (c) PCC(S)A 2000, s. 37(6) (electronic monitoring); (d) PCC(S)A 2000, sch. 3 (enforcement of community orders).

10 DRUG TREATMENT AND TESTING ORDER

| An order requiring the offender to submit to treatment for drug dependency or a propensity to misuse drugs, together with a testing requirement that the offender shall provide samples during the period of the order. The offender is also under supervision. | All offences except those for which the sentence is fixed by law or falls to be imposed under the PCC(S)A 2000, ss. 109–111 | The minimum age is 16. There is no maximum age. | (a) Procedural requirements (a), (b) and (f) in relation to CROs also apply here. (b) A pre-sentence report is required before the order is made unless the court is of the view that it is 'unnecessary' to obtain one. (c) The offender must express his willingness to comply with the order. | The court fixes the period of the order. The minimum period is 6 months and the maximum is 3 years. The order must provide for review by the court which made the order at intervals of not less than one month. | An offender who is in breach of a DTTO may be fined up to £1,000, or be made subject to a CPO. Alternatively the order may be revoked and the offender re-sentenced. A person subject to a DTTO who commits a further offence may be dealt with (in addition to the sentence for the new offence) by revocation of the order and re-sentencing. | (a) PCCS(A) 2000, s. 35 (community orders); (b) PCC(S)A 2000, s. 52 (general powers); (c) PCC(S)A 2000, sch. 3 (enforcement of community orders). |

Nature of punishment	Offences for which imposable	Age groups for which imposable	Procedural requirements	Maximum and minimum terms	Sanctions for failure to comply with order	Statutory Authorities
11 ATTENDANCE CENTRE ORDER An order which requires the offender to attend a centre (usually for sessions of two or three hours at weekends) under the supervision of the police or probation service, to take part in physical exercise and constructive activities.	All imprisonable offences except those for which the sentence is fixed by law or falls to be imposed under PCC(S)A 2000, ss. 109–111.	Offenders aged between 10 and 20 inclusive.	(a) Procedural requirements (a) and (b) in relation to CROs are also applicable here. (b) A pre-sentence report is not required. (c) The court must ensure that there is an attendance centre available to receive the offender, which is within reasonable travelling distance.	The number of hours of attendance must be specified by the court. The normal minimum number is 12, except where the offender is aged between 10 and 13 inclusive and a lesser minimum is appropriate. The normal maximum number of hours is also 12, except where that is inadequate, in which case the maximum is 24 hours where the offender is 10–15 inclusive, and 36 hours where the offender is aged 16–20 inclusive.	An offender who is in breach of an attendance centre order may be fined up to £1,000, or the order may be revoked and the offender re-sentenced.	(a) PCC(S)A 2000, s. 35 (community orders); (b) PCC(S)A 2000, s. 35 (general powers); (c) PCC(S)A 2000, sch. 5 (enforcement of attendance centre orders).

12 SUPERVISION ORDER

An order which requires the offender to be supervised for a period of time which is specified by the court. Various requirements may be written into the order (such as a requirement of residence or a requirement that the offender participate in various schemes of treatment).	Any offence except those where the sentence is fixed by law.	Offenders aged between 10 and 17 inclusive.	(a) Procedural requirements (a) and (b) in relation to CROs are also applicable here. (b) A pre-sentence report is required before additional requirements are added to the order, unless the court is of the view that it is 'unnecessary' to obtain a report. (c) A supervision order may be made by a youth court or the Crown Court but not by an adult magistrates' court.	(a) The duration of the order must be specified by the court. There is no minimum period. The maximum period is 3 years. (b) Requirements of 'attendance' and of 'participation in specified activities' may last for a maximum of 90 days. A night restriction requirement cannot be imposed in respect of more than 30 separate days, or continue in operation for longer than three months.	An offender who is in breach of a supervision order may be fined up to £1,000, or may be made the subject of an attendance centre order or a curfew order. The court may revoke the order and impose any sentence which it could have imposed if dealing with him for the original offence.	(a) PCC(S)A 2000, s. 63 (general power); (b) PCC(S)A 2000, sch. 6 (requirements in supervision orders); (c) PCC(S)A 2000, sch. 7 (breach of supervision orders).

Nature of punishment	*Offences for which imposable*	*Age groups for which imposable*	*Procedural requirements*	*Maximum and minimum terms*	*Sanctions for failure to comply with order*	*Statutory Authorities*
13 ACTION PLAN ORDER						
An order placing the offender under supervision and requiring him to comply with any of a range of requirements.	Any offence expect those where the sentence is fixed by law.	Offenders between 10 and 17 inclusive.	(a) Procedural requirements (a), (b), (c) and (f) in relation to CROs also apply here. (b) A pre-sentence report is not required but the court must obtain and consider a written report.	The court must direct a further hearing not more than 21 days after the making of the order to receive a report from the supervisor.	An offender who is in breach of an action plan order (by failure to comply with one of its requirements) may be fined up to £1,000 or be made subject to a curfew order or an attendance centre order. Alternatively the action plan order may be revoked and the offender re-sentenced. A person subject to an action plan order who commits a further offence may be dealt with by revocation of the order and re-sentencing.	(a) PCC(S)A 2000, s. 35 (community orders); (b) PCC(S)A 2000, s. 69 (general powers); (c) PCC(S)A 2000, sch. 3 (enforcement of action plan orders).

14 FINE Payment to the state of a sum of money fixed by the court — normally payment must be made within a stated time or by instalments.	All offences except those for which the sentence is fixed by law or falls to be imposed under PCC(S)A 2000, ss. 109–111.	All ages. The court must normally order that fines imposed on a person aged between 10 and 15 inclusive should be paid by that person's parent or guardian. The court has a discretion to do this where the offender is aged 16 or 17.	The court must have regard to the offender's ability to pay the fine, whether this has the effect of increasing or decreasing the amount to be paid.	Indictable offences are punishable with an unlimited fine; the maximum fine for a summary offence is fixed by reference to a standard scale of fines. Special rules govern the fining of juveniles.	Various enforcement procedures are available. The ultimate sanction for non-payment is custody in default.	(a) PCC(S)A 2000, s. 127 (fines for indictable offences); (b) CJA 1982, s. 37 (standard scale); (c) PCC(S)A 2000, s. 137 (payment by parent); (d) PCC(S)A 2000, s. 128(3) (requirement to have regard to means of offender).
15 DISCHARGE An absolute discharge discharges the offender with no conditions or qualifications. A conditional discharge discharges the offender subject to the condition that he does not commit a further offence during the period of the discharge.	All offences except those for which the sentence is fixed by law or falls to be imposed under PCC(S)A 2000, ss. 109–111. The court must consider that it is inexpedient to inflict punishment.	Offenders of any age may be discharged.	(a) The court must consider that it is inexpedient to inflict punishment. No punishment can be combined with a discharge. (b) A discharge does not count as a 'conviction' for certain purposes.	The court fixes the period of a conditional discharge. The maximum period is three years; there is no minimum period.	An offender who commits an offence while subject to a conditional discharge may be sentenced for the original offence, in which case the discharge ceases to have effect.	(a) PCC(S)A 2000, s. 12 (general powers); (b) PCC(S)A 2000, s. 13 (breach of conditional discharge); (c) PCC(S)A 2000, s. 14 (limited effect of conviction).

Nature of punishment	Offences for which imposable	Age groups for which imposable	Procedural requirements	Maximum and minimum terms	Sanctions for failure to comply with order	Statutory Authorities
16 REPARATION ORDER An order requiring the offender to make reparation for the offence to the victim, or to the community more generally, otherwise than by the payment of compensation.	All offences except those for which the sentence is fixed by law.	Offenders aged 10 to 17 inclusive.	(a) Although the reparation order is not a community order, the restrictions on liberty imposed by the order should be commensurate with the seriousness of the offence. (b) A pre-sentence report is not required but the court must obtain and consider a report indicating the form of reparation proposed and the attitude of the victim. The order cannot be made without the agreement of the victim. (c) The court must explain the effect of the order, the consequences of non-compliance and the possibility of review.	A reparation order cannot require the offender to work for more than 24 hours in total, and the reparation must be complete within 3 months of the order.	An offender who is in breach of a reparation order (by failure to comply with its requirements) may be fined up to £1,000 or be made subject to a curfew order or an attendance centre order. Alternatively the reparation order may be revoked and the offender re-sentenced. A person subject to a reparation order who commits a further offence may be dealt with by revocation of the order and re-sentencing.	(a) PCC(S)A 2000, s. 73 (general powers); (b) PCC(S)A 2000, sch. 8 (enforcement of reparation orders).

17 HOSPITAL ORDER AND GUARDIANSHIP ORDER

MHA 1983, s. 37.

An order authorising an offender's admission to and detention at a (mental) hospital specified in the order. His subsequent discharge from hospital is a matter for the doctor treating him. He also has a right to apply at specified intervals to a MHRT which may order his discharge. A guardianship order is similar to a hospital order but places the offender under the guardianship of the local authority or other named person.

All imprisonable offences except those for which the sentence is fixed by law or falls to be imposed under PCC(S)A 2000, s. 109.

Offenders of any age may be made the subject of a hospital order. Guardianship orders are available for offenders of at least 16 years of age.

(a) There must be oral or written evidence from two doctors (one a specialist in mental disorders) that the offender is suffering from mental illness, psychopathic disorder, mental impairment or severe mental impairment.
(b) Arrangements must be made to ensure that the offender can be received at the hospital which is specified in the order.

The hospital order is for an indeterminate period, initially for six months, renewal for a further six months, and at yearly intervals thereafter. A guardianship order lasts for 12 months, but may be renewed.

An offender who is absent without leave from the hospital may be taken into custody and returned to the hospital, unless he has been absent for more than 28 days, in which case the order ceases to have effect and he is no longer liable to be detained.

Nature of punishment	*Offences for which imposable*	*Age groups for which imposable*	*Procedural requirements*	*Maximum and minimum terms*	*Sanctions for failure to comply with order*	*Statutory Authorities*
18 RESTRICTION ORDER Where the Crown Court makes a hospital order, it may, in order to protect the public from the risk of serious harm, attach a restriction order. This makes discharge from the hospital subject to the decision of a MHRT.	As for 17.	As for 17.	(a) As for 17. (b) The restriction order must be justified by the need to protect the public from the risk of serious harm.	As for 17, but discharge subject to the decision of a MHRT.	As for 17.	MHA 1983, s. 41.
19 COMPENSATION ORDER An order requiring the offender to pay the victim of his offence a sum of money to compensate him for personal injury, loss or damage resulting from the offence.	Any offence. Compensation may be imposed as an ancillary order or may stand alone.	Offenders of any age can be ordered to pay compensation. The court must normally order that compensation imposed on a person aged between 10 and 15 inclusive should be paid by that person's parent or guardian. The court has a discretion to do this where the offender is aged 16 or 17.	(a) A compensation order should be made only if the offender agrees he is liable to compensate the victim in the sum to be specified in the order *or* if there is material before the court clearly establishing liability to compensate in that sum. (b) The court must have regard to the offender's means before making a compensation order. (c) A compensation order should not be made where there are difficulties in assessing the size of the loss. (d) The court should give reasons for *not* awarding compensation. (e) Compensation takes priority over a fine. (f) The victim need not apply to the court for compensation.	Magistrates' courts are restricted to a maximum of £5,000 compensation for each offence. There is no limit in the Crown Court, subject only to the extent of the loss and the offender's ability to pay.	The court orders the offender to pay the compensation as a lump sum or by instalments. Various enforcement procedures are available. The ultimate sanction for non-payment is custody in default.	PCC(S)A 2000, ss. 130–134.

20 RESTITUTION ORDER				
An order requiring a person in possession of stolen goods to restore them to the owner (or anyone else entitled to possession of them). A restitution order may be made only when there has been a conviction 'with reference to the theft' of the stolen goods to which the order relates. 'Stolen goods' include goods obtained by deception and by blackmail.	Offenders of any age may be ordered to make restitution.	(a) Restitution orders should not be made in cases of doubt where the money or property might belong to some third party (i.e. not to the offender or to the proposed recipient under the order). (b) In some cases the victim need not apply to the court for restitution.	Non-compliance with a restitution order amounts to a contempt of court and is punishable as such.	PCC(S)A 2000, s. 148.
21 DEPRIVATION ORDER				
An order for the forfeiture of goods used in the course of an offence committed by the offender or intended for such use. Any offence.	Offenders of any age.	(a) A deprivation order must be based on proper evidence. (b) Other persons claiming true ownership of the property may apply to the court for return of the property, showing that they did not realise that the property would be put to unlawful use. (c) After passage of a period of time, property forfeited may be sold, and the proceeds paid to the victim of the offence.		PCC(S)A 2000, s. 143; other specific powers of forfeiture exist under other statutes.
22 CONFISCATION ORDER: DRUG TRAFFICKING				
An order made by the Crown Court for the confiscation of profits derived by the offender from drug trafficking offences. A drug trafficking offence, as defined in DTA 1994, s. 1.	Offenders of any age.	(a) The court must determine whether the defendant has benefited from drug trafficking. If so, the court must determine the amount, and then order the defendant to pay that sum, or such lower sum as can actually be realised. (b) The issue of confiscation should normally be resolved before sentence is imposed.	There is no maximum or minimum sum which may be recovered.	DTA 1994.

Nature of punishment	*Offences for which imposable*	*Age groups for which imposable*	*Procedural requirements*	*Maximum and minimum terms*	*Sanctions for failure to comply with order*	*Statutory Authorities*
23 CONFISCATION ORDER: OTHER OFFENDING						
An order for the confiscation of profits derived by the offender.	Any indictable offence other than a drug trafficking offence, and a restricted range of summary offences.	Offenders of any age.	As for 22.	There is no maximum or minimum sum which may be recovered.	Various enforcement procedures are available. The ultimate sanction for non-payment is custody for default.	CJA 1988, Part VI, as amended by CJA 1993 and PCA 1995.

TABLE 3   OFFENDERS SENTENCED BY TYPE OF COURT, TYPE OF SENTENCE OR ORDER AND TYPE OF OFFENCE

England and Wales — Number of offenders (thousands) and percentages

Type of sentence or order	1998	1999						
		Number of offenders				Percentage of total offenders sentenced		
	Total	Total	Indictable offences	Summary offences		Indictable offences	Summary offences	
				Offences (excluding motoring offences)	Motoring offences		Offences (excluding motoring offences)	Motoring offences
Magistrates' courts								
Absolute discharge	17.7	15.8	1.9	4.2	9.6	1	1	2
Conditional discharge	112.0	111.4	54.8	47.7	8.9	20	11	1
Fine	1,057.5	989.7	90.0	334.7	565.0	34	78	89
Community penalties								
Probation order	49.8	50.6	31.6	9.3	9.8	12	2	2
Supervision order	11.6	11.8	8.4	3.0	0.5	3	1	0
Community service order	39.5	41.1	22.5	8.9	9.7	8	2	2
Attendance centre order	8.0	8.6	5.7	2.7	0.2	2	1	0
Combination order	17.3	17.3	9.1	2.7	5.5	3	1	1
Curfew order	0.9	1.5	0.8	0.3	0.4	0	0	0
Secure training order	0.1	0.2	0.1	0.0	0.0	0	0	0
Young offender institution	13.1	14.5	9.0	2.8	2.7	3	1	0
Imprisonment								
Fully suspended	1.2	1.2	0.6	0.2	0.4	0	0	0
Unsuspended	39.4	43.3	24.3	6.3	12.7	9	1	2
Otherwise dealt with	20.6	23.9	8.9	8.2	6.8	3	2	1
Total	1,388.6	1,330.8	267.7	431.1	632.0	100	100	100
The Crown Court								
Absolute discharge	0.1	0.1	0.1	0.0	–	0	0	–
Conditional discharge	2.7	2.6	2.1	0.5	0.0	3	20	1
Fine	3.3	2.7	2.1	0.3	0.2	3	15	28
Community penalties								
Probation order	8.3	7.7	7.4	0.3	0.1	10	11	13
Supervision order	0.9	0.9	0.8	0.0	0.0	1	1	0
Community service order	9.1	8.5	8.0	0.4	0.1	11	18	6
Attendance centre order	0.1	0.1	0.1	0.0	–	0	0	–
Combination order	3.9	3.4	3.3	0.1	0.0	4	4	4
Curfew order	0.0	0.1	0.1	0.0	1.0	0	0	0
S53 C&YP Act 1933	0.6	0.6	0.6	*	*	1	*	*
Secure training order	0.0	0.0	0.0	–	–	0	–	–
Young offender institution	10.4	10.3	10.1	0.2	0.1	14	7	8
Imprisonment								
Fully suspended	2.2	2.0	2.0	0.0	0.0	3	1	1
Unsuspended	36.9	36.4	35.6	0.4	0.3	48	19	34
Otherwise dealt with	1.8	1.7	1.6	0.1	0.0	2	4	4
Total	80.4	77.2	74.0	2.3	0.9	100	100	100

TABLE 3 — *continued*

England and Wales					Number of offenders (thousands) and percentages			
Type of sentence or order	*1998*			*1999*				
			Number of offenders			*Percentage of total offenders sentenced*		
	Total	*Total*	*Indictable offences*	*Summary offences*		*Indictable offences*	*Summary offences*	
				Offences (excluding motoring offences)	*Motoring offences*		*Offences (excluding motoring offences)*	*Motoring offences*
All courts								
Absolute discharge	17.8	15.9	2.0	4.2	9.6	1	1	2
Conditional discharge	114.7	114.0	56.9	48.2	8.9	17	11	1
Fine	1,060.7	992.4	92.1	335.0	565.3	27	77	89
Community penalties								
Probation order	58.2	58.4	38.9	9.6	9.9	11	2	2
Supervision order	12.4	12.7	9.2	3.0	0.5	3	1	0
Community service order	48.6	49.6	30.5	9.4	9.7	9	2	2
Attendance centre order	8.1	8.7	5.8	2.7	0.2	2	1	0
Combination order	21.2	20.7	12.4	2.8	5.5	4	1	1
Curfew order	1.0	1.6	0.9	0.3	0.4	0	0	0
S53 C&YP Act 1933	0.6	0.6	0.6	*	*	0	*	*
Secure training order	0.1	0.2	0.2	0.0	0.0	0	0	0
Young offender institution	23.5	24.8	19.1	3.0	2.8	6	1	0
Imprisonment								
Fully suspended	3.4	3.2	2.5	0.2	0.4	1	0	0
Unsuspended	76.3	79.7	59.9	6.8	13.0	18	2	2
Otherwise dealt with	22.4	25.6	10.5	8.3	6.8	3	2	1
Total	1,468.9	1,408.0	341.7	433.5	632.9	100	100	100

Source: *Criminal Statistics England and Wales 2000*, table 7.1.

1.2.2 Age categories of offenders

A matter which may well have a crucial impact upon where the offence is to be tried and sentenced, and the powers available to the sentencing court, is the offender's age. Several age groups need to be distinguished. The terminology which is used in this book is as follows:

> *Adult offenders*
> aged 21 or over   adults
> aged 18, 19 or 20   young adults
>
> *Juveniles*
> aged 14, 15, 16 or 17   young persons
> aged 10, 11, 12 or 13   children

For the purposes of determining the method of trial and the appropriate sentencing court, the crucial dividing line is between adult offenders and juveniles. Adult offenders are dealt with in the Crown Court or in a magistrates' court, depending upon the seriousness of the offence charged. Juveniles are dealt with in the youth court. The CJA 1991 included 17-year-olds within the category of young persons (rather than adults) for a range of criminal justice purposes, so that 17-year-olds appear in youth courts. For the sentences available for various age categories of offenders see Table 2 on pp. 15 to 29.

What happens when the defendant's birthday occurs during the course of the proceedings? The determining factor in sentencing is normally the age of the offender on the date when he or she is convicted or found guilty. Thus if an offender is aged 15 when charged with an offence but is aged 16 when he is convicted or pleads guilty, the court's powers to deal with 16-year-olds but not 15-year-olds (such as a community punishment order) are available. So a birthday between charge and conviction will make a difference. On the other hand, a birthday between conviction and sentence will not make a difference. If an offender is aged under 18 when convicted but turns 18 before being sentenced, he or she should be treated as being under the age of 18 for sentencing purposes. This would mean that the appropriate custodial sentence would be a detention and training order, rather than detention in a young offender institution: see *Cassidy* [2000] All ER (D) 1200 and *Robinson* [1993] 1 WLR 168. When a court needs to determine the age of an offender before passing sentence it may consider any evidence which is available to it (PCC(S)A 2000, s. 164(1)). If the court imposes sentence on an assumption which subsequently turns out to be incorrect, the sentence is not rendered invalid by that mistake (*Brown* (1989) 11 Cr App R (S) 263). If there is a dispute about the offender's age, the best course is to adjourn until the matter can be resolved (*Steed* (1990) 12 Cr App R (S) 230). It is, of course, quite wrong, and would be regarded as an abuse of the process of the court, to adjourn a case simply so that an offender can attain a particular age in the meantime (*Arthur v Stringer* (1986) 8 Cr App R (S) 329).

1.2.3 Categories of offences

It is crucial to distinguish between sentencing for:

(a) offences triable only on indictment,
(b) offences triable either way, and
(c) offences triable summarily.

Offences triable only on indictment must be dealt with in the Crown Court. Such offences include murder, manslaughter, rape and robbery.

Offences triable either way can, as their name implies, be dealt with either in the Crown Court or in a magistrates' court. Such offences include burglary, theft and assault occasioning actual bodily harm. The decision over where an offence triable either way will be dealt with is known as the *mode of trial* decision. Basically, an offence triable either way will be dealt with on indictment if *either* the accused relies upon his right to trial in Crown Court *or* the magistrates come to the view that the case is too serious for them (i.e. that if the accused is convicted of the offence charged a sentence will be required which is in excess of the magistrates' sentencing powers). When determining mode of trial, magistrates must make the decision on the basis of what has been alleged about the gravity of the offence(s) charged. If they think that their powers would be adequate to sentence the accused, then they should give the accused the option of summary trial. If they think that their powers would not be adequate, then they should embark upon committal proceedings with a view to trial on indictment.

A matter of terminology which often causes confusion is that in English law the term 'indictable offence' means an offence which is triable only on indictment *or* an offence which is triable either way (Interpretation Act 1978, sch. 1). So both murder and burglary are indictable offences. Similarly, a conviction in Crown Court is referred to as a 'conviction on indictment' whether or not the offence involved was an offence triable only on indictment or an offence triable either way.

Summary offences are (with certain exceptions dealt with below) dealt with exclusively in the magistrates' courts. These are the least serious offences and include many road traffic matters, regulatory offences and other assorted minor offences. Some offences which are triable only summarily cannot, however, be dismissed as trivial. Driving (or being in charge) of a vehicle while unfit through drink or drugs, driving with excess alcohol, taking a motor vehicle without consent and assaulting a police officer in the execution of his duty are all summary offences. Several of these offences were formerly triable either way and have been converted into summary offences in an attempt by Parliament to lighten the load of business in the Crown Court. There are two exceptions to the general rule that summary offences are tried and sentenced in the magistrates' court. First, if the magistrates are committing the offender for an offence triable either way, they may also commit for a summary offence at the same time, so as to avoid splitting the sentencing function between the magistrates' court and the Crown Court. This can only be done if the summary offence is punishable with imprisonment and arose out of circumstances which were connected with the offence triable either way (CJA 1988, s. 41). Secondly, certain summary offences (at present restricted to common assault, taking a motor vehicle without consent, driving while disqualified and criminal damage of £5,000 or less) may be included by the prosecution in the indictment along with the indictable offence to be dealt with in the Crown Court. The summary offence must be founded on the same facts or evidence as the indictable offence or be part of a series of offences of the same character as, or a similar character to, the indictable offence (CJA 1988, s. 40).

Summary offences are sometimes referred to as 'purely summary offences'. The word 'purely' adds nothing, but is sometimes included to reinforce a distinction being drawn between summary offences and offences triable either way. 'Summary conviction' means conviction in a magistrates' court, whether for a summary offence or for an offence triable either way.

The overall effect of the arrangements just described is that the great bulk of crime is dealt with in the magistrates' courts, serious crime is for the Crown Court, and crime of intermediate gravity is shared between the Crown Court and the magistrates' courts. A good picture of the distribution of sentencing responsibility is given by the *Criminal Statistics for England and Wales*. In 1999 magistrates' courts sentenced some 1,330,800 offenders; 267,700 of those had committed indictable offences, 632,000 had committed summary traffic offences and 431,100 had committed other summary offences. The Crown Court sentenced only 77,200 offenders, all but 3,200 of whom had committed indictable offences. Thus, approximately 5.5 per cent of offenders were sentenced in the Crown Court and 94.5 per cent were sentenced by magistrates. Even as regards indictable offences, 78 per cent of offenders were dealt with in the magistrates' courts and 22 per cent in the Crown Court. However, when one turns from sheer quantity of sentencing to the type of sentence passed, it is the work of the Crown Court which becomes the more significant. Sixty-six per cent of offenders aged 21 and over sentenced in the Crown Court for indictable offences received an immediate custodial sentence, while in the magistrates' courts, the figure was 15 per cent. Moreover the average length of sentence of immediate custody imposed on adult males by the Crown Court for indictable offences was around 24 months, as compared with 2.6 months in the magistrates' courts. When dealing with summary offences, magistrates very rarely pass custodial sentences. In fact, most offenders sentenced by magistrates are fined — 34 per cent of those sentenced for indictable offences (as compared with 3 per cent in the Crown Court), 89 per cent of those sentenced for summary road traffic offences and 78 per cent of those sentenced for other summary offences (all statistics taken from Home Office, *Criminal Statistics England and Wales* 2000).

1.2.4 Courts sentencing adults

Adult offenders are sentenced either by the Crown Court or by a magistrates' court. An adult offender convicted on indictment will be sentenced by a Crown Court judge. The range of powers available to a Crown Court are set out in Table 2 on p. 15. An adult offender who is summarily convicted will normally be sentenced by the magistrates. The various limitations upon the sentencing powers of magistrates will be explained in the relevant parts of this book, but an overview can usefully be given here.

When magistrates convict an adult offender summarily of an offence triable either way they may pass a sentence of up to six months' imprisonment and/or a fine of up to £5,000. If the offender is aged under 21 neither the Crown Court nor a magistrates' court can pass a prison sentence. When they convict an adult summarily of two offences triable either way magistrates may sentence to an aggregate term of up to 12 months' imprisonment (or detention in a young offender institution) and/or a fine of up to £5,000 for each offence. Other methods of dealing with adult offenders are available to the magistrates in broadly the same circumstances as they are available to the Crown Court, except that magistrates cannot add a restriction order to a hospital order, or make a compensation order of more than £5,000 in respect of any one offence.

The decision over mode of trial has already been referred to. The level of gravity at which magistrates should refuse jurisdiction in respect of an offence triable either way is not susceptible to precise definition, but it is possible to gauge the kind of conduct which can properly be punished with a sentence of six months' imprisonment or less. Section 19 of MCA 1980 requires magistrates to have regard to the following matters in deciding whether an offence is more suitable for summary trial or trial on indictment:

(a)   the nature of the case,

(b)   whether the circumstances make the offence one of serious character,

(c)   whether the punishment which a magistrates' court would have power to inflict for it would be adequate,

(d)   any other circumstances which appear to the court to make it more suitable for the offence to be tried in one way rather than the other, and

(e)   any representations made by the prosecution or the defence.

A practice note containing national mode of trial guidelines has been issued: *Practice Note (Mode of Trial: Guidelines)* [1990] 1 WLR 1439, which was revised and reissued in 1995. The Guidelines are designed to assist magistrates with their decision. They apply to all defendants aged 18 and over. General guidance given there on mode of trial is as follows:

(a)   the court should never make its decision on the grounds of convenience or expedition;

(b)   the court should assume for the purpose of deciding mode of trial that the prosecution version of the facts is correct;

(c)   the fact that offences are alleged to be sample counts is a relevant consideration, but the fact that the defendant if convicted will be asking for other offences to be taken into consideration is not;

(d)   where cases involve complex questions of fact or difficult questions of law, the court should consider transfer for trial;

(e)   where two or more defendants are jointly charged with an offence each has an individual right to elect his mode of trial;

(f)   in general, except where otherwise stated in the Guidelines, offences triable either way should be tried summarily unless the court considers that the particular case has one or more of the features set out *and* that its sentencing powers are insufficient;

(g)   the court should also consider its powers to commit an offender for sentence, under PCC(S)A 2000, s. 3, if information emerges during the course of the hearing which leads them to conclude that the offence is so serious, or the offender such a risk to the public, that their powers to sentence him are inadequate.

The Guidelines then give specific advice on mode of trial for various individual offences. This advice is set out in relation to each of the offences considered in Chapter 12, where the sentencing pattern for a range of commonly encountered offences is explained.

If a person aged 18 or over is dealt with summarily, pleads guilty or is found guilty after summary trial, the magistrates will normally pass sentence. Sometimes, however, where the offender is convicted of an offence triable either way, the magistrates may commit to Crown Court for sentence. It will be remembered that the magistrates' decision on mode of trial was based on their view that their sentencing powers would be adequate in the event of conviction. Even so, further information may emerge during the course of the trial, or from the information received by the court after conviction, which inevitably affects the magistrates' provisional view and makes the offence(s) now seem more serious than at first sight. The magistrates may then commit for sentence to the Crown Court. This will normally be done under PCC(S)A 2000, s. 3, though there are other provisions which provide this power. The only justification for committal for sentence under s. 3 is that the offence(s) are more serious than at first appeared. Following a committal under s. 3, the Crown Court may deal with the offender as if he had just been convicted of the relevant offence(s) on indictment (PCC(S)A 2000, s. 5).

Section 3 applies where a person who is aged 18 or over has been convicted at summary trial of an offence which is triable either way. In order to commit to Crown Court for sentence the magistrates must be of the opinion that the offence is so serious that proper punishment for it would exceed their powers or, in the case where the offender has committed a violent offence or a sexual offence, a longer sentence than they can impose is required to protect the public from the offender. The usual reasons for committing for sentence under s. 3 are:

(a)   where the offender's previous convictions (which, of course, the magistrates will not have known about until they come to sentence him) place the offender in a less favourable light than if this had been his first offence, or they make the current offence seem more serious in the light of what has gone before, or

(b)   he asks for offences to be taken into consideration at that stage, the additional punishment for those taking the case above the magistrates' limit.

Magistrates should always think carefully before accepting a case which on the face of it seems likely to require a sentence close to their limit, not least because accepting it will lead the offender to expect to be sentenced in accordance with the lower court's powers. Having accepted jurisdiction, however, the magistrates can still change their minds about the case and commit for sentence. See *North Sefton Magistrates' Court, ex parte March* (1995) 16 Cr App R (S) 401, in which it was stated that the justices had an 'open-textured discretion' in the matter, a case which departed from the earlier more rigid approach in *Manchester Magistrates' Court, ex parte Kaymanesh* (1994) 15 Cr App R (S) 838.

Section 4 of the PCC(S)A 2000 deals with the case where there are several either-way offences charged against the defendant, to some of which he pleads guilty and some of which he intends to contest at trial. If the magistrates commit the defendant to Crown Court for trial, they can also commit for sentence the offences to which he pleads guilty, even though those offences standing alone would not have been serious enough to justify committal for sentence under s. 3.

1.2.5 Courts sentencing juveniles

Juveniles (i.e. persons who have not attained the age of 18) are normally sentenced by a youth court. Sometimes, however, they may be sentenced by an adult magistrates' court or by the Crown Court. As with adults, the general rule is that they are sentenced by the court in which they pleaded guilty or were found guilty but, again, this is subject to several exceptions.

When a juvenile charged with an offence is the only accused involved in the proceedings (or when any other accused are juveniles as well), he (or they) must be tried in a youth court unless either (i) the offence charged is murder, manslaughter or causing death by dangerous driving or (ii) the magistrates in the youth court consider that the prosecution allegations are such that, if convicted on indictment, the Crown Court could order the offender to be detained under PCC(S)A 2000, s. 91. Section 91 empowers the Crown Court to order that juveniles convicted of certain grave crimes be detained for a period of time not exceeding the maximum prison term which could be imposed upon an adult for the offence (see **4.3.9**). Orders under s. 91 are appropriate only in very serious cases. Thus, provided no adult is involved in the offence, juveniles will be tried in a youth court unless the charge is a very serious one, in which event they must be tried on indictment.

A juvenile who has a finding of guilt recorded against him in a youth court is also sentenced there. The sentencing powers of youth courts are almost as great as those of the Crown Court in respect of juveniles. The only major limitation is that a youth court cannot order detention under PCC(S)A 2000, s. 91, but youth court magistrates have power to order a detention and training order on a juvenile for up to two years. This is the same power as the Crown Court in respect of juveniles, and stands in sharp contrast to the limit of six months' imprisonment for magistrates' courts in respect of those aged 18 or over.

When a juvenile pleads guilty or is found guilty on indictment, all the sentencing powers available by law in respect of juveniles are at the Crown Court's disposal. However, PCC(S)A 2000, s. 8 provides that, except in cases of homicide, if a juvenile is convicted otherwise than in a youth court he shall be remitted to that court unless the convicting court is 'satisfied that it would be undesirable to do so'. The rationale of s. 8 is that the magistrates sitting in a youth court have greater experience in sentencing juveniles than do Crown Court judges. Accordingly Crown Court judges used to be encouraged to remit to a youth court for sentence, unless it was thought that the juvenile should be given a sentence which a youth court had no power to impose or (at the other extreme) that the case could be dealt with leniently, such as by way of a discharge, and that prolonging the proceedings by remitting was pointless. In *Lewis* (1984) 6 Cr App R (S) 44, however, the Court of Appeal qualified its earlier approach. Lord Lane CJ regarded the idea that the youth court was the only court in which juveniles should be sentenced as out of place, and expressed the view that Crown Court judges would be justified in not remitting juveniles for sentence for, among others, the following reasons:

(a)   where the judge, having presided over the juvenile's trial, feels that he is better informed as to the facts and circumstances of the case than a youth court could be;

(b)   where an adult has been convicted as well as the juvenile, and remitting the juvenile might lead to disparity through co-offenders being sentenced in different courts;

(c)   where remitting the juvenile would lead to delay, duplication of proceedings and fruitless expense.

The last of these reasons could apply to virtually any case, so Lord Lane appears to have advocated that, notwithstanding s. 8, Crown Court judges should, as a general rule, themselves sentence juveniles convicted on indictment and should not remit them to a youth court for sentence.

Since s. 8 does not apply to cases of homicide, juveniles convicted of murder, manslaughter or causing death by dangerous driving will always be sentenced in the Crown Court.

Where a juvenile is convicted in an adult magistrates' court, that court's powers of dealing with the juvenile are very limited. The magistrates may make a referral order, impose a fine or a discharge, bind over the juvenile's parents, disqualify the juvenile from driving or endorse his licence, and make certain ancillary orders as to costs or compensation (s. 8(7) and (8)). Should these options not be appropriate, it will be necessary to remit to the youth court. An adult magistrates' court cannot remit a juvenile to the Crown Court.

1.2.6   Sentencers in the Crown Court

Sentence in the Crown Court is pronounced by a Crown Court judge. Normally the judge alone will conduct the trial and deal with sentencing, but there are some occasions on which the judge must, or may, sit with up to four lay justices. If the offender comes before the Crown Court as a result of being committed there for sentence, the Crown Court judge must normally sit with two lay magistrates (Supreme Court Act 1981 (SCA 1981), s. 74(1)) and may sit with up to four. If the appeal or committal for sentence is in respect of a juvenile, the justices must be members of a youth court panel and the court must include both a man and a woman. A magistrate who adjudicated in the same matter in the lower court cannot sit with the judge in the Crown Court. Lay justices will not normally be present at a trial on indictment, since the *Practice Direction (Crown Court: Allocation of Business)* [1995] 1 WLR 1083 indicates that justices should not sit with a High Court judge in any case where the matter is listed for a plea of not guilty.

In those cases where justices may sit (proceedings listed for hearing by a circuit judge or a recorder and not listed for a plea of not guilty), the justices should play a full part in the decisions of the court, including the decision as to sentence (*Newby* (1984) 6 Cr App R (S) 148). In the event of disagreement, the majority view prevails (s. 73(3)). Thus, at least in theory, the justices can outvote the judge, but if an even-numbered court is evenly divided the judge has a casting vote. Also, the justices must accept directions from the judge on any questions of law relevant to a decision the court has to take (*Orpin* [1975] QB 283). The role the justices play as part of the court is the same whether their presence is optional or compulsory.

There are, if one excludes for the moment lay magistrates, five varieties of Crown Court judge:

(a) *High Court judges* Section 8(1)(a) of SCA 1981 provides that any High Court judge may sit in the Crown Court. On average, about 20 High Court judges will be sitting in the Crown Court at any one time. Normally a High Court judge asked to do Crown Court work will be one of the judges attached to the Queen's Bench Division, and will probably (but not necessarily) have gained knowledge of criminal practice during practice at the Bar.

High Court judges are asked to deal with the most serious criminal cases. The *Practice Direction (Crown Court: Allocation of Business)* [1995] 1 WLR 1083 provides a complex classification of Crown Court business for these purposes. A Class 1 offence must be tried by a Crown Court judge. These offences are treason, murder, genocide, torture, hostage-taking, an offence under the War Crimes Act 1991, an offence under the Official Secrets Acts and incitement, conspiracy or attempt to commit any of those offences. Exceptionally, a case of murder (or incitement, conspiracy or attempt to commit murder) may be tried by a circuit judge approved by the Lord Chief Justice. A Class 2 offence may be tried by a High Court judge or an approved circuit judge. The most important of these offences are manslaughter, infanticide, child destruction, rape, sexual intercourse with a girl under 13, incest with a girl under 13 and incitement, conspiracy or attempt to commit any of those offences. Offences which are neither necessarily reserved for High Court judges nor prima facie reserved for them (Class 3 and Class 4 offences) may none the less be put into a High Court judge's list if the facts alleged by the prosecution are particularly grave or a difficult issue of law is likely to arise.

(b) *Circuit judges* The office of circuit judge was created by the Courts Act 1971 (CA 1971), at the same time as the Crown Court itself. Together with recorders (see below) they handle the great bulk of Crown Court work. They also sit in the county courts, though the way a judge's time is split will vary from one to another. Like High Court judges (but unlike recorders), circuit judges are full-time judges appointed by the Queen on the Lord Chancellor's recommendation. Retirement is normally at the age of 72, although occasionally circuit judges are allowed to continue in office until they reach 75 (CA 1971, s. 17).

(c) *Recorders* Barristers or solicitors who have a 10-year Crown Court or county court qualification may be appointed to sit in the Crown Court as recorders. Again the appointment is by the Queen on the Lord Chancellor's recommendation, but the appointment is a part-time one for a certain period or for a specified number of days during the course of a year (CA 1971, s. 21(3)). When not sitting the recorder may, and usually does, revert to private practice. Retirement is at the age of 72 (CA 1971, s. 21(5)). Despite the fact that a solicitor is eligible for appointment as a recorder and is eligible to be appointed as a circuit judge after completing three years as a recorder, the great majority of circuit judges and recorders are drawn from the ranks of the Bar.

(d) *Deputy circuit judges and assistant recorders* Section 24 of CA 1971 empowers the Lord Chancellor to appoint retired Lord Justices of Appeal, retired High Court judges or retired circuit judges to act as deputy circuit judges. The Lord Chancellor may also appoint barristers or solicitors of at least 10 years' standing to act as assistant recorders. The purpose of such appointments is essentially to enable the Crown Court to cope with an unexpected rush of work or with an accumulated back-log of cases. For the period of appointment, a deputy circuit judge or an assistant recorder carries out the same functions as a circuit judge or recorder, as the case may be.

The effect of the above arrangements is that a small minority of very serious cases must be tried, or will normally be tried, by a High Court judge, while the great bulk of trials on indictment, sentencing following conviction on indictment and committals for sentence will be distributed between the other Crown Court judges as convenience dictates. Administrative staff at Crown Court locations exercise a discretion to direct the more serious and/or complicated cases towards an experienced circuit judge rather than an inexperienced assistant recorder.

More generally from the sentencing point of view, however, it is clear that even in the Crown Court an offender may be dealt with by a relatively inexperienced sentencer. This raises the question: what training do Crown Court judges receive in sentencing? The Judicial Studies Board provides training for the judiciary in the criminal field and in the civil and family jurisdictions. The Board has always given special prominence to training in matters related to sentencing. Induction seminars are now compulsory for all newly appointed assistant recorders, and refresher seminars are available for experienced circuit judges and recorders. A one-day conference, focussing primarily on sentencing, is run for all members of the full-time and part-time judiciary on each court circuit each year.

1.2.7 Sentencers in magistrates' courts

Sentence in the magistrates' courts is, of course, passed by magistrates. Most magistrates are lay men or women, often referred to as lay justices on account of their more formal title, 'justice of the peace'. 'Lay', in this context, simply means unpaid. Magistrates are entitled to an allowance for travelling and subsistence, and to compensation for loss of earnings (Justices of the Peace Act 1997, s. 10). Many lay justices are in full-time employment away from the court and so their availability to sit as justices is strictly limited. Normally magistrates are required to sit once a fortnight, but in some busy courts it may be once a week.

A small minority of magistrates, formerly known as stipendiary magistrates, but now properly described as District Judges (Magistrates' Courts), are appointed to act full-time. Unlike lay justices, district judges are qualified lawyers who are paid a salary. District judges are appointed by the Queen on the advice of the Lord Chancellor. They must be barristers or solicitors of at least seven years' standing. Provisions regarding their appointment, removal, remuneration etc. can be found in the Justices of the Peace Act 1997, ss. 10A to 10E.

For the purposes of summary trial and sentencing, a magistrates' court is duly constituted if it consists of a district judge or at least two lay justices (MCA 1980, s. 121(1)). A single lay justice cannot conduct a trial or pass sentence. Benches of three magistrates are preferable to benches of two because an uneven-numbered court is permitted to reach decisions by a majority, whereas if an even-numbered bench is split the case has to be remitted to a different bench.

The great majority of the business of the magistrates' courts is conducted by lay magistrates. They are appointed by the Lord Chancellor on the advice of local committees. Any person or organisation (e.g. a local political party) may submit to the secretary of the local advisory committee the name of a person who, in the view of the person or organisation, would make a good magistrate. The only significant category of persons to be excluded from appointment is undischarged bankrupts. Efforts are made to draw magistrates from as wide a range of ages, backgrounds, employments and ethnic groups as possible. The requirement that magistrates be available regularly for court duties which are unpaid does, however, result in a less than fully representative sample of people on the bench. Magisterial law, not least in the area of sentencing, is becoming more and more complex, and a certain intellectual standard is clearly required. At the age of 70 a magistrate in effect retires. Technically, their name is placed on the 'supplemental list', which means that, although retaining the status of justice of the peace, they cannot exercise jurisdiction. District judges also retire at 70.

A magistrate is appointed to be a justice of the peace for the county in which he or she resides (in London there are six commission areas instead of counties). The counties are divided into petty sessional divisions (PSDs), with a magistrates' court in each one. Although a magistrate could in theory sit at any court in the county, magistrates are in practice assigned to the bench for the petty sessional division in which they live or work, and they would normally only sit in that division. Bench sizes have varied considerably throughout the country. There is a trend towards larger courts, by amalgamation, for reasons of economy.

At each sitting of a magistrates' court, the magistrates are assisted by a clerk. The duties of the clerk include putting the charge to the accused, noting down the evidence, explaining the procedure of the court to a party who is not legally represented and, most importantly, advising lay magistrates on matters of law. There is usually one justices' clerk for each PSD. The clerk must be a barrister or solicitor of at least five years' standing who has served for at least five years as assistant to a justices' clerk (Justices of the Peace Act 1997, s. 43). The justices' clerk will be aided by a deputy and by assistant clerks. The justices' clerk is required to carry out a range of administrative and managerial duties (these duties have increased considerably in recent years), and may be able to sit in court only infrequently. If the assistant clerks are to act as 'clerks in court' they must have certain minimum qualifications, but they are not required to have a law degree or to be professionally qualified. Despite the relatively low formal qualifications needed to be a clerk in court, lay magistrates rely heavily on their advice. In respect of sentencing, the *Practice Direction (Justices: Clerk to Court)* [2000] 1 WLR 1886 has summarised the duties of the clerk in court. The clerk must:

> . . . provide the justices with any advice they require to properly perform their functions whether or not the justices have requested that advice, on: (a) questions of law (including ECHR jurisprudence and those matters set out in s. 2(1) of the Human Rights Act 1998); (b) questions of mixed law and fact; (c) matters of practice and procedure; (d) the range of penalties available; (e) any relevant decision of the superior courts or other guidelines; (f) other issues relevant to the matter before the court; (g) the appropriate decision making structure to be applied in any given case.

Thus the clerk will often be asked by the magistrates whether a particular form of sentence is open to the bench, or whether they have power to commit for sentence. The proper practice now is for the advice to be given in open court so that the parties can hear what is said. Sometimes the clerk is asked by the justices to retire with them when they leave to consider their decision. Case-law stresses that the clerk's task is to *advise* the magistrates on matters of sentencing law and procedure, and not to *influence* their decision on the facts. In practice, however, this sharp distinction is a rather difficult one to achieve and, in drawing to the attention of the bench any relevant sentencing guidelines, as the Practice Direction requires, the clerk may seem to be advocating a particular sentencing outcome.

When lay magistrates are appointed they undertake to complete, within one year, a course of basic training. The training is organised by the magistrates' courts committee for the relevant county or district. Although it is the function of the Lord Chancellor's Department to oversee the training of magistrates, in practice the training officer is almost always one of the justices' clerks in the county, who enjoys considerable discretion over the matters to be covered. Training falls into two stages. The first stage, which must be completed before a new magistrate is allowed to take part in court work, consists of attending court sittings as an observer, listening to talks on the nature of a magistrate's duties and reading recommended literature. During the first stage a magistrate will be told about the sentencing options at the court's disposal and the kinds of situation in which each option is appropriately used. The second stage takes place after the magistrate has begun sitting in court. New magistrates from several PSDs may join together for lectures, discussions and practical exercises. A considerable proportion of the second stage is devoted to sentencing. A common teaching technique is the sentencing exercise, where magistrates are given details of imaginary sentencing cases, divided into groups and asked to report back their views on the appropriate sentences. Discussion then follows on differences which may have emerged. There are also required visits to custodial institutions and probation service facilities. In addition to the training on sentencing just described, there will be follow-up talks and exercises in subsequent years.

1.2.8   Sentencers in youth courts

Trial in a youth court is simply a special form of summary trial, so that the sentencers in youth courts are magistrates. Not all magistrates are entitled to sit in a youth court, however. Every three years the magistrates of a PSD meet together to elect on to the youth court panel those of their number whom they consider to be especially well suited for handling cases involving juveniles (CYPA 1933, sch. 2). Only members of the youth court panel may sit in the youth court.

A youth court must consist of two or three magistrates, preferably with both sexes represented. A district judge will be a member of the local youth court panel and he or she may sit alone in a youth court. Upon election to the youth court panel a magistrate is given training in the work of that court because the training given upon appointment as a magistrate does not cover youth court work. When dealing with a juvenile offender, the magistrates do not 'convict' but 'record a finding of guilt' and, rather than 'sentencing', they 'make an order upon a finding of guilt' (CYPA 1933, s. 59). While this might be seen as an important issue of principle, nothing of practical importance turns on it.

1.3   AIMS OF SENTENCING

There has been much discussion in recent years concerning the proper aims of sentencing. Several different aims have been identified. Traditionally, sentencers were largely free to pursue the sentencing approach which seemed to them most appropriate, on a case by case basis, and there was little attempt to regulate this. Indeed it has often been argued by sentencers themselves that the formulation of sentencing policy is a matter peculiarly within the remit of the judiciary. There has been a view that sentencing is 'an art not a science', that it has to be absorbed through the experience of doing it, rather than being addressed by way of a set of principles. This approach is still adhered to by some sentencers (the very words quoted were used by a member of the Court of Appeal in *Graham* [1999] 2 Cr App R (S) 312).

There are very few discussions at appellate level about the aims of sentencing. An exception is *Sargeant* (1974) 60 Cr App R 74, where Lawton LJ took advantage of a run-of-the-mill appeal against sentence to expound what he took to be the functions of, and the justifications for, sentencing. Giving the judgment of the Court of Appeal, Lord Justice

Lawton referred to the 'classical principles of sentencing', which he said could be summed up in the four words 'retribution', 'deterrence', 'prevention' and 'rehabilitation'. The Court of Appeal, however, offered no explanation of how these aims were to be reconciled when they were in conflict with one another.

In a government White Paper, *Crime, Justice and Protecting the Public*, issued in 1990, the government addressed sentencing aims in a more systematic fashion, with the avowed purpose of achieving greater uniformity of approach amongst sentencers. The White Paper endorsed 'desert' (or retribution) as the guiding criterion in sentence selection. In making a number of clear statements on this matter, it is evident that the government intended that desert should be the dominant sentencing aim, ahead of deterrence, prevention and rehabilitation. Specifically, the White Paper was sceptical about relying upon deterrence as the basis for determining sentence. The principles in the White Paper formed the basis for the CJA 1991 but, in a number of respects, later developments have compromised the basic approach. In summer 2001 the government is expected to publish a wide ranging Review of the Sentencing Framework, and this may signal further moves away from the 1991 Act principles.

The imposition of punishment by the state will involve to one extent or another, depending on its precise nature, the imposition of hardship upon offenders. Another way of saying this is that sentences handed down by the court impose varying degrees of restriction of liberty upon offenders. Starting at the top of the range of punishments currently available to the courts in this country, custodial sentences obviously impose the most severe restrictions upon liberty. Lesser, though still significant, restrictions are involved in the various community orders. A community punishment order, for example, restricts liberty by requiring the offender to give up a proportion of leisure time to perform demanding unpaid work on a specified project of benefit to the community. A community rehabilitation order (at its most basic) requires the offender to report to a supervising officer at regular specified times, and keep the officer informed of any change of circumstances. This may seem a minimal restriction, but for an immature and disorganised individual it may impose a significant burden. Various conditions, more or less stringent, may be inserted into a community rehabilitation order by the sentencer, such as requiring the offender to undergo treatment for a mental condition or for addiction to alcohol or drugs, or to attend a centre for education, practical advice or counselling (which may be designed to force the offender to face up to his offending behaviour). These requirements can be very demanding. Even financial penalties, designed to be a tax on an offender's spare income, are restrictions on liberty in the sense that the offender is deprived of cash which he or she would much have preferred to have spent on something else. For those on low incomes a fine can be a severe penalty, and sentencers are required to ensure that an offender's means are properly taken into account whenever a fine is imposed (see Chapter 6).

Once it is agreed that sentencing involves the infliction of hardship upon offenders, in the sense of restriction of liberty, the second step is to recognise that this practice stands in need of justification. How can the infliction of punishment by the courts, acting as instruments of the state, be justified? This is a question with which philosophers have grappled for many years. Broadly, two sets of ideas have emerged. They may be described as the reductivist approach and the desert approach.

1.3.1 The reductivist approach

The reductivist approach is that the imposition of hardship through punishment is justified whenever certain benefits are achieved by that punishment, and where those benefits outweigh the hardship and make its imposition, on balance, worthwhile. This is the principle of utility, expounded by Jeremy Bentham and others. In particular, the imposition of punishment is here designed to reduce the overall incidence of offending within society. The offender is thus being used as an instrument in an effort to achieve this beneficial result.

A number of distinct approaches shelter under the reductivist umbrella, and so a sentencer might impose a reductivist sentence by following one (or a mixture) of different lines of thought. The first line is that the punishment will act to deter the person sentenced (individual deterrence), so that the person will desist from offending through fear of repetition of the penalty in future. The second line is that the punishment will deter other like-minded people (general deterrence). They will decide not to commit an offence when they see what penalty has been inflicted on the offender on this occasion for doing so. The third line is that by imposing a sentence of a particular type, such as a lengthy prison term or a driving disqualification, the offender will be prevented from committing further offences in the future (incapacitation), at least for a limited period of time. The fourth line is that the sentence handed down by the court will bring about a change of attitude (reform, rehabilitation) on the part of the offender, so that he will desist from offending in future, not through fear of further punishment, but through a deeper realisation of the anti-social nature of offending.

All these arguments are offered by reductivists as justification for the practice of punishment generally and in individual cases. While it is helpful to draw distinctions between them, and there is a very substantial legal and philosophical literature on each, it will be apparent that a sentencer might, perfectly coherently, pursue more than one of these goals at the same time when passing a single sentence. What they have in common is the attempt, by the passing of the sentence, to reduce the general level of offending in society. The reductivist objective is, at least in theory, empirically testable. It might be possible to demonstrate that the passing of a particular sentence, or a policy of sentencing in a particular way, has 'worked', in that it has achieved a net benefit in terms of the number of offences which have thereby been prevented. In practice, however, it is extremely difficult to measure the impact of a particular sentencing decision or group of decisions.

Sentencers sometimes claim that a particular form of offending has been 'stamped out' by severe deterrent sentences handed out to a few people who have offended in that way. Can such a claim be substantiated? Let us take house burglary as an example. Suppose that the official criminal statistics record a downturn for that offence in the months which follow a new practice of markedly more severe sentencing for burglary. It would be tempting to assume that the downturn was the result of the new sentencing policy. Such temptation should be resisted. For one thing, any such impact could not be measured by the official criminal statistics. These relate only to offences reported to the police and which are recorded by them. Unreported crime (a very much larger figure) is not recorded. So a decrease in reported house burglaries might conceal a real rise in the number of burglaries, or vice versa. The problem of the inadequacy of the statistics for recorded crime might in part be overcome by conducting regular victim surveys (such as the British Crime Survey) which would give a clearer picture of whether the decline in reported burglary was mirrored by a fall in the real level of such offending. Even if this could be shown to have happened, however, it would still be dubious to assume that the sentencing decision had brought about the change. The downturn may have been occasioned by some other factor, quite independent of sentencing, such as the growth of neighbourhood watch schemes, an advertising campaign for home security, a change in the economic climate of the country or simply a change in the fashions of offending. Further reflection reveals the lack of plausibility of claims that sentencing has a deterrent impact upon the real level of offending.

The argument presupposes that burglars make choices about committing burglary based upon their knowledge of current sentencing practice. This may be true in some cases and, certainly, there is an important element of rational choice in the selection of targets for house burglary, particularly by so-called professional offenders. The general picture, however, is that most burglaries are committed by young men, often after drinking, without much forward planning and with little or no consideration of penalty levels. The criminological literature tells us that many young offenders tend to 'live for the moment' and rarely plan ahead or weigh the consequences of being caught against the excitement of breaking the law. In any event a burglar sufficiently well-informed to have read the sentencing reports will also know that the police clear-up rate for house burglary is very low. Penalty levels must become even less significant to offenders when they believe that they have little or no chance of being caught.

The argument about reductivist sentencing is not, however, solely about whether it can be shown to work. Let us take the burglary example again. Suppose a Crown Court judge imposes an exceptionally severe sentence upon a burglar in an attempt to deter. There is then the issue of the injustice of imposing a sentence which is more severe than this offender deserves (in comparison with sentences which have been imposed on others for doing the same) in an attempt to achieve a general effect. The moral point is a strong one. Some people may feel that even if the sentence's effectiveness could be convincingly demonstrated, and even if it could be shown that news of the severe sentence had travelled fast and had prevented, say, ten burglaries which would otherwise have taken place, the severe sentence should still be struck down on the ground that it is unjust to the sentenced offender. The fact that all reductivist strategies rely upon using the sentence imposed on the offender as a tool to achieve a wider social impact gives rise to a further criticism of reductivist approaches: they all contain a danger that the enthusiastic pursuit of the social goals may result in grave injustice to those few offenders who are caught, prosecuted and convicted. If severe sentences, contrary to expectation, do not appear to be having the desired effect of reducing crime, then this may result in even more severe sentences.

There has been some disillusionment with reductivist sentencing goals, particularly reform and rehabilitation, because the reductivist approach, which seemed in the 1960s and 1970s to be capable of achieving those goals, has largely failed to do so. As we have seen, reductivist goals are somewhat amenable to empirical testing, and this is particularly so in the case of reform. A number of large-scale surveys which were carried out in the 1970s have been widely, though somewhat inaccurately, summarised with the dictum that 'nothing works' in fact the evidence is that rehabilitative programmes do sometimes 'work', by having a discernible impact upon the reconviction rates of those made subject to them, but often only for highly selected 'good risk' offenders (who might not have reoffended anyway), in rather specialised situations and over rather short follow-up periods. Rehabilitation has been out of fashion as the central aim of sentencing, but it remains an important element in the appropriate use of community sentences and in the educational and training opportunities which ideally ought to be available as part of a custodial sentence. More recently there has been a considerable reawakening of interest in the efficacy of rehabilitative programmes with the government investing large sums in a new 'what works' programme for both community and custodial sentencing, but the reductivist goal which has attained most prominence in recent years is that of offender incapacitation. The CJA 1991, although having desert as its principal approach, also permits custody to be used, and longer-than-normal sentences to be imposed, on offenders convicted of violent or sexual crimes who appear to represent a serious risk to the public. It is incapacitation as a sentencing goal which leads to the promotion of electronic monitoring of offenders, and it was this objective which former Home Secretary Michael Howard had in mind when he insisted that 'Prison works'. The policy has produced the so-called 'three strikes' laws in the United States and has been influential in the introduction of the presumptive minimum sentences in the Crime (Sentences) Act 1997. Of course it is true that, for the period of incapacitation, reoffending by the offender is minimised, but claims in the United States that 'selective incapacitation' of high-risk offenders will have a significant impact on crime rates have so far promised much more than they have delivered. There are also substantial ethical questions about incapacitation which do not admit of easy answers. The main problem is that incapacitative sentencing requires a prediction to be made by the sentencer about the offender's future lawbreaking, on the basis of reports about him and what he has done in the past. Such predictions are, however, unreliable, with research evidence suggesting that risk assessments are, at best, as likely to be wrong as they are to be right.

We can perhaps say of those who adhere to reductivist sentencing strategies that they do so often in the absence of convincing empirical evidence, and sometimes in the face of considerable ethical doubts. On the other hand, sentencers want to see some beneficial results from the sentences handed down by the courts. Punishment in itself seems rather backward-looking and negative, whereas reductive strategies at least seem to offer ways of making the world a better or safer place in which to live. To abandon reductivist sentencing goals, then, may seem to make sentencing a more mechanical, or even pointless, exercise and reductivist views may be (and are) strongly held by many sentencers.

1.3.2   The desert approach

A second view can be set in contrast to the reductivist one. The desert approach to sentencing emphasises the moral requirement of maintaining a proper proportion between offence and punishment. It states that punishment involves censuring the offender for his wrongful behaviour. Thus the prime determinant of sentencing should be to ensure that the punishment imposed is that which is deserved for the offence, having regard to the seriousness of the harm caused or risked by the offender and the degree of the offender's culpability. It should be understood that, in contrast to the various reductivist approaches, desert principles do not require that sentencing practice should affect overall crime levels. Although desert theorists would, of course, welcome any reduction in the incidence of crime generally, desert theory treats the sentencing of offenders as an issue distinct from tackling the roots of offending in the community. The view is that the 'crime problem' in society can and should be tackled by a combination of strategies including economic policy, social policy, housing policy, environmental design and education, but only to a rather limited extent through sentencing practice.

Desert theory has, at its heart, proportionality between the seriousness of the offence and the severity of the penalty imposed. This sounds a simple idea and, in some ways and in general terms, it is. But the working out of desert theory in the kind of rigorous and detailed way which is required in a complex sentencing system, such as that in England and Wales, brings with it considerable difficulty. 'Seriousness' is an elusive idea. What makes one offence more serious than another? A good starting point would be the kind of harm, and the amount of harm, occasioned to the victim. If the victim's life is taken that is clearly more serious than if the victim is injured but survives. That, in turn, is more serious than a case where the victim suffers only loss of property, or is merely inconvenienced or distressed by the offence. Various empirical studies of the public's perception of the relative seriousness of various crimes display a fair degree of consensus.

Most people would agree that robbery is a more serious offence than theft. Indeed the legal definitions of the two crimes tell us that robbery is an aggravated form of theft: theft with the use of force or fear. But further reflection reveals that not all robberies are more serious than all thefts. A bag snatch involving minimal force and the loss of little of value would be regarded by most people as less serious than the theft of £1 million from a bank. Many existing criminal offences describe criminal conduct in rather broad terms, and offences overlap with each other. This makes it difficult to draw up a hierarchy of offences for sentencing. One response might be to have more subdivision of existing offences. This subdivision need not be recognised in formal criminal law, but it could become accepted that a particular offence contained within it two or three seriousness bands, which should be kept distinct for sentencing purposes. As we will see, the offence of burglary is now formally divided for sentencing purposes into two: burglary of dwellings and burglary of other buildings, such as offices or shops. This distinction in relative seriousness was developed through courts' sentencing practice and only later reflected in legislation by the creation of different maximum sentences for the two forms of the offence (see **12.4.5**). There are other complications. One victim may suffer substantially more, or substantially less, harm from a crime than might have been expected. An elderly person, for example, might incur considerable hardship and distress from a house burglary from which a more resilient, and perhaps better insured, person would recover relatively quickly. How far should this differential impact affect our assessment of crime seriousness?

There is more to seriousness of crime than the harm incurred by the victim. The culpability of the offender is also of great importance. Criminal law *mens rea* terms such as intention, recklessness and negligence may play a further role here, but the offender's responsibility for the offence requires a fuller analysis at the sentencing stage. Sentencers distinguish a carefully planned crime from one committed on the spur of the moment, and between the ringleader in the offence and others who played a lesser role. Weight is given to other factors, such as provocation before the offence, and some regard can be given to the pressures which the offender may have been under at the time of the crime which, while not excusing it, may place what happened in a fuller and more revealing context. A further important point is that the two elements of crime seriousness, harm and culpability, do not operate independently. Each impinges on the other. To return to the earlier example, if the elderly victim of a burglary suffers very greatly, that may affect our view of the crime, but if it turns out that the offender targeted the house because he *knew* the householder was elderly, that may well affect it again. What is clear is that desert principles in sentencing force us to think in a systematic way about the relative seriousness of crime (both when comparing one category of offence with another, and one instance of an offence compared with a different instance).

Offence seriousness is on one side of the scale. On the other side is penalty severity. Again, most people would agree that five years' imprisonment is a more severe sentence than a community punishment order of 100 hours. But devising a scale of penalties in terms of severity is beset with difficulties just as acute as those of comparing the seriousness of offences. Penalties are very different. How can one compare imprisonment with a community rehabilitation order or a fine? A useful starting point is to gauge all the various sentences in terms of their relative impact upon the average offender, or perhaps the extent to which they can be expected to impinge upon and restrict the average offender's liberty. This rough kind of scaling amongst sentences has always been part of the sentencing system in England and Wales, and it formed the basis of the description of the various sentencing powers available to the courts which was given earlier in this chapter. It is referred to in some of the texts on sentencing as the sentencing 'tariff', reflecting, in a rather non-specific way, that more serious offences require more severe penalties. The traditional picture of sentencing is more complex than this, however. First, there is a degree of ambiguity about the meaning of the 'tariff'. Sometimes the term has been used to mean that an offender should progress up the sentencing ladder in the event of offence repetition. Thus a burglar who was sentenced to a community sentence last time he was convicted of burglary must expect to receive something more severe if he reoffends. This approach, however, has much more to do with reductivist ideas of sentencing than with desert principles. Secondly, some of the available sentences have traditionally not been regarded as punishments at all. The community rehabilitation (in its former title, probation) order is a clear example. CRO was not regarded as occupying any particular place in the tariff. Indeed, until the CJA 1991 it was not strictly in law a 'punishment' or 'sentence' at all. It was an individualised measure addressed to the offender's needs, rather than to the seriousness of the offence. The strongly reductivist base of community sentences such as the CRO led probation officers to urge them upon sentencers in their pre-sentence reports as being 'alternatives to custody', likely to produce a more beneficial (or at least less harmful) effect than imprisonment.

The apparent failure of rehabilitation to deliver on the promise it seemed to offer in the 1970s was mentioned earlier in this chapter. At around the same time in the United States there emerged other concerns about reductivist goals in sentencing, which prompted a resurgence of interest in the principle of desert. The main concern was that, in the pursuit of reductivist goals, sentencers were imposing long and often indeterminate custodial terms. The new desert movement protested at the injustice of incarcerating offenders for periods of time which bore no relationship to the seriousness of the offence which they had committed. In the wake of the American developments, and for similar reasons, many other countries have re-thought their sentencing principles. There have been important initiatives in Canada, Australia and several European countries, including Sweden and Eire.

In England and Wales, as we have seen, comparable changes were signalled by the CJA 1991. The best way of understanding that Act is to see it as laying down a basic framework for sentencing. It dealt with custodial sentences, community sentences, fines, and discharges and other measures, and these, as now consolidated into the PCC(S)A 2000, should be seen as occupying more or less distinct levels in the sentencing scheme, with custodial sentences at the top and discharges at the bottom. Selection of the appropriate sentence is dependent, first and foremost, on the seriousness of the offence committed. A diagram representing the sentencing framework is set out at figure 1 on p. 52, and that framework is the subject of Chapter 2.

There have been numerous legislative developments in sentencing since the 1991 Act, although the framework remains basically intact. These changes are dealt with where appropriate in this book, but it may be helpful to summarise the main ones here. The CJA 1993 represented something of a reversal of policy in sentencing after the 1991 Act. The 1993 Act abolished the system of 'unit fines' in magistrates' courts which had been introduced by the 1991 Act, and it also recast s. 29 of that Act, which dealt with the relevance to offence seriousness of the offender's previous convictions or his failure to respond to previous sentences. This issue is discussed at **2.2.5**. The Criminal Justice and Public Order Act 1994 made a number of important changes to sentencing provision. It placed on a statutory footing the circumstances in which a court should take account of an offender's guilty plea, it substituted a revised definition of 'sexual offence' in the 1991 Act, and relaxed the requirement that a pre-sentence report should be obtained before imposing a custodial sentence or certain community sentences. That CJPOA 1994 also lowered the age at which a sentence of long-term detention could be passed on a juvenile, from 14 to

10, and increased the maximum sentence of detention in a young offender institution which could be imposed on a 15, 16 or 17-year-old from 12 months to 24 months. The CJPOA 1994 introduced a new custodial sentence for juvenile offender, the secure training order. Powers to make these orders, however, became available only in 1998, and they were repealed shortly thereafter. Further important changes were occasioned by the Crime (Sentences) Act 1997. These were the introduction of an 'automatic' life sentence for the second serious offence committed by the offender (such offences being defined and set out in the Act), a presumptive minimum sentence of seven years for the third Class A drug trafficking offence, and a presumptive minimum sentence of three years for the third 'domestic burglary'. The first two of these three sections came into force in October 1997, but implementation of the burglary provision was delayed until December 1999. The 1997 Act also abolished the requirement that the offender should consent to the imposition of a range of community orders, including probation and community service. The Crime and Disorder Act 1998 introduced a new custodial sentence for young offenders, the detention and training order. This sentence replaced the secure training order and the sentence of detention in a young offender institution for offenders aged under 18. Two new community sentences were introduced, the drug treatment and testing order and the action plan order, together with a further non-custodial sentence for juveniles, the reparation order. The Act also placed a specific duty on the Court of Appeal to issue new sentencing guidelines and revise existing ones, and it established the Sentencing Advisory Panel to advise and assist the Court in that task.

In the year 2000, as a result of a Law Commission project, the 1991 Act framework and nearly all of the above changes to sentencing legislation since that date were consolidated into one statute — the Powers of Criminal Court (Sentencing) Act 2000. Most sentencing provisions, especially as they affect the Crown Court, can now be found in that single statute, which is a great improvement over the previous situation where sentencing provisions were widely scattered. Any hope that this consolidation would signal an end to sentencing change was soon dashed, however. The Criminal Justice and Court Services Act 2000 amended the consolidation statute in a number of significant ways, and introduced further changes. The most important is the projected abolition of the sentence of detention in a young offender institution for the remaining group of young offenders to whom it applied, the 18, 19 and 20-year-olds. At the time of writing, this amendment has not been brought into force, but when it is offenders in this age group will become eligible for imprisonment (and, by implication, suspended sentences of imprisonment). This is an important change because it brings to an end the traditional sentencing demarcation of 'young adult offenders' from those aged 21 and over. The CJCSA 2000 also made rather pointless changes to the names of well established community sentences — the probation order became a community rehabilitation order, the community service order became a community punishment order, and the combination order became a community punishment and rehabilitation order.

FIGURE 1
OUTLINE OF THE SENTENCING SCHEME

CUSTODIAL SENTENCES

Imprisonment (21 +)*

Detention in a young offender institution (18–20)**

Detention and training order (12–17)

Detention under PCC(S)A 2000, s. 91 (10–17)

↑   **CUSTODY THRESHOLD** : 'so serious'   ↑
offence seriousness (s. 79(2)(a))
or
public protection following conviction for violent
or sexual offence (s. 79(2)(b))

COMMUNITY SENTENCES	FINES
CPRO (16+)	
CPO (16+)	
Drug treatment and testing (16+)	
CRO (16+)	
Curfew order (10+)	
Attendance centre order (10–20)	all age
Supervision order (10–17)	groups
Action plan order (10-17)	

↑ **COMMUNITY SENTENCE**
THRESHOLD
'serious enough' (s. 6(1))

NON-CUSTODIAL SENTENCES

Reparation order (10–17)

Bind over (all age groups)

Discharge (all age groups)

---

*Reduced to 18 + when the CJCSA 2000, s. 61 is brought into force.
**Sentence abolished when the CJCSA 2000, s. 61 is brought into force.

SERIOUSNESS OF OFFENCE ↑

2 Sentencing Law and Sentencing Principles

2.1 HOW SHOULD THE SENTENCER ARRIVE AT THE SENTENCE?

This entire book could be regarded as an explanation of how a sentencer arrives at the sentence. Yet by outlining, at this early stage, the major factors which should govern the sentencer's decision in a particular case, it will be possible to set in context the detailed discussion of sentencing procedure, powers and policy which follow in later chapters.

It is helpful to think of a sentencer asking himself or herself a sequence of four questions (see **2.1.1** to **2.1.4**):

2.1.1 Is the sentence for the offence fixed by law?

If statute prescribes a mandatory sentence for the offence of which the offender has just been convicted, the sentencer's task is simple. The sentence fixed by law is pronounced. Sentence is so fixed in very few cases.

(a) For murder, the sentence must be one of life imprisonment (or detention at Her Majesty's pleasure, depending upon the age of the offender). The sentence for murder is considered at **4.5.2**, where the sentencer's retention of a degree of influence over a murderer's eventual release date is explained.

(b) The PCC(S)A 2000, s. 109, requires the Crown Court to impose a life sentence where an offender has been convicted of a second 'serious offence' as defined in the Act. Where an offender has been convicted for the third time of a Class A drug trafficking offence, s. 110 requires the Crown Court to impose a custodial sentence of seven years or more and, where an offender has been convicted for the third time of a domestic burglary, s. 111 requires the Crown Court to impose a custodial sentence of three years or more. However, none of these sentences is truly a 'mandatory' sentence, in that the court has a discretion to pass a different sentence if it finds that there are 'exceptional circumstances' in a case falling under s. 109 and, in a case falling under s. 110 or s. 111, it need not impose the prescribed sentence if there are 'specific circumstances' which would render such a sentence unjust.

Statutes empowering the courts to deal with offenders by some means other than imprisonment often use a form of words to the effect that the sentence may be imposed for any offence not being an offence the sentence for which is fixed by law or which falls to be imposed under ss. 109–111 of the 2000 Act. This formula makes explicit the fact that the sentencing power is not available to the court in the cases just described.

2.1.2   What powers are at the court's disposal?

Assuming that sentence is not fixed by law, the sentencer considers the sentencing options which are at the court's disposal. This exercise can raise numerous sub-questions, such as 'What is the maximum penalty for the offence permitted by law?', 'What is the offender's age?' and 'Have reports on the offender been prepared?' Magistrates must bear in mind the special restrictions on the sentencing powers of magistrates' courts to impose custody (see **4.1**) or to impose a fine (see **6.1**). A Crown Court judge dealing with an offender on a committal for sentence should ascertain the particular statutory provision under which the committal took place, for in some cases the Crown Court's powers are limited to those which the magistrates would have had if they had not committed for sentence.

As to the maximum penalties available, if the offence is statutory the relevant statute will specify the longest term of imprisonment which may be imposed or, by not referring to imprisonment, shows that the offence is non-imprisonable. Common law offences are punishable with imprisonment for life (i.e. the judge may pass a life sentence or may impose the appropriate fixed-term sentence or some lesser punishment). Offenders under 21 may not be sentenced to imprisonment. All offences (apart from murder) and offenders of any age may be dealt with by way of a fine. If the offence is summary, the statute creating it specifies the maximum amount of the fine: if it is indictable the potential fine is unlimited. All this is subject to the restrictions on the powers of magistrates to fine and the special rules relating to the fining of juveniles. For maximum penalties see Table 1 on pp. 7–14. The availability of other forms of sentence depends primarily upon the age of the offender, and upon whether the offence of which the offender has been convicted is imprisonable (i.e. punishable with imprisonment in the case of an adult).

The matters mentioned above are covered in detail in later chapters, and the courts' sentencing powers are conveniently summarised in Table 2 on pp. 15–32. The main point to appreciate here is that the maximum penalty available for an offence in the Crown Court is usually well in excess of anything the sentencer would wish to impose, except in a very small batch of cases where the offender's crime is just about the most serious of its type.

2.1.3   How serious is the offence?

Given that the sentencer is unlikely to want to pass the maximum sentence, the next question is: what level of sentence would properly reflect the seriousness of the offence? It is very difficult to define 'seriousness' in the abstract, and no attempt is made to do so in existing sentencing law. It is of great importance, however, for the sentencer to gauge the seriousness of one offence in relation to another, and to distinguish within each offence, for example one case of burglary from another case of burglary. Distinctions also need to be drawn between the respective roles played by co-defendants in a particular case. This is a demanding task for the sentencer, but it is central to the sentencing decision. It is perhaps not so difficult as it might sound. In assessing seriousness, the sentencer should have regard to the immediate circumstances of the offence, and the degree of the offender's culpability in relation to that offence. Sentencers are not entirely on their own in this task. They do not need to start from a blank sheet in every case. They will derive guidance on the assessment of offence seriousness, particularly where sentence is being imposed in the Crown Court, from the guideline judgments of the Court of Appeal and, where sentence is being imposed by magistrates, from the Magistrates' Association Guidelines (2000) and, perhaps, guidelines and norms produced by the particular bench. This guidance relates to sentencing for particular offences, and is set out where appropriate in Chapter 12, which deals with sentencing for a range of individual crimes.

In determining the seriousness of the offence, the sentencer must always take into account any aggravating or mitigating factors which impinge upon the question of offence seriousness. Some of the factors apply across a range of offences. An example of a factor which tends to make an offence more serious is where the offender has committed the offence in 'breach of trust'. This has relevance in theft and deception offences, for example where a senior employee abuses his position of responsibility to embezzle funds or provide an outside team of offenders with a key to the stockroom. It also has relevance in sexual offences, for example where a schoolteacher or a social worker abuses that position of authority to commit a sexual offence on a child. An example of a general factor which tends to make an offence less serious is where there was provocation immediately before the offence. This factor may be relevant in a range of offences against the person or against public order. There are other factors which are relevant to seriousness in a more restricted range of offending. Thus, if the offence is one involving dishonesty, the court, as well as considering any breach of trust, will also be influenced by matters such as whether the offence was carefully planned or was committed on impulse, the value of the property involved and whether any, or how much, of it has been recovered. If the offence is one of violence, the court will be influenced by the severity of the injuries caused to the victim, the extent to which the victim has recovered, the offender's intention (or lack of it) to cause serious injury and the nature of the weapon (if any) which was used. By weighing up such factors as these, the sentencer will be able to reach a view on offence seriousness, and hence a provisional view on the appropriate sentence. According to the CJA 1991 (and now the PCC(S)A 2000), offence seriousness is the key factor in determining whether the sentence will be a financial, community or custodial penalty. As we shall see, it is also a crucial factor in determining the size of the fine, the nature of the community sentence and the duration of any period of incarceration.

2.1.4 What personal mitigation is there?

The final matter for the sentencer's consideration is whether there are matters of mitigation personal to the offender which it is appropriate to take into account, even though these do not impinge upon the seriousness of the offence as such. Commonly encountered examples are where the sentencer gives credit for the offender's guilty plea, or the offender's clean (or nearly clean) criminal record. There are many other mitigating factors which may be considered, in the court's discretion. Information about the offender's personal circumstances might emerge from the facts of the offence, from the pre-sentence report or from the plea in mitigation advanced by the defence.

2.1.5 Consideration of the questions together

Of course a sentencer does not actually jump through the hoops of answering each of the above questions every time sentence is passed. The question at **2.1.1** is so basic that it answers itself. The question at **2.1.2** will, at least where an experienced Crown Court judge is concerned, require little more consideration, though it should not be thought that mistakes over the court's powers are never made. Sentencing law has become much more voluminous and complex in recent years, and there have been many changes, so that mistakes are perhaps not infrequent. The Court of Appeal has said on several occasions recently that it is the duty of counsel to correct the sentencer if it looks as if a mistake is about to be made. If nobody notices the error until after sentence is passed, but it emerges later, the court has 28 days in which to rectify it and re-sentence. A lay bench of magistrates will often need help from their clerk as to their available powers.

The questions posed at **2.1.3** and **2.1.4** are the difficult ones. Many sentencers in the past would not have separated them, but would have asked themselves something like: what is the range or bracket of sentences generally considered by the courts to be appropriate for persons of a background and character similar to those of this offender, who have committed offences roughly similar to that committed by him? From that range the sentencer would then select the sentence, influenced by his own personal attitude towards the aims of sentencing, and by the impression which defence mitigation makes on him on the day. The two-stage approach, of determining the penalty appropriate to the gravity of the offence, and then reducing it to allow for mitigation which is not related to the offence was, however, advocated by the Court of Appeal in *Fraser* (1982) 4 Cr App R (S) 254. Its great advantage is to emphasise that the sentence should not be out of proportion to the gravity of the crime for which the offender is being sentenced, however appalling the offender's character and record might be. Thus good character and other meritorious aspects of the offender's life which are placed before the court might serve to mitigate the sentence but his bad character should not aggravate it.

2.2   THE STATUTORY FRAMEWORK OF SENTENCING

The outline of the process by which the sentencer should approach the sentencing decision given above is based upon the statutory framework for sentencing decisions laid down in the CJA 1991 (and now the PCC(S)A 2000). It is now time to say something more about that framework.

2.2.1   The key concept of offence seriousness

Figure 1 on p. 52 is an attempt to represent in pictorial form the sentencing structure which is currently in place. It tries to show the way in which the groups of criminal penalties are now related to each other. It will be seen that these groups are related more or less hierarchically, with custodial sentences at the apex and community sentences immediately below. At the lower levels are fines and discharges. The PCC(S)A 2000 requires that (with an exception relating to violent offences and sexual offences) a custodial sentence can be imposed only where the offence committed by the offender is 'so serious that only such a sentence can be justified' (s. 79(2)(a)). This makes it clear that custodial sentences should be reserved for the most serious crimes, and that on every occasion when a sentencer is considering using custody he must ask himself whether 'only such a sentence can be justified': in other words that no lesser penalty, such as a community order, will do. The exception referred to above, that a sentencer may impose custody where the offender has committed a sexual offence or a violent offence, requires that 'only such a sentence would be adequate to protect the public from serious harm from him' (s. 79(2)(b)). The 2000 Act also provides that a sentencer must justify the imposition of a community sentence (rather than something less severe) and the criterion here is that the offence committed by the offender is 'serious enough to justify such a sentence' (s. 35(1)). This makes it clear that community sentences should be reserved for that 'middle band' of offending which is serious enough to justify that approach but which is not so serious that the only possible sentence is a custodial one. The sentencing hierarchy is, then, primarily fixed by offence seriousness. It is offence seriousness which mainly determines the outcome at both the 'custody threshold' and the 'community sentence threshold'. The provisions relating to community sentences are described in more detail in Chapter 5. Fines and other non-custodial sentences are dealt with in Chapters 6 and 7, respectively.

When the sentencer is determining the seriousness of the offence, he is obliged by s. 81(4) to 'take into account all such information as is available to him about the circumstances of the offence (including any aggravating or mitigating factors)'. This must be done whenever the sentencer is considering the imposition of a custodial sentence (s. 81(4)) or a community sentence (s. 36(1)). It should be noted that the language of the Act in this respect is mandatory, and imposes a *duty* upon the sentencer to give proper weight to factors relevant to offence seriousness. In addition, and by contrast, s. 158(1) states that nothing shall prevent the court having regard to any other matters in mitigation which are personal to the offender. Such matters will not relate to the seriousness of the offence, as such.

A sentencer might be expected to take into account a range of factors as being relevant to the seriousness of an offence. It is not possible (and it would be rather tedious to try) to give an exhaustive list. What follows is an outline of what the sentencing cases indicate to be the most important of these matters. Importance in this context can be measured both in terms of the range of offences to which they may be regarded as relevant, and to the extent of their likely impact upon sentence levels.

2.2.2   Factors which aggravate offence seriousness

(a)   *Where the victim is especially vulnerable*   It is widely accepted that where the offender has taken advantage of a relatively helpless person (i.e., someone very young, very old or handicapped) this aggravates the seriousness of the offence. An example is *Allen* (1988) 10 Cr App R (S) 466, where a custodial sentence of six years was upheld on offenders who robbed an 82-year-old woman in her own home. Another type of case is where confidence tricksters take advantage of elderly people to overcharge them for work done. An example is *Richards* (1989) 11 Cr App R (S) 286, where Hutchison J said that 'where victims selected are elderly or for some other reason vulnerable' offenders can expect custody 'despite youth or good character'. An issue of principle here is whether the offence is only to be regarded as aggravated where it can be shown that the offender actually knew that the victim was vulnerable, and had targeted him or her for that reason, or whether the offence is also aggravated when, say, an elderly householder suffers severe nervous shock when confronting a burglar in her home. It seems not unreasonable to take the view that any burglar may be assumed to know that victims may suffer distress, and must take the consequences of a greater than average degree of injury resulting from the offence. The Court of Appeal guideline case on house burglary, *Brewster* [1998] 1 Cr App R (S) 181, draws no sharp distinctions here, but it can safely be assumed that the offence is at its worst when a victim was targeted because of their vulnerability.

There is a category of people whose employment puts them in a position where they are more likely to be the victims of assault than the average person. Where persons such as police officers, taxi drivers, traffic wardens, late-night bus drivers and landlords of licensed premises are the victims of crime, this is often regarded by the courts as enhancing the seriousness of the offence. In *Tremlett* (1983) 5 Cr App R (S) 199 Kenneth Jones J said that 'What very substantially increases the seriousness of these offences is that they were directed towards a bus conductor doing his ordinary job on a bus shortly after midnight'. In *Robertson* (1990) 12 Cr App R (S) 278 the Court of Appeal observed that traffic wardens 'deserve the protection of the courts in carrying out their sometimes unpopular duties'. In *Rankin* (1993) 14 Cr App R (S) 636 the Court said that 'cab drivers are recognised as being vulnerable to attack and . . . sentences upon those who attack cab drivers have to reflect their vulnerability'.

(b) *Breach of trust* This is a key aggravating factor. It is encountered in two main contexts.

First, it arises in sexual offences, where an offender has taken advantage of a person for whose care they were responsible. In *Usher* (1980) 2 Cr App R (S) 123 a schoolteacher, aged 30, was convicted of two counts of unlawful sexual intercourse and one of abduction of a pupil, aged 14, with whom he had formed an association. The Court of Appeal said that a custodial sentence was inevitable in this case and that 'it has to be made clear to persons occupying similar positions of trust, and to the parents of girls who are the recipients of that trust, that an abuse of it will receive stern treatment from the courts'. Many similar comments in later cases can be found. See, for example, *B* [1997] 2 Cr App R (S) 96, where the sexual offences were committed on a vulnerable child and 'were in gross breach of trust', and *Baker* (1989) 11 Cr App R (S) 513.

Secondly, it is relevant in offences of dishonesty, where a person has taken advantage of his office or employment to abuse trust which has been reposed in him. In *Dawson* (1987) 9 Cr App R (S) 248, when upholding a custodial sentence for theft of £64,000 by a stockbroker but reducing it from four years to three years for other reasons, Stephen Brown LJ said that breaches of trust 'undermine public confidence, because the matters of financial dealing with which this man was involved cannot be carried out unless confidence is reposed in those who carry out these transactions on behalf of members of the public'. For the guideline decision on theft in breach of trust see *Barrick* (1985) 7 Cr App R (S) 143 and **12.4.1**.

(c) *Premeditation and professionalism* This aggravating factor suggests that, where the offence was committed after careful planning and/or by an offender experienced in perpetrating such offences, the offender's culpability is very high. The carefully planned offence stands at the other end of the scale of seriousness from offences which are committed on the spur of the moment and in response to immediate temptation (see **2.2.3**). A good contrast is between 'one-off' cases of pickpocketing, which are almost always dealt with by way of a fine or a conditional discharge, and carefully planned campaigns of pickpocketing (see *Tillett* (1987) 9 Cr App R (S) 411). A similar distinction is drawn in practice in shoplifting. See the cases discussed at **12.4.1**.

Planned offending may betoken the 'professional' offender, i.e. one who is committed to a criminal way of life, rather than one who drifts in and out of law-breaking. The fact that an offence is committed in the course of so-called organised crime is clearly an aggravating factor, but one problem of focussing on 'professionalism' as an aggravating factor in sentencing is that it is often difficult to distinguish it from simple persistence in offending. The conduct of the petty persistent offender lacks the elements of seriousness which characterise the professional, but it is unclear precisely when the sentencer may draw an inference from the pattern of an offender's criminal history that he displays the aggravating element of professionalism.

(d) *Gratuitous violence and injury* Where an offender has deliberately caused harm over and above that which is normally intrinsic in the commission of the particular offence, this is regarded as an aggravating feature of the case. In giving sentencing guidelines for rape in *Billam* (1986) 8 Cr App R (S) 48, for example, Lord Lane CJ indicated that in any case where violence was used over and above the force necessary to commit the rape, or where a weapon was used, or where the victim was subjected to sexual indignities apart from the fact of the rape, all those matters would aggravate the offence significantly. See further **12.3.1**. Such aggravating factors can also be identified in relation to the various types of assault, such as where the offender kicks and inflicts further injury on a victim who is already on the ground and is unable to defend himself. In *Ivey* (1981) 3 Cr App R (S) 185 Griffiths LJ said that 'The degree of injury likely to be caused by kicking a man in the head when he is down is of a wholly different degree to that which is likely to be suffered in the course of a fist fight.' Gratuitous violence and injury was at its worst in *Legge* (1988) 10 Cr App R (S) 208, where the offender forced the victim to remove his clothes before beating and kicking him, stabbing him in the leg and urinating on him. In that case a sentence of seven years' imprisonment was upheld. The matter is also relevant in house burglary, where ransacking, soiling and gratuitous damage in the house all make the offence more serious (*Brewster* [1998] 1 Cr App R(S) 181).

(e) *Group offending* Where an offence is committed by several people acting together, this is often regarded as a matter which aggravates the seriousness of the offence. This issue is most prominent in public order offences, where the offence label itself may well reflect the group nature of the offending. In *Rogers-Hinks* (1989) 11 Cr App R (S) 234, a sentence of eight years' imprisonment was upheld on an offender who took a leading part in inciting a disturbance by football supporters on a North Sea ferry. Fighting lasted for 45 minutes, damage to the value of £24,000 was caused, property worth a further £6,000 was stolen, and many passengers were put in fear. For other examples see **12.6.3**. The level of public fear generated by group offending is highly significant here, and group dynamics may lead to greater harm or damage being caused.

(f) *Offending whilst on bail* In *Baverstock* [1993] 1 WLR 202 it was established that where the offence had been committed while the offender was on bail awaiting trial for another offence, that factor should be regarded as aggravating the later offence. Section 151(2) of the PCC(S)A 2000 now provides: 'In considering the seriousness of an offence committed while the offender was on bail, the court shall treat the fact that it was committed in those circumstances as an aggravating factor.' This provision is expressed in mandatory terms, but it has to be set against a further rule which states that consecutive sentences should be given for offences which are linked in this way. See further on this, **4.4.4**.

(g) *Offence prevalence* It is possible to find comments in sentencing cases that the prevalence of an offence may justify an increased sentence, or that severe sentencing for a particular type of offence is appropriate in an area where it is presenting a special problem, on grounds of general deterrence. An example is *Bennett* (1995) 16 Cr App R (S) 438 ('joyriding' by juvenile offenders). In *Masagh* (1990) 12 Cr App R (S) 568, however, a case dealing with pickpocketing, Lloyd LJ doubted whether prevalence should be taken into account. In *Cunningham* [1993] 1 WLR 183, Lord Taylor CJ said that prevalence of a particular form of offending, and public concern about such offences, would be regarded as an aggravating factor when sentencing for an example of such an offence. His lordship gave the example of violent sexual attacks being prevalent in a particular neighbourhood. Each such offence, he said, affects not only the immediate victim, but women generally in that area, putting them in fear and limiting their freedom of movement. Accordingly, in such circumstances, the sentence commensurate with the seriousness of the offence may need to be higher than had the offence taken place elsewhere. The point was restated in *Cox* [1993] 1 WLR 188. In fact, his lordship's comments may have less to do with prevalence as such, and more to do with the need for sentencing to reflect levels of community concern about a form of offending.

(h)   *Racially motivated offending*   The Court of Appeal has said in the past on several occasions that where an offence is shown to have been racially motivated that is an important aggravating feature of the offence. Examples are *A-G's References (Nos. 29, 30 and 31 of 1994)* (1994) 16 Cr App R (S) 698, and *Craney* [1996] 2 Cr App R (S) 336. The Magistrates' Association Guidelines (2000) make the same point. Parliament has now taken a hand in this area, and the PCC(S)A 2000, s. 153(1) states that if an offence is racially aggravated the court must treat that as a factor which increases the seriousness of the offence. The section further requires that the court must state in open court that the offence was so aggravated (s. 153(2)). In this context 'racial aggravation', as defined in the CDA 1998, s. 28, may take the form either of racial motivation or the demonstration towards the victim of hostility based on their membership of a racial group. In *Morrison* [2001] 1 Cr App R (S) 12 the Court of Appeal said that the appropriate additional punishment to reflect racial aggravation would depend on all the circumstances, but in that case approved the enhancement by two years of a nominal sentence of four and a half years for burglary committed in circumstances of racial aggravation. Section 153 is of general application in sentencing, except that it does not apply when the court is passing sentence for one of the specific 'racially aggravated offences' which were created by the CDA 1998. These are certain racially aggravated assaults, racially aggravated criminal damage, certain racially aggravated public order offences, and racially aggravated harassment. These offences all carry higher maximum penalties than their equivalent non-aggravated form (see the Table at pp. 7–14 above). In *Saunders* [2000] 2 Cr App R (S) 71, a case of racially aggravated actual bodily harm, Rose LJ said that '. . . [R]acism must not be allowed to flourish . . . The courts must do all they can, in accordance with Parliament's recently expressed intention, to convey that message clearly by the sentences which they pass in relation to racially aggravated offences'. His lordship indicated that it would be helpful if a sentencer dealing with a racially aggravated offence under the CDA 1998 considered what the appropriate sentence would have been in the absence of the racial aggravation, and then added a further term, bearing in mind the enhancement to the maximum penalty which Parliament had provided. Even if the basic offence would not have crossed the custody threshold, the aggravated offence might well do so. The Sentencing Advisory Panel proposed to the Court that it should issue sentencing guidelines on racial aggravation, both in respect of the specific racially aggravated offences under the CDA 1998, and more generally under the PCC(S)A 2000, s. 153, and the Court adopted (in part) the Panel's advice in *Kelly and Donnelly* [2001] Crim LR 411.

2.2.3   Factors which mitigate offence seriousness

(a)   *Offender has acted under provocation*   While provocation is recognised in English law as a partial defence to murder (reducing that crime to manslaughter), in respect of all other offences it is relevant solely as a matter in mitigation. It is widely accepted offender's culpability for, say, an assault, may be significantly affected by his received provocation before the act was committed. A sudden and impulsive violent r‿‿tion is regarded as less blameworthy than planned retaliation. The strength of the evidence of the provocation, of course, varies from case to case. In *Haley* (1983) 5 Cr App R (S) 9 the offender was a man of 45 and was of previous good character. He learned that, while he had been ill in hospital, his wife had formed an association with another man. The offender went to the man's house and, when he answered the door, he stabbed him four times. A sentence of three years' imprisonment was reduced to 18 months on a 'mild, inoffensive and unspectacular man suddenly . . . overwhelmed by circumstances and driven to do something which is wildly out of character' (per Lord Lane CJ). Another example is *Brookin* (1995) 16 Cr App R (S) 78 where the victim had attacked the offender's girlfriend and taunted him before the offender struck him. A custodial sentence was suspended in the light of the provocation. Where provocation is used as a mitigating factor, rather than as a partial defence to murder, it is more loosely interpreted by the courts and shades into cases where the offender has acted against a background of emotional stress.

(b) *Offender has acted under duress* Duress is a defence recognised in English law, but it is tightly circumscribed. In a case where an offender has been unable to found a defence of duress at his trial, it may nonetheless be possible to take those circumstances into account on sentence. In *Taonis* (1974) 59 Cr App R 160, for example, the offender was convicted of unlawful importation of cannabis. He had been forced into acting as a drug courier because of threats to beat and torture the woman he was living with and that he would be falsely accused of having stolen a considerable amount of money. The sentence was reduced from four years' imprisonment to two years, Scarman LJ commenting that 'The experience [the defendant] has gone through was described in the court below as truly terrifying'. Taonis could not on the facts avail himself of the defence of duress, since there was an interval between the time of the threats and the commission of the offence during which time he could have gone to the police, but the pressure he was under did significantly reduce his culpability.

(c) *Offender has been tricked by the authorities into committing the offence* The House of Lords in *Sang* [1980] AC 402 made it clear that circumstances of entrapment did not amount to a defence in English law, though on appropriate facts 'its mitigating value may be high'. In *Chapman* (1989) 11 Cr App R (S) 222 the offender pleaded guilty to conspiracy to supply amphetamine sulphate. Chapman had been in custody with respect to a different matter when he was placed in the same cell as a detective posing as a drug dealer. Later the detective met Chapman again and offered him £20,000 if Chapman could obtain amphetamine for him. Chapman undertook to do so, but subsequently withdrew from the agreement. Chapman's sentence of four years' imprisonment was reduced on appeal. Similarly, in *Mackey* (1993) 14 Cr App R (S) 53 sentence was reduced from seven years to five years on an offender who pleaded guilty to supplying heroin, since the offender had been encouraged to commit the offence by an informer.

(d) *Offender acted under a mistake or ignorance of the law* The offender's mistake or ignorance of the law may sometimes provide powerful mitigation. A good example is *Universal Salvage v Boothby* (1983) 5 Cr App R (S) 428, where the offending company's fine for breaching road traffic regulations was reduced to take account of the fact that they had reasonably relied upon a letter from the appropriate government department informing them (incorrectly, as it turned out) that they were exempt from the regulations. Another example is *Surrey County Council* v *Battersby* [1965] 2 QB 194, discussed at **7.1.1**.

(e) *Offender was intoxicated* Surprisingly, there are few reported cases which deal with the relevance of an offender's intoxication at the time of the offence to his culpability and, hence, to the seriousness of the offence. The difficulty is that while the offender's intoxication may in some circumstances show that the offence was not a calculated one, and that the offender is therefore less blameworthy than he might otherwise have been, there is a clear element of culpability inherent in the fact of voluntary intoxication which tends to cancel this out or, in the eyes of some, make matters even worse.

One or two Court of Appeal decisions indicate that intoxication is *not* relevant. In *Kirkland* (1975) CSP C3-2D01 the offender, after having drunk 16 pints of beer, set fire to an unoccupied hostel and caused damage estimated at £440. Lawton LJ, in upholding a sentence of three years' imprisonment, said that 'The truth of the matter is that this offence came to be committed because the appellant had far too much to drink. The courts do not normally take drunkenness into account as a mitigating factor for criminal offences.' See also *Bradley* (1980) 2 Cr App R (S) 12. Despite these authorities, there are other examples where the offender's intoxication at the time of the offence has been interpreted by the courts to mean that there was less culpability on his part than there would have been if there had been a sober decision to commit the offence. An example is *Abrahams* (1980) 2 Cr App R (S) 10, where the theft of a plastic dinghy by the offender was described by the Court of Appeal as a 'drunken frolic rather than a premeditated crime of dishonesty'. So construed, the offence was not serious enough to require the activation of a suspended sentence imposed upon the offender in earlier proceedings. Another example is *Spence* (1982) 4 Cr App R (S) 175.

2.2.4 Personal mitigation

Offenders are rarely so bad that nothing can be said on their behalf. Usually the counsel or solicitor for the defence puts forward a plea in mitigation (see **3.6.1**), and even where the offender is unrepresented he is entitled to mitigate for himself. Once the sentencer has heard and considered the mitigation, sentence will often be reduced from the penalty which was originally in mind, to give credit for what the sentencer considers to be good mitigation. It must be remembered, however, that unlike matters which are relevant to offence seriousness, which *must* be taken into account by the sentencer under PCC(S)A 2000, s. 81(4), allowance for matters of personal mitigation is not an entitlement; these matters *may* be taken into account at the sentencer's discretion, under PCC(S)A 2000, s. 158(1).

The cases indicate that sometimes an offence is so serious that mitigation can have no effect, or have only a marginal effect. This was stated in *Inwood* (1974) 60 Cr App R 70, where the offender, a man of previous good character, pleaded guilty to various counts of deception. Referring to the 'personal tragedy' of the offender, Scarman LJ said that:

> We have listened, I hope with sympathy and understanding, to the mitigating factors urged upon us . . . But in the balance that the court has to make between the mitigating factors and society's interest in marking its disapproval for this type of conduct, we come to the irresistible though unpalatable conclusion, that we must not yield to the mitigating factors.

In respect of particular offences, matters in mitigation may be largely ignored for public policy reasons. An example is the general irrelevance of the offender's good character and clean record when sentencing drug couriers (see *Aramah* (1982) 4 Cr App R (S) 407). The reason is that, according to the Court of Appeal in that case, it is generally people of good character who are targeted for recruitment as couriers.

The cogency of certain forms of mitigation may vary from offence to offence. For example the tendering of a guilty plea is given special weight in sexual offences, since the victim is thereby spared the further ordeal of having to give evidence in court (*Billam* (1986) 8 Cr App R (S) 48). Assistance given by the offender to the police in catching the 'prime movers' justifies a substantial reduction when sentencing drug offenders who have played a role lower down the scale (*Aramah*). These special cases apart, normally the eventual sentence reflects such mitigating factors as the defence have been able to put before the sentencer.

Personal mitigation can affect the sentence in one of two ways. Sometimes it reduces the quantum of punishment, as when the offender is sent to prison for a shorter term, is given a smaller fine or ordered to perform fewer hours of community service than would have been the case had there not been mitigation. Sometimes mitigation will persuade the sentencer to impose a different form of sentence, such as a suspended sentence of imprisonment rather than an immediate term (though the circumstances in which this is appropriate must be exceptional) or a community sentence rather than a custodial one.

Section 158(1) provides that:

(1) Nothing . . . shall prevent a court from mitigating an offender's sentence by taking into account any such matters as, in the opinion of the court, are relevant in mitigation of sentence.

On the face of it, this subsection gives sentencers complete freedom to have regard to any matter, or combination of matters, in mitigation when they think it appropriate to do so. It was confirmed in *Cox* [1993] 1 WLR 188 that in a case where the sentencer had decided that the seriousness of the offence was such that only a custodial sentence could be justified for it, it was still possible that the sentencer could avoid the imposition of custody by having regard to the offender's personal mitigation (see **4.2.4**). This decision underlines the importance of the two-stage form of reasoning outlined in **2.1.2**.

It is important to note that s. 158(1) does not allow for 'personal aggravation', allowing factors unrelated to offence seriousness to increase the sentence. It is wrong, for example, for a sentencer to increase sentence because (as in *Spinks* (1980) 2 Cr App R (S) 335) the offender has chosen to contest the case, or (as in *Evans* (1986) 8 Cr App R (S) 197) because of the manner in which he has conducted his defence (although of course the offender will not have the benefit of any discount which he would have received had he pleaded guilty). It was said in *Loosemore* (1980) 2 Cr App R (S) 172 that a sentencer must deal with an offender on the basis of his offence and not on the basis of his 'feckless character and general behaviour'. A more plausible claim, perhaps, is that an offender's sentence may be aggravated by his record of previous offending. This issue is considered in **2.2.5**.

Some of the many factors which may, at the court's discretion, be taken into account as mitigation are dealt with below.

(a) *Offender is relatively young* The effect of youth as a mitigating factor is somewhat unpredictable. An offender's relative youth might tend to reduce culpability (along with the matters mentioned at **2.2.3**). This might be reflected in the substantive sentencing rules, such as the lower maximum custodial sentences which are available for offenders under 18. It seems though, that youth cannot *per se* affect culpability, and so it is more appropriately seen as a mitigating factor. It was said in *A-G's Reference (No. 42 of 1996)* [1997] 1 Cr App R (S) 388 and in *Howells* [1999] 1 WLR 307 that it will often be right to pass a shorter custodial sentence on a young offender than would be passed on an adult for the same offence. The age difference will be of less importance when the offence is a very serious one. In *Dodds* (1996), *The Times*, 28 January 1997, the Court of Appeal said that some earlier authorities exaggerated the importance of youth as a mitigating factor, and that if the offence was very serious, little or no reduction in sentence should be made for that reason. Youth is more significant as a mitigating factor when associated with other personal characteristics, such as a clean record and good character (see, for example, *Cox* [1993] 1 WLR 188). Where the offender is very young, the principle contained in CYPA 1933, s. 44(1) has still relevance: 'Every court in dealing with a child or young person who is brought before it, either as an offender or otherwise shall have regard to [his or her] welfare.' See *Secretary of State for the Home Department, ex parte Furber* [1998] 1 Cr App R (S) 208.

(b)   *Offender is relatively old*   In *Varden* [1981] Crim LR 272 the Court of Appeal upheld a reduction in sentence on a 71-year-old offender of low intelligence because his advanced years would probably make a term of imprisonment all the more unpleasant for him. In *Wilkinson* (1974) CSP C2-2B01 the offender pleaded guilty to various charges of indecent assault, indecency with a child and unlawful sexual intercourse with a girl aged under 13. All the offences were committed on the offender's grandnieces. Prison sentences of four years were reduced, 'as an act of mercy', to two and a half years, Roskill LJ stating that 'No court willingly sentences a man of 60 to spend a large part of the remainder of his life in prison.' See also *Nicholson* (1992) 14 Cr App R (S) 311, at (k) below. On occasions (such as where there is evidence of senility, or disordered thinking) it is arguable that the offender's relative age might tend to reduce culpability together with the matters mentioned at **2.2.3**. Ordinarily, though, age does not affect culpability, so that it is better regarded as personal mitigation.

(c)   *Offender has a good character, a clean record or relatively few previous convictions*   One of the most powerful matters which can be advanced in mitigation is the offender's good character and clean record. For such a person, the fact of conviction itself may be a sufficient penalty. Even where the offence is so serious that a custodial sentence is inevitable, there is an argument for reducing such a sentence for a first offender since 'for a man of good character undergoing his first prison sentence, conviction and a prison sentence are in themselves a substantial punishment' (per Lord Lane CJ in *Vinson* [1982] Crim LR 192). Lawyers try to mitigate on behalf of an offender who does have previous convictions by trying to show those convictions in a better light, such as by pointing out that they were committed some years ago (such as in *Cole* (1983) 5 Cr App R (S) 218, where the offender was aged 27 and the Court of Appeal said that a conviction as a juvenile 'can be disregarded for present purposes'), or were relatively trivial (in *Silver* (1982) 4 Cr App R (S) 152, a record of road traffic offences was said to be irrelevant when the current offence was manslaughter), or were of a quite different type to the current offence (in *Williams* (1983) 5 Cr App R (S) 244, an earlier conviction for rape not relevant to an offence of dishonesty). It seems that even a substantial list of convictions can be offset by evidence of a gap in the offending prior to the most recent offence, such a gap being indicative of an attempt by the offender to 'go straight'. In *Bleasdale* (1984) 6 Cr App R (S) 177 Hobhouse J commented that: 'What has to be said in favour of this appellant is that since serving the sentence [in 1978] he has kept out of trouble. This is an important feature in his favour.'

(d)   *Offender has rendered substantial assistance to the police*   Mitigation is appropriate, and may in some cases be very substantial, where an offender has disclosed information to the authorities which has led to the apprehension of others and the bringing against them of serious charges. The extent of the discount varies, depending on the degree of assistance given, the seriousness of the offender's offence and the seriousness of the other crimes cleared up. In *Lowe* (1977) 66 Cr App R 122 the offender pleaded guilty to four counts of robbery and other offences. He was sentenced to 10 years' imprisonment, with a suspended sentence of 18 months activated consecutively. The Court of Appeal held that he should have been given greater credit for his statements made to the police, in which he implicated no fewer than 45 other people in armed robbery, burglary, theft and handling offences. The sentence was reduced to a total of five years. In *King* (1985) 7 Cr App R (S) 22 a sentence of six years on a man who pleaded guilty to robbery and eight counts of burglary was reduced to four and a half years to give credit for the offender's assistance to the police, which had resulted in the conviction of 17 other offenders, and in *Saggar* [1997] 1 Cr App R (S) 167 sentence was reduced from seven years to four and a half years because of the help given by the offender, including testifying for the prosecution in related matters. On the other hand, in *Debbag* (1991) 12 Cr App R (S) 733 no discount was appropriate. The information had not been given to the police until after the offender, who vigorously contested the case, had been convicted and sentenced. The information, when produced, was already known to the police in any event.

(e)   *Offender has performed some meritorious act unrelated to the offence, which shows him in a good light*   This category of mitigation is a classic example of the court having regard to matters which are totally unrelated to the offence, and engaging in a kind of 'moral accounting'. Sentences have been reduced where the offender has failed in a valiant attempt to rescue three children from a burning house (*Reid* (1982) 4 Cr App R (S) 280), gone to the assistance of a wounded police officer (*Playfair* [1972] Crim LR 387), raised the alarm after prisoners escaped from a bus transporting them (*Dawn* (1993) 15 Cr App R (S) 720), and has previously shown great courage in apprehending armed men who had been carrying out a robbery (*Alexander* [1997] 2 Cr App R (S) 74).

(f)   *Offender has shown remorse*   The offender's remorse for the offence committed, particularly where it is more than a mere expression of sorrow but involves some more practical demonstration of contrition, may afford a degree of mitigation.

One difficulty with this head of mitigation is that statements of remorse are easy to make and their genuineness or otherwise is difficult for the court to assess. In some cases the offender's remorse will be associated with an early guilty plea, or with assistance to the authorities, in which case the combination becomes a more persuasive one. A frank admission to the police when questioned about the offence produced some mitigation in *Moores* (1980) 2 Cr App R (S) 317, but a stronger case is *Claydon* (1994) 15 Cr App R (S) 526, where the offender confessed to a scout leader and then gave himself up. The Court of Appeal indicated that sentence should be reduced by up to half in such a case.

It may be that by the time of sentence the offender has already made voluntary restitution to the victim. The strength of this mitigation will vary according to the relative difficulty for the offender in making such a payment, rather than the amount of compensation which the offender actually makes. It can also give rise to a danger that such mitigation will thereby be available only to offenders who have the money to pay. The Court of Appeal was aware of this dilemma in *Crosby* (1974) 60 Cr App R 234 and pointed out that to impose a custodial sentence on one co-defendant but to suspend sentence on the other since he had managed to find £3,600 to pay to the victim 'does not seem to us to be a firm foundation for the administration of justice'.

(g)   *Offender has pleaded guilty*   Undoubtedly the most important and most frequently relied upon matter in mitigation is the offender's guilty plea. It has importance in respect of all offences, both in the Crown Court and in magistrates' courts, but it has particular relevance in cases involving sexual offences, if it saves the victim the distress of having to give evidence (see *Billam* (1986) 8 Cr App R (S) 48, the guideline case on rape, at **12.3.1**). In some cases a guilty plea may be evidence of genuine remorse on the part of the offender (see (f) above). In the great majority of cases, however, the reason why the courts grant a substantial discount on sentence for a guilty plea is that, by cooperating in the smooth running of the criminal justice system, defendants who plead guilty help to shorten trials, reduce court backlogs and save the costs of legal aid. The authorities suggest that a guilty plea typically results in a sentence reduction in the Crown Court of between one quarter and one third in the length of a custodial sentence. Its effect in each particular case is a matter within the discretion of the sentencing court, and in an appropriate case the discount may be reduced or denied altogether. The Magistrates' Association Guidelines (2000) include sentence guides for offences dealt with summarily which are based on a first-time offender pleading not guilty. The Guidelines state that 'A timely guilty plea may attract a sentencing discount of up to one third but the precise amount of discount will depend on the facts of each case and a last-minute plea of guilty may attract only a minimal reduction'. The leading Court of Appeal decision is *Costen* (1989) 11 Cr App R (S) 182, where it was confirmed that the guilty plea discount might be lost in any of the following circumstances:

(i)   If the protection of the public makes it necessary that a long sentence, possibly the maximum sentence, be passed, then the discount may be lost. An example is *McLaughlin* (1979) 1 Cr App R (S) 298, which involved a robbery committed at knifepoint. But there is a powerful counter-argument that the maximum sentence should not be imposed if there is significant mitigation in the case, such as a guilty plea. See, for example, *Greene* (1993) 14 Cr App R (S) 682.

(ii)   Discount can be reduced or lost in cases of 'tactical plea', where the offender has delayed his plea until the final moment in a misguided attempt to secure some tactical advantage. In such a case, of course, much of the expense involved in arranging the trial has already been incurred. An example is *Hollington* (1985) 7 Cr App R (S) 364, where the offender had delayed his plea so as to enjoy the somewhat more congenial surroundings while on remand awaiting trial than he would have done if he had pleaded guilty from the start and been sent to prison.

(iii)   If the offender has been caught red-handed and a plea of guilty is inevitable, the discount may be lost. This was the case in *Landy* (1995) 16 Cr App R (S) 908. The offender pleaded guilty to aggravated vehicle taking. After being pursued by the police at 90 mph he crashed the car into a fence and turned it upside down. Police officers pulled him out through the rear window.

There are other situations in which it seems that the discount can be reduced or lost. In *Byrne* [1997] 1 Cr App R (S) 165 it was held that an offender who had absconded and remained at large for 19 months was not entitled to expect a discount for his guilty plea when he was rearrested and brought back before the court. Also, some or all of the discount may be lost if the offender admits guilt but adduces a version of the facts at odds with the prosecution, requiring the court to conduct a *Newton* hearing (see **3.3.2**) to determine exactly what happened. Examples are *Stevens* (1986) 8 Cr App R (S) 297 and *Williams* (1991) 12 Cr App R (S) 415, in each of which the Court of Appeal accepted that some of the discount should be lost, not least because the victim was still required to give evidence.

The above principles are well established in the case law, but the PCC(S)A 2000, s. 152, makes specific provision as to reductions in sentences for guilty pleas:

(1) In determining what sentence to pass on an offender who has pleaded guilty to an offence in proceedings before that or another court, a court shall take into account—

(a) the stage in the proceedings for the offence at which the offender indicated his intention to plead guilty; and

(b) the circumstances in which this indication was given.

(2) If as a result of taking into account any matter referred to in subsection (1) above, the court imposes a punishment on the offender which is less severe than the punishment it would otherwise have imposed, it shall state in open court that it has done so.

(3) In the case of an offence the sentence for which falls to be imposed under subsection (2) of section 110 or 111 above, nothing in that subsection shall prevent the court, after taking into account any matter referred to in subsection (1) above, from imposing any sentence which is not less than 80 per cent of that specified in that subsection.

Sections 110 and 111 of the 2000 Act are considered at **4.3.2** and **4.3.3** below. The reference to 'the stage of the proceedings' and the 'circumstances' in which the plea was tendered are sufficiently broad to be regarded as incorporating the case law described above, and so far there have been no Court of Appeal decisions to indicate any change in practice as a result of the section. It should be noted that this provision is not confined to custodial sentences. It seems to be relevant to any sentence. The Magistrates' Association Guidelines (2000) state that 'Discounts apply to fines, periods of community sentences and custody'. It is clear that a guilty plea, particularly where associated with other mitigation, may form the basis for passing a community sentence rather than a custodial one (see, for example, *Cox* [1993] 1 WLR 188, described at **4.2.4**). On the other hand, reduction from an immediate prison sentence to a suspended sentence on the basis of a guilty plea is not permissible, since even an early guilty plea cannot amount to the 'exceptional circumstances' required before a prison sentence may be suspended (see **4.6.3**).

Section 152 places an obligation on judges and magistrates to state in open court that, in consequence of the guilty plea, the court has imposed a less severe sentence than it would otherwise have done. In *Fearon* [1996] 2 Cr App (S) 25 the Court of Appeal stressed that sentencers must always make it clear whether or not a reduction has been given but in *Bishop* [2000] 1 Cr App R (S) 432, where the sentencer had not done so, the Court of Appeal declined to reduce the sentence on appeal, saying that it was possible to tell that the plea had been taken into account.

(h) *Adverse effects of sentence on offender have been especially severe* In general the Court of Appeal has taken the view that the collateral effects upon the offender of conviction and sentence are not in themselves sufficient reason for mitigating the penalty normally appropriate for the offence. Thus in many cases of serious theft in breach of trust (see **12.4.1**) the offender may well lose his reputation, employment and the prospects of future employment in any position of responsibility. The general approach is to say that the offender should have considered those risks before embarking on the offending. Sometimes, however, where the collateral effects are particularly harsh and the original offence is not so serious as to preclude it, some mitigation will be available. In *Richards* (1980) 2 Cr App R (S) 119 the offender was a 57-year-old general medical practitioner, who was convicted of obtaining money from the health authority by submitting false expenses claims. The sum involved was £600. He was sentenced to 30 months' imprisonment. It was urged on the Court of Appeal that the sentence was too high, and that the sentencer had given insufficient weight to the fact that Richards faced professional disciplinary proceedings, would surely never work as a doctor again, would lose his pension rights and, given his age, would be unable to find comparable work. There were other tragic personal circumstances, such as that his wife had committed suicide. Sentence was reduced to 12 months. In contrast in *Lowery* (1993) 14 Cr App R (S) 485, where 'catastrophic consequences' ensued after the offender, a police officer, was convicted of false accounting, the Court of Appeal felt unable to suspend the prison sentence. In *Barbery* (1975) 62 Cr App R 248 sentence was reduced on a man who had been involved in an affray, during the course of which his own hand had been severed. In *Rees* (1982) 4 Cr App R (S) 71 it was accepted that the sentencer might take into account the fact that, as a result of his conviction, the offender would be discharged from military service, but a harder line was taken in *Ranu* [1996] 2 Cr App R (S) 334.

(i)   *Offender's serious illness*   The general view seems to be that the offender's illness is not a reason for mitigation, and should not form the basis for avoiding a custodial sentence which is otherwise merited. In *Moore* (1993) 15 Cr App R (S) 97 and in *Stark* (1992) 13 Cr App R (S) 548 the offenders had been diagnosed as HIV positive. In the former case the medical evidence as to the offender's condition was unclear, but in the second case it was accepted that he had recently developed AIDS and that his life expectancy was between one and two years. In both cases the Court of Appeal held that the correct sentences had been imposed and that the illness was a matter for the executive authorities and the Home Office, but not the courts. Nevertheless, in other cases, such as *Varden* [1981] Crim LR 272 the Court of Appeal has upheld a sentence reduction and, after reviewing the earlier authorities, the Court of Appeal in *Bernard* [1997] 1 Cr App R (S) 135 said that an offender's serious illness may exceptionally, as an act of mercy, allow the imposition of a lesser sentence than would otherwise be required.

(j)   *Severe adverse effect of sentence on offender's family*   There is authority that, in principle, the adverse effect upon the offender's family of the offender's conviction and sentence is not in itself a ground for mitigation. In *Ingham* (1974) CSP C4-2A01 Lord Widgery CJ said that '. . . imprisonment of the father inevitably causes hardship to the rest of the family . . . The crux of the matter is that part of the price to pay when committing a crime is that imprisonment does involve hardship on the wife and family, and it cannot be one of the factors which can affect what would otherwise be the right sentence.' On the other hand, such matters are regularly invoked in pleas in mitigation and, certainly where the effects upon the family would be unusually severe, they have been permitted to mitigate sentence.

The Court of Appeal has on occasions varied a custodial sentence so as to allow an offender's immediate release where there is evidence of acute hardship. In *Haleth* (1982)

4 Cr App R (S) 178, for example, the offender was convicted of affray and sentenced to 12 months' imprisonment. After sentence the offender's wife died from a kidney disease leaving their son, who was also very ill, uncared for. Sentence was varied to allow immediate release. In *Bellikli* [1998] 1 Cr App R (S) 135 a prison sentence was suspended by the Court of Appeal because the offender's child was very ill and would require major surgery in the near future. Another aspect of the same problem is where a custodial sentence on a woman will have the effect of leaving her children with nobody to look after them. Again, in principle, this factor is not relevant, but the Court of Appeal has adjusted sentence on some occasions to achieve a merciful outcome. *Vaughan* (1982) 4 Cr App R (S) 83 is one such case. More recently in *Whitehead* [1996] 1 Cr App R (S) 111 the Court of Appeal observed that there was always a reluctance to send the mother of small children to prison, although sometimes there was no choice. In this case, where both parents were given short prison terms, it was possible to vary the sentence on the mother so that she could be returned to her three young sons.

(k) *Lapse of time since the commission of the offence* Lapse of time since the commission of an offence has been taken into account in mitigation of sentence in several cases. It seems to be relevant for two reasons. The first is that where the offence is 'stale', the offender may, in a sense, be thought of as a different person from the one who committed it. An example is *Dashwood* (1994) 16 Cr App R (S) 733, where the offender was sentenced at the age of 29 for offences committed when he was 14. Second, the offender may have suffered considerable stress in having the matter hanging over him for so long. The argument for mitigation will be much less strong where the offence was a very serious one, and/or where the offender has taken active steps to avoid detection. It will be stronger where these factors are missing and/or there has been an unusually long delay in the prosecution and trial process. In *Tierney* [1982] Crim LR 53 there was a delay of some 18 months between the offender's arrest and his trial for burglary. Part of the delay was due to his being involved in a road accident and having to spend time in hospital. During the interval the offender had married and found a job. The Court of Appeal reduced the sentence of nine months' imprisonment to one of six months, suspended for two years, and said that the offender should be sentenced on the basis of his situation at the time of sentence and not at the time of the offence.

There are some offences, such as sexual offences committed within the family, the facts of which may not emerge until long after they have been committed. This, together with the serious nature of the offences themselves, means that any discount for the delay is likely to be minimal. In *Nicholson* (1992) 14 Cr App R (S) 311 the 64-year-old offender was being sentenced for a series of violent and sexual offences committed on his stepchildren 20 years before. A total sentence of nine years was reduced to seven years, to take account of the lapse of time and the age of the offender.

2.2.5 Relevance of previous convictions

The significance of the offender's previous convictions to the current sentence is a complex matter. Everyone accepts that the offender's record can often be of considerable importance in selecting the sentence, but there is little appellate discussion of the point, and it is not clear precisely what aspects of the offender's previous record should properly be regarded as relevant. The most settled point is that an offender who has a clean, or relatively clean, record is generally entitled to a degree of mitigation in that respect. Section 158(1) of

PCC(S)A 2000, as we have seen, would allow mitigation in such a case. No precise formula as to the extent of such mitigation can be arrived at, but it seems obvious that the more serious the offence the less scope there will be for mitigation (see **2.2.4**). A more difficult issue is the extent to which a sentencer is entitled to pass a more severe sentence on an offender who does have a record. Some Court of Appeal decisions, such as *Galloway* (1979) 1 Cr App R (S) 311 and *Bailey* (1988) 10 Cr App R (S) 231, displayed a general acceptance of the view that it is wrong to impose a sentence which is longer than would be indicated by the seriousness of the offence purely on the basis of previous record. A poor record should not, on that view, be regarded as an aggravating factor relevant to offence seriousness (see **2.2.2**).

One of the clearest statements of this principle can be found in *Queen* (1981) 3 Cr App R (S) 245. There the offender pleaded guilty to theft and related offences. Queen, who had a long list of offences of dishonesty going back 25 years, was given a prison sentence of 18 months. In the Court of Appeal Kenneth Jones J said that it was clear that the offender had been sentenced 'not merely for the offences which he committed, but for his record'. Such an approach was 'wrong in principle':

> Of course no prisoner is to be sentenced for the offences which he has committed in the past and for which he has already been punished. The proper way to look at the matter is to decide a sentence which is appropriate for the offence for which the prisoner is before the court. Then in deciding whether that sentence should be imposed or whether the court can extend properly some leniency to the prisoner, the court must have regard to those matters which tell in his favour, and equally to those matters which tell against him; in particular his record of previous convictions. Then matters have to be balanced up to decide whether the appropriate sentence to pass is one at the upper end of the bracket or somewhere lower down.

The sentence was varied so as to allow Queen, who at the time of the appeal had served a little over nine months of his sentence, immediate release from custody. This approach to previous convictions, often referred to as the 'theory of progressive loss of mitigation', holds that while a first offender may present a good case for mitigation in light of his record, the accumulation of previous convictions results in the progressive loss of that mitigation so that, by the time of (say) the fourth or fifth conviction, all mitigation for a clean (or fairly clean) record is lost and the offender is sentenced in accordance with the seriousness of the offence. It also entails, however, that an offender's sentence should never be increased to a level disproportionate with the seriousness of the current offence simply because of his poor record. Despite the Court of Appeal authority listed above, this principle has never been fully accepted by sentencers who undoubtedly do still tend in practice to regard a list of previous convictions as an aggravating factor and, at least to some extent, to sentence offenders 'on their records'.

The relevant statutory provision is PCC(S)A 2000, s. 151(1), which states that:

> In considering the seriousness of any offence, the court may take into account any previous convictions of the offender or any failure of his to respond to previous sentences.

Section 151(2) is concerned with offending while on bail, and was considered in **2.2.2(f)**. Subsections (3) to (6) of s. 151 provide that for the purposes of the section the court may take into account previous convictions of the offender which have been dealt with by way of a community rehabilitation order, or by the grant of a discharge. They also provide that the court may take into account any failure by the offender to respond to an earlier community rehabilitation order or conditional discharge. These provisions are there to make it clear that such disposals do count as previous convictions, despite s. 14 of the PCC(S)A 2000, which states that they are convictions only for certain purposes. Section 14 is considered further at **7.1.4** and need not detain us here.

It can be seen that s. 151(1) provides the sentencer with a power to take into account the offender's previous convictions, where these impinge upon the seriousness of the offence to be sentenced. Unfortunately the subsection gives no indication of *when* the previous record is relevant for this purpose. Without delving too far into the history of this provision, it is helpful to realise that this is the second version of this provision, which was originally to be found in the CJA 1991, and that the original version, in contrast, stated that an offence should *not* be regarded as more serious by reason of the offender's previous convictions or failures to respond to previous sentences, although there was a narrow exception in cases where the previous convictions revealed an aggravating feature of the new offence which otherwise might not have been apparent, such as a history of racially motivated offending. This original version was in line with desert theory in giving a very limited relevance to previous convictions, but it was subjected to sustained criticism when the 1991 Act was implemented. Despite the new version of the subsection having been on the statute book since 1993 (when the CJA 1993 substituted the new wording), there has been no guidance from the Court of Appeal on its meaning. It is sometimes said that the new version, as set out in s. 151(1), gives sentencers complete flexibility to take account of previous convictions when sentencing, so that offenders can now be sentenced 'on their record'. This claim, however, ignores the fact that s. 151(1) is still tied to the concept of offence seriousness, and so the question still unanswered by Parliament and the Court of Appeal is: *When* can it properly be said that previous convictions of the offender, or previous failures of his to respond to past sentences, actually affect the *seriousness* of the new offence? The Magistrates' Association Guidelines (2000) advise magistrates to 'identify any convictions relevant for this purpose and then consider to what extent they affect the seriousness of the present offence'. It may also be noted that the *Practice Direction (Crime: Antecedents)* [1998] 1 Cr App R 213 states that 'In the Crown Court the police will provide brief details of the circumstances of the last three similar convictions, and/or of convictions likely to be of interest to the court, the latter being judged on a case by case basis.'

2.3 THE DUTY TO AVOID DISCRIMINATION

Article 14 of the ECHR provides that enjoyment of the rights set out in the Convention shall be secured 'without discrimination on any ground such as sex, race, colour, language, religion, political or other opinion, national or social origin, association with a national minority, birth or other status'. Several of the rights in the ECHR are, of course, highly relevant to sentencing, especially Article 3, which prohibits inhuman or degrading treatment or punishment, and Article 6, concerning the right to a fair trial. Article 14 apart, there is no statutory sentencing principle relating to non-discrimination. Section 95 of the CJA 1991, however, places a duty on the Secretary of State 'each year to publish such information as he considers expedient . . .' for the purpose of enabling criminal justice agencies to 'avoid discriminating against any person on the ground of race or sex or any other improper ground'. Publications designed to fulfil this duty have been published on a regular basis since then.

In *Statistics on Race and the Criminal Justice System* (Home Office, 1998) material relevant to sentencing includes information on the racial origin of offenders given probation, community service and combination orders. Those of ethnic minority origin made up 7 per cent, 10 per cent and 10 per cent of those orders, respectively (1997–8 figures). As far as custodial sentencing is concerned, ethnic minorities accounted for 18 per cent of the male prison population (12 per cent black, 3 per cent Asian and 3 per cent other) and 25 per cent of the female prison population (20 per cent black, 1 per cent Asian and 4 per cent other) (June 1997 figures). These figures compare starkly with the overall population figures for England and Wales (again in 1997–8), where 2 per cent of population was of black ethnic origin, 3 per cent was of Asian origin and 1 per cent was of 'other' non-white ethnic origin. The report also shows that ethnic minorities remained under-represented in the police service, the prison service, the lay magistracy and senior posts in all the criminal justice agencies.

In *Statistics on Women and the Criminal Justice System* (Home Office, 2000), there is much information relevant to sentencing. The report shows that women were more likely than men to be discharged or given a community sentence for an indictable offence and were less likely to be fined or given a custodial sentence (1998 figures). Women accounted for 12 per cent of offenders supervised by the probation service in 1998, but they were less likely to have previous convictions, or to have served a previous custodial sentence, than the men given a community sentence. Women made up only 5 per cent of the total prison population in 1999, but this reflected a 100 per cent rise in their numbers since 1993, as compared to a 43 per cent rise in the number of men in custody over that period. Fifteen per cent of female prisoners were foreign nationals, and three quarters of those were being held for drugs offences. Forty-two per cent of women in prison have committed theft, handling stolen goods, fraud or forgery. Fifty-five per cent of all women in prison have a child under the age of 16 and one third of mothers in prison have a child under five.

2.4   COSTS OF SENTENCING MEASURES

Section 95 of CJA 1991 also requires the Secretary of State to publish regularly such information as he considers expedient for the purpose of 'enabling persons engaged in the administration of criminal justice to become aware of the financial implications of their decisions'.

2.4.1   Average costs of various sentences

According to the most recent government figures available, the costs of different sentencing disposals are in order of:

custodial sentence	£2,700 per month
community punishment and rehabilitation order	£270 per month
community rehabilitation order	£190 per month
supervision order	£150 per month
community punishment order	£140 per month

These figures should be treated with a degree of caution, since experience has shown that actual expenditure resulting from a particular disposal varies considerably from case to case. The figures given for prison sentences do not include costing for the mandatory element of supervision where relevant, but they do make an allowance for capital as well as running costs. Breach costs in respect of community sentences are not included. What is clear beyond doubt is the totally different scale of costs involved in custodial sentences, as compared to other forms of disposal.

3   Sentencing Procedure

Before selecting the appropriate sentence, the sentencer will require further information about the offence and about the offender. From the moment when the offender pleads guilty or is found guilty to the moment when the judge or bench of magistrates passes sentence, there is a period of time in which this information will be adduced. In simple, straightforward cases, particularly in magistrates' courts, the decision on sentence may be reached almost immediately. In more complex cases, the procedure between conviction and sentence may take several hours, involving the calling of witnesses and the close investigation of disputed facts. It may seem odd, at first sight, that an accused can be found guilty of an offence when important factual issues remain unresolved. It should be remembered, however, that where the accused has pleaded guilty, there will have been no trial and hence no examination of the circumstances of the offence in court. Even where there has been a full trial, it will have been confined to issues relevant to guilt. Other matters, not relevant to that issue, may still require examination before the proper sentence can be fixed. Consider offences of strict liability. Whether the accused committed the offences knowingly or not is irrelevant to liability, but it is of central importance when fixing the punishment. An example is *Lester* (1975) 63 Cr App R 144, where the offender pleaded guilty to strict liability offences under the Trade Descriptions Act 1968 and was sentenced on the assumption that he had *mens rea*. The Court of Appeal said that the assumption should not have been made without the offender having been given a chance to give evidence on the matter, and reduced the sentence from six months' imprisonment to a fine of £280. See also *Yorkshire Water Services* (1994) 16 Cr App R (S) 280.

The procedure between conviction and sentence is markedly different from that which pertains to the trial itself. The role of the judge or bench of magistrates changes from that of an umpire to one of a collector of information about the offence and the offender. Rules relating to the admissibility of evidence are somewhat relaxed, and the combative or adversarial style of the opposing lawyers is less marked. The judge takes a more central and active role in the gathering of information, which comes from a variety of sources, in reaching the sentencing decision. In fact there are relatively few legal rules governing the procedure between conviction and sentence: many of the practices discussed below have grown up through the day-to-day workings of the courts. Their operation is governed by a few statutory provisions, scattered appellate decisions, Practice Statements and administrative guidance, especially a number of Home Office circulars.

The procedure between conviction and sentence may usefully be divided into three main stages, namely the determination of the facts of the offence and the hearing of evidence about the offender's character and antecedents; the reading by the court of reports prepared on the offender; and the presentation of defence mitigation. Before considering these three stages in detail, two preliminary matters must be mentioned: advance indications of sentence and adjournment before sentence.

3.1 ADVANCE INDICATIONS OF SENTENCE

In what circumstances may a Crown Court judge give an indication, in advance of the indictment being put to the accused, of the sentence the accused may expect to receive? This is a complex and difficult matter.

All lawyers (and many defendants) know that an accused who pleads guilty to a charge will, ordinarily, receive a lower sentence than he would receive if he were to contest the case and then be convicted. The reasons for this are threefold. First, to plead guilty saves a good deal of court time and public money. Second, in some cases, such as alleged sexual assault, witnesses will be spared the distress of reliving their experience in court. Third, at least in some cases, a decision to plead guilty will indicate the offender's regret for the offence (for discussion of the sentencing 'discount' for pleading guilty, see **2.2.4**). About two-thirds of accused in the Crown Court plead guilty and nine out of every ten accused in magistrates' courts do so. It is generally assumed that if the incentive to plead guilty were removed there would be many more contested trials, and some people claim that the administration of criminal justice would grind to a halt. Clearly it is one of the tasks of the defence lawyer to explain the sentencing discount fully and fairly to the accused (*Herbert* (1991) 94 Cr App R 233). The Code of Conduct of the Bar confirms that defence counsel should explain to the accused the advantages and disadvantages of pleading guilty. Strong advice to enter a guilty plea is permissible (*Peace* [1976] Crim LR 119). It should not, however, be so strong as to effectively deprive the accused of his free choice as to how he pleads (*Inns* (1975) 60 Cr App R 231). The danger, of course, is that an innocent accused may feel under great pressure to plead guilty believing that the plea will make the difference between a custodial sentence and a community sentence. Such pressure is all the greater if the accused, rightly or wrongly, gets the impression that the judge is involved as well.

The law in this area is governed by *Turner* [1970] 2 QB 321. That case states that the only circumstance in which the judge may give an advance indication of sentence is to say that the sentence will (or will not) take a particular form *regardless of how the accused pleads*. Usually defence counsel will go to see the judge in his private room and will ask him if he is prepared to give any indication of the type approved in *Turner*. In reply the judge may say that, regardless of plea, he is not considering a custodial penalty, or that the sentence will, in any event, be a fine, or will be one of the community orders. The judge may, on the other hand, decline counsel's request and he certainly should do so if he is not in possession of all the material facts (*Winterflood* (1978) 68 Cr App R 291). If an indication is given it is vital that it is not made conditional upon the plea. Where the judge indicates a community sentence in the event of a guilty plea but is silent as to the sentence which would follow conviction by a jury, this amounts to such an indication (*Ryan* (1977) 67 Cr App R 177). It will be seen that the judge may still take the plea into account, along with the range of other matters, in fixing custodial sentence *length* and in deciding what *level* of fine or *which* community sentence will be imposed. An indication from the judge that the sentence will be a community sentence, regardless of how the accused pleads may, then, be very helpful in a case where defence counsel suspects that his client really wants to plead guilty but is terrified that he will receive a custodial sentence. If the judge indicates that he is not considering a custodial sentence in any event, the accused may pluck up the courage to plead guilty.

A further point made in *Turner* is that anything the judge says privately to counsel must be passed on to the accused. It is inappropriate for matters of this sort to be communicated 'in confidence' between the judge and counsel (*Bird* (1977) 67 Cr App R 203). Indeed, the Court of Appeal has said that no discussion of this sort should take place in the judge's private room without the presence of a shorthand writer or tape recordist to record exactly what is said (*Smith* [1990] Crim LR 354). Also, whenever defence counsel goes to see the judge privately, counsel for the prosecution should be present and the accused's solicitor may also be there. The accused is never present at these discussions but, again according to *Turner*, defence counsel may refer to any mitigating consideration, including something of which the accused is ignorant (such as the fact that the accused has a serious illness and may not have long to live). It seems that, apart from the limited circumstances specified in *Turner*, the rule is that any approach made by counsel to the judge for an indication of likely sentence is quite wrong (*Coward* (1979) 70 Cr App R 70). The judge should certainly never initiate a private meeting for this purpose (*Llewellyn* (1977) 67 Cr App R 148).

If a judge fails to comply with *Turner* and promises a community sentence in the event of a guilty plea, and either expressly says that the promise would not apply were the accused to be convicted by a jury, or simply gives no indication of what would happen in that event, then the accused is placed under intolerable pressure to plead guilty. A plea of guilty tendered in such circumstances would, on appeal, be treated as a nullity. The Court of Appeal would quash the conviction and order a re-trial at which, presumably, the accused would plead not guilty. Examples of such cases are *Ryan* (1977) 67 Cr App R 177 and *James* [1990] Crim LR 815.

An important implication of *Turner* is that any sentencing undertaking which is made by the judge must subsequently be honoured. The point is well illustrated by *Moss* (1983) 5 Cr App R (S) 209. Moss and two other young women were charged with shoplifting. Counsel asked to see the judge privately. The judge indicated that, regardless of what the pleas might be he was not considering a custodial sentence. In the event all three accused pleaded not guilty and were convicted by a jury. The judge adjourned for reports to be prepared. At the end of the period of adjournment the offenders appeared before a different judge to be sentenced. Although the reports recommended various community sentences, and although the sentencer was told of the first judge's inclination as to sentence, he still passed custodial sentences on all three young women. Since they each had several previous convictions for dishonesty, the sentences were in themselves not objectionable. The first judge had promised community sentences, however, and the Court of Appeal held that the promise was binding and substituted community rehabilitation orders for the custodial sentences. See also *Keily* [1990] Crim LR 204. The situation may be different, though, where the sentence indication given by the judge, and subsequently followed, is appealed by the Attorney-General on the basis that it was too lenient. If the Court of Appeal agrees that the sentence was unduly lenient it may increase it, despite the original sentence indication given (*A-G's Reference (No. 40 of 1996)* [1997] 1 Cr App R (S) 357). In *A-G's Reference (Nos 80 and 81 of 1999)* [2000] 2 Cr App R (S) 138, however, the Court of Appeal said that on the facts it would not grant leave to the Attorney-General to appeal non-custodial sentences imposed for fraud which were undoubtedly lenient. This was because at the trial counsel for the Crown had been fully supportive of the judge's proposal to pass non-custodial sentences. It would be wrong now to re-open the sentences, at the behest of the Crown and to the likely detriment of the offenders.

The discussion of this topic has been entirely concerned with the Crown Court. No advance indications of sentence can be given in magistrates' courts. This is because magistrates, prior to the plea being tendered, are permitted to know nothing about the details of the prosecution case or the character and record of the offender, so obviously they are in no position to give undertakings about the sentence. A Crown Court judge, on the other hand, can familiarise himself with the case in advance by reading through the committal statements. The judge is also entitled before the plea is entered to see the accused's antecedents and list of previous convictions, which magistrates are not. Thus, the papers in the case may well give the judge an adequate basis for giving an indication as to sentence.

3.2 ADJOURNMENT BEFORE SENTENCE

The court does not necessarily sentence the offender on the day on which he or she pleads guilty or is found guilty. It has power to adjourn prior to passing sentence. This is, in fact, frequently done, for a range of reasons discussed below. Of course, adjournments are administratively inconvenient and can be disruptive and expensive. It is also quite likely, particularly in magistrates' courts, that the sentencer who ordered the adjournment will not be the same as the one who deals with the matter after adjournment, and this on occasions can cause difficulty. Such matters must, however, be outweighed by the need to take extra time in securing a just sentence.

The Crown Court's power to adjourn is one which it possesses by virtue of common law. It is distinct from its statutory power to defer sentence (see *Annesley* (1975) 62 Cr App R 113 and **3.10**). A magistrates' court's power to do so is governed by MCA 1980, s. 10(3). which permits a magistrates' court to adjourn 'for the purpose of enabling inquiries to be made or of determining the most suitable method of dealing with the case'. Adjournment for some other purpose, such as to put off making a difficult decision, or to allow the passage of time so that a young offender will become eligible for a prison sentence (as in *Arthur* v *Stringer* (1986) 8 Cr App R (S) 329), is unlawful. During the period of an adjournment before sentence, the offender will be remanded in custody or on bail. There is a prima facie right to bail by reason of the Bail Act 1976 (BA 1976), s. 4, but bail may be refused on any one of several grounds specified in that Act. In the present context all the grounds which may justify a refusal of bail before conviction apply here also, but an additional ground applies — that the adjournment is for the purpose of preparing a report and that it would be impracticable to do so if the offender were at liberty (BA 1976, sch. 1, Part 1, para. 7). Where an offender remanded for reports is granted bail the court may, in its discretion, include a condition that the offender makes himself available 'for the purpose of enabling inquiries or a report to be made to assist the court in dealing with him for an offence' (BA 1976, s. 3(6)(d)).

3.2.1 Adjournment for reports

Independent reports on offenders are often a vital factor in the sentencing decision. The most frequently encountered reports are pre-sentence reports (PSRs) and medical reports (see further on these **3.5.1** and **3.5.2**). Where the accused indicates an intention to plead guilty and it seems likely that the court will need reports before passing sentence, the reports are prepared before the hearing if possible. If, however, the accused is pleading not guilty it is unlikely that reports will be prepared. This is because an important element, in the pre-sentence report in particular, is consideration of the accused's attitude to the offence. If the accused is pleading not guilty then obviously this aspect cannot be investigated. Even if the accused is pleading guilty, the preparation of reports is not automatic. The circumstances in which the court is bound in law to obtain a pre-sentence report or a medical report are laid down by statute.

(a)   *Pre-sentence reports*   Broadly speaking, the Crown Court or a magistrates' court should normally obtain a pre-sentence report whenever the imposition of a custodial sentence is under consideration, or when the court is considering any of the following community sentences: a community rehabilitation order which includes additional requirements, a community punishment order, a community punishment rehabilitation order, a supervision order which includes additional requirements, or a drug treatment and testing order. The role of pre-sentence reports is considered in detail in **3.5.1**. Apart from these specified cases where the court should not normally proceed to sentence without a pre-sentence report, there is a range of other circumstances where to pass the sentence without a report would not be good sentencing practice. In these circumstances, too, the court should adjourn for reports to be prepared.

When magistrates adjourn for reports it must be for not more than four weeks if the offender is remanded on bail, and not more than three weeks if he is remanded in custody (MCA 1980, s. 10(3)). The Crown Court can in theory adjourn for any period of time, but in practice adjournments are normally for two or three weeks. *National Standards* (Home Office 2000) state that a pre-sentence report should be prepared within, at most, 15 working days of request, or such shorter period as has been agreed in protocols with the court. Clearly, all reports should be prepared as speedily as possible, with priority being given to offenders who are being held in custody.

(b)   An alternative to a pre-sentence report, a specific sentence report (SSR) may be made available to the court more speedily, usually on the day of request. The purpose of such a report is to provide information about the offender to assist the court in deciding whether he or she is suitable for a specific sentence envisaged by the court. According to the *National Standards* (2000) a specific sentence report is most likely to be ordered where the court is considering a community punishment order of up to 100 hours or a community rehabilitation order without additional requirements.

(c)   *Medical reports*   The circumstances in which a court can adjourn for a medical report are as follows. Written or oral evidence of two medical practitioners that the offender is suffering from mental disorder within the meaning of the Mental Health Act 1983 (MHA 1983) must be obtained before a court can make a hospital order under MHA 1983, s. 37(1), an interim hospital order under s. 38 or a hospital or limitation direction under s. 45A. One of the doctors making a report must be a psychiatrist approved by the Home Office (MHA 1983, s. 54). A report from at least one medical practitioner is required before a probation order with a requirement of treatment for a mental condition may be made (PCC(S)A 2000, sch. 2, para. 5). Whenever a Crown Court or a magistrates' court is considering imposing a custodial sentence upon an offender who is, or who appears to be, mentally disordered, the court should obtain and consider a medical report before passing a custodial sentence, and should consider the likely effect of a custodial sentence on that condition and on any treatment which may be available for it (PCC(S)A 2000, s. 82). Further, under MCA 1980, s. 30, a magistrates' court can adjourn for a medical report even before convicting the accused, if it is satisfied that the accused 'did the act or made the omission charged'. Under this provision the accused can be remanded for up to three weeks in custody or four weeks on bail. If the accused is granted bail, it must be made a condition of bail that he cooperates in the preparation of the report (MCA 1980, s. 30(2) and BA 1976, s. 3(6)(d)). Provisions in MHA 1983, ss. 35 and 36 allow the Crown Court or a magistrates' court to remand offenders to a hospital (rather than in custody or on bail) for reports to be prepared.

3.2.2 Adjournments where there are several offenders

There is a strong argument to be made that offenders who have jointly committed an offence, or offenders who have committed separate offences which arose out of the same circumstances or were otherwise factually linked, should be sentenced together by one judge on one occasion. To do so should ensure consistent treatment for them all, with any differences in the sentences received being justified by the different degrees to which they were involved in the criminal conduct, or by other material differences between them.

The procedural rules on joinder of defendants in one indictment make it likely that alleged confederates in crime will be charged in a single indictment and so initially will appear together to plead to that indictment. If they all plead guilty, or all plead not guilty, there is no problem about having them sentenced together. If, however, A pleads guilty and B pleads not guilty, then difficulties arise. Clearly B cannot be sentenced unless and until he is convicted by a jury. Jury trials are sometimes lengthy affairs. Nonetheless, the desirability of dealing with A and, if convicted, B together has led to a general rule that the sentence on A should be postponed until after the trial of B. This has the additional advantage of allowing the judge to hear the evidence called at B's trial, and proportion his sentences according to which, if either, of the accused played the leading role in the offence or offences. This general rule was established in *Payne* [1950] 1 All ER 102. In that case, however, Lord Goddard CJ stated that there was an exception to the general rule, where A was to 'turn Queen's evidence' and be called by the prosecution as a witness in the trial of B. In such a case, it was said, A should be sentenced straight away, so that there should be no suspicion of his evidence being coloured by the fact that, undoubtedly, he would hope for a lighter sentence as a reward for cooperating with the authorities and giving evidence against B.

While the general rule in *Payne* still represents the law, the scope of exception has been challenged in more recent cases. In *Weekes* (1980) 2 Cr App R (S) 377, in particular the Court of Appeal expressly stated that the prosecution's intention of calling A at the trial of B is not a sufficient reason for the Crown Court departing from the normal practice of sentencing A after B's trial is over. The statement in the case was, however, obiter. It is submitted that the decision as to when to sentence A should be left to the discretion of the trial judge, who is in the best position to balance the interests of B (that A, when he testifies, should have no motive for giving false evidence) against the wider interests of justice (that confederates in crime should be sentenced together so as to avoid unjustified differences in sentence). The existence of such a discretion is supported by the comments of Lord Denning MR in *Sheffield Crown Court, ex parte Brownlow* [1980] QB 520, where he suggested that the following matters (amongst others) might be relevant to whether or not to adjourn sentence upon A:

(a) A would have a very long wait before sentence could be passed, such as where B absconded; or

(b) A's offence was trivial in comparison with the charge against B; or

(c) there were more than usually strong reasons to think that A would perjure himself in giving evidence against B.

The situation discussed in this section also creates difficulty when the sentencer comes to determine the factual basis for passing sentence on the two offenders. Comments adverse to A's role in the offence may be made at B's trial which A may have little opportunity to refute. This issue is considered at **3.3.4**.

3.2.3   Adjournments where there are outstanding charges

It is desirable that an accused with several charges outstanding against him should be sentenced on one occasion for all matters in respect of which he is ultimately convicted. If he is sentenced piecemeal by different judges (or even by the same judge on different occasions) there is a danger that the aggregate sentence will be out of proportion to the overall gravity of the offending. There is also a danger that the first judge, dealing perhaps with the less serious offences, will pass a community sentence and thus create a dilemma for the second judge. The latter may feel that a custodial sentence is necessary for the offences with which he is dealing, but to pass such a sentence might prevent the earlier community sentence running its natural course. To avoid such difficulties, it is better that one sentencer should deal with everything on one occasion, even if this means adjournments and extra administrative work behind the scenes. Adjournment in these circumstances is entirely at the discretion of the court, and the accused may be remanded in custody or on bail (SCA 1981, s. 81(1)(c)).

Occasionally various charges against an accused may not have been consolidated into one indictment, perhaps because they are insufficiently linked to go into one indictment or simply because it is not realised at the time the first indictment is preferred that the accused is also to be indicted for trial on other charges. In *Bennett* (1980) 2 Cr App R (S) 96 Watkin J stressed that there was an obligation 'on solicitors, counsel and judges alike to do all within their power to ensure that as far as possible all outstanding charges against a defendant are dealt with in the same court, by the same judge upon a single occasion'. If it becomes known that there are charges against the accused other than the ones before the court, application should be made to the judge to have the accused's case adjourned to be dealt with later at that Crown Court or to be transferred to another Crown Court where the outstanding charges lie.

3.2.4   Sentence promises on adjournment for reports

Where the Crown Court or a magistrates' court adjourns for reports in circumstances which justifiably lead the offender to think that, if the report turns out to be favourable, a community sentence will be passed, then the court is bound by the implied promise which it has given. To resile from the promise would leave the offender with a legitimate sense of grievance.

This principle was first stated in *Gillam* (1980) 2 Cr App R (S) 267. The offender, who was nearing the end of a prison sentence, was before the court to be sentenced for two burglaries and one offence of reckless driving. It appeared likely that he would receive a further custodial sentence, but the judge adjourned so that Gillam's suitability for community service could be assessed. He also ordered that the offender should be released on bail once the custodial term he was serving came to an end. According to Watkins LJ, in the Court of Appeal, the main reason for the adjournment was 'to ascertain whether community service was available for such a person as the offender and whether he was a fit subject to perform that service'. In the event Gillam was assessed to be suitable for community service.

Nonetheless the judge passed a sentence of six months' imprisonment. Watkins LJ indicated that the proper sentence in Gillam's case would have been immediate custody of about 15 months, but the appeal was allowed, since (at p. 269):

> . . . an important principle of sentencing is involved in this case . . . When a judge in these circumstances purposely postpones sentence so that an alternative to prison can be examined and that alternative is found to be a satisfactory one in all respects, the court ought to adopt the alternative. A feeling of injustice is otherwise aroused.

Gillam has been followed in several later cases. In *Ward* (1982) 4 Cr App R (S) 103, for example, the judge adjourned for three weeks so that Ward could stay at a probation hostel with a view to the making of a probation order with a condition of residence at that hostel. The report was favourable, and a custodial sentence, which was imposed by the judge despite that report, was quashed by the Court of Appeal. In *Wilkinson* (1988) 9 Cr App R (S) 468, on very similar facts, the offender came before a different judge after the adjournment. He took the view that the offence committed had been so serious that he was not prepared to incur public anger by taking such a lenient course. The Court of Appeal quashed the custodial sentence, saying that there was no alternative but to honour the first judge's promise, no matter what the public might think. Although these sentences were all imposed in the Crown Court, exactly the same principle applies to adjournments in magistrates' courts. An example is *Gutteridge* v *DPP* (1987) 9 Cr App R (S) 279.

The cases so far discussed all depend upon 'there having been something in the nature of a promise, express or implied, that if a particular proposal is recommended, it will be adopted' (per Croom-Johnson J in *Moss* (1983) 5 Cr App R (S) 209). So, if the judge ordering the adjournment makes it clear to the offender that no promise is being made, even if the report turns out to be favourable, then the offender can have no sense of grievance if the eventual outcome is a custodial sentence. Thus in *Horton* (1985) 7 Cr App R (S) 299 the offenders had been found guilty of snatching a handbag. The judge adjourned for three weeks for a social inquiry report and community service assessment to be compiled, but stated that he thought that custody would be the likely outcome. Community service was recommended, but the judge nevertheless imposed a custodial sentence. This sentence was upheld by the Court of Appeal. In many cases it is necessary for the court to obtain a pre-sentence report before passing a custodial sentence, so it is clearly not in every case where an adjournment is made for reports that the judge is making a promise of a community sentence to the offender. The judge in *Horton* seems to have struck the correct balance: ordering the report, warning the offender not to expect too much, but leaving open the possibility of a community disposal should something exceptional in the report cause him to change his mind. This was the approach approved in *Chamberlain* (1994) 16 Cr App R (S) 473, where the Court of Appeal recommended that to avoid the sense of injustice referred to in *Gillam* the defendant must be told that he should not assume that he is likely to receive any form of treatment, or that a custodial sentence is ruled out, whatever the further report or inquiry may reveal.

3.3 THE FACTS OF THE OFFENCE

Having dealt with advance indications of the sentence and the procedure of adjournment, the remainder of this chapter is devoted to an examination of the proceedings between conviction and sentence. Although the description relates principally to proceedings in the

Crown Court, the arrangements are little different in magistrates' courts; relevent differences are mentioned where appropriate.

3.3.1 Prosecution statement of facts

If the accused pleads guilty, the first stage in the procedure between conviction and sentence is the summary by the prosecutor of the facts of the offence. In the Crown Court this will be done by counsel for the prosecution, and in the magistrates' court by a representative of the Crown Prosecution Service (the CPS). This summary is designed to assist the court and to inform the offender and the public of the basis of the prosecution case. If the accused has pleaded not guilty this summary is dispensed with, since the facts of the offence will have emerged during the trial and will already be well known to the court.

An account will be given of the salient features of the offence. If it is an offence of theft, the value of the property taken should be pointed out and the amount of property recovered, if any, should also be mentioned. If it is an offence of violence, the injuries to the victim, whether the victim required hospital treatment and whether the victim made a full recovery should be stated. If it is an offence involving breach of trust, the position held by the offender should be indicated. If the offence involves drugs, their weight or quantity and the offender's role in the offence should be explained. If it is a sexual offence, any previous relationship between the offender and the victim should be explained, and whether force was used over and above the force inherent in the offence itself should be made clear. The degree of planning which preceded any offence is relevant, as is any other aggravating factor such as the use of a weapon or the selection of a vulnerable victim. The circumstances of the offender's arrest, and his reaction, will be noted. If the offender cooperated with the police and promptly admitted guilt, this may tell in his favour on sentence.

The impact of the offence upon the victim is clearly an important consideration when the court is gauging the seriousness of the offence and in *Nunn* [1996] 2 Cr App R (S) 136, a case where the offender pleaded guilty to causing death by dangerous driving, the Court of Appeal said that it was an elementary principle of sentencing that the damaging and distressing effects of a crime upon the victim or, where the victim had been killed, the impact on the victim's family, should be made known to, and taken into account by, the sentencer. It is part of the duty of the prosecution to draw that impact to the sentencer's attention, but it will rarely be appropriate to call the victim as a witness (*Ashmeil* (1988) 10 Cr App R (S) 127). In *Hobstaff* (1993) 14 Cr App R (S) 605 the offender pleaded guilty to three counts of indecent assault, the offences having being committed on his neighbour's young daughters, who were aged between five and eight years. When opening the case, counsel for the prosecution said that the effects on the children had been 'horrific': one had suffered from nightmares and both had required treatment from a child psychologist. The sentencer made it clear when imposing sentence that he had borne that information in mind. The Court of Appeal said that while taking account of information about the victim's suffering was normally entirely appropriate, in this particular case it was improper, since there was no evidence before the court on the matter. Such evidence must be in proper form, whether as an expert's report or a witness statement or in some other appropriate form. The defence should, of course, see any such evidence in advance, and evidence of the victim alone should be approached with care especially if it relates to matters the defence cannot easily investigate or rebut. The Court of Appeal reviewed and summarised the guidelines given on this matter in *Perks* [2001] 1 Cr App R (S) 66. It was said that the court must pass the sentence appropriate to the facts of the offence and the circumstances of the offender.

The court should not accede to a plea for vengeance from the victim or the victim's relatives. It also had to be very cautious about pleas for mercy from the victim, although some allowance might be made where (a) the sentence originally imposed on the offender was aggravating the victim's distress (see *Roche* [1999] 2 Cr App R (S) 105), or (b) where the victim's forgiving attitude indicates that their physical or mental suffering must be significantly less than might have been expected (see *Mills* [1998] 2 Cr App R (S) 252).

The main point to notice is that, in principle, the prosecution is bound to take a *neutral* attitude during the stage between conviction and sentence. They are not concerned to influence the sentencer towards a heavy sentence; indeed to do so would be quite improper. On the other hand, if the offender in his statement to the police or in mitigation puts forward a version of the facts of the offence which does not accord with the evidence available to the prosecution, counsel should indicate that the defence version is not accepted by them. Further, according to Lord Bingham CJ in *A-G's Ref (Nos. 80 and 81 of 1999)* [2000] 2 Cr App R (S) 138, although 'in this country prosecutors to not behave like persecutors', there is never any 'obligation to acquiesce in an indication given by the judge to which the Crown takes exception'. The Code of Conduct of the Bar states that whilst the prosecution have a duty to point out any aggravating features of the case, they are also duty bound to draw to the court's attention any matters, of which they are aware, which reflect to the offender's credit. This is particularly the case where the offender is unrepresented (see **3.11**). While the neutrality of the prosecutor is an essential feature of the English criminal justice system, and stands in contrast to the role of the prosecutor in other jurisdictions, the neutrality card can sometimes be overplayed. First, the prosecutor does have an important indirect influence upon sentencing outcome, through the initial selection of the charges to be brought and through any negotiations with the defence as to charges. Secondly, there is a recent trend in judicial decisions and statutory development towards the greater involvement of the prosecutor at the sentencing stage. The most obvious change was the introduction in the CJA 1988 of a prosecution power to draw the attention of the Attorney-General to an example of excessively lenient sentencing in the Crown Court, with a view to the Attorney-General referring the matter to the Court of Appeal. That development is considered further below (see **13.3**), but a number of other smaller, but collectively significant, changes have also taken place, and it is convenient to deal with those here.

(a) In any case where the court is likely to make an order ancillary to the sentence, such as a compensation order under PCC(S)A 2000, s. 130, a restitution order under PCC(S)A 2000, s. 148 or a deprivation order under PCC(S)A 2000, s. 143, it seems that prosecution counsel must be ready to provide all the relevant information for the court. None of these orders can be made without an adequate factual basis being laid for them. In the case of a compensation order, for example, since the victim is not a party to the proceedings and may well not even be present in court, it will, in practice, fall to the prosecutor to provide the necessary facts. If personal injury, loss or damage has been occasioned to the victim, the onus is upon the prosecutor to adduce the amount, quantifying the loss so far as possible and producing evidence to substantiate the amount, such as receipts showing the cost of repairing property damaged by the offender (*Horsham Justices, ex parte Richards* (1985) 7 Cr App R (S) 158). The case of *Pemberton* (1982) 4 Cr App R (S) 328, dealing with a deprivation order, contains a clear statement on the point. According to Kilner Brown J:

It is incumbent upon the prosecution to justify the application and it is incumbent upon the trial judge to put the prosecution to proof if they simply state baldly, without any supporting evidence, that they seek an order for forfeiture.

It is not, however, the duty of the prosecutor to investigate the offender's means (*Johnstone* (1982) 4 Cr App R (S) 141; *Phillips* (1988) 10 Cr App R (S) 419). If the victim's loss has not been quantified, or is in dispute, the court may adjourn so that further inquiries can be made.

Where the question of confiscation of the offender's assets arises, on his conviction of an offence of drug trafficking under the Drug Trafficking Act 1994 (DTA 1994) or his conviction of an offence of a relevant description under the CJA 1988, the statutes impose responsibility upon the prosecution to adduce full information about the offender's assets and to demonstrate the extent to which the offender has benefited from the offending before such an order can be made (for confiscation orders, see Chapter 9).

(b) In a number of different circumstances the practice has been developing for sentencers to consult both defence and prosecution counsel, and invite submissions from them, before imposing a particular form of sentence. Both counsel may, for example, be invited to address the judge on the appropriateness of imposing a discretionary life sentence upon the offender (*Virgo* (1988) 10 Cr App R (S) 427). The judge may also seek the views of both counsel before embarking on a *Newton* hearing into disputed facts (see further **3.3.2**) and, of course, during such a hearing the prosecution will be put to proof of its version of the contested facts.

(c) Court of Appeal decisions have made it clear that it is the duty of both prosecution and defence counsel to make themselves aware of any legal limitations on the court's sentencing powers so as to be in a position to assist the judge if necessary. In *Kennedy* [1976] Crim LR 508 it was said that 'It is the duty of counsel to inform themselves what are the permissible sentences for the offences with which a defendant is charged, so as to be in a position to assist the judge if he makes a mistake.' This point was reinforced in *Komsta* (1990) 12 Cr App R (S) 63, and in *Richards* (1993) *The Times*, 1 April 1993, it was said to be 'particularly' the duty of counsel for the Crown to inform himself of the maximum sentence available for the offence being dealt with, and to correct the judge if he was about to make an error by exceeding it. Following these last-mentioned exhortations from the Court of Appeal, the Code of Conduct of the Bar indicates a more general duty upon prosecuting counsel to assist the sentencer in avoiding error. This goes beyond reminding the judge of maximum sentencing powers and extends to the increasingly complex range of statutory provisions on sentencing, and to Court of Appeal guideline judgments. The Code of Conduct suggests that such advice should be given either if asked for by the sentencer, or on counsel's initiative if it seems that a mistake of sentencing law is about to be made. In *Panayioutou* (1989) 11 Cr App R (S) 535 Hodgson J said that the time had come when judges were entitled to have guideline cases brought to their attention by counsel for the prosecution though, of course, the prosecutor could not ask for any particular penalty.

3.3.2   Establishing the facts after a guilty plea

By pleading guilty the offender does not necessarily admit that the prosecution case against him is correct in its entirety. He admits, of course, that he committed the offences described in each of the counts of the indictment to which he enters a guilty plea, and if defence counsel says anything in mitigation which is inconsistent with the plea then the judge will either ignore it or will invite the defence to consider whether the plea should be changed. A change of plea may be accepted by the court at any time before sentence is passed, but whether the court should do so is a matter within its discretion. The main issue here, however, is that many modern criminal offences are broadly drafted, and the particulars given in an indictment about an offence are likely to reveal little about whether the offence is a serious one, or a trivial one of its type. Thus, it sometimes happens that an offender quite properly pleads guilty and then, after the facts have been presented by prosecuting counsel, denies that his crime was as grave as has been alleged or might be assumed. Examples of such disputes, taken from decided cases, are: whether offenders had abandoned a conspiracy to rob before the police intervened to make commission of the robbery impossible anyway; whether an offence of unlawful wounding had been committed by the use of a knife or by fists alone; and whether a man who had caused grievous bodily harm to his wife had first been gravely provoked by taunts. It will be noted that in each of the examples given the accused, even on his own version of the events, was guilty as charged, but the sentence would be significantly affected by whether the judge accepted the prosecution statement of facts or the defence mitigation.

The leading case in this area is *Newton* (1982) 4 Cr App R (S) 388. The accused pleaded guilty to an offence of buggery, committed upon his wife. The prosecution summary of the facts stated that the offence had been committed without her consent. At the time of the case the offence was subject to a maximum sentence of life imprisonment, irrespective of consent, but clearly a case involving consent was far less serious than one where consent was absent. Defence counsel made it clear in mitigation that, according to his client, the wife had consented but the judge did not hear any evidence on the matter either from Newton or from the wife. He passed a sentence of eight years, which was clearly based upon an acceptance of the prosecution version of the facts. The Court of Appeal reduced the sentence to one year, to result in Newton's immediate release from custody (he had by that time already served ten months in prison). Lord Lane CJ said (at p.15):

On his own story Newton had to plead guilty to buggery, which left the vital issue of consent unresolved . . . There are three ways in which a judge in these circumstances can approach his difficult task of sentencing. It is in certain circumstances possible to obtain the answer from a jury . . . The second method which could be adopted by the judge in these circumstances is himself to hear the evidence on one side and another, and come to his own conclusion, acting so to speak as his own jury on the issue which is the root of the problem. The third possibility is for him to hear no evidence but to listen to the submissions of counsel and then come to a conclusion. But if he does that . . . then where there is a substantial conflict between the two sides . . . the version of the defendant must so far as possible be accepted.

On the facts of *Newton* the first option was unavailable, since this was a guilty plea rather than a conviction after a trial, but the judge had failed to adopt either of the other two courses which had been open to him. He had simply sentenced the offender on the basis that the acts were non-consensual, without hearing any evidence on the point at all.

The basic propositions in *Newton* have been elaborated in later decisions of the Court of Appeal, and the procedure advocated by Lord Lane has become known as a '*Newton* hearing'. The following main points have emerged:

(a) In *Newton* cases the burden of proof rests upon the prosecution to establish its version of the facts beyond reasonable doubt. One authority on the point is *Ahmed* (1984) 6 Cr App R (S) 391, where Parker LJ referred to 'the broad principle, which is so clearly recognised in *Newton*, that the accused should be given the benefit of the doubt', and then added:

The accused is given the benefit of the doubt (if there is one) by the necessity for the Crown Court to direct itself (or any jury) that the accused's account must be accepted *unless that court is sure that it is untrue.* (emphasis added)

In *Kerrigan* (1993) 14 Cr App R (S) 179 it was accepted to be 'clear beyond any argument' that the criminal standard was the appropriate one. In that case it was also said that it was better for the judge to direct himself openly as to the relevant burden and standard of proof, although failure to do so was not necessarily fatal. It is the duty of the defence to notify the Crown in advance that a plea of guilty will be tendered but that the prosecution version of the facts will be disputed at the sentencing stage. This will enable the prosecution to take steps to ensure that the necessary witnesses are present in court (*Mohun* (1993) 14 Cr App R (S) 5).

(b)   In *Newton* Lord Lane CJ said that the principles were applicable where there was a 'a substantial conflict between the two sides'. It follows that where the factual difference is insignificant and would make no real difference to the sentencing outcome, there is no need for a *Newton* hearing to resolve it. An example is *Bent* (1986) 8 Cr App R (S) 19, where the offender received a sentence of six months' youth custody for assaulting a store detective who was trying to arrest him. The prosecution stated that B had struck the detective with a stick, whilst Bent claimed that he had only threatened the victim with it. The sentencer took the view that the gravamen of the charge was the resisting of arrest and that it mattered little whether the stick had actually struck the detective or not. In a case such as this, for the avoidance of doubt, it is probably better for the sentencer to make it clear that he is sentencing on the basis of the defence version of the facts, as was recommended by Lincoln J in *Hall* (1984) 6 Cr App R (S) 321 at p. 324.

(c)   A series of cases following *Newton* have made it clear that there are some situations in which the defence version of the facts is so implausible that the judge may reject it out of hand rather than being obliged to conduct a *Newton* hearing into the matter. In *Hawkins* (1985) 7 Cr App R (S) 351, the offender's account of his involvement as the get-away driver in a joint offence of burglary, committed by himself and two others, was that he was unaware until the very end of the incident why the others had asked him to drive them to specified premises and then collect them an hour later. The judge declined to hear evidence on the matter and sentenced Hawkins on the prosecution version of the facts, which was that Hawkins had been a knowing participant throughout. The Court of Appeal upheld the decision, agreeing that H had made an 'incredible assertion'. (See also the situation dealt with at the end of **3.6.1.**) The judge's decision to reject the defence version out of hand must not, however, be taken lightly. In *Costley* (1989) 11 Cr App R (S) 357 C pleaded guilty to inflicting grievous bodily harm. The prosecution claimed that C had struck the victim about the head and body with a piece of wood. The defence version was that fists only had been used, and that there had been very considerable provocation. The Court of Appeal said that the defence version of the facts should not have been rejected out of hand, that there was a difference of importance between the sides, and that this should have been resolved by a *Newton* hearing.

(d)   Where there is a dispute over the relevant facts, the initiative to raise the matter normally rests with the defence, who should draw the matter to the attention of the prosecution and the court (*Tolera* [1998] Crim LR 425). In a case where a *Newton* hearing is appropriate, the judge is under a duty to hold one. The judge may hear submissions from counsel as to the appropriateness of that course, but the decision is then one for the judge. Thus a hearing may go ahead even if the defence is against that course (*Williams* v *Another*

(1983) 5 Cr App R (S) 134). The parties are given the opportunity to call witnesses, if they wish to do so, and to cross-examine the witnesses of the other side. The offender is a competent witness for the defence at the sentencing stage (Criminal Evidence Act 1898, s. 1(1) and *Wheeler* [1917] 2 KB 283), but cannot be called by the prosecution. The defence may, of course, sit back and wait to see if the prosecution can discharge its burden of proof. The whole *Newton* hearing procedure has more in common with trial procedure than the normal arrangements between conviction and sentence. The hearing itself should follow adversarial lines (*McGrath* (1983) 5 Cr App R (S) 460, at p. 463). The judge should preside over the matter and direct himself as if he were directing a jury (*Gandy* (1989) 11 Cr App R (S) 564). He should not assume an inquisitorial role and, if asking questions of the offender, should normally wait until both counsel have completed their questioning (*Myers* [1996] 1 Cr App R (S) 187). It is unclear how many of the other familiar rules of criminal evidence would also apply to *Newton* hearings, but *Gandy* indicates that, where identification is in issue, the judge should direct himself in accordance with the guidelines in *Turnbull* [1977] QB 224, which would have been applicable at trial.

(e)   It will be clear from the last paragraph that a *Newton* hearing may be ordered by the sentencer even where the prosecution and defence are agreed upon the facts on which the plea was based. In *Beswick* [1996] 1 Cr App R (S) 343 the judge was not prepared to accept the factual basis which had been agreed by the two sides. On appeal the Court of Appeal said that sentence should always be passed on a factual basis which is true. The prosecution must not lend itself to any agreement with the defence which was based on an unreal set of facts. If that had occurred, the judge could properly order a *Newton* hearing, and it was the duty of the prosecution to assist the judge by presenting the prosecution evidence and challenging the defence version.

(f)   One result of contesting the facts by way of a *Newton* hearing is that the offender may lose some of the discount which he would otherwise have received for pleading guilty (see **2.2.4 (g)**). The offender ought to be told about this, but the judge should be careful not to give the impression of having already decided against the offender's version of the facts (*Satchell* [1997] 2 Cr App R (S) 258).

It is one of the most fundamental principles of sentencing that an offender who has pleaded guilty to an offence must only be sentenced for *that* offence. Where the prosecution accepts a plea of guilty to a lesser offence, or accepts a plea of guilty to one of several counts which were originally preferred against the accused, the judge must be careful to sentence only for the matters admitted or specifically proved against the offender. In *Lawrence* (1981) 3 Cr App R (S) 49 the offender pleaded guilty to possession of cannabis and a count for possession with intent to supply was not proceeded with. The Court of Appeal varied a short prison sentence to a fine because it was felt that the sentencer had failed to 'banish from his mind' the possibility that L was growing the cannabis in order to sell it. *Lawrence* was followed and applied in *O'Prey* [1999] 2 Cr App R (S) 83.

A difficult problem is posed by the bringing of sample counts against an accused. After a period of some uncertainty, it is now clearly established by the Court of Appeal in *Canavan* [1998] 1 Cr App R 79 that the sentencer is bound to impose sentence purely on the basis of the sample counts proved against the offender or admitted by him, unless the defence concede that the counts are merely part of a wider pattern, or ask for the other offences to be taken into consideration. For further discussion of sample counts see **3.9.**

3.3.3   Establishing the facts after a verdict of guilty

Post-conviction disputes about the circumstances of the offence are not limited to cases
where the offender pleads guilty, for a jury's verdict of guilty after a not guilty plea is not
necessarily a total vindication of the prosecution's case. Consider, for example, the position
if an accused denies a charge of assault occasioning actual bodily harm. The victim gives
evidence for the prosecution that he was attacked with a knife, and the accused admits
striking the victim but says that he was acting in reasonable self-defence and did not use a
weapon. A verdict of guilty will merely show that, in the jury's view, the admitted assault
was not a justified act of self-defence. It will not resolve the issue, highly relevant to
sentence, of whether a weapon was used.

In such cases it is for the judge to form his own view of the evidence adduced before the
jury, and decide what the facts of the offence were. In general, it seems, he should not ask
the jury the reasons for their verdict or ask them what facts they find proved. In earlier times
it was common practice for the judge to ask a jury to elaborate on the factual basis for its
decision, to deliver a 'special' rather than a 'general' verdict. A case often cited as authority
that this practice is now improper is *Larkin* [1943] KB 174, although examples of trial
judges doing it may be found in later cases, such as *Lamb* [1967] 2 QB 981 (at p. 984),
Frankum [1984] Crim LR 434, *Baldwin* (1989) 11 Cr App R (S) 139 and *McGlade* (1990)
12 Cr App R (S) 105. With the exception of *McGlade*, these are all cases of manslaughter,
a crime which may be legally established in a number of different ways. It may be that
manslaughter cases represent an exception to what the Court of Appeal in *Stosiek* (1982) 4
Cr App R (S) 205 (at p. 208), called 'the usual and proper practice' of 'refrain[ing] from
inviting juries to explain their verdicts'. The reason for doubting this practice in England is
the rather strange ground that investigation by the judge into the precise reason for the jury's
verdict may reveal that different members of the jury have based their conviction on
materially different versions of the facts. If it emerges that this has happened, the accused's
conviction must be quashed (see *Brown* (1984) 79 Cr App R 115). In *McGlade* the relevant
issue was the same as in *Newton*: whether an act of buggery had been consensual or not.
The judge invited the jury to add a rider to their verdict to indicate their finding on this
matter, and the Court of Appeal did not indicate any disapproval of what the judge had done.
Seeking guidance from the jury was said to be 'not necessarily wrong' in *Cranston* (1993)
14 Cr App R (S) 103. There remains the possibility that the jury may, unsolicited, volunteer
their reasoning to the judge (as in *Jama* (1968) 52 Cr App R 498) or make their opinion
clear in some other way, such as by adding a rider to the verdict.

One way of avoiding the practice of the judge questioning the jury to determine the facts
is for the prosecution to anticipate the problem, and insert an additional count in the
indictment, which is designed to resolve the ambiguity on the main count. While this is often
possible in theory, in practice it is difficult to achieve. Thus, it has been suggested that if in
Newton (see **3.3.2**) the prosecution had included an additional count of assault occasioning
actual bodily harm, the jury's verdict on that count might have resolved the issue of whether
the sexual offence was consensual or not. Even so, on the prosecution version of the facts,
the wife had received other injuries consistent with an attempt to escape from her husband,
so it seems that a verdict of guilty on the assault charge would not necessarily have settled
the 'vital issue of consent'. In *Efionayi* (1995) 16 Cr App R (S) 380, however, such a course
should have been possible. There the defendants were charged with neglect of a child 'on
a day between the 1st and 14th day of September'. The prosecution resisted a defence
request to include a further count of neglect relating to a particular day or days. The jury

convicted and sentence was passed on the basis that neglect occurred throughout the period, but the Court of Appeal said that the indictment could and should have been amended so as to secure the jury's finding on that point.

The view of the facts which the judge adopts must be consistent with the jury's verdict. If the jury refuse to find the accused guilty as charged but convict him of a lesser offence, the sentence must be appropriate to that lesser offence, notwithstanding that the judge is convinced that there should have been a conviction for the more serious offence (*Hazelwood* (1984) 6 Cr App R (S) 52). In *Baldwin* (1989) 11 Cr App R (S) 139 the Court of Appeal reduced sentence on the offender, who was indicted for murder but convicted of manslaughter after stabbing the victim in the chest with a lock-knife, from ten years to seven years, to be faithful to the jury's 'perplexing' view that Baldwin had no intent to inflict grievous bodily harm.

Where several interpretations of the jury's verdict are possible, the judge is not bound to accept that version of events which is most favourable to the offender. In *Triumph* (1984) 6 Cr App R (S) 120 the jury found the offender not guilty of attempted murder but guilty of causing grievous bodily harm with intent. The defence claimed that injuries to the victim's legs had been caused when the gun had gone off accidentally, and that a stab which the victim had also received had been inflicted by another offender without Triumph's knowledge. The judge rejected the defence version in favour of a finding that the offender had shot the victim deliberately, even though he had not intended to kill him. This decision was upheld by the Court of Appeal. This case must, however, be read in the context of other decisions, particularly *Stosiek* (1982) 4 Cr App R (S) 205, which make it clear that the sentencer must be 'extremely astute' to give the benefit of any doubt about the facts of the offence to the offender. In *Stosiek* the offender was convicted of an assault upon a plain-clothes police officer. A prison sentence of 12 months was imposed, on the basis that Stosiek realised that his victim was a police officer. In fact, as the Court of Appeal explained, there was a 'reasonable possibility' that he had not realised that, and had overreacted to what he took to be a member of the public picking a quarrel with him. The custodial sentence was quashed and a fine was substituted.

3.3.4 Establishing the facts after a verdict of guilty, where a co-accused pleads guilty

The development of the procedures outlined above has generated difficulty in the case where A has pleaded guilty but is not sentenced and B, who has pleaded not guilty, is convicted at his trial. The problem is that when sentencing B the judge is, of course, under a duty to determine the proper factual basis for sentencing both offenders.

In *Smith* (1988) 10 Cr App R (S) 271 the offender pleaded guilty to involvement in the supply of stolen credit cards to the three co-accused. One of the co-accused pleaded guilty, while the other two were found guilty by a jury after their defence, that they were acting under duress from Smith, was rejected. At sentence, the judge stated that he had taken the view that Smith was the ringleader in the enterprise, based in part upon the evidence which the two co-accused had given in their own defence. The judge offered Smith the opportunity to testify in his own defence at the sentencing stage, but this was turned down. A sentence of 21 months' imprisonment was imposed upon Smith, while the three co-accused were all given community service orders. The Court of Appeal upheld the sentences, saying that the sentencer was entitled to take account of all the evidence he had heard at the trial of B in fixing the appropriate sentence on A. It was important that A be given the chance to give evidence about the extent of his involvement, and this had been done. Lord Lane CJ said that it was important that the sentencing judge should bear in mind the obvious risk that self-serving statements made by the offenders might be untrue. A *Newton* hearing might offer a way of resolving any significant factual dispute, but in the case the offender had turned down the opportunity to present his version of events on oath. The judge had, therefore, 'handled this difficult situation impeccably'. In *Winter* [1997] 1 Cr App R (S) 331 six offenders were charged with conspiracy to cause grievous bodily harm with intent. One offender pleaded guilty while the others were convicted after a trial and received eight-year or six-year sentences. The offender who had pleaded guilty appealed against his six-year term on the basis that he had been given no credit for his plea and that the factual basis for that plea, which was that he had used no violence against the victim, had been ignored. The Court of Appeal, reducing the sentence from six years' imprisonment to five, said that the offender should at least have been given the opportunity to give evidence if he had wished. This had not been done.

3.4   ANTECEDENTS EVIDENCE AND CRIMINAL RECORD

After the prosecution summary of the facts or, in the case of a not guilty plea, immediately after the verdict of guilty, the prosecution will provide information on the 'character and antecedents' of the offender. Antecedents evidence covers general information about the offender's background and circumstances, and is prepared in advance by the police in a standard form. On a separate sheet, attached to the antecedents evidence, is a list of the offender's previous convictions, if there are any. In the Crown Court, the prosecutor will summarise the accused's antecedents and record in his opening of the facts, provided that no dispute is anticipated. If some material in the antecedents is in dispute, a police officer is usually called to give evidence, and is then cross-examined by the defence. In the magistrates' courts a list of previous convictions is prepared, and this is handed by the prosecution to the bench.

3.4.1   Antecedents

The antecedents material is now on a set of standard forms which are prepared in advance by the police, and are subject to guidance provided by the *Practice Direction (Crime: Antecedents)* [1998] 1 Cr App R 213. The Practice Direction lays down minimum standards applicable for the provision of this information in the Crown Court and magistrates' courts and these were agreed between the Lord Chancellor's Department, the CPS and the Association of Chief Police Officers. Where local practice has been to provide fuller information it is intended that that practice should continue. The antecedents must contain personal and other details relating to the defendant, most of which will be completed by the police on the basis of information supplied by the defendant, such as to the custody officer on arrest, or upon committal by the magistrates to Crown Court. This information would normally include the defendant's date of birth rather than just his age (especially where the defendant is a juvenile and his age will crucially affect the sentencing options available), his address, home circumstances and employment details, together with date of arrest. The antecedents must also contain information about the defendant's previous convictions and previous findings of guilt, if any, derived from the Police National Computer (see further **3.4.2**). Where appropriate, in the Crown Court these should contain brief details of the facts of the last three similar convictions. Spent convictions should be specially marked as such, but spent convictions are not erased from the record itself (see **3.4.4**). Details of any previous formal caution, warning or reprimand will appear on a separate sheet (**3.4.3**). Seven copies of the antecedents documents are prepared in the Crown Court. Two copies are sent directly to the CPS, and the remainder are sent to the court which will be dealing with the case. The court then sends one copy of the antecedents to the defence and one to the probation service. Case law indicates that the defendant should see a copy of the antecedents as soon as possible, especially where the document contains material which is likely to be disputed (*Wilkins* (1977) 66 Cr App R 49). The remaining copies are for the court's use, including one for the note-taker. The antecedents documents must be served within 21 days of committal in every case. Any points of dispute arising from the information in the antecedents should be raised with the police, by the defence, at least seven days before the hearing, so that wherever possible the matter can be cleared up before the hearing itself. Seven days before the listed hearing date the police will check the conviction information against their computer-held data and will supply information to the court on any additional convictions, together with any other outstanding matters. The antecedents should also contain information on the date of last discharge from prison or other custodial institution, any court orders to which the defendant is currently subject, any outstanding offences, and liability for driving disqualification. Outstanding fines, however, are not shown. Where relevant, information should be given on the time which has been spent by the defendant on remand in custody on the impending matter.

Some portion of the antecedents material is quite often read out in court. As explained above, the material should have been supplied or verified by the defendant and in most cases proves to be entirely uncontroversial. In the past, problems have arisen where the police have included material in the antecedents which has gone well beyond that indicated in the Practice Direction. An illustrative case is *Sargeant* (1974) 60 Cr App R 74, where the defendant disputed a suggestion in the antecedents that he had been dismissed from his last employment for drunkenness. Lawton LJ said that if it was thought that the information really would help the sentencer, information in support of the allegation should have been provided for the court. Another example is *Bibby* [1972] Crim LR 513, where the Court of Appeal said that it was unfair for the antecedents material to contain a general statement that the defendant 'mixed with criminals'. The basic principle to be derived from these cases is that, should the defence challenge information in the antecedents, the prosecution are required to prove the matter according to the normal criminal standard. If they are unable to do so, the sentencer should make it clear that he has disregarded the disputed material (*Campbell* (1911) 6 Cr App R 131). It follows that if there is no proper proof of an allegation prejudicial to the defendant, it should not be made in the first place.

3.4.2 Previous convictions

Evidence of the offender's previous convictions, if there are any, is always made available to the court when it turns to consider sentence. There is no doubt that information about previous convictions, and the offender's response to previous sentences, is highly influential in sentence decision-making. If an offender has no previous convictions, or is lightly convicted, or has a conviction-free gap prior to the commission of the latest offence, these are matters which the court may (and usually will) weigh in the offender's favour in the court's discretion under PCC(S)A 2000, s. 158(1). If the offender does have a poor record, however, its precise relevance is more difficult to state. Certainly the offender is not entitled to the mitigation which he could have claimed on the basis of a clean record. It is not clear, however, in what circumstances, or to what extent, the court may view the offender's poor record as making the new offence more serious, and therefore deserving of a heavier punishment. Section 151(1) of the 2000 Act simply states that 'the court may take into account any previous convictions of the offender or any failure of his to respond to previous sentences' when considering the seriousness of the latest offence. This provision, and the background to it, was considered at **2.2.5**.

Attached to the antecedents form will be the list of the offender's previous convictions. This list also contains previous 'findings of guilt'. A finding of guilt is the equivalent of a conviction, but made against a juvenile who has pleaded guilty or has been found guilty in a youth court or in a magistrates' court (CYPA 1933, s. 59). For each conviction, the previous convictions form gives the court at which the offender was convicted, the date of the conviction, the offences of which the offender was convicted, the sentence passed (generally including the amount of any fine, the duration of any custodial or community sentence and the number of hours of any community service ordered) and any alteration made as the result of an appeal. The date of release from the last custodial sentence, if any, is also given.

Previous convictions are taken to be those in existence before the commission of the offence for which the offender is now to be sentenced. Any convictions between the commission of the offence and the hearing relating to that offence should, technically, not appear in the list of previous convictions, but should still appear in the antecedents. There must, of course, never be mention on the form of any arrests, charges or prosecutions which have not ended in conviction (*Burton* (1941) 28 Cr App R 89). Offences taken into consideration are not convictions, and those incurred by the offender on previous occasions should be listed separately (see **3.8**). Formal cautions, warnings or reprimands (**3.4.3**) are not convictions, but any which have been incurred by the offender during the last three years will appear on a separate list. The payment of a fixed penalty without prosecution under the Road Traffic Offenders Act 1988 does not count as a conviction and so should not appear in the convictions list. No order should appear in the list of previous convictions which was not made consequent upon conviction (Rehabilitation of Offenders Act 1974, s. 7(5)). The best example of such an order would be where a person is bound over to keep the peace, without having been convicted of any offence (see **7.2.1**). It may be thought that a conviction followed by an absolute or conditional discharge should not be included in the list of previous convictions because of the effect of PCC(S)A 2000, s. 14, which states that, for a range of purposes, an offender who is so sentenced is deemed not have been convicted of the offence (see **7.1.4**) but ROA 1974, s. 1(4), defines 'conviction' so as to include conviction followed by discharge.

The list of the previous convictions will also include, where this is known to the police or CPS, information about any breaches of a suspended sentence, probation order, conditional discharge or breach of licence conditions following an offender's early release from custody, provided that these have been the subject of court proceedings. Where breach proceedings are brought against an offender following his failure to comply with the requirements of a probation order, for example, no further offence has been committed and so the matter might not be known about by the police or CPS. If it is apparent from the evidence of previous convictions that the offender committed his present offence during the operational period of a conditional order such as a suspended sentence or a conditional discharge, then he should be asked whether he admits the breach of the sentence. Assuming that he does so, the court can then deal with him for that matter as well as for the current offence, in accordance with the statutory provisions dealing with breach and revocation of the particular conditional order. If the offender refuses to admit the breach, or indeed if he challenges any of the evidence about previous convictions, the prosecution must prove beyond reasonable doubt that the evidence challenged is correct. Otherwise it should be ignored by the judge when sentence is passed, and the judge should make it clear that this is being done (*Butterwasser* [1947] 2 All ER 417). An offender who admits a previous conviction but wishes to be allowed to explain it more fully should be permitted by the court to do so (*Metcalfe* (1913) 9 Cr App R 7). This may perhaps be more conveniently done in the plea in mitigation, rather than by challenging the antecedents.

In most cases, the information about previous convictions is clear and is not disputed by prosecution or defence. Sometimes, however, there can be difficulties. The prosecution may wish to show that the offender has other convictions, such as very recent ones, which do not appear on the record. The records are sometimes inaccurate or incomplete in other ways, and for other reasons. In *Brumwell* (1980) *The Guardian*, 17 November 1980 the offender was given a sentence of six months' imprisonment but was released when it came to light that an error on his record had credited him with eight previous convictions while, in fact, he had only two. There is also concern over a lack of awareness among some practitioners of the requirements of the Practice Direction (see in *Re A Barrister (Wasted Costs Order) (No. 1 of 1999)* (2000) *The Times*, 18 April 2000, *per* Clarke LJ).

An alleged previous conviction which is disputed by the offender will normally be proved by:

(a)   producing a certificate of conviction signed by the clerk of the court in which the conviction took place (PACE 1984, s. 73 and, where the conviction was for an offence relevant to ss. 109–111 of the PCC(S)A 2000, s. 113 of that Act), and

(b)   adducing evidence to show that the person named in the certificate is the person whose conviction it is sought to establish.

It will thus be for the prosecution to prove that the offender before the court is the person named in the certificate of conviction that has been produced. For previous convictions on indictment, the certificate of conviction will give the substance of the indictment upon which the conviction took place. For summary convictions, it will consist of a copy of the document recording the conviction (PACE 1984, s. 73(2)). In addition, there is a special provision to cater for proof of previous convictions of a person convicted of a summary offence where that person does not attend court. A notice must be served on the person, not less than seven days before the hearing, stating the alleged previous convictions which it is proposed to bring to the attention of the court. The court may, if the offender does not dispute the convictions, then take account of them in the offender's absence. Endorsements on a driving licence may be produced as prima facie evidence of the matters endorsed (Road Traffic Offenders Act 1988 (RTOA 1988), ss. 31(1) and 44(1)). An order of disqualification from driving may be proved by the production of an extract from the court register certified by the clerk of the court.

3.4.3   Formal cautions, warnings and reprimands

As an alternative to initiating a prosecution the police may decide to issue a formal caution. A formal caution should be distinguished from an informal warning given to the person by a police officer as part of the officer's 'on the street' discretion. The practice of administering a formal caution is subject to guidelines set out in a series of Home Office circulars, the most recent being Home Office Circular 18/1994. Sections 65 and 66 of the

CDA 1998 provided for a new system of reprimands and warnings to replace the current system of formal cautions for those aged under 18. A formal caution involves four elements. First, the person cautioned must fully admit guilt. Second, there must be enough evidence against the person at that time to provide a realistic prospect of conviction if a prosecution were brought. Third, the person must consent to being formally cautioned rather than being prosecuted; the effect of the person's consent to accepting a caution must be explained to him, and he must be told that cautions may be cited in court in the event of future offending. Fourth, certain procedural requirements must be complied with, such as that the caution must normally be administered at a police station, by an officer of at least the rank of inspector.

For those aged under 18, a police officer may issue a reprimand where the young person has not been reprimanded or warned before, where there is sufficient evidence to provide a realistic prospect of conviction, where the young person admits the offence and has not previously been convicted of any offence, and where it is in the public interest not to prosecute. The next more serious step is for the police officer to issue a warning. This can be done only where no previous warning has been given or, exceptionally, where at least two years has elapsed since the last warning. A young person who receives a warning is also referred to a youth offending team.

It should be noted that the cautioning power rests with the police and not the prosecuting authorities, although, of course, the CPS have an important discretion to discontinue proceedings against a person, even where the police have passed the papers to them with a view to prosecution.

The rapid growth in the use of formal cautioning, rather than prosecution, especially for juvenile offenders, has been an important feature of modern criminal justice policy. There are thought to be strong policy reasons for delaying a juvenile's entry into the criminal justice system for as long as possible, in the hope that he will grow out of his offending behaviour and never enter the system at all. The percentage of males aged 10–11 inclusive cautioned for indictable offences in 1999 (as a percentage of those found guilty or cautioned) was 87 per cent. The equivalent figure for those aged 12–14 inclusive was 69 per cent, for those aged 18–20 inclusive it was 29 per cent and for those aged 21 and over it was 16 per cent. The cautioning rate for adults varies considerably across the country.

Before a formal caution, warning or reprimand is administered, the position of the victim should be considered, by obtaining his views about the offence, and considering the extent of any loss or damage. One factor to be borne in mind is that if a suspect is so dealt with rather than prosecuted there is no opportunity for a court to make a compensation order.

Formal cautions are not convictions, and so should not appear in the list of previous convictions. All police forces, however, record cautions administered locally. Previous cautions which were issued for offences committed by the offender (whether a juvenile or an adult) within the three years preceding the current offence may be cited in court (Home Office Circular 59/1990). That Circular also makes it clear that cautions and convictions, although presented to the court at the same time, should not appear on the same sheet, so as to preserve a distinction between them. Section 66 of the CDA 1998 provides that a reprimand or a warning, 'may be cited in criminal proceedings in the same circumstances as a conviction of the person may be cited'.

3.4.4 Spent convictions

The Rehabilitation of Offenders Act 1974 (ROA 1974) was passed with the aim of helping ex-offenders to 'live down' the stigmatising effect of previous convictions. The main effect of the Act is that, once a certain time (the 'rehabilitation period') has elapsed from the date of the offender's conviction, the conviction becomes 'spent' and the offender, in respect of that conviction, is a 'rehabilitated person' (ROA 1974, s. 1(1)). As a rehabilitated person he is, for most purposes, treated as if he had never committed or been convicted of the offence (s. 4(1)). 'Conviction' is, for the purposes of the ROA 1974, widely defined to include 'any finding in criminal proceedings other than one linked with a finding of insanity' (s. 1(4)). It includes 'findings of guilt' made against juveniles.

On its face, the ROA 1974 does not apply to a wide range of judicial proceedings, including criminal proceedings (s. 7(2)). This is misleading. In the case of criminal proceedings, *Practice Direction (Crime: Spent Convictions)* [1975] 1 WLR 1065 endorsed the spirit of the Act in stating that neither counsel nor judge should refer to a spent conviction where 'such reference can reasonably be avoided'. Mention of a spent conviction requires the judge's authority and that authority should be given only where the interests of justice so require. At the sentencing stage, the list of previous convictions given to the court should mark those which are spent. They are usually stamped over with the word 'SPENT' (though what is written underneath remains readable). When passing sentence the judge should say nothing about spent convictions unless it is vital to do so to explain the penalty decided upon. *Practice Direction (Crime: Spent Convictions)* has no direct application to magistrates' courts but, following advice issued by the Secretary of State (in Home Office Circular 98/1975) comparable practice is followed in the lower courts.

Whether a previous conviction is capable of becoming spent and, if so, the length of the rehabilitation period, are governed by the sentence imposed for the offence. Thus, if the offender serves a sentence of more than 30 months' imprisonment or detention in a young offender institution (including a life sentence) the conviction can never become spent. If he serves a sentence of more than six months but not more than 30 months, the conviction becomes spent after 10 years. At the other end of the scale, if he is given an absolute discharge the rehabilitation period is only six months. A full list of rehabilitation periods is given at **13.6.1**, together with some of the other provisions in the Act, such as the reduced rehabilitation periods for some sentences which apply to offenders who were under 18 years of age when convicted.

It is important to realise that for a conviction to become spent the rehabilitation period must be conviction-free. If an offender is convicted of an offence (other than a purely summary offence) during the rehabilitation period for an earlier conviction, then (unless the later conviction can never become spent) the two convictions both become spent on the later of the two relevant rehabilitation dates (s. 6(4)). This usually means that the earlier conviction does not become spent until the date on which the later conviction becomes spent. It follows that regular offenders tend to have no spent convictions, since the rehabilitation periods for early convictions are extended by the later convictions. The ROA 1974 has its main practical effect then where a person collects a conviction early in life and this is followed by a long conviction-free period.

A further complexity of the ROA 1974 lies in the wide range of exceptions to its out-of-court application. These were first set out in the Rehabilitation of Offenders Act 1974 (Exceptions) Order 1975 and have been added to since. See **13.6.2**.

3.5 REPORTS

Once evidence has been given concerning the offender's antecedents and previous convictions the sentencer will turn to consider any reports which have been prepared on the offender. In general terms, the purpose of reports is to provide additional factual information for the sentencer about the circumstances of the offence and the character of the offender. Sometimes sentence may properly be passed without the benefit of reports, but there are now many occasions upon which the court is placed under an obligation to obtain and consider them, and other cases in which it is good sentencing practice to do so.

The relevant reports may have been obtained prior to conviction or hearing, in which case, in the Crown Court, they will probably have been read by the judge in advance. If they have not been obtained, it may be appropriate for the sentencer to adjourn for them to be prepared (see **3.2.1**). A pre-sentence report (see below) on an accused who intends to plead not guilty will not generally be prepared in advance. This is because to do so would be a wasted effort if the accused is acquitted, and because important matters which should appear in the report, such as the extent of the accused's culpability and the accused's attitude to the offence, cannot be investigated. In these cases, adjournment after conviction is the general rule.

In the discussion which follows the main emphasis is placed upon the pre-sentence report because this is the document most commonly encountered in practice and in many cases will be the only report which the court will have. Depending on the issues raised by the case, however, the pre-sentence report may be supplemented by other reports.

3.5.1 Pre-sentence reports

Section 162(1) of PCC(S)A 2000 provides that a pre-sentence report (or PSR) is a report in writing which:

(a) with a view to assisting the court in determining the most suitable method of dealing with an offender, is made or submitted by an appropriate officer; and

(b) contains information as to such matters, presented in such manner, as may be prescribed by the Secretary of State.

Where the offender is aged 18 or over, the report is prepared by a probation officer or a social worker of a local authority social services department. If the offender is under 18, additionally a pre-sentence report can be prepared by a member of a youth offending team (s. 162(2)). Whenever a court requests a report, it is the duty of the relevant service to provide one. A copy of the pre-sentence report must be given to the offender or to his lawyer so that any controversial matters in it can be challenged and a further copy should be given to the prosecutor (PCC(S)A 2000, s. 156). Ordinarily the court should not read out a pre-sentence report in full (*Smith* (1968) 51 Cr App R 376). If matters in the report are in dispute the writer should be called. Otherwise, and particularly if it is uncontroversial, the report may be presented by a court liaison officer rather than by the person who has written it. Any matters relating to the report should be dealt with before counsel for the defence enters the plea in mitigation, so that counsel can question the report writer if necessary and refer to the content of the report in the mitigation (*Kirkham* [1968] Crim LR 210). In practice, lawyers often base their pleas in mitigation on material in the report. This is natural enough, but has sometimes occasioned criticial comment.

The PCC(S)A 2000 gives little information about the form and content of pre-sentence reports. The Home Office *National Standard* (Home Office, 2000) fills in much of the detail. A pre-sentence report must be 'in writing'. This excludes the possibility of presentation of an oral 'stand-down' inquiry in any of the cases where a pre-sentence report is referred to by statute (see below). Perhaps an oral report could still be given, in appropriate circumstances, where a pre-sentence report is not otherwise required. Where the court has a specific sentence in mind, such as a short CPO or a CRO without additional requirements, it may order a specific sentence report instead of a pre-sentence report. A specific sentence report will normally be made available to the court on the day requested. A specific sentence report is a pre-sentence report for the purposes of the PCC(S)A 2000.

Important provisions in the PCC(S)A 2000 require a sentencing court to obtain and consider a pre-sentence report in the following circumstances. As far as custodial sentences are concerned, it should be borne in mind when looking at (a) and (b) below that, subject to the normal requirement that the court 'shall obtain and consider a pre-sentence report' (PCC(S)A 2000, s. 81(1)), the court may dispense with such a report if, in the circumstances of the case, the court is of the opinion that it is unnecessary to obtain one (s. 81(2)). The discretion to dispense with a report is subsequently narrowed in respect of an offender who is under the age of 18. Unless the offence is one which is triable only on indictment, the court cannot decide that a pre-sentence report on a juvenile is unnecessary unless a report was prepared earlier and the court has seen it (s. 81(3)). Section 81(5) provides that no sentence shall be invalidated by failure of the court to comply with s. 81(1), but on appeal against a custodial sentence passed without the court having obtained and considered a pre-sentence report, the appellate court must obtain and consider one unless, in accordance with s. 81(6), that court thinks that the court below was justified in not calling for a report or, even if it was not justified, in the circumstances of the case at the time the matter is before the appellate court, it is unnecessary to obtain one. Again, however, the appellate court cannot take this line with a juvenile not convicted of an offence triable only on indictment. In such a case the appellate court must order a report, or have sight of a recent one prepared on the juvenile (s. 81(7)).

(a) *When making a decision whether a custodial sentence is justified.* In assisting the sentencer to make this decision the report should address, and the sentencer should have regard to, those matters which the sentencer is bound to consider under PCC(S)A 2000, s. 79(2)(a) (whether the offence was 'so serious' that only a custodial sentence can be justified for it) or, under s. 79(2)(b) (where the offence was a violent offence or a sexual offence, whether only a custodial sentence would be adequate to protect the public from serious harm from the offender). The court must take into account all such information as is available to it, '. . . about the circumstances of the offence (including any aggravating or mitigating factors' (s. 81(4)(a)). The pre-sentence report is a prime source for this information. Where the court is dealing with an offender convicted of a violent offence or a sexual offence, it may 'take into account any information about the offender which is before it' (s. 81(4)(b)). More generally, PCC(S)A 2000, s. 158(1) provides that nothing 'shall prevent a court mitigating an offender's sentence by taking into account any such matters as, in the opinion of the court, are relevant in mitigation of sentence', and s. 151(1) permits the court to have regard to the offender's previous convictions and any failure of his to respond to previous sentences as is available to it. Material in the pre-sentence report may be relevant to all of these matters.

(b) *When making a decision on the appropriate length of a custodial sentence.* The court must take into account 'all such information . . . about the circumstances of the offence (including any aggravating or mitigating factors (s. 81(4)(a)). Where the court is dealing with an offender convicted of a violent offence or a sexual offence, it may 'take into account any information about the offender which is before it' (s. 81(4)(b)). Again, s. 158(1) provides that nothing 'shall prevent a court mitigating an offender's sentence by taking into account any such matters as, in the opinion of the court, are relevant in mitigation of sentence', and s. 151(1) permits the court to have regard to the offender's previous convictions and any failure of his to respond to previous sentences. Material in the pre-sentence report may be relevant to all of these matters.

(c)   *When making a decision to impose one of the more onerous community orders.*   In this context, PCC(S)A 2000, s. 36(3), identifies:

(i)   a CRO which includes additional requirements authorised by sch. 2 to the 2000 Act;

(ii)   a CPO;

(iii)   a CPRO;

(iv)   a drug treatment and testing order; or

(v)   a supervision order which includes requirements authorised by sch. 2.

The 2000 Act states that a court should not impose a community sentence unless it is of the opinion that the offence 'was serious enough to warrant such a sentence' (s. 35(1)) and that the restrictions imposed upon the offender by the community sentence 'are commensurate with the seriousness of the offence' (s. 35(3)(b)). When imposing a community sentence the court is also bound, by s. 35(3)(a), to select that sentence which is the 'most suitable for the offender'. Section 158(1), referred to above in relation to custodial sentences, also applies to community sentences, so that the court may consider any matter in mitigation which is drawn to its attention, and s. 151(1) permits the court to have regard to the offender's previous convictions and any failure of his to respond to previous sentences.

As far as the orders listed here are concerned, it should be borne in mind that, subject to the normal requirement that the court 'shall obtain and consider a pre-sentence report' (s. 36(4)), the court may dispense with such a report if, in the circumstances of the case, the court is of the opinion that it is unnecessary to obtain one (s. 36(5)). The discretion to dispense with a report is, as with custodial sentences considered above, subsequently narrowed in respect of an offender who is under the age of 18.

Even for those community sentences where a pre-sentence report is not normally required it will often be good sentencing practice to obtain one, in order to consider further information both about the offence and the offender.

In what circumstances could a sentencer properly take the view that a pre-sentence report is unnecessary? Home Office research published in 1997 found that it was rare for either the Crown Court or magistrates' courts to pass a community sentence without a pre-sentence report, but in both courts around 15 per cent of cases involved the imposition of a custodial sentence without a report. Sentencers pass sentence without a report where it seems unlikely that a report could make a difference to the outcome — such as where the offender is inevitably facing a long custodial sentence, or where the offender has already spent time on remand in custody and where a sentence is passed which will result in the offender's immediate release.

The Home Office *National Standard* requires that reports should be prepared as quickly as possible, and should, in any event, normally be completed within 15 working days.

The *National Standard* (2000) states that every pre-sentence report must set out the basic factual information on the offender and the offence(s) and list the sources used to prepare the report. Every pre-sentence report should contain an 'offence analysis', including the offender's attitude to the offence(s) and awareness of its consequences for the victim; an 'offender assessment', including any 'relevant personal background, such as accommodation or employment problems, or substance misuse; and an 'assessment of the risk to the public and the likelihood of reoffending'. The pre-sentence report should conclude by making a 'clear and realistic proposal for sentence'. The making of sentence recommendations has always been controversial, and in some Court of Appeal decisions probation officers have been criticised for making 'unrealistic' proposals (e.g. *James* [1982] Crim LR 59). The offender 'should be interviewed on one or more occasions' to provide information for the report. The pre-sentence report should be objective, impartial, free from discriminatory language and stereotype, balanced, verified and factually accurate. The report should contain only information which is relevant to the sentencing decision and should provide a clear indication of the source of main facts and whether they have been verified.

3.5.2 Medical reports

There is a range of circumstances in which a court will have before it a medical report prepared upon the offender. Medical reports are generally prepared in advance on any offender charged with murder or manslaughter, a serious violent or sexual offence or arson. Apart from these cases, a request for a medical report may be initiated by the defence, or sometimes by the sentencer. A court must obtain medical reports before it can make a hospital order or a guardianship order under MHA 1983, s. 37 or before it can insert into a CRO or a supervision order a requirement of medical treatment (see Chapter 11).

A court must order a medical report to be prepared on any offender who is, or appears to be, mentally disordered, before a custodial sentence (apart from a mandatory life sentence for murder or a sentence under PCC(S)A 2000, s. 109) is passed on him (s. 82(1)). Failure to comply with this requirement does not render the sentence invalid but, if there is an appeal, the appellate court must obtain a medical report (s. 82(4)). The court need not obtain a report if it thinks this is 'unnecessary' (s. 82(2)). In any event, before passing a custodial sentence on such an offender, the court must consider any information before it (whether in a medical report, a pre-sentence report or otherwise) which relates to the offender's mental condition and the likely effect of a custodial sentence on that condition and the availability of treatment for it (s. 82(3)). A medical report may be submitted orally or in writing by a registered medical practitioner who is duly approved for the purposes of MHA 1983, as having special experience in the diagnosis and treatment of mental disorder (s. 82(5)). Section 82 does not affect the decision of the Court of Appeal in *Hook* (1980) 2 Cr App R (S) 353, which was to the effect that a sentencer cannot recommend that an offender serve a custodial sentence at the psychiatric prison, Grendon Underwood.

The court may adjourn for the preparation of a medical or psychiatric report on the offender. Adjournment for reports is considered in **3.2.1**. When the report has been prepared, a copy should be given to the clerk of the court and to the defence lawyer. The offender will not see the report, but if he is not legally represented he should be told the gist of what is in it (MHA 1983, s. 54(3)). Although the report should not be read out in court, there may be discussion in court of its contents. The defence may require the report writer to be called to give evidence, and evidence can be called to rebut what is in the report. In the Crown Court, the vast majority of requests for reports came from the defence, in the context of providing material for mitigation. Reports seemed to be given considerable weight by sentencers. Clear recommendations for psychiatric disposal are overridden by the sentencer in only a very few cases with custody being imposed instead because of the seriousness of the offence.

3.5.3 Other reports

Information may on occasion be derived from other reports. Custodial establishments may submit a report to the Court of Appeal which relates to the offender's behaviour while in custody. Sometimes information about an offender's reaction to his first few weeks of custody is a factor which weighs with the appellate court in reducing sentence (see further **13.2**).

Before passing any one of a range of non-custodial sentences, the court must have an assessment of the offender's suitability for that disposal. So whether in addition to a pre-sentence report or not, there will be a short report from a probation or other appropriate officer indicating whether the offender seems to have the necessary skills and motivation to perform work under the order. For details see the discussion of the various non-custodial sentences in Chapters 5 and 7. By PCC(S)A 2000, s. 157, where report (other than a pre-sentence report) is made by a probation officer or member of a youth offending team to a Crown Court or adult magistrates' court with a view to helping the court select a suitable disposal, the court must give a copy of that report to the offender or his legal representative.

3.6 DEFENCE MITIGATION AND OTHER REPRESENTATIONS

After the judge has read and considered the reports, the defence has the opportunity to present the 'plea in mitigation' on behalf of the offender. The prosecution, on the other hand, has no opportunity to present a 'plea in aggravation'. It was explained earlier that sentencing procedure is quite different from trial procedure, and the lack of an adversarial approach here is a further illustration of that point.

3.6.1 The plea in mitigation

There is no set pattern for mitigation. According to Comyn J in *Gross* v *O'Toole* (1982) 4 Cr App R (S) 283, mitigation is 'purported to be the province of the most junior of counsel' but 'is in fact amongst the most difficult tasks any barrister can ever face'. The purpose of the plea in mitigation is to make known to the sentencer any aspects of the case which tend to reduce its gravity, whether this relates to the precise facts of the offence (any significant differences between prosecution and defence versions of the facts should already have been resolved: **3.3**), the offender's attitude to the offence, his individual circumstances, any feelings of remorse, willingness to make reparation or other mitigating factors. On the other hand, it is important that the lawyer advancing mitigation should be 'realistic' about his client's case, and be frank about the aggravating features of the case as well. In a case where the judge may have in mind a sentence which counsel may not have considered, the judge should give the lawyer notice of that fact before mitigation is begun, so that he may address that specific point. Examples are where the judge is considering imposing a life sentence on the offender (*Morgan* (1987) 9 Cr App R (S) 201) or a longer-than-normal custodial sentence under PCC(S)A 2000, s. 79(2)(b) (*O'Brien* (1995) 16 Cr App R (S) 556). Another is disqualification from driving for life, rather than for a fixed term of years (*Scott* (1989) 11 Cr App R (S) 249). A fourth is where the judge is considering imposing a separate custodial sentence for failure to surrender to bail (*Woods* (1989) 11 Cr App R (S) 551).

The plea in mitigation generally takes the form of a single address, but it is open to the defence to call witnesses to speak to the offender's generally good character (e.g. an employer who says that he is willing to continue employing the offender), or to comment upon the circumstances of the offence. This evidence may be called at the beginning, in the middle, or at the end of the speech (per Comyn J in *Gross* v *O'Toole*). The offender will not normally be called at this stage unless there is a dispute about the facts of the offence, or if it is a road traffic case and the offender is subject to mandatory disqualification unless he shows special reasons for not being disqualified from driving (see **10.1**). If the lawyer decides to call his client at this stage, it is not appropriate for the judge to discourage it (*Cross* [1975] Crim LR 591). It is perfectly proper for counsel to cite guideline sentencing decisions of the Court of Appeal when giving the speech in mitigation (*Ozair Ahmed* (1993) 15 Cr App R (S) 286). There is in fact great variation in the style, length and content of pleas in mitigation. What ought to be said will obviously vary considerably from case to case, and the lawyer's common sense and experience will be the guide as to what is better left unsaid. Even where there appears to be little which can be said in favour of the offender, it is the lawyer's duty to present whatever mitigation can be found, and the sentencer's duty to listen to those representations, without excessive interruption (*Jones* [1980] Crim LR 58). The plea in mitigation will normally be heard in open court, but there is power to clear the court of members of the public to hear sensitive matters of mitigation in camera. This is a 'wholly exceptional' course to take (*Ealing Justices, ex parte Weafer* (1981) 3 Cr App R (S) 296). Where a matter is to be put forward in mitigation which the offender does not wish to have made public, the information may be written down and handed to the sentencer, with a copy being given to the prosecution (*Ealing Justices* (above); *Beckett* (1967) 51 Cr App R 180). If the defendant contested the case but was convicted, it is wrong for counsel to repeat the defendant's claim to be innocent in the speech in mitigation (*Wu Chun-piu* v *The Queen* [1996] 1 WLR 1113). During the speech in mitigation, counsel must not make statements which are 'merely scandalous or intended or calculated to vilify, insult or annoy' any person (Code of Conduct of the Bar, para. 610(e)). Section 58 of the Criminal Procedure and Investigations Act 1996 states that the judge may make an order to prevent the reporting by the press of any false or irrelevant assertions made during a speech in mitigation. Of particular concern here are suggestions made in the speech that the victim of the offence was a person of less than upright character, or was at least partly responsible for what happened.

As we have seen, offence seriousness is the key criterion under the PCC(S)A 2000 when determining both the form of sentence (custodial, community or financial penalty) and the appropriate degree of restriction of liberty, if a custodial or community sentence is selected. This approach is often reflected in pleas in mitigation. The lawyer will tend initially to address matters of offence seriousness, pointing out in particular those matters which make the offence less serious than other examples of the particular offence committed. Perhaps the offence was committed on the spur of the moment, rather than planned, or, if several offenders were involved, the offender's role was a peripheral one or, if the offender has committed an assault, this followed a degree of provocation from the victim. After the circumstances of the offence and the offender's degree of involvement have been discussed, the lawyer may then turn to more general matters in mitigation. Of particular importance will be credit for a guilty plea, for a clean record and for full co-operation with the police. In a case where the seriousness of the offence indicates that a community sentence is the likely outcome, the offender's attitude to the offence and his willingness to comply with any community penalty would be important matters. Recent or impending changes in the offender's circumstances may be brought to the court's attention. In all these matters the lawyer may refer the sentencer to relevant passages in the pre-sentence report. All these matters are discussed further in Chapter 2.

Sometimes difficulties arise where an assertion is made in the plea in mitigation which is hard for the sentencer to accept, since it conflicts with other information which has been received. In *Gross v O'Toole*, the offender was convicted of offering his services as a driver at Heathrow Airport contrary to a by-law. In mitigation it was contended that he had offered his services innocently, and free of charge. Before passing sentence the magistrates commented that they disbelieved the mitigation, no doubt because the offender had many previous convictions for the same sort of offence. One of the points argued on appeal against sentence was that the bench should have given the defence warning that they were minded to reject the mitigation. The Divisional Court said that the prime responsibility was on the defence advocate to 'make good the submission', whether by a speech or by calling evidence. The bench was not obliged to warn the lawyer of its provisional view, but it might be 'good practice' to do so.

As was explained in **3.3**, where conflicting versions of the facts of the offence are advanced by prosecution and defence, and acceptance of one version rather than the other would result in a material difference to the sentence, the sentencer is required to make a choice between them, and a *Newton* hearing should be held for this purpose. Suppose, however, that the prosecution is not in a position to refute mitigation urged by the defence, such as where it relates to matters not directly connected with the commission of the offence. In *Ogunti* (1987) 9 Cr App R (S) 325, for example, the defence claimed that the offender had committed the offence (possession of drugs with intent to supply) because a stranger who had given him the drugs had threatened him with violence if he did not comply. Even though the mitigation was consistent with Ogunti's statements to the police, the Court of Appeal held that the sentencer was certainly not bound to accept the defence assertion. In such a case the burden is on the defence to prove their version of events, on the balance of probabilities (*Guppy* [1994] Crim LR 614). This may be contrasted with a 'true' *Newton* case, where the prosecution is positively involved in asserting a different version of facts from the defence and the burden of proof rests upon them to establish their version beyond reasonable doubt.

3.6.2   Other representations to the sentencer

(a)   *The Jury*   The jury has no direct role to play in sentencing. Their task is to return a verdict of guilty or not guilty or, where appropriate, guilty of a lesser offence. The traditional view is that the jury should be discouraged, in cases where they convict, from trying to influence the judge's decision on sentence. In *Sahota* [1980] Crim LR 678, for example, the Court of Appeal criticised a Crown Court judge who simply wrote 'yes' on a note he had been sent by the jury, which asked if they could add a rider to their verdict recommending leniency. The accused had been charged with causing grievous bodily harm to his wife. The evidence had shown that he had been provoked by her, and the jury were clearly reluctant to convict unless they could be assured that the offender would not be dealt with too harshly. None the less, the Court of Appeal said that the jury should have been told that sentencing was not their concern. The effect of this rule is that a jury may be tempted to acquit perversely; if this happens, there is no method of appeal. Alternatively the jury may, perversely, convict of a lesser offence. A different line was taken by the Court of Appeal on this matter in *A-G's Reference (No. 8 of 1992)* (1993) 14 Cr App R (S) 130. The jury convicted the offender, who was aged 17 at the time of the offence, of manslaughter on an indictment for murder, but asked that the judge be made aware that they had 'great sympathy' for the offender. A probation order was imposed. It was accepted by the

Attorney-General for the purposes of the sentencing reference to the Court of Appeal, and by the appellate court itself, that 'the judge was right to give effect to the recommendation of mercy, or at least of sympathy, expressed by the jury'. Lord Taylor CJ said that the sentencer had been 'absolutely correct' in his view that he 'had to have regard to the jury's recommendation'. None the less the Court of Appeal felt that the sentence was unduly lenient in all the circumstances, and increased it to one of two years' detention in a young offender institution. See also **3.3.3**.

(b) *The victim* The Court of Appeal stated clearly in *Perks* [2001] 1 Cr App R (S) 66 that the opinion of the victim or members of the victim's family about the appropriate level of punishment for the offender could not provide a sound basis for sentencing. Otherwise, cases with identical features would be dealt with in widely differing ways. It has been held in Scotland that it is wrong for a sentencer to seek the views of the victim of an offence as to the appropriate sentence for the offender (*HM Advocate* v *McKenzie* 1990 SLT 28). The reason given by the court in that case was that it would be 'invidious to expose the complainer to a risk of public pressure by passing any comment on matters that lie outside her expertise'. Although some other jurisdictions do allow victims to have their say on sentence, there are obvious dangers in that approach. The victim is hardly likely to bring the necessary degree of detachment required to reach a proper sentencing decision, and the criminal offence is a wrong against society as a whole as well against an individual victim. Sometimes, however, the views of the victim of the offence will become known to the court. For example, the victim may have forgiven the offender and now be urging leniency. If so, there may be some scope to take account of the victim's representations in mitigation of sentence, but the court may properly pass a sentence which disregards those views if the seriousness of the offence dictates otherwise (*Hutchinson* (1993) 15 Cr App R (S) 124). In the unusual circumstances that the sentence passed by the judge has had the effect of increasing the anguish occasioned to the victim or his family, the sentence can be reduced on appeal (see *Nunn* [1996] 2 Cr App R (S) 136, where the offender and the victim had been friends and the custodial sentence had made the victim's death harder to bear, and *A-G's Reference (No. 8 of 1994)* (1995) 16 Cr App R (S) 327). Conversely, the victim's interest in the offender receiving a severe sentence may be apparent from evidence given at trial or, perhaps, from an application to the court for compensation from the offender. Again, the court's prime concern is to fix a sentence appropriate to the seriousness of the offence and the culpability of the offender. For compensation orders see **8.1**.

(c) *The offender* When the plea in mitigation is concluded, it is the habit of some sentencers to ask the offender whether he (rather than his lawyer) has anything to say to the court.

3.7 PRONOUNCING SENTENCE

A Crown Court judge sitting alone will normally pronounce sentence immediately after defence mitigation is concluded. If the judge is sitting with lay magistrates (e.g. on a committal for sentence) and the decision is a difficult one, they sometimes retire to consider the sentence. Similarly, a lay bench of magistrates may wish to retire to consider the sentence. They may ask their clerk to retire with them to advise them on their sentencing powers (see **1.2.7**). In a magistrates' court the decision on sentence may be taken by a majority but it is pronounced by the chairman of the bench, without any mention of the fact that it is not unanimous.

In a number of situations courts are now required to justify their sentencing decision by reference to specific statutory sentencing criteria. Examples are:

(a)   Whenever a magistrates' court or the Crown Court imposes a custodial sentence (including a suspended sentence, but excluding a case where custody results from the offender's failure to express his willingness to comply with a condition in a community order which requires an expression of such willingness) it is the court's duty to state in open court its view that custody is justified under either or both of the criteria in PCC(S)A 2000, s. 79(2), to explain why it is of that opinion and to explain to the offender in open court and in ordinary language why it is passing a custodial sentence (s. 79(4)). For magistrates' courts, this must be specified in the warrant of commitment and entered in the register (s. 79(5)). See further **4.2.3**.

(b)   Whenever a magistrates' court or the Crown Court imposes a custodial sentence which is for a term longer than is commensurate with the seriousness of the offence(s) (including a discretionary life sentence, a sentence of custody for life or a sentence of detention under PCC(S)A 2000, s. 91), the court must state that in its view the criterion in s. 80(2)(b) applies, explain why it is of that opinion and explain to the offender in open court and in ordinary language why the sentence is for such a term. See further **4.2.6**.

(c)   A court which is dealing with an offender who is in breach of a suspended sentence and which chooses not to activate the sentence in full must give reasons for taking a more lenient approach (PCC(S)A 2000, s. 119(2)). See further **4.2.6**.

(d)   A court which has power to make a compensation order on the offender must, if it does not do so, explain why compensation has not been ordered (PCC(S)A 2000, s. 130(3)).

(e)   Section 152 of the PCC(S)A 2000 requires sentencers to state in open court that the sentence imposed has been reduced in consequence of the offender's guilty plea. See **2.2.4(g)**.

(f)   When sentencing a juvenile aged under 16 the court should normally bind over the parent or guardian of that offender and, if it does not do so, explain why not (PCC(S)A 2000, s. 150(1)). See **7.2.5**.

(g)   By the PCC(S)A 2000, s. 73(8), where the court has power to make a reparation order and did not do so, the court must explain why it did not make such an order. See **7.4.1**.

(h)   Where a court, for 'special reasons', exercises its discretion not to disqualify the offender from driving or not to order endorsement, it must state its grounds for doing so in open court and if it is a magistrates' court it must enter these reasons in the register. The same requirements apply if, because of 'mitigating circumstances', a court does not disqualify, or disqualifies for a period shorter than six months. See further **10.1**.

Apart from these specific cases, sentencers have been encouraged wherever possible to give reasons for deciding upon a particular sentence. They should certainly give reasons when the sentence on the face of it may seem unduly severe (*Newman* (1979) 1 Cr App R (S) 252) or unduly lenient, given the circumstances of the case. In *A-G's Reference (No. 23 of 1992)* (1993) 14 Cr App R (S) 759 the Court of Appeal, dealing by way of an Attorney-General's Reference with a Crown Court sentence alleged to be unduly lenient, criticised the sentencer for not specifying reasons or explaining the process by which a 'derisory' sentence had been arrived at. As the Court of Appeal pointed out in that case, not only does the requirement of giving reasons make it easier, in the event of an appeal, for the appellate court to understand the thought processes of the sentencer, it also tends towards greater clarity in the initial sentencing decision. The increasing number of statutory requirements to give reasons should prompt sentencers to give fuller explanations for sentence in all cases, even apart from the overarching obligations under the fair trial provisions of Article 6 of the ECHR. In addition to the requirement to give reasons, there are also numerous provisions in sentencing legislation where courts are required to explain the import of the sentencing decision to the offender in ordinary, non-technical language. There are also a few cases in which an expression of willingness to comply with the order of the court must be expressed by the offender before a particular sentence may lawfully be passed. Again, these require that the court explain the implications to the offender in ordinary language.

Occasionally the sentencer's comments when passing sentence reveal that an irrelevant or inappropriate consideration has been taken into account. This may then form the basis for an appeal. There are occasionally cases which are seized upon by the press, where a judge expresses himself inappropriately, such as by stating that a female hitch-hiker who was raped was guilty of 'contributory negligence', thereby justifying a lower sentence for the offender (see now the guideline case of *Billam* (1986) 8 Cr App R (S) 48, discussed at **12.3.1**, which makes it clear that sentence should not be reduced in such cases). In earlier times it was quite common for judges to deliver sentencing 'homilies' upon the offender, in which the judge might express a view about the offender's general moral character and suggest ways in which he ought to adjust his life-style to avoid further conflict with the criminal law. Some odd statements are still made from time to time by judges, but sentencing homilies are now very much rarer than they were.

3.8 TAKING OTHER OFFENCES INTO CONSIDERATION

One of the most fundamental sentencing principles, which emerges from the material in this chapter, is that the offender must only be sentenced for those offences for which he has been found guilty or to which he has pleaded guilty. There is a limited exception to this principle, which applies where other offences are taken into consideration.

Other offences taken into consideration when sentence is passed (or 't.i.c.'s as they are generally known) are offences of which the offender is never convicted, but which are admitted by him in court and, at his request, are borne in mind by the judge when sentence is passed for the offences in respect of which there is a conviction (hereinafter referred to as the 'conviction offences'). The sequence of events leading up to offences being taken into consideration will vary from case to case, and the procedure is a matter of convention and court practice rather than statutory regulation (*Walsh* (1973) CSP L3.3A01). The practice is one of long standing (see, for example, *Syres* (1908) 1 Cr App R 172) and it has been referred to in several statutory provisions, such as PCC(S)A 2000, s. 161(1). Typically, it will involve a suspect, who has been arrested on suspicion of one or more crimes, admitting at the police station that he committed the crimes alleged and making it obvious that he intends to plead guilty. The police may then ask him about other similar offences which they believe he might have committed, but which, in the absence of an admission from him, they would find difficult to prove. Since he is resigned to having to plead guilty to the offences for which he was arrested, the suspect often decides to make a clean breast of everything on the understanding that some or all of the offences he is now being asked about will not be the subject of separate charges but will merely be taken into consideration. A list is then drawn up of the offences to be taken into consideration, and the suspect signs the list. The offences for which he was arrested and with which he was charged are then prosecuted in the normal way. Copies of the list are given to the prosecutor and to the defence. In *Wheeldon* (1988) *The Times*, 13 May 1988, one of the grounds for allowing an appeal against sentence was that the defence had not been provided with the list.

At court, the accused duly pleads guilty. Then, at some stage during the prosecution's statement of the facts, the prosecutor will mention to the sentencer that the offender wants to have other matters considered. The sentencer will then be handed the list of the offences signed by the offender and the sentencer, or the court clerk, will ask the offender in open court whether he admits them, and whether he wants them taken into consideration (*Anderson* v *DPP* [1978] AC 964). If the offender answers 'yes' to both questions the sentencer may, and probably will, comply with the request. Agreement must come from the offender, rather than his lawyer (*Davis* [1943] KB 274). The offender should admit the offences in open court (*Griffiths* (1932) 23 Cr App R 153). It is not necessary to put the particulars of the offences to the offender one by one. Usually the offender is asked whether he signed the list, whether he agrees that he committed the offences and whether he wants them taken into consideration. It is essential that the offender fully understands what is being done. In *Walsh* (1973) CSP L3.3A01 it emerged later that some of the 259 't.i.c.'s which W had admitted had in fact been committed at a time when Walsh was in prison. Any offences which the offender denies must be deleted. In *Burfoot* (1990) 12 Cr App R (S) 252 an appeal against sentence was allowed where B had been sentenced on the basis of a list of no less than 600 't.i.c.'s which B had signed at the police station but subsequently denied at court.

The prosecution should be in a position to provide the sentencer with brief details of any offence taken into consideration. The sentence which is eventually passed will be somewhat more severe than it would have been in the absence of the 't.i.c.'s (*Batchelor* (1952) 36 Cr App R 64). The addition to the sentence will, however, be considerably less than the penalty would have been if they had been prosecuted separately. If, in a magistrates' court, the new information about the 't.i.c.'s now makes the case one which should attract a punishment greater than the magistrates are empowered to impose, and provided the offence is triable either way and the offender is aged 18 or over, the case may be committed to the Crown Court for sentence (PCC(S)A 2000, s. 3: see also **1.2.9**).

It will be seen that the system of taking offences into consideration has advantages for offenders. It allows the offender to 'clear the slate' and to receive a lesser sentence than might otherwise have been the case. It also has advantages for the police, because they 'clear up' offences which might otherwise have remained unsolved. The following additional points about taking offences into consideration should be noted:

(a)   When the sentencer is deciding whether an offence is, or offences are, so serious that only a custodial sentence can be justified, the court may consider the conviction offences or a combination of the conviction offences and the offences taken into consideration (PCC(S)A 2000, s. 79(2)(a): see also **4.2.3**). If the sentencer decides that a custodial sentence is justified on this ground, then all the conviction offences and all the 't.i.c.'s should be weighed when determining the appropriate sentence length (PCC(S)A 2000, s. 80(2)(a): see also **4.4**). If, on the other hand, the sentencer decides that the offence is, or the offences are, not so serious as to require custody, a community sentence may be imposed, but only where serious enough to justify that course, rather than a financial penalty or a discharge. When deciding whether the offence is, or offences are, so serious that a community sentence is required, the court may similarly have regard to the 't.i.c.'s as well as the conviction offences (PCC(S)A 2000, s. 35(1): see also **5.1**). If the sentencer decides that a community sentence is justified on this ground, then all the conviction offences and all the 't.i.c.'s should be weighed when determining the appropriate degree of restriction upon the offender's liberty (PCC(S)A 2000, s. 35(3)(b): see also **5.1**).

(b)   The sentence the court may pass is restricted to the maximum permissible for the offence(s) of which the offender has been convicted (*Hobson* (1944) 29 Cr App R 30 and, for custodial sentences, PCC(S)A 2000, s. 80(2)(a)). In practice it is almost always possible to add something to the sentence for the conviction offences to reflect the existence of the 't.i.c.'s, without approaching the maximum sentence.

(c)   Which offences to charge and which to refrain from charging in anticipation of their eventually being taken into consideration is a matter within the discretion of the police and prosecution authorities. It is common for there to be up to ten 't.i.c.'s, but on occasions the 't.i.c.'s may vastly outnumber the conviction offences. In *Oyediran* [1997] 2 Cr App R (S) 277 the offender had claimed social security benefit for three years without revealing that he was also in receipt of a student grant. He pleaded guilty to five counts of false accounting and asked for 68 additional offences to be taken into consideration. Each time Oyediran had signed the benefit form he had committed a further offence. Another common situation in which there will often be a large number of 't.i.c.'s is credit card and chequebook fraud, where each dishonest use of the card or chequebook is a further offence. The sentencer should state, when passing sentence, how many offences have been taken into consideration.

(d)   Since the taking of an offence into consideration does not, as a matter of law, amount to a conviction, the offender would not be able to resist a subsequent prosecution for the offence by reliance upon a plea of *autrefois convict* (that he has already been convicted of that charge, and so cannot be charged again) (*Nicholson* [1947] 2 All ER 535). In practice, however, prosecutions should never be brought for offences which have been taken into consideration. In a case where, by error, one was brought, the Court of Appeal recommended that there be 'no additional penalty' for it (*North* (1971) CSP L3.1B01).

(e)   Although the 't.i.c.' system is designed primarily for offenders pleading guilty, there is nothing to stop the prosecution requesting a short adjournment after the accused has been found guilty, following a not guilty plea, to ask him whether, given the outcome of the trial, he would now like other offences considered.

(f)   The court is not obliged to comply with a request to take offences into consideration. Magistrates should not take offences into consideration which are triable only on indictment (*Simons* [1953] 1 WLR 1014). More generally, it is bad practice to take offences into consideration which are more serious than the conviction offences; nor should the 't.i.c.'s be of a different type from the conviction offences. The court should never take offences into consideration which carry endorsement or disqualification unless the conviction offences are also so punishable (*Collins* [1947] KB 560) because the sentencing powers of the court are limited to those it possesses in respect of the conviction offences.

(g)   A compensation order may be passed by the court in respect of an offence taken into consideration (PCC(S)A 2000, s. 130(1)). In a magistrates' court, the total sum which may be ordered by way of compensation where the offender has 't.i.c.'s must not exceed the maximum which could be ordered for the offences, apart from the 't.i.c.'s (PCC(S)A 2000, s. 131(2)). (The maximum compensation which may be ordered for any offence by magistrates is £5,000.) A restitution order may be passed in respect of an offence taken into consideration (PCC(S)A 2000, s. 148(1)). A deprivation order may be imposed, *inter alia*, where the offender asks to have an offence taken into consideration which involves unlawful possession of property which has since been lawfully seized from him or was in his possession or under his control when he was apprehended (PCC(S)A 2000, s. 143(2)).

3.9   SAMPLE COUNTS

Where the prosecution alleges that the offender has committed a large number of very similar offences over a substantial period of time, they may wish to proceed on the basis of 'sample counts'. A few of the alleged offences will be charged and then the sentencer will be invited to pass sentence on the basis of the whole scale of the offending. This may be seen as an alternative to presenting a list of 't.i.c.'s. Provided that the defence accepts the wider allegations and the offender pleads guilty to the sample counts, the sentencer may pass sentence on that basis. If, however, the defence says that the charges brought represent the total of the offending, the sentencer is not entitled to hear evidence from either side as to which version is correct. To do so would involve sentencing the offender for offences with which he has not been charged, which is quite improper.

The leading authority is *Canavan* [1998] 1 Cr App R 79, where the Court of Appeal dealt with a number of appeals giving rise to the same issue. Lord Bingham CJ said that it was 'inconsistent with principle that a defendant should be sentenced for offences neither admitted nor proved by verdict'. His lordship could find nothing to support any contrary interpretation of the law (indeed ss. 80(2)(a) and 161(1) of the PCC(S)A 2000 both indicate that the court should not take into account offences other than those of which the offender has been convicted or which he has had taken into consideration), and nor could his lordship see any relevant difference between the approach to be taken after a trial or when sentencing after a guilty plea. Thus, in respect of one appellant, a sentence of two years' imprisonment imposed on the basis that there had been repeated intimidation of a witness could not be sustained where the offender had been convicted of a single count of intimidation. Noting the common practice of prosecutors to proceed by way of specimen counts, his lordship continued: 'prosecuting authorities will wish, in the light of this decision . . . to include more counts in some indictments. We do not think this need be unduly burdensome or render the trial unmanageable.' The Court of Appeal approved earlier decisions to the same effect in *Hutchison* [1972] 1 WLR 398 and *Clark* [1996] 2 Cr App R (S) 351, and disapproved other cases, especially *Bradshaw* [1997] 2 Cr App R (S) 128, which suggested that the judge might pass sentence on the basis that the offending was in reality far more extensive than that revealed by the sample counts. In *Huchison* [1972] 1 WLR 398 the offender pleaded guilty to one count of incest with his daughter. The daughter's statement to the police indicated that sexual intercourse had taken place regularly over a period of years, but the defence claimed that it was limited to the one occasion alleged in the indictment. The judge passed a sentence of four years' imprisonment on the basis that the offence had been repeated, but the Court of Appeal halved the sentence. The judge was bound to sentence only on the offence admitted; the only other course open to him might have been to adjourn so that counts for the other occasions could be added to the indictment.

3.10   DEFERMENT OF SENTENCE

Both magistrates' courts and the Crown Court have powers to adjourn before passing sentence (see **3.2**). A comparable, though distinct, power to defer sentence is provided for both courts by PCC(S)A 2000, s. 1. Section 1(1) provides that a court may defer passing sentence on an offender for the purpose of enabling it:

> to have regard, in dealing with him, to his conduct after conviction (including, where appropriate, the making by him of reparation for his offence) or to any change in his circumstances.

The exercise of this power is subject to the offender giving his consent (s. 1(2)). The deferment must not exceed six months (s. 1(3)) and, subject to one exception mentioned in a moment, sentence may be deferred only once. The date to which sentence is deferred should be announced at the time of the deferment, but if the offender is not dealt with on that date the court does not thereby lose its power to sentence (*Ingle* [1974] 3 All ER 811). Should the offender be convicted of a further offence during the period of the deferment, the court which deferred sentence may issue a summons or warrant for arrest immediately (i.e. the court need not wait until the deferred sentence date) so as to bring him before it to be dealt with for the deferred sentence offence. Alternatively, the court dealing with the new offence may also deal with the deferred sentence offence, except that a magistrates' court cannot deal with an offence in respect of which the Crown Court deferred sentence (s. 2(3)(a)). If the Crown Court deals with an offence in respect of which a magistrates' court deferred sentence, the Crown Court is limited to the sentencing powers of the magistrates (s. 2(3)(b)). At the end of a period of deferment, a magistrates' court may commit the offender to the Crown Court to be sentenced in preference to dealing with him themselves (s. 1(5)(b)) and if it wishes, the Crown Court may then itself defer sentence (s. 1(7)); this is the one exception to the rule that sentence may be deferred only once. When deferring sentence the court may not remand the offender (s. 1(4)), it simply allows him to go free on the understanding that he will return on the day to which sentence has been deferred. If he fails to do so, a summons or warrant can be issued to secure his attendance. Whenever an offender is dealt with in respect of an offence for which sentence was deferred, the court may deal with him in any way the court which deferred sentence could have dealt with him (s. 1(5)). The court should always make it clear that it is deferring sentence under these powers rather than simply adjourning (*Fairhead* [1975] 2 All ER 737).

In the case of *George* [1984] 1 WLR 1083 Lord Lane CJ gave important guidance on how the courts should use the power to defer sentence. The case provides a useful summary of points made in several earlier decisions and these are outlined below:

(a) A court deferring sentence should make it clear to the offender what its purposes in doing so are and what conduct is expected of the offender during the period of the deferment. A careful note of these matters must be made for the assistance of the court which eventually passes sentence. Ideally, a copy of the note should be given to the offender. Common reasons for deferring sentence are to establish whether the offender will make genuine efforts to find work or will stay in work, will save money so as to be in a position to make reparation to the victim of the offence, will give up drinking to excess or will contact and take advice from a probation officer. The reasons given for deferring sentence must always come within the terms of PCC(S)A 2000, s. 1(1); deferment should not be used as a device for substantially restricting the offender's control over his own life during the period of deferment (e.g. by requiring that the offender reside at a mental hospital as a voluntary patient: *Skelton* [1983] Crim LR 686).

(b) When the offender appears to be sentenced at the end of the period of deferment, the court passing sentence will know what the reasons for deferring were (if necessary, the sentencer may refer to the note which was made at the time sentence was deferred). If the material before the sentencing court (e.g. a pre-sentence report and the defence mitigation) shows that the offender has substantially complied with the requirements or expectations of the deferring court, then an immediate custodial sentence should not be imposed. If he has not, then the court is not so restricted, but it must state precisely how the offender failed. If this explanation is not given, any custodial sentence which is imposed may be quashed on appeal (even though otherwise justified by the seriousness of the offence), because of the unfairness to the offender (*Glossop* (1981) 3 Cr App R (S) 347).

(c)   Whenever possible the judge or the magistrates who deferred sentence should make themselves available to pass sentence (*Gurney* [1974] Crim LR 472). Counsel who represented the offender at the deferment should also strive to attend at sentencing (*Ryan* [1976] Crim LR 508). It is precisely because this will not always (or often) be possible, that the elaborate requirements in (a) and (b) have been devised by the Court of Appeal. Every effort should be made to sentence the offender on the deferred date but, in exceptional circumstances, an adjournment (rather than a deferment) even to a date more than six months from the date of deferment is permissible (*Anderson* (1984) 78 Cr App R 251). The sentence eventually passed should be reduced to take account of the delay.

(d)   Deferring sentence is not meant to be 'an easy way out for a court which is unable to make up its mind about the correct sentence' (Lord Lane CJ in *George*). In particular, the court should consider carefully whether the objectives of deferment could not be more efficiently achieved by passing an immediate sentence, such as a probation order with certain specific requirements included within it (see **5.2.3**). Deferment should be preserved for those cases where the court needs to know how the offender will behave in the near future, but its expectations of him (e.g. that he will try hard to find employment) are too imprecise to be put into a probation order. It should also be remembered that statutory restrictions introduced since the decision in *George* upon the proper use of a probation order mean that probation can now be appropriate only in a case where the passing of community sentence is justified by the seriousness of the offence(s) committed.

3.11   LEGAL REPRESENTATION

An unrepresented offender may, of course, put forward his own plea in mitigation. Such a person is likely to be at a disadvantage, however, because of ignorance as to the relevance of mitigating factors which may weigh with the court. Legal representation is of especial importance where the offender is at risk of a custodial sentence. There is special legislative provision in PCC(S)A 2000, s. 83, therefore, that, subject to an exception mentioned below, when a magistrates' court or the Crown Court is dealing with an offender who is not legally represented in court, the court must give that person an opportunity to apply for legal representation before doing any of the following:

(a)   passing a sentence of imprisonment if the offender has never before received such a sentence;

(b)   passing a sentence of detention in a young offender institution;

(c)   passing a sentence of custody for life under PCC(S)A 2000, s. 93 or 94;

(d)   making an order for detention under PCC(S)A 2000, s. 90 or 91;

(e)   making a detention and training order.

Paragraph (a) above also applies to the passing of a suspended sentence, but a suspended sentence imposed on the offender in the past which never took effect is ignored when deciding whether the offender has previously received a prison sentence (PCC(S)A 2000, s. 83(5)). Note that in paras (b) to (e) the requirement of legal representation before sentence is passed is not restricted to the first occasion upon which the sentence is passed on the offender.

The exception set out in PCC(S)A 2000, s. 83(3) applies to the person to be sentenced if either:

(a) he was granted a right to representation funded by the Legal Services Commission as part of the Criminal Defence Service but the right was withdrawn because of his conduct; or

(b) having been informed of his right to apply for such representation and having had the opportunity to do so, he refused or failed to apply.

For these purposes a person is to be treated as legally represented if he has the assistance of counsel or a solicitor to represent him at some time after he is found guilty and before he is sentenced. The offender's legal representation may relate to the whole proceedings or just in relation to sentence.

If a magistrates' court imposes a custodial sentence without complying with these provisions and the offender appeals to the Crown Court against sentence, it was held in *Birmingham Justices, ex parte Wyatt* [1976] 1 WLR 260 that the Crown Court must pass a sentence which the lower court could lawfully have passed, which must necessarily be a non-custodial sentence. On the other hand, where the Crown Court proceeded without complying with the provisions, it was held that the Court of Appeal might uphold the custodial sentence if it thought that it was the correct one in all the circumstances (*McGinlay* (1975) 62 Cr App R 156; *Hollywood* (1990) 12 Cr App R (S) 325). These cases were followed in *Wilson* (1995) 16 Cr App R (S) 997 where the problem was that the defendant sacked one firm of lawyers after another.

3.12 COMMENCEMENT AND VARIATION OF SENTENCE

A sentence imposed by the Crown Court takes effect from the beginning of the day on which it is imposed, unless the court directs otherwise (PCC(S)A 2000, s. 154). The court cannot order a sentence to take effect earlier than the day on which it was pronounced (*Gilbert* [1975] 1 WLR 1012). There is, however, a discretion to order the sentence to begin at a specified later date, usually at the expiration of another period of custody to which the offender is already subject. An unusual example of the use of this power arose in *Fairbrother and Hughes, The Times,* 29 June 1991 (news item) where the judge passed custodial sentences (of two months and six weeks) on company directors who had pleaded guilty to revenue offences. In an attempt to avoid the collapse of the business, the sentencer ordered the custodial sentence on one offender to commence at such time as the other offender was released.

The Crown Court may vary or rescind a sentence imposed or other order made within 28 days of its being passed (PCC(S)A 2000, s. 155). The variation must be made by the Crown Court judge who originally passed the sentence (s. 155(4)). If he was then sitting with lay justices they need not be present for the variation. If the offender was jointly indicted with other accused, the period is 56 days from the passing of the sentence or 28 days from the conclusion of the joint trial, whichever expires the sooner (s. 155(2)). The offender should be present in court when sentence is varied (*Cleere* (1983) 5 Cr App R (S) 465) unless there is some good reason for his absence, such as in *McLean* (1988) 10 Cr App R (S) 18, where the good reason was that McLean had absconded. Any variation should be made in open court, so that nobody can be left in doubt as to what sentence has been passed; it should not be done behind the scenes, or by sending a message (*Dowling* (1988) 88 Cr App R 88). It is clear that the power to vary sentence may be used to correct an error in the original sentence. Thus, in *Iqbal* (1985) 7 Cr App R (S) 35, an unlawful sentence of 30 months' youth custody imposed upon a juvenile was replaced by an equivalent term of detention under the PCC(S)A 2000, s. 91. It may also be used to replace one form of sentence with a quite different one. In *Sodhi* (1978) 66 Cr App R 260 a prison sentence of six months was replaced by a hospital order plus restriction order.

The extent to which a sentence may be varied substantially to the offender's detriment is less clear. In *Grice* (1978) 66 Cr App R 167 the Court of Appeal's view was that a susbstantial increase to the original sentence was not permissible. The judge had passed a suspended sentence upon receiving an undertaking from the offender that he would not go near his adopted daughter, with whom he had committed unlawful sexual intercourse. Grice did in fact contact his daughter and, since the contact took place within the 28-day period, the judge varied the sentence to one of immediate imprisonment. The Court of Appeal restored the sentence to what it had originally been. However, other cases suggest that *Grice* takes a too restrictive view of the power to vary. In *Hart* (1983) 5 Cr App R (S) 25, for example, Hart was given a suspended prison sentence, partly on the basis of evidence that he was leaving the country to start a new life abroad. Shortly afterwards a newspaper reported Hart as saying that this story had been a lie, told to the judge to trick him into passing a lenient sentence. The judge brought Hart back to court and replaced the suspended sentence with immediate custody. The variation had to be quashed because it was done outside the 28-day period, but the Court of Appeal said that, had it been done in time, this was 'one of the plain cases for which [the section] is designed'.

Magistrates' courts may also vary or rescind a sentence under MCA 1980, s. 142. Again the variation must be made within 28 days of the sentence being passed. The court varying sentence must either be identical to the original court or, where the original court consisted of three or more justices, a majority of those must be present for the variation. In *Jane v Broome* (1987) *The Times*, 2 November 1987 the Divisional Court held that magistrates were entitled to exercise their powers under s. 142 in a case where they had originally found special reasons for not disqualifying J from driving, but had later come to the view that their findings of fact could not amount in law to special reasons. They reconvened the court and disqualified J for 12 months.

Once the statutory period for variation has expired, a court may not vary its sentence even if, through inadvertence, it has failed to include in the sentence an order which it really should have made (*Menocal* [1980] AC 598). In *Stillwell* (1992) 13 Cr App R (S) 253 the sentencer rescinded the original sentence within the time limit but did not impose a new one until the period had expired. It was held that no valid sentence was in place and the offender was released on appeal. The court may, however, correct the terms of an order which is lawful in substance though defective in form (*Saville* [1981] 1 QB 12), since it has an inherent jurisdiction to remedy minor mistakes.

3.13 REWARDS

The Crown Court has power to order the payment of a sum of money to any person who has been 'active in or towards the apprehension of any person charged with an arrestable offence' (Criminal Law Act 1826, s. 28). The amount of any such reward should be sufficient to compensate that person for any 'expenses, exertion and loss of time' involved in that apprehension. Such an award might well be made at the time of sentencing an offender. For an example see *Alexander* [1997] 2 Cr App R (S) 74.

4   Custodial Sentences

The imposition of custodial sentences, whether by a magistrates' court or the Crown Court, is governed by the general statutory sentencing framework originally laid down in the CJA 1991 and now consolidated in the PCC(S)A 2000, and a range of specific statutory provisions and case-law dealing with particular forms of custodial sentencing. For a discussion of the general sentencing framework see Chapter 2. This chapter describes in detail the law which governs the imposition of custodial sentences.

For offenders aged 21 and over the appropriate custodial sentence is imprisonment. When s. 61 of the CJCSA 2000 is brought into force, this will be reduced to 18. A sentence of imprisonment cannot be passed on anyone aged under 21 (PCC(S)A 2000, s. 89). There is no upper age limit for imprisonment. Those aged under 21 cannot be sentenced to imprisonment for any reason, even, for example, the non-payment of a fine, but if a person under 21 is remanded in custody or committed for trial or sentence in custody and there is no remand centre available, he may be committed to prison for the period before the case is disposed of (s. 89(2)). The custodial sentences which are available for offenders aged under 21 are a detention in a young offender institution, the detention and training order and detention under PCC(S)A 2000, s. 91. In determining a person's age, and the sentence available, the relevant date is the date of conviction. Where there is doubt about the age of an offender before the court, PCC(S)A 2000, s. 164(1) provides that:

> For the purposes of any provision of this Act which requires the determination of the age of a person by the court or the Secretary of State his age shall be deemed to be that which it appears to the court or (as the case may be) the Secretary of State to be after considering any available evidence.

When a court imposes a sentence on an assumption of the offender's age made under s. 164(1), the sentence is not rendered unlawful if it is discovered subsequently that the assumption was incorrect (*Brown* (1989) 11 Cr App R (S) 263). In *Harris* (1990) 12 Cr App R (S) 318 the offender appeared to the judge to be 21 and he imposed a suspended sentence of imprisonment on that basis. In this case, however, the wording of the antecedents form which was before the judge indicated that the offender was only 20 and, in those circumstances, s. 164(1) could not rescue the sentence and it was quashed. If there is a dispute about the offender's age, the best course is for the court to adjourn until the matter can be resolved (*Steed* (1990) 12 Cr App R (S) 230).

4.1   FORMAL REQUIREMENTS BEFORE CUSTODY MAY BE IMPOSED

Whenever the court is considering the imposition of a custodial sentence, it must abide by the following statutory requirements.

4.1.1   Offence must be imprisonable

The most obvious limitation on the availability of a custodial sentence is that the offence must be an imprisonable offence in the case of an adult. All common law offences are punishable with imprisonment. A statutory offence is so punishable if the statute creating it specifies imprisonment as one of the methods of dealing with offenders who commit the offence. Thus, if the statute mentions only a fine, or perhaps a fine plus disqualification from driving, as the penalties for the offence, it is non-imprisonable. Virtually all indictable offences are imprisonable; offences under the Forgery and Counterfeiting Act 1981, ss. 18 and 19, which proscribe the putting into circulation of imitation currency notes and coins without permission, are two exceptions. The more serious summary offences are also imprisonable. Drink/driving offences carry up to six months' imprisonment (Road Traffic Offenders Act 1988, sch. 2) assaulting a police officer in the execution of his duty carries six months (Police Act 1996, s. 89) and interfering with a motor vehicle carries three months (Criminal Attempts Act 1981, s. 9). Most summary road traffic offences (such as careless driving, speeding, using a vehicle without insurance and failing to stop after an accident) are non-imprisonable. A great mass of minor offences, such as dropping litter, are non-imprisonable.

If an offence is not imprisonable in the case of an adult, a custodial sentence cannot be imposed upon an offender aged under 18.

4.1.2   Legal representation

Section 83 of PCC(S)A 2000 provides that a court shall not pass a sentence of imprisonment on an offender who is not legally represented, and who has not previously been so sentenced, unless he was granted a right to legal representation but the right was withdrawn because of his conduct, or he has been informed of his right to apply for such representation and has failed to make any application. Lord Bridge of Harwich explained the importance of this matter for the unrepresented defendant in *McC (A Minor)* [1985] AC 528:

> No one should be liable to a first sentence of imprisonment . . . unless he has had the opportunity of having his case in mitigation presented to the court in the best possible light. For an inarticulate defendant, such presentation may be crucial to his liberty.

It should be noted that s. 83 applies to the imposition of a suspended prison sentence as well as to immediate custody. Where a person has in the past received a suspended prison sentence, which was not activated, such sentence must be disregarded when deciding whether the offender is now facing the prospect of his first prison sentence.

Section 83 also applies whenever the court is considering imposing a custodial sentence on an offender aged under 21. There is a difference, however, in that for young offenders s. 83 is *not* limited to the imposition of the *first* custodial sentence, as it is for imprisonment. Compliance with it is thus a prerequisite for passing any custodial sentence on an offender aged under 21. Custodial sentences on offenders under 21 cannot be suspended, so there is no equivalent provision in their case. See further s. 3.11.

4.1.3 Compliance with statutory criteria

Before passing a custodial sentence, the court must be satisfied that it is justified in doing so in accordance with the criteria in PCC(S)A 2000, s. 79(2). Put shortly, these criteria are that the custodial sentence is justified either on the basis of the seriousness of the offence committed or, where a violent or sexual offence has been committed, on the ground of public protection. See further **4.2**.

4.1.4 Pre-sentence report

In order to determine whether the statutory criteria in s. 79(2) are satisfied, the court must obtain and consider a pre-sentence report, unless the court considers that to obtain such a report is 'unnecessary' (s. 81). Material in the report is also relevant when deciding upon custodial sentence length. Although no sentence is invalidated by a failure to comply with s. 81, in the event of an appeal against a custodial sentence imposed without one, the appellate court should normally obtain and consider one. Pre-sentence reports are considered in detail at **3.5.1**.

4.1.5 Other relevant material

In addition to considering the pre-sentence report, the court must 'take into account all such information about the circumstances of the offence (including any aggravating or mitigating factors) as is available to it' (s. 81(4)), and may take into account any matter of mitigation personal to the offender (s. 158(1)). These matters are discussed further below.

4.1.6 Stating reasons

It is a basic requirement of justice that proper reasons be given for sentencing decisions. Apart from the general desirability of sentencers giving reasons (a matter the importance of which has been stressed by the Court of Appeal on numerous occasions, such as in *A-G's Reference (No. 23 of 1992)* (1993) 14 Cr App R (S) 759), the number of situations in which courts are required by statute to give their reasons for sentence has been increasing in recent years. Any court passing a custodial sentence is now required by s. 79(4) to state in open court that such a sentence is justified under either s. 79(2)(a) (offence seriousness) or s. 79(2)(b) (public protection), or both. It must explain why it has come to that view. The court must also, by s. 79(4)(b), explain to the offender in open court and in ordinary language why it is imposing a custodial sentence. There is a further requirement in a magistrates' court that the reason must be recorded in the warrant of commitment and in the court register.

In *Baverstock* [1993] 1 WLR 202 the Court of Appeal said that in general a two-stage process of explanation by the sentencer is not necessary to comply with s. 79(4). In most cases the judge should be able at one and the same time to explain in ordinary language the reasons for his conclusion and tell the offender why he is passing a custodial sentence. Lord Taylor CJ said that, when complying with the second of these requirements, the judge would be addressing the offender directly and if, in complying with s. 79(4)(a) he had not used ordinary language, it would be necessary for him to do so in order to comply with subsection s. 79(4)(b). The Court of Appeal stressed that the precise words used by the judge were not critical, and that the statutory provisions 'are not to be treated as a verbal tightrope for judges to walk'. Provided that the judge's approach is in accord with the statutory provisions, the Court of Appeal will not be sympathetic to appeals based upon 'fine linguistic analysis' of the sentencing remarks.

4.2 JUSTIFYING THE IMPOSITION OF CUSTODY

Section 79 of the PCC(S)A 2000 creates a set of criteria to assist the courts in determining when the imposition of a custodial sentence is appropriate. The key provision is s. 79(2), which restricts the powers of the Crown Court and magistrates' courts to impose a custodial sentence to cases where the court is of the opinion either:

(a) that the offence, or the combination of the offence and one or more offences associated with it, was so serious that only such a sentence can be justified for the offence; or

(b) where the offence is a violent or sexual offence, that only such a sentence would be adequate to protect the public from serious harm from him.

These provisions have general application in the Crown Court and in magistrates' courts, and they apply to all 'custodial sentences'. This expression is defined in s. 76. For a person of or over 21, 'custodial sentence' means 'a sentence of imprisonment', which includes discretionary life imprisonment and a suspended sentence of imprisonment (but it does not include a committal or attachment for contempt of court). For a person under 21 it means detention in a young offender institution, a detention and training order, or detention under PCC(S)A 2000, s. 91.

These custodial sentences are dealt with, in turn, in the following paragraphs. First, however, it should be noted that there are two exceptions to the application of PCC(S)A 2000, s. 79(2).

4.2.1 Murder cases and custodial sentences falling to be imposed under ss. 109, 110 or 111 of the PCC(S)A 2000

Section 79(2) of the 2000 Act naturally does not apply where the sentence for the offence is fixed by law (s. 79(1)(a)). This, in practice, means the offence of murder, where the penalty is fixed at imprisonment for life for an offender aged 21 or over. Detention at Her Majesty's pleasure (PCC(S)A 2000, s. 90) is the equivalent sentence in the case of an offender aged under 18 who is convicted of murder. Nor does s. 79(2) apply where the Crown Court is, subject to exceptional circumstances, obliged by s. 109 to impose a life sentence on an offender for his 'second serious offence' (see **4.3.5**) or is, subject to specific circumstances which would make the sentence unjust, required to impose a custodial sentence of at least seven years on an offender for his third Class A drug trafficking offence under s. 110 or one of at least three years on an offender for his third domestic burglary under s. 111.

4.2.2 Offender failing to express willingness to comply with requirement in community sentence

In a limited range of cases, before a community sentence may be imposed on an offender, he must express his willingness to comply with a requirement which the court intends to insert into that order. If the offender is not willing to do so, s. 79(3) states that nothing in s. 79(2) shall prevent the court from passing a custodial sentence instead. The relevant cases in which an expression of willingness to comply are so required are:

(a)   where the court proposes to insert into a CRO a requirement that the offender undergo treatment for a mental condition;

(b)   where the court proposes to insert into a CRO a requirement that the offender undergo treatment for drug or alcohol dependency;

(c)   where the court proposes to insert into a supervision order, a requirement that an offender aged 14 or over undergo treatment for a mental condition; and

(d)   where the court proposes to make a drug treatment and testing order (see **5.6**).

More general requirements in the earlier law that the offender must consent to the imposition of a range of community orders, including CROs and CPOs, were abolished by the C(S)A 1997. Earlier case law indicated that an offender should be given a fair opportunity to choose whether to consent to the community sentence (see, for example, *Marquis* [1974] 1 WLR 1087). This surely still holds good under the new provisions, as does the observation of the Court of Appeal in *Barnett* (1986) 8 Cr App R (S) 200 that the offender's agreement is not vitiated by his knowledge that, if he does not agree, a custodial sentence might be imposed instead. In these circumstances, a grudging consent is an adequate legal consent.

4.2.3   Justifying a custodial sentence under s. 79(2)(a)

We turn now to consider the criteria for imposing a custodial sentence in s. 79(2), on the assumption that neither of the exceptions discussed in the last two paragraphs apply to the case. The first alternative ground is:

(a)   that the offence, or the combination of the offence and one or more offences associated with it, was so serious that only such a sentence can be justified for the offence.

This paragraph is best seen as a custody threshold provision (see Chapter 2). It provides the key justification in the 2000 Act for a sentencer to select a custodial sentence rather than a community sentence. The Act also requires the sentencer to have regard to aggravating and mitigating factors of the case which impinge upon the seriousness of the offence, and permits the sentencer to take account of any other mitigating (but not aggravating) factor. It is clear from the decision in *Cox* [1993] 1 WLR 188 that factors which are *not* associated with offence seriousness may operate to save the offender from custody, by pulling the offender back from the custody threshold, but can never provide the impetus for custody if the offence is not in itself sufficiently serious to justify it. See **4.2.4**.

4.2.4   Seriousness and the single offence

Under PCC(S)A 2000, s. 79(2)(a), the offender must have been convicted of at least one offence, and this of course covers both conviction after a trial and a guilty plea (*Cole* [1965] 2 QB 388). Taking first the case of an offender being dealt with for a single offence, in *Cox* [1993] 1 WLR 188 Lord Taylor CJ adopted the following words of Lawton LJ in the pre 1991 Act case of *Bradbourn* (1985) 7 Cr App R (S) 180, as providing an indication of the meaning of the phrase 'so serious that only such a sentence can be justified for the offence':

The kind of offence which . . . would make all right thinking members of the public, knowing all the facts, feel that justice had not been done by the passing of any sentence other than a custodial one.

In *Bradbourn*, Lawton LJ formulated even this degree of guidance with reluctance, commenting that 'courts can recognise an elephant when they see one, but may not find it necessary to define it'. In *Howells* [1999] 1 WLR 307, however, Lord Bingham CJ accepted that the *Bradbourn* test was unhelpful and said that in reality a court was bound in each case to give effect it its own judgment of what justice required. When dealing with cases which were on or near the custody threshold, it would normally be helpful to consider the nature and extent of the defendant's criminal intention and the nature and extent of injury or damage caused.

In addition to these general considerations relating to the custody threshold, there is a substantial and important body of case law, developed by the Court of Appeal in guideline judgments, which determines in what circumstances the commission of particular offences could properly be regarded as so serious that only a custodial sentence can be justified. This case law is considered in the context of sentencing for particular offences in Chapter 12. The decisions tend to discuss the seriousness of a particular offence category in the context of a range of aggravating and mitigating factors which might apply, generating a series of 'starting points' for different levels of seriousness within a particular offence. Thus, in *Billam* (1986) 8 Cr App R (S) 48, the Court of Appeal stressed that the offence of rape calls for a custodial sentence other than in wholly exceptional circumstances, and then proceeded to describe three broad categories of the offence with appropriate starting points. A number of aggravating and mitigating factors were then spelt out. In *Aramah* (1987) 9 Cr App R (S) 360, a case amended and refined in several later decisions, the Court of Appeal indicated appropriate starting points for sentences for importation, supply and possession of Class A, B and C drugs. In *Barrick* (1985) 7 Cr App R (S) 142, updated in *Clark* [1998] 2 Cr App R (S) 95, Lord Lane CJ said that offenders who steal or obtain property by deception in the course of their employment should, notwithstanding their previous good character, be given a custodial sentence unless the sum involved is small. The court then proceeded to indicate three starting points, determined by reference to the amount of money involved. In *Brewster* [1998] 1 Cr App R (S) 181 the Court of Appeal explained why an offence of house burglary is normally so serious that only custody can be justified, and then proceeded to spell out the major aggravating and mitigating factors which tend to arise in such cases.

Whenever a court decides, under s. 79(2)(a), whether to impose a custodial sentence, s. 81(4) requires that the court 'shall take into account all such information about the circumstances of the offence or (as the case may be) of the offence and the offence or offences associated with it (including any aggravating or mitigating factors) as is available to it'. A range of aggravating and mitigating factors relevant to offence seriousness have developed through the case law, and these factors were discussed at **2.2.2** and **2.2.3** above. Additionally, s. 158(1) provides that 'Nothing in this Part shall prevent a court from mitigating an offender's sentence by taking into account any such matters as, in the opinion of the court, are relevant in mitigation of sentence'. The more commonly encountered matters of personal mitigation were considered at **2.2.4** above.

It is clear that although an offence may be regarded as so serious that only a custodial sentence can be justified, mitigating factors which are personal to the offender may mean that the offender can still be dealt with in a less severe way, and custody can be avoided. Such mitigation may pull the offender back from the custody threshold. An example is *Cox*

[1993] 1 WLR 188. There the offender pleaded guilty to theft and reckless driving. He had been riding a motor cycle without lights and carrying a pillion passenger. In attempting to avoid a pursuing police car, he mounted the pavement, which he drove along for 50 metres, executed a dangerous manoeuvre in front of a car, ignored a 'Give way' sign, and then lost control of the cycle and fell off. He had with him various items of stolen property, which he had taken from a garage earlier in the evening. The Court of Appeal agreed with the sentencer that the offences were so serious that only a custodial sentence could be justified, but also found that the sentencer had given insufficient attention to personal matters of mitigation, such as the offender's age (he was 18 at the time of the offence), the fact that there was only one previous court appearance on his record and the suggestion of probation in the pre-sentence report. A CRO for 12 months was substituted.

4.2.5 Seriousness and multiple offences

The preceding discussion of s. 79(2)(a) has been based on the assumption that the offender has been found guilty of, or has pleaded guilty to, one offence. Section 79(2)(a) also refers to the judgment of seriousness being made on the basis of 'the combination of the offence and one or more offences associated with it'. When considering the gravity of a combination of offences, s. 161(1) provides that one offence is to be regarded as 'associated with' another offence if the offender is convicted of the offences in the same proceedings, or is sentenced for the offences at the same time, or when convicted and sentenced he asks to have one or more other offences taken into consideration. Obviously, a custodial sentence may be justified when the court is looking at more than one offence when it would not be so justified in respect of any one of the offences standing alone.

The limitations inherent in the phrase 'associated with' are important ones. In *Baverstock* [1993] 1 WLR 202 the offender was being dealt with for two offences. The second had been committed while the offender was on bail in respect of the first. Since the offender was being sentenced for the two offences on the same occasion, they were 'associated' offences for the purposes of s. 161(1). It was established in *Godfrey* (1993) 14 Cr App R (S) 804 that where a sentencer is sentencing for a new offence and, at the same time, revokes a community sentence and resentences the offence for which it was imposed, the new offence and the earlier offence are associated offences. This is also true where the sentencer sentences for a new offence and resentences for breach of a conditional discharge. On the other hand, in *Crawford* (1993) 98 Cr App R 297 the offender was committed to the Crown Court for sentence for an offence of theft from a supermarket. The commission of that theft had placed him in breach of a suspended sentence of imprisonment imposed for an earlier offence of theft. The Court of Appeal held that these two offences were not 'associated'. The sentencer, when deciding whether a custodial sentence was appropriate for the second theft, should have left the first theft out of account. The sentencer should have sentenced for the new offence standing alone, and then turned to consider what effect the new sentence should have on the suspended sentence. This case was followed and applied in *Cawley* (1994) 15 Cr App R (S) 25. Finally, in *Canavan* [1998] 1 Cr App R 79 it was clearly established that where the offender has been convicted on an indictment charging him with offences alleged to be representative of other similar offences (sample counts), the offender cannot be sentenced for offences of which he has not been convicted or which he has not asked to have taken into consideration. As Lord Bingham of Cornhill CJ put it, 'unindicted, unadmitted offences' cannot be 'associated' offences. See further, on the issue of sample counts, **3.9**.

Once the court has decided that a custodial sentence is justified, the next question is how long that custody may properly be. That matter is discussed at **4.4** below.

4.2.6   Justifying a custodial sentence under s. 79(2)(b)

A custodial sentence may be justified under PCC(S)A 2000, s. 79(2)(b), if the court is of the opinion:

> (b)   where the offence is a violent or sexual offence, that only such a sentence would be adequate to protect the public from serious harm from [the offender].

This provision permits the Crown Court or a magistrates' court to impose a custodial sentence on an offender convicted of a violent or sexual offence, on the basis of a prediction of the offender's future predilection to commit violent or sexual offences. It is thus a 'predictive' rather than a 'desert' based test, and may be regarded as an exception to the general sentencing framework (see further Chapter 2). The 2000 Act provides a definition of 'serious harm', as well as definitions of 'violent offence' and 'sexual offence' (see below).

The great majority of custody decisions are made under the 'seriousness' criterion in s. 79(2)(a) rather than under s. 79(2)(b). In particular, there are very few cases where it will be appropriate for a magistrates' court to impose custody on the basis of s. 79(2)(b). This is because the relative shortness of custodial sentences available to magistrates could rarely achieve the envisaged public protection. Presumably the legislature anticipated that there would be some such cases, for it would not otherwise have given this power to the lower courts. The inclusion of s. 79(2)(b) in the statutory scheme presupposes that there are some violent or sexual cases where the offence or offences committed by the offender are not in themselves sufficiently serious to justify custody under s. 79(2)(a). If that were not so, s. 79(2)(b) would be superfluous. A case where s. 79(2)(b) might be used is where the offender has committed an offence not in itself requiring custody (such as a minor indecent assault), but information about the offender, including details of his previous convictions and perhaps a psychiatric report, leads the court to believe that custody is required in order to protect the public from the risk of future offending.

4.2.7   Meaning of 'violent offence' and 'sexual offence'

Section 79(2)(b) must be interpreted in the light of s. 161(3), which provides that a 'violent offence' means an offence:

> which leads, or is intended or likely to lead, to a person's death or to physical injury to a person, and includes an offence which is required to be charged as arson (whether or not it would otherwise fall within this definition).

This provision covers cases which range from those where death or physical injury is actually caused by the offender, even where that outcome was not intended or even likely to occur, to cases where no harm at all is occasioned but where such harm was a likely consequence of the offender's conduct. There is no requirement that the physical injury caused or risked need be 'serious', but an offence which results, or is likely to result, only in psychological harm is not a violent offence for these purposes.

In respect of many criminal offences the application of these criteria will be perfectly clear. Other offences, however, will sometimes qualify as 'violent' offences, but sometimes not. The Court of Appeal in *Robinson* [1993] 1 WLR 168 confirmed that whether a particular offence falls within the definition of a 'violent offence', thereby permitting the sentencer to consider the imposition of custody under s. 79(2)(b), depends not upon the offence category as such but rather upon the individual facts of each case. This has given rise to a number of rather strange decisions. In *Bibby* (1995) 16 Cr App R (S) 127, for example, the Court of Appeal doubted whether an offender who had threatened staff in building society branches with a knife, and had demanded cash, had committed a 'violent offence', since the evidence was that Bibby had neither used the knife nor had any intention of doing so. In *Khan* (1995) 16 Cr App R (S) 180 the carrying of an unloaded firearm in the course of a robbery was held not to constitute a violent offence. Using an imitation firearm to threaten the victim in the course of a raid on a sub-post office was held not to constitute a violent offence in *Palin* (1995) 16 Cr App R (S) 88.

Apart from robbery, another offence giving rise to problems in this context is that of threatening to kill. In *Richart* (1995) 16 Cr App R (S) 977 the offender made numerous telephone threats to the victim, threatening to kill her, and also sent her a bullet with her name on it through the post. The Court of Appeal found that in this case no 'violent offence' had been committed, since there was no physical injury or evidence that the threats were intended or likely to lead to physical injury. The Court invited Parliament to amend the definition, so as to include cases which, on the face of it, would lead to a reasonable apprehension of violence.

Section 161(3) states that 'an offence which is required to be charged as arson' (i.e., the offence of criminal damage when committed by fire) always qualifies as a 'violent offence'. It was held in *Guirke* [1997] 1 Cr App R (S) 170 that all offences of *attempted* arson are also included. This seems doubtful, since attempted arson is not mentioned in s. 161(3) and so it can qualify as a violent offence only where it leads, or is intended or likely to lead, to death or physical injury.

It is clear from the decision in *Robinson* [1993] 1 WLR 168 that the categories of 'violent offence' and 'sexual offence' overlap, and are not mutually exclusive. That case involved a rape committed by a 16-year-old offender on an elderly woman after he had tricked his way into her home. The judge had proceeded on the basis that this was both a 'violent' and a 'sexual' offence, and his view was upheld by the Court of Appeal.

Section 161(2) of the 2000 Act provides that 'sexual offence' means:

(a) an offence under the SOA 1956, other than an offence under ss. 30, 31, or 33 to 36 of that Act;

(b) an offence under s. 128 of the MHA 1959;

(c) an offence under the Indecency with Children Act 1960;

(d) an offence under s. 9 of the Theft Act 1968 of burglary with intent to commit rape;

(e) an offence under s. 54 of the CLA 1977;

(f) an offence under the Protection of Children Act 1978;

(g) an offence under s. 1 of the CLA 1977 of conspiracy to commit any of the offences in paras (a) to (f) above;

(h) an offence under s. 1 of the Criminal Attempts Act 1981 of attempting to commit any of those offences;

(i) an offence of inciting another to commit any of those offences.

It will be seen that Parliament has adopted a quite different approach in defining 'sexual offence' from that used to define 'violent offence'. Whether an offence counts as a 'sexual offence' or not turns entirely on the category of offence with which the offender is convicted. The Court of Appeal in *Wrench* [1996] 1 Cr App R (S) 145 noted that the offence of child abduction under the Child Abduction Act 1984 was not a 'sexual offence' within the meaning of s. 161(2), and described this as a 'grave omission'. As later pointed out in *Newsome* [1997] 2 Cr App R (S) 69, that offence might, depending on the precise facts, nonetheless amount to a 'violent offence'. The list of offences includes within category (a) most serious sexual offences, including rape, incest, sexual intercourse with under-age females, and indecent assault. It excludes offences such as living on the earnings of prostitution (SOA 1956, s. 30), and offences related to the keeping of brothels (ss. 31 and 33 to 36 of the 1956 Act). The offence referred to in (b) is unlawful sexual intercourse with a mental patient by a member of staff; the offence in (c) is the commission of an act of gross indecency with or towards a child; the offence in (e) is a form of incest; and offences under (f) are taking, permitting to be taken, or distributing indecent photographs of a child.

Reliance upon s. 79(2)(b) requires an assessment by the court that, in the light of the offender's conviction for a violent or sexual offence, only a custodial sentence would be adequate to 'protect the public from serious harm from him'. It is clear from this wording that the sentencer must consider that the public require protection from this particular offender, rather than just from offenders of his type. 'Serious harm' is defined for these purposes by s. 161(4) to mean 'death or serious personal injury, whether physical or psychological, occasioned by further such offences' committed by the offender. The reference to 'further *such* offences' makes it clear that it is the commission of further violent or sexual offences by the offender from which the public need to be protected. While the statute makes it clear that there must be a risk of serious harm, there is no indication of how substantial that risk must be perceived to be to justify sentencing under s. 79(2)(b). It will be seen that while the causing of psychological harm cannot amount to a violent offence, the prospects of causing such harm in the future may be included when considering the risk to the public posed by the offender. Section 81(4) allows the court to take into account any information about the offender when making this assessment. The court will normally have obtained and considered a pre-sentence on the offender by this stage. If the offender is, or appears to be, mentally disordered, a medical report must be obtained (PCC(S)A 2000, s. 82(1)). In making its assessment of the offender's dangerousness the court may take the offender's previous convictions into account. These issues are considered further in **4.4.3**.

In *Baverstock* [1993] 1 WLR 202 the Court of Appeal established the important principle that a sentencer should not pass a sentence in reliance upon s. 79(2)(b) without giving an express indication to counsel that this was being considered.

4.3 VARIETIES OF CUSTODIAL SENTENCES

4.3.1 Determinate sentences of imprisonment

A determinate sentence of imprisonment is the normal custodial sentence for offenders aged 21 or over. It should be noted that when the CJCSA 2000, s. 61 comes into force, imprisonment will become available for offenders aged 18 or over.

The maximum term of imprisonment which may be imposed for a statutory offence is almost always laid down by the statute which creates that offence. For summary offences and for offences triable either way which are tried summarily, general limits on the power of magistrates' courts to impose imprisonment are specified by the PCC(S)A 2000, s. 78(1) and MCA 1980, ss. 31 and 32. The minimum prison sentence which may be imposed by a magistrates' court in any case is five days (MCA 1980, s. 132). The maximum in respect of any one offence is six months, unless the statute which creates the offence prescribes a lower maximum or the offence is non-imprisonable. The maximum aggregate term which magistrates can impose is also six months, unless two of the terms imposed are for offences triable either way, in which case the maximum aggregate term is 12 months (MCA 1980, s. 133). Thus the maximum term of imprisonment which a magistrates' court can impose for an offence triable either way is less, indeed often much less, than the Crown Court can impose following conviction on indictment.

A table of maximum prison terms available for a range of commonly encountered offences is set out at Table 1 on pp. 7–14. Table 1 does not reveal a rational pattern; the Advisory Council on the Penal System conducted a review of maximum penalties in 1978 and commented that:

> The system of maximum penalties is not the product of a rational and consistent scheme, but rather the result of piecemeal legislation over more than a century, in response to many different pressures such as, for example, transient Parliamentary concern with a specific crime.

It will be seen from Table 1 on pp. 7–14 that the available maxima are generally very high. For many offences nothing like the maximum sentence is approached in day-to-day Crown Court sentencing practice. There are exceptions, so that very long determinate sentences or life sentences are not uncommon for very grave crimes such as rape or armed robbery. Generally speaking, however, the average length of prison terms actually imposed for offences is well below half the maximum term which may lawfully be imposed. For males aged 21 and over who were sentenced for indictable offences in the Crown Court and received a sentence of immediate imprisonment in 1999, the average sentence length for burglary was 22.3 months (maximum either 10 or 14 years depending on the nature of the premises burgled), for theft/handling stolen goods it was 11.3 months (maximum for theft seven years, and for handling 14 years) and for robbery it was 46 months (maximum life). Related to the point that maximum sentences are, in general, very high, is the point that the maximum term available for a given offence is only a very approximate guide to its gravity relative to other offences. The maximum sentence for perjury, for example, is seven years, which is significantly less than the maximum of 14 years for handling stolen goods. The Court of Appeal has said on several occasions that a custodial sentence is almost inevitable for an offence of perjury (see, for example *Hall* (1982) 4 Cr App R (S) 153) whereas that is certainly not the case for handling. The reduction in the maximum penalty for theft from 10 years to seven years by CJA 1991 made the maximum sentence of 10 years for obtaining property by deception (given the substantial overlap between the two offences, especially since *Gomez* [1993] AC 442) look rather anomalous. The maximum sentence for non-consensual buggery of a man over 16 was, prior to the CJPOA 1994, 10 years. That Act extended the legal definition of rape so as to include so-called 'male rape', thereby in effect increasing the maximum sentence for the former offence to life imprisonment.

The maximum penalty available for dealing with a particular offence is no real guide at all to the normal sentencing bracket for that offence. The Court of Appeal has stated that imposition of the maximum sentence is appropriate only when sentencing for 'the worst example of that offence which is likely to be encountered in practice' (*Byrne* (1975) 62 Cr App R 159). Even so, when the sentencer is considering whether a particular offence is one of the worst examples of its kind, regard should be had to the range of cases actually encountered in practice, rather than to unlikely or hypothetical examples (*Ambler and Hargreaves* (1971) CSP A1-4C01). A second proposition which follows from the general principle mentioned above is that, if there is substantial mitigation present in a case, imposition of the maximum prison sentence must be incorrect (*Thompson* (1980) 2 Cr App R (S) 244). Sometimes sentencers have chafed against this principle, usually because they have been confronted in a particular case with an available maximum sentence which seems anomalously low. This was the case in *Carroll* (1995) 16 Cr App R (S) 488, where the judge, after imposing the maximum sentence of two years' detention in a young offender institution on an offender who had pleaded guilty to aggravated vehicle-taking, commented that the maximum sentence provided was too low. The Court of Appeal, in reducing the sentence to 18 months, said that sentencers must abide loyally by the maximum sentences provided, that the maximum sentence should be reserved for the most serious examples of that offence and that an appropriate discount (such as for a guilty plea) should be made from the sentence which was commensurate with the seriousness of the offence. The case is one of several which makes it clear that the maximum sentence should not be imposed where the offender has pleaded guilty. In *Greene* (1993) 14 Cr App R (S) 682 the maximum sentence of five years' imprisonment for violent disorder was reduced to three years for this reason, and in *Barnes* (1983) 5 Cr App R (S) 368 a maximum sentence for attempted rape was reduced on the grounds of the guilty plea and saving the victim from the further ordeal of giving testimony.

It is an important principle that an offender who falls to be sentenced after the maximum penalty for the offence has been increased, but in respect of an offence committed before that increase, must be sentenced on the basis that the former maximum applies, unless there is a clear legislative intent that the new maximum should apply retrospectively (*Penwith Justices, ex parte Hay* (1979) 1 Cr App R (S) 265). Article 7 of the ECHR states that no heavier penalty shall be imposed that the one applicable at the time the offence was committed (see *Welch* v *UK* (1995) 20 EHRR 247). In *Street* [1997] 2 Cr App R (S) 309 the 73-year-old offender pleaded guilty to several counts of indecent assault on a girl committed many years earlier. The Court of Appeal reduced the custodial sentences imposed because the sentencer had overlooked the fact that the offences had been committed before the maximum penalty for indecent assault was increased from two years to 10 years by the CJA 1988. In *S* (1991) 13 Cr App R (S) 306 the offender was convicted of indecent assault. It was unclear on what day the assault had taken place and the period within which it was alleged by the prosecution that the offence had taken place covered the period before and after the increase in the maximum penalty came into force. The Court of Appeal held that the offender must be sentenced on the basis of the former maximum penalty. If the reverse problem occurs and the maximum penalty has been reduced, the court should seek guidance from the relevant statute or commencement order. See *Shaw* [1996] 2 Cr App R (S) 278.

There are a number of special rules relating to maximum penalties:

(a) *Statutory offence: no maximum specified* If a person is convicted on indictment of a statutory offence and is liable to be sentenced to imprisonment, but the sentence is not limited to a specified term by that statute, the maximum prison sentence is deemed to be two years (PCC(S)A 2000, s. 77). This provision does not, however, apply to common law offences, such as kidnapping, perverting the course of justice and incitement, where the penalty is at the discretion of the court.

(b) *Statutory conspiracies* Under the Criminal Law Act 1977 (CLA 1977), s. 3, a person guilty of conspiracy to commit murder, conspiracy to commit any offence for which the maximum penalty is life imprisonment or conspiracy to commit any indictable offence punishable with imprisonment where no maximum term is specified is subject to a maximum penalty of life imprisonment. The maximum penalty for other statutory conspiracies is the same as the maximum period provided for the relevant offence. These provisions do not apply to common law conspiracies (preserved by CLA 1977, s. 5), which are subject to a penalty at the discretion of the court. By the CJA 1987, s. 12, however, the maximum penalty for conspiracy to defraud is 10 years.

(c) *Attempts*   Section 4 of the Criminal Attempts Act 1981 provides that the maximum penalty for attempted murder is life imprisonment; other indictable offences are subject to the same maximum as applies on conviction on indictment for the offence attempted. If the offence is triable either way, the maximum penalty on summary conviction is the same as the maximum penalty available for that offence tried summarily. Certain exceptions are provided for in s. 4(5). By reference to the Sexual Offences Act 1956, s. 37 and sch. 2, a maximum sentence of two years is provided for attempted incest by a man with a female over the age of 13 and for attempted incest by a woman; in each case the maximum penalty for the full offence is seven years. A maximum sentence of seven years is specified for attempted sexual intercourse with a girl aged under 13, where the maximum penalty for the full offence is life imprisonment.

4.3.2   Detention in a young offender institution

Detention in a young offender institution has been the most commonly imposed custodial sentence for offenders aged under 21. The impending abolition of this sentence by s. 61 of the CJCSA 2000 will coincide with the extension of the sentence of imprisonment to those aged 18, 19 or 20.

4.3.3   Minimum of seven years for a third Class A drug trafficking offence

Section 110 of the PCC(S)A 2000 states that where a person has been convicted of a Class A drug trafficking offence and, at the time of that offence he was aged 18 or over, and he had previously been convicted of two other Class A drug trafficking offences, and one of those had been committed after he was convicted of the other, the Crown Court *must* impose a custodial sentence of at least seven years. The relevant custodial sentence will be imprisonment or detention in a young offender institution, and 'drug trafficking offence' is defined in the DTA 1994 (see **9.1.1**). The relevant provision (new PCC(S)A 2000, s. 110) came into force in October 1997 and the third qualifying offence must be committed after 30 September 1997. It is irrelevant whether the two earlier offences took place before or after that date.

This provision is, however, not mandatory, since the court may impose a lesser sentence if it finds that there are 'particular circumstances' which relate to any of the offences or to the offender which would make the imposition of the seven-year sentence 'unjust . . . in all the circumstances' (s. 110(2)). If the court takes this line, it must explain in open court why it is of that opinion and what the particular circumstances are which would make the sentence unjust (s. 110(3)). In *Harvey* [2000] 1 Cr App R (S) 368, the Court of Appeal rejected an argument that such a sentence would be unjust in all the circumstances if it would be considered manifestly excessive for the latest offence. Lord Bingham CJ noted that the section clearly required a court to pass a sentence of at least seven years where, before the implementation of that section, the court might well not have done so. His lordship declined to provide further guidance on the kind of circumstances which might make the minimum sentence unjust. Nothing in s. 110 prevents a hospital order being imposed on an offender where that would be a more suitable disposal (MHA 1983, s. 37(1A)).

If the offender pleads guilty, there is a question over how credit for the plea can be reflected in a minimum sentence prescribed by statute. This matter has been resolved by Parliament amending the PCC(S)A 2000, s. 152 (see **2.2.4** at (g)) so as to permit a discount of up to 20 per cent of the sentence of seven years or more which would otherwise have been imposed by the sentencer under s. 110. In these circumstances it is apparent from the decision of the Court of Appeal in *Brown* [2000] Crim LR 496 that it will not be enough for the sentencer simply to announce the final sentence. He or she should indicate what the sentence of at least seven years imposed under s. 110 would have been (without the guilty plea), and then demonstrate that an appropriate reduction of up to 20 per cent has been made from that figure.

It should be noted that if either of the earlier Class A drug trafficking offences were dealt with by way of a discharge or (if the conviction was imposed before 1 October 1992, when the CJA 1991 came into force) a probation order, that conviction will not count for the purposes of s. 110. See further **7.1.4**.

4.3.4 Minimum of three years for third domestic burglary

Section 111 of the PCC(S)A 2000 states that where a person has been convicted of a domestic burglary and, at the time of the offence, was aged 18 or over and had been convicted in England and Wales of two other domestic burglaries, and one of those burglaries was committed after he had been convicted of the other then, provided that *all three* domestic burglaries were committed after 30 November 1999, the Crown Court *must* impose a custodial sentence of at least three years. The relevant custodial sentence will be detention in a young offender institution or imprisonment. For the purposes of s.111, 'domestic burglary' means a burglary committed in respect of a building or part of a building which is a dwelling (s. 111(5)). The section does not mention attempted burglary, so it would appear that it must be confined to commission of three separate instances of the full offence.

This provision is, however, not mandatory, since the court may impose a lesser sentence than three years if it finds that there are 'particular circumstances' which relate to any of the offences or to the offender which would make the imposition of the three year sentence 'unjust . . . in all the circumstances' (s. 111(2)). If the court takes this line, it must explain in open court why it is of that opinion and what the particular circumstances are which would make the sentence unjust (s. 111(3)). There is at the time of writing no appellate guidance as to what kind of circumstances might make the imposition of the minimum sentence unjust, but see **4.3.3** above for emerging case-law on the closely related minimum custodial sentence for the third Class A drug trafficking offence. Nothing in s. 111 prevents a hospital order being imposed on an offender where that would be a more suitable disposal (MHA 1983, s. 37(1A)).

Where the offender pleads guilty the sentencing court is required by PCC(S)A 2000, s. 152 to take into account the stage at which he indicated his intention to plead guilty and the circumstances in which this indication was given. In the case of an offender falling to be sentenced under s. 111, s. 152 states that the maximum reduction for a guilty plea shall be 20 per cent of the determinate sentence of at least three years which would have been imposed. See the discussion at **4.3.3** above.

It should be noted that if either of the earlier domestic burglaries was dealt with by way of a discharge then that conviction will not count for the purposes of s. 111. See further **7.1.4**.

4.3.5 Mandatory life sentences for murder

Life imprisonment is the mandatory sentence for murder when committed by an offender aged 21 or over (Murder (Abolition of Death Penalty) Act 1965, s. 1(1)). The sentence for an offender under the age of 21 who is convicted of murder has been custody for life under the PCC(S)A 2000, s. 93, unless the offender was under the age of 18 at the time the offence was committed, in which case the sentence is detention at Her Majesty's pleasure, under the PCC(S)A 2000, s. 90. These three sentences are all mandatory sentences, so that the judge has no discretion whatever over choice of sentence when sentencing for murder. Murder is the only crime which is subject to a mandatory sentence in this way. The mandatory sentence does not even apply to closely related crimes, such as attempted murder or conspiracy to murder. The sentence of custody for life will be abolished when s. 61 of the CJCSA 2000 is brought into force. From that date murderers aged 18, 19 or 20 will be sentenced to life imprisonment. A sentence under s. 90 of the PCC(S)A 2000 is served 'in such place and under such conditions as the Secretary of State may direct or arrange', which is likely to be a specialised secure unit for young offenders.

The existence of the fixed penalty for murder is clearly anomalous in our sentencing system, and it has been the subject of considerable criticism from the judiciary and from commentators in recent years. The sentence can be attacked on the basis that it fails to allow judicial discretion in the sentencing of a crime where offender culpability can vary significantly, and where that ought to be reflected in the sentence passed by the court. The arrangements for early release of mandatory life sentence prisoners have also been heavily criticised, mainly because they give a politician, the Home Secretary, a decisive influence over judicial matters. The report of the House of Lords select committee, *Murder and Life Imprisonment* (House of Lords Papers, Session 1988–89, 78), recommended that the mandatory penalty should be abolished, and the House of Lords in its legislative capacity voted to abolish it during the passage through Parliament of the Bill which became the CJA 1991. Lord Bingham CJ, when considering an application by the Moors murderer Myra Hindley for judicial review of the Home Secretary's decision that she should never be released from prison, commented that:

> There [is] room for serious debate whether the task of determining how long convicted murderers should serve in prison as punishment for their crimes should be undertaken by the judiciary, as is the case of discretionary life prisoners or, as now, by the executive. That [is] in large measure a political and constitutional debate, not a question for decision by the court. The applicant clearly felt that she was held hostage to public opinion, condemned to pass the rest of her life in prison, although no longer judged a danger to anyone, because of her notoriety and the public obloquy which would fall on any Home Secretary who ordered her release. (*Secretary of State for the Home Department, ex parte Hindley* [1999] 2 WLR 1253).

The present arrangements for adult murderers have also been subject to challenge under the Human Rights Act 1998 in *Secretary of State for the Home Department, ex parte Anderson* (2001) *The Times*, 27 February 2001, but the argument that the fair trial provisions of Article

6 of the ECHR applied to the setting of the tariff, such that it ought properly to be a function of the sentencing court and not the Home Secretary, was rejected by the Divisional Court. According to Rose LJ in that case the mandatory life sentence for murder was an 'automatic penalty' and the fixing of the tariff was an administrative procedure.

Although these three sentences are mandatory, they rarely require the offender to serve the rest of his or her life in custody. At some point during the sentence the offender will probably be released back into the community, although remaining under supervision and recall. For this reason, these sentences are perhaps better referred to as 'indeterminate' rather than 'life' sentences, but because the latter term is in general usage it will also be used in this book. When a sentencer passes a sentence of life imprisonment for murder on an adult the period of time to be served in custody is determined by the Home Secretary as advised by the Parole Board (see C(S)A 1997, s. 29), but the sentencing judge has some influence over that issue. The court is empowered under s. 1(2) of the Murder (Abolition of Death Penalty) Act 1965, to 'declare the period which it recommends to the Secretary of State as the minimum period which in its view should elapse' before licence. This recommendation is not strictly binding on the executive authorities, who will actually determine the date of release and, since it is not a sentence in itself, there is no right of appeal against this recommendation (*Leaney* [1996] 1 Cr App R (S) 30). It was said in *Flemming* [1973] 2 All ER 401 that if the sentencer would be content to see the offender at liberty in under 12 years he should make no recommendation. Apart from the power to make a recommendation in each case, which is in fact quite rarely used, the sentencing judge is required to indicate in writing the 'tariff' period which in his view is necessary to meet the requirements of retribution and deterrence in the case. This report goes to the Lord Chief Justice, who also records his views, and then to the Home Secretary. These indications do not, however, bind the Home Secretary, who may set a lower or higher tariff than is indicated by the judges. Such a change should be made only exceptionally, and may be challenged by judicial review in the courts by the prisoner to whom it relates (*Secretary of State for the Home Department, ex parte Doody* [1994] 1 AC 531. The House of Lords held in *Secretary of State for the Home Department, ex parte Hindley* [1999] 2 WLR 1253, that the Home Secretary is entitled to fix a 'whole life tariff', which would mean that the offender would never be released from prison, but the decision could not be made in such a way as to prevent its being reopened, either by the same Home Secretary at a later date, or by a successor in that office.

If the murder was committed by an offender who was under 18 at the time of the offence, the appropriate mandatory sentence is detention at Her Majesty's pleasure under PCC(S)A 2000, s. 90. Twenty-four young offenders were so sentenced during 1999. There have been important changes to this sentence in recent years. As a result of the decision of the European Court of Human Rights in *V* v *UK* (2000) 30 EHRR 121, the practice whereby the tariff period to be served by the detainee before first becoming eligible for consideration for early release was ultimately set by the Home Secretary, has been abolished. The CJCSA 2000, s. 60, which is in force, now requires the sentencer imposing a sentence of detention at Her Majesty's pleasure normally to specify in open court the tariff period. The sentencer will do this in accordance with PCC(S)A 2000, s. 82A, which already operates where a discretionary life sentence, or an automatic life sentence for the second serious offence, is passed. The House of Lords in *Secretary of State for the Home Department, ex parte Venables* [1998] AC 407 stressed that when passing such a sentence on a very young offender the welfare of that child or young person is also of great importance, and there should be flexibility in the early release arrangements so that the executive authorities could review the case in the light of progress during the period of detention. See further on s. 28 **4.5.2**.

4.3.6 Automatic life sentence for the second serious offence

Under the PCC(S)A 2000, s. 109, the Crown Court is required to impose a life sentence on an offender who is convicted of a 'serious offence' which has been committed after 30 September 1997 (when s. 109 came into force) if, at the time when that offence was committed, the offender was aged 18 or over and had already been convicted of another 'serious offence'. Where the offender is aged 21 or over the relevant life sentence is life imprisonment, and where the offender is aged from 18 to 20 inclusive the relevant life sentence is custody for life but, when CJCSA 2000, s. 61 is brought into force, the sentence of custody for life will be abolished and the relevant sentence will in all cases be life imprisonment. Automatic life sentences are not mandatory life sentences in the same sense as mandatory life sentences imposed for the crime of murder (see **4.3.5**). The sentencing court may pronounce a different sentence if it finds that there are 'exceptional circumstances' relating to either of the offences, or to the offender, which justify its not imposing a life sentence. If the court does not impose a life sentence, it must state what the 'exceptional circumstances' are which it has relied upon.

It will be seen from the wording of s. 109 that the first serious offence may have been committed before that section was brought into force. The age of the offender when he committed that first offence is irrelevant, and there is no requirement that the two offences be of the same kind, nor any restriction on the period of time which must have elapsed between them. It is possible, however, that such matters may be relevant when a judge is deciding whether there are 'exceptional circumstances' applicable to the case.

'Serious offence' has a particular meaning here. The offences which qualify as 'serious offences' for the purposes of s. 109 are listed in s. 109(5). They are:

(a) attempted murder, conspiracy to murder or incitement to murder;
(b) soliciting murder;
(c) manslaughter;
(d) wounding or causing grievous bodily harm with intent;
(e) rape or attempted rape;
(f) sexual intercourse with a girl under 13;
(g) an offence under s. 16 (possession of a firearm with intent to injure), 17 (use of a firearm to resist arrest) or 18 (carrying a firearm with criminal intent) of the Firearms Act 1968; and
(h) robbery where, at some time during the commission of the offence the offender had in his possession a firearm or imitation firearm within the meaning of the 1968 Act.

All these offences already carry life imprisonment as their maximum penalty. It is clear, therefore, that Parliament is not providing additional powers for the Crown Court in s. 2 but, rather, is seeking to ensure that ('exceptional circumstances' apart) the courts will impose such a sentence where a 'serious offence' has been committed by the offender for the second time. A *discretionary* life sentence (see **4.3.7**) cannot be passed unless the offence which has been committed is a violent or a sexual offence, and in nearly every case where an offence qualifies as a serious offence it will also qualify as a 'violent offence' or a 'sexual offence' as defined in PCC(S)A 2000, s. 161 (see **4.2.7**). One possible exception is an offence of robbery using an imitation firearm, which qualifies as a 'serious offence', but was held not to amount to a 'violent offence' on the particular facts of *Palin* (1995) 16 Cr App R (S) 888.

A number of other observations can be made about the offences listed in s. 109(5). Specific reference is made in (e) to attempted rape as well as to the full offence, so that it can almost certainly be inferred that attempts not referred to in other sub-paragraphs are not covered. For example, an attempted wounding with intent, or an attempted robbery, would not be 'serious offences'. Of the three Firearms Act offences listed in (g), the second and third can be committed using an imitation firearm, but the subparagraph does not specifically say whether such cases would be qualifying offences for the purposes of s. 109. The Court of Appeal in *Buckland* [2000] 1 WLR 1262 held that the paragraph did extend to imitation firearms. The offence of robbery in (h) is a qualifying offence only where the offender had with him a firearm or imitation firearm at the time. In *A-G's Reference (No. 71 of 1999)* [1999] 2 Cr App R (S) 369 the Court of Appeal said that it was a 'serious offence' where the offender had not actually carried a firearm during the robbery but where a co-defendant did so. In another case, *Brownbill* [1999] 2 Cr App R (S) 331, the offender had threatened a shopkeeper with a knife. This did not make the offence a 'serious offence' as such, but the fact that the offender knew that his co-defendant was carrying a non-working air pistol brought him within the terms of the section.

It should also be noted that if the earlier 'serious offence' was sentenced by way of a conditional or absolute discharge (unlikely though not impossible — conditional discharges for manslaughter, for example, are not unheard of), then the conviction is not a qualifying conviction for the purposes of s. 109. This is because a conviction followed by a discharge counts for limited purposes only (see PCC(S)A 2000, s. 14 and **7.1.4**). A similar rule used to apply to probation orders (now community rehabilitation orders), so if the offender was placed on probation for the earlier serious offence before 1 October 1992 that conviction would not count either. In *Frost* [2001] Crim LR 143 the offender, aged 25 at the time of the relevant hearing, had been convicted for his first serious offence when he was 15, and had then been given a supervision order by the youth court. It was argued that, had he been slightly older at the time of that offence, the likely sentence would have been a probation order, which would have meant that the conviction did not count for the purposes of s. 109. The Court of Appeal accepted that this odd legal outcome amounted to an 'exceptional circumstance' relating to the offender which justified the passing of a sentence other than a life sentence.

The Court of Appeal has considered the meaning of 'exceptional circumstances' in relation to s. 109 on a number of occasions. In *Kelly* [1999] 2 Cr App R (S) 176 Lord Bingham CJ said that it was clearly Parliament's intention that life sentences should be passed under s. 109 in a range of circumstances where the criteria for passing a discretionary life sentence were not made out. His lordship went on to indicate that in the nature of things 'exceptional circumstances' would be rarely encountered, and the sentencer was not relieved of the duty to pass an automatic life sentence even where he or she thought that such a sentence would be quite unjust. 'Exceptional circumstances' were, however, found in *Buckland* [2000] 1 WLR 1262, where the offender was convicted of an attempted robbery and possession of an imitation firearm on arrest. The latter was the 'serious offence'. He was involved in a bizarrely amateurish crime. He handed the cashier a note demanding money, the note being signed by the offender and bearing his own name and address. The cashier asked the offender to wait at the customer service desk, and he remained there until the police arrived and arrested him, at which time the imitation firearm was discovered.

Lord Bingham CJ said that it was very unusual for a bank robbery to be carried out with the incompetence and lack of aggression shown by Buckland. The sentence was varied to a determinate prison sentence of four and a half years. The meaning of 'exceptional circumstances' was reconsidered by the Court of Appeal, this time under Lord Woolf CJ, in *Offen* [2001] 1 WLR 253, and this is now the leading decision on s. 109. His lordship stressed that the real rationale of the automatic life sentence under s. 109 was the protection of the public, so that:

[i]t could therefore be assumed that the section was not intended to apply to someone in relation to whom it was established that there would be no need for protection in the future. In other words, if the facts showed the statutory assumption was misplaced, then that, in the statutory context, was not the normal situation and, in consequence, for the purposes of the section the position was exceptional.

The effect of this decision is, it would seem, to broaden considerably the meaning of 'exceptional circumstances', and to bring much closer together the rationale for the automatic life sentence under s. 109 with that of the discretionary life sentence. For the automatic life sentence, however, there is still a statutory requirement to pass such a sentence unless the offender can be shown to pose no significant risk to the public and, if the sentencer decides that there are indeed 'exceptional circumstances', the reasons for reaching this view still have to be given in open court.

In *Kelly*, Lord Bingham CJ had declined to decide whether the automatic life sentence provisions infringed the provisions of the ECHR, but in *Offen* the Court of Appeal held that s. 109 did not infringe Article 7 (retrospective penalties). Further, according to Lord Woolf CJ in that case, although s. 109 could on the face of it be taken to infringe either or both of Article 3 (inhuman or degrading treatment or punishment) and Article 5 (right to liberty and security), provided that 'exceptional circumstances' was given the more flexible meaning advocated by the Court of Appeal, these Articles would not be infringed either.

Whether the life sentence imposed under s. 109 is a sentence of life imprisonment or a sentence of custody for life, the sentencer may exercise the power under PCC(S)A 2000, s. 82A, to specify what part of the sentence must expire before the offender is to be considered for early release, and normally should do so. See further on s. 82A, **4.5.2**.

4.3.7 Discretionary life imprisonment

A discretionary life sentence may be passed in respect of any offence for which life imprisonment is provided as the maximum penalty (see Table 1 on pp. 7–14 for examples of such offences). The relevant discretionary life sentence for an offender aged 21 or over is life imprisonment. For an offender aged from 18 to 20 inclusive the relevant sentence is custody for life and, if the offender is under 18, the relevant sentence is detention for life under PCC(S)A 2000, s. 91. When CJCSA 2000, s. 61 is brought into force the sentence of custody for life will be abolished, and the relevant sentence for 18, 19 or 20-year-olds will become life imprisonment. The statutory criteria in the PCC(S)A 2000 for determining whether the imposition of a custodial sentence is justified, and, if so, for fixing its length, apply to discretionary life sentences as they do to determinate sentences. Since the life sentence is an indeterminate sentence, it is very difficult to see how its imposition, rather than that of a determinate sentence of imprisonment, could be justified in terms of s. 80(2)(a) as being 'commensurate with the seriousness of the offence'. A discretionary life sentence may now be justified only under s. 80(2)(b), as being 'necessary to protect the public from serious harm from the offender'. It therefore follows that an indeterminate sentence can be passed only where the offender has committed a violent offence or a sexual offence (as defined in s. 161). In *Robinson* [1977] 2 Cr App R (S) 35, where the offender pleaded guilty to possessing an imitation firearm with intent to commit a burglary, a discretionery life sentence was quashed on the basis that the offence was neither a sexual offence nor, on the facts, a violent offence. See also *Meek* (1995) 16 Cr App R (S) 1003. Statutory criteria apart, there are several offences punishable with life imprisonment which never in practice result in such a sentence. This is especially true of common law offences, which carry life as the maximum penalty unless statute provides to the contrary. The offences most likely to lead to a sentence of discretionary life imprisonment are manslaughter, rape and arson.

It might be thought that the principle that the maximum penalty should be reserved for the gravest instances of an offence reasonably likely to occur would lead to the conclusion that the most serious offences of rape, robbery, arson or manslaughter would be punished with life imprisonment while those which are less serious would merit a fixed-term sentence. That is not, however, the approach of the courts. Crimes which, though grave, are not necessarily the gravest of their type sometimes result in a life sentence for the offender. Conversely, unless the conditions outlined below are satisfied, even the gravest examples are normally dealt with by determinate sentences, albeit very long ones. Thus in *Wilson* (1964) 48 Cr App R 329, better known as the 'Great Train Robbery', in which the Glasgow to London mail train was held up and £2,600,000 in used notes was stolen, only a fraction of which was ever recovered, life sentences were not passed. Concurrent terms of 30 years (for the robbery) and 25 years (for the associated conspiracy) were imposed by the judge. If life imprisonment was not seen as appropriate in such a case, when could it be appropriate? The Court of Appeal has developed several important sentencing principles over the years which relate to the imposition of the discretionary life sentence. These principles are well known and appear in the main to be well settled.

The starting point is that 'life sentences for offences other than homicide should not be imposed unless there are exceptional circumstances in the case' (per Lawton LJ in *Pither* (1979) 1 Cr App R (S) 209). What constitutes such exceptional circumstances? From leading cases such as *Hodgson* (1968) 52 Cr App R 113, *De Havilland* (1983) 5 Cr App R (S) 109 and *O'Dwyer* (1986) 86 Cr App R 313, it can be seen that life imprisonment has been deemed to be appropriate only where the following conditions have been satisfied:

(a)   the offence or offences are in themselves serious enough to require a very long sentence;

(b)   it appears from the nature of the offences, or from the offender's criminal history, that he is a person of mental instability who, if at liberty, would probably reoffend and present a grave danger to the public;

(c)   the offender will remain unstable and a potential danger for a long and/or uncertain period of time.

The continuing relevance of these criteria was confirmed in *J* (1992) 14 Cr App R (S) 500 and *A-G's Reference (No. 34 of 1992)* (1994) 15 Cr App R (S) 167. Although in *Hodgson* (1968) 52 Cr App R 113 it was said that a life sentence was proper only where the offence was itself grave enough to justify a very long sentence, and in *A-G's Reference (No. 32 of 1996)* [1997] 1 Cr App R (S) 263 it was stated that there could be 'no question' of a life sentence unless a very serious offence had been committed, in *Chapman* [2000] 1

Cr App R (S) 377 the Court of Appeal recognised that this requirement had not always been adhered to in the past.

The second condition for the imposition of a life sentence is evidence of mental instability such that the offender is perceived as a real danger to the public. Life sentences have been imposed in the past following psychiatric evidence of the offender's 'immaturity and sexual maladjustment' in a case of repeated rape (*Thornett* (1979) 1 Cr App R (S) 1), psychopathic disorder not susceptible to treatment (*De Havilland* (1983) 5 Cr App R (S) 109), personality disorder (*Finney* (1979) 1 Cr App R (S) 301), latent schizophrenia and a long history of eccentric and inconsequent behaviour (*Scott* (1981) 3 Cr App R (S) 334) and paedophilia not susceptible to treatment (*Hatch* [1997] 1 Cr App R (S) 22). On the other side of the line are cases such as *Blackburn* (1979) 1 Cr App R (S) 205, where a life sentence for conspiracy to rob was varied to one of eight years' imprisonment; the offender was described in medical reports as having 'a severe personality problem', as 'impulsive' and 'capable of dishonesty', but the evidence did not point to mental instability. In *Wilkinson* (1983) 5 Cr App R (S) 105, the Court of Appeal held that, in the absence of evidence of mental instability, the accused, who had carried out numerous burglaries, sometimes threatening occupants with violence, had to be sentenced like any other 'bad burglar or robber', a term of 11 years being substituted for the life sentence. The fact that an offender is of 'borderline subnormal intelligence' has been held not of itself to be enough to fulfil the mental instability criterion (*Laycock* (1981) 3 Cr App R (S) 104), nor is the fact that the offender is a chronic alcoholic (*Stewart* (1989) 11 Cr App R (S) 132). In *Roche* (1995) 16 Cr App R (S) 849, a case involving attempted murder and indecent assault on a woman, the medical evidence did not disclose any abnormal mental state, and so the Court of Appeal held that a life sentence could not be justified. Medical evidence should normally be considered by the court when an assessment of dangerousness is being made (*Pither* (1979) 1 Cr App R (S) 209) although it is not necessary to show that the offender is suffering from a specific mental disorder within the meaning of the MHA 1983. In an exceptional case the sentencer may impose a life sentence without hearing any medical evidence at all (*Stevenson* (1993) 14 Cr App R (S) 22).

Whether the third condition, that there must be a potential danger, exists may be ascertained by the court from the facts of the offence, details of the offender's previous convictions and the medical evidence. The danger in question will usually be a danger to the public generally, but a specific threat to a particular person may be sufficient. In *A-G's Reference (No. 32 of 1996)* [1997] 1 Cr App R (S) 261 the offender was convicted of causing grievous bodily harm with intent, an offence committed the day after he had been released on home leave from a life sentence for murder. Imposing a further life sentence for the assault the Court of Appeal stressed that the offender would pose a serious danger for an indefinite period of time. This test has been applied in later cases, including *McPhee* [1998] 1 Cr App R (S) 201. The offender's dangerousness will justify a life sentence where the medical evidence is that the offender's condition will not improve through treatment or the passage of time (*Virgo* (1988) 10 Cr App R (S) 427). Conversely, where there is evidence that the offender's mental state will improve during a specified period, and a sentence proportionate to the seriousness of the offence would thereby provide sufficient protection for the public, that sentence, rather than a life sentence, should be passed (*Hercules* (1980) 2 Cr App R (S) 156).

Even in cases where the above three conditions are met it is quite likely that the court will have available an alternative which may be seen as more suitable than life imprisonment. The alternative is a hospital order made under the provisions of the MHA 1983, s. 37

(see **11.3**). The effect of a hospital order, in the case of a dangerous offender, would be his compulsory detention in a mental hospital. It is likely that special restrictions would, by s. 41 of the Act, be placed upon his discharge from hospital. The following conditions must, however, be satisfied if a court is to make a hospital order:

(a)   the offender must be diagnosed as suffering from one or more of the forms of mental disorder specified in the MHA 1983;

(b)   there must be a suitable hospital prepared to offer him admission; and

(c)   the court must consider that treatment rather than punishment is appropriate in view of the extent to which the offender was responsible for his actions.

A mentally unstable offender will not necessarily be suffering from mental disorder within the meaning of the MHA 1983; even if he is, there may not be room for him in hospital. In such circumstances the court may be thrown back upon what is regarded as the 'least wrong' sentence in the circumstances, life imprisonment.

If the judge is considering imposing a discretionary life sentence, he should as a matter of good practice alert counsel to that fact, so that the matter may be addressed in argument by them. This is clearly of particular importance for defence counsel (*McDougall* (1983) 5 Cr App R (S) 78), but in *Virgo* (1988) 10 Cr App R (S) 427 the judge heard submissions from both counsel. While warning counsel in this way is good practice, it should not be regarded as an absolute requirement, since there may be cases where the passing of a life sentence is an obvious possibility to all concerned in the case (*Allen* (1987) 9 Cr App R (S) 169).

A life sentence and a fixed-term sentence may run concurrently. In *Nugent* (1984) 67 Cr App R 93 the imposition of two determinate prison sentences to run consecutively but concurrently with a life sentence was approved by the Court of Appeal. A fixed-term sentence may not run consecutively to a life sentence (*Foy* [1962] 1 WLR 609) and an implication of this is that life sentences cannot run consecutively to each other. Neither may a life sentence run consecutively to a fixed term (*Jones* v *DPP* [1962] AC 635).

4.3.8   Custody for life

As was explained in **4.3.5**, an offender under the age of 21 who is convicted of murder *must* be sentenced to custody for life (PCC(S)A 2000, s. 93), unless he was under the age of 18 at the time of commission of the offence, in which case the proper sentence is detention at Her Majesty's pleasure. An offender aged 18, 19 or 20 who is convicted of an offence which is punishable in the case of an adult with a maximum sentence of life imprisonment *may* be sentenced to custody for life (PCC(S)A 2000, s. 94). In many respects this sentence is parallel to the discretionary life sentence for adult offenders. When the CJCSA 2000, s. 61 is brought into force, the sentence of custody for life will be abolished and offenders aged 18, 19 or 20 for whom a discretionary life sentence is the appropriate sentence will henceforth be sentenced to life imprisonment.

4.3.9   Detention for life under PCC(S)A 2000, s. 91

An offender aged under 18 who is convicted of an offence which is punishable in the case of an adult with a maximum sentence of life imprisonment may be sentenced to detention for life under the PCC(S)A 2000, s. 91. In many respects the sentence is parallel to the discretionary life sentence for adult offenders and the sentence of custody for life under s. 93 for those aged 18, 19 or 20. In *Bryson* (1973) 58 Cr App R 464 a sentence of detention for life was upheld on a 14-year-old who pleaded guilty to arson causing damage worth £20,000 and considerable risk to life. In *Carr* [1996] 1 Cr App R (S) 191 the defendant was a 15-year-old girl who pleaded guilty to causing grievous bodily harm with intent, having stabbed another schoolgirl in the back with a knife. Two other offences, in which she had tried to strangle other schoolgirls, were taken into consideration. Reports revealed other instances of disturbed and aggressive behaviour and indicated that the defendant was 'exceptionally dangerous'. An indeterminate sentence under s. 53(2) was upheld. See also *Lomas* (1995) 16 Cr App R (S) 955 and *Secretary of State for the Home Department, ex parte Furber* [1998] 1 Cr App R (S) 208 both manslaughter cases.

Five young offenders were sentenced to detention for life under PCC(S)A 2000, s. 91 during 1999.

4.3.10   Detention for a fixed term under PCC(S)A 2000, s. 91

Section 91 of the PCC(S)A 2000 gives the Crown Court a discretionary power to sentence juveniles convicted of certain grave offences to detention for a term not exceeding the maximum prison term carried by the offence in question. A striking contrast may be made with the detention and training order where the maximum sentence which may be imposed is 24 months. In contrast sentences imposed under s. 91 may sometimes be for life (see 4.3.9) and are rarely for less than two years, although a number of shorter sentences are imposed under s. 91.

While the proportion of offenders given sentences under s. 91 is still relatively small (607 such sentences were passed in 1999 compared to 24,800 sentences of detention in a young offender institution), s. 91 is very important because it gives the Crown Court power to deprive a young offender of his or her liberty for a substantial period of time. Of the 607 cases, 258 followed conviction for robbery, 111 were for offences of violence, 58 for sexual offences, 101 for burglary and 29 for arson. The use of this sentence has been increasing sharply in recent years. Only 102 such orders were made in 1991.

The availability of the sentence under s. 91 depends upon a complex interlocking of s. 91 with various other provisions. The first point to note is that the power is reserved to the Crown Court after the young offender has been convicted on indictment. A youth court cannot pass such a sentence in any circumstances, nor may the Crown Court do so if the offender is remitted there for sentence after a finding of guilt in a youth court (*McKenna* (1985) 7 Cr App R (S) 348). In a case where the offence merits a greater penalty than is permitted by the 24-month maximum detention and training order, or where the offender is aged under 12 and so is ineligible for a detention and training order in any event, the proper course is for the magistrates in the youth court to commit to Crown Court for trial. An error was made in *Learmonth* (1988) 10 Cr App R (S) 229, where the 16-year-old offender pleaded guilty before the youth court to assault with intent to rob. He was committed by that court to the Crown Court for sentence, where three years' detention under s. 91 was ordered. This sentence had to be quashed on appeal, since Learmonth had not been convicted of the offence on indictment. The Court of Appeal has stressed the importance of this point on several occasions, such as in *Billam* (1986) 8 Cr App R (S) 48, in respect of offences of rape committed by juveniles, and again more generally in *AM* [1998] 1 WLR 363.

The second point is that the offender must be aged from 10 to 17 inclusive. Since no offender aged under 12 can receive a detention and training order it will be apparent that, the sentence of detention under s. 91 is the only available custodial sentence for offenders aged under 12. To qualify for a detention and training order, an offender aged 12, 13 or 14 must be a 'persistent offender'. There is no such requirement in relation to detention under s. 91. See *Jenkins-Rowe and Glover* [2000] Crim LR 1022.

The third point is that the young offender must have been convicted of one of the range of offences specified in s. 91. This list of 'relevant offences' now comprises:

(a)   any offence punishable in the case of an adult with imprisonment for 14 years or more, but not murder;

(b)   an offence of indecent assault, whether committed on a man or on a woman;

(c)   if the defendant is aged between 14 and 17 inclusive, an offence of causing death by dangerous driving (RTOA 1988, s. 1) or causing death by careless driving while under the influence of drink or drugs (RTOA 1988, s. 3A).

Relevant offences include, therefore, manslaughter, arson, wounding with intent, robbery, burglary committed in a dwelling and handling stolen goods, but not theft, obtaining by deception, burglary committed other than in a dwelling (see *Brown* (1995) 16 Cr App R (S) 932), aggravated vehicle taking (even where death results) unlawful wounding, or assault occasioning actual bodily harm. Offences in (b) and (c) above are specially listed since, although they may attract a sentence under s. 91 in an appropriate case, they carry a maximum sentence of less than 14 years' imprisonment in the case of an adult.

The fourth and final point is that s. 91 expressly provides that the sentence should not be imposed unless no other method of dealing with the offender (such as a detention and training order) is appropriate. This requirement is considered further below.

The maximum term of detention which may be ordered under s. 91 is the maximum prison term which could be ordered for the relevant offence if committed by an adult. If the offence carries imprisonment for life, then detention for life may be ordered (*Abbott* [1964] 1 QB 489 and **4.3.9**). There is no minimum term fixed by statute, but it is obvious from the restricted circumstances in which the sentence is available that detention under s. 91 is only meant to be used in those rare cases in which a juvenile deserves to lose his liberty for a substantial period of time. The effect of the sentence is that the detainee is liable to be kept 'in such a place and under such conditions' as the Secretary of State considers appropriate. Depending on the age of the detainee, that place might be local authority secure accommodation, a young offender institution or a prison. If the offender is suffering from a mental disorder, he might be sent to a suitable hospital.

The Court of Appeal has stated clearly on several occasions that the power to order detention under s. 91 is to be used sparingly, as a last resort, reflecting the language of s. 91 that it should be used only where 'none of the other methods in which the case may legally be dealt with is suitable'. Traditionally, long-term detention has been used for offences involving grave violence or where there is danger to the public. Thus in *Storey* [1973] 1 WLR 1045 the Court of Appeal upheld 20 years' detention for the 16-year-old ringleader of a group of youngsters who had, for no reason, set upon a man in the street. Storey had dragged the man into an alley, hit him and kicked him in the head. The group left him lying there, but on two occasions later in the evening returned to him and Storey kicked him again repeatedly and hit him with a brick. The victim's injuries were very severe. The Court of Appeal decided that Storey must be detained until such time as he had matured, and could be trusted not to behave in such an appalling way again. Another example is *Taylor* (1995) 16 Cr App R (S) 570, where seven years' detention was reduced to six years for robbery committed with great violence by a 17-year-old on a 70-year-old man, and *K* (1995) 16 Cr App R (S) 966, where a six-year term of detention was appropriate for an offender aged 16 who raped his six-year-old sister. The medical report in the latter case 'gave a disturbing picture of sexual fantasising' and indicated that the offender would remain a risk to the public for at least the next decade.

The circumstances in which s. 91 detention is appropriate for non-violent but serious offences of dishonesty has not been entirely clear. In *Oakes* (1983) 5 Cr App R (S) 389 the Court of Appeal said that Parliament did not intend s. 91 to be used for simple offences of dishonesty, however despicable they might be. In that case the Court of Appeal substituted a sentence of 12 months' detention in a young offender institution for 30 months' detention under s. 91 in a case where a 16-year-old had been convicted of burgling the homes of several old people by tricking his way in and then stealing any items of value while his accomplice kept the victim occupied. In *Simmons* (1995) 16 Cr App R (S) 801, however, five years' detention was upheld in the case of a 16-year-old who pleaded guilty to seven counts of house burglary and asked for a large number of offences to be taken into consideration, including 67 burglaries and attempted burglaries. It was held by the Court of Appeal that the sentence was appropriate to reflect both the gravity of the offending and its persistence.

A sentencing problem is posed where an offender who stands convicted of more than one offence, but where only one of those offences is punishable under s. 91. This issue was clarified by the Court of Appeal in *Walsh* [1997] 2 Cr App R (S) 210, where there were five offenders, all girls aged 14 or 15. They pleaded guilty to false imprisonment and unlawful wounding, committed while carrying out a sustained and violent attack on another girl aged 14. Sentences of detention under s. 91 were imposed for terms varying between three and a half years and three years and 11 months. It was argued on appeal that the sentences were wrong, since the real gravity of the offending lay in the unlawful wounding of the victim, but that was an offence for which s. 91 was not available. The Court of Appeal, however, said that the two offences were 'associated offences' (see **4.2.4**) and, since s. 91 was available in respect of the false imprisonment, it was also available when the two offences were being dealt with together. The approach taken in *Walsh* was endorsed in *AM* [1998] 1 WLR 363.

Long-standing general guidance on the use of the power under s. 91 was provided by the Court of Appeal in *Fairhurst* [1986] 1 WLR 1374, in which Lord Lane CJ stated that, '. . . it is not good sentencing practice to pass a sentence of detention under s. 91 simply because a [24] months' sentence seems to be on the low side for the particular offence committed'. Subsequently this was interpreted by the Court of Appeal in *Wainfur* [1997] 1 Cr App R (S) 43 to mean that for offenders within this age group, the court should be satisfied before imposing a sentence under s. 91 that a sentence 'substantially greater' than 24 months is appropriate. In the important case of *AM* [1998] 1 WLR 363, however, the Court of Appeal signalled a different approach. Lord Bingham CJ stated that the earlier law had the effect of creating a 'sentencing no-man's land' between the maximum sentence of detention in a young offender institution and the shortest term which might appropriately be imposed under s. 91. Accordingly, his lordship said that while a Crown Court sentencer should not exceed the 24-month limit without careful thought, if it was concluded that a longer term, even if not much longer, was needed, then the court should impose whatever it considered the appropriate period of detention under s. 91 to be.

The imposition of a sentence under s. 91 is subject to the statutory criteria for determining the imposition of custodial sentences, and for determining their length, which are laid down in PCC(S)A 2000. The cases discussed above illustrate that there are some occasions on which recourse to s. 91 is justified by the seriousness of the offence and others where the protection of the public is the triggering factor. All the decided cases on s. 91 must, however, be read with the statutory limitations in mind. Clearly, unless the term is being imposed for the protection of the public, the duration of detention under s. 91 should be in proportion to the seriousness of the offence. Indeed, for a very young person, it is well recognised that the sentence should be shorter than that which would be appropriate for an adult.

4.3.11   Detention and training order

The detention and training order was introduced by the CDA 1998 and the relevant provisions can now be found in the PCC(S)A 2000, ss. 100–107. The powers were brought into force on 1 April 2000 and, from that date the DTO became the principal custodial sentence for offenders under the age of 18. From the same date the secure training order was abolished (for details of that sentence see the previous edition of this work) and the sentence of detention in a young offender institution became applicable just to offenders aged 18, 19 or 20. The DTO applies to offenders aged from 12 to 17 inclusive. There is provision in s. 100(2)(b) for the Secretary of State to extend the DTO to 10 and 11-year-olds, but no such order has so far been made. Where an offender is aged 17 at the time of the offence but is aged 18 when sentenced, it is clear that the sentence now takes effect as a sentence of detention in a young offender institution (*Cassidy* [2000] All ER (D) 1200). As was explained earlier, when the CJCSA 2000, s. 61 is brought into force, the sentence of detention in a young offender institution will be abolished for 18, 19 and 20-year old offenders as well as for those under 18, so that from that date the relevant custodial sentence for those aged 18 and over will be imprisonment.

The DTO is available to the youth courts and to the Crown Court for young offenders convicted of an offence punishable with imprisonment in the case of an adult. The DTO is a 'custodial sentence' for the purposes of the PCC(S)A 2000, ss. 79 and 80, so that the imposition of a DTO, and determination of its length, must be in accordance with the seriousness of the offence or, in the case of a violent or sexual offence committed by the offender, the need to protect the public from the commission of further such offences committed by him. In most cases the first half of the DTO will be served in custody (in a young offender institution, a secure training centre, or in local authority secure accommo-dation, depending on the age and needs of the particular young offender). The second half of the sentence will be served under supervision and on licence in the community. There are limited powers conferred on the Secretary of State to order release at a point earlier than half-way through the term of the order. For this sentence, unlike any other custodial sentence on the statute books, the legislation requires that the court selects a DTO for one of the terms specified in s. 101(1). These terms are 4, 6, 8, 10, 12, 18 or 24 months. No other sentence lengths are possible. A sentence of 14 months would be an unlawful sentence, but the statute does not expressly say what would be the effect of passing such a sentence. It might take effect as a term of 12 months. The selection of even-numbered terms is designed to make calculation of the two distinct parts of the sentence easy to do and, more importantly, easier for the young offender to understand at the time of sentence. It also assists in the tailoring of rehabilitative schemes within the custodial part of the DTO, since the authorities will know exactly how long the young offender will be with them before release into the community. It is not clear on this rationale, however, why sentences of 14, 16 or 20 months could not be passed. It may have something to do with the traditional predilection of sentencers for the terms listed in s. 101(1). Historically sentences of 12 or

18 months have been common, but terms of 14 or 16 months relatively rare. The formal restriction to the seven terms listed in the subsection has, however, given rise to practical problems early in the history of this order, as explained below.

It can be seen that four months is the minimum term of a DTO. In a case where the proportionate sentence for the offence would have been four months, but there is significant mitigation in the case, such as a guilty plea, which would take the sentence below that figure, a DTO cannot be passed at all. In such a case, a community sentence would be the appropriate outcome. Formerly the minimum sentence of detention in a young offender institution which could be ordered for an offender under 18 had been two months, and it was pointed out by the Divisional Court in *Inner London Crown Court, ex parte N and S* [2001] 1 Cr App R (S) 343 that one effect of the introduction of DTOs in April 2000 had been to raise the custody threshold for young offenders. It is clear that the minimum sentence of four months cannot be reached by a sentencer by passing shorter DTO terms to run consecutively. This must be the case, since the shorter terms would themselves be unlawful. A comparable rule applied in relation to sentences of detention in a young offender institution (*Kent Youth Court, ex parte Kingwell* [1999] 1 Cr App R (S) 263). The maximum available term for a DTO is 24 months. This term is available for the Crown Court and (surprisingly enough) for the youth courts. It seems rather odd that a youth court may order a custodial sentence for up to 24 months on a young offender, while a magistrates' courts is of course limited to a maximum of six months' imprisonment on an adult for a single offence. It is important to note that if the Crown Court or a youth court passes a DTO for more than 24 months, the effect of s. 101(5) is that the 'excess shall be treated as remitted'. This is an automatic effect of the statute — any surplus length simply disappears. Before the introduction of DTOs there was a similar rule which existed in relation to sentences of detention in a young offender institution where, for offenders aged 15, 16 or 17, the maximum term was 24 months. Crown Court sentencers were sometimes caught out by the provision. They passed a sentence of 'detention' for (say) three years on a 17-year-old offender. This could be a lawful sentence if the 'detention' was actually long-term detention under PCC(S)A 2000, s. 91. If, however, the sentencer failed to make his intentions clear, there was a risk that the sentence would be construed as an unlawful sentence of detention in a young offender institution, with the third year being automatically remitted. The problem is explained in some detail by Lord Bingham CJ in *AM* [1998] 1 WLR 363. Comparable problems may arise at the top end of the DTO scale if sentencers fail to explain whether they are passing a DTO or a term of long-term detention under s. 91. It has been confirmed by the Court of Appeal that a maximum term of DTO can be lawful even where there has been a guilty plea or other significant mitigation. This can arise where the offence is one which can attract a sentence under s. 91, the proportionate term would be more than 24 months, but when the mitigation is taken into account the sentence just comes within the DTO range (see, for example, *Smith* [2001] 1 Cr App R (S) 62).

Consecutive terms of DTO may be ordered, and the principles would seem to be the same as are applicable to consecutive sentences of imprisonment. Consecutive DTOs must not, however, exceed 24 months since, once again, any excess over that period will be automatically remitted. Section 101(13) states that where consecutive DTOs are ordered these 'shall be treated as a single term'. This phrase could be construed as meaning 'a single term which is one of those terms set out in s. 101(1)'. The Court of Appeal in *Norris* [2001] 1 Cr App R (S) 401, however, has held that the statute should not be construed in this way and, provided that each of the individual DTO terms is lawful in itself, the terms need not add up to one of the terms listed. Thus consecutive terms of eight months may be imposed, giving 16 months overall, despite the fact that 16 months would not be lawful as a single term. It must also follow that two unlawful terms (say, five months each) cannot be run consecutively to reach a sentence of ten months, which is in the list. The sentence would be unlawful because its constituent terms are unlawful.

Where the young offender is aged 12, 13 or 14 at the time of the conviction, s. 100(2)(a) provides that a DTO may be imposed by the court only where 'it is of the opinion that he is a persistent offender'. 'Persistent offender' is not defined in the PCC(S)A 2000, and the courts have been left to develop their own guidelines. In a batch of early cases the appellate courts have construed the phrase very widely. First, the courts have held that a sentencing court may have regard to formal cautions as well as previous findings of guilt (*D* [2001] 1 Cr App R (S) 202). This seems right, given that a formal caution can only be given where the youngster has admitted guilt to a police officer in a formal setting, and records of formal cautions are kept and form part of the antecedents (though not, technically, part of the list of previous convictions). Formal cautions for juveniles are now replaced by a scheme of warnings and reprimands under the CDA 1998, but the point remains good for these as well. Second, the decision in *Smith* [2001] 1 Cr App R (S) 62 established that a young offender could be a 'persistent offender' even though he had no previous findings of guilt (or formal cautions). In that case the 14-year-old offender Smith pleaded guilty to three counts of robbery, two of possession of an offensive weapon (a kitchen knife) and one count of false imprisonment. The offences all took place over a two-day period and were committed in the company of other youths. The victims were slightly younger boys. In view of the range of 'appalling' offences before the court, the Court of Appeal said that Smith was a persistent offender, and passed a DTO sentence of 24 months. The wide interpretation has been endorsed in later cases, including *C (Young Person: Persistent Offender)* (2000) *The Times*, 11 October 2000. This case also involved a 14-year-old offender, who had committed a burglary and an offence of allowing himself to be carried on a vehicle without consent of the owner. While on bail for these offences he had committed two further burglaries and an offence of aggravated vehicle taking. The court said that the young offender 'had burgled and then had done it again' and so was a persistent offender despite the lack of a formal criminal record at the time of sentence. In contrast, in *D* [2000] All ER (D) 1496 the young offender's latest offence was affray. He had a caution and a previous finding of guilt for handling and was awaiting sentence in a youth court for riding a stolen motorcycle. This time the Court of Appeal, while endorsing the earlier authorities in principle, said that the different nature of the earlier offending meant that he could not be regarded as 'persistent'. This decision suggests that persistence will more readily be found where there is repetition of the same kind of offending. The 'persistent offender' requirement is specific to the DTO. It does not apply to sentences of long-term detention under PCC(S)A 2000, s. 91. In *Jenkins-Rowe and Glover* [2000] Crim LR 1022 two 14-year-olds were involved. One pleaded guilty to robbery and the other was convicted after a trial. They had chased another 14-year-old walking home from school and had grabbed him, punched him and threatened him with a pen-knife so that he has handed over his school bag. Neither of the offenders had any previous findings of guilt. The sentencer imposed terms of long-term detention under s. 91, of 20 months and three years, respectively. It was argued on appeal that since neither offender was a 'persistent offender', terms of detention should not have been ordered. The Court of Appeal rejected that argument, saying that the powers under s. 91 co-existed alongside the DTO. In the present case since neither offender qualified as 'persistent', the only available custodial sentence was detention under s. 91 (robbery is a qualifying offence for that section). The terms were, however, reduced to 15 months and 30 months, respectively.

There is an important requirement that whenever a DTO is passed the sentencer 'shall take account of any period for which the offender has been remanded in custody in connection with the offence' (s. 101(8)). The DTO is the only custodial sentence where the sentencer is required to adjust the term of the sentence to take account of time spent on remand (although he is also required to do so when fixing the period under s. 28 of the C(S)A 1997 to determine the relevant period in respect of a discretionary life sentence). For all other custodial terms, including long-term detention under s. 91, the period spent on remand is deducted automatically in accordance with CJA 1967, s. 67. 'Remanded in custody' is defined, for these purposes, to include police detention, remand or committal to custody, remand or committal to local authority secure accommodation under the CYPA 1969, s. 23, and admission to hospital. Since the DTO falls into two distinct halves, with only the first half being spent in custody, it follows that the period which the sentencer should deduct from the term of the DTO should normally be *twice* the period which was actually spent on remand. This requirement to adjust the sentence to take into account time spent on remand creates a problem in relation to the terms specified in s. 101(1). It has been argued that, where a court is minded to pass a sentence of 18 months DTO, but the offender has served some time on remand (even a few days) the sentencer is bound to give effect to that and reduce sentence to the next available term, which is 12 months. The Divisional Court in *Inner London Crown Court, ex parte I* (2000) *The Times*, 12 May 2000, decisively rejected this argument. It was held that the requirement to 'take account' of the time spent on remand did not require the sentencer to 'reflect such time . . . reducing the term of the DTO by that period'. An automatic and proportionate adjustment was not necessary. The approach of the court in this case has been approved in several later cases, including *Inner London Crown Court, ex parte N and S* [2001] 1 Cr App R (S) 343. In that case the young offender had spent three days on remand in custody and Lord Justice Rose said that it was impossible to fine-tune a DTO by reference to a few days. This is clearly right in practical terms, but difficult to square with the wording of s. 101(8), which requires the court to 'take account of *any period*'.

4.4 FIXING THE LENGTH OF CUSTODIAL SENTENCES

4.4.1 Statutory criteria

Once the court has reached a decision that the particular case before it has to be dealt with by a custodial sentence in accordance with the criteria indicated in PCC(S)A 2000, s. 79, the next decision for the court is to fix the length of the custodial sentence. Prior to the 1991 Act there was no statutory guidance on this matter. It is worth mentioning the landmark Court of Appeal decision in *Bibi* [1980] 1 WLR 1193 at this point, however. That case articulated the important general principle that, where loss of liberty is inevitable, the custodial sentence should be kept as short as possible. As Lord Lane CJ said:

> It is no secret that our prisons are at the moment dangerously overcrowded. So much so that sentencing courts must be particularly careful to examine each case to ensure, if an immediate custodial sentence is necessary, that the sentence is as short as possible, consistent only with the duty to protect the interests of the public and to punish and deter the criminal. Many offenders can be dealt with equally justly and effectively by a sentence of six or nine months' imprisonment as by one of 18 months' or three years.

The principle enunciated in that case was reinforced by the CJA 1991. Much more recently, the Court of Appeal in *Ollerenshaw* [1999] 1 Cr App R (S) 65 said that the comments in

Bibi were no less valid today than they were at the time they were made. *Bibi* was further endorsed in *Howells* [1999] 1 WLR 307.

The PCC(S)A 2000 provides statutory criteria for determining sentence length, which are set out in s. 80 of the Act. They apply to all custodial sentences, including discretionary life sentences and suspended sentences, whether imposed by the Crown Court or by magistrates' courts and whether passed on adults or on young offenders. Any sentence imposed must, of course, be within the statutory maximum provided for the offence and, if sentence is being imposed in a magistrates' court, must accord with the restrictions on the powers of that court to pass custodial sentences of a particular length. The different statutory maxima which apply to young offenders (see Table at pp. 7–14) must also be borne in mind. Section 80(2) of the 2000 Act excludes from the ambit of the section cases where the sentence for the offence is fixed by law (i.e. murder) and cases where sentence falls to be imposed under s. 109–111 of that Act (see **4.3.3** to **4.3.6**). Section 80 further provides as follows:

(2)　. . . the custodial sentence shall be—

(a)　for such term (not exceeding the permitted maximum) as in the opinion of the court is commensurate with the seriousness of the offence, or the combination of the offence and one or more offences associated with it; or

(b)　where the offence is a violent or sexual offence, for such longer term (not exceeding that maximum) as in the opinion of the court is necessary to protect the public from serious harm from the offender.

(3)　Where the court passes a custodial sentence for a term longer than is commensurate with the seriousness of the offence, or the combination of the offence and one or more offences associated with it, the court shall—

(a)　state in open court that it is of the opinion that subsection (2)(b) above applies and why it is of that opinion; and

(b)　explain to the offender in open court and in ordinary language why the sentence is for such a term.

(4)　A custodial sentence for an indeterminate period shall be regarded for the purposes of subsections (2) and (3) above as a custodial sentence for a term longer than any actual term.

Section 81 of the 2000 Act requires that, for the purposes of forming an opinion under s. 80(2)(a) or (b) as to the appropriate length of a custodial sentence, the court 'shall obtain and consider a pre-sentence report' unless, in the circumstances of the case, the court is of the opinion that it is unnecessary to obtain one (s. 81(2)). For pre-sentence reports generally, see **3.5.1**. Section 81(4)(a) states that the court must have regard to any information about the circumstances of the offence (including any aggravating or mitigating factors) which have a bearing on the seriousness of that offence. The court may also have regard to any relevant mitigating (but not aggravating) factor which does not impinge upon offence seriousness but which relates to the offender (s. 158(1)). Where the criteria under consideration by the court are those in s. 80(2)(b), the court 'may take into account any information about the offender which is before it' (s. 81(4)(b)). For discussion of these general provisions see Chapter 2.

4.4.2　Custodial sentence length under PCC(S)A 2000, s. 80(2)(a)

Turning first to s. 80(2)(a), it will be seen that the criterion for sentence length embodies the key principle derived from the CJA 1991 that sentence length should be commensurate with the seriousness of the offence. In the great majority of cases where custodial sentences are imposed, sentence length will be determined in accordance with s. 80(2)(a) rather than s. 80(2)(b). Section 80(2)(a) may be relied upon even where the offence is a violent or sexual offence, since s. 80 merely gives an option to the sentencer of justifying custodial sentence length under s. 80(2)(b) in these cases, but does not require the sentencer to do so. Given the emphasis in s. 80(2)(a) upon the requirement that the sentence be 'commensurate with the seriousness of the offence', and the wording of s. 80(4), it is difficult to see how the imposition of a discretionary life sentence could be justified under s. 80(2)(a).

In *Cunningham* [1993] 1 WLR 183, Lord Taylor CJ said that the purpose of a custodial sentence had primarily to be to punish and deter, and the phrase 'commensurate with the seriousness of the offence' in s. 80(2)(a) meant 'commensurate with the punishment and deterrence which the seriousness of the offence' required. The reference here to deterrence is potentially misleading, and it is important to understand the implications of Lord Taylor's remark. It permits reference by the sentencer to deterrence (whether individual or general deterrence) as an objective in sentencing only insofar as a deterrent effect may be achieved by imposing the commensurate custodial sentence. It does *not* permit the sentencer to exceed the commensurate sentence in an attempt to achieve a greater deterrent impact. Indeed Lord Taylor stated specifically in *Cunningham* that the wording of s. 80(2)(a) prohibits adding extra length to the commensurate sentence so as to make a special example of the defendant (so-called 'exemplary sentencing'). Prevalence of the offence is, however, a legitimate factor in determining the length of a custodial sentence (see **2.2.2(g)**).

Section 80(2)(a) states that the court may have regard to 'the combination of the offence and one or more offences associated with it' when determining the length of a custodial sentence. Section 161 makes provision as to when one offence may properly be regarded as for these purposes as 'associated with' another, and was considered at **4.2.5**. Where the offender is being sentenced for several offences (and perhaps asks for several others to be taken into consideration), the danger of sentencing on the basis of the totality of the offending is that it could lead to a total sentence which is disproportionate to the nature of the offending behaviour. The PCC(S)A 2000, s. 158(2), in an attempt to avoid this, declares that nothing shall prevent a court 'in a case of an offender who is convicted of one or more other offences, from mitigating his sentence by applying any rule of law as to the totality of sentences'. This rather obliquely worded provision gives statutory recognition to the 'totality principle', which has been developed over the years by the Court of Appeal. For discussion of this principle see **4.4.4**.

The offender's previous convictions and response to previous sentences are relevant when the court is considering sentence length. For a discussion of this see **2.2.5**.

4.4.3 Custodial sentence length under PCC(S)A 2000, s. 80(2)(b)

Section 80(2)(b) deals with the extent to which the court is permitted to depart from the general principle of commensurability set out in s. 80(2)(a). The court may impose a longer-than-normal sentence, but not one which exceeds the statutory maximum for the offence, in the case of a custodial sentence passed for a violent offence or a sexual offence, where the court is of the opinion that a custodial sentence of that length is necessary to protect the public from serious harm from the offender. Definitions of 'violent offence', 'sexual offence' and 'serious harm' are provided in s. 161 of the PCC(S)A 2000 and were considered at **4.2.6**. The longer sentence which is imposed in reliance upon s. 80(2)(b) may be a determinate sentence which is longer than could be justified in reliance upon s. 80(2)(a) or, when sentencing for an offence which carries life imprisonment as its maximum penalty when committed by an adult, it may be a discretionary life sentence. Only where a violent offence or a sexual offence has been committed, where the public protection criterion is made out, and where the further criteria for the imposition of a discretionary life sentence have been made out (see **4.3.7**) may such a sentence be passed.

It should be clear that s. 80(2)(b) provides the court with a *power* to impose a custodial sentence which is longer than that which would be commensurate with the seriousness of the offence. It does not require the court to do so, and in the ordinary run of sentencing for violent offences or sexual offences a sentence commensurate with the seriousness of the offence imposed under s. 80(2)(a) will be a perfectly appropriate response. Given the statutory language of 'public protection', the circumstances in which it would be appropriate for an adult magistrates' court (which is, of course, normally limited to a maximum custodial sentence of six months) to rely upon s. 80(2)(b) will arise very rarely, if ever. The Crown Court may, however, impose a sentence under s. 80(2)(b) on an offender convicted in the magistrates' court and committed to Crown Court for sentence. An example is *Etchells* [1996] 1 Cr App R (S) 163.

Where reliance is placed upon s. 80(2)(b), s. 80(3) requires that the sentencer must state in open court that the court is of the opinion that s. 80(2)(b) applies and why it is of that opinion. The sentencer must explain to the offender in open court and in ordinary language why the sentence is for such a term. These requirements may be compared to those which apply in respect of a decision to impose a custodial sentence (see **4.1.6**). In that context, in *Baverstock* [1993] 1 WLR 202, Lord Taylor CJ said that a two-stage process of explanation was not strictly necessary and that the precise words used by the judge when doing so were not critical. The Court of Appeal would not be sympathetic to appeals based upon a fine linguistic analysis of the judge's sentencing remarks. A magistrates' court is additionally required to specify in the warrant of commitment, and to enter in the register, its reason for passing a custodial sentence (s. 79(5)), but it is not strictly required to specify its reasons for determining the length of the custodial sentence.

The general rule in sentencing (violent and sexual offences included) remains that the sentence should be proportionate to the seriousness of the offence but, exceptionally, the court may impose a longer-than-normal sentence where special risk to the public is made out and where the imposition of a proportionate sentence would not provide adequate protection for the public. In *Crow* (1995) 16 Cr App R (S) 409 the Court of Appeal said that if the offence was an isolated example, or there was no good reason to fear a substantial risk of further offending, s. 80(2)(b) would not be applicable. This point is also clear from *Bestwick* (1995) 16 Cr App R (S) 268, where two offenders had been involved in a series of arson offences. One was given a proportionate sentence of 30 months' detention in a young offender institution, but the other received five years' imprisonment, passed as a longer-than-normal sentence. An appeal on the basis of disparity between the two sentences was dismissed, the Court of Appeal noting that the offender who received the longer sentence had a seriously disturbed personality and an obsession with lighting fires and represented a real risk to the public. The other offender had a normal personality and hence fell to be sentenced in accordance with the seriousness of his offending.

Although the imposition of a longer-than-normal sentence should not, then, be regarded as the normal course for the sentencer to take when dealing with a violent or sexual offence, it is well established that, where a defendant is clearly eligible for a longer-than-normal sentence, the court's decision not to impose one (or its failure to appreciate that it might have done so) may be regarded as the imposition of an unduly lenient sentence. In *A-G's*

Reference (No. 9 of 1994) (1995) 16 Cr App R (S) 366, for example, the Court of Appeal upheld a prosecution appeal and said that a longer-than-normal sentence of 10 years, rather than a commensurate sentence of six years, should have been passed. The offender had committed a series of sexual offences against young boys, and he represented a real and continuing danger. Another example is *A-G's Reference (No. 47 of 1998)* [1999] 1 Cr App R (S) 464, where a sentence of two years' imprisonment for a series of indecent assaults was varied to a longer-than-normal sentence of six years.

Before imposing a sentence under s. 80(2)(b) the court must be sure that it is basing its decision on accurate information about the offender, if necessary by holding a *Newton* inquiry into any important factual issue (*Oudkerk* (1995) 16 Cr App R (S) 172). The evidential basis for passing a longer-than-normal sentence under s. 80(2)(b) will normally be found in a psychiatric report prepared on the offender, or in his previous convictions, or both. Normally both these elements will figure in the court's consideration, but it seems that an offender who has no previous convictions may still receive a longer-than-normal sentence provided that the medical evidence is clear (*Crow* (1995) 16 Cr App R (S) 409). On the other hand, in a case where the previous convictions speak eloquently of the offender's dangerousness, a longer-than-normal sentence may be passed without obtaining a medical report (*Hashi* (1995) 16 Cr App R (S) 121). Where the previous convictions are being relied on, the court must of course ensure that the information which it has about the circumstances of those earlier offences is accurate, and it may be necessary to investigate the previous offences to see whether the offender really does represent a serious risk or whether he can properly be sentenced on a proportionate basis (*Samuels* (1995) 16 Cr App R (S) 856). It seems from the cases that information about the current offence standing alone, without inferences drawn from previous offences and without the benefit of a psychiatric report, is unlikely to be enough to justify a longer-than-normal sentence.

A number of important principles have emerged from the Court of Appeal decisions on the appropriate use of longer-than-normal sentences under s. 80(2)(b). It should be recalled that the subsection states that a longer-than-normal sentence shall be for such longer term (not exceeding the maximum available for the offence) '. . . as in the opinion of the court is necessary to protect the public from serious harm from the offender'. The first point, then, is that the court must be clear that it is *this offender* who poses the risk — the threat must come from him. So, the court cannot use a longer-than-normal sentence simply to mark its disapproval of a particularly serious offence, or to register concern at the type of offending involved. The court must base its view on the information which it has concerning the offence and the offender. Thus, in *Walsh* (1995) 16 Cr App R (S) 204, a longer-than-normal sentence was held to be inappropriate in a case where the offender had committed sexual offences on a 13-year-old boy, but where the offence was 'out of character' for the offender and repetition was unlikely. Secondly, it must be shown to be necessary to protect *the public* from serious harm from the offender. While in the ordinary case the risk will be to members of the public generally, it has been accepted in some cases that a longer-than-normal sentence can properly be passed for the protection of a small group of individuals or a particular person. In *Hashi* (1995) 16 Cr App R (S) 121 the threat posed by the offender was to his ex-wife and any male friends that the offender might see her with. In *Nicholas* (1994) 16 Cr App R (S) 381 the offender had in the past persistently assaulted his wife but had never assaulted anyone else. Although the principle was accepted in *Nicholas* that a longer-than-normal sentence could be imposed in such a case, on the facts it was not justified since the wife now had a court order restraining the offender from molesting her and the offender had apparently now accepted that their marriage was over. Another aspect of this issue arose in *L* (1994) 15 Cr App R (S) 501, where the offender admitted sexually abusing his stepdaughters, aged 10 and 12, over a period of 20 months. The Court of Appeal quashed a longer-than-normal sentence of seven years and substituted a proportionate term of three years on the basis that the offending had been confined within the family, that the offender had no other convictions and would have no future contact with the victims. In the circumstances the court did not think that the offender represented a risk 'to the public'. Thirdly, it has to be shown that in the particular case before the court the public needs to be protected from *serious harm* from the offender. As we have seen, the 2000 Act states that this phrase should be 'construed as a reference to protecting members of the public from death or serious personal injury, whether physical or psychological, occasioned by further such offences committed by the offender' (s. 161(4)). What matters here is not so much the likelihood of further offences occurring, nor necessarily the seriousness of the current or previous offences committed by the offender (though both of these will of course weigh with the court), but rather the anticipated seriousness of future offending. Also, that the sentencer must anticipate the commission of 'further *such* offences', i.e., further violent or sexual offences, being committed by the offender. In *Creasey* (1994) 15 Cr App R (S) 671 the offender pleaded guilty to indecent assault on a 13-year-old boy, attempting to masturbate him by rubbing his hand on the boy's trousers. Creasey had previous convictions for similar offences, but the Court of Appeal quashed a longer-than-normal sentence of five years and substituted a proportionate sentence of 21 months. The offending was 'unpleasant and distressing' but, in the view of the court, did not require the protection of the public from serious harm. The case may be contrasted with *Bowler* (1994) 15 Cr App R (S) 78, where the defendant pleaded guilty to indecent assault, having put his hand up a young girl's skirt and fondled her. He had eight previous convictions for very similar offences, committed on women and girls. In this case a longer-than-normal sentence of six years was upheld by the Court of Appeal, on the basis that the court must bear in mind the possibility of future victims more vulnerable to such conduct than the average, who might suffer psychological harm. The distinction between these two cases is difficult to see. *Bowler* was distinguished in *Fishwick* [1996] 1 Cr App R (S) 359, where the offender had a history of relatively minor physical assaults of a non-sexual nature, and where the Court of Appeal felt that there was no basis to conclude that future victims were likely to suffer serious psychological injury. A longer-than-normal sentence of three years was, accordingly, reduced to a proportionate sentence of 18 months.

The question of the appropriate additional length to be added to a custodial term under s. 80(2)(b), to take account of the risk to the public, has been considered in several Court of Appeal decisions, but no clear pattern has emerged. In *Mansell* (1994) 15 Cr App R (S) 771 the Court of Appeal said that in each case the sentencer had to try to balance the need to protect the public on the one hand, with the need to look at the totality of the offending on the other. It was, the Court of Appeal said, impossible to provide more precise guidance. In *Crow* (1995) 16 Cr App R (S) 409 it was said that, when fixing the length of a longer-than-normal sentence, account should be taken of the age of the offender (in that the risk which the offender represented to the public might be expected to decline over time), some allowance should normally be made for a guilty plea (even in the worst case) and a sentence imposed under s. 80(2)(b) should still bear a 'reasonable relationship' to the offence for which it was imposed, but in *Bowler* (1994) 15 Cr App R (S) 78 the Court of Appeal said that when a sentence is being passed to protect the public, matters of mitigation, such as a guilty plea, the impulsive nature of the offence and the offender's limited intelligence, would carry less weight than in the case of a proportionate sentence. The decisions in

Campbell [1997] 1 Cr App R (S) 119 and *Gabbidon* [1997] 2 Cr App R (S) 19 make it clear that, in cases where a very long proportionate sentence imposed under s. 2(2)(a) would in any event be justifiable on the facts of the offence (proportionate custodial terms of 15 years would have been appropriate for rape in the former case and for robbery in the latter case), the court may still pass a longer-than-normal sentence under s. 2(2)(b) where the criteria for such a sentence are made out, even though commensurate sentences of such length would already contain a significant element of public protection. Care should be taken, however, to ensure that the balance referred to in *Mansell* is preserved: the need to protect the public should not produce a sentence which is out of all proportion to the offending behaviour. A total sentence of 20 years was reduced to 17 years in *Campbell*, and 27 years reduced to 20 years in *Gabbidon*. In *De Silva* [2000] 2 Cr App R (S) 408 the Court of Appeal again indicated that some reasonable proportion between the total sentence and the nature of the offending had to be maintained.

4.4.4   Concurrent and consecutive custodial sentences and the totality principle

When an offender is convicted on more than one count, the court should pass separate sentences on each count. If custodial sentences are passed in respect of two or more offences the court may order that the sentences must be served either at the same time as, or successively to, each other. In the former case the sentences are said to be *concurrent*; in the latter case they are said to be *consecutive*. Where sentences are concurrent, the aggregate term will be the longest of the individual terms passed. Where sentences are consecutive, the aggregate term will be the total of the individual terms. These principles apply to sentences of imprisonment, to terms of detention in a young offender institution and to the detention and training order. It is open to the sentencer to make some terms run concurrently with each other but consecutively to other terms. In some cases this may lead to a complex sentencing pattern (see, for example, *Prime* (1983) 5 Cr App R (S) 127, below). If a sentencer fails to state when passing sentence whether a term is to be served concurrently or consecutively to another term, the sentences are presumed to be concurrent. Similarly, if an offender is already serving a custodial sentence when he appears to be sentenced for a further offence, the court may make any further custodial sentence it imposes for the new offence concurrent or consecutive to the term being served, though this is subject to PCC(S)A 2000, s. 116 (see **4.5.1**).

A determinate custodial sentence may not run consecutively to a life sentence (*Foy* [1962] 1 WLR 609) nor vice versa (*Jones* v *DPP* [1962] AC 635). Where sentence is passed on an offender under s. 80(2)(b), a custodial sentence (whether a proportionate or longer-than-normal term) imposed at the same time for other matters must be ordered to run concurrently with and not consecutively to it (*Walters* [1997] 2 Cr App R (S) 87; *Johnson* [1998] 1 Cr App R (S) 126). Terms of imprisonment may be made to run consecutively to each other even though the result is that the aggregate term exceeds the maximum which could have been imposed for any one of the offences concerned. Thus in *Blake* [1962] 2 QB 377 the offender was convicted of five offences under the Official Secrets Act 1911, and an aggregate sentence of 42 years was upheld, even though the maximum sentence available for a single offence was 14 years. Similarly, in *Prime* an aggregate sentence of 38 years was passed (on one indictment) for seven offences contrary to the Official Secrets Act 1911 and (on a second indictment) three offences of indecent assault. The offender was sentenced to 14 years on each of two counts on the first indictment, to run consecutively, and to seven years on each of the remaining five counts, to run concurrently with each other but consecutively to the other terms. The total sentence on the first indictment was, therefore, 35 years. On the second indictment the total sentence was three years, made to run consecutively to the 35 years, making a grand total of 38 years.

It will be recalled that the maximum term for a detention and training order is 24 months (see **4.3.11**). This restriction cannot be circumvented by imposing shorter consecutive sentences whose total exceeds 24 months. Section 101(4) of the 2000 Act states that a court shall not pass a detention and training order where its effect is to impose a total term in excess of that period. In the event of such a sentence or sentences being passed, so much of the total term as exceeds 24 months is treated as remitted (s. 101(5)).

It is wrong in principle to pass consecutive custodial terms for two or more offences if to do so would, in effect, punish the offender twice for what was really one crime. Thus in *Coker* [1984] Crim LR 184 the offender attacked a young woman as she was walking across a field. He struck her repeatedly about the face, and indecently assaulted her. He was sentenced to two years' imprisonment for the indecent assault and three years consecutive for assault occasioning actual bodily harm. The Court of Appeal held that, as the facts of the two offences were inextricably linked, the terms should have been concurrent. Even where, unlike *Coker*, the offender has committed two quite distinct offences, sentences imposed should still be concurrent where the offences arise out of the same set of facts: the 'same occasion' or the 'same transaction', as it is sometimes put. Thus in *Jones* (1980) 2 Cr App R (S) 152 the Court of Appeal held that consecutive terms of 12 months and six months respectively for driving while disqualified and driving with excess alcohol could not be justified, since the two offences were committed on the same occasion. The decisions in this area are not consistent, however. In *Wheatley* (1983) 5 Cr App R (S) 417, a sentence of 12 months for driving while disqualified was ordered to run consecutively to a sentence of six months for driving with excess alcohol. The reasoning behind the sentence was that, if the sentences were concurrent, Wheatley, who was a persistent offender, might think that he could drive with excess alcohol and incur no additional penalty for the breach of disqualification. This case was followed and applied in *Jordan* [1996] 1 Cr App R (S) 181.

It is well established that sentencers must have regard to the total length of the sentence passed, particularly where consecutive sentences have been imposed, to ensure that the sentence properly reflects the overall seriousness of the behaviour. This effect will not be achieved merely by adding the sentences of a multiple offender together, for this will soon result in a total sentence out of all proportion to the kind of offending which has taken place. This principle, which has its clearest application in relation to custodial sentences, has achieved oblique recognition in PCC(S)A 2000, s. 158(2)(b), which states that nothing shall prevent a court 'in the case of an offender who is convicted of one or more other offences, from mitigating his sentence by applying any rule of law as to the totality of sentences'. The Court of Appeal's development of the totality principle has been most associated with custodial sentencing, but the statutory provision clearly also applies to fines and to community orders.

If offences are committed on different occasions, or are not part of the 'same transaction', there is no objection to imposing consecutive sentences, but this approach should not be regarded as inevitable. Bearing in mind the totality principle, it may be more convenient for the sentencer, particularly when sentencing for a series of similar offences, to pass a proportionate sentence for the most serious offence, coupled with shorter, concurrent terms for the less serious matters. In that way the various terms reflect the relative seriousness of the offences for which they are imposed, but the overall punishment remains in proportion to the overall gravity of the offender's criminal conduct. There are some situations, however, in which the Court of Appeal has stressed the need to impose consecutive custodial terms. This approach should be taken, *inter alia*, where the offender has used violence to resist arrest for another offence (e.g. *Wellington* (1988) 10 Cr App R (S) 384) or has used violence against a householder to make good his escape from the scene of a burglary (e.g. *Bunch* (1971) CSP A5-2C01). Sentences should also normally be consecutive where the offender carries a firearm while committing another offence (*French* (1982) 4 Cr App R (S) 57). In *A-G's Reference (No. 1 of 1990)* (1990) 12 Cr App R (S) 245, the Court of Appeal said that consecutive sentences for indecent assault and perverting the course of justice should have been imposed in a case where the offender had written to the victim of the indecent assault from prison, while on remand, in an attempt to dissuade him from giving evidence. A custodial sentence imposed for escaping from custody should run consecutively to the sentence which was being served at the time of the escape (*Clarke* (1994) 15 Cr App R (S) 825). According to *Whittaker* [1998] 1 Cr App R (S) 172, consecutive sentences should normally be passed where the offender commits one offence on bail which was granted in respect of the other offence. It is not clear how this squares with the statutory principle that the second offence must be regarded as more serious by virtue of it having been committed by an offender on bail (see **2.2.2(f)**).

4.4.5 Taking account of time served on remand

A sentencer passing a custodial sentence on an offender may not infrequently be dealing with a person who has already spent days, weeks or months on remand in custody awaiting trial and/or sentence. Section 67 of the Criminal Justice Act 1967 (CJA 1967) provides that, if an offender spends time in custody awaiting trial and/or sentence, the term of any sentence of imprisonment ultimately passed on him shall be treated as reduced by the period in custody; 'shall be treated as reduced' means that the relevant period is automatically taken off the sentence. If an offender is remanded in custody by magistrates prior to summary trial or committal proceedings, and/or is committed for trial or sentence in custody, and/or is remanded in custody after conviction and before sentence, the period for which he is thus detained is deducted from the sentence which he eventually has to serve. Occasionally this can mean, in a case where the sentence is short, that the term has already been served by the date on which it is imposed, so that the offender is entitled to release immediately after sentence.

Although CJA 1967, s. 67 is expressed in terms of the effect of time spent on remand upon a sentence of imprisonment, it is clear that it also counts towards a sentence of detention in a young offender institution and a determinate sentence imposed under s. 91 of the 2000 Act. Section 67 does *not* apply to the detention and training order, where the sentencer is required to make the appropriate adjustment before passing sentence. It should also be noted that a suspended sentence is a sentence of imprisonment, so a sentencer passing a suspended sentence should take account of any time spent by the offender in custody on remand when fixing the length of the term which is to be suspended (*Practice Direction (Crime: Suspended Sentence)* [1970] 1 WLR 259). In one sense this has no direct impact on the offender, but if the suspended sentence were subsequently to be activated, the reduction would have practical effect.

Of course CJA 1967, s. 67 does not apply if the offender would have been in custody anyway for the relevant period, such as where he was serving a custodial term for an earlier offence. Nor does it apply to time spent in custody in a foreign country awaiting extradition to this country in respect of the offence being dealt with. The sentencer has a discretion to take such period, or part of such period, into account when fixing sentence length. In *Scalise*

(1985) 7 Cr App R (S) 395 this was said by Lawton LJ to be the 'normal' approach, but in *Vincent* [1996] 2 Cr App R (S) 6 and *De Simone* [2000] 2 Cr App R (S) 332 only part of the period was credited because the offender had chosen to challenge the extradition proceedings. In recent cases it has been held that allowance under s. 67 should be made for periods spent by the offender in local authority secure accommodation (*Secretary of State for the Home Department, ex parte A* [2000] 2 WLR 293) and a lengthy period on remand in a bail hostel under restrictive conditions (*Watson* [2000] 2 Cr App R (S) 301). CJA 1967, s. 67 does not extend to a case where the offender is held in custody in respect of an offence which is subsequently taken into consideration, though in *Towers* (1987) 9 Cr App R (S) 333 it was said to be appropriate to make some allowance in those circumstances.

In *Governor of Brockhill Prison, ex parte Evans* [1997] 1 Cr App R (S) 282, the Divisional Court held that where concurrent or consecutive sentences are imposed on a defendant in respect of offences for which he has spent separate periods on remand in custody, the term which he is required to serve will be reduced by the remand time relating to the first offence *plus* the remand time relating to the second offence, provided that these remand periods do not overlap. An overlapping period would count once, not twice.

The PCC(S)A 2000 contains provisions which, if brought into force, will repeal CJA 1967, s. 67 and replace it with new arrangements for the crediting of periods of remand in custody under ss. 87 and 88 of the 2000 Act. These provisions are not in force.

4.5 SENTENCING AND EARLY RELEASE

While the sentencer is responsible for fixing the length of the custodial sentence and for announcing that term in open court, the actual period to be served by the offender is affected by the operation of early release arrangements and, in some cases, by subsequent decisions made by the Parole Board. Traditionally, the view was that sentencing decisions and early release decisions were entirely separate matters, the former for the judiciary and the latter for the executive authorities, and that the sentencer should put considerations about early release out of his mind when sentencing for the offence (*Maguire* (1956) 40 Cr App R 92). This was true whether the adjustment which the sentencer was minded to make would involve shortening or lengthening the sentence. Thus in *Kenway* (1985) 7 Cr App R (S) 457, Taylor J said that 'it is well established that to take account of parole when passing sentence is improper'. The main reason for this was that since the operation of remission and parole was highly discretionary, there was no certainty whether an offender being sentenced would subsequently benefit from them.

The CJA 1991 brought about a radical overhaul of the arrangements for early release. As a result, subject to their good behaviour when in custody, most offenders who receive custodial sentences now know at the time of their sentence what their actual release date will be. There is much greater correlation for short-term prisoners between the sentence imposed and the time served. On the other hand, some discretion over the release date for long-term prisoners remains in the hands of the executive authorities.

After the 1991 Act was implemented, Lord Taylor issued a *Practice Statement (Crime: Sentencing)* [1992] 1 WLR 948, in which he explained that it would henceforth be necessary for sentencers to have regard to the period in custody which would actually be served by the offender in consequence of the early release provisions of the 1991 Act, as compared to the period in custody which the offender would have served before the Act. In *Cunningham* [1993] 1 WLR 183, however, Lord Tayler CJ warned that the Court of Appeal would be unmoved 'by nice mathematical comparisons' on the effective length of custodial sentences. The Court of Appeal in *Ensley* [1996] 1 Cr App R (S) 294 said that there was no issue of disparity where one co-defendant received a sentence of less than four years and the other received a sentence of more than four years (this qualifying them as 'short-term' and 'long-term' prisoners subject to different early release provisions.

Practice Direction (Custodial Sentences: Explanations) [1998] 1 WLR 278 requires Crown Court sentencers to explain in every case the practical effect of any custodial sentence passed. The Practice Direction was, apparently, issued mainly in response to Home Office research indicating widespread misconceptions about sentencing, which were said to be undermining public confidence in the sentencing system:

> It was desirable that when sentence was passed the practical effect of the sentence should be understood by the defendant, any victim and any member of the public who was present in court or read a full report of the proceedings.
>
> In future, whenever a custodial sentence is imposed on an offender, the court should explain the practical effect of the sentence in addition to complying with existing statutory requirements. That would be no more than an explanation; the sentence would be that pronounced by the court.
>
> Sentencers should give the explanation in terms of their own choosing, taking care to ensure that the explanation is clear and accurate. No form of words is prescribed. Annexed are short statements which might, adapted as necessary, be of value as models.

In the following paragraphs the current system for early release from custodial sentences is outlined, and attention is drawn to the implications of these matters for sentencing.

4.5.1 Determinate sentences and the PCC(S)A 2000, s. 116

Adult determinate sentence prisoners fall into one of three categories:

(a)   offenders serving a sentence of less than 12 months;
(b)   offenders serving terms of 12 months or more but less than four years (short-term prisoners);
(c)   offenders serving terms of four years or more (long-term prisoners).

For an offender serving a sentence of less than 12 months, release is automatic after half the sentence has been served, unless release is delayed because additional days have been added. There is no supervision on licence. For short-term prisoners, release is automatic after serving half the sentence, again, unless release is delayed because additional days have been added, but there is supervision under licence by a probation officer for these offenders, which will last until the three-quarter point of the sentence. Failure by a short-term prisoner to comply with the conditions of a licence is a summary offence but it may also be dealt with by termination of the licence and recall to prison. A long-term prisoner must be released after serving two thirds of the sentence, and there may be discretionary release at a point somewhere between one half and two thirds of the sentence, to be determined in accordance with a recommendation made in each case by the Parole Board. Supervision on licence will last from the point of release until the three-quarter point of the sentence. In the event of breach of licence conditions by a long-term prisoner, the Home Secretary may revoke the licence and recall the prisoner to custody where it appears to be expedient to do so. This may be done with or without the recommendation of the Parole Board.

For any prisoner, whether short-term or long-term, who commits a further offence punishable with imprisonment during the period from the date of release from custody until the expiry of the full term of the sentence, the sentencing court dealing with the new offence 'may, whether or not it passes any other sentence on him, order him to be returned to prison' (PCC(S)A 2000, s. 116). Section 116 has been the subject of much judicial interpretation, and subsection (1) to (6) are set out here in full. It provides that:

(1)   This section applies to a person if—

(a)   he has been serving a determinate sentence of imprisonment which he began serving on or after 1st October 1992;

(b)   he is released under Part II of the Criminal Justice Act 1991 (early release of prisoners);

(c)   before the date on which he would (but for his release) have served his sentence in full, he commits an offence punishable with imprisonment ('the new offence'); and

(d)   whether before or after that date, he is convicted of the new offence.

(2)   Subject to subsection (3) below, the court by or before which a person to whom this section applies is convicted of the new offence may, whether or not it passes any other sentence on him, order him to be returned to prison for the whole or any part of the period which—

(a)   begins with the date of the order; and

(b)   is equal in length to the period between the date on which the new offence was committed and the date mentioned in subsection (1)(c) above.

(3)   A magistrates' court—

(a)   shall not have power to order a person to whom this section applies to be returned to prison for a period of more than six months; but

(b)   subject to section 25 of the Criminal Justice and Public Order Act 1994 (restrictions on granting bail), may commit him in custody or on bail to the Crown Court for sentence to be dealt with under subsection (4) below.

(4)   Where a person is committed to the Crown Court under subsection (3) above, the Crown Court may order him to be returned to prison for the whole or any part of the period which—

(a)   begins with the date of the order; and

(b)   is equal in length to the period between the date on which the new offence was committed and the date mentioned in subsection (1)(c) above.

(5)   Subsection (3)(b) above shall not be taken to confer on the magistrates' court a power to commit the person to the Crown Court for sentence for the new offence, but this is without prejudice to any such power conferred on the magistrates' court by any other provision of this Act.

(6)   The period for which a person to whom this section applies is ordered under subsection (2) or (4) to be returned to prison—

(a)   shall be taken to be a sentence of imprisonment for the purposes of Part II of the Criminal Justice Act 1991 and this section;

(b)   shall, as the court may direct, either be served before and be followed by, or be served concurrently with, the sentence imposed for the new offence; and

(c)   in either case, shall be disregarded in determining the appropriate length of that sentence.

Section 116 applies only where the original sentence was a determinate sentence of imprisonment, a term of detention in a young offender institution, or a term of detention under PCC(S)A 2000, s. 91. A provision equivalent to s. 116 is applicable to offenders who commit a further offence during the period of supervision of a detention and training order (s. 105). Section 116 is not applicable where the original sentence was an indeterminate one. It should be noted that s. 116 applies whether or not the conviction for the new offence takes place after the expiry of the full term of the original sentence; what matters is whether the new offence was committed before that date. The exercise of the power to return the offender to prison is discretionary, and the court may order the offender to be returned for the full period indicated in the section, a lesser period, or not at all. Helpful general guidance on the operation of the s. 116 was given in *Taylor* [1998] 1 Cr App R (S) 312. It was explained by the Court of Appeal that the sentencer should first decide what was the proper sentence for the new offence. The possibility of an order under s. 116 should be disregarded when making this decision. Then, in considering whether an order should in addition be made under s. 116, it would usually be appropriate to have regard to the nature and extent of any progress made by the offender since his release, and the nature and gravity of the new offence (especially whether it called for a custodial sentence). It would then be necessary to look at the totality of the custodial terms, both when deciding whether an order should be made under s. 116 at all and, if so, whether it should be for all or only part of the relevant period.

It was held in *Harrow Justices, ex parte Jordan* [1997] 1 Cr App R (S) 410 that, where an offender who is liable to be returned to custody under s. 116 is convicted in a magistrates' court, the magistrates should deal with both the sentence for the new offence and the order for return to custody, or should commit the offender to the Crown Court in respect of both matters. Lord Bingham CJ, in the Divisional Court, stated that committal to the Crown Court would be appropriate where the new offence is one of any gravity and where a significant part of the licence period is unexpired. In *Worthing and District Justices, ex parte Varley* [1998] 1 Cr App R (S) 175 the issue arose whether a magistrates' court could both make an order returning an offender to custody under s. 116 and impose the custodial sentence for the new offence to run consecutively to it where the aggregate exceeded the maximum aggregate term of imprisonment which that court could impose (normally six months: PCC(S)A 2000, s. 78). The Divisional Court held that it could do so, since an order that the offender be returned to custody under s. 116 is not, in any ordinary sense, a sentence of imprisonment, but is an order to reactivate custody from which the offender had been prematurely released. Section 116(6)(a), which states that a period of return ordered under s. 116 'shall be taken to be a sentence of imprisonment' is not relevant. Its purpose is to deem the reactivated term to be a term of imprisonment for purposes of the early release provisions of the 1991 Act. If a custodial sentence is imposed for the new offence, the section makes it clear that the sentence may run concurrently with, or consecutively to, the reinstated period, but that the reinstated period cannot run consecutively to the sentence for the new offence (s. 16(6)(a) and *Clerkenwell Crown Court, ex parte Feely* [1996] 2 Cr App R (S) 309). If the sentence imposed for the new offence is a sentence passed for a violent or sexual offence under s. 80(2)(b), any reinstated period required to be served under s. 116 should run concurrently with the sentence for the new offence. This is because a sentence under s. 80(2)(b) is imposed for reasons of public protection, and it makes no sense to order such a sentence to start from a future date (*Johnson* [1998] 1 Cr App R (S) 126); though a different view was taken in *Blades* [2000] 1 Cr App R (S) 463.

4.5.2 Life sentences and the PCC(S)A 2000, s. 82A

It is necessary to distinguish between the early release arrangements for offenders aged 18 and over serving a mandatory life sentence for murder, and those serving other forms of life sentence. The mandatory sentence of life imprisonment (currently for those of 21 and over) and the mandatory sentence of custody for life for murder (currently for those aged 18, 19 or 20) were discussed at **4.3.4**, and will not be further considered here.

When imposing any other form of life sentence the sentencer is given power under the PCC(S)A 2000, s. 82A, to specify the period which must elapse before the offender serving the life sentence can be considered for early release. The life sentences in respect of which the power under s. 82A may be exercised are, then, an automatic life sentence imposed under PCC(S)A 2000, s. 109 for the second 'serious offence' (see **4.3.6**), a discretionary sentence of life imprisonment (see **4.3.7**), a discretionary sentence of custody for life (see **4.3.8**), a sentence of detention for life under the PCC(S)A 2000, s. 91 (see **4.3.9**) and (although that sentence is applicable only in murder cases) a sentence of detention during Her Majesty's pleasure under PCC(S)A 2000, s. 90.

The part of the sentence specified in the order shall, by s. 82A(3), be:

. . . such part as the court considers appropriate, taking into account—

(a)   the seriousness of the offence, or the combination of the offence and other offences associated with it, and

(b)   the effect of any direction which it would have given under s. 87 below [not yet in force] if it had sentenced him to a term of imprisonment, and

(c)   the provisions of this section as compared with those of sections 33(2) and 35(1) of the 1991 Act.

The effect of specifying part of the sentence under s. 82A is that the life prisoner will not become eligible to be considered for early release until the expiry of that period. If exceptionally, the sentencer orders that because of the seriousness of the offence no order should be made under s. 82A in respect of the life prisoner, 'the Secretary of State shall at the appropriate stage direct that the early release provisions shall apply to him as soon as he has served a part of his sentence specified in the direction'.

The power in s. 28 of the C(S)A 1997 to specify a part of the sentence to be served by a discretionary life sentence offender before he can be considered for early release was replaced by the equivalent power in s. 82A (inserted by the CJCSA 2000, s. 60).

The sentence of detention at Her Majesty's pleasure was brought within the terms of s. 82A by the CJCSA 2000, s. 60, which is now in force. See further **4.3.5**.

In *Practice Direction (Crime: Life Sentences)* [1993] 1 WLR 223, Lord Taylor CJ said that the sentencer should normally specify the relevant period, the only exception being the rare case where the sentencer thinks that the offender should never be released, and that if the judge decided not to specify a period he should state this in open court when passing sentence. A decision not to specify might be the subject of an appeal (*Hollies* (1995) 16 Cr App R (S) 463). When specifying the relevant period the judge should have regard to the specific terms of the section, and should indicate the reasons for the decision. Before specifying the relevant period the sentencer should permit counsel for the defence to address the court on the appropriate length of the relevant part. An order under s. 82A may be the subject of an appeal (*D* (1995) 16 Cr App R (S) 564) or might constitute an unduly lenient sentence (*A-G's Reference (No. 65 of 2000)* [2000] Crim LR 701).

In *Lundberg* (1995) 16 Cr App R (S) 948 the Court of Appeal emphasised that, when having regard to the seriousness of the offence, or the combination of the offence and other offences associated with it, as required by s. 82A(3)(a) the section permitted the sentencer to look at the totality of the associated offences, rather than just the offence for which the life sentence was being passed, and to consider whether, if a life sentence had not been given, the sentences for the associated offences would have been consecutive to the main sentence. See also *Haan* [1996] 1 Cr App R (S) 267.

Section 82A(3)(b) makes reference to the PCC(S)A 2000, s. 87. Section 87 is not in force. If it is brought into force, s. 87 will replace CJA 1967, s. 67 (effect of time spent in custody on remand: see **4.4.5**). Whether or not s. 87 is brought into force, s. 82A(3)(b) requires the sentencer to take account of any period spent by the offender in custody on remand. In *M* [1999] 1 WLR 485, the Court of Appeal said that the sentencer should normally give full credit for the period spent on remand, but there is a discretion in the matter.

Section 82A(3)(c) requires the sentencer to take account of the fact that under ss. 33(2) and 35(1) of the 1991 Act a prisoner who receives a long-term determinate sentence is entitled to be released at some part between one-half and two-thirds of the term. In *M* [1999] 1 WLR 485 the Court of Appeal stated that sentencers were now required to state what the determinate sentence would have been (if a life sentence had not been passed) and should then normally fix the specified period at *one-half* of that notional term. Exceptionally, a longer period might be selected, up to two-thirds of the notional term.

The power conferred by s. 82A of the 2000 Act is not, on the face of it, confined to cases where the discretionary life sentence is imposed for a violent or sexual offence within the meaning of s. 161 of the 2000 Act. It is now clear that a discretionary life sentence can only be imposed for a violent or sexual offence (see **4.3.7**) but, in the case of an automatic life sentence imposed for the 'second serious offence', under the s. 109 of the 2000 Act, there is no specific requirement that the offences which, subject to exceptional circumstances, will trigger the automatic life sentence, need be violent or sexual offences within the meaning of s. 161 (see **4.3.7**).

4.5.3 Sexual offences committed before 30 September 1998: extension of licence period

Where an offender is sentenced to imprisonment, detention in a young offender institution or a determinate sentence under PCC(S)A 2000, s. 91, the sentence is for 12 months or more and the whole or part of the custodial sentence is imposed for a 'sexual offence' (as defined in PCC(S)A 2000, s. 161: see **4.2.7**), and where that sexual offence was committed before 30 September 1998, the sentencer may, at the time of passing sentence, also make an order under the PCC(S)A 2000, s. 86 (formerly CJA 1991, s. 44). Its effect is that the offender, after release from custody, will remain on licence for the whole term of the sentence, rather than such licence expiring (as would otherwise be the case) at the three-quarter point of the sentence.

In making such an order, the court must have regard to the need to protect the public from serious harm and the desirability of preventing the commission by the offender of further offences and of securing his rehabilitation. The restriction to sentences of 12 months or more means that this power is effectively confined to Crown Court sentencers. The Court of Appeal has indicated the appropriate use of the power under s. 86 in a number of cases. In particular, in *A-G's Reference (No. 7 of 1996)* [1997] 1 Cr App R (S) 399 it increased a sentence of seven years' imprisonment together with an order under s. 86 for burglary with intent to rape, which had been imposed as a commensurate sentence under PCC(S)A 2000, s. 80(2)(a), to a sentence of 12 years, passed as a longer-than-normal sentence under s. 80(2)(b) of that Act. The offender had a long record of serious offending, including two convictions for rape. The Court also upheld the trial judge's order under s. 86 and applied it to the whole of the increased sentence, Lord Bingham CJ commending its use in appropriate cases to sentencers. His lordship stated that this was a section which gave the authorities additional control over an offender, since it affected both the period which an offender will serve if he is recalled to prison after release on licence and the period for which a prisoner will be supervised after release on licence. He added that in some parts of the country it was too little used. Other cases in which orders under s. 86 have been upheld are *Kennan* [1996] 1 Cr App R (S) 1 and *Samuels* (1995) 16 Cr App R (S) 856.

4.5.4   Sexual or violent offences committed on or after 30 September 1998: extended sentences

Since the relevant provisions of the Crime and Disorder Act 1998 were brought into force, the power under s. 44 of the CJA 1991 described in **4.5.3** has been superseded by new powers to impose 'extended' custodial sentences on offenders convicted either of sexual or violent offences now contained in PCC(S)A 2000, s. 85. The terms 'violent' and 'sexual' offences have the same meanings as in the PCC(S)A 2000, s. 161 (see **4.2.6**). The purpose of the new provision is to allow the court to pass an 'extended sentence' in a case where the offence was committed on or after 30 September 1998 and in which it thinks that the offender would otherwise be subject to a licence period which is inadequate for the purposes of (a) preventing the commission by him of further offences and (b) securing his rehabilitation. That extended sentence is the sum of the custodial term which the court would otherwise have passed ('the custodial term') and a further period ('the extension period') during which the offender will be subject to a licence and which is itself of a length necessary to achieve the purposes (a) and (b) indicated above. The effect of s. 85 is to add a licence period to the end of the custodial sentence which the court would have imposed anyway, either as a proportionate sentence under s. 80(2)(a) or as a longer-than-normal sentence for a violent or sexual offence under s. 80(2)(b). If the offence is a violent offence, the court shall not pass an extended sentence which is less than four years, and the extension period (i.e., the additional licence period) must not exceed five years. If the offence is a sexual offence there is no specified minimum for the length of the custodial term, but the extension period must not exceed 10 years (s. 85(3) and (4)). In no case can the extended sentence exceed the maximum sentence for the offence committed (s. 85(5)).

If the offender would otherwise have been released unconditionally (i.e., the extended term is for less than 12 months), the effect of an order under s. 85 will be that his release will be on licence until the end of the extension period. If the offender would otherwise have been released on licence (i.e., the extended term is for 12 months or more), the effect of an order under s. 85 is that the licence period, rather than ending at the three-quarter point of the sentence, will last until the end of the extension period. If the offender commits a new offence while on licence and the court, in addition to dealing with him for the new offence, decides to return the offender to custody under PCC(S)A 2000, s. 116 (see **4.5.1**) the extension period must be included when determining the duration of the period to be reinstated. This means that an order under s. 116 can be made if the new offence is committed at any time within the entire licence period, including the 'extension period'.

The reason for imposing an extended sentence is clearly to do with considerations relating to the offender, rather than just to the seriousness of the offence. In many cases the Crown Court will be required to choose whether to deal with a dangerous sexual or violent offender by the imposition of a longer-than-normal sentence under s. 80(2)(b) of the 2000 Act, or to pass an extended sentence. In *Hennessey* [2000] 2 Cr App R (S) 480 a sentence of six years' imprisonment passed on an offender who had numerous previous convictions for a knife attack on his wife was upheld by the Court of Appeal, together with an extension period of three years. The offender represented a serious risk that he would be violent towards persons with whom he formed a close relationship. The effect of the sentence was that after four years he would be entitled to be released on licence, but would then be subject to recall at any time during the licence period and the extension period, to serve in custody a further period extending to the end of the extension period. In *Gould* [2000] 2 Cr App R (S) 173 the sentencer passed a sentence of five years' detention in a young offender institution together with a five-year extension period on an offender who pleaded guilty to wounding with intent. The Court of Appeal endorsed the extended sentence in light of the offender's abuse of drink and drugs and history of violence, but reduced the extension period to two years.

In *Nelson*, 13 March 2001 (unreported) the Court of Appeal referred to the Sentencing Advisory Panel the question of when it is appropriate to impose an extended sentence and the length of sentences appropriate in such cases.

4.6 THE SUSPENDED SENTENCE

A suspended sentence of imprisonment is one which will not be brought into effect unless the offender is convicted of an imprisonable offence committed during a period of time fixed by the court when it suspends the sentence. It is very important to notice that only a determinate sentence of imprisonment may be suspended: it is not possible to suspend any other custodial sentence, such as a detention and training order. Currently, then, the suspended sentence is confined to cases involving offenders aged 21 and over. When CJCSA 2000, s. 61 is brought into force, the sentence of detention in a young offender institution will be abolished, offenders aged 18, 19 or 20 will become eligible for sentence of imprisonment, and hence the suspended sentence will become available for that age group as well. Since suspended sentences are treated in law as sentences of imprisonment (PCC(S)A 2000, s. 118(1)), and since all the statutory restrictions upon the imposition of immediate imprisonment also apply to them, it is appropriate to describe them in the part of this book dealing with custodial sentences. It will be apparent, however, that these sentences are merely *potentially* custodial. The court's hope when it suspends a sentence of imprisonment is that the question of activating it will never arise, because the offender will be deterred from further offending by the knowledge that he is subject to the suspended sentence. As we shall see, conviction for a further imprisonable offence during the operational period of a suspended sentence normally means that the suspended sentence is activated and served in full.

Suspended sentences were introduced in 1967. The present legislation on suspended sentences is contained in PCC(S)A 2000, ss. 118–125. Suspended sentences used to be popular with sentencers but since 1991 their use has been confined to cases where there are 'exceptional circumstances'. In 1998 the Crown Court imposed a suspended sentence in only 3 per cent of indictable offences. The main difficulty is that the suspended sentence, rooted as it is in a theory of achieving compliance through deterrence, sits uneasily within the current desert-based sentencing framework.

4.6.1 The term which is to be suspended

The maximum term of imprisonment which may be suspended is *two years* or the maximum immediate term which the court could impose, whichever is the less (PCC(S)A 2000,

s. 118(1)). Thus a magistrates' court is normally limited to the imposition of a suspended sentence of no more than six months in length, since that is the normal maximum term of imprisonment which such a court can impose. There is no minimum fixed for the length of a prison sentence which may be suspended, but since the minimum sentence of immediate imprisonment which can be imposed by a magistrates' court is five days (MCA 1980, s. 132), this must also represent the shortest suspended sentence which can lawfully be passed by that court. In practice, the 'exceptional circumstances' requirement has meant that the suspended sentence has more or less died out in the magistrates' courts.

Where a court is dealing with an offender for several offences and it passes consecutive sentences of imprisonment for two of those offences, it may suspend the sentences only if the total term is less than two years. This is because PCC(S)A 2000, s. 125(1) states that consecutive terms of imprisonment, and terms which are wholly or partly concurrent, shall be treated as single terms unless the context otherwise requires. In *Arkle* (1972) 56 Cr App R 722 the offender had been sentenced to three terms of nine months, all to run consecutively, and the court had purported to suspend the aggregate term of 27 months. It was held that the suspension was a nullity, with the consequence that commission of a further offence by the offender did not put him at risk of having the sentence activated. It seems that if a sentencer purports to suspend a sentence which he has no power to suspend, the sentence takes effect as a sentence of immediate imprisonment (*Arkle*). Oddly enough, it appears that a term of imprisonment imposed under the Vagrancy Act 1824, s. 10 may not be suspended, since the condition of being an incorrigible rogue is a status and not an offence (*Theophile* (1975) CSP A11-2B01).

The length of the term which is to be suspended must be that length which would have been appropriate had an immediate sentence of imprisonment been imposed instead. Thus a sentencer should not lengthen (nor, presumably, shorten) the term merely because it is to take effect as a suspended rather than an immediate sentence of imprisonment. This point was underlined in *Mah-Wing* (1983) 5 Cr App R (S) 347. Since sentence length has to be justified in terms of the criteria laid down in PCC(S)A 2000, s. 80 (primarily the seriousness of the offence), it follows that the length of the suspended term must also reflect the seriousness of the offence.

When fixing the length of the term, the sentencer should take into account any period of time already spent in custody by the offender in respect of that offence (*Practice Direction (Crime: Suspended Sentence)* [1970] 1 WLR 259). In a case where the offender has already been held in custody on remand for a period equivalent to the appropriate term of imprisonment for the offence, the sentence should be such as to secure his immediate release (*McCabe* (1988) 10 Cr App R (S) 134). Indeed, it is wrong in these circumstances to impose a suspended sentence at all (*Peppard* (1990) 12 Cr App R (S) 88).

4.6.2   The operational period

The operational period of the suspended sentence is that period during which commission of a further imprisonable offence will put the offender at risk of having the suspended sentence activated. That period must be not less than one and not more than two years (s. 118(2)). The precise length of the operational period is fixed by the court when it passes the suspended sentence. The period runs from the date of the sentence. In practice, operational periods tend to be three months, six months, 12 months, 18 months or two years. There appears to have been no appellate discussion of what principles might underlie the selection of operational period length. It is not clear, therefore, whether this period should reflect primarily the seriousness of the offence (as should the length of the term), or whether other matters, such as the sentencer's perception of the likelihood of the offender remaining conviction-free during a lengthy operational period, may properly be taken into account.

4.6.3 Justifying the imposition of a suspended sentence

PCC(S)A 2000, s. 118(4) and (5), provides as follows:

(4) A court shall not deal with an offender by means of a suspended sentence unless it is of the opinion —
(a) that the case is one in which a sentence of imprisonment would have been appropriate even without the power to suspend the sentence; and
(b) that the exercise of that power can be justified by the exceptional circumstances of the case.
(5) A court which passes a suspended sentence on any person for an offence shall consider whether the circumstances of the case are such as to warrant in addition the imposition of a fine or the making of a compensation order.

Subsection (4)(a) contains an important principle of sentencing in relation to the use of suspended sentences. A suspended sentence must not be imposed by a court unless the imposition of an immediate prison sentence would have been available to the sentencing court, and would have been appropriate for use in the particular case, in the absence of the power to suspend. A suspended sentence cannot be ordered unless all the statutory provisions as to the imposition of a sentence of immediate imprisonment, have been complied with. The court must be clear that it would have passed a sentence of immediate imprisonment in the absence of the power to suspend, and that such sentence would have been for a term of two years or less. It is important to remember that the power to impose a suspended sentence in a magistrates' court is limited just as the magistrates' powers to impose a sentence of immediate imprisonment are limited.

The question of whether a particular case would properly have been dealt with by an immediate custodial sentence in the absence of the power to suspend is, of course, a matter of judgment. The key question which must be asked is whether the offence, or the combination of the offence and one or more offences associated with it, was so serious that only a prison sentence could be justified. As Lord Parker CJ explained in *O'Keefe* [1969] 2 QB 29 (at p. 32):

it seems to this court that before one gets to a suspended sentence at all, the court must go through the process of eliminating other possible courses such as absolute discharge, conditional discharge, probation order, fines, and then say to itself: this is a case for imprisonment, and the final question, it being a case for imprisonment, should be: is immediate imprisonment required, or can a suspended sentence be given?

This principle still holds good.

The Court of Appeal has on numerous occasions quashed a suspended sentence because it did not accept that immediate imprisonment would have been correct on the facts of the particular case and considered that the imposition of a suspended sentence was therefore wrong. In *Watts* (1984) 6 Cr App R (S) 61, for example, a sentence of three months' imprisonment, suspended for two years, was reduced on appeal to a conditional discharge for 12 months; the offender had allowed her premises to be used for smoking cannabis in circumstances which, according to the Court of Appeal, were 'not by any means the gravest for this sort of offence', she had no previous convictions involving cannabis and none at all for 15 years. In *Jeffrey* (1985) 7 Cr App R (S) 11 a suspended sentence was said to be 'wholly inappropriate' in respect of a man with a clean record who stole an electric fire from his landlady. In *Bedborough* (1984) 6 Cr App R (S) 98 the Court of Appeal quashed a sentence of 18 months' imprisonment, suspended for two years, where the offender pleaded guilty to buggery committed in a public lavatory with a consenting adult; since immediate imprisonment has been held to be generally wrong in such cases (see *Tosland* (1981) 3 Cr App R (S) 365), suspended imprisonment was also wrong. A striking case is *Smith* (1990) 12 Cr App R (S) 85, in which the sentencer imposed a suspended sentence so as to ensure that the offender, who had obtained employment as a supply teacher by using the name and qualification of a friend without her knowledge, would be prevented from obtaining further employment as a teacher. The Court of Appeal said that a fine was the proper sentence for the deception. A suspended sentence ought never to have been passed, the sentencer having disregarded the statutory restrictions. It was also said to be improper to pass a suspended sentence in an attempt to deny the offender future employment.

It is contrary to principle to impose a suspended sentence in a case where a fine is the proper sentence, solely because the offender lacks the means to pay. In *Whitehead* (1979) 1 Cr App R (S) 187 a conditional discharge was substituted for a sentence of six weeks' imprisonment, suspended for one year, for shoplifting. The suspended sentence was 'quite wrong in principle'; the offender was a woman with a clean record who was dependent upon social security benefits and there were other mitigating factors of substance. Conversely, a suspended sentence should not be imposed for an offence for which a fine would normally be the correct penalty, solely on the ground that the offender is well-off and the fine would have little impact upon him (*Hanbury* (1979) 1 Cr App R (S) 243). While this decision still holds good today, the issue is now less likely to arise since PCC(S)A 2000, s. 128(4), permits courts to vary the level of a fine upwards to increase its impact on a well-to-do offender (see **6.1.5**).

Section 118(4)(b) restricts the sentencer to imposing a suspended sentence only in a case where that can be 'justified by the exceptional circumstances of the case'. This phrase was inserted by the CJA 1991, and was designed to ensure that the suspended sentence 'should be used far more sparingly than it had been in the past' (*Lowery* (1993) 14 Cr App R (S) 485). The statute provides no hint of what might be regarded as 'exceptional circumstances'. In *Okinikan* [1993] 1 WLR 173, the first occasion on which the Court of Appeal was able to consider the matter, Lord Taylor CJ declined to lay down a definition of the phrase, stating that what amounted to exceptional circumstances would depend on the facts of each case. He did say, however, that 'taken on their own or in combination, good character, youth and an early plea' were *not* exceptional circumstances justifying a suspended sentence, since they were common features of many cases and hence could not be characterised as 'exceptional'. In *Armstrong* [1997] 1 Cr App R (S) 255 Simon Brown LJ commented that where the offence itself was of a particularly serious nature, circumstances to justify suspending the inevitable prison sentence would have to be not merely 'exceptional', but 'unique'.

There has been a steady trickle of appeals to the Court of Appeal on the question of 'exceptional circumstances', but the Court has continued to deal with the matter on a case-by-case basis with little attempt to formulate more general principles. Indeed in *Thomas* (CA unreported, 6 February 1995) Lord Taylor CJ expressly declined an opportunity to elaborate further:

It might be thought helpful if we were to give guidance as to the circumstances in which it would be appropriate to suspend a sentence. However, the provisions . . . make it clear that it has to be considered on a case-by-case basis. What amounts to exceptional circumstances has to be considered in relation to all the facts of the case. The circumstances which could produce a justification for suspension may not be any one particular matter but a combination of matters. It must be left open to individual judges in individual cases to decide when the circumstances contemplated by the section have arisen.

The result is that the cases are very hard to reconcile with one another.

One case in which no 'exceptional circumstances' could be found is *Sanderson* (1993) 14 Cr App R (S) 361, where the offender pleaded guilty to an offence of unlawful wounding, and the sentence of six months' imprisonment was upheld, the Court of Appeal stating that the offender's good character, family circumstances and a measure of provocation before the offence were all relevant to sentence length, but not to suspension of the sentence. A second example is *Frow* (1995) 16 Cr App R (S) 609, where the court declined to suspend a prison term of nine months for dangerous driving, despite the fact that the offender had incurred serious leg injuries in the accident which he had caused. A third is *Murti* [1996] 2 Cr App R (S) 152, where suspension of a sentence of eight months' imprisonment was inappropriate in the case of a Post Office counter assistant who had permitted other women to cash DSS benefit vouchers which she knew had been stolen, despite the fact that the offender was the mother of two small children, had suffered from post-natal depression at the time of the offence, and had cooperated fully with the prosecuting authorities.

In contrast, a case in which 'exceptional circumstances' were found so as to justify suspending the sentence is *Cameron* (1993) 14 Cr App R (S) 801, where the offender pleaded guilty to assault occasioning actual bodily harm on his five-year-old son. The Court of Appeal suspended the prison sentence of 12 months in the light of a decision made by social workers to try to rehabilitate the family under supervision. In *French* (1994) 15 Cr App R (S) 194 exceptional circumstances were found in the offender's financial and emotional difficulties before the offence, which was a conspiracy relating to an insurance fraud, and the fact that the offender was now undergoing treatment for depression. In *Oliver* [1997] 1 Cr App R (S) 125 the relevant exceptional circumstances were that the offender, who pleaded guilty to possession of amphetamine with intent to supply, had been the victim of a multiple shooting awaiting trial. His life was still in danger from one of the bullets, which could not be surgically removed. In *Bellikli* [1998] 1 Cr App R (S) 135 the offender was convicted of facilitating illegal entry, but the sentence of two years' imprisonment was suspended by the Court of Appeal on the basis that the offender's child was very ill and would probably require major surgery in the near future. In *Brookin* (1995) 16 Cr App R (S) 78, where the offender pleaded guilty to unlawful wounding, there was found to be sufficient provocation both before and at the time of the offence to justify suspension of a sentence of six months' imprisonment. Finally, in *Snelling* [1996] 2 Cr App R (S) 56, where the offender agreed to help a physically handicapped friend to move to another area by burning down her house, and as a result was trapped in the burning house and suffered burns to her back and legs, the case fell 'four square' within the power to suspend. According to Leggatt LJ in the Court of Appeal, in this case suspension 'not only could but should have been exercised' by the sentencer.

4.6.4 Concurrent and consecutive suspended sentences

If an offender is already serving a prison sentence, it is wrong to pass a suspended sentence upon him, whether this is intended to run concurrently with, or consecutively to, it (*Baker*

(1971) 55 Cr App R 182). Where two suspended sentences are passed on the same occasion, the court must make it clear whether they are to run concurrently or consecutively (*Wilkinson* [1970] 1 WLR 1319). If they are to run consecutively, they constitute a single suspended sentence (PCC(S)A 2000, s. 125(1)). If an offender is already under a suspended sentence, and the sentencer passes a further suspended sentence on him, the sentencer should give no indication whether, if activated, the sentences are to run concurrently or consecutively, since that is for the sentencer ordering the activation on a later occasion to decide (*Blakeway* [1969] 1 WLR 1233).

More generally, it is bad sentencing practice to allow suspended sentences to accumulate in respect of an offender. In a case where more than one suspended sentence is activated in respect of an offender at the same time, the overall term is subject to the totality principle (*Smith* (1971) CSP A11-6C01) and see **4.4.4**.

4.6.5   Combining a suspended sentence with other sentences or orders

An immediate prison sentence and a suspended sentence should not be imposed on the same occasion (*Sapiano* (1968) 52 Cr App R 674) nor should a suspended sentence be passed in respect of a person already serving a prison sentence (*Baker* (1971) 55 Cr App R 182).

A suspended sentence and a community order may not be imposed by the court on an offender, whether or not the offences are charged in the same indictment (PCC(S)A 2000, s. 118(6)). The effect of combining a suspended sentence with a CRO may be achieved by passing a suspended sentence supervision order (see **4.6.6**).

A fine may be combined with a suspended sentence; indeed this is a combination specifically encouraged by PCC(S)A 2000, s. 118(5). It is important to remember, however, that it is wrong to combine them where a fine standing alone would have been the proper sentence. To do so would conflict with the principle in s. 118(4)(a), discussed in **4.6.3**. Another way of stating this is to say that 'a fine may be added to a suspended sentence, but a suspended sentence may not be added to a fine'. The correct reasoning was explained in *Genese* [1976] 1 WLR 958 at p. 964:

> if the court decides that there is no other appropriate method of dealing with the offender than imprisonment and imposes a prison sentence, the court can then, in the appropriate case, go on to consider that the sentence should be suspended. . . . If the court does go on to consider that the sentence should be suspended . . . the court can also consider whether an additional penalty by way of a fine is justified.

In such a case, the fine is added as a kind of 'sting in the tail' of the suspended sentence, so that the offender has an immediate penalty to pay for the offence as well as the deterrent threat of the suspended sentence hanging over him. If a fine is added to a suspended sentence the court must, of course, have proper regard to the means of the offender (*King* [1970] 1 WLR 1016).

A suspended sentence cannot be combined with a discharge when sentencing for a single offence because a discharge is imposed only 'where it is inexpedient to inflict punishment', but a discharge could be given for one offence when a suspended sentence was passed in respect of another offence sentenced on the same occasion.

A compensation order may be imposed in addition to any other sentence, so such an order may be mixed with a suspended sentence, whether in respect of a single offence or for different offences sentenced on the same occasion. The combination of suspended sentence and compensation order is expressly encouraged by s. 118(5). It should be borne in mind, however, that it would be contrary to principle to pass a suspended, rather than an immediate, custodial sentence, merely because of the offender's ability to pay compensation. Regard should also be had to the fact that if the offender reoffends within the operational period of the suspended sentence, the activation of that sentence may well bring to an end any prospect of compensation being paid (*McGee* [1978] Crim LR 370).

Apart from compensation, other ancillary orders may be combined with a suspended sentence, such as a forfeiture order, a restitution order, or an order to pay costs. If the offence is so punishable, a suspended sentence may be combined with an order for disqualification from driving.

4.6.6 Suspended sentence supervision orders

Section 122(1) of the PCC(S)A 2000 provides that where a court passes a suspended sentence of more than six months for a single offence it may order that, for a period not exceeding the operational period of the suspended sentence, the offender shall be placed under the supervision of a probation officer. The probation officer will be one assigned to work in the petty sessions area in which the offender lives (s. 122(2)). The offender is under a duty to keep in touch with the officer in accordance with the latter's instructions and notify him of any change of address (s. 122(3)). If he fails to do so, a summons or warrant for arrest may be issued to bring him before the magistrates' court for the relevant petty sessions area, and the magistrates may fine him up to £1,000 (s. 123). Where the offender is fined by the magistrates for failing to keep in touch with the probation officer, the supervision order is unaffected and there is, of course, no question of activating the suspended term. Should the offender be convicted of an imprisonable offence committed during the operational period of the suspended sentence supervision order, the normal rules about activation of the suspended sentence still apply (see **4.6.7**). If the sentence is brought into effect the supervision order automatically terminates.

There is provision in s. 124 for the early discharge of a suspended sentence supervision order on application of the offender or the probation officer concerned. Application would normally be made to the magistrates' court, but to the relevant Crown Court if that Court reserved to itself the power of discharge when it passed the sentence.

In some ways the suspended sentence supervision order provides a means of combining a suspended sentence and a CRO, a mix which is otherwise prohibited. In contrast to a CRO, however, where several different kinds of requirements may be included within it, a suspended sentence supervision order may include only the basic requirement of keeping in touch with the probation officer. The Home Office National Standards state that supervision of an offender under a suspended sentence supervision order should be conducted in accordance with the standard on CRO supervision (see **5.2.2**). The provision that a supervision order may be attached to a suspended sentence only where the latter is for a term of more than six months for one offence has the effect that magistrates have no power to pass a suspended sentence supervision order. In *Seafield* (1988) *The Times*, 21 May 1988, the Court of Appeal stressed that the power was not available where a term of exactly six months had been suspended, and noted that this mistake had required correction by the Court of Appeal on several occasions. It was held in *Baker* (1988) 10 Cr App R (S) 409 that a suspended sentence supervision order may not be passed where sentences which are each shorter than six months are imposed consecutively to make an aggregate sentence of more than six months.

Relatively few suspended sentence supervision orders are made each year and there is no appellate guidance to speak of. In *Terry* (1992) 156 JP 795, the Court of Appeal observed that a suspended sentence supervision order should not be used as an alternative to a CRO, nor should it be seen as a 'CRO with teeth'. Clearly this is correct since, as we have seen, the sentencer must have regarded the offence as so serious that a custodial sentence was the only appropriate means of dealing with it, and hence rejected all community orders (including the CRO), before the option of the suspended sentence came into view.

4.6.7 Breach of suspended sentences

An offender who is convicted of an imprisonable offence during the operational period of a suspended sentence is thereby in breach of the suspended sentence, and is at risk of being ordered to serve the suspended term in prison. In 1999, 14 per cent of suspended sentences imposed by the courts were breached.

It is important to note that conviction for a non-imprisonable offence will not constitute breach. Thus, in *Melbourne* (1980) 2 Cr App R (S) 116, activation of a suspended sentence was overturned by the Court of Appeal where the defendant was convicted before magistrates during the operational period of a suspended sentence of two offences which were punishable only by a fine on summary conviction. It was said to be irrelevant that the offences could have attracted a prison sentence on conviction on indictment. It is also clear that conviction for an offence committed *before* the offence for which the offender was given the suspended sentence will not suffice to justify activation of the suspended sentence (*Daurge* (1972) CSP A13-2A01). On the other hand, conviction for an imprisonable offence committed during the operational period does amount to a breach even if the conviction is not until after the expiry of the operational period. In such circumstances, however, it is likely that the court would exercise its discretion not to activate the suspended sentence. In what follows, the offence for which the suspended sentence was passed is referred to as the 'original offence' and the offence which puts the offender in breach of the suspended sentence is referred to as the 'subsequent offence'.

The options which are available to a court dealing with an offender for breach of a suspended sentence are listed in PCC(S)A 2000, s. 119(1):

(a)   to order that the suspended sentence shall take effect with the original term unaltered; or

(b)   to order that the sentence shall take effect with a lesser term substituted for the original term; or

(c)   to vary the original suspended sentence by making the operational period run until a date not more than two years from the date of the variation; or

(d)   to make no order with respect to the suspended sentence.

The court *must*, however, activate the suspended sentence with its term unaltered (that is, choose (a) above) unless it is of the opinion that, in all the circumstances, including the facts of the subsequent offence, it would be unjust to do so (s. 119(2)). Where it is of the opinion that it would be unjust to activate the sentence with its term unaltered, the court must state its reasons. This applies both to the Crown Court and to magistrates' courts. In 1999, breaches of suspended sentence were dealt with by immediate imprisonment in 79 per cent of cases.

Before looking at these options in detail, two points should be made about the powers of the court dealing with the subsequent offence. First, if that court were to impose a discharge for the subsequent offence, there is then no power to deal with the suspended sentence at all, since (by PCC(S)A 2000, s. 14), there is deemed to have been no 'conviction' in respect of the subsequent offence (*Moore* [1995] QB 353 and see **7.1.4**). Secondly, if the court defers sentence for the subsequent offence there is no power to deal with the suspended sentence in that situation either, since it remains open to the court to deal with the subsequent offence by way of a discharge at the end of the period of deferment (*Salmon* (1973) 57 Cr App R 953).

There are four steps in a court's consideration of the options available to it under s. 119 when dealing with an offender who is in breach of a suspended sentence. The first step is that the sentencer must consider the appropriate penalty for the subsequent offence (*Ithell* [1969] 1 WLR 272). If the appropriate penalty is a custodial sentence, then the second step is to determine the appropriate length of that sentence. The third step is to consider whether the suspended sentence should be activated. Bearing in mind that s. 119 requires the sentencer to bring the suspended sentence into effect with its term unaltered unless it would be unjust to do so, this will probably be the appropriate course to take. According to Russell J in *Craine* (1981) 3 Cr App R (S) 198, 'it cannot be made too plain that when suspended sentences of imprisonment are imposed they mean what they say. In *Chuni* [2000] 2 Cr App R (S) 64 the Court of Appeal stressed that a prison sentence was suspended only in exceptional circumstances, and if there was a breach of the suspended sentence there would have to be good reason to do other than activate it in full. The fourth and final step is to consider whether the suspended term should run consecutively to, or concurrently with, the term for the subsequent offence. In *Ithell* Edmund Davies LJ said (at pp. 273-4) that 'unless there are some quite exceptional circumstances, the suspended sentence should be ordered to run consecutively to the sentence given for the current offence'. The sentencer must make sure, however, that the overall effect of the sentence is not too severe and does not breach the totality principle (see **4.4.4**). To avoid that effect, the sentencer may either reduce the term which he originally had in mind for the subsequent offence, or may substitute a lesser term for that originally suspended (that is, choose option (b) rather than (a) (*Bocskei* (1970) 54 Cr App R 519).

The rule in s. 119 that upon breach of a suspended sentence the term suspended should be activated in full has, on the whole, been strictly endorsed by the Court of Appeal. The Court has not been easily convinced on appeal that activation in full was unjust and, in particular, has held on several occasions that the subsequent offence being different in type from the original offence does not by itself render activation of the full term unjust. In *Clitheroe* (1987) 9 Cr App R (S) 159 the offender was subject to a sentence of six months' imprisonment, suspended for two years, imposed for handling stolen goods. The subsequent offence, committed 14 months after the suspended sentence was passed, was for wounding with intent. The sentencer imposed a sentence of four years for the subsequent offence and activated the suspended sentence in full and consecutively. The Court of Appeal upheld the sentence. Lord Lane CJ observed that 'the mere fact that the subsequent offence was wholly unrelated to the earlier is no ground for not activating the suspended sentence in full and consecutively'. An offender is more likely to succeed where he argues against activation on the basis that the subsequent offence was a relatively trivial one, so that if he is required to serve the whole suspended term plus a short term for the subsequent offence the overall penalty will be out of proportion to the gravity of the conduct. Such an argument will be all the stronger if it can be shown that the subsequent offence was both relatively trivial *and* dissimilar to the original offence (*Moylan* [1970] 1 QB 143). In such a case, it seems, the sentencer might consider either not activating the suspended sentence at all or activating it but with a much reduced term. An example is *Abrahams* (1980) 2 Cr App R (S) 10, where the offender was in breach of a suspended sentence of 18 months which had been imposed for burglary. The subsequent offence involved theft of a plastic dinghy whilst on holiday and in 'a drunken frolic'. Here the Court of Appeal quashed the order for activation of the suspended sentence. Another good argument for non-activation is that the subsequent offence was committed right at the end of the operational period of the suspended sentence. In *Carr* (1979) 1 Cr App R (S) 53 the offender had completed 22 months of the two-year period of suspension before being convicted of a subsequent offence, for which he received two years' immediate imprisonment. The activation of the 12-month suspended sentence in full and consecutively was disapproved by the Court of Appeal, which ordered that it should run concurrently with the new sentence.

The sentencer may decide that the subsequent offence is not so serious that only custody can be justified for it. If the sentencer selects a community order as the appropriate means of dealing with the subsequent offence, the general rule seems to be that activation of the suspended sentence is not appropriate. One reason for this is that it is generally illogical and undesirable to mix together custodial and community sentences. In *Brooks* (1990) 12 Cr App R (S) 756 the offender pleaded guilty to possession of a small quantity of cannabis resin. He was then in breach of a sentence of nine months' imprisonment, suspended for two years, for possession of cannabis with intent to supply. The sentencer passed a sentence of imprisonment of one month for the subsequent offence and activated the suspended sentence in full. The Court of Appeal said that the proper way to have dealt with the subsequent offence was by way of a fine and that, in those circumstances, activation of the suspended sentence was inappropriate. Auld J commented that:

> the fact that a subsequent offence does not warrant a custodial sentence is a strong argument for not activating the suspended sentence . . . this is not a matter of principle but a matter of strong argument for counsel when mitigating in such a case . . . Whilst the argument is particularly strong when a later offence is of a different character from the earlier one as well as being comparatively trivial . . . it is not confined to such a case.

In *Brooks* the main reason for not activating the suspending sentence was not the incompatibility of the sentence for the subsequent offence with the activated term of imprisonment, but an acceptance that where the subsequent offence can properly be dealt with by way of a fine, activation of the suspended sentence is generally inappropriate. *Brooks* has been followed in later cases, such as *Burnard* (1994) 15 Cr App R (S) 218, but in other cases the Court of Appeal has upheld implementation of the suspended sentence in full. See, for example, *Calladine* (1994) 15 Cr App R (S) 345 and *Stacey* (1994) 15 Cr App R (S) 585.

A court activating a suspended sentence is not empowered to suspend part of it (*Senior* (1984) 6 Cr App R (S) 15).

4.6.8 When a court may deal with breach of suspended sentence

If an offender appears before the Crown Court to be sentenced for an offence, whether following conviction on indictment or following a committal for sentence from the magistrates, and he is in breach of a suspended sentence, the Crown Court may deal with the breach whether the suspended sentence was originally imposed in the Crown Court or in a magistrates' court (PCC(S)A 2000, s. 120(1)). On the other hand, a magistrates' court can deal with breach of a suspended sentence only if that sentence was imposed by itself or another magistrates' court.

If a magistrates' court deals summarily with an offender for an offence which puts him in breach of a suspended sentence imposed by the Crown Court, the magistrates may choose one of two options under s. 120(2). The first and more usual course is to commit the offender to Crown Court to be dealt with for the breach. If this option is chosen the magistrates will also commit the offender to be sentenced by the Crown Court for the subsequent offence. In this way the Crown Court will deal with both matters at the same time. The second option is to give written notice to the Crown Court that the conviction has occurred. If this option is chosen, the magistrates will sentence for the subsequent offence, thereby hinting strongly their view that the suspended sentence should not be activated. Once the Crown Court receives notice, it may issue a summons or warrant for arrest to secure the offender's appearance before it. Difficulties may then arise if the Crown Court is of the view that the suspended sentence should be activated, particularly if the magistrates have imposed a sentence for the subsequent offence which is generally incompatible with activation. First, if the magistrates have dealt with the subsequent offence by granting a discharge in respect of it, there is no power in the Crown Court to deal with the suspended sentence at all, since by PCC(S)A 2000, s. 14(1), there is deemed to have been no 'conviction' in respect of the subsequent offence (*Moore* [1995] QB 353 and see further **7.1.4**). Second, it is undesirable for the magistrates to impose a community order for the subsequent offence (as happened in *Stewart* (1984) 6 Cr App R (S) 166), or to pass a second suspended sentence (as happened in *Hamilton* (1984) 6 Cr App R (S) 451), since that renders the task of the Crown Court dealing with the original suspended sentence much more difficult. In such cases it is better for the magistrates to select the first option, and commit the offender to the Crown Court so it may deal with the whole matter.

5 Community Sentences

Community sentences lie within a central band of available sentencing options, appropriate in cases where the offender has committed an offence of an intermediate degree of seriousness. Community sentences are imposed where the sentencer takes the view that the nature of the offence is not such as to require custody, but that it does require something more than the mild penalty of a bind over or a discharge. A community sentence is a sentence which includes one or more community orders (though these may, in turn, be mixed with other measures, particularly fines and compensation). The various community orders are a diverse group, since they have been introduced by legislation at different times during the century, against a changing penological background. It is possible to see in all of the community orders the twin ideas of rehabilitation of the offender and punishment in the community. In the past the former of these ideas was predominant, particularly in measures such as the community rehabilitation order (formerly the probation order), which was regarded as lying outside the 'tariff', an individualised measure geared towards rehabilitation of the offender away from crime. Until 1991 the probation order was not even legally a 'sentence' and could not be combined with any other order of the court which contained a punitive element within it (such as a fine). The emphasis was shifted significantly by the CJA 1991, and the probation order has been brought within the tariff, but the conflicting underlying objectives still remain.

5.1 COMMUNITY SENTENCES IN GENERAL

It must be appreciated that not all sentences that are by nature non-custodial, are 'community sentences'. The latter phrase is now a term of art, defined in PCC(S)A 2000, s. 33(1) so as to encompass the community rehabilitation order (formerly probation order), the community punishment order (formerly community service order), the community punishment and rehabilitation order (formerly combination order), the curfew order, the attendance centre order, the supervision order, the exclusion order, the drug treatment and testing order, the drug abstinence order and the action plan order. Other sentencing options, particularly fines and discharges, are not technically community sentences; they are considered in Chapters 6 and 7. While community orders display a large degree of diversity, the 2000 Act ensures that they share a common legal framework. This framework relates both to the circumstances in which they may be selected by the sentencer in a particular case and, for the most part, to the consequences for an offender who finds himself in breach of a community order. This common framework is described next, and then the legal provisions and principles of sentencing applicable to the individual community orders are dealt with in the remainder of this chapter.

The PCC(S)A 2000 requires that the imposition of any community order must be justified by the court in accordance with certain statutory criteria. Section 35(1) provides that:

> (1) A court shall not pass a community sentence on an offender, unless it is of the opinion that the offence, or the combination of the offence and one or more offences associated with it, was serious enough to warrant such a sentence.

The requirement in s. 35(1) that the court must consider 'the offence, or the combination of the offence and one or more offences associated with it' mirrors the provision in s. 79(2)(a), which relates to the court's requirement to justify the imposition of custody (see **4.2.3**). A definition of the phrase 'associated with' is provided by s. 161(1), and was considered at **4.2.3**. An offence which is taken into consideration at the time of sentence may count as an offence to be weighed in accordance with s. 161(1). Unlike the justification for imposing a custodial sentence, however, the seriousness of the offence, or offences, is here the sole criterion for imposing a community sentence. There is no equivalent provision to s. 79(2)(b) (which permits the imposition of a custodial sentence on the basis of public protection following the offender's conviction for a violent offence or a sexual offence).

It will be noted that while s. 35(1) states that a community sentence may be imposed only where the offence is 'serious enough' to warrant such a sentence, the imposition of a custodial sentence requires that the offence be 'so serious that only' a custodial sentence can be justified. This is a significant difference in wording. It means that at the lower threshold of the community sentence band there is some degree of overlap between community sentences and fines. A particular offence may be 'serious enough' to qualify for a community sentence but, in all the circumstances of the case, the court may still properly impose a fine. A further complication is provided by PCC(S)A 2000, s. 59, relating to 'persistent petty offenders', whereby a community punishment order or a curfew order can be imposed instead of a fine on an offender who already has outstanding fines (see **6.6**).

Section 35(3) provides that:

> (3) Subject to subsection (2) above and to section 69(5) below (which limits the community orders that may be combined with an action plan order), where a court passes a community sentence—
> (a) the particular order or orders comprising or forming part of the sentence shall be such as in the opinion of the court is, or taken together are, the most suitable for the offender; and
> (b) the restrictions on liberty imposed by the order or orders shall be such as in the opinion of the court are commensurate with the seriousness of the offence, or the combination of the offence and one or more offences associated with it.

It will be noted that, in parallel with the criteria relating to custodial sentence length, the court may look at the whole pattern of offending in determining whether to impose a community order and, if so, which community order or orders to impose (see **4.4.2**). Where several offences are involved, a danger of this approach is that it could lead to a total sentence which is disproportionate to the overall seriousness of the offending behaviour. Section 158(2) of the PCC(S)A 2000, in an attempt to avoid this, makes reference to the totality principle (see **4.4.4**) by stating that the sentencer may mitigate the sentence by 'applying any rule of law as to the totality of sentences' and this applies to community sentences as well as custodial ones. There is a good deal of potential difficulty with s. 35(3).

The twin objectives of 'suitability' and 'seriousness' are likely on some occasions to conflict, and the statute gives no indication of which objective should prevail where that is the case.

In forming its opinion that a community sentence is justified under s. 35, and in determining the appropriate restrictions on liberty imposed by the community order or orders comprising the community sentence, s. 36(1) requires the court to 'take into account all such information about the circumstances of the offence (including any aggravating or mitigating factors) as is available to it'; and, by s. 36(2)), in forming an opinion about the suitability of the community order or orders for the offender, the court 'may take into account any information about the offender which is before it'. Further, by s. 158(1) nothing shall prevent a court from 'mitigating an offender's sentence by taking into account any such matters as, in the opinion of the court, are relevant in mitigation of sentence' and, by s. 158(2) and without prejudice to the generality of s. 158(1), the court may mitigate any penalty included in an offender's sentence by taking into account any other penalty included in that sentence. For discussion of mitigation and aggravation, see **2.2**; for the rules relating to combining individual community orders with other sentences or orders see the detailed discussion of the particular community orders below.

By PCC(S)A 2000, s. 36(4), the obtaining of a pre-sentence report is normally required whenever the court is considering imposing:

(a) a community rehabilitation probation order which includes additional requirements authorised by sch. 2 to the 2000 Act;

(b) a community punishment order;

(c) a community punishment and reparation order;

(d) a drug treatment and testing order.

(e) a supervision order which includes requirements authorised by sch. 6 to the 2000 Act; or

It follows that a pre-sentence report is not normally required whenever the court is considering imposing:

(f) a community rehabilitation order which does not include additional requirements;

(g) a supervision order which does not include the specified requirements;

(h) a curfew order;

(i) an attendance centre order;

(j) an action plan order;

(k) an exclusion order; or

(l) a drug abstinence order.

In many of the cases falling within (f) to (l), however, it would no doubt constitute good sentencing practice to obtain a pre-sentence report before passing such a sentence.

Section 36(4) is made subject to s. 36(5), which states that the court may dispense with a pre-sentence report in any case where the offender is aged 18 or over and the court considers such a report to be 'unnecessary'. For those under the age of 18, s. 36(6) says that, in a case where the offence is punishable only on indictment the court may dispense with a pre-sentence report, but if the offence is not so punishable the court should not dispense with a report unless there exists an earlier pre-sentence report on the offender and the sentencer has seen that and taken it into account.

Even in those cases where the obtaining of a pre-sentence report is normally required, s. 36(7) states that no community sentence shall be invalidated by the failure of the court to order a report, but, in the event of an appeal being brought against a community sentence passed without the court having obtained and considered such a report, the appellate court must then obtain and consider one unless it believes that the sentencer was justified in not calling for one or that, although proceeding without a report was not justified at the time, in light of the current circumstances it is unnecessary to obtain one.

When s. 52 of the CJCSA 2000 is brought into force, a new section 36B will be inserted into the PCC(S)A 2000, relating to electronic monitoring. This provision is of general application to community sentences, and states that a community order may include by order of the court a requirement of electronic monitoring of the offender's compliance with any other requirement or requirements imposed by the order. Electronic monitoring has been used for some years now (although initially only on a pilot basis) for securing compliance with curfew orders. When the relevant parts of the CJPOA 2000 are fully in force, the use of electronic monitoring will be significantly extended, to play a role in the compliance and enforcement of community orders generally.

Former provisions requiring that an offender must consent to the imposition of certain community sentences before they could be imposed were abolished by the C(S)A 1997, s. 38. For further discussion, see the text relating to specific community orders.

The number of community sentences passed by the courts is rising steadily year by year. In 1999 nearly 152,000 community sentences were passed, compared to under 95,000 in 1988.

5.2 COMMUNITY REHABILITATION ORDERS

5.2.1 The probation service and the community rehabilitation order

The origins of the probation service go back to the latter part of the nineteenth century when voluntary church societies appointed 'police court missionaries' to assist in the reformation of drunkards and others who appeared in the inner city courts. The practice then grew up of magistrates releasing petty offenders without sentencing them, on the understanding that they would accept help from the missionary. The practice was put on a statutory footing by the Probation of Offenders Act 1907, which enabled courts to make probation orders in a form rather similar to that of the basic CRO which is still used today. Also, magistrates' courts were allowed to appoint probation officers who, instead of being supported by voluntary societies, would be paid by the local authority.

Probation officers today are officers of the court. In addition to supervising offenders sentenced to probation (now community rehabilitation) orders, they have a wide (and increasing) range of other duties. They supervise offenders under early release from custody, they organise the work performed by offenders under community punishment orders, they run probation centres and probation hostels and prepare pre-sentence reports for the courts.

The role of central government in the organisation and funding of the probation service has increased greatly since 1907, and it now exercises a dominant control. During the 1960s the social work or welfare ideology was clearly dominant in probation practice, and there has always been an important element of offering practical help to the offender, by assistance in finding employment, for example. More recently the service has been required to implement clearer management objectives and to accept national standards to govern the ways in which the community orders are administered, and in the preparation of pre-sentence reports for the courts. Independent external review is provided by HM Inspectorate of Probation.

Between 1988 and 1998 the proportionate use of CROs for indictable offences has been increasing steadily. This holds true for nearly all the main categories of offending, though in some of these there was a greater use in the proportionate use of the CRO during the early 1990s which appears now to have tailed off. The percentage change in the use of CROs between 1988 and 1999 for the main categories of offending is as follows:

		1988	*1999*
(1)	violence against the person	6 per cent	12 per cent
(2)	sexual offences	12 per cent	17 per cent
(3)	burglary	13 per cent	12 per cent
(4)	robbery	3 per cent	4 per cent
(5)	theft and handling	11 per cent	14 per cent
(6)	fraud and forgery	13 per cent	16 per cent
(7)	criminal damage	13 per cent	13 per cent
(8)	drug offences	5 per cent	9 per cent
(9)	motoring offences	6 per cent	5 per cent
	All offending	9 per cent	11 per cent

This in fact translates into a modest increase in the numbers of offenders receiving CROs (38,900 in 1999 as compared with 36,400 in 1988) but this should be seen against a marked decline in the overall number of offenders being sentenced by the courts.

5.2.2 Power to make a community rehabilitation order (CRO)

With effect from April 2001, the probation order has been re-named the community rehabilitation order (CRO) (CJCSA 2000, s. 43).

A CRO may be made by the Crown Court, by an adult magistrates' court or by a youth court. Its effect is that the offender is required to be under the supervision of a probation officer for a period specified in the order, of not less than six months nor more than three years. If the offender is aged under 18, the supervision may be by a member of a youth offending team instead. During that period the offender must keep in touch with the supervising officer, follow such instructions as he is given by that officer and notify him of any change of address (PCC(S)A 2000, s. 41(11)). This is the 'basic' CRO. The government requires that CRO's should be seen to be more demanding than has sometimes been the case in the past, when the measure was dismissed by some as a 'soft option'; the order should require the offender to face up to his offending, and should be more rigorously and consistently enforced. The Home Office National Standard (2000) states that the purposes of supervision in the community are to (i) address and reduce offending behaviour; (ii) challenge the offender to accept responsibility for the crimes committed and their consequences; (iii) contribute to the protection of the public; (iv) motivate and assist the offender towards a greater sense of personal responsibility and discipline; and (v) aid reintegration as a law-abiding member of the community.

The National Standards for CROs require that there be frequent meetings between the supervisor and the offender (at least 12 appointments in the first 12 weeks of supervision, together with a home visit, and then at least six appointments within the next 12 weeks). The National Standards envisage that the offender and the supervisor will, at the first meeting, together draw up in writing a 'supervision plan' based upon the requirements of the order and any assessment and outline proposals made in the pre-sentence report. This plan should identify the offender's motivation and pattern of offending, his or her relevant problems, the risk of reoffending or serious harm to the public and the requirements of the order. It should then set out an individual programme designed to tackle these issues, identifying the appropriateness of individual or group work for the offender, referral to a specialist probation team or facility (such as a probation centre or drug or alcohol group) and referral to, or involvement with, other resources and opportunities in the community (such as employment, training, education, health, social services, housing and community groups). A time-scale for achieving these objectives should be set and records must be kept of all meetings.

In practice, most CROs are for a period of between 12 months and two years. The criteria for fixing the length of a CRO are unclear, but presumably its duration would be affected both by the court's perception of the seriousness of the offence and the needs of the offender. A short CRO might be appropriate where the offender has immediate problems (such as financial difficulty) which require resolution, but a comparatively short order may make more severe demands on some offenders than more severe orders would on others. Where appropriate, a CRO may be discharged early (see **5.2.10**). In addition to this 'basic' CRO, the court may choose to insert various specific requirements into the order. These are considered at **5.2.3**.

The conditions which must be established before a CRO may be made by the court are as follows.

(a) Since a CRO is a 'community order' within the meaning of PCC(S)A 2000, s. 33(1), the imposition of a CRO in any case requires justification by the court in terms of the seriousness of the offence, or the offence and one or more offences associated with it. This general requirement for all community orders is dealt with at **5.1**.

(b) The offender must be aged 16 or over. The age requirement was lowered from 17 to 16 by the CJA 1991. As a result of this change, offenders aged 16 or 17 are eligible for both CROs *and* supervision orders (as to the latter see **5.11**). There is as yet no statutory or appellate guidance on the appropriate choice between these measures for such offenders. The National Standards suggest that in practice the supervision order should normally be preferred for offenders aged 16 and 17. There is no upper age limit for the CRO.

(c) The CRO is available for offenders convicted of any offence, subject only to the crime of murder and to the three presumptive minimum sentences under PCC(S)A 2000, ss. 109–111. The offence does not need to be imprisonable. On the other hand, the requirement that the offence, or the offence and one or more offences associated with it, must be sufficiently serious, together with the limited resources of the probation service, mean that the imposition of a CRO by the court for a trivial offence is inappropriate.

(d) If the court has it in mind to include within the CRO any of the requirements specified in the PCC(S)A 2000, sch. 2, it should normally first obtain a pre-sentence report (PCC(S)A 2000, s. 36(4) and **5.1**). Even if no such additional requirements are proposed, it would seem that before a basic CRO is passed, it will often be good sentencing practice to obtain a pre-sentence report.

(e) The court must be of the opinion that supervision of the offender is desirable in the interests of securing the rehabilitation of the offender, protecting the public from harm from him or preventing the commission by him of further offences (s. 41(1)).

(f) The court must explain to the offender in ordinary language the effect of the order (including the effect of any additional requirements to be included in it), the consequences for the offender of breach of the order and that the court has power to review the order later, on the application either of the offender or the supervising officer (s. 41(7)).

(g) The court must give copies of the order to the probation officer in attendance at the court, who must then pass on copies to the offender, the officer who will supervise the offender and the person in charge of any hostel or other institution in which the order obliges the offender to live (s. 41(9)). It is unlikely that a failure to comply precisely with these requirements would invalidate the probation order (see, by analogy, *Walsh* v *Barlow* [1985] 1 WLR 90, considered at **5.3.1**).

Once the CRO is made by the court, the Home Office National Standard indicates that supervision should commence promptly: normally within five working days. If practicable, the first appointment should be made before the offender leaves court.

On making a CRO the court may, if it thinks it expedient for the purpose of reformation of the offender, allow any person who agrees to do so to give financial security for the good behaviour of the offender (s. 41(8)). This option seems to be very rarely used by the courts.

5.2.3 Requirements in community rehabilitation orders

The court may require that, during the whole or part of the CRO, the offender must comply with such additional requirements in the order as the court considers desirable in the interests of securing the offender's rehabilitation, protecting the public from harm from him or preventing the commission by him of further offences (PCC(S)A 2000, s. 42). This is a generally expressed provision, so that it would seem that any reasonable condition might be inserted by the sentencing court. One example would be the inclusion by the court of a requirement that the offender shall not, during the period of the CRO, possess, use or carry a firearm: Firearms Act 1968, s. 52. The generality of s. 42(1) is subject, however, to s. 42(3), which states that the payment of compensation to the victim must not be included as a requirement of a CRO (though there is no objection to making a compensation order and a CRO at the same time and, indeed, this is commonly done). In *Rogers* v *Cullen* [1982] 1 WLR 729 Lord Bridge indicated that no requirement should be included in a probation order (now a CRO) which would 'introduce a custodial or other element', and that any discretion conferred on the supervisor to regulate the offender's activities should be 'confined within well defined limits'. In a *Practice Note* (1952) 35 Cr App R 207 Lord Goddard CJ deprecated 'vague' conditions being written into such orders. There is no power to include in a CRO a condition that the offender leave the country never to return (*McCartan* [1958] 1 WLR 923).

Schedule 2 to the 2000 Act provides statutory authority for a number of specific requirements which may be inserted into the basic CRO. It should always be remembered that to the extent that the insertion of such requirements makes the CRO more onerous for the offender, it may only be justified in accordance with the terms of s. 35(3): that the particular order or orders comprising the community sentence must be such as in the opinion of the court is, or are, the most *suitable* for the offender, *and* the restrictions on liberty imposed by the order or orders are commensurate with the seriousness of the offence, or the combination of the offence and one or more offences associated with it. In particular, complex and onerous conditions should not be included within a CRO unless they are justified by the relative degree of seriousness inherent in the offence for which the CRO is imposed.

In practice about two-thirds of CROs are made without the insertion of specified requirements.

5.2.4 Requirements as to residence

A CRO may require the offender to live at a certain private address, or in an approved probation hostel, or in some other named institution (PCC(S)A 2000, sch. 2, para. 1). A probation hostel provides supervised accommodation for offenders on a CRO, as well as for those on licence following early release from custody and defendants who are on bail. Some are operated by the probation service and some by the voluntary sector. The Home Office National Standards set requirements for the management, rules and regime, induction and record-keeping of such hostels. According to the National Standards (2000), the purpose of approved hostels is to provide an enhanced level of supervision to enable bailees and offenders to remain under supervision in the community. Hostel residents are normally expected to go to work or to attend projects, training courses or treatment facilities in the community, but they are subject to a supervised night-time curfew.

A residence requirement may last for the whole or part of the duration of an order; but the period for which it will last must be stated in the order. Often the residence period is several months shorter than the full term of the order, to allow a reasonable period of supervision after residence in the hostel has ceased. Before inserting a residence condition into a CRO, the court must consider the home surroundings of the offender, the pre-sentence report being the obvious source for such information. A requirement of residence at a hostel might be appropriate where the offender's home environment is particularly bad, or where he represents more of a risk to the public than the average probationer, so that requiring him to live in approved accommodation supervised by the probation service is some additional safeguard for the public. It is clear that approved hostels should thus be reserved for those who require this enhanced degree of supervision, and that they are not meant simply as convenient accommodation for homeless offenders. They should provide a structured and supportive environment within which their residents can be supervised effectively. They are not secure, however, and so cannot provide the same degree of protection for the public as do most custodial establishments.

5.2.5 Requirements as to activities, etc.

A CRO may require an offender to report to a person specified in the order, at a place specified in the order (such as a centre run by the probation service or an associated agency such as NACRO), to participate in specified activities (PCC(S)A 2000, sch. 2, para. 2). This provision makes it possible to require the offender to participate in a variety of schemes and activities offered by the probation service. Alternatively, or in addition, the condition may require that the offender refrain from participating in specified activities (such as attending football matches, where the offending arose from violence at such events).

A requirement of participation in activities may not involve the offender for more than a total of 60 days. Before making such a requirement, the court must be satisfied that it is feasible to secure the offender's compliance (para. 2(2)) and that he can attend at times which do not interfere with work or school commitments, if applicable. The place specified in the order must be one approved by the relevant probation board as providing facilities suitable for persons subject to CROs (para. 2(5)) though, of course, persons who are not subject to CROs may be attending at the same time. In any case where an activity will involve a person other than the offender and the supervising officer, the consent of that person to the arrangement should be obtained. A requirement that the offender refrain from a particular activity may be imposed in respect of a certain day or days within the currency of the order, or extend for a portion of the order, or the whole of it (para. 2(1)(b)).

Where an offender has been convicted of a sexual offence (as defined in PCC(S)A 2000, s. 161(2): see **4.2.7**), the normal limit (60 days) for attendance for participation in specified activities under para. 2 does not apply. The duration may, in the case of such an offender, be for 'such greater number of days as may be specified in the direction' and thus may extend for the full duration of the CRO.

5.2.6 Requirement of attendance at community rehabilitation centre

The offender may be required, during the CRO, to attend at a community rehabilitation centre specified in the order (PCC(S)A 2000, sch. 2, para. 3). A 'community rehabilitation centre' is described in para. 3(8) as:

premises—
(a) at which non-residential facilities are provided for use in connection with the rehabilitation of offenders; and
(b) which are for the time being approved by the Secretary of State as providing facilities for persons subject to CROs.

Before making a requirement of attendance at a community rehabilitation centre, the court must consult a probation officer, ensure that arrangments can be made for the offender's attendance and that the manager of the centre agrees to the inclusion of the requirement (para. 3(2) and (3)). A requirement imposed under para. 3(1) may involve attendance at the centre for a maximum of 60 days during the course of the order, during which the offender must comply with the instructions of staff at the centre (para. 3(3)). Attendance arrangements must, so far as possible, avoid times when the offender would otherwise be at work or school.

Where an offender has been convicted of a sexual offence (as defined in PCC(S)A 2000, s. 161(2): see **4.2.7**), the normal limit (60 days) for attendance at a community rehabilitation centre under para. 3 does not apply. The duration may, in the case of such an offender, be for 'such greater number of days as may be specified in the direction' and thus may extend for the full duration of the CRO. It is clear that the purpose of this is to encourage the courts to deal with offenders convicted of the less serious sexual offences by closer supervision in the community, rather than by custody.

5.2.7 Requirement as to treatment for mental condition etc.

The imposition of a requirement of this kind is provided for in PCC(S)A 2000, sch. 2, para. 5. Community rehabilitation orders containing such a requirement are considered, together with other sentencing provisions for mentally disordered offenders, at **11.1**.

5.2.8 Requirements as to treatment for drug or alcohol dependency

Under PCC(S)A 2000, sch. 2, para. 6, a CRO may include a requirement of treatment for drug or alcohol dependency where the court is satisfied (para. 6(1)):

(a) that the offender is dependent on drugs or alcohol;

(b) that his dependency caused or contributed to the offence in respect of which the order is proposed to be made; and

(c) that his dependency is such as requires and may be susceptible to treatment.

A CRO is often seen as the appropriate sentence where an offender convicted of an offence of intermediate seriousness has exhibited a willingness to receive treatment for alcohol or drug abuse. Before such a requirement can be imposed the court must ensure that arrangements can be made for the treatment to be carried out, and the offender must express his willingness to comply with the requirement (para. 6(5)).

In these provisions 'dependency' is widely construed, and includes cases where the offender has 'a propensity towards the misuse of drugs or alcohol' (para. 6(9)). Treatment for the dependency must be of a kind specified in the order (para. 6(4)). It may continue for the whole period of the CRO or for such specific part of it as is required by the court (para. 6(3)). Clearly the treatment is the main purpose of the order, and the probation officer's normal supervision duties are relevant only insofar as is necessary for the purpose of revocation or amendment of the order (para. 6(6)). It would seem from the words 'caused or contributed to the offence' in para. 6(1) that the court is not confined in the use of these powers to cases where the offender has been convicted of an offence which was committed when the offender was affected by alcohol or drugs or which is otherwise directly related to alcohol or drugs. The powers could, for example, be used where an offender has committed theft or assault in order to obtain money to purchase a supply of alcohol or drugs, or has committed burglary or robbery in a chemist's shop in order to obtain drugs. Of course, in any of these cases, the court might properly regard the offence as being so serious that only a custodial sentence could be justified.

It should be noted that, with the nationwide introduction of drug treatment and testing orders, para. 6(2) provides that as soon as these orders become available in the local area they will supersede the power to order treatment for drug (not alcohol) dependency in that area.

5.2.9 Requirements as to drug abstinence, curfew and exclusion

When sections 49, 50 and 51 of the CJCSA 2000 are brought into force, the courts will be given additional powers to insert requirements into CROs. These are drug abstinence, curfew and exclusion requirements. Where certain conditions are made out, the court must include a drug abstinence requirement into a CRO.

(a) *Drug abstinence requirement*   Section 49 will amend subsection (2) of s. 42 of the PCC(S)A 2000 and place new subsections (2A) to (2F) into that section. These provisions will create a new power to insert a requirement into a CRO where:

(i)   the offender is aged 18 or over;

(ii)   is dependent on, or has a propensity to misuse, specified Class A drugs; and

(iii) where the misuse of such a drug caused or contributed to the offence.

If these three conditions are satisfied and, in addition, the offence with which the offender has been convicted is a 'trigger offence', then the court must include a drug abstinence requirement in the CRO. For the meaning of 'trigger offence', see the CJCSA 2000, sch. 6

and **5.7.1** below. Subsection (2D), however, provides that a drug abstinence requirement shall not be inserted into the CRO if either the CRO includes a requirement of treatment for alcohol or drug dependency under sch. 2, para. 6 of the PCC(S)A 2000 (see **5.2.8** above) or the CRO is part of a community sentence which includes a drug treatment and testing order.

(b)   *Curfew requirement*   Section 50 will add a new para. 7 to sch. 2 of the PCC(S)A 2000, so as to permit a court to insert into a CRO a requirement that the offender remain, for periods specified in the order, at a place so specified (a curfew requirement). In most cases this is likely to involve electronic monitoring (see **5.5.5**). The court cannot insert such a condition if the CRO forms part of a community sentence which includes a curfew order.

(c)   *Exclusion requirement*   Section 51 will add a new para. 8 to sch. 2 of the PCC(S)A 2000, so as to permit a court to insert a CRO a requirement prohibiting the offender from entering a place specified in the requirement for a period so specified of not more than two years (an exclusion requirement). In most cases this is likely to involve electronic monitoring (see **5.5.5**). The court cannot insert such a condition if the CRO forms part of a community sentence which includes an exclusion order.

5.2.10   Combining community rehabilitation orders with other sentences or orders

It is not permissible to combine a CRO with a sentence of immediate custody, whether in respect of the same offence or for different offences sentenced on the same occasion (*Mullervy* (1986) 8 Cr App R (S) 41 and *Duporte* (1989) 11 Cr App R (S) 116). It is also impermissible to combine a CRO with a suspended sentence (PCC(S)A 2000, s. 118(6)); the suspended sentence supervision order (see **4.6.6**) provides a means of mixing a suspended sentence with an element of supervision. A CRO may be combined with a fine when sentencing for a single offence, or when sentencing for different offences sentenced on the same occasion. A CRO may not be combined with a community punishment order when sentencing for a single offence (s. 35(2)), except where imposed in a specified mix to form a community punishment and rehabilitation order. Nor can a CRO and a CPO be imposed for different offences which are sentenced on the same occasion (*Gilding* v *DPP* (1998) *The Times*, 20 May 1998). A CRO may, however, be combined with a curfew order whether in respect of the same offence or different offences sentenced on the same occasion. A CRO may not be be combined with a conditional discharge or an absolute discharge when sentencing for a single offence, since a discharge is appropriate only when 'it is inexpedient to inflict punishment' (s. 12(1)) but a CRO and a discharge may be used for sentencing different offences on the same occasion.

A CRO may be combined with a compensation order or an order for costs (s. 148(2)), or an order for disqualification from driving (RTOA 1988, s. 46(1)). It may also be combined with an order for deportation (Immigration Act 1971, s. 6(3)), or an exclusion order in respect of licensed premises (Licensed Premises (Exclusion of Certain Persons) Act 1980, s. 1(2)). A CRO may be combined with an order for deprivation of property under the PCC(S)A 2000, s. 143 or a restitution order under s. 148.

When combining sentencing measures, regard should always be had to s. 158(2) which states that 'nothing shall prevent a court from mitigating any penalty included in an offender's sentence by taking into account any other penalty included in that sentence'. It may also be useful to refer to the White Paper (Home Office, 1990), in which it was stated that 'For most offenders only one of these orders will be necessary, or justified by the seriousness of their offences. For more serious offenders, however, more than one community penalty could be imposed.'

5.2.11 Early termination of CRO

According to the Home Office National Standards, early termination of a CRO should be considered whenever the offender has made good progress in achieving the objectives set out for the order, and where there is not considered to be a significant risk of reoffending and/or of serious harm to the public. An application for early termination should not normally be sought before half-way through the term of the order, but such action should be considered by the time two-thirds of the term has elapsed, unless there are clear reasons for not doing so. There are two possible procedures here.

The first is where an application is made to a magistrates' court or the Crown Court (whichever made the CRO) by the offender with the support of the supervising officer, under sch. 3, para. 10 or 11. During the application the officer will present a report outlining the offender's good progress under the order. It is desirable, though not apparently essential, that the offender be present at this time. The magistrates' court, if it made the order, and having taken into account the extent to which the offender has complied with the order, may now decide to revoke it (para. 10). If the Crown Court made the order, it follows a parallel procedure (para. 11).

The second procedure is under sch. 3, para. 12, where application is made to the court which imposed the CRO for the CRO to be discharged and for a conditional discharge to be substituted. Application under this section is appropriate where it is felt that the CRO can serve no further useful purpose but where it is too early in the term of the order to seek revocation. Application cannot be made while any appeal against the CRO is pending (para. 12(7)). Under para. 12 the offender is not required to attend court provided that the supervising officer can assure the court that the offender consents to the application being made and understands what the effect of the order will be. A person in respect of whom an order under para. 12 has been made is to be treated, for so long as the conditional discharge continues, in all respects (and especially for the purposes of commission of a further offence) as if the original order had been a conditional discharge and not a CRO. The reason for this is that the powers of the court when dealing with a breach of a conditional discharge are different from those when dealing with revocation of a CRO after commission of a further offence. The conditional discharge expires at the time when the CRO would otherwise have expired (para. 12(4)). Presumably the discharge counts as a 'conviction' only for limited purposes (PCC(S)A 2000, s. 14(1); see **7.1.4**).

5.3 COMMUNITY PUNISHMENT ORDERS

5.3.1 Power to make a community punishment order

With effect from April 2001, the 'community service order' has been re-named the 'community punishment order' (CPO) (CJCSA 2000, s. 44).

A CPO is a 'community order' and the court cannot impose one unless the conditions which apply to the passing of a community order are first satisfied. In particular, by PCC(S)A 2000, s. 35(1), the court must be satisfied that the offence committed is serious enough to warrant a community order (see **5.1**).

Community service orders were introduced into English law in 1972. The relevant powers of the courts to pass CPOs are now to be found in the PCC(S)A 2000, s. 46. A CPO is an order that requires the offender to perform unpaid work in the community. Its main purposes, according to the Home Office National Standards are to 're-integrate the offender into the community through (i) positive and demanding work, keeping to disciplined requirements, and (ii) reparation to the community by undertaking socially useful work which, if possible, makes good damage done by offending'. The work should be physically, emotionally or mentally demanding. It should be noted that the court does not have power to order that the offender shall perform community service for any particular victim injured by his offence. Reparation here is meant in the sense of reparation to society generally for the offence committed. Appropriate work may include the amelioration of damage which has been criminally caused, e.g. by the removal of grafitti from walls.

Between 1988 and 1999 the proportionate use made by the courts of CPOs for sentencing for indictable offences has remained steady across most of the main categories of offending. Increased use of CPOs in burglary cases during the early 1990s has since tailed off. The percentage change in the use of CPOs for indictable offences between 1988 and 1998, for the main categories of offending is as follows:

		1988	1999
(1)	violence against the person	7 per cent	15 per cent
(2)	sexual offences	1 per cent	2 per cent
(3)	burglary	13 per cent	9 per cent
(4)	robbery	5 per cent	4 per cent
(5)	theft and handling	8 per cent	8 per cent
(6)	fraud and forgery	7 per cent	18 per cent
(7)	criminal damage	7 per cent	8 per cent
(8)	drug offences	3 per cent	6 per cent
(9)	motoring offences	12 per cent	10 per cent
	All offending	8 per cent	9 per cent

This represents an almost unchanged level of use over that period with 30,400 offenders being so sentenced in 1988 and 30,500 in 1999. The CPO is used in fewer cases than the CRO (38,900 in 1999), but in more cases than the other community orders put together.

A CPO may be made by the Crown Court, by an adult magistrates' court or by a youth court. The offender must be aged 16 or over. There is no upper age limit, but in practice this measure tends to be used mainly for offenders in their late teens or twenties. The offender must have committed an offence which is punishable with imprisonment in the case of an adult. The total number of hours to be worked must be specified in the order, and must be between 40 and 240 hours. The number of hours ordered by the court should reflect primarily the seriousness of the offence committed. Normally, according to the Home Office National Standard, the first work session should be under way within ten days of the making of the order. A minimum work rate of five hours per week should be achieved throughout the order, but normally no more than 21 hours should be worked in any one week. Work must be completed within the period of 12 months from the date of the order but, unless revoked, the order remains in force until all the hours are in fact completed. The 12-month period may be extended by application to the court under PCC(S)A 2000, sch. 3, para. 22. If the offender is in employment the CPO must be arranged for evenings or weekends or such other times as do not clash with the offender's working hours. If the offender is unemployed, the order should not conflict with his or her entitlement to welfare benefits, and should not prevent the offender from being available to seek or take up employment.

The court should not normally impose a community punishment order without first obtaining a pre-sentence report (s. 36(4) and **5.1**).

When s. 49 of the CJPOA 2000 is brought into force, there will be a new power to insert a drug abstinence requirement into a CPO where:

(a)   the offender is aged 18 or over;

(b)   is dependent on, or has a propensity to misuse, specified Class A drugs; and

(c)   where the misuse of such a drug caused or contributed to the offence.

If these three conditions are satisfied and, in addition, the offence with which the offender has been convicted is a 'trigger offence', then the court must include a drug abstinence requirement in the CPO. For the meaning of 'trigger offence', see the CJCSA 2000, sch. 6 and **5.7.1** below. It is further provided, however, that such a requirement shall not be included in a CPO if the CPO forms part of a community sentence which includes a drug treatment and resting order or a drug abstinence order.

Before making the order the court must be satisfied that the offender is a suitable person to perform a CPO (for example, that he is physically fit enough to do so) and that there is work available locally. Formerly there was a legal requirement that the offender must consent before the order was made, but that requirement was abolished by the C(S)A 1997, s. 38, the government arguing that the requirement was 'anomalous . . . and a derogation from the authority of the court' (Consultation Document, *Strengthening Punishment in the Community* (1995)). There were two reasons for the consent requirement. One was that to pass a CPO when an offender is not motivated to comply with it merely stores up trouble for the future. The second was that without the requirement of consent it was thought that the CPO could infringe the ECHR, Article 4(2) which states that 'No one shall be required to perform forced or compulsory labour'. Although Article 4(3) goes on to exempt work 'required to be done in the ordinary course of detention . . . or during conditional release from such detention', it does not exempt work done under sentence in the community. According to its Consultation Document (1995) the government does not believe that removal of the requirement of consent will be regarded as a breach of the Article since 'a community sentence does not involve detention and is, therefore, less restrictive' than work required of a sentenced prisoner.

The CPO must specify the petty sessions area in which the offender lives. The court must explain to the offender in open court and in ordinary language the purpose and effect of the CPO, the consequences of failure to comply with it and the fact that the court has power to review the order subsequently on the application of either the offender or the responsible officer (s. 46(9) and (10)). The court must then give copies of the order to the probation officer and the offender. Non-compliance with these provisions does not, apparently, invalidate the order. In *Walsh* v *Barlow* [1985] 1 WLR 90 it was argued by the offender, unsuccessfully, that a CPO imposed upon him was ineffective, since no copy of it had been delivered to him. The Court of Appeal held that such delivery was not a prerequisite of the coming into force of the order.

5.3.2   Community punishment order arrangements

Community punishment orders are administered by the probation service. That service is reponsible for all the administrative arrangements, including liaison with a wide range of local groups to which offenders on CPOs are attached from time to time. For this purpose many probation service areas have a designated unit or a number of officers organised into the community punishment order team. The work itself may be directed by supervisors employed by the probation service, or by a local voluntary or public body. Some tasks involve offenders working alongside volunteers. The Home Office National Standards require that the probation service should arrange a variety of community punishment order work placements, which should be 'demanding in the sense of being physically, emotionally or intellectually taxing, of benefit to the community and, if possible, personally fulfilling for offenders and designed to secure public support for the supervision of offenders in the community'. The sort of work available varies considerably but examples include helping in outdoor conservation or reclamation projects, refurbishing community facilities, building adventure playgrounds, making toys which are then sold to raise money for charity, decorating flats and houses for the elderly or handicapped, and helping disabled people. Work done under a CPO should not be of a type which a business might be interested in carrying out on a paid basis; community punishment orders must not be permitted to undercut ordinary commercial enterprise. Community punishment orders are imposed 'as punishment' not 'for punishment', so it is not the intention that the work 'should deliberately be made unpleasant in the expectation that this will deter'. The probation service is also made responsible by the National Standards for ensuring that the risk to the public of placing offenders on CPOs is minimised. Work may be undertaken in individual placements, which should be designed to emphasise to the offender his or her own personal responsibility, or group placements which allow offenders to take part in a team project.

The probation service is responsible for enforcing the order and securing the offender's compliance with its terms. An offender's failure to comply with the terms of the order must be investigated by the probation officer. If there is no adequate explanation for the failure to comply, the incident must be recorded. According to the National Standards, action to breach the order may be taken after one unacceptable failure but, if it is not taken on that occasion, the offender will receive a warning letter and be permitted only one warning in the 12-month period. The offender is not actually under supervision during the period of the order, but there will be times where personal contact between the probation service and the offender is appropriate in order to deal with problems arising during the time of the order and to help the offender maintain a commitment to completion of the order. By s. 47(1), the offender is required to keep in touch with the relevant probation officer and notify him of any change of address. A failure to do so would be a failure to comply with the order. If an offender requires a more formal element of supervision in addition to the CPO, this may be achieved by the court passing a community punishment and rehabilitation order.

5.3.3 Concurrent and consecutive community punishment orders

Section 46(8) of the PCC(S)A 2000 allows for the possibility of the court passing CPOs in respect of two or more offences, and specifying that those orders shall either run concurrently with, or consecutively to, each other. It seems clear that the principles underlying the choice between concurrent and consecutive sentencing are the same as those which inform the choice between concurrent and consecutive custodial sentencing (see **4.4.4**). Section 46(8) also requires that the total number of work on the CPO to be completed by the offender must not exceed the maximum which could be imposed for a single offence, which is 240. This provision has direct application where the court is imposing two community service orders on the same occasion. In *Siha* (1992) 13 Cr App R (S) 588 the Court of Appeal said that while s. 46(8) did not actually apply to the case where an offender is already serving a CPO and subsequently has a further CPO imposed upon him, sentencers imposing a second CPO on an offender in such circumstances should remember that Parliament had prescribed 240 hours as the maximum to be imposed on a single occasion. In *Anderson* (1989) 11 Cr App R (S) 147 it was made clear that it was the total number of hours imposed on the offender (rather than the number of hours which remained to be served) which must not exceed 240.

5.3.4 Combining community punishment orders with other sentences or orders

A CPO should not be imposed on the same occasion as an immediate custodial sentence, whether the sentences relate to different counts or to separate indictments (*Starie* (1979) 69 Cr App R 239) and a CPO should not be combined with a suspended sentence of imprisonment (*Ray* (1984) 6 Cr App R (S) 26). A CPO may be combined with a fine. A CPO and a CRO may not be combined for a single offence except in the form of a CPRO (s. 35(2)). Nor can a CPO and a CRO be imposed for different offences sentenced on the same occasion (*Gilding* v *DPP* (1998) *The Times*, 20 May 1998). It is possible to combine a CPO with a curfew order. It is clear from s. 148(2) that a CPO may be combined with an order for costs, a disqualification of any kind imposed on the offender, a compensation order or a forfeiture order made under s. 143. A CPO cannot be combined with an absolute or conditional discharge when sentencing for a single offence, since a discharge can be imposed only where 'it is inexpedient to inflict punishment' (s. 12), but these two measures may, of course, be used for sentencing different offences on the same occasion.

When combining sentencing measures regard should always be had to s. 158(2), which states that 'nothing shall prevent a court from mitigating any penalty included in an offender's sentence by taking into account any other penalty included in that sentence'. Regard may also be had in this context to the White Paper (Home Office, 1990), where it was stated that 'For most offenders, only one of these orders will be necessary, or justified by the seriousness of their offences. For more serious offenders, however, more than one community penalty could be imposed.'

5.3.5 Community punishment orders: sentencing principles

The Court of Appeal has endorsed the use of CPOs for some younger offenders who have committed offences which lie close to the custody threshold, such as non-residential burglary. In *Brown* (1981) 3 Cr App R (S) 294 a CPO was said to be 'tailor-made' for a 19-year-old offender with no previous convictions who, in breach of trust, and together with a co-defendant, had committed burglary of his employer's premises, with loss of goods to the value of £2,850. In *Lawrence* (1982) 4 Cr App R (S) 69 the offender, together with three others, had taken a car without authority and driven to another town. There they had broken the window of a shop and stolen television sets, video recorders and tape recorders. The Court of Appeal took account of a period of five years without convictions which preceded the current offences, and the fact that the offender was 'a man who really has all the marks of someone who, at this stage in his life, is capable of settling down and remaining a good and useful member of the community'. The offender was 'ideally suited' to a CPO of 190 hours, though this was varied to 150 hours to take account of time which he had already spent in custody. There are few recent decisions on the use of CPOs in burglary cases. In *Tetteh* (1994) 15 Cr App R (S) 46 the offender was seen coming out of the cellar at a YMCA club, where the spirits store was found to have been broken open. Nothing had been stolen.

Despite the defendant's poor record the Court of Appeal thought that this case did not cross the custody threshold and that a CPO would have been appropriate. A similar case is *Carlton* (1994) 15 Cr App R (S) 335. Where the property involved is a house, rather than a factory, office or shop, the offence will normally be regarded by the courts as being above the custody threshold (for the relevant guideline case, see **12.4.5**). A CPO will then only be appropriate where the offender has a clean record, has played a peripheral role, or where there is other substantial mitigation. One example is *Mole* [1991] Crim LR 220, where the offender, a youth of 17 with no previous convictions, acted as lookout while two others ransacked a house and stole valuables. A sentence of three months' detention in a young offender institution was quashed and a CPO for 100 hours was substituted. See also *Suker* (1990) 12 Cr App R (S) 290, where the 19-year-old offender, affected by drink and looking for money to pay his taxi fare home, attempted to climb through the bathroom window of a house in the early hours of the morning and was detained by the householder.

Occasionally a CPO has been upheld for less serious offences of violence. An example is *McDiarmid* (1980) 2 Cr App R (S) 130, where an offender, aged 18 and of previous good character, threw a beer glass at a man in the course of a disturbance in a public house. A custodial sentence was varied to a CPO of 75 hours by the Court of Appeal. A CPO is not a suitable sentence for offences involving serious violence, however. In *A-G's Reference (No. 49 of 1996)* [1997] 2 Cr App R (S) 144, the offender pleaded guilty to causing grievous bodily harm with intent after attacking a man in the street with a bottle and then punching and kicking him on the ground. The Court of Appeal said that a CPO was unduly lenient and varied it to nine months' imprisonment. Another example is *A-G's Reference (No. 30 of 1993)* (1995) 16 Cr App R (S) 318, where the offender, a man with a bad record for violence, had struck a man in the face with a pool cue and had then tried to kick him when he fell to the ground. After having been convicted of wounding with intent the sentence was a CPO for 240 hours together with a compensation order. The Court of Appeal said that the sentence would 'undermine public confidence in the administration of justice' and increased it to 18 months' imprisonment. A CPO of 150 hours imposed for robbery in a contested case was held to be unduly lenient in *A-G's Reference (No. 39 of 1996)* [1997] 1 Cr App R (S) 355. The offender and a co-defendant had encountered a youth riding a mountain bike. They kicked and punched the victim several times and took the bike, abandoning it at the side of the road shortly afterwards. The Court of Appeal increased the sentence to 12 months' imprisonment. A CPO was also said to be wrong in *A-G's Reference (No. 6 of 1994)* (1995) 16 Cr App R (S) 343, where robbery of an 18-year-old victim was committed at night by threatening to use a knife. A sentence of 18 months' imprisonment was substituted.

Community punishment orders may be appropriate in a wide range of property crimes. It is this group which seems to form the main catchment area for CPO sentencing, whether or not offenders have previous convictions. In *Graham* (1988) 10 Cr App R (S) 352 the offender continued to draw unemployment benefit for 12 months after gaining employment. The total sum involved was over £1,500, and 120 hours' CPO was said to be appropriate. In a case where offenders sprayed paint on carriages at a London Underground depot (*Ferreira* (1988) 10 Cr App R (S) 343) the Court of Appeal replaced custodial sentences with a CPO of 120 hours, Farquharson J commenting that the CPO was 'designed' for such a case. A sentence of 60 hours' CPO was said to be correct in *Hamilton* (1988) 10 Cr App R (S) 383, where the offender stole goods and property worth £180 and the same sentence was approved in *Zaman* (1992) 12 Cr App R (S) 657, where a 19-year-old stole a radio from a car. In *Small* (1993) 14 Cr App R (S) 405 the 19-year-old offender pleaded guilty to three counts of theft, committed while he was employed as operations manager by a firm supplying pizzas. He failed to pay into the bank three sums of money totalling just over £1,000. The sentencer passed a sentence of three months' detention in a young offender institution but the Court of Appeal, bearing in mind the offender's youth and inexperience, his good record and the fact that, in the view of the court, too much responsibility had been placed on him at work without adequate supervision, varied the sentence to a CPO.

A CPO may be appropriate for some road traffic offences. In *Eynon* (1988) 10 Cr App R (S) 437 the offender, a man of good record, pleaded guilty to dangerous driving after his car, pursued by a police car, mounted a pavement and nearly knocked down pedestrians. A sentence of 180 hours' CPO, together with disqualification from driving and orders for compensation and costs, was upheld. The case may be contrasted with *A-G's Reference (No. 36 of 1994)* (1995) 16 Cr App R (S) 723 where a CPO of 240 hours together with disqualification from driving for three years was imposed on a goods driver, a man with a clean record, for causing death by careless driving having consumed alcohol above the prescribed limit. The defendant's vehicle had mounted a verge at the side of a dual carriageway after dark and had struck and killed a young man walking on the verge. Sentence was varied to two years' imprisonment.

5.4 COMMUNITY PUNISHMENT AND REHABILITATION ORDERS

With effect from April 2001, the combination order has been re-named the community punishment and rehabilitation order (CPRO) (CJCSA 2000, s. 45.) By PCC(S)A 2000, s. 51, magistrates' courts and the Crown Court have power to pass a CPRO on an offender who is of or over the age of 16 in any case where the offence is punishable with imprisonment. This sentence is a mix between a CRO and a CPO. A CPRO is a 'community order', and the court cannot impose one unless the conditions which apply to the passing of a community order are satisfied. In particular, by s. 35(1), the court must be satisfied that the offence is serious enough to warrant the passing of a community order (see **5.1**).

The combination order was introduced by the 1991 Act. The White Paper (Home Office, 1990) suggested that the order 'would enable the courts to introduce an element of reparation but, at the same time, to provide the probation service with an opportunity to work with offenders, to reduce the likelihood of future offending'.

The courts have made good use of this sentencing option, with CPROs as sentences for indictable offences increasing sharply from 900 cases in 1992 (the first year in which the measure was available to the courts) to over 6,000 cases in 1993 and 12,400 in 1999. This total is still small, however, compared with CROs and CPOs standing alone.

5.4.1 Power to make a community punishment and rehabilitation order

The sentence is a mix of a CPO and a CRO. The legislation provides that the supervision element shall be dealt with in law as if it were a CRO and the community work element as if it were a CPO (PCC(S)A 2000, s. 51(4)). The supervision element within the order may last for a period of between one year and three years (as compared to between six months and three years for a CRO) and the community work element of the order must require the completion of between 40 and 100 hours (as compared to between 40 and 240 hours for a CPO standing alone). The court may also insert into the CPRO any of the additional requirements provided for in sch. 2 to the 2000 Act, which might be added to a CRO standing alone, though this must be subject to the proviso that these requirements are not inconsistent with the performance of the community work part of the order. For these requirements see **5.2.3**.

Unlike a CRO, a CPRO may be imposed only in a case where the offender has been convicted of an offence punishable with imprisonment. The court should normally consider a pre-sentence report before passing a combination order (PCC(S)A 2000, s. 36(4) and **5.1**). Formerly, the offender's consent was required before a CPRO could be imposed, since such consent was needed before either a CPO or a CRO could be made. The consent requirement for those sentences was abolished by the C(S)A 1997, s. 38. Section 35(2) states that 'a community sentence shall not consist of or include both a CRO and a CPO'. The effect of this is to ensure that the supervision and work elements can be mixed together only in the form of a CPRO.

5.4.2 Combining community punishment and rehabilitation orders with other sentences or orders

In principle, since a CPRO is itself a complex order which may involve a range of requirements, it is submitted that it will generally be undesirable to combine it with other sentences or orders. There seems little doubt that it should not be mixed with custody, whether immediate or suspended. It would seem to be illogical to mix it with a CRO or a CPO. It can be assumed that it could be mixed with a fine, with a compensation order, with a disqualification or with an order for forfeiture, since either CPO or a CRO standing alone may be so mixed. A CPRO could be mixed with a curfew order. A CPRO may not be combined with a conditional discharge or an absolute discharge when sentencing for the same offence, since a discharge is appropriate only where 'it is inexpedient to inflict punishment' (PCC(S)A 2000, s. 12(1)), but a CPRO and a discharge may be used for sentencing different offences on the same occasion.

When combining sentencing measures regard should always be had to s. 158(2) which states that 'nothing shall prevent a court from mitigating any penalty included in an offender's sentence by taking into account any other penalty included in that sentence'. Regard may also be had in this context to the White Paper (Home Office, 1990), where it was stated that 'For most offenders, only one of these orders will be necessary, or justified by the seriousness of their offences. For more serious offenders, however, more than one community penalty could be imposed.'

5.4.3 Community punishment and rehabilitation order: sentencing principles

The aim of this sentence is to provide a demanding community sentence to cater for some offenders who otherwise would receive immediate custody. The White Paper (Home Office, 1990) specifically mentioned 'persistent property offenders . . . sentenced for burglary, theft, handling, fraud and forgery [who] have three or more previous convictions'. According to PCC(S)A 2000, s. 51(3), a CPRO should be imposed where it is desirable in the interests of 'securing the rehabilitation of the offender' or 'protecting the public from harm from him or preventing the commission by him of further offences'. These are the same statutory objectives as for a CRO (s. 41(1)). It would seem that a CPRO is most likely to be regarded as suitable for an offender who has committed an offence which is amongst the most serious for which a community sentence may be imposed; has clearly identified areas of need that have contributed to the offending and which can be dealt with by supervision; and has a realistic prospect of completing such an order, including both the supervision and community work elements.

Offenders who might not be regarded as suitable for a CPRO would be those whose lifestyle is particularly chaotic (as a result of drug or alcohol addiction, for example) and who might have particular difficulty in keeping to a programme of community work. Conversely, also excluded might be offenders with well ordered lifestyles who have little need of, or little prospect of responding to, supervision. Orders which contain additional requirements within the supervision element are likely to be particularly onerous, and are likely to prove to be difficult to complete, especially for younger offenders.

The National Standards (2000) stress that for a CPRO the standards for both the CRO and the CPO apply i.e. a minimum of 12 supervision appointments, one work assessment and 11 work sessions to be arranged in the first 12 weeks. The two elements in the sentence must be managed together, and any unacceptable absences from either element will be treated cumulatively.

There is little guidance from the Court of Appeal on the appropriate use of the CPRO. Such a sentence was held to have been an unduly lenient sentence for robbery by mugging in *A-G's Reference (No. 74 of 1995)* [1996] 2 Cr App R (S) 436. The offender and a co-defendant, wearing overalls and balaclavas, attacked the 17-year-old victim and stole his pay packet. The Court of Appeal increased the sentence to 12 months' detention in a young offender institution. Another case of robbery where the Court of Appeal varied a CPRO to a custodial sentence is *A-G's Reference (No. 2 of 1994)* (1995) 16 Cr App R (S) 117.

5.4.4 Early termination of community punishment and rehabilitation order

The procedures for application for early termination of a CPRO are the same as those for a CRO, for which see **5.2.10**. Practice seems to be that early termination may be considered only after completion of the community work element of the order, and then in accordance with the criteria for early termination of CROs.

5.5 CURFEW ORDERS

By PCC(S)A 2000, s. 37, magistrates' courts and the Crown Court have power to impose a curfew order on an offender of any age who is convicted of any offence except murder or an offence attracting a prescribed custodial sentence under ss. 109–111 of the 2000 Act. A curfew order is a 'community order' and the court is not able to impose a curfew order unless the conditions relating to the passing of a community order are satisfied. In particular, by s. 35(1), the court will have to be satisfied that the offence committed is serious enough to warrant the passing of a community order (see **5.1**). A curfew order should not be confused with the power to attach a curfew condition to the grant of bail; a curfew order is a final disposal, not a measure pending trial or sentence. It should also be distinguished from home detention curfew, which may form part of an offender's early release arrangements from custody.

The history of curfew orders has been closely associated with the use of electronic monitoring. Although the powers to impose curfew orders date from the CJA 1991, they were not brought into force until January 1995, by the CJPOA 1994. That Act allowed for the introduction of pilot trials on the use of curfew orders enforced by electronic monitoring, on an area-by-area basis, before being made available nationwide from 2000. In 1999 900 offenders dealt with for indictable offences were given a curfew order.

5.5.1 Power to impose a curfew order

A curfew order may be imposed by the Crown Court, by an adult magistrates' court or by a youth court on an offender who is convicted of any offence, subject only to the crime of murder and the three prescribed custodial sentences under ss. 109–111 of the 2000 Act. A previous restriction on the use of curfew orders to offenders aged 16 or over was removed by the C(S)A 1997, s. 43, and the order is now also available for offenders aged from 10 to 15 inclusive. The curfew order may specify different places of curfew or different periods of curfew on different days, but the curfew order cannot last for longer than six months from the date of the making of the order or, in the case of an offender under the age of 16, three months from the date of the order (s. 37(3) and (4)). It must not involve curfew periods of less than two hours' duration, or more than twelve hours' duration, in any one day during that period (s. 37(3)). The curfew arrangements must not, so far as possible, interfere with the times when the offender attends work or school, or conflict with the requirements of any other community order to which he may be subject (s. 37(5)). The order must name a person who is to be responsible for monitoring the offender's whereabouts during the periods of curfew (s. 37(6)).

The court must explain to the offender in ordinary language the effect of the order and the consequences of failure to comply with its requirements (s. 37(10)). A former require-ment that the offender must consent before a curfew order could be imposed was removed by the C(S)A 1997, s. 38. The court must have information about the place or places to be specified in the order, including information about the attitudes of persons likely to be affected by the enforced presence there of the offender under curfew (s. 37(8)) and in the case of an offender aged under 16 the court is required to obtain additional information about the young offender's family circumstances and the likely effect of such an order on those circumstances (s. 37(9)). The obtaining of a pre-sentence report is not normally required before a curfew order is passed (see **5.1**) but, since the court must have the information referred to in s. 37(8) and (9) the obtaining of such a report is likely to be regarded as good sentencing practice.

The government explained in the White Paper (Home Office, 1990) that it was not the purpose of curfew orders to keep people at home for most of the day. The aim is:

> to enable them to go to work, to attend training courses or probation centres, to carry out community service or to receive treatment for drug abuse. Curfews could be helpful in reducing some forms of crime, thefts of and from cars, pub brawls and other types of disorder. A curfew order could be used to keep people away from particular places, such as shopping centres or pubs, or to keep them at home in the evenings or at weekends.

A subsequent White Paper (Home Office, 1996a) noted that 'the curfew order is a significant restriction on liberty with the courts empowered to sentence for up to 2,000 hours over a period of six months'.

It may be noted in this context that courts currently have other powers to prevent offenders from frequenting specified places, such as licensed premises (see **10.4**), or football matches (see **10.5**). More specifically in relation to juveniles a 'night restriction order' (a form of curfew) may be included as a condition of a supervision order (see **5.11.4**), though these conditions are little used in practice.

5.5.2   Combining a curfew order with other sentences or orders

It seems clear from the observations in the White Paper cited in the last paragraph that the curfew order can operate in tandem with other community orders, such as a CRO or a CPO, although it can stand on its own. If a curfew order is being considered as part of a package of measures, the court should always remember that the overall effect should be to pass a total sentence which is proportionate to the seriousness of the offence committed. When combining sentencing measures, PCC(S)A 2000, s. 158(2) states that 'nothing shall prevent a court from mitigating any penalty included in an offender's sentence by taking into account any other penalty included in that sentence'. A curfew order can be combined with a fine, a compensation order, an order for disqualification from driving or an order for forfeiture. In practice, perhaps because of the difficulties of ensuring compliance with a curfew, such orders routinely carry a requirement of electronic monitoring (see **5.5.3**).

It can safely be assumed that a curfew order could not be combined with an immediate custodial sentence and that the restrictions upon the use of suspended imprisonment means that a combination with it is unlikely. A curfew order could not be combined with an absolute or conditional discharge since a discharge cannot be combined with a punitive measure for the same offence (s. 12), though there would be nothing to prevent a curfew order being imposed in respect of one offence and a discharge in respect of another offence sentenced on the same occasion.

The general provisions as to mitigation (s. 158(1)) and the White Paper's comments on combining community sentences (see **5.4.2**) should be borne in mind in addition to the matters mentioned above.

5.5.3 Electronic monitoring

A curfew order imposed under s. 37 may include requirements for securing the electronic monitoring of the offender's whereabouts during the curfew periods specified in the order. Electronic monitoring is not a sentence in its own right, but solely a means of enforcing a curfew order which is imposed under s. 37. The difficulties of ensuring compliance with a curfew order without including a condition of electronic monitoring were referred to above.

The issue of electronic monitoring of offenders has attracted a good deal of interest. The Home Office ran three experimental schemes of electronic monitoring during 1990, though it was then used as a means of reinforcing bail conditions rather than as part of the sentencing exercise. Further trials, to test the electronic monitoring of curfew orders, ran in pilot areas from 1995, in order to test further the technical arrangements and costs of general introduction of the measure. The government has said in its White Paper, *Protecting the Public* (Home Office, 1996a) that it is convinced of the:

> value of electronic monitoring as a highly flexible, restrictive community sentence with a part to play in punishing offenders and reducing crime . . . The technology has so far proved successful in monitoring offenders whom the courts want off the streets, and has ensured that the courts' sentences cannot be evaded without serious consequences. The slightest breach of a curfew order or attempt to tamper with the equipment is detected, and investigated by the contractors immediately. No violations are ignored, with warnings given for the most minor infringement. Offenders who continue not to comply are returned to court.

This statement misleads in suggesting that electronic monitoring is in itself a sentence — as we have seen, it is not.

At the time of writing, electronic monitoring is available to the courts only in respect of curfew orders. The relevant powers are to be found in the PCC(S)A 2000, s. 38. When s. 52 of the CJCSA 2000 is brought into force, s. 38 will be repealed and a new s. 36B will be inserted into the PCC(S)A 2000. This will extend the power to order electronic monitoring to offenders who are given any community order, or any combination of community orders. It will then become possible to use electronic monitoring as a means of ensuring complicance with a curfew order, an exclusion order, CRO, a CPO, a CPRO, a drug treatment and testing order, a drug abstinence order, an attendance centre, a supervision order, or an action plan order.

5.6 DRUG TREATMENT AND TESTING ORDERS

Sections 52–58 of the PCC(S)A 2000 provide for the drug treatment and testing order, a community sentence originally introduced on a pilot basis by the CDA 1998. The DTTO is a 'community order', and the court can not impose such an order unless the conditions relating to the passing of a community order are satisfied. In particular, by s. 35(1) the court will have to be satisfied that the offence committed is serious enough to warrant the passing of a community order (see **5.1**). The court should not normally impose a DTTO without first obtaining a pre-sentence report (s. 36(4)).

5.6.1 Power to impose a drug treatment and testing order

A DTTO may be imposed by the Crown Court, by an adult magistrates' court or a youth court on an offender aged 16 or over who is convicted of any offence, subject only to the crime of murder and to the three presumptive custodial sentences under ss. 109–111 of the 2000 Act. The court may, by s. 52(3) make such an order where it is satisfied:

(a) that [the offender] is dependent on or has a propensity to misuse drugs; and

(b) that his dependency or propensity is such as requires and may be susceptible to treatment.

For the purposes of s. 52(3) the court may require the offender to provide samples, in order to establish whether the offender has any drug in his body. This requirement cannot be made unless the offender expresses his willingness to comply with it (s. 52(4)). Before making a DTTO the court must explain to the offender in ordinary language the effect of the order and the consequences of failure to comply with its requirements (s. 52(6)), and the order itself cannot be made unless the offender expresses his willingness to comply with it. Copies of the order must be provided for the offender, the person who will provide the treatment under the order and the probation officer (s. 57(1)). It is unlikely, however, that non-compliance with this last requirement would be fatal to the order: see *Walsh* v *Barlow* [19851 1 WLR 90, considered at **5.3.1**. The order will have effect for a period specified in the order of not less than six months nor more than three years (s. 52(1)).

The DTTO has two elements to it. The first is the 'treatment requirement', which is that the offender should, during the whole time of the order undergo treatment with a view to tackling the offender's dependency on, or propensity to misuse, drugs. Such treatment may be as a resident at a place specified in the order, such as a hospital or clinic, or as an out-patient (s. 53(2)). The second element is the 'testing requirement', which is the provision of further regular samples by the offender during the course of the order (s. 53(4)). During the order the offender will be under the supervision of a probation officer (s. 54(2)). The offender is required to keep in regular contact with the probation officer and to provide the officer with the results of the tests carried out on the samples which the offender has supplied, but supervision is carried out by the officer only to the extent necessary to enable reports on the offender's progress to be made to the court, and to deal with any questions of amendment or revocation of the order which may arise (s. 54(5)).

Section 54(6) makes the important and novel requirement that periodic reviews of an offender's progress under a DTTO be made by the court at intervals of not less than one month. These reviews, at least initially, will involve the offender's attendance at a 'review hearing' in court, at which the offender's test results, the supervising officer's report on his progress, and the views of the person providing the treatment will be considered by the court (s. 54(6)). If, at a review hearing, it appears that the offender's progress is satisfactory, subsequent reviews may be carried out by the court without a full review hearing (in the case of the Crown Court, by a judge, and in the case of a magistrates' court, by a justice of the peace) but, if progress subsequently becomes unsatisfactory, a further review hearing in court must be convened (s. 55(7)). At the review hearing the court may revoke the order and resentence the offender, giving credit for any period of the order which has been successfully completed (s. 55(4)) or, with the agreement of the offender, amend any requirement or provision of the order, but not so as to make the length of the order less than six months or more than three years. Any amendment to the treatment or testing requirements of the order require the offender's willingness to comply.

The court cannot make a drug treatment and testing order unless arrangements have been made in that court area for the treatment to be specified in the order to be carried out (s. 52(5)).

The DTTO may be compared with a requirement as to treatment for drug or alcohol dependency which may be inserted as a requirement of a CRO (see **5.2.8**). Clearly the two orders are very similar. The differences seem to be (a) that the CRO requirement extends to alcohol misuse, whereas the DTTO is confined to misuse of drugs; (b) that the DTTO has the 'testing requirement' which the CRO does not; and (c) that the provisions for the CRO state that the offender's dependency should have 'caused or contributed to the offence', while no such causal link is specified for the DTTO.

It should be noted that, with the nationwide introduction of DTTOs, sch. 2, para. 6(2) of the 2000 Act provides that as soon as these orders become available in the local area they supersede the power to order treatment for drug (not alcohol) dependency in a CRO in that area.

5.7 DRUG ABSTINENCE ORDERS (not yet in force)

The CJCSA 2000, s. 47 inserts ss. 58A and 58B into the PCC(S)A 2000. Section 58A provides a power for the courts to impose a new community order, to be known as an 'drug abstinence order'. A drug abstinence order is a community order within the meaning of PCC(S)A 2000, so that (in particular) the imposition of a drug abstinence order requires justification in terms of the seriousness of the offence, or the offence and one or more offences associated with it (s. 35(1)). A pre-sentence report is not required before such an order is made, but no doubt there will be occasions where the obtaining of such a report will be desirable sentencing practice.

5.7.1 Power to impose a drug abstinence order

By PCC(S)A 2000, s. 58A(1), where a person aged 18 or over is convicted of an offence, the adult magistrates' court or Crown Court by or before which he is convicted may make an order which requires him:

(a)   to abstain from misusing Class A drugs and
(b)   to provide, when instructed to do so by the responsible officer, any sample for the purpose of ascertaining whether he has any specified Class A drug in his body.

The order lasts for a period specified in the order of not less than six months nor more than three years (s. 58A(7)). The court shall not make such an order unless (s. 58A(3)):

(a)   in the opinion of the court the offender is 'dependent on, or has a propensity to misuse' specified Class A drugs, and
(b)   the offence in question is a 'trigger offence' or, in the opinion of the court, the misuse of any Class A drug caused or contributed to the offence in question.

The reference to a 'trigger offence' in s. 58A(3)(b) is a reference to a special list of offences provided in the CJCSA 2000, sch. 6. The list comprises offences under the Misuse of Drugs Act 1971 (production and supply, possession, or possession with intent to supply a controlled drug) where committed in respect of a Class A drug, and various offences under the Theft Act 1968 (theft, robbery, burglary, aggravated burglary, taking a motor vehicle without authority, aggravated vehicle-taking, obtaining property by deception, or going equipped for stealing).

A drug abstinence order must provide that, for the period for which the order has effect, the offender shall be under supervision by a responsible officer. The order shall include provision for making a person responsible for monitoring the offender's whereabouts during the periods when the prohibition operates; and a person who is made so responsible shall be of a description specified in an order made by the Secretary of State (s. 58A(4)). In due course this is likely to involve electronic monitoring (see **5.5.3**). It is important to note that drug abstinence orders are in force on a pilot basis only, and a court should not make a drug abstinence order unless it has received notification from the Secretary of State that arrangements for implementing such orders are available in the area proposed to be specified in the order and the notice has not been withdrawn (s. 58A(9)).

Before making an drug abstinence order, the court must explain to the offender in ordinary language the effect of the order and of the requirements proposed to be included in it, the consequences which may follow upon failure to comply with the order, and that the court has power to review the order (s. 58B(1)).

Clearly, the drug abstinence order bears close resemblance to the drug treatment and testing order (or DTTO: see **5.6**). There are, however, a number of important differences. The drug abstinence order is available only iii respect of misuse of Class A drugs, whereas the DTTO applies whatever the class of the drug. The drug abstinence order lacks the treatment requirement which is integral to the latter. The drug abstinence order applies to offenders aged 18 and over, while the latter is available for offenders aged 16 and over and thus extends to the youth court. The drug abstinence order is available only where a 'trigger offence' has been committed or where misuse of the Class A drug is found to have 'caused or contributed to the offence', while the DTTO is available whatever the offence, and without the formal need to establish a causal connection between the drug misuse and the offending.

5.7.2   Breach, revocation and amendment of drug abstinence orders

Schedule 3 to the PCC(S)A 2000 makes provision for breach, revocation and amendment of certain community orders, and sch. 3 applies to drug abstinence orders (s. 58B(3)). See **5.9**.

5.8 EXCLUSION ORDERS (not yet in force)

The CJCSA 2000, s. 46 inserts new ss. 40A–40C into the PCC(S)A 2000. Section 40A provides a power for the courts to impose a new community order, to be known as an 'exclusion order'. An exclusion order is a community order within the meaning of the PCC(S)A 2000 so that, in particular, the imposition of an exclusion order requires justification in terms of the seriousness of the offence, or the offence and one or more offences associated with it (s. 35(1)). A pre-sentence report is not required before an exclusion order is made.

5.8.1 Power to impose an exclusion order

By PCC(S)A 2000, s. 40A(1), where a person is convicted of an offence, the youth court, adult magistrates' court or Crown Court by or before which he is convicted may make an order prohibiting him from entering 'a place' (which includes 'an area': s. 40A(12)) specified in the order for a period so specified of not more than two years (or not more than three months if the offender is aged under 16: (s. 40A(4)). The order may provide for the prohibition to operate only during the periods specified in the order or may specify different places for different periods or days (s. 40A(3)).

The requirements in an exclusion order shall, as far as practicable, be such as to avoid any conflict with the offender's religious beliefs, with the requirements of any other community order to which he may be subject, and any interference with the times, if any, at which he normally works or attends school or any other educational establishment (s. 40A(5)). The order shall include provision for making a person responsible for monitoring the offender's whereabouts during the periods when the prohibition operates; and a person who is made so responsible shall be of a description specified in an order made by the Secretary of State (s. 40A(6)). In due course this is likely to involve electronic monitoring (see **5.5.3**). It is important to note that exclusion orders are in force on a pilot basis only, and a court should not make an exclusion order unless the court has been notified by the Secretary of State that arrangements for monitoring the offender's whereabouts are available in the area in which the place proposed to be specified in the order is situated and the notice has not been withdrawn (s. 40A(8)).

Before making an exclusion order in respect of an offender who on conviction is under 16, the court shall obtain and consider information about his family circumstances and the likely effect of such an order on those circumstances (s. 40A(9)). In any case the court, before making the order, must explain to the offender in ordinary language the effect of the order (including any additional requirement of electronic monitoring), the consequences which follow upon failure to comply with the order, and that the court has power to review the order (s. 40A(10)).

The exclusion order overlaps significantly with other community sentences. A very similar effect may be achieved by the insertion into a community rehabilitation order, or a supervision order, of various requirements set out in sch. 2 or sch. 6, respectively, to the PCC(S)A 2000. There is also an overlap with the curfew order. The difference is that the curfew order confines the offender to a certain place for certain periods of time, while the exclusion order prevents the offender from being in a certain locality or localities for the duration, or part of the duration, of the order. Section 40C provides that the Secretary of State may make rules for regulating the monitoring of offenders subject to exclusion orders, and this will involve electronic monitoring where appropriate.

5.8.2 Breach, revocation and amendment of exclusion order

Schedule 3 to the CJCSA 2000 makes provision for breach, revocation and amendment of certain community orders, and sch. 3 applies to exclusion orders (s. 40B). See **5.9**.

5.9 BREACH, REVOCATION AND AMENDMENT OF CERTAIN COMMUNITY ORDERS

The arrangements for enforcement (breach, revocation and amendment) of several of the community orders are to be found in the PCC(S)A 2000, sch. 3. The community orders so dealt with are the CRO, the CPO, the CPRO, the curfew order, the DTTO, the drug abstinence order and the exclusion order. The provisions for enforcement of the three other community orders — attendance centre orders, supervision orders and action plan orders — are somewhat different, and are dealt with as part of the description of each of those orders, at **5.10.4**, **5.11.10** and **5.12.3** respectively. The provisions dealing with breach of conditional discharge and breach of reparation orders are different again, since neither of these orders is a community order. For breach of conditional discharge see **7.1.5** and for breach of reparation orders see **7.4.3**.

An important distinction should be drawn at the outset between breach, revocation and amendment of community orders. 'Breach' refers to the situation where enforcement action is taken against an offender in consequence of a failure to comply with one of more of the requirements of the relevant community order, such as a failure to notify the supervisor of a change of address or a failure to carry out properly the work specified under a CPO. 'Revocation' refers to the situation where application is made to the court to bring the relevant community order to an end. This may be for one of a number of reasons, such as early termination where progress under the order has been good. It also covers the case, however, where the offender has committed a further offence during the currency of the order. As part of the court's response when dealing with the new offence, it may decide to revoke the original community order. An example would be where a custodial sentence is passed for the new offence, a sentence generally incompatible with the continuance of the community order. Commission of a further offence is thus relevant to revocation, rather than to breach. In contrast to breach and to revocation, either the offender or the relevant officer may make application to the court for amendment of a community order. This covers cases where some change of circumstance has occurred since the order was imposed, and an adjustment to the terms of the order is thus requested.

The Home Office National Standards suggest that, in general, action should be taken to return an offender to court for breach of the relevant community order where there have been no more than *three* unacceptable failures to comply with the requirements of the order. For details, see the text relating to each of the specific community orders.

Before turning to consider the enforcement arrangements for community sentences in more detail, it may be worth indicating what percentage of offenders given various community sentences are subsequently returned to court, and how frequently the court then imposes a custodial sentence. According to the *Criminal Statistics* (Home Office, 2000), during 1999, 18 per cent of offenders given CROs were subsequently returned to court and, of those, 28 per cent received a custodial sentence instead. Of offenders given CPOs, 30 per cent were returned to court, of whom 18 per cent received custody, and 29 per cent of those given CPROs were returned to court, with 30 per cent of those returned receiving custody. No figures are provided for other community orders. The *Statistics* compare the rate of recall to court and the percentage use of custody across the last 10 years. While the percentage rate of recall to court for all three sentences has remained quite steady over the years, the percentage of those given immediate custody has been falling, from 26 per cent to 18 per cent for CPOs, 49 per cent to 28 per cent for CROs and 41 per cent to 30 per cent for CPROs. Care should be taken with these figures, since the relevant table in the *Criminal Statistics* (Table 7.24) refers to the rate of 'breach' of community orders, but it appears that the figures also include cases where the order has been 'revoked' for commission of a further offence, a distinction which was explained above.

5.9.1 Breach of certain community orders

Where there is evidence of breach of the terms of a CRO, a CPO, a CPRO, a curfew order, a DTTO, a drug abstinence order or an exclusion order, a justice of the peace may issue a summons or warrant for the offender's appearance. The offender must appear before a magistrates' court acting for the petty sessions area concerned or, in the case of a drug treatment and testing order, the court responsible for the order. The Crown Court has no jurisdiction to deal with breach of a community order unless the matter has first come before the magistrates. Any breach must be admitted by the offender or be formally proved. The prosecution must be in a position to put before the court the facts of the original offence as well as the circumstances of the alleged breach (*Clarke* [1997] 2 Cr App R (S) 163). If it is proved to the magistrates' court before which the offender appears that he has failed without reasonable excuse to comply with the requirements of the order the court may then adopt any one of four courses of action set out in the PCC(S)A 2000, sch. 3, para. 4(1)(a) to (d).

(a) It may impose a fine on the offender not exceeding £1,000. The original community order would continue.

(b) Where the offender is aged 16 or over, it may make a CPO of not more than 60 hours. The original community order would continue. If the offender is being dealt with for breach of an existing CPO, this option is still available, but the total number of hours under both orders must not exceed 240 hours (para. 7(3)). It can perhaps be assumed that this total of 240 refers to the total number of hours ordered, rather than the total number which remain to be served, by analogy with *Anderson* (1989) 11 Cr App R (S) 147 (see **5.3.3**).

(c) Where the offender is in breach of a CRO, or a CPRO, and is under 21, or is in breach of a curfew order and is aged under 16, the court may make an attendance centre order (para. 3(1)(c)). The original community order would continue.

(d) Where the original order was made by a magistrates' court (for cases where the original court was the Crown Court, see below), the court may revoke the order and deal with the offender, for the offence in respect of which the community order was passed, in any manner in which it could deal with him if he had just been convicted by the magistrates' court of that offence.

Options (a) to (c) are without prejudice to the continuation of the original order. They are simply penalties for the offender's failure to comply with the order's requirements, and do not amount to sentencing the offender for the original offence. In principle there seems no reason why a court might not exercise options (a) to (c) more than once in respect of subsequent breaches of the same community order. If, however, the offender can be said to have 'wilfully and persistently failed to comply' with the order, the court may choose to follow option (d). Note also that the court has no power, when dealing with breach of a community order, to extend the operational period of that order.

Under option (d), the court may revoke the community order in the light of the breach, and pass sentence again for the original offence. When dealing with an offender under para. 4(1)(d) the court, according to para. 4(2):

(a)   shall take into account the extent to which the offender has complied with the requirements of the relevant order; and

(b)   in the case of an offender who has wilfully and persistently failed to comply with those requirements, may impose a custodial sentence (where the relevant order was made in respect of an offence punishable with such a sentence) notwithstanding anything in section 79(2).

There is perhaps an assumption that, once the court turns to para. 4(1)(d), the offender will then be facing a custodial sentence. This is likely, but not inevitable, particularly where, having regard to para. 4(2)(a), the offender has in fact completed a substantial part of the community order. PCC(S)A 2000 gives statutory recognition to the principle developed in earlier cases on breach of CPOs that the court should have regard to the offender's progress under the order when considering how to deal with the breach. In *Paisley* (1979) 1 Cr App R (S) 196 six months' custody, consequent upon breach and revocation, was varied to allow an offender's immediate release, where he had completed 61 of his 100 hours, although he had on three occasions failed to comply with the order's requirements. Even if good progress under the order cannot dissuade the court from revoking the order and imposing custody, it should properly serve to reduce the length of the term imposed. While the desirability of giving credit is most compelling when the offender has completed a high proportion of the order, in *Whittingham* (1986) 8 Cr App R (S) 116 the Court of Appeal said that some credit should have been given where only a third of the hours of a CPO had been completed successfully. Apparently, hours completed after breach proceedings have been initiated may still be of some value in mitigation (*Tebbutt* (1988) 10 Cr App R (S) 88).

If a custodial sentence is imposed consequent upon breach of a community order, the court must, of course, have regard to the normal limitations upon the imposition of custodial sentences (such as the restriction on the maximum custodial sentence which can be imposed by a magistrates' court). It seems that the breach court should normally also observe the statutory restrictions in PCC(S)A 2000, s. 79(2) on the imposition of custodial sentences. This means that custody should only be given consequent upon breach where the original offence was so serious that only custody could be justified for it. It was explained by the Court of Appeal in *Oliver* [1993] 1 WLR 177 that the mere fact that the offender has received a community sentence does not mean that the offence itself was below the custody threshold. The court which imposed the community sentence may have taken into account matters of personal mitigation which, at the time, saved the offender from custody, but these may seem less persuasive now in light of his failure to comply with the community order. If, however, the court is relying on para. 4(2)(b), that the offender has 'wilfully and persistently failed to comply' with the requirements of the community order, it is clear from the wording of that sub-paragraph that the court is not required to justify custody in accordance with s. 79(2) of the 2000 Act.

Whenever a custodial sentence is imposed following breach of a community order, allowance should be given for any period of time which was spent by the offender in custody on remand before the community sentence was passed, although the extent of the allowance is a matter for judicial discretion. This point has been made on a number of occasions by the Court of Appeal. In *Henderson* [1997] 2 Cr App R (S) 266, Stuart White J in the Court of Appeal added that the breach court should always indicate the extent to which the time served on remand has been taken into account.

In the preceding discussion of court proceedings for breach of a community order, the assumption has been that the magistrates' court will be dealing with the breach itself. All breaches of community orders must come before a magistrates' court initially, but that court has discretion to send the offender to be dealt with in the Crown Court whenever the community order was originally passed by the Crown Court (sch. 3, para. 4(4)). The Crown Court's powers on breach are identical to those stated above in relation to magistrates' courts except that, in a case where the Crown Court chooses to revoke the order and exercise the power equivalent to that in para. 4(1)(d) (which for the Crown Court can be found in para. 5(1)(d)), the Crown Court is empowered to deal with the offender in any manner in which it could deal with him if he had just been convicted by the Crown Court of that offence. The upshot of this is that there is little point in magistrates sending an offender to the Crown Court to be dealt with for breach of a community sentence originally imposed by the higher court unless the magistrates expect the Crown Court to revoke the order and sentence for the original offence. The Crown Court, in dealing with an offender under para. 5(1)(d) must have regard to matters equivalent to those in para. 4(2) (see above).

A person sentenced by magistrates under para. 4(1)(d) may appeal to the Crown Court against the sentence (para. 4(6)).

It should be noted that, when s. 53 of the CJCSA 2000 is brought into force, sch. 3 to the PCC(S)A 2000 will be amended in a number of important respects. The responsible officer will henceforth be able to warn an offender only once for a breach of the order, and thereafter must take the offender back to court for the breach to be dealt with. The discretion of the court dealing with breach will be narrowed. Where it is proved that an offender who is aged 18 or over and who is subject to one of these orders has failed without reasonable excuse to comply with it, the court must imposed a custodial sentence. This applies unless it is of the opinion that the offender is likely to comply with the requirements for the remainder of the order, or that there are exceptional circumstances which justify the court in not imposing a custodial sentence. These changes are applicable both to magistrates' courts and to the Crown Court. The changes apply to the community orders listed in **5.9**, and so do not affect attendance centre orders, supervision order or action plan orders. Further, the obligation to impose a custodial sentence does not apply to a DTTO or a drug abstinence order where the breach related to the requirement to abstain from misusing drugs.

5.9.2   Revocation of certain community orders

A CRO, a CPO, a CPRO, curfew order, a DTTO, a drug abstinence order or an exclusion order may be revoked for any one of a number of reasons relating to the offender's change of circumstances since the order was imposed. A CRO may be revoked, for example, in the light of the offender's good progress. A CPO may be revoked because the offender can no longer carry out the work required under the order (e.g. since he has injured his back: *Fielding* [1993] Crim LR 229). A community order may also be revoked as a consequence of breach (see **5.9.1**). Commission of a further offence also forms the factual basis for revocation of the order, and the following discussion concentrates on this aspect of revocation. The use of revocation in contexts other than commission of a further offence must, however, be borne in mind when looking at the following provisions.

A magistrates' court acting for the petty sessions area concerned may revoke any of the community orders listed above (except for the DTTO), or deal with the offender in some other way for the offence, where, on the application of the offender or the responsible officer, it appears to be in the interests of justice to do so. In the case of a DTTO, however, this function can only be performed by the court which actually made the order. Unless the offender is making the application, the court must summon the offender to appear or, if he does not appear, issue a warrant for his arrest. By sch. 3, para. 10(3), a magistrates' court, if the original community order was made in a magistrates' court, may either, under para. 10(3)(a), simply revoke the order or, under para. 10(3)(b), revoke it and deal with the offender for the offence in respect of which the order was made in any manner in which it could have dealt with him if he had just been convicted by that court. In the latter case the magistrates must take into account the extent to which the offender has complied with the terms of the original order (e.g. the number of hours of community service which the offender has completed successfully, para. 10(5)). This principle is parallel to the rule discussed at **5.9.1** in relation to breach of community orders.

The issue of revocation of one of the relevant community orders may come before the Crown Court in one of three different ways. First, an offender in respect of whom a relevant community order is in force may be convicted before the Crown Court of a further offence. Second, the offender may have been convicted of a further offence by a magistrates' court and committed for sentence to the Crown Court. Third, the magistrates may have committed the offender to Crown Court because the original order was made by the Crown Court, and a magistrates' court may not revoke a Crown Court order. In any of these situations the Crown Court may either (a) simply revoke the community order or (b) revoke the community order and resentence for the original offence, para. 11(2). If it resentences, the Crown Court must take into account the extent to which the offender has complied with the requirements of the order (para. 11(4)).

It was at one time unclear whether the Crown Court, when revoking and resentencing an offender in respect of a community order which was originally imposed by a magistrates' court, is restricted to the powers of the lower court. After a series of conflicting decisions on this point the Court of Appeal ruled in *Ogden* [1996] 2 Cr App R (S) 386 that it is so restricted, and the wording of para. 11(2) reflects this position. Where a custodial sentence is passed consequent upon revocation of a community order, allowance should be made for any period spent by the offender on remand in custody before the community order was passed, though the extent of such allowance is a matter for judicial discretion (*McDonald* (1988) 10 Cr App R (S) 458 and the decision in *Henderson* [1997] 2 Cr App R (S) 266, see **5.9.1**). The case law indicates that where a community order is revoked in consequence of the commission of a further offence, it is almost always desirable for the court to deal fully and finally with the original offence for which the community order was passed (see *Rowsell* (1988) 10 Cr App R (S) 411). If custodial sentences are imposed both for the new offence and in consequence of resentencing for the original offence, such custodial terms may run consecutively, but subject to the usual totality principle (*Cook* (1985) 7 Cr App R (S) 249 and, for an explanation of this principle, see **4.4.4**).

A couple of further complications have arisen in the cases. One is where the offender commits a further offence during the operational period of a community order but has completed all the requirements of that order before being convicted of the new offence. Here the answer is straightforward: the court has no power to revoke the order or to deal with the offender for the original offence (*Cousin* (1994) 15 Cr App R (S) 516). The second is where the offender is convicted of an offence during the operational period of a community order but it turns out that the offence was in fact committed before the community order was imposed. The Court of Appeal has wavered on this one, but the prevailing view is that, although the court dealing with the new offence may revoke the community order, it is wrong to resentence for the original offence, since the offender did not break the terms of the community order by committing a further offence while he was subject to it (*Saphier* [1997] 1 Cr App R (S) 235, but see *Day* [1997] 2 Cr App R (S) 328).

5.9.3 Amendment of certain community orders

There is a range of circumstances in which application may be made to amend one or other of the relevant community orders. Such application should be made to the local magistrates' court, by the offender or by the relevant officer except for the DTTO, where application must be made to the court responsible for the order. Paragraph 18 allows for amendment of a relevant community order to take account of a change in the offender's area of residence. Paragraph 19 deals with the possibility of making amendments to the conditions or duration of a CRO, a CPRO or a curfew order. Paragraph 20 relates to CROs or CPROs which contain a condition of mental treatment or a condition of treatment for alcohol or drug dependency and provides for variation or cancellation of that requirement. Paragraph 21 allows for amendments to be made to requirements in a DTTO. Paragraph 22 allows for the extension of the period of a community sentence order beyond 12 months, for reasons such as the ill-health or changed work commitments of the offender.

5.9.4 Reciprocal enforcement of certain community orders

Schedule 4 to the PCC(S)A 2000 deals with certain detailed matters relating to the carrying out of community orders made by the courts in England and Wales by offenders who will be resident after sentence in either Scotland or Northern Ireland and the transfer to England and Wales of corresponding orders made in Scotland or Northern Ireland.

5.10 ATTENDANCE CENTRE ORDERS

An attendance centre order may be imposed on an offender between the ages of 10 and 20 inclusive. It may be made by the Crown Court, an adult magistrates' court or a youth court. It requires the offender to attend at a specified attendance centre for a specified number of hours. An attendance centre order is a 'community order' and the court cannot impose an attendance centre order unless the conditions relating to the passing of a community order are satisfied. In particular, by PCC(S)A 2000, s. 35(1), the court must be satisfied that the offence committed is serious enough to warrant a community order (see **5.1**).

Between 1988 and 1999 the proportionate use made by the courts of attendance centre orders when sentencing for indictable offences has remained steady at 2 per cent, but of the total number of offenders being sentenced, the number receiving attendance centre orders has risen slightly from 5,500 to 5,800 over that period.

5.10.1 Power to impose an attendance centre order

Power to pass an attendance centre order derives from PCC(S)A 2000, s. 60. Such an order may be made by the Crown Court, an adult magistrates' court or a youth court, in any case where an offender aged between 10 and 20 inclusive is being sentenced for an offence punishable with imprisonment in the case of an adult. One exceptional case where an offender over 20 but under 25 may be given an attendance centre order is considered below.

The number of hours for which the offender must attend the centre is fixed by the court when it makes the order. The minimum number of hours is 12, except in a case where the offender is aged under 14 and the court is of the opinion that 12 hours would be excessive (s. 60(3)). The maximum number is 24, where the offender is aged under 16, or 36 hours where the offender is 16 but under 21 (s. 60(4)). Where an offender is dealt with for several offences on one occasion by means of two or more attendance centre orders, it is the aggregate number of hours which must be not less than 12 nor more than 24 or 36. If, on the other hand, an offender is already subject to an attendance centre order made on a previous occasion and the court dealing with him for a further offence also wishes to make such an order, the number of hours which he is to attend under the second order may be fixed without taking into account the hours he still has to attend under the first order (i.e. the combined total may exceed 24 or 36) (s. 60(5)). This rule stands in contrast to that which applies in relation to community punishment orders (see **5.3.3**).

Both the centre which the offender must attend and the time of his first attendance are specified by the court when it makes the order (s. 60(1) and (8)). Thereafter he has to attend in accordance with the direction of the person in charge of the centre (s. 60(9)). Interference with school or working hours must, as far as practicable, be avoided, and the offender may not be ordered to attend for more than three hours on any one occasion or more than one occasion on any one day (s. 60(10)). Periods of two or three hours on each occasion are normal, with periods of two hours being favoured for offenders aged under 18. A copy of the order should be provided for the offender and another for the officer in charge of the centre (s. 60(11)).

Not all areas have attendance centres, so the court must have been notified that an attendance centre is available in the relevant area to receive a person of the age and sex of the offender, and it must be satisfied that the attendance centre which is named in the order is reasonably accessible to the offender (s. 60(1) and (6)). The Home Office has recommended that an order should not be made if the offender would have to travel more than 15 miles to reach the centre or if the journey would take him more than an hour and a half (if the offender is under 14, the recommended maxima are 10 miles and an hour's journey).

5.10.2   Attendance at the centre

An attendance centre is defined in PCC(S)A 2000, s. 62(2) as 'a place at which offenders aged under 21 may be required to attend and be given, under supervision, appropriate occupation or instruction'. Most centres are run by police officers, prison officers or teachers in their off-duty hours, at premises such as schools, youth clubs and church halls. They are usually open on alternate Saturday mornings or afternoons, and the effect of a typical attendance centre order is that the offender has to go to the centre named by the court for a number of three-hour sessions on separate Saturdays. Thus, the offender is punished by having his normal Saturday activities interfered with. One obvious use of the attendance centre order is to keep a young person convicted of disorder connected with football matches away from such matches. This possibility was specifically referred to in Home Office Circular 69/1990, where using an attendance centre order in conjunction with a football exclusion order (now a football banning order: see **10.5**) was advocated as an appropriate means of dealing with such cases. The object of an attendance centre order is not, however, entirely punitive. According to the Home Office, attendance at an attendance centre should benefit the offender by 'bringing him under the influence of representatives of the authority of the state' and 'teaching him something of the constructive use of leisure'. Firm discipline, periods of strenuous physical exercise and instructions in handicrafts, citizenship, first aid, motor-cycle maintenance or such like are typical of the attendance centre regime. Each scheme of activities must be approved by the Secretary of State.

The imposition of an attendance centre order does not require the consent of the offender. The obtaining of a pre-sentence report before the passing of such a sentence is not required but, no doubt, there is a range of such cases where the obtaining of a report would constitute good sentencing practice.

In the past most attendance centres have catered for male juveniles. The government has in recent years encouraged the opening of more attendance centres for juvenile males and for girls.

As well as being used as a community sentence for an offence, attendance centre orders can be used as a means of enforcement in respect of breach of a range of other sentencing measures. The importance of this role for attendance centre orders has increased significantly in recent years. An attendance centre order may now be used:

(a) for those who default in payment of a fine, a compensation order etc., who are aged under 25 (PCC(S)A 2000, s. 60(1)) — formerly this option was restricted to offenders aged under 21, but the age limit was raised to under 25 by the C(S)A 1997 and is the only circumstance in which offenders over 20 may be sent to an attendance centre. Payment of the whole sum discharges the attendance centre order, and payment of a proportion of the sum reduces the number of hours to be served by the same proportion, rounded down to the nearest complete hour (s. 60(12));

(b) for breach of a CRO, where the offender is aged under 21 (sch. 3, para. 4);

(c) for breach of a CPRO, where the offender is aged under 21 (sch. 3, para. 4);

(d) for breach of a curfew order, where the offender is aged under 16 (sch. 3, para. 4);

(e) for breach of a supervision order (sch. 7, para. 2);

(f) for breach of an action plan order (sch. 8, para. 2); and

(g) for breach of a reparation order (sch. 8, para. 2).

5.10.3 Combining attendance centre orders with other sentences or orders

It is inappropriate to combine an attendance centre order with any form of custodial sentence. Since an attendance centre order is one of the methods open to the court when dealing with an offender aged under 21 who is in breach of one of a range of community sentences, it would seem that such orders when imposed on a person under that age should not be made at the same time as an attendance centre order. There is no objection to imposing a fine, a compensation order, an order for disqualification from driving or an order for forfeiture at the same time as an attendance centre order. Adding a football exclusion order to an attendance centre order will be an attractive option in appropriate cases. An attendance centre order cannot be combined with an absolute or conditional discharge when sentencing for a single offence, since discharges are imposed only where 'it is inexpedient to impose punishment' (PCC(S)A 2000, s. 12), but these two measures may certainly be used when sentencing for different offences dealt with on the same occasion.

When combining sentencing measures regard should always be had to s. 158(2) which states that nothing shall prevent a court 'from mitigating any penalty included in an offender's sentence by taking into account any other penalty included in that sentence'.

Regard may also be had in this context to the White Paper (Home Office, 1990), where it was stated that 'For most offenders, only one of these [community] orders will be necessary, or justified by the seriousness of their offences. For more serious offenders, however, more than one community penalty could be imposed.'

5.10.4   Revocation and amendment of attendance centre order

An attendance centre order can be discharged early, either on application by the officer in charge of the attendance centre, or on the application of the offender, to a magistrates' court acting for the petty sessions area in which the centre is situated or to the court which actually made the order (sch. 5, para. 4(1)). The Crown Court may reserve to itself the power to discharge the order. The power of discharge includes the option of dealing with the offender, for the original offence, in any manner in which he could have been dealt with by the court which made the attendance centre order (sch. 5, para. 4(3)). This might allow the court, for instance, to impose an alternative penalty where there has been a change in the offender's circumstances (e.g. he has obtained employment which includes Saturday working) which mean that he is no longer able to carry out the order. Further, the relevant magistrates' court may, on application by the officer in charge or the offender, vary the starting day or hour of the order (para. 5(1)), or may substitute a different attendance centre. This will be appropriate if the offender changes his address or if the attendance centre named in the order closes.

There is no provision in sch. 5 for dealing with the attendance centre order consequent upon the commission of a further offence.

5.10.5   Breach of attendance centre order

If the offender has failed to attend, or has committed a breach of the rules for the regulation and management of attendance centres made under s. 62(3) which cannot adequately be dealt with under those rules, proceedings for breach of the attendance centre order may be initiated. A justice of the peace acting for the petty sessions area in which the attendance centre named in the order is situated, or, if the order was made by a magistrates' court, the petty sessions area for which that court was acting, may issue a summons requiring the offender to appear, or may issue a warrant for his arrest, requiring him to be brought before the court (sch. 5, para. 1).

If the order was made by a magistrates' court, the magistrates' court before which the offender is brought has power to impose a fine not exceeding £1,000 and continue with the order, or to revoke the order and deal with the offender for the original offence in any manner in which he could have been dealt with for that offence by the court which made the order (sch. 5, para. 2). If the order was made by the Crown Court, the magistrates' court may commit him in custody or release him on bail until he can appear before the Crown Court. The magistrates' court should provide a certificate signed by a justice of the peace giving details of the case, though this is not conclusive of the breach, which must be specifically proved before the Crown Court. The Crown Court has powers to revoke the order and to deal with the offender for the original offence. In reaching its decision on the appropriate action to deal with the breach, the court must always take into account the extent to which the offender has complied with the requirements of the attendance centre order (sch. 5, para. 3(3)(a)), such as the number of hours successfully completed prior to the breach. Further, if the court finds that the offender has 'wilfully and persistently failed to comply' with the requirements of the order, the purpose of para. 3(3)(b) is to allow the court to deal with the offender by way of a custodial sentence.

5.11 SUPERVISION ORDERS

Supervision orders are broadly equivalent to community rehabilitation orders but cater for younger offenders. A supervision order may be passed by the Crown Court or a youth court (but not an adult magistrates' court) on an offender aged between 10 and 17 inclusive. For offenders aged 16 or 17, both orders are available. While both a supervision order and a CRO are intended to assist an offender to become more responsible and to keep out of trouble, the clearest feature distinguishing them is that the supervision order is also intended to help a young person to develop into an adult, whereas a CRO is more appropriate for someone who is already emotionally, intellectually, socially and physically an adult. Since many 16 and 17-year-olds are still very much in the stage of transition into adulthood, the supervision order may often in practice be the more suitable form of supervision. Other relevant matters are the degree of offenders' independence from parents, whether they lead an independent life or have their own family reponsibilities, how they might be influenced by other offenders whom they may meet at group sessions and whether assistance is currently being received, or is needed, from social services.

In 1999 some 9,200 supervision orders were made; the number made has increased steadily from 5,100 in 1989.

Supervision orders are designed to provide a demanding but constructive sentencing option for young people. Section 44 of CYPA 1933 sets out the principle that all courts must have regard to the welfare of the child or young person who appears before them. The CJA 1991 brought 17-year-old offenders within the scope of this provision, but it is clear that the younger the offender the more important the welfare requirement is.

A supervision order is a 'community order' and the court will not be able to impose a supervision order unless the conditions relating to the passing of a community order are satisfied. In particular, by PCC(S)A 2000, s. 35(1), the court will have to be satisfied that the offence committed is serious enough to warrant a community order (see **5.1**). A pre-sentence report is normally required before imposing a supervision order which includes requirements authorised by sch. 6 (s. 36(3)), and in any other case where a supervision order is made it may be considered good sentencing practice to obtain a report. A supervision order does not require the offender's consent, but the court may not insert a requirement of treatment for a mental condition under sch. 6, para. 6 on an offender who has attained the age of 14 unless the offender expresses his willingness to comply with it.

5.11.1 Power to impose basic supervision order

By the PCC(S)A 2000, s. 63, a supervision order may be made by a youth court or by the Crown Court but not by an adult magistrates' court, where an offender under 18 is found guilty of any offence. This is subject to s. 90 (mandatory sentence of detention during Her Majesty's pleasure for murder committed by an offender aged under 18). For this, and for long-term detention of juveniles convicted of other serious crimes, see **4.3.5** and **4.3.10**. The youth court is the court in which the great majority of supervision orders are made.

A supervision order will last for three years from the date on which it was made, or for such shorter period as may be specified in the order (s. 63(7)). In practice supervision orders tend to be for one year or two years. There is no minimum period. The order places the juvenile under the supervision of either a local authority social worker, a probation officer or member of a youth offending team (s. 63(1)). A local authority must not be designated as a supervisor unless the person to be supervised resides in that area (s. 64(1)). Where a probation officer is the supervisor, he will be one of those working in the petty sessions area where the juvenile lives. In every case the supervisor's duty is to 'advise, assist and befriend the offender' (s. 64(4)). A local authority carries out this task through the social workers in its employment. The Home Office National Standards 2000 envisage that supervision should start within five working days of the making of the order, should involve frequent appointments (where practicable and appropriate, there should be 12 in the first three months), accurate and timely record-keeping of appointments and prompt and effective action to enforce the order, including breach action where behaviour is unacceptable. The National Standards state that wherever possible the supervisor should work together with the offender and the offender's parent or guardian and should involve them at all stages of the order.

The order described above may be characterised as a 'basic supervision order'. A range of further special requirements may be included within the order at the court's discretion. These are dealt with next.

5.11.2   Requirement as to residence

A supervision order may require the juvenile to reside with an individual who is named in the order (sch. 6, para. 1). The person so named must agree to the requirement being made. Any residence requirement imposed under sch. 6, para. 1 is subject to the supervised person being obliged from time to time to reside elsewhere by virtue of a requirement imposed under one of the other paragraphs of sch. 6.

5.11.3   Requirement to comply with directions of supervisor

The effect of a requirement made under sch. 6, para. 2 is that, for a certain number of days, the person supervised is liable to be directed by the supervisor to:

(a)   live at a place specified by the supervisor; and/or
(b)   attend (but not live at) a place specified; and/or
(c)   take part in specified activities.

The number of days in respect of which the supervisor may give directions is specified by the court when the order is made, up to a maximum of 90 days, which need not necessarily be consecutive (para. 2(5)). By these requirements, the supervisor may ensure that for a short time the person supervised is taken away from his home environment, or at least is kept usefully occupied while still at home. Typically, these requirements involve individual counselling or group discussion; there is an educational and skills-based approach. Particular projects may be used by supervisors to put the persons supervised into situations where they face new challenges and have the opportunity to develop their abilities and to be involved in worthwhile activities. Juveniles might be directed to take part in a course to learn a new skill (such as horse riding or canoeing) or might be sent on an adventure-type holiday, such as walking the Pennine Way or, more mundanely, might be required to attend a youth club on a certain number of evenings a week. It will be seen that these requirements are not envisaged as punitive as such. The aim is to give juvenile offenders the opportunity to develop more constructive use of their leisure time which does not involve the committing of criminal offences. The implementation of requirements under para. 2 is very much within the discretion of the supervisor.

5.11.4 Requirements as to activities, reparation, night restrictions etc.

Requirements may, alternatively but not additionally, be included within a supervision order by virtue of sch. 6, para. 3. In such a case, the court itself may require the offender to do anything which the supervisor might have required the supervised person to do under para. 2; for example, it may nominate where the juvenile is to live or which activities he is to take part in. The maximum number of days is again 90, and the court must consult with the proposed supervisor to ensure that it will be feasible to ensure compliance with the proposed scheme. Additionally, the court may require the offender to refrain from participating in activities on specified days or for a specified period.

By sch. 6, para. 3(2)(d), the court has power to require that the offender shall make specified reparation to the victim of the offence (the offender's consent to this is required) or to the community at large. Before making an order under para. 3(2)(d) the court must be satisfied that securing compliance with the order is feasible and, if the person is aged under 16, the court must obtain and consider information about his family circumstances and the effect of the order on those circumstances.

By sch. 6, para. 3(2)(e) the court may require the offender, on not more than 30 separate occasions within the first three months of the supervision order, to be indoors by a certain hour in the evening and not thereafter to go out until the next morning. The periods specified must be between 6 p.m. and 6 a.m. and must not require the offender to remain at a place for longer than ten hours on any one night (sch. 6, para. 4). The place, or one of the places, specified in the order must be the home of the offender. The offender may only leave the place during the relevant period if accompanied by his parent, guardian, supervisor or some other person specified in the order.

Before making an order under para. 3(2) the court must be satisfied that securing compliance with the order is feasible but the fact is that, in many cases, night restriction requirements are in practice unenforceable and, in contrast to curfew orders (see **5.5**), there is no provision of electronic monitoring of juveniles under night restriction requirements. Before making any order under para. 3(2) on a person under 16, the court must consider the likely effect of it upon the offender's home circumstances.

5.11.5 Requirement as to residence in local authority accommodation

By sch. 6, para. 5, where certain conditions are satisfied (see below), a supervision order may contain a requirement that a juvenile live for a specified period in local authority accommodation. The order must specify the local authority in whose area the offender lives and the authority must be consulted first (para. 5(3) and (4)). The maximum period of residence is six months (para. 5(6)). A residence requirement may also specify that the juvenile may *not* live with a particular person (para. 5(5)).

The conditions which must be met before a requirement of residence in local authority accommodation can be imposed are, by para. 5(2):

   (a)   that a supervision order has previously been made in respect of the offender;

   (b)   that the previous order imposed a requirement under para. 1, 2, 3 or 7 of sch. 6 or a local authority residence requirement;

(c)   that the offender fails to comply with that requirement or is found guilty of an offence which was committed while that supervision order was in force; and

(d)   that the court is satisfied that the behaviour which constituted the offence was due, to a significant extent, to the circumstances in which he was living and the imposition of a local authority residence requirement will assist in his rehabilitation.

The first part of condition (d) does not have to be satisfied if the offender is already subject to a residence requirement.

A requirement of residence in local authority accommodation should not be made unless the juvenile is legally represented or, if not so represented, unless he has had the opportunity to apply for legal aid (para. 5(7)). A supervision order imposing a requirement of residence in local authority accommodation may also include any requirement imposed under para. 2, 3, 6 or 7 of sch. 6 (para. 5(9)).

5.11.6   Requirement as to treatment for a mental condition etc.

Under sch. 6, para. 6, a requirement of treatment for a mental condition may be inserted into a supervision order. The supervised person, if aged 14 or over, must consent to the insertion of such a requirement. This requirement is fully discussed at **11.2**.

5.11.7   Requirement as to education

Where the supervised person is of compulsory school age, a requirement may be inserted into the basic supervision order requiring that person to comply, for as long as he is of that age and the order remains in force, 'with such arrangements for his education as may from time to time be made by his parent, being arrangements for the time being approved by the local education authority' (para. 7(2)). The court must secure the agreement of the education authority (para. 7(3)). The consent of the offender is not required.

5.11.8   Revocation and amendment of supervision order

Provision as to the discharge or variation of supervision orders is contained in sch. 7 para. 5.

During the currency of a supervision order in respect of a person who has not yet reached the age of 18, a youth court (or, in the case of a person who has reached that age, an adult magistrates' court) may, on the application of the supervisor or the supervised person, make an order for early termination by discharging the supervision order (para. 5(1)). The Home Office National Standards suggest that early termination of a supervision order should be considered where the offender has made good progress in achieving the objectives set out in the order and where there is not considered to be a significant risk of reoffending and/or of serious harm to the public. An application for early termination should normally be considered by the time two-thirds of the term of the order has elapsed unless there are clear reasons for not doing so.

The relevant court may also vary the supervision order by cancelling any requirement included in it under sch. 6 or by inserting any provision into the order which could have been included in the original order. The relevant court is not empowered, however, to insert a requirement under para. 3(2)(e) (night restriction order: see **5.11.4**) in respect of any day which falls outside the period of three months beginning with the date on which the order was made. There are also limitations on the court's powers to vary a requirement under para. 6, relating to medical treatment (see **11.2**).

5.11.9 Breach of supervision order

The powers of the court to deal with breach of supervision orders may be found in sch. 7, para. 2.

Any apparent failure to comply with requirements in a supervision order should be followed up promptly by the supervising officer, normally within two working days. If the offender's explanation (or lack of one) is not considered acceptable, the incident must formally be recorded as an instance of failure to comply. Immediate action in respect of a breach may be appropriate in some cases of failure to comply, such as a failure to notify a change of adddress when it is clear that the failure was an attempt to avoid carrying out the order. In other cases the supervising officer should normally take such action after no more than *three* instances of failure to comply. When action is taken the supervising officer has an important role in the process of proving the breach before the court and advising the court on further action. The officer should be clear as to what action he or she would like the court to take. This advice should be contained, as required, in an oral or written report to the court, which should also include an account of the offender's response to supervision thus far, and the extent to which the offender has successfully completed the order. If thought necessary, the officer may complete a further pre-sentence report prior to the breach hearing.

If breach action is brought against a supervised person who has not yet attained the age of 18 the appropriate court to deal with the breach is the youth court. By para. 2, where it is proved to the satisfaction of the youth court, on the application of the supervisor, that a supervised person who has not attained the age of 18 has failed to comply with any of the requirements of the order then, whether or not it also revokes the supervision order (see **5.11.8**), the court may order payment of a fine not exceeding £1,000, or may make a curfew order, or an attendance centre order.

If breach action is brought against a supervised person who has attained the age of 18, the appropriate court to deal with the breach is the adult magistrates' court. Alternatively, if the original order was made by a magistrates' court, it may revoke the order and deal with the offender in any way in which he could have been dealt with by the court which made the order, or, if the original order was made by the Crown Court, he may be committed to that court. The Crown Court may deal with him in any way in which he could have been dealt with by the Crown Court when the order was made.

The relevant court must always take account of the extent to which the person supervised has complied with the requirements of the supervision order (para. 2(7)).

5.12 ACTION PLAN ORDERS

The Crime and Disorder Act 1998 created a community order applicable to offenders under the age of 18 — the action plan order. The relevant provisions are now to be found in the PCC(S)A 2000, ss. 69 and 70. In the White Paper, *No More Excuses* (Home Office, 1997), the government described the action plan order as 'a short intensive programme of community intervention combining punishment, rehabilitation and reparation to change offending behaviour and prevent further crime. The order is available for 10–17-year-olds and imposes requirements designed to address the specific causes of offending. Each order lasts for three months.'

The action plan order is a 'community order', and the court will not be able to impose such an order unless the conditions relating to the passing of a community order are satisfied. In particular, by PCC(S)A 2000, s. 35(1), the court will have to be satisfied that the offence committed is serious enough to warrant the passing of a community order (see **5.1**). The court may pass an action plan order without first obtaining a pre-sentence report, but the court is required, before making such an order, to obtain and consider a written report by a probation officer, a social worker or a member of a youth offending team. The report must indicate the requirements which that person proposes to include in the action plan order, the benefits to the offender which those requirements are designed to achieve, the attitude of a parent or guardian of the young offender to the proposed requirements and, where the offender is under the age of 16, information about the young offender's family circumstances and the likely effect of the order on those circumstances.

5.12.1   Power to impose an action plan order

An action plan order may be imposed by the Crown Court or a youth court on any offender aged under 18 who is convicted of any offence, subject only to the law on sentencing for the crime of murder and the three presumptive sentences under the PCC(S)A 2000, ss. 109–111. The court may make an action plan order if it is of the opinion that this is desirable in the interests of securing the young offender's rehabilitation, or of preventing the commission by him of further offences (s. 69(3)). The order will (a) require the young offender for a period of three months, commencing with the date of the order, to comply with the specified action plan (which is a series of requirements with respect to his actions and whereabouts during that time); (b) place him under supervision; and (c) require him to comply with directions given by the supervisor (who will be a probation officer, a social worker or a member of a youth offending team) as to the implementation of the action plan (s. 69(1)). Requirements to be made of the young offender, any or all of which may be included by the court in a particular action plan (s. 70(1)), are:

(a)   to participate in specified activities at specified times;
(b)   to present himself to a specified person at a specified place and time;
(c)   to attend at an attendance centre for a specified number of hours;
(d)   to stay away from a place or places specified in the requirements;
(e)   to comply with any specified arrangements for his education;
(f)   to make reparation to a specified person or to the community at large; and
(g)   to attend any hearing fixed by the court under s. 71.

Requirement (c) above cannot be included unless the offence committed by the young offender is punishable with imprisonment in the case of an adult (s. 70(2)), and requirement (f) cannot be included unless a person has been identified as a victim of the offence or a person otherwise affected by it and that person consents to the reparation being made (s. 70(4)). The requirements included in the action plan order must, so far as possible, not interfere with the times when the offender attends school or conflict with his religious beliefs or with the requirements of any other community order to which he may be subject (s. 70(5)). The White Paper (Home Office, 1997) indicated that the requirements in the action plan order will be tailored to the individual young offender, reflecting consultation with the offender, his family and perhaps the victim, and 'it may include elements such as motor projects, anger management courses, alcohol or drug treatment programmes or help with problems at home or at school or in finding accommodation, training or employment'.

The court must explain to the offender in ordinary language the effect of the order and the requirements to be inserted into it and the consequences of failure to comply with the order (s. 79(11)). For the powers of the court on breach of the order see **5.12.3**. Immediately after making an action plan order the court may fix a further hearing for a date not more than 21 days after the date of the order (s. 71(1)) at which time the supervising officer will submit a progress report, indicating the extent to which the order has been implemented and its effectiveness. In the light of that report the court may cancel any of the existing requirements or insert new ones. The young offender may be required to attend that hearing.

5.12.2 Combining an action plan order with other sentences or orders

Section 69(5) of the PCC(S)A 2000 states that an action plan order shall not be made if the offender is already the subject of such an order, or if the court proposes to pass a custodial sentence, a CRO, a CPO, a CPRO, a supervision order, an attendance centre order or a referral order. Reparation orders are not included in this list but, since an element of reparation may be included within an action plan order, mixing the two orders together would seem to be undesirable. There is nothing to prevent an action plan order being combined with a fine, a compensation order, a deprivation order or a restitution order but, more generally, the compendious nature of the action plan order makes it unlikely that courts would wish to combine it with other sentences or orders.

5.12.3 Revocation and amendment of an action plan order

Arrangements for discharge or variation of an action plan order (or a reparation order) are set out in the PCC(S)A 2000, sch. 8. Para. 5 provides that while an action plan order is in force the young offender or the supervisor may make application to the youth court for an order to discharge that order, or to vary it by cancelling any provision within it or by inserting any fresh provision. Ordinarily the young offender should be present in court at the time the application is made (para. 6), but his attendance is not necessary where, for instance, the court is discharging the action plan order or cancelling a requirement in it (para. 6(9)). If an application for discharge is made, and is dismissed by the court, no further application for discharge can be made without the consent of the court.

5.12.4 Breach of an action plan order

Arrangements for dealing with failure to comply with the terms of an action plan order (or a reparation order) are set out in the PCC(S)A 2000, sch. 8. When dealing with the young offender for breach of an action plan order the relevant court must take into account the extent to which he has complied with the order (para. 2(7)). The young offender should be present in court (para. 6(1)).

Paragraph 2 provides that where it is proved that the young offender has failed to comply with any of the requirements of the order the youth court (a) whether or not it also revokes the order, may fine the offender an amount not exceeding £1,000, or make an attendance centre order, or a curfew order on him, or (b) if the original order was made by a youth court, may discharge the order and deal with the young offender in any manner in which he could have been dealt with for the offence, or (c) if the original order was made by the Crown Court, the youth court may commit the young offender in custody or on bail until he can appear before the Crown Court (para. 2(2)). The Crown Court must then revoke the action plan order and deal with the young offender in any manner in which he could have been dealt with by that court for the offence (para. 2(4) and (5)).

6 Fines and Deprivation Orders

A fine is an order that the offender shall pay a sum of money to the state, and it is the most commonly imposed penalty in the courts. In 1999 the fine was the selected sentence in 34 per cent of indictable offences in magistrates' courts and 3 per cent of such offences in the Crown Court. It was used in 78 per cent of summary (non-motoring) cases in magistrates' courts and for summary motoring cases heard there it was used in 89 per cent of cases. Although these figures appear to be very high, the importance of the fine in sentencing should not be overstated. These figures are skewed because of the almost exclusive use of the fine as the sentence for minor offences, regulatory offences and road traffic offences. Crimes of violence, sexual offences and serious crimes against property are unlikely to be dealt with by way of a fine, since their seriousness renders the fine an unsuitable punishment. Figures for the relative use of different sentencing options, for a range of different offences, are given in Chapter 12. The proportionate use of the fine has declined over the last ten years. The percentage of male offenders aged over 21 who were sentenced for indictable offences and received a fine has decreased from 42 per cent of the total in 1988 to 31 per cent in 1999. For male offenders aged 18 but under 21 the percentage fined has fallen from 42 per cent in 1988 to 29 per cent in 1999. The decline in the rate of use of the fine for female offenders, in both these groups, has been even more marked. This change seems to be taking place at the same time as a substantial increase in the proportionate use by the courts of custody, the conditional discharge and, to a lesser extent, community sentences.

In terms of the sentencing structure created by the CJA 1991, the fine occupies a somewhat ambivalent position. It is clear that if the offence committed is so serious that only a custodial sentence would be an adequate penalty then a fine cannot be used. In general, too, the fine can be regarded as occupying a lower tier in the sentencing framework than the community orders, but that will not always be the case. It will be recalled that PCC(S)A 2000, s. 35(1) requires that a community sentence shall not be imposed unless the offence is serious enough for that approach to be justified, but it does not require that the offence be too serious for it to be dealt with by way of a fine. There is thus a degree of overlap between the fine and the community sentences, so that the court will sometimes have to make a choice between them. It is submitted that in making a choice between a community order and a fine the main criterion for the court to consider will be whether a simple financial penalty ('hitting the offender in the pocket') is a proper and adequate response to the case, or whether the nature of the offence and the character of the offender requires more intensive intervention by the state in the life of the offender, by requiring his supervision, community work or whatever. For special provision in relation to persistent petty offenders, see **6.6**.

When a fine is imposed, payment is normally made, whether by cash or a cheque, to the clerk of the appropriate magistrates' court, who at periodical intervals accounts for the revenue which has been received to the Secretary of State (Justices of the Peace Act 1979, s. 61). The fine is one of the very few sentencing options that actually generates income for the state.

All offences, apart from those attracting a mandatory life sentence (murder) or a sentence under PCC(S)A 2000, ss. 109–111, are punishable by fine. The great majority of summary offences, as they were originally drafted, provided for punishment by way of a fine not exceeding a certain stated sum. Changing these sums across a myriad of summary offences, to take account of changes in the value of money, was a complex matter. As a result of the CJA 1982, all statutes creating summary offences which provide for a financial penalty have been amended, so as to permit a fine to be imposed which does not exceed the amount shown at a certain level on a 'standard scale' of fines (i.e. the statutes no longer refer to a sum of money). The standard scale is set out at **6.2.1**. The advantage of this development is that changes over time to the value of money may be taken into account by adjustment to the standard scale, rather than by having to amend all the individual provisions so affected. If a statute mentions only imprisonment as a means of dealing with offenders for a summary offence, a fine not exceeding level 3 may none the less be imposed as an alternative (MCA 1980, s. 34(3)). In the case of indictable offences, PCC(S)A 2000, s. 127 empowers the Crown Court, following conviction on indictment, to fine the offender in lieu of, or in addition to, dealing with him in any other way. This power does not apply, however, where:

(a)   the sentence is fixed by law, i.e. after conviction for the offence of murder; or

(b)   the sentence falls to be imposed under ss. 109–111; or

(c)   where the use of some other power precludes the use of the fine (e.g. a discharge, or a hospital order).

6.1   FINES IN THE CROWN COURT

6.1.1   Maximum fines in the Crown Court

Where an offender has been convicted on indictment, there is no statutory limit to the amount of the fine which may be imposed by the Crown Court (CLA 1977, s. 32(1)). In *Ronson* [1991] Crim LR 794 the Court of Appeal upheld a fine of £5 million (in addition to a prison sentence). Nor is there a limit if the offender has been committed to the Crown Court for sentence under PCC(S)A 2000, s. 3, following summary conviction in a magistrates' court of an offence triable either way.

There are, however, some circumstances in which the maximum fine which the Crown Court can impose is restricted to the maximum fine which is available in the magistrates' courts. These circumstances are:

(a)   where the offender is convicted on indictment of a summary offence dealt with on indictment by virtue of CJA 1988, s. 40 (see further **1.2.3**);

(b)   where an offender is committed for sentence for a minor offence under CJA 1967, s. 56 (various minor offences);

(c)   where the Crown Court resentences an offender for an offence for which he was previously sentenced by a magistrates' court to a community sentence or previously conditionally discharged by a magistrates' court (see further **5.9.2** and **7.1.5**); and

(d)   where a fine is imposed on the disposal of an appeal against conviction or against a sentence passed in a magistrates' court.

6.1.2   Crown Court's duty to fix term in default

A term of imprisonment or detention to be served in default must be fixed in every case where the Crown Court imposes a fine (PCC(S)A 2000, s. 139(2)), unless the offender is under 18 years of age. If the offender is aged between 18 and 20 inclusive, the term in default takes the form of a term of detention under PCC(S)A 2000, s. 108. If such an offender eventually has to serve the term, he may be detained in a prison, young offender institution or remand centre at the discretion of the authorities (s. 108(5)). No term of detention in default can be ordered in respect of a person under 18 (*Basid* [1996] 1 Cr App R (S) 421).

Despite the apparently mandatory nature of the duty to fix a term in default, it has been held that a failure to fix such a term does not invalidate the fine itself (*Hamilton* (1980) 2 Cr App R (S) 1). The term which is fixed by the court should relate to the whole sum of the fine, rather than to any instalment (*Power* (1986) 8 Cr App R (S) 8). Where fines are imposed in respect of more than one offence, the terms to be served in default may be ordered to run concurrently or consecutively (*Savundra Nayagan* [1968] 1 WLR 1761). Also, the court may order that the term(s) to be served in default can run concurrently with, or consecutively to, any term of imprisonment (or detention in a young offender institution) to which the offender is sentenced at that time by the court, or which he is currently serving (PCC(S)A 2000, s. 139(5)). A term of imprisonment in default may be imposed consecutively to a maximum prison sentence imposed for the same offence (*Carver* [1955] 1 WLR 181). Consecutive custodial terms are, however, subject to the totality principle (*Savundra Nayagan* and *Benmore* (1983) 5 Cr App R (S) 468), and the total term (i.e. the term of imprisonment for the offence plus the term in default) should not be disproportionate to the overall gravity of the offending. This principle is discussed at **4.4.4**.

Where the Crown Court imposes a fine on committal for sentence from a magistrates' court, in circumstances where the powers of the Crown Court are limited to those of the magistrates' court (see **6.1.1**), the Crown Court must nevertheless specify the term to be served in default (s. 139(7)).

The maximum terms of imprisonment or detention which may be ordered by the Crown Court are set out in s. 139(4).

Size of fine	*Maximum term in default*
Not exceeding £200	7 days
Over £200, not exceeding £500	14 days
Over £500, not exceeding £1,000	28 days
Over £1,000, not exceeding £2,500	45 days
Over £2,500, not exceeding £5,000	3 months
Over £5,000, not exceeding £10,000	6 months
Over £10,000, not exceeding £20,000	12 months
Over £20,000, not exceeding £50,000	18 months
Over £50,000, not exceeding £100,000	2 years
Over £100,000, not exceeding £250,000	3 years
Over £250,000, not exceeding £1 million	5 years
Over £1 million	10 years

These are maximum periods and, of course, the Crown Court has discretion to fix shorter terms. An appropriate period from within the band should be selected (*French* (1995) 16 Cr App R (S) 841).

6.1.3 Crown Court fines: allowing time to pay

When imposing a fine (or forfeiting a recognisance, or making an order for the payment of compensation or costs), the sum becomes due for payment immediately and some offenders pay before leaving the court, by cash or cheque. Whether a cheque is accepted as payment is, of course, at the clerk's discretion. The Crown Court (and magistrates' courts) are, however, usually under a duty to give the offender 'time to pay'. This might be done by fixing a date by which the whole sum must be paid or, more likely, by making arrangements for the payment of the sum by instalments. Even where it is not strictly under such a duty, the court always has a discretion to allow time to pay (PCC(S)A 2000, s. 139(1)). If time to pay is granted, and it almost invariably is, enforcement is the responsibility of the magistrates' court (see **6.5**). The only occasions on which the Crown Court (or a magistrates' court) may refuse to allow an offender time to pay are when, by s. 139(3):

(a)   the offence is punishable with imprisonment and the offender appears to have sufficient means to pay the sum forthwith, i.e. in practice, on the same day;

(b)   it appears to the court that the offender is unlikely to remain long enough at a place of abode in the United Kingdom to enable payment of the sum to be enforced by other methods; or

(c)   the offender is already serving a custodial sentence or a term of detention under s. 108, or is given a custodial sentence by the court at the same time as it imposes the fine.

The court may order that the offender be searched (by a police officer of the same sex as the offender), so that money found on him can be used to pay the fine (s. 142(1)). Such money cannot be used if the court is satisfied that the money does not belong to the offender. When a court grants time to pay, it either fixes a period within which the entire sum must be paid or it orders that the sum be paid by fixed instalments.

Where a court allows payment of a fine by instalments, the general rule is that the fine should be capable of being paid off by the offender within 12 months (*Knight* (1980) 2 Cr App R (S) 82 and *Nunn* (1983) 5 Cr App R (S) 203). This is certainly not a rigid rule, however, and in *Olliver* (1989) 11 Cr App R (S) 10 Lord Lane CJ said:

> . . . there is nothing wrong in principle with the period of payment being longer, indeed much longer than one year, providing it is not an undue burden and so too severe a punishment having regard to the nature of the offence and the nature of the offender. Certainly it seems to us that a two-year period will seldom be too long, and in an appropriate case three years will be unassailable, again of course depending on the nature of the offender and the nature of the offence.

Where payment is fixed by instalments, the offender is in default as soon as he fails to meet any one of the instalment payments.

On the rare occasions when a Crown Court refuses time to pay and the offender does not produce the money at once, the offender will be detained, first at court, and then by committal to prison until he pays or has served the term which was fixed in default.

6.1.4 Crown Court fines: fine should reflect the seriousness of the offence

The first principle of sentencing in relation to the use of the fine in the Crown Court is that the selection of the fine rather than some other punishment, and the determination of the appropriate level of the fine, if selected, should reflect, primarily, the seriousness of the offence (PCC(S)A 2000, s. 128(2)).

Clearly, a fine is an inappropriate penalty where the seriousness of the offence requires an immediate custodial sentence. An example is *A-G's Reference (No. 41 of 1994)* (1995) 16 Cr App R (S) 792, where fines totalling £350 had been imposed on the offender, who had pleaded guilty to wounding with intent to cause grievous bodily harm. He had struck the victim on the head with a bottle, causing a wound which required stitches, and subsequently threatened him with a knife. The Court of Appeal held that the sentence was 'absurd', unduly lenient, and substituted a custodial term of 30 months. On the other hand, there are cases where the facts do not disclose a degree of seriousness sufficient to justify a fine. A discharge may well be the proper sentence in that case. In *Jamieson* (1975) 60 Cr App R 318 the offender, who had a clean record and substantial personal mitigation, was convicted of theft of a half bottle of whisky from a supermarket and fined £300 with £100 costs. The Court of Appeal varied the sentence to a conditional discharge and an order to pay costs not exceeding £50.

As far as the level of the fine is concerned, this should also reflect primarily the seriousness of the offence (s. 128(2)). In parallel to the principle which applies in relation to custodial sentences, it is clear that the imposition by the court of the maximum fine should be reserved for the most serious instances of the offence which are reasonably likely to occur. An illustration of this point is *Universal Salvage* v *Boothby* (1983) 5 Cr App R (S) 428 which, although a magistrates' court decision, is certainly applicable to the Crown Court as well. In that case the company was fined for breach of regulations requiring it to have in its lorry proper equipment to record the journeys made by the lorry. It was accepted that, in reliance on a letter from the relevant government department, the company had reasonably believed that the lorry was a 'specialised breakdown vehicle', and as such was not required to carry the recording equipment. The offence being one of strict liability the company was none the less guilty. The magistrates imposed the maximum available fine, which was £200. The Divisional Court, on an appeal by way of case stated, held that the circumstances surrounding the offence, particularly the reasonable reliance upon the letter, provided considerable mitigation. In a case where such mitigation was present it was an error of law for the magistrates to have imposed the maximum sentence.

In all cases involving fines it is the 'first duty' of the sentencer to 'measure that fine against the gravity of the offence' (per Kenneth Jones LJ in *Messana* (1981) 3 Cr App R (S) 88), having regard to all relevant matters in aggravation and mitigation. As with custodial sentences, there is no precise tariff, only a degree of consensus over how large or how small particular fines should be. In *Cleminson* (1985) 7 Cr App R (S) 128 the offender pleaded guilty to handling stolen goods, some jewellery which had been stolen in a burglary. The jewellery was recovered. She was fined £1,000. According to Boreham J, 'judged by the gravity of the crime itself, this was a penalty which, in our judgment, was excessive . . . the appropriate fine is £150'. At the other end of the scale, in *F. and M. Dobson Ltd* (1995) 16 Cr App R (S) 957, a fine of £25,000 had been imposed on a confectionery manufacturer for failing to detect the blade of a Stanley knife in one of its products. The Court of Appeal said that the relevant considerations were the level of culpability involved plus the need to reflect an element of deterence. The fine was reduced to £7,000. In *Fairbairn* (1980) 2 Cr App R (S) 315, where the offender was convicted of seven counts of theft from his employers of goods estimated to be worth between £600 and £700, and received a prison sentence of nine months together with fines totalling £7,500, the Court of Appeal, while not disapproving the custodial sentence, pointed out that 'the amount of the fine was over 10 times the value of the goods stolen, and . . . is out of scale in relation to the gravity of the offence of which he was convicted'. This last case should certainly not be taken to say that the amount of the fine should equate to the value of the property taken, but there will be many cases in which a rough equivalence will be appropriate. In any event, these cases must now be read subject to PCC(S)A 2000, s. 128(4), which requires the Crown Court to adjust the level of a fine to take account of the offender's means. In the case of a well-off offender convicted, say, of a minor theft, the level of the fine is likely to be significantly more than the value of the property stolen. In *Roberts* (1980) 2 Cr App R (S) 121, where the judge apparently calculated the fine on the basis of the compensation which would have been received if the victim had made application to the Criminal Injuries Compensation Board, the Court of Appeal disapproved that approach.

6.1.5 Crown Court fines: amount of the fine should be adjusted to take account of means

The court is required by PCC(S)A 2000, s. 128(1) and (3) to inquire into the financial circumstances of the offender, and take those into account when fixing the level of the fine. Of course, a fine is meant to be a punishment, and it is perfectly proper that the offender should have to endure a degree of 'hardship', as Lord Lane CJ put it in *Olliver* (1989) 11 Cr App R (S) 10, since 'one of the objects of the fine is to remind the offender that what he has done is wrong'. Such hardship might properly involve the offender giving up other expenditure and leisure activities or postponing the purchase of some item in order to pay. But a fine which is so large that the offender will not be able to pay it and, at the same time, provide for the necessities of life, is counter-productive. The offender may, indeed, be tempted into more crime in order to pay the fine. The main point, however, is that if a court imposes a fine at an unrealistically high level it is not in reality imposing a fine at all — it is really imposing a custodial sentence, since the offender may end up going to prison in default of payment. To take this course is wrong in principle because the seriousness of the offence did not require custody in the first place. Clearly, the principle of adjusting the fine to meet an offender's ability to pay will, on occasions, conflict with the principle expressed at **6.1.4**, and great care is needed in its exercise.

A number of important sentencing principles should be noted here. Where the offender lacks the means to pay the fine proportionate to the seriousness of the offence, it is clearly contrary to principle to impose a custodial sentence instead. According to Roskill LJ in *Reeves* (1972) 57 Cr App R 366, where the offender had pleaded guilty to obtaining £600 by deception and had received a prison sentence of nine months, the comments made by the sentencer 'must plainly have indicated to the appellant . . . that he was being sent to prison not because the offence itself merited a sentence of immediate imprisonment but because he had not the financial wherewithal to pay a substantial fine. That . . . is, of course, completely wrong.' The same principle applies to the imposition of a suspended prison sentence in these circumstances, since such a sentence should be passed only where a prison sentence would have been appropriate in the absence of a power to suspend (see **4.6.3**). Whenever the use of custody is inappropriate for this reason, there are three alternatives which the court might consider. The first is to ask whether the offender's lack of means might in some cases justify the selection of a community sentence instead. This might be appropriate so long as the offending is 'serious enough to warrant such a sentence' (PCC(S)A 2000, s. 35(1)). If so, the court should then select that community order which is the 'most suitable for the offender' (s. 35(3)(a)) and which involves a level of restriction upon the offender's liberty which is commensurate with the seriousness of the case (s. 35(3)(b)). See further the provisions on persistent petty offenders (see **6.6**). A second possibility is to move to a conditional discharge instead. A third is to adjust the level of the fine downwards, to a sum which the offender can reasonably afford to pay. A good example of consideration of these options was provided by the Court of Appeal in *Ball* (1981) 3 Cr App R (S) 283. The 18-year-old offender had been convicted of shoplifting. The Court of Appeal disapproved, as too severe a punishment, the suspended prison sentence which had been passed by the sentencer. The pre-sentence report which had been prepared did not recommend a probation order because, its author said, the offender was 'a basically honest young woman' and was not, apparently, in need of supervision. In this case a conditional discharge was not appropriate either, since the offender was, as a result of her conviction for shoplifting, now in breach of a conditional discharge imposed for her only other previous offence, handling stolen goods. The Court of Appeal therefore selected 'the least wrong course which is open to us', imposing a £25 fine, with six months in which to pay. There is no precise formula to determine the sum to which the fine should be reduced in such circumstances.

Where the offender is well-off and the fine appropriate to the offence would create little inconvenience for him, it is clearly contrary to principle to impose a custodial sentence for that reason (*Gillies* [1965] Crim LR 64). It is, however, right to raise the level of the fine in such a case, so as to increase its penal 'bite'. Section 128(4) of the PCC(S)A 2000 makes it clear that the level of the fine should be adjusted to reflect the offender's means whether this has the 'effect of increasing or reducing the amount of the fine'. Punishment does not lie in the amount of a fine but in the degree of hardship and inconvenience caused by the need to pay it. Section 128(4) does not, of course, affect the principle that an offender who is well-off should not be dealt with by financial penalty where the offence itself merits custody and a person who is less well-off would have gone to prison (*Markwick* (1953) 37 Cr App R 125). The principle that a rich offender must not be seen to 'buy his way out of prison' is a fundamental one, and it applies equally where the offender has friends or family who are able to meet a substantial fine (*Curtis* (1984) 6 Cr App R (S) 250).

The principle that the level of the fine should be adjusted according to the offender's means entails that the court should not assume that somebody else will pay the fine. In *Charambous* (1984) 6 Cr App R (S) 389, where a fine was imposed on a married woman who had limited income of her own, the Court of Appeal stressed that the fine must reflect the offender's means and was not a fine on their family.

Section 128(1) of the PCC(S)A 2000 requires the court to inquire into the offender's financial circumstances before fixing the level of the fine. Section 126 provides that a court may, for that purpose, make a 'financial circumstances order' requiring him to provide for the court a statement of his financial circumstances. Failure to comply without reasonable excuse is an offence, as is furnishing a statement known to be false in a material particular.

6.1.6 Crown Court fines: the totality principle

In *Chelmsford Crown Court, ex parte Birchall* (1989) 11 Cr App R (S) 510 the offender, an independent haulage contractor, pleaded guilty before a magistrates' court to ten offences of using a goods vehicle whose gross weight exceeded the weight shown on the plating certificate, the degree of overweight varying on these occasions between 15 per cent and 25 per cent. He was fined a total of £7,600. The fines were calculated by a formula which took a basic fine of £400 as a starting point, then added a further £20 for each 1 per cent by which the overweight exceeded the permitted maximum. The offender's appeal against this sentence to the Crown Court was dismissed. He applied for judicial review of the Crown Court's decision (see **13.1.3**) The Divisional Court said that it found the sentence 'truly astonishing'. The appropriate sentence for the total wrongdoing was said to be a fine of £1,300, allotted between the different offences by imposing a fine £400 on one and £100 on each of the others, the fine to be paid at the rate of £55 per month. The court emphasised that the application of a 'rigid formula' was incorrect when imposing a fine, even for a single offence, and it was wrong to apply it to each of ten offences and then add the sentences up. The court had to consider all the circumstances and apply the principles of sentencing which, it said, were 'well known'. The main importance of this decision is its clear endorsement of the 'totality principle' in relation to fines: that the sentencer must review the total sentence, and ensure that it remains proportionate to the totality of the offending, as well as being within the offender's capacity to pay.

Since that decision the totality principle has received statutory recognition and the PCC(S)A 2000, s. 158(2)(b) reinforces the common law by stating that nothing shall prevent a court 'in a case of an offender who is convicted of one or more other offences, from mitigating his sentence by applying any rule of law as to the totality of sentences'.

6.2. FINES IN MAGISTRATES' COURTS

6.2.1 Maximum fines in magistrates' courts

Where an offender has been summarily convicted of an offence triable either way which is listed in MCA 1980, sch. 1, the magistrates may fine him an amount not exceeding the 'prescribed sum' (MCA 1980, s. 32(1)). By s. 32(9), 'the prescribed sum' means £5,000. If the offender has been summarily convicted of an offence triable either way and the statute creating the offence prescribes a maximum penalty upon summary conviction which is greater than £5,000, the magistrates may fine him an amount not exceeding that higher maximum (s. 32(2)), and subject to the exception of certain drug offences listed in s. 32(5). There are also some 'continuing offences', where a fine prescribed in the relevant statute may be levied for each day on which the offence continues after the conviction (s. 32(4)). Where the maximum penalty indicated in the statute creating the offence is expressed to be 'the statutory maximum', that maximum shall be the prescribed sum, i.e. £5,000. In the case of an offender under 18 years of age, a special maximum fine applies (see **6.3**). Where magistrates are dealing with an offender for two or more offences (whether triable either way or triable summarily), there is no objection to them imposing fines which in the aggregate exceed what they could have imposed for any one offence, subject to their statutory duty to have regard to the offender's means and the totality principle.

The maximum fine which may be imposed for a summary offence is normally set out in the statute which creates the offence. If the statute refers only to punishment by means of imprisonment, a fine not exceeding level 3 may, nevertheless, be imposed as an alternative (MCA 1980, s. 34(3)). The 'standard scale' of maximum fines for summary offences is contained in CJA 1982, s. 37(2), and is as follows:

Level on the scale	*Amount of fine*
1	£200
2	£500
3	£1,000
4	£2,500
5	£5,000

A fine which is punishable at level 1 on the standard scale is generally known as a 'level 1' offence, and so on. Examples of *level 1* offences are: dog being on a designated road without being on a lead; holding on to a vehicle in order to be towed or carried; and pedestrian failing to give his name and address to a constable directing traffic after failing to stop. Examples of *level 2* offences are: not wearing a seat belt; riding a motor cycle without a helmet; and removing a fixed penalty notice attached to a vehicle. Examples of *level 3* offences are: speeding; failing to provide a specimen of breath for a breath test; misuse of a disabled person's badge; and cycling when unfit through drink. Examples of *level 4* offences are: careless driving; dangerous cycling; driving after making a false declaration as to physical fitness to drive. Examples of *level 5* offences are: driving with excess alcohol; driving while disqualified; and fitting of defective or unsuitable vehicle parts.

6.2.2 Magistrates' courts: normal requirement not to fix term in default

When a magistrates' court imposes a fine it should not normally fix a term of imprisonment (or detention under PCC(S)A 2000, s. 108) in default. This is in sharp contrast to the Crown Court duty to fix such a period (see **6.1.2**). If, however, the case is of a kind where the court is not obliged to allow the offender any time to pay (and by MCA 1980, s. 82(1) and (2), these are the same as the occasions set out in s. 139(3) in respect of the Crown Court: see **6.1.3**), it should fix such a term.

6.2.3 Magistrates' courts: sentencing principles

The sentencing principles applicable in relation to the use of the fine in magistrates' courts are the same as those which apply in the Crown Court, and which were described in **6.1.4** to **6.1.6**.

6.3 FINING JUVENILES

There are special provisions relating to the appropriate level of fines for juveniles, and in some circumstances the parents or guardian of a juvenile may be ordered to pay a fine imposed in respect of an offence committed by that juvenile.

Where a person under 18 years of age pleads guilty or is found guilty by a magistrates' court of an offence in respect of which the court would normally be empowered to impose a fine exceeding £1,000, the amount of the fine imposed must not exceed £1,000 (PCC(S)A 2000, s. 135(1)). If the offender is under the age of 14 and the court could otherwise have imposed a fine exceeding £250, the amount of the fine imposed shall not exceed £250 (s. 135(2)). There is no limit upon the fine which may be imposed by a Crown Court upon a juvenile convicted on indictment.

The parent or guardian of a person under 18 may be ordered to pay a fine (or a compensation order or costs) imposed upon the juvenile, by virtue of PCC(S)A 2000, s. 137. If such an order is made it is, of course, the means of the parent rather than the means of the juvenile, which are taken into account in determining the level of the fine (s. 138(1)). If the juvenile is aged under 16, however, it is the *duty* of the court to order that the fine, compensation or costs is paid by the parent or guardian rather than by the juvenile himself. The court *may* make such an order (or, in the case of a juvenile under 16, *must* make such an order), unless the court is satisfied either:

(a)   that the parent or guardian cannot be found; or

(b)   that it would be 'unreasonable to make an order for payment, having regard to the circumstances of the case'.

The power under s. 137 to order a parent or guardian to pay the fine imposed on a juvenile also applies where the fine has been imposed in consequence of breach of a community order or breach of supervision of a detention and training order. The court may also require an order for costs or a compensation order against a juvenile to be met by the juvenile's parent or guardian. Many 16 and 17-year-old offenders are in a position to pay the fine or compensation themselves, and it is appropriate that they should. If not, the parent should pay, especially where the order is for compensation and the victim would otherwise lose out. In respect of younger offenders, who are clearly unable themselves to pay, the court should not simply make the order and assume that a parent will pay. It is right that the parent should by order be required to pay, since this should have the effect of bringing home to them 'the reality of the consequences of their children's behaviour, and the implications for their own actions'. The *Criminal Statistics* show that, in 1999, 10 per cent of parents were ordered by the court to a pay a fine imposed on their child for an offence, and 23 per cent of parents were so ordered in respect of a compensation order. These are overall figures, and for younger juveniles the percentage of parents ordered to pay is much higher. For juveniles aged at least 10 but under 14, the equivalent figures were 32 per cent and 44 per cent.

The court should not make an order under s. 137 against a parent without first considering their means (*Lenihan* v *West Yorkshire Metropolitan Police* (1981) 3 Cr App R (S) 42) or without giving the parent an opportunity of being heard (s. 137(4)). It may in the circumstances be 'unreasonable' for the court to make an order under s. 137 in a case where the parent has done all that he or she reasonably could to prevent the offending. In *Sheffield Crown Court, ex parte Clarkson* (1986) 8 Cr App R (S) 454 it was held that any assessment made by the court about the financial position of the parents, or of the extent to which they had been neglectful of their offspring, must be made on the basis of properly admissible evidence. The Court of Appeal said that it was wrong simply to draw inferences about these matters from the pre-sentence report which had been prepared on the young offender. In *TA* v *DPP* [1997] 1 Cr App R (S) 1 a mother was required by the court to pay £100 compensation for criminal damage committed by her daughter, when she kicked the door panel of a police car. The Court of Appeal heard that the incident occurred at a local authority home. The daughter was living there temporarily, as the mother was unable to control her behaviour. Since the mother had, in practice, no control over what her child was doing at the relevant time, the order under s. 137 was incorrect and was quashed.

In the last-mentioned case the daughter was not in care, but in any case where a local authority has 'parental responsibility' for a juvenile within the meaning of the Children Act 1989, s. 3 and the juvenile is in their care or is provided with accommodation by them, that local authority will come within the scope of s. 137. Where the local authority is required to pay a fine (or a compensation order or costs), the usual requirement that the court must have regard to the offender's means does not apply but the court still has a discretion not to make an order where, having regard to the circumstances of the case, it would be unreasonable to do so. Accordingly, the Divisional Court in *D* v *DPP* (1995) 16 Cr App R (S) 1040 said that orders under s. 137 should not have been made where the relevant authority had, on the facts, done all it reasonably and properly could to keep the young offender from criminal ways and to protect the public. In *Bedfordshire County Council* v

DPP [1996] 1 Cr App R (S) 322 the Divisional Court stated that before ordering the authority to pay it was normally necessary to establish some causal link between any fault proved against the council and the commission of the particular offences. The court also stressed that, where a youth court was considering making an order that a local authority should pay a fine or compensation, the relevant authority must be given notice and informed of its right to make representations to the court.

An appeal against an order made by a magistrates' court under s. 137 lies to the Crown Court (s. 137(6)), and an appeal against an order made by the Crown Court lies to the Court of Appeal (s. 137(7)).

6.4 COMBINING FINES WITH OTHER SENTENCES OR ORDERS

Apart from the restrictions referred to in PCC(S)A 2000, s. 127 (enactment requiring offenders to be dealt with in a particular way), there is no general restriction on combining fines with imprisonment or other custodial sentences, whether in respect of the same offence or different offences sentenced on the same occasion, but in practice this will often not be a desirable combination, since incarceration may well deprive the offender of the means to pay the fine. In any event a fine and a custodial sentence will be an inappropriate combination where the offender lacks the means to pay the fine, and hence will serve the term fixed in default of payment (*Maunde* (1980) 2 Cr App R (S) 289), or where the offender will be saddled with a significant financial burden on his release from prison.

In several cases in the 1980s the Court of Appeal approved the addition of a fine to an immediate custodial sentence as a means of removing a 'substantial financial benefit' made by the offender from his offending (*Forsythe* (1980) 2 Cr App R (S) 15). In *Garner* (1985) 7 Cr App R (S) 285 Hodgson J described the fine in these cases as 'a rough and ready method of confiscating the profits of crime'. A more sophisticated approach to the removal of the proceeds of offending, which was not available to the courts at the time of these decisions, is to make a confiscation order: see Chapter 9.

A court which imposes a suspended sentence of imprisonment may also impose a fine for the same offence, but the offence must be one which would have been properly dealt with by way of immediate custody in the absence of a power to suspend the sentence (see **4.6.3**). A fine imposed in such circumstances is usually added by the court as a 'sting in the tail' of the suspension, and to provide an immediate penalty to counter any suggestion that the offender has received a complete 'let-off'. In every case in which a suspended sentence is imposed the court is required to consider 'whether the circumstances of the case are such as to warrant in addition the imposition of a fine or the making of a compensation order' (s. 118(5)). There are, however, dangers inherent in this combination (see **4.6.3**). Where the fine is being so used (as a subsidiary part of punishment), it is difficult to know how the court should gauge the proper level of the fine. One thing is clear, however. The court, as always, must have proper regard to the offender's means (*King* [1970] 1 WLR 1016).

It seems clear that a fine may, in principle, be combined with any of the community orders individually, or with any mix of community orders. Statutory restrictions which once existed on combining a fine with a CRO, or with a CPO, have been removed. A fine may not be combined with an absolute or conditional discharge, however, since a discharge may only be imposed where it is 'inexpedient to inflict punishment' (and see *McClelland* [1951] 1 All ER 557), but a fine and a discharge may be imposed on the same occasion for different offences.

A fine and a compensation order may be combined. The PCC(S)A 2000, s. 130(12) provides that, where the offender has insufficient means to pay both the appropriate fine and appropriate compensation, the court shall give preference to compensation. In a particular case this will mean that the level of the fine is reduced to enable the full compensation order to stand, or that no fine is ordered and the compensation order stands alone (see further **8.1.8**). Fines may be combined with other financial orders, such as an order to pay the costs of the prosecution, though the court must consider the total effect of the orders it is making and should ensure that the whole sum the offender has to pay is not beyond his means. According to the case of *Northallerton Magistrates' Court, ex parte Dove* [2000] 1 Cr App R (S) 136, the court should fix the level of the fine first, then consider awarding compensation, and then determine the costs. If the total sum exceeds the defendant's means the order for costs should be reduced rather than the fine. There is authority to the effect that a small fine should not be combined with a large order for costs (*Whalley* (1972) 56 Cr App R 304). A fine may also be combined with a restitution order under the PCC(S)A 2000, s. 148, a deprivation order under s. 143, or an order for disqualification from driving where the vehicle was used for the purposes of crime under s. 147.

A fine cannot be combined with a hospital order (MHA 1983, s. 37(8)).

6.5 ENFORCEMENT OF FINES

Enforcement of all fines rests with magistrates' courts, whether the fine was originally imposed in a magistrates' court or in the Crown Court. When ordering a fine, the Crown Court must fix a term to be served in default but a magistrates' court should not normally do so (see **6.1.2** and **6.2.2**). The procedure for enforcement of fines is contained in MCA 1980, ss. 75 to 91. As a result of the wide definition of 'fine' in MCA 1980, s. 150, the same procedures also apply to enforcement of compensation orders.

The magistrates' court responsible for enforcement is that court which imposed the fine or, if the fine was imposed by the Crown Court, the court specified in the fine order or, if none was specified, the court which committed the offender for trial or sentence to the Crown Court. Where the offender is now residing in a different petty sessions area, a transfer of fine order may be made (MCA 1980, s. 89).

When a fine is imposed it becomes due for payment immediately. The court may, however, allow time for payment or order payment by instalments (s. 75(1)). Subsequently, further time may be given (s. 75(2)). If the court orders payment by instalments, default in any one instalment is taken to be a default of all instalments then unpaid (s. 75(3)). Where a magistrates' court allows time (or further time) for payment, it may fix a day on which the offender must appear in person (unless he is serving a custodial sentence) to enable a means enquiry to be conducted (MCA 1980, s. 86). The offender must be present at such an inquiry, and his attendance can be secured by summons or by issuing a warrant for his arrest. Offenders cannot be imprisoned for default without such further inquiry into their means and full consideration of other methods of enforcement.

6.5.1 Immediate enforcement of fines

The magistrates' court may use the following methods to enforce *immediate* payment of the sum:

(a) The court may order the offender to be searched for money to meet the fine, with any balance being returned to the offender (s. 80(1)). Such money, which includes money found on the offender at the time of his arrest or at the time of his reception into prison or detention (s. 80(2)), must not be used for payment of the fine if the court is satisfied that the money does not belong to the offender, or if it is satisfied that 'the loss of the money would be more injurious to his family than would be his detention' (s. 80(3)).

(b)   Where the offence is punishable with imprisonment, the court may order the offender to be *detained* at a police station until 8 a.m. of the following day (s. 136).

(c)   The court, on the occasion of the conviction or on a subsequent occasion, may make a *money payment supervision order* (MCA 1980, s. 88), which should specify the terms of the payment. Such an order places the defendant under the care of a person, usually a probation officer, whose duty is to 'advise and befriend the offender with a view to inducing him to pay and thereby avoid imprisonment' (Magistrates' Courts Rules 1981, r. 56). There is no requirement that the offender consent to the making of the order. A money payment supervision order may be imposed on a juvenile as well as an adult, and in the case of an offender aged under 21 it must be used before committing to detention, unless it is undesirable or impracticable to do so (s. 88(4)). If the court commits an offender under 21 to detention without having first issued a money payment supervision order, it shall state in the warrant of commitment the reasons for so doing (s. 88(5)). The court shall not commit to prison in default a person in respect of whom a money payment supervision order has been made before taking reasonable steps to obtain a report from the supervisor (s. 88(6)).

(d)   The magistrates may issue a *warrant of distress*, authorising the seizure and sale of goods belonging to the offender, using the proceeds to meet the sum outstanding (s. 76). Where it appears that the offender has assets available to satisfy the sum outstanding, a distress warrant should be used rather than committal to prison (*Birmingham Justices, ex parte Bennett* [1983] 1 WLR 114). The court may also postpone the issue of a warrant if it thinks it expedient to do so, until such time and on such conditions as the court thinks just (s. 77).

(e)   The court may order the offender's *immediate imprisonment* (or, in the case of an offender aged 18 or over but under 21, detention under the PCC(S)A 2000, s. 108) for the term specified as being the time to be served in default or, if no such time was specified, a term specified by the court having regard to the table in the MCA 1980, sch. 4. This table corresponds to the first seven entries listed in the PCC(S)A 2000, s. 139(4), which is set out at **6.1.2**. It should be noted that the periods specified in the table are the maximum periods which may be ordered, and shorter periods may be ordered at the discretion of the court. The minimum period of imprisonment which can be imposed in any case is five days (s. 132). By MCA 980, s. 82(1), immediate committal to custody cannot be ordered unless:

(i)   in the case of an offence punishable with imprisonment, the offender appears to the court to have sufficient means to pay the sum forthwith, or

(ii)   whether the offence is punishable with imprisonment or not, it appears to the court that the offender is unlikely to remain long enough at a place of abode in the United Kingdom to enable payment of the sum to be enforced by other methods, or

(iii)   the offender is being sent to prison or detention on the same or another charge, or if the offender is already serving a prison sentence or sentence of detention.

The court should announce its reason(s) for making an immediate committal and the reason(s) should be entered in the court register and on the committal warrant. Failure to specify reasons may result in the committal being challenged successfully by way of judicial review (*Oldham Justices, ex parte Cawley* [1996] 1 All ER 464). If, even at this stage, the defendant tenders payment of the fine to court staff or other officials, payment should be received from him, and he is entitled to be released.

The default period can be ordered to be served concurrently with or consecutively to another sentence already being served. If ordered to run consecutively it is not unlawful for the addition of the default period to the custodial term already imposed to exceed the statutory maximum for magistrates' courts (*Green* [1977] 1 All ER 353), but consecutive terms are subject to the totality principle (see **4.4.4**). If more than one fine is being enforced, the periods of imprisonment or detention in default may run consecutively to each other, except that the total period to be served must not exceed the maximum stated in the table in sch. 4 to the 1980 Act as being appropriate for the aggregate sum and, again, this is subject to the totality principle (*Southampton Justices, ex parte Davies* [1981] 1 All ER 722).

Where the offender serves the whole of the term in default this has the effect of expunging the fine. Payment of the sum in default means that the person must be released (s. 79(1)). Part payment of the sum by the offender will result in a proportionate reduction in the term to be served in default (s. 79(2) and (3)).

6.5.2 Enforcement pursuant to means inquiry

If the offender fails to pay the whole or any part of the sum within the time allowed by the court, the magistrates' court may issue a summons or warrant requiring the offender to appear or issue a warrant to arrest him and bring him before the court to conduct a means inquiry to investigate the defendant's ability to pay (s. 83). The court may require that the defendant produce evidence of his income and outgoings. If the court orders the defendant to produce a statement of means and the defendant fails to do so, such failure is an offence punishable by a fine not exceeding £1,000 (s. 84(2)). If the offender knowingly or recklessly furnishes a statement which is false in a material particular, or knowingly fails to disclose any material fact, this is an offence punishable with imprisonment not exceeding four months, a fine not exceeding £1,000, or both (s. 84(3)).

In the light of information received by the court at the means inquiry, the magistrates may grant further time to the offender for payment of the fine, or arrange payment by instalments, or reduce the amount of each instalment (s. 75). The court may remit the whole or any part of the fine having regard to any change in his circumstances since the offender's conviction (s. 85(1)). The court may also remit or reduce the fine where the fine was imposed in the absence of adequate information about his means either because he was convicted in his absence or failed to comply with an order to furnish information concerning his means. In no circumstances can the court increase the fine in consequence of holding a means inquiry. If the Crown Court imposed the fine, the magistrates may only remit the fine in whole or in part if they first obtain the consent of the Crown Court. It should be noted that the power to remit is restricted to fines, and there is no equivalent power in respect of compensation orders (s. 85(2)).

Pursuant to a means inquiry, the magistrates' court may enforce payment by the following methods:

(a) to (d)   The methods which are set out at (a) to (d) in **6.5.1** are available.

(e)   In the case of an offender who is employed, the court may make an *attachment of earnings order*, directing that the employer make deductions from the offender's wages after deduction of tax and remit them to the court. This procedure is governed by the Attachment of Earnings Act 1971, s. 14. Such an order can be imposed on a person aged under 18 as well as on a person aged 18 or over.

(f) In respect of offenders aged 18 or over, the court may make an order for the *deduction from the offender's income support payments* in accordance with the Criminal Justice Act 1991, s. 24. The court makes application to the appropriate district office of the Department of Social Security for this to be done. Detailed arrangements are set out in the Fines (Deduction from Income Support) Regulations 1992 (SI 1992/2182).

(g) In respect of offenders under the age of 25, the court may make an attendance centre order (PCC(S)A 2000, s. 60 and see **5.10.2**).

(h) In respect of offenders aged 16 or over the court may, by the C(S)A 1997, s. 35, make a community service order. The minimum number of hours community service which may be ordered under s. 35 is 20 (s. 35(5)). By s. 35(6), in the case of a sum in default not exceeding £200 the number of hours of community service shall not exceed 40, for a sum exceeding £200 but not exceeding £500 the number of hours shall not exceed 60, and for a sum exceeding £500 the number of days shall not exceed 100. A magistrates' court shall not make an order under this section unless notified by the Secretary of State that arrangements for implementing such orders are available in the relevant area (s. 35(11)). On payment of the whole sum in default the order ceases to have effect and on a payment of part of the sum the number of hours shall be reduced proportionately (s. 35(13)).

(i) In respect of an offender aged 16 or over the court may, by the C(S)A 1997, s. 35, make a curfew order. By s. 35(9), in the case of a sum in default not exceeding £200 the number of days to which the curfew order may relate shall not exceed 20, for a sum exceeding £200 but not exceeding £500 the number of days shall not exceed 30, for a sum exceeding £500 but not exceeding £1,000 the number of days shall not exceed 60, for a sum exceeding £1,500 but not exceeding £2,500 the number of days shall not exceed 90, and for a sum exceeding £2,500 the number of days shall not exceed 180. A magistrates' court shall not make an order under this section unless notified by the Secretary of State that arrangements for implementing such orders are available in the relevant area (s. 35(11)). On payment of the whole sum in default the order ceases to have effect and on a payment of part of the sum the number of hours or days shall be reduced proportionately (s. 35(13)).

(j) By the C(S)A 1997, s. 40, the court may order the person in default to be disqualified from holding or obtaining a driving licence for such period, not exceeding 12 months, as the court thinks fit. A magistrates' court shall not make an order under this section unless notified by the Secretary of State that the power to make such orders is exercisable by the court (s. 40(3)). On payment of the whole sum in default the disqualification ceases to have effect and on a payment of part of the sum the period of disqualification shall be reduced proportionately (s. 40(4)).

(k) The court may order the offender's *immediate imprisonment* (or, in the case of an offender aged 18 or over but under 21, detention under the PCC(S)A 2000, s. 108) for the term originally specified as being the time to be served in default or, if no such time was specified, a term specified by the court having regard to the table in the MCA 1980, sch. 4. This table corresponds to the first seven entries listed in the PCC(S)A 2000, s. 139(4), which is set out at **6.1.2**. An immediate committal to custody can only be ordered where since the conviction the court has inquired into the offender's means in his presence on at least one occasion and where:

(i) in the case of an offence punishable with imprisonment the offender appears to the court to have sufficient means to pay the sum outstanding forthwith, or

(ii)   the court is satisfied that the default is due to the offender's wilful refusal or culpable neglect and the court has considered or tried all other methods of enforcing payment of the sum and it appears to the court that they are inappropriate or unsuccessful (1980 Act, s. 82(4)).

Further restrictions on the use of immediate committal to prison are set out in s. 82(5) to (5F). The court must have 'considered or tried' all other methods of enforcement: these words must be complied with and allow no room for the exercise of discretion (*Norwich Magistrates' Court, ex parte Lilly* (1987) 151 JP 689). The warrant of commital should state the grounds on which the court was satisfied that it was undesirable or impracticable to use the other methods of enforcement (*Oldham Justices, ex parte Cawley* [1996] 1 All ER 464). For offenders aged over 18 but under 21, the PCC(S)A 2000, s. 108(4) further requires the justices to specify in the warrant their reasons for concluding that detention is the only appropriate method of dealing with the defaulter. 'Wilful refusal', which means a deliberate defiance of the court order, or 'culpable neglect', which means a reckless disregard of the court order, must be established by proof beyond reasonable doubt (*South Tyneside Justices, ex parte Martin* (1995) *The Independent*, 20 September 1995).

6.6   PERSISTENT PETTY OFFENDERS

The PCC(S)A 2000, s. 59 provides powers for magistrates' courts and the Crown Court applicable in a case where, ordinarily, the court would have imposed a fine on the offender as the penalty commensurate with the seriousness of the offence, but where the evidence is that the offender already has outstanding fines against his name. In these circumstances it may seem pointless to impose a further financial burden on the offender, so s. 59 permits the court to impose a CPO, or a curfew order, instead. Both CPO and curfew order have the same meaning in this context as they have when used as straightforward community orders, except that while a curfew order used as a community sentence may be imposed on an offender under 16 here it applies only to those aged 16 and over. CPOs are, of course, only available to those aged 16 and over in any event.

The term 'persistent petty offenders' is not used in the section itself, but appears in the section heading and must be intended to give some indication of the audience at which these measures are meant to be targeted. Operation of the provision, by s. 59(2), requires that:

(a)   one or more fines imposed on the offender in respect of one or more previous offences have not been paid; and

(b)   if a fine were imposed in an amount which was commensurate with the seriousness of the offence, the offender would not have sufficient means to pay it.

Paragraph (a) is a rather token attempt to capture the element of 'persistence', requiring that the offender has now committed at least three offences, and the meaning of 'petty' is also contentious. It clearly means that these offences are ordinarily punishable by way of fine, but is says nothing about the level of the fine. If s. 59 is really confined to 'petty' cases, why is it made available to the Crown Court? Objection might be made to the section that it breaches the important principle deriving from the 1991 Act, that a community sentence should be imposed only where the offence is 'serious enough' to justify it. This is presumably why s. 59(2) states that the community order may be imposed on a petty persistent offender 'notwithstanding anything in subsections (1) and (3)(b) of section 35 above'. As explained earlier, however, there has always been a degree of overlap between fines and community sentences and, provided that the community order does not create onerous obligations out of all proportion to the nature of the offending, it is not objectionable to use that alternative where extracting fines from the offender has proved very difficult in the past. As we have seen, these same community sentences may now be used as methods of fine enforcement (**6.5.2**). Section 59 could be viewed as a more honest approach to the problem, avoiding the complexity and delay of fine enforcement procedures, which may have led to the same result in any event.

6.7   DEPRIVATION ORDERS UNDER THE PCC(S)A 2000, s. 143

The main power of the courts to order the forfeiture of property which has been connected with the commission of an offence is created by PCC(S)A 2000, s. 143. In addition, there is a range of other powers of forfeiture which arise only upon conviction for certain offences; these are considered at **6.8**. The power under s. 143 may be exercised by the Crown Court, a magistrates' court or a youth court in respect of any offence. Unlike a compensation order or a restitution order, which are orders ancillary to sentence, a deprivation order is part of sentence. It is best regarded as a species of fine, which takes the form of removal of an item of the offender's property (which was connected with the offence) rather than a sum of money. The order operates to deprive the offender of his rights in the property, and the property is required to be taken into police possession, if it is not already there. In many cases it will be quite clear that the property in question has been used for the criminal purpose. The sawn-off shotgun and the house-breaking implements can clearly be forfeited as 'tools of the trade'. The powers extend somewhat further than this, however.

Deprivation orders are used in a relatively small percentage of cases (apart from their use in drug-related offences, where separate powers exist: see **6.8.1**). Deprivation orders were made in 6 per cent of robbery cases, 9 per cent of cases involving violence against the person and only 2 per cent of burglary cases sentenced in the Crown Court in 1999.

6.7.1   Power to make deprivation order

Power to make a deprivation order arises where a person has been convicted of any offence. It may be made in respect of any property which has been lawfully seized from the offender or was in the offender's possession or under his control, either at the time when he was apprehended for the offence or when a summons in respect of it was issued. The property must have been used for the purpose of committing, or facilitating the commission of, any offence, or must have been intended by the offender to be so used (s. 143(1)). The power does not extend to real property, such as the offender's home (*Khan* (1982) 4 Cr App R (S) 298).

In a typical case, the property will have been used for the purposes of the offence which has led to the offender's conviction, but s. 143 clearly contemplates the offender being deprived of property which he used for a quite different offence. The power does not extend, however, to property which was associated with an offence committed by some person other than the offender (*Neville* (1987) 9 Cr App R (S) 222). On the other hand, in *Coleville-Scott* (1992) 12 Cr App R (S) 238 it was held that the power did extend to £125,000 which was found on the offender when he was arrested, and which had been paid to him as a reward for his involvement in the offences with which he had been convicted. 'Facilitating the commission of an offence' includes taking steps after the offence has been committed to dispose of the proceeds or to avoid detection (s. 143(8)). When considering whether to make a deprivation order, the court must always have regard to the value of the property and the likely financial and other effects on the offender of making the order (s. 143(5)).

6.7.2 Deprivation orders and motor vehicles

Deprivation orders have been used in a number of cases to confiscate an offender's car. Under s. 143(6) and (7), in any case where the offender has been convicted of an offence involving 'driving, attempting to drive, or being in charge of a vehicle' (which may include any offence under the RTA 1988 which is punishable with imprisonment, manslaughter and an offence of wanton and furious driving (under the OAPA 1861, s. 35), or failing to provide a specimen for analysis (RTA 1988, s. 7) or failing to stop and give information or report an accident (RTA 1988, s. 170), the vehicle involved is to be regarded as having been used for the purpose of committing the offence. Subsections (6) and (7), however, in no way limit the courts' power to order forfeiture of the offender's car under the general provision in s. 143. The main issue there is whether the use of the car was merely peripheral to the offence, in which case there is no power to order forfeiture, or whether it can fairly be said that it was used for the purpose of the offence. In *Lucas* [1976] Crim LR 79 the offender offered a woman a lift in his car and drove her to a place near some wasteland. They left the car and had sexual intercourse, apparently with the woman's consent. He then indecently assaulted her in a manner to which she did not consent. He was convicted of indecent assault and deprived of his car. The Court of Appeal quashed the order on the basis that the use of the car was part of the background to the offence, but it had not been used to commit or facilitate the offence. A comparable case is *McDonald* (1990) 12 Cr App R (S) 408, where the offender indecently assaulted a young girl on the street and tried to drag her to his car. An order for forfeiture of the car was quashed, since there was insufficient connection between the vehicle and the offence. By contrast, in *Buddo* (1982) 4 Cr App R (S) 268 the offender had driven himself and his accomplice to a chemist's shop, with the intention of breaking in and stealing drugs. The vehicle used was a motor caravan which belonged to the offender. The Court of Appeal found that the 'use of the motor caravan was an integral part of the offence of burglary' (though the order was quashed for other reasons: see **6.7.4**).

6.7.3 Deprivation orders: procedural matters

In deciding whether to make an order under s. 143, the court may proceed on its own initiative, or the prosecution may apply for the order to be made (*Pemberton* (1982) 4 Cr App R (S) 328). Evidence must be laid before the judge on the issue of forfeiture, and 'full and proper investigation' must be made (*Pemberton*). Where any item of substantial value is to be made the subject of an order, the sentencer must have proper information about its value. The use of forfeiture orders should be confined to 'simple, uncomplicated cases'; in *Troth* (1980) 71 Cr App R 1 it was held that an order should not have been made in respect of property which was subject to joint ownership. In that case the offender was convicted of theft of coal, using a tipper lorry which was co-owned by himself and his partner and used in the course of their joint business as coal merchants; there was no suggestion that the partner was involved in the theft.

The effect of an order under s. 143 is to deprive the offender of his rights in the property (s. 143(3)). It does not affect the rights of any other person, who may apply to the court for recovery of that property. The normal avenue of redress would be the Police (Property) Act 1897, but no such application may be made more than six months from the date of the making of the forfeiture order. The claimant must satisfy the court either that he had not consented to the offender having possession of the property or, where the order was made under s. 143(1)(a), that he did not know, and had no reason to suspect, that the property was likely to be used for criminal purposes.

Section 145 allows the court, where the offender has been convicted of an offence which has resulted in a person suffering 'personal injury, loss or damage' or where such an offence is taken into consideration by the court, to order that any proceeds which accrue from the disposal of the forfeited property shall (up to a certain specified sum) be paid to that person. The court should exercise this power only in a case where it would have made a compensation order (of that specified sum) in that person's favour, but was unable to do so because of the offender's lack of means. This special provision apart, it must be remembered that a deprivation order is a penalty in its own right, and cannot be used as security for the payment of a fine or compensation (*Kingston Justices, ex parte Hartung* (1981) 72 Cr App R 26).

An offender in respect of whom a deprivation order has been made may appeal against the order in the same way as against any other order or sentence of the court.

6.7.4 Deprivation orders: sentencing principles

When considering whether to make a deprivation order, the court must always have regard to the value of the property, and to the likely financial and other effects on the offender of making the order (s. 143(5)). In *Highbury Corner Justices, ex parte Di Matteo* (1990) 12 Cr App R (S) 594, the Court of Appeal found that no proper inquiry as to the likely financial or other effects of making the order had been undertaken by the sentencer, and hence the order was quashed. It must always be remembered that the deprivation order forms part of the sentence for the offence, and other component elements of the punishment must be adjusted accordingly if deprivation, especially of a substantial item, is also ordered.

This important principle has been applied by the Court of Appeal in several cases. In *Buddo* (1982) 4 Cr App R (S) 268, in addition to a total prison sentence of two years, the offender was deprived of his rights in a motor caravan in which he and an accomplice had driven to the scene of a burglary. The Court of Appeal said that although such an order could properly be made on the facts, to do so in this case was 'overdoing the punishment' and the order was accordingly quashed. A similar case is *Joyce* (1989) 11 Cr App R (S) 253. Where the order would have a disproportionately severe impact upon an offender, it should not be made. In *Tavernor* [1976] RTR 242 an order depriving an offender of his rights in a car, imposed in addition to a suspended sentence and a fine, was quashed in view of the offender's physical disability and the fact that his car was specially adapted for his use.

In a case where several offenders are equally implicated in an offence and receive comparable sentences, it is wrong to impose a deprivation order on only one of them (*Ottey* (1984) 6 Cr App R (S) 163). This may be contrasted with the principle applicable to ancillary orders, such as compensation orders where only one offender has the means to pay compensation (see *Beddow* (1987) 9 Cr App R (S) 235, at **8.1.5**). The main purpose of a deprivation order is to punish the offender, rather than to compensate the victim.

6.7.5 Combining deprivation orders with other sentences or orders

It seems that a deprivation order may be combined with any other punishment, provided that the sentencing principle described in the last paragraph is observed by the court. A deprivation order cannot be combined with an absolute discharge (*Hunt* [1978] Crim LR 697) or a conditional discharge (*Savage* (1983) 5 Cr App R (S) 216) since a discharge may only be used where it is 'inexpedient to inflict punishment'. A deprivation order may be combined with a compensation order, and provision is made under s. 145 to allow the sale of property connected with the offence to finance the compensation (see **6.7.3**).

6.8 DEPRIVATION ORDERS UNDER OTHER STATUTES

Several statutes empower the criminal courts to make deprivation orders with respect to their subject matter.

6.8.1 Misuse of drugs

By the Misuse of Drugs Act 1971 (MDA 1971), s. 27(1), the court by or before which a person is convicted of an offence under the MDA 1971 (or a drug trafficking offence, as defined in the DTA 1994, s. 1(3)) may order anything shown to the satisfaction of the court to relate to the offence to be forfeited, and either destroyed or dealt with in such manner as the court may order. 'Anything', in this context, is restricted to tangible items of personal property, including money, of which physical possession can be taken by persons authorised to do so (*Cuthbertson* [1981] AC 470). The power does not extend to seizure of real property such as a house (*Pearce* [1996] 2 Cr App R (S) 316). It does not extend to intangibles, such as money in bank accounts, nor to personal property which is situated abroad. The item to be forfeited must be shown to relate to the offence with which the offender has been convicted, and it is not enough to show that it relates to some other offence, whether planned or already committed (*Ribeyre* (1982) 4 Cr App R (S) 165; *Boothe* (1987) 9 Cr App R (S) 8). It does not apply to offenders convicted of a conspiracy to contravene the provisions of the MDA 1971, since conspiracy is not an offence under the Act (*Cuthbertson*). The court must adopt a judicial rather than a whimsical approach when determining how the items seized are to be disposed of (*Beard*).

The court has a duty to hear evidence before making an order under s. 27(1) (*Churcher* (1986) 8 Cr App R (S) 94). Provided the other requirements of s. 27(1) are made out, property may be forfeited even though it belongs to a person other than the offender (*Menocal* [1980] AC 598). In that case, however, any such person claiming ownership may apply to the court to be heard (s. 27(2)).

Orders under s. 27(1) are limited in their scope. If the court wishes to make an order designed to remove the profits of drug offending, a more appropriate option is to make a confiscation order under the DTA 1994 (see **9.1**). That power, however, is not available in magistrates' courts. There is no power under s. 27(1) to order compensation to be paid from any proceeds of property seized.

In 1999, 52 per cent of offenders sentenced for indictable drug-related offences in magistrates' courts had deprivation orders made against them, and 64 per cent of offenders so sentenced in the Crown Court. The number of deprivation orders has increased dramatically between 1989 and 1999 (from 6,300 to 19,415 in magistrates' courts and from 906 to 7,232 in the Crown Court).

6.8.2 Firearms and other weapons

Section 52 of the Firearms Act 1968 applies where a person:

(a)   is convicted of an offence under that Act; or

(b)   is convicted of any other offence for which he is given a custodial sentence; or

(c)   has been ordered to enter into a recognisance to keep the peace or be of good behaviour, on condition that he shall not possess, use or carry a firearm; or

(d)   is subject to a probation order which contains a requirement that he shall not possess, use or carry a firearm.

In any such case, the court by or before which the person is convicted, or by which the order is made, may make such order as to the forfeiture or disposal of any firearm or ammunition found in his possession as it thinks fit, and may cancel any firearms certificate or shot-gun certificate held by him.

The wording of s. 52 is broad, and it does not require that the offender was in possession of the firearm at the time of the offence nor, indeed, that the firearm was in any way related to the offence.

By the Prevention of Crime Act 1953, s. 1(2), when any person is convicted of an offence under s. 1(1) (possession of offensive weapon in a public place without lawful authority or reasonable excuse), the court may make an order for the forfeiture or disposal of any weapon in respect of which the offence was committed. A person convicted under the Crossbows Act 1987 may be liable to the forfeiture and disposal, as the court thinks fit, of any crossbow or part of a crossbow in respect of which the offence was committed (Crossbows Act 1987, s. 6(3)) as may a person convicted of an offence under CJA 1988, s. 139, of having an article with a blade or a sharp point in a public place or on school premises.

6.8.3   Written material

A range of forfeiture provisions exist in relation to offences involving written material:

(a)   A court may, on a conviction for seditious libel, make an order for the disposal of all copies of the libel seized (Criminal Libel Act 1918, s. 2).

(b)   Under the Incitement to Disaffection Act 1934, s. 3, the court may order any documents connected with an offence under that Act to be destroyed, or otherwise disposed of.

(c)   Where articles are seized under the Obscene Publications Act 1959, s. 1(4), and a person is convicted of having those publications for gain, the court must order forfeiture of those goods.

(d)   Where indecent photographs of children are seized, under the Protection of Children Act 1978, the Indecency with Children Act 1978, s. 5 or the CJA 1988, s. 160, the photographs must be seized and destroyed. 'Photographs' now includes computer-generated images.

(e)   Under the Public Order Act 1986, where a person is convicted of specified offences relating to the incitement of racial hatred, the court must order written material or recordings relating to the offence to be seized.

Note that in several of these examples the court, subject to certain conditions specified in the statutes, is under a duty, rather than merely given a power, to seize the material.

6.8.4   Other statutes

There are a number of other powers of forfeiture, including the following. A person convicted of certain offences under the Forgery and Counterfeiting Act 1981 is liable to have any property which is shown to the satisfaction of the court to relate to the offence to be forfeited and either destroyed or dealt with in such other manner as the court may order (Forgery and Counterfeiting Act 1981, ss. 7(3) and 24). A person convicted on indictment of an offence of assisting illegal entry into the UK, if he is at that time the captain or the owner (or director or manager of a company which is the owner) of a ship, aircraft or vehicle used or intended to be used in connection with that offence, may be subject to forfeiture of that ship, aircraft or vehicle, in the discretion of the court (Immigration Act 1971, s. 25 and Customs and Excise Management Act 1979, ss. 49 and 68).

7 Discharge, Bind Over, Reparation and Parenting Orders

In Chapters 4, 5 and 6 of this book the sentences which appear in the three key levels of the sentencing framework created by the CJA 1991 were described. We turn now to consider the non-custodial penalties of discharge and bind over, which have their place towards the foot of the sentencing structure. These measures are appropriate in cases where the offence is not sufficiently serious to justify the imposition of a community sentence. Courts are then often faced with a choice between a fine and a non-custodial order. Another non-custodial sentence, but one relevant only to juveniles, is the reparation order, considered at **7.4**. Finally in this chapter, court orders, directed at the parents of out-of-control youngsters are considered.

7.1 ABSOLUTE AND CONDITIONAL DISCHARGE

The court's power to pass absolute or conditional discharges may be found in PCC(S)A 2000, s. 12. The power to discharge is available whatever the age of the offender and whatever the offence committed, subject only to the crime of murder and where PCC(S)A 2000, ss. 109–111 apply. There are also three situations in which statute prevents the courts from passing a *conditional* discharge. These are dealt with below. It is a power enjoyed by the Crown Court, an adult magistrates' court and a youth court. Powers of discharge are not community orders. There is no requirement that the court obtain a pre-sentence report. The only effective limitation on the use of the discharge is the requirement in s. 12(1) that the court, having had regard to the circumstances, including the nature of the offence and the character of the offender, must conclude that it is 'inexpedient to inflict punishment' before a discharge can be ordered. A discharge is not, then, technically a punishment at all (although a conditional discharge might perhaps be characterised as a 'mild' penalty). There is no reported judicial consideration of the phrase 'inexpedient to inflict punishment'. One effect of it, however, is to restrict the other sentences or orders with which a discharge may be combined (see **7.1.3**).

7.1.1 Use of the absolute discharge

Where a court grants an absolute discharge, the offender leaves court with no effective penalty at all. The absolute discharge must, of course, be distinguished from an acquittal, since in the latter case no conviction has been recorded. An absolute discharge is a sentence imposed upon conviction, and will be recorded in the offender's list of previous convictions. Two qualifications to that statement should, however, be noted. First, an absolute discharge may be granted by a criminal court in a case where a person has been charged with an offence and has not been convicted, but has either been found unfit to plead or not guilty by reason of insanity. This matter is dealt with in **11.3.7**. Second, by PCC(S)A 2000, s. 14, wherever a conviction is followed by a discharge (whether absolute or conditional) that conviction counts as a conviction for a limited range of purposes only (see **7.1.4**).

Absolute discharges are infrequently awarded by the courts. Taking the figures for all courts for 1999, the absolute discharge was used in 1 per cent of indictable offences, 1 per cent of non-motoring summary offences and 2 per cent of summary motoring offences. It may be tempting to think of the absolute discharge simply as being the sentence appropriate in trivial cases. This is true to some extent, but there are perhaps three different types of case in which an absolute discharge has been seen as appropriate:

(a)   In cases where the offence is trivial, and/or the offender is virtually blameless for what has occurred and/or the public interest does not require that the offender should suffer any penalty beyond the recording of guilt. In *Surrey County Council* v *Battersby* [1965] 2 QB 194 the Divisional Court recommended that magistrates should absolutely discharge a woman convicted of the offence of failing to register a fostering arrangement because, before entering into the arrangement in question, she had sought, and received, official advice that no such registration was required in her case. An absolute discharge was held to be appropriate in a case of possession of a small amount of a controlled drug, where the offender originally had acquired the drug lawfully and subsequently forgotten its where-abouts (*King* [1977] Crim LR 627). Where a defendant company had committed an offence of strict liability without any degree of culpability, and where it was doubtful if the public interest had been served in prosecuting, an absolute discharge was appropriate (*Smedleys Ltd* v *Breed* [1974] AC 839).

(b)   Where the court wishes to register its disapproval of police methods used in the particular case, and the discharge is addressed as much to the police as to the offender. In *Willcock* v *Muckle* [1951] 2 KB 844 an absolute discharge was 'emphatically approved' where the police had exercised special powers to demand identity documents from the offender in inappropriate circumstances. It was also upheld in *Browning* v *Watson* [1953] 1 WLR 1172, where the offenders had been trapped by the police into committing the offence. Criticism may also be directed by the court at the prosecuting authorities, such as where charges for very trivial, stale or technical offences have been brought. It may be noted in this context that the Code for the Crown Prosecution Service, issued pursuant to POA 1985, s. 10, indicates that, where the circumstances of an offence are not particularly serious and a court would be likely to impose a purely nominal penalty, Crown Prosecutors should consider carefully whether the public interest would be better served by dropping the prosecution.

(c)   The absolute discharge is also employed as an administrative measure by some courts when dealing with an offender convicted of a number of offences on a single occasion. In road traffic cases particularly, the court may pass the 'real' sentence for the most serious of the offences, and deal with a number of other lesser offences by way of absolute discharge. Other courts use the device of 'no separate penalty' to achieve the same effect, though this seems to have no statutory or judicial authority (*Burnham Justices, ex parte Ansorge* [1959] 1 WLR 1041). Yet another method is to adjourn the proceedings 'sine die'.

7.1.2 Use of the conditional discharge

When a discharge is conditional, the sole condition is that the offender should commit no further offence during the period of the conditional discharge. No other condition or requirement may be inserted. The period of the conditional discharge is fixed by the court, up to a maximum of three years. In practice conditional discharges are usually for periods of six months or 12 months. If an offender is convicted of an offence during that period, he will be in breach of the conditional discharge and will be liable to be sentenced for the offence in respect of which he received the discharge as well as being sentenced for the new offence. Before making an order for conditional discharge, the sentencing court must explain the consequences of breach to the offender in ordinary language (s. 12(4)). In *Wehner* [1977] 1 WLR 1143 it was said to be sound practice for the court to explain this to the offender personally, but delegation of that task to the offender's lawyer was not prohibited, provided that the court was satisfied that the explanation had been made and understood before the order was made. The Court of Appeal adopted this approach when substituting a conditional discharge on an offender who had appealed against sentence (*Whitehead* (1979) 1 Cr App R (S) 187).

A conditional discharge cannot be passed where the offender has been convicted of breaching an anti-social behaviour order or a sex offender order or (exceptional circumstances apart) where he is convicted of an offence within two years of receiving a warning from a police officer (CDA 1998, s. 65).

The conditional discharge is widely used by the courts. Taking the figures for all courts for 1999, the conditional discharge was used in 17 per cent of indictable offences, 11 per cent of summary non-motoring offences and 1 per cent of summary motoring offences.

The conditional discharge is the most important sentencing option, apart from the fine, lying beneath the community sentence threshold. There is very little appellate authority on the choice between the fine and the conditional discharge, or indeed on the conditional discharge at all. It would seem that where the offence is not serious enough to warrant the use of a community sentence, a fine will continue to be the first choice for sentencers. Indeed, in magistrates' courts, the fine is often regarded as the presumptive penalty. Despite the requirement in s. 12(1) that it should be used only where 'it is inexpedient to inflict punishment', the conditional discharge may also usefully be regarded as a penalty, albeit a mild one, in the form of a warning. In *Whitehead* (1979) 1 Cr App R (S) 187 the offender was convicted of shoplifting a tin of ham, a tin of steak and a pair of tights. She had an 'unblemished character' and was living in difficult domestic and financial circumstances. She was bringing up on her own two children, one of whom was mentally handicapped, and she was reliant upon social security payments. The Court of Appeal said that the appropriate sentence in such a case was a conditional discharge for 12 months, not least because of the offender's straitened circumstances. In *McGowan* [1975] Crim LR 113 the Court of Appeal approved the use of the conditional discharge where a fine would otherwise have been the proper sentence, but the offender lacked the means to pay. The threat inherent in the conditional discharge, that the offender will be sentenced for the original offence if he fails to keep out out of trouble during the period of the discharge, is clearly an important aspect of the sentence. In *Watts* (1984) 6 Cr App R (S) 61 the Crown Court judge had imposed a suspended prison sentence of three months on the offender, who had allowed her premises to be used for the purposes of smoking cannabis. It was accepted that she did not smoke cannabis herself, but had allowed a friend of hers to do so when he visited her. She had some previous convictions, but none during the last 15 years, during which time she had led 'an honest and perfectly respectable life'. The Court of Appeal said that the suspended sentence was contrary to principle since the offence was not serious enough to justify custody, but that 'some sanction to prevent her from permitting any repetition of the offence in her house' was required. A conditional discharge for 12 months would supply that requirement, and was the proper sentence for the judge to have imposed.

On making an order for conditional discharge, the court may, if it thinks it expedient for the purpose of the offender's reformation, allow any person who consents to do so to give security for the offender's good behaviour (s. 12(6)). It is thought that this power is rarely exercised.

7.1.3 Combining a discharge with other sentences or orders

It has been held that a discharge, whether absolute or conditional, cannot be combined with a punitive measure for the same offence (*Savage* (1983) 5 Cr App R (S) 216), except where such a mix is expressly permitted by statute. Thus a discharge cannot be combined with any custodial sentence, any community sentence or a fine. The incompatibility of the fine and the discharge was made clear in *McClelland* [1951] 1 All ER 557 and was confirmed in *Sanck* (1990) 12 Cr App R (S) 155. These restrictions on combining a discharge with other sentences are not so restrictive as they might at first appear, however, since where an offender is being dealt with for more than one offence, the court is free to discharge for one offence and exercise its normal sentencing powers with respect to other offences (*Bainbridge* (1979) 1 Cr App R (S) 36). A discharge can in any event be combined with a compensation order, an order for costs, a deprivation order, a restitution order or any disqualification (s. 12(7)).

7.1.4 Limited effect of conviction where discharge is granted

Where an offender pleads guilty or is convicted of an offence and is dealt with by way of discharge, he is deemed not to have been convicted of the offence unless and until he is subsequently sentenced for it, i.e. where the discharge is a conditional one and he is later in breach of it (PCC(S)A 2000, s. 14 and *Moore* [1995] QB 353). The rule in s. 14 has the effect, for example, that a person granted a discharge for a particular offence would not be debarred from holding an office from which persons convicted of that offence are normally barred.

Another (perhaps unintended) effect is that, if a person commits an imprisonable offence during the operational period of a suspended sentence, and receives an absolute or conditional discharge for that new offence, the offender cannot be dealt with for breach of the suspended sentence since power to activate a suspended sentence arises only where there has been a 'conviction' for the subsequent offence (*Tarry* [1970] 2 QB 561). In practice a court which imposed a discharge for the new offence might well be minded not to activate the suspended sentence in any event, but the authorities indicate that the relative triviality of the new offence is not, in itself, sufficient reason for not activating the suspended sentence. In respect of other sentences which become available only where the offender is shown to have relevant previous convictions, an earlier discharge will not count for this purpose. Thus, in relation to PCC(S)A 2000, s. 111, which normally requires the passing of a custodial sentence of at least three years for the third domestic burglary, an earlier conviction for that offence which was dealt with by way of a discharge would not count as a qualifying conviction (see **4.3.4**).

It should be noted that, quite apart from s. 14, the operation of the Rehabilitation of Offenders Act 1974 may mean that an offender can deny that he has been convicted of an offence once his conviction becomes 'spent' (see **13.6.1**).

Section 14 does not prevent a person who is granted a discharge from appealing against conviction or against sentence (MCA 1980, s. 108(1A) and CAA 1968, s. 50(1A)).

7.1.5 Breach of conditional discharge

A conditional discharge can be breached only by the conviction of the offender of a further offence committed during the period of the discharge (PCC(S)A 2000, s. 13). In every case the breach must be clearly admitted by the offender or be proved (*Devine* (1956) 40 Cr App R 45). This will normally present no problem, since the date of the offender's conviction for the further offence will be a matter of record. Breach must always be dealt with by sentencing for the original offence. The percentage of offenders originally dealt with by way of conditional discharge who are subsequently dealt with for the original offence in consequence of breach has remained remarkably consistent over the last ten years. It has stayed at around 10 per cent throughout that period. It has been said that the sentence for the original offence should normally be more than a nominal one (*Stuart* [1964] 1 WLR 1381). No detailed breakdown of disposals following breach of conditional discharge is available, but it may perhaps be assumed that the most frequently used penalty in these circumstances is a fine. The criminal statistics do, however, record the proportionate rate of use of custody following breach of conditional discharge. Over the last ten years the annual figure has declined from 20 per cent to 15 per cent. Sentencing for the original offence always terminates the conditional discharge, but any order for compensation or for costs which was made at the time of the conditional discharge remains valid (*Evans* [1963] 1 QB 979).

If a magistrates' court is sentencing for the new offence, it should sentence for the original offence either if it imposed the discharge or if a different magistrates' court imposed the discharge and the agreement of that court is obtained. If the discharge was imposed by the Crown Court the magistrates may commit the offender to the Crown Court. If the Crown Court is sentencing for the new offence it may sentence for the original offence whether the discharge was imposed by the Crown Court or by a magistrates' court.

When dealing with the breach, the court may sentence the offender for the original offence in any manner in which it could have dealt with the offender if he had just been convicted before the court of that offence (s. 13(6)) except that the Crown Court dealing with a person conditionally discharged by a magistrates' court is limited to the lower court's powers (s. 13(7)).

If an offender aged under 18 has been conditionally discharged by a magistrates' court for an offence which is triable only on indictment in the case of an adult, any court dealing with him for the original offence consequent upon breach of the conditional discharge after he has attained the age of 18 may impose a fine not exceeding £5,000 or deal with him in any way in which a magistrates' court could deal with him.

7.2 BINDING OVER TO KEEP THE PEACE

There is a range of powers available to English sentencers which are conveniently grouped together under the heading of 'binding over'. All these powers take the form of a suspended financial penalty, on the basis of an undertaking by the person bound over to comply with certain (sometimes rather vague) requirements of the court.

The powers which a magistrates' court possesses to bind over a person to keep the peace derive from two different sources. The first is where an action in the form of a complaint is brought before the court, pursuant to MCA 1980, s. 115. If the court finds the complaint to have substance, it may bind over the person in respect of whom the complaint was brought (and, incidentally, if the court finds cause, the complainant as well: *Wilkins* [1907] 2 KB 380). The procedure is more closely analogous to civil rather than criminal procedure and cannot in any circumstances result in a conviction and sentence. This form of bind over is, accordingly, not considered further here. The second form of bind over to keep the peace stems from an ancient common law power, the existence of which has been recognised in several statutes, notably the Justices of the Peace Act 1361. These powers arise only in criminal proceedings. They are very wide and, in addition to being used as part of a sentence, may be exercised by the justices at any time before the conclusion of the proceedings. The Justices of the Peace Act 1968, s. 1(7) makes it clear that 'any court of record having a criminal jurisdiction has, as ancillary to that jurisdiction, the power to bind over to be of good behaviour'. The Crown Court is a court of record (Supreme Court Act 1981, s. 45), and hence possesses power to bind over, and it has been established that this power also extends to the Court of Appeal (*Sharp* [1957] 1 QB 552).

7.2.1 Scope of power to bind over

Common law powers to bind over to keep the peace may be exercised whenever the court considers that the conduct of a person before the court has been such that there might be a breach of the peace in the future, whether committed by that person or by others. The traditional explanation for the breadth of these powers has been the court exercising 'preventive justice' (*Veator* v *Glennon* [1981] 1 WLR 567). A common law bind over may be used against a witness before the court (*Sheldon* v *Bromfield Justices* [1964] 2 QB 573) or upon a defendant who has been acquitted (*Inner London Crown Court, ex parte Benjamin* (1986) 85 Cr App R 267) as well as on sentence. It may not, however, be used against a person who came to court as a witness but was not called (*Swindon Crown Court, ex parte Pawittar Singh* (1983) 5 Cr App R (S) 422).

The effect of the order is that the person bound over is required to enter into an undertaking (or, as it is normally called, a recognisance) that he will keep the peace for a specified period or forfeit a certain sum of money if he fails to do so. The period for which a bind over to keep the peace may run is entirely within the court's discretion but periods of 12 months are common. A bind over may name a person or persons for whose special protection the bind over is made (*Wilson* v *Skeock* (1949) 65 TLR 418); otherwise, the cases indicate that courts should not insert specific conditions into bind overs. In *Randall* (1986) 8 Cr App R (S) 433, a condition that the person bound over did not teach, or try to teach, anyone under the age of 18 was held to be invalid. In *Goodlad* v *Chief Constable of South Yorkshire* [1979] Crim LR 51 a condition forbidding the possession, carrying or use of a firearm was held to be invalid, but this cannot be squared with the Firearms Act 1968, s. 52, which specifically envisages that such an order may be made (see **6.8.2**). In any event, such conditions must be reasonable, and it has been held that there is no power to bind over a person on condition that they leave the jurisdiction and do not return (*Ayu* [1958] 1 WLR 1264), though see **7.3**. The sum of money to be forfeited upon breach of the bind over is also within the court's discretion. There appears to be no limit, save that the sum should be reasonable in all the circumstances. It is clear, for instance, that a person may be bound over in a sum which is greater than the maximum fine available for the offence of which he stands convicted (*Sandbach Justices, ex parte Williams* [1935] 2 KB 192).

Powers to bind over to keep the peace may be imposed after conviction, on sentence. The powers exercisable at that stage appear to be indistinguishable from those which may be exercisable at earlier stages of the proceedings. Remarkably, it is unclear whether a convicted offender may be dealt with by way of a bind over to keep the peace standing alone on sentence, or whether the passing of some other sentence upon him is required in addition. The wording of the Justices of the Peace Act 1968, s. 1(7) (see **7.2**) indicates that the bind over is 'ancillary' to the court's criminal jurisdiction, and this may mean that a court should determine the penalty for the offence before the ancillary power of binding over to keep the peace is considered.

Formerly there was power to bind over a person 'to be of good behaviour' instead of binding over to keep the peace, in cases where the misbehaviour did not amount to a breach of the peace but was found to be *contra bonos mores*. Such behaviour was described by the Divisional Court in *Hughes* v *Holley* (1988) 86 Cr App R 130 as conduct which was 'wrong, rather than right, in the judgment of the majority of contemporary citizens'. In *Hashman and Harrup* v *UK* (2000) 30 EHRR 241, the European Court of Human Rights said that the nature of the requirements imposed on a person bound over to be of good behaviour were too vague to qualify as a 'restriction prescribed by law' under the ECHR, Article 10(2).

When the court proposes to bind over a person convicted of an offence in anything other than a trivial sum, the court should have regard to his means and other personal circumstances, and should allow him to make representations in respect of those matters (*Central Criminal Court, ex parte Boulding* [1984] QB 813). The court should fix the period of the recognisance and the sum of money to be forfeited upon breach at the time when it imposes the bind over.

Under the Magistrates' Courts (Appeals from Binding Over) Act 1956, there is a right of appeal to the Crown Court against a bind over to keep the peace made by a magistrates' court. Where the bind over is imposed by the Crown Court on sentence, a right of appeal lies to the Court of Appeal by virtue of CAA 1968, s. 50(1).

7.2.2   Use of bind over to keep the peace

Little is known about the actual operation of the power to bind over to keep the peace, and it is very difficult to disentangle the use of the power as a sentencing option from use at earlier stages of the criminal process. Speaking generally, there seem to be three areas of law-breaking where the courts tend to favour the use of bind overs:

(a)   the less serious matters of violence and public disorder;
(b)   relatively minor matters involving annoyance and distress, including certain forms of sexual behaviour in public; and
(c)   neighbour and domestic disputes.

The Criminal Statistics for 1999 indicate that magistrates' courts use their powers to bind over on sentence almost entirely in respect of summary, rather than indictable, offences. The summary offences are broken down no further in the statistics, but the bulk of the indictable offences dealt with by way of bind over on sentence were offences of violence against the person.

Since the rationale for the use of powers to bind over to keep the peace is 'preventive justice', it follows that such powers should not be used where there is no reasonable apprehension by the court of such conduct in the future. It may be argued that binding over should not be used where a person is convicted of matters unconnected with violence or public disturbance, actual or potential. In *Middlesex Crown Court, ex parte Khan* (1997) 161 JP 240 the Divisional Court said that before binding over an acquitted defendant the court should be satisfied beyond reasonable doubt that the defendant posed a threat to other persons and was a man of violence.

7.2.3 Refusal or failure to enter into recognisance

Whenever the court requires a person to be bound over to keep the peace, that person must consent to being so dealt with. The sanction for refusal to enter into a recognisance proposed by the court is imprisonment. There appears to be no limit to the duration of the term of custody which may be imposed where the court acts under its common law powers, but the normal limitations upon magistrates' courts powers to impose custody would surely apply where the bind over was imposed by magistrates upon a convicted offender.

Provided that there is consent, it seems that an offender of any age may be bound over. Problems have arisen where the court has sought to bind over an offender whom it had no power to imprison, but who refused to consent. There is no power to order detention of a person under the age of 18 in these circumstances, but an attendance centre order could be made (PCC(S)A 2000, s. 60(1)). The Crown Court may otherwise deal with a refusal to be bound over as a contempt of court.

7.2.4 Failure to comply with bind over

If a person who has been bound over by the Crown Court is adjudged to have failed to comply with the conditions of the order, the court may deal with him by forfeiting the whole or part of the recognisance in its discretion, together with costs. It may allow time for payment, or direct payment by instalments of the sum forfeited (PCC(S)A 2000, s. 139(1)). It is important to realise that the court is *not* empowered to impose custody for failure to comply with the conditions of a bind over (*Finch* (1962) 47 Cr App R 58; *Gilbert* (1974) CSP D10-3A01). This is in contrast to the court's powers to impose custody where a person refuses to be bound over. The Crown Court, when forfeiting a recognisance, must fix a term of imprisonment or detention not exceeeding 12 months, to be served in the event of default of payment (PCC(S)A 2000, s. 139(2)). It seems that in a magistrates' court a recognisance can be declared to be forfeit only by way of an order on complaint (MCA 1980, s. 120), irrespective of the power which the court was exercising when the bind over was first imposed.

Proceedings for breach of bind over are civil in character and require only the civil standard of proof (*Marlow Justices, ex parte O'Sullivan* [1984] QB 381). The person concerned should, nevertheless, be told the nature of the breach alleged and be given an opportunity to present evidence, call witnesses or adduce an explanation (*McGregor* [1945] 2 All ER 180). There appears to be no right of appeal against an adjudication of forfeiture (*Durham Justices, ex parte Laurent* [1945] KB 33), although there is the possibility of making an application for judicial review.

7.2.5 Binding over parent or guardian of young offender

The PCC(S)A 2000, s. 150(1) places an obligation upon magistrates' courts and the Crown Court to bind over the parent or guardian of an offender who is under the age of 16, whenever the court is satisfied that to do so would be desirable in the interests of preventing the commission by the young offender of further offences. If the court is not satisfied of that, on the facts of the particular case, it should state in open court that it is not so satisfied, and give reasons for its view. In contrast to the obligation imposed here in respect of offenders under 16, the court has a discretionary power to bind over the parent or guardian of an offender aged 16 or 17. The bind over will normally be imposed on parents at the same time as a sentence (such as a supervision order) is imposed on the juvenile. In such a case, the court may include a requirement in the recognisance that the parent or guardian ensure the young offender's compliance with the community sentence.

By s. 150(3), the court is empowered to order the parent or guardian to enter into a recognisance, in a sum not exceeding £1,000, to take proper care of the offender and exercise proper control over him. The maximum duration of the recognisance is until the offender reaches the age of 18, or for a period of three years, whichever is the shorter period (s. 150(4). Entry into the recognisance requires the consent of the parent or guardian, but if consent is refused and the court considers the refusal to be unreasonable, the parent or guardian may be punished by a fine not exceeding level 3 on the standard scale (s. 150(2)). In fixing the level of the recognisance, the court should take into account, among other things, the means of the parent or guardian, whether such consideration has the effect of increasing or reducing the level of the recognisance fixed upon (s. 150(7)).

As far as forfeiture of the recognisance is concerned, s. 150(5) states that MCA 1980, s. 120 shall apply in relation to a recognisance under s. 150 as it does to a recognisance to keep the peace (see **7.2.4**). The court may, therefore, order forfeiture of the whole or part of the recognisance in its discretion, together with costs. A right of appeal to the Crown Court against an order made under s. 150 which is made by a magistrates' court is created by s. 150(8); where the order is made by the Crown Court, there is a right to appeal to the Court of Appeal (s. 150(9)).

7.3   BINDING OVER TO COME UP FOR JUDGMENT

A common law power enjoyed by the Crown Court (but not a magistrates' court or a youth court) is to bind over a person to come up for judgment to be sentenced on a certain later day, or on a day to be specified to him later, on recognisance on certain specified conditions. If the offender breaks one or more of the conditions, he will be brought back before the court for sentencing for the original offence but, if he does not break any of the conditions within the specified period, he will either not be sentenced for the original offence at all, or will receive a nominal penalty for it.

A bind over to come up for judgment is made in lieu of sentence and it is therefore wrong to impose it in addition to the sentence (*Ayu* [1958] 1 WLR 1264). An offender should consent to the bind over, although such consent is not vitiated by a reasonable expectation of a custodial sentence in the alternative (*Williams* [1982] 1 WLR 1398). It is a 'sentence' made on conviction on indictment (*Abrahams* (1952) 36 Cr App R 147), and therefore an appeal against it lies to the Court of Appeal (CAA 1968, s. 50(1)).

This power is anomalous and would appear to have very limited use. It has a long history, pre-dating all the modern non-custodial disposals. The power bears some similarity to the courts' powers to defer sentence (see **3.10**), but deferment is a statutory power and really ought to be used in preference. In many cases the effect of binding over to come up for judgment may be achieved by imposing a probation order, where the offence is serious enough to justify that course, or a conditional discharge. The sentence may also be compared to the bind over to keep the peace or be of good behaviour, the main difference lying in the Crown Court's power to impose a range of conditions within a bind over to come up for judgment. It is in the possibility of such conditions that the residual usefulness of this power may be found. From time to time it has been used in respect of offenders who are prepared to leave the country, where the sentencer also wishes that course to be followed but cannot make a recommendation for deportation because the offender is a British subject.

If the offender is in breach of a bind over to come up for judgment, he is liable to forfeit the recognisance as well as being sentenced for the original offence. Where a person is brought back before the court on the ground that a recognisance entered into by him has been broken, the breach must be proved beyond reasonable doubt (*McGarry* (1945) 30 Cr App R 187). The person bound over is entitled to be heard on the matter (*David* [1939] 1 All ER 782).

7.4 REPARATION ORDERS

Reparation to the victim is obviously the central feature of this order, although it will be recalled that a reparation requirement may be included as one element within an action plan order or a supervision order. Unlike the CPO, the reparation is designed to allow the young offender to make reparation in some tangible form to the victim of the offence, other than by the payment of compensation. The victim must always agree to being involved in this way and, if so agreeing, the victim will have some say in what form the reparation should take. In a case where the victim does not agree to become involved, or perhaps where there is no obvious victim, the reparation may be made to the community at large. In that form the reparation order runs very close to a CPO, although the maximum number of hours for a reparation order is 24, while for a CPO it is 240. It is important to note that the reparation order (unlike the action plan order) is not a 'community order'. The reparation order may, therefore, be used in respect of an offence which is not serious enough to justify the passing of a community sentence although there seems no reason why, in an appropriate case, it might not be used as an alternative to one of the less onerous forms of community sentence. See further **7.4.2**. Section 74(2) states that the number of hours of work required of the young offender and, presumably, the nature of that work, must be such as in the opinion of the court are commensurate with the seriousness of the offence or offences committed. The court may pass a reparation order without first obtaining a pre-sentence report but, by s. 73(5), before making a reparation order the court must obtain and consider a report from a probation officer, a social worker or a member of a youth offending team indicating the type of work that is suitable for the young offender and the attitude of the victim or victims to the requirements to be included in the order.

7.4.1 Power to impose a reparation order

A reparation order may be imposed by the Crown Court or a youth court on any offender aged under 18 who is convicted of any offence, subject only to the crime of murder. The order requires the young offender to make reparation specified in the order either to a named victim or victims of the offence (subject to their agreement), or to the community at large (s. 73(1)). The order shall not require the offender to work for more than 24 hours in total (s. 74(1)). The reparation must be carried out under the supervision of a probation officer, a social worker, or a member of a youth offending team (s. 74(8)). Presumably where the reparation is to be made to the community at large the relevant community service team will make arrangements for suitable work to be found.

The requirements in the reparation order must not, so far as possible, interfere with the times when the young offender works or attends school, or conflict with his religious beliefs or with the requirements of any other order to which he may be subject (s. 74(3), and on this see **7.4.2**).

The court must explain to the offender in ordinary language the effect of the order and the requirements to be inserted into it and the consequences of failure to comply with the order (s. 73(7)). For the powers of the court on breach of the order see **7.4.3**. If the court does not make a reparation order in a case where it had power to do so, s. 73(8) requires the court to give reasons why it did not do so. This requirement is similar to that which operates in relation to compensation orders.

7.4.2 Combining a reparation order with other sentences or orders

Section 73(4) states that a reparation order shall not be made if the court proposes to pass a custodial sentence, a CPO, a CPRO, a supervision order which includes requirements under sch. 6 to the 2000 Act, an action plan order or a referral order. This restriction seems to apply not just to mixing the orders when sentencing for a single offence, but also to imposing the orders at the same time for separate offences. In addition to the measures listed in s. 73(4), it is clear that a reparation order could not be combined with an absolute or conditional discharge since a discharge cannot be combined with a punitive measure for the same offence (s. 12), though there would be nothing to prevent a reparation order being imposed in respect of one offence and a discharge in respect of another offence sentenced on the same occasion. The list envisages that a reparation order might in an appropriate case be imposed on an offender at the same time as a CRO, a supervision order which does not contain the particular requirements referred to, a DTTO, an attendance centre order, a fine, a compensation order, a deprivation order or a restitution order.

7.4.3 Breach, revocation and amendment of a reparation order

Arrangements for breach, revocation and amendment of a reparation order are set out in the PCC(S)A 2000, sch. 8 (see **5.10.4** and **5.10.5**).

7.5. PARENTING ORDERS

Under ss. 8–10 of the CDA 1998, the Crown Court and youth courts have *power* to impose a parenting order on a parent or guardian of a person under 18 who, *inter alia*, has been convicted of an offence, to attend counselling or guidance sessions and to comply with certain specified requirements. The parent can be required to attend the counselling or guidance sessions, in accordance with instructions given by the responsible officer (who will be a probation officer, social worker or member of the youth attending team specified in the order), not more than once a week and for no longer than three months overall. The specified requirements, however, may remain in force for up to 12 months. These can take whatever form the court considers to be desirable in the interests of preventing the child from re-offending, and might commonly include requirements that the parent ensure that the child is accompanied to school each day and is indoors by a certain hour in the evening.

While there is power to make a parenting order where the young offender is aged 16 or 17, by s. 9, if a child under the age of 16 has been convicted of an offence and the court is satisfied that a parenting order would help to prevent a recurrence of the child's offending behaviour, the court is under a *duty* to make such an order against the parent or guardian, unless the court thinks that to make an order would not help prevent the commission of further offences by the juvenile, in which case there is an obligation to explain why the order has not been made. This is clearly an important area of discretion for the court, and a pre-sentence report or other report will have to be made available so that the court can make an informed decision. There will certainly be cases where the court will take the view that the home circumstances of the young offender are such that a parenting order is either unnecessary or will be counter-productive. Before making a parenting order on the parent of a juvenile under 16 convicted of an offence, the court must take into account information about the family circumstances and shall explain the effect and consequences of the order, including the consequences which may flow from breach of the order, to the parent or guardian in ordinary language.

The parenting order may subsequently be discharged or varied by the court, on the application of the parent or the responsible officer. The order can be cancelled, such as in the case of good progress, or varied by cancelling a requirement or adding a fresh requirement. Breach of the parenting order, which is constituted by failure by the parent without reasonable excuse to comply with any requirement in the order, is punishable by a fine not exceeding level 3 on the standard scale. Commission of a further offence by the juvenile would not constitute a breach of the order. Section 10(4) provides that the parent or guardian may appeal against the making of a parenting order in the same way as they could appeal against a conviction or sentence.

8   Compensation and Restitution

While the great bulk of this book is concerned with the legal framework of punishments which may be imposed upon an offender in consequence of his offence, this chapter is concerned with what many perceive to be an equally important task to be undertaken at the sentencing stage: providing for appropriate compensation for the victim of crime.

Since most criminal offences are also civil wrongs, victims, at least in theory, will often be able to sue their offender in a civil court for damages. In reality, however, this is rarely done. A civil remedy is, of course, not available where the perpetrator of the crime has not been identified. Even where he has been caught, however, relatively few people who have been the victims of crime are prepared to take on the considerable further burden of pursuing that person for redress through the civil courts. In a case where the perpetrator has been prosecuted and convicted and the facts of the matter are before the criminal court, it would seem to be an unnecessary duplication to require in addition that the victim sue the offender for compensation. It makes good sense, at least in cases which are factually clear and straightforward, for the criminal court to make an award of compensation to the victim at the same time as it imposes appropriate punishment on the offender. The power to make compensation orders is contained in PCC(S)A 2000, ss. 130–134. Section 130 provides that, instead of or in addition to dealing with the offender in any other way, the Crown Court, an adult magistrates' court or a youth court may require the offender to pay compensation to the victim for any 'personal injury, loss or damage resulting from the offence'. It should be clear from the explanation given here that the punishment and compensation functions of the criminal court are in principle quite separate, being designed to achieve different objectives. In practice, however, they are not always so clearly distinguished.

The compensation order is one of the ways in which the victim of an offence may be compensated for the crime which has been committed against them. The other main avenue is for the victim to make an application for compensation under the state-funded Criminal Injuries Compensation Scheme. That scheme, which has been in existence since 1964 but was re-established on a statutory basis by the Criminal Injuries Compensation Act 1995, is confined to cases where the victim has suffered physical injury as a result of a 'crime of violence'. There are restrictions on applicants, such as that the applicant must have cooperated fully with the investigating authorities and must not have contributed to the crime himself. There are further restrictions in respect of domestic violence cases, especially where the victim is a child, which are designed to ensure that the payment of compensation does not fall into the hands of the perpetrator. Clearly this scheme offers compensation to a narrower range of claimants than compensation orders, being confined to victims of violent crime. In another way, though, it is more extensive than compensation orders, since under the state scheme the victim may receive compensation even though the perpetrator has never been caught. The principal drawback of compensation orders is that they are restricted to cases where offenders have been caught, prosecuted and convicted, and where it is established that they have the means to pay the victim. If the perpetrator of the offence has received a formal caution, warning or reprimand, rather than being prosecuted and convicted, no opportunity to make a compensation order arises. On the other hand, compensation may be ordered in respect of offences which are taken into consideration. In those cases where a criminal court is able to make a compensation order, to take that approach may be seen as particularly appropriate, and properly reflective of personal responsibility, since it is the offender himself who is being required to pay compensation to the victim, rather than the State being relied upon to do that job.

In a case where a victim for whose benefit a compensation order has been made does not feel that the order reflects the true extent of his loss, there is nothing to prevent the victim also making application to the Criminal Injuries Compensation Authority or claiming damages against the offender in a civil court. Clearly, however, the rules cannot permit the victim to recover twice, so the award of damages will be reduced by the amount actually paid under the compensation order, and a plaintiff victim may enforce judgment for an amount by way of a compensation order only where the civil court gives leave. Similarly, any award which a victim receives from the State scheme, or any payment which a victim receives via any relevant insurance policy, will be reduced by the amount of the compensation order.

The percentage of offenders sentenced for indictable offences during 1999 who were also required to pay compensation to their victim is recorded in the criminal statistics and is shown in the Table below:

Offence category	*Magistrates' court*	*Crown Court*
violence against the person	43 per cent	17 per cent
sexual offences	28 per cent	1 per cent
burglary	27 per cent	4 per cent
theft and handling	15 per cent	7 per cent
fraud and forgery	31 per cent	12 per cent
criminal damage	51 per cent	16 per cent

8.1 COMPENSATION ORDERS

8.1.1 Power to make a compensation order

The central aim of making a compensation order was explained by Scarman LJ in *Inwood* (1975) 60 Cr App R 70, when he said that it was to provide victims of crime with 'a convenient and rapid means of avoiding the expense of resorting to civil litigation, when the criminal clearly has means which would enable the compensation to be paid'. Since the compensation order is ancillary to sentence, it should not be regarded as part of the punishment for the offence (even though the offender who is required to pay may not always appreciate the difference between compensation and a fine), and hence its imposition does not require any adjustment in the sentence per se. In particular, compensation orders should not provide an escape route by which wealthy offenders may buy their way out of the normal consequences of their crime (see *Barney* (1989) 11 Cr App R (S) 448, discussed at **8.1.4**).

Also, compensation orders are not an appropriate device for depriving an offender of the fruits of his crime. In a case where the court has this aim in mind, a confiscation order (see Chapter 9) or a fine are the appropriate options to pursue.

There is no limit to the amount of compensation which the Crown Court may order, though it is an important principle of sentencing that the sentencer must always have regard to the offender's ability to pay compensation (PCC(S)A 2000, s. 130(11): see further **8.1.5**). In a magistrates' court, PCC(S)A 2000, s. 131(1) provides that the maximum sum which may be ordered by way of compensation for any offence is £5,000. Section 131(2) also places a limit on the total sum which may be ordered by way of compensation in a magistrates' court where the offender asks for offences to be taken into consideration. The total amount ordered must not exceed the maximum which could be ordered for the offences in respect of which the offender has been formally charged and convicted. It seems that the court should make clear which amounts of compensation relate to which offences. Thus the fixing of a 'global figure' for compensation is normally inappropriate (*Oddy* [1974] 1 WLR 1212). The only exception seems to be where the offences were all committed against the same victim (*Wharton* [1976] Crim LR 520). Where there are competing claimants for available funds, the total compensation available should normally be apportioned on a pro rata basis (*Miller* (1976) 63 Cr App R 56). This approach seems preferable to that adopted in *Amey* (1982) 4 Cr App R (S) 410, where the court selected some claimants for compensation and excluded others. Where there are co-defendants, it is preferable to make separate orders against each of them (*Grundy* [1974] 1 WLR 139).

Compensation may be ordered for 'any personal injury, loss or damage' resulting from the offence. This phrase has been liberally construed by the courts. Although, as was mentioned above, many criminal offences are also civil wrongs and the main aim of making a compensation order is to save the victim the inconvenience of pursuing a civil claim, it has been held that it is not a prerequisite of making a compensation order that the offender would be liable in civil law for the loss (*Chappell* (1984) 80 Cr App R 31). 'Personal injury, loss or damage' has been taken to include distress and anxiety (*Bond* [1983] 1 WLR 40, where an order for £25 was upheld in respect of a householder who had been terrified when the offender threw a stone through her window). 'Loss' has been held to include a sum by way of interest (*Schofield* [1978] 2 All ER 705), but it seems that calculation of interest will be appropriate only where the sum involved is substantial and the relevant period is a lengthy one. A compensation order may be made whenever it can fairly be said that a particular loss results from the offence (*Rowlston* v *Kenny* (1982) 4 Cr App R (S) 85). A common sense test should be applied in deciding such cases, without having regard to technical issues of causation (*Thomson Holidays* [1974] QB 592). Thus in *Taylor* (1993) 14 Cr App R (S) 276 it was held to be appropriate to require the offender to pay £50 compensation to a man who had been kicked in the course of an affray, in which the offender and four others had accosted another group of men and a fight developed. It could not be established that Taylor had kicked the victim, but it was said to be 'artificial and unjust to look narrowly at the physical acts of each defendant' (see also *Denness* [1996] 1 Cr App R (S) 159). A case which fell on the other side of the line was *Derby* (1990) 12 Cr App R (S) 502 where the offender had threatened the victim with a knife and his co-defendant had seriously injured the victim by attacking him with a piece of wood. It was held that a compensation order for £4,000, made against the offender, was improper, since the offender had clearly not been responsible for inflicting the injuries.

In cases where no injury, loss or damage can be established (such as where a stolen article has been recovered, returned undamaged, and is of no less value to the owner than before it was taken), no compensation order can be made (*Hier* (1976) 62 Cr App R 233). Conversely, where there has been damage or loss to the victim, a compensation order is not precluded by the fact that the offender has made no profit from the offence.

A compensation order in respect of bereavement may only be made for the benefit of a person who could claim damages for bereavement under the Fatal Accidents Act 1976, s. 1A (i.e. the spouse of the deceased or, in the case of a deceased minor, his parents, or mother if the minor is illegitimate), and the amount of that compensation shall not exceed the sum specified in the Fatal Accidents Act 1976, s. 1A(3) (currently £7,500) (s. 130(10)). A compensation order in respect of funeral expenses may be made for the benefit of anyone who incurred the expenses (s. 35(3B)).

The victim does not have to apply to the court before a compensation order can be made; in fact victims relatively rarely do so. The court is required by s. 130(3) to consider awarding compensation in every case, and if it does not do so, reasons why no order has been made should be given.

8.1.2 Procedural requirements

Section 130(4) states that compensation shall be of such amount as the court considers appropriate, 'having regard to any evidence and to any representations that are made by or on behalf of the accused or the prosecutor'. Thus the amount of the victim's loss should either be agreed by the defendant, or be established by the evidence. In *Horsham Justices, ex parte Richards* (1985) 7 Cr App R (S) 158, Neill LJ said:

> in my judgment the court has no jurisdiction to make a compensation order without receiving any evidence where there are real issues raised as to whether the claimants have suffered any, and if so what, loss.

In practice, however, courts do sometimes proceed on fairly flimsy evidence in their anxiety to provide compensation for victims wherever possible. Where the case raises complex factual issues, the court should not embark on a complex inquiry into the scale of loss, since compensation orders are designed to be used only in clear, straightforward cases: see further **8.1.7**.

In the case of an offence under the Theft Act 1968 where the property in question is recovered, any damage to the property occurring while it was out of the owner's possession is normally treated as having resulted from the offence, however and by whomsoever it was caused (s. 130(5), applied in *Quigley v Stokes* [1977] 1 WLR 434). In *Ahmad* (1992) 13 Cr App R (S) 212, however, an 18-year-old offender pleaded guilty to taking a conveyance, reckless driving and driving while disqualified. A compensation order for £99, for repairing damage done to the vehicle was upheld, but insofar as the order related to the loss of property which had been in the vehicle (valued at £300) it was quashed, as the offender had not been found guilty of theft. A compensation order may only be made in respect of injury, loss or damage which was due to an accident arising out of the presence of a motor vehicle on a road (other than loss suffered by a person's dependants in consequence of his death), if either it is damage which falls within s. 130(5) or it is in respect of injury, loss or damage for which the offender is uninsured in relation to the use of the vehicle and compensation is not payable under any arrangements to which the Secretary of State is a party, i.e. the Motor Insurers' Bureau Agreements (s. 130(6)). Under that scheme the first £175 of loss is not covered, and so in an appropriate case a compensation order in that amount can be made (see *Austin* [1996] 2 Cr App R (S) 191). In the exceptional cases where a compensation order can be made in respect of such an accident, the compensation may include a sum representing the whole or part of any loss of or reduction in preferential rates of insurance attributable to the accident, i.e. the victim's no claims bonus (s. 130(7)). A vehicle which is exempted from insurance (e.g. a vehicle which belongs to the Crown) is not uninsured for these purposes (s. 130(8)).

The victim of the offence will not receive any compensation until there is no further possibility of an appeal by which the order could be varied or set aside (s. 132(1)). By s. 133(3), at any time before the offender has paid into court the whole amount due under the order, the magistrates' court having power to enforce the order may, on application of the offender, discharge the order or reduce it on the ground that:

(a)   the injury, loss or damage in respect of which the order was made has been held in civil proceedings to be less than it was taken to be for the purposes of the order;

(b)   property the loss of which was the subject of the order has now been recovered;

(c)   the means of the offender are insufficient to satisfy both the compensation order and a confiscation order made against him in the same proceedings under CJA 1988 (see **9.2** for confiscation orders); or

(d)   the offender's means have suffered a substantial reduction which was unexpected at the time of making the order.

Before the magistrates may act under (c) or (d) to discharge or reduce a Crown Court order, they must have the consent of that court.

Section 130(3) contains a further important procedural requirement, which is that in every case where a court has power to make a compensation order but does not do so, it must give reasons why no such order has been made. Such reasons might include the incompatibility of the sentence imposed for the offence (see **8.1.8**), the offender's lack of means (**8.1.5**), or the complexity of the case (**8.1.7**).

8.1.3   Enforcement of compensation orders

Enforcement of compensation orders is the function of magistrates' courts. The maximum terms of imprisonment which a magistrates' court may impose in default of payment of compensation orders are specified in MCA 1980, sch. 4. These are the same periods which apply in the case of fines (set out at **6.1.2**) and, as with fines, magistrates have no power to specify a term in default in excess of 12 months. Magistrates have discretion to fix a lower term. The Crown Court is not empowered to make an order fixing the term to be served in default of payment of a compensation order (in contrast to its duty to do so in respect of fines: *Komsta* (1990) 12 Cr App R (S) 63 and see **6.1.2**). The maximum terms indicated in sch. 4 will thus normally also apply in default of payment of compensation orders imposed by the Crown Court. Exceptionally, however, if the Crown Court makes a compensation order for an amount in excess of £20,000 and considers that a maximum default term of 12 months is inadequate, it may fix a longer period, not exceeding the term specified for the equivalent amount in PCC(S)A 2000, s. 139(4). As with fines, part payment of the compensation order will result in proportionate reduction in the term to be served in default.

Where a child or young person is convicted of an offence and the court makes an order for compensation, it may, under s. 137 of the 2000 Act, order the parent or guardian of the child or young person to pay the compensation order. See **6.3** for further information on this provision, which also operates in respect of fines imposed on a child or young person.

8.1.4 Compensation orders are not to be regarded as punishment

As has been explained above, the making of a compensation order should not in principle affect the punishment imposed for the offence. In particular, it would be quite wrong that the payment of compensation should 'permit the offender to buy his way out of a custodial sentence'. This principle has been stated on many occasions, and is well illustrated in *Barney* (1991) 11 Cr App R (S) 448. In that case the sentencer said to the offender 'Were you in a position to pay compensation, I would reduce the sentence for that . . .'. In the Court of Appeal, Ognall J stated that the impression given by that remark was incorrect and that:

> It must never be thought that the convicted criminal can buy his way out of imprisonment or any part of it. The significance of an offer to pay compensation is that it may be treated as some token of remorse on the defendant's behalf as well as redressing the private loss of the victim. To that extent and no further it sounds in the sentencing exercise. But it must be clearly recognised that compensation orders are otherwise wholly independent of that exercise.

This important principle is not, however, always rigidly followed by the courts, and there have been cases where, for example, a sentence of imprisonment has been suspended on the basis that if the offender goes to prison he will thereby be deprived of the means of paying compensation to the victim of the offence. This point was conceded in *Huish* (1985) 7 Cr App R (S) 272 by Croom-Johnson LJ, but its importance was re-emphasised by Lord Taylor CJ in *A-G's Reference (No. 5 of 1993)* (1993) 15 Cr App R (S) 201.

The general principle that compensation should not displace punishment is, in any event, subject to PCC(S)A 2000, s. 130(12), which applies in a case where the court decides that the appropriate penalty for the offence is a fine but wishes to make a compensation order in addition. If the offender would have insufficient means to meet his obligations under both orders, s. 130(12) requires the court to give priority to the imposition of a compensation order. This, in a strict sense, permits the offender to 'buy his way out of the penalties for crime', but it may be regarded as a legitimate exception allowing, as it does, for the offender's limited resources to be channelled towards the victim rather than the state. Section 130(12) has no application to sentences other than fines.

8.1.5 Compensation orders and the means of the offender

The next important principle is that a compensation order should be made only where the sentencer is satisfied that the offender has the means to pay. This principle may be found in PCC(S)A 2000, s. 130(11) but is sometimes overlooked by the courts, to judge from the number of occasions upon which the Court of Appeal has had to quash or reduce compensation orders on that ground. Part of the trouble stems from a failure to follow the general principle expressed at **8.1.4**. The defence in mitigation often stresses the offender's willingness to pay compensation, in the hope that this will lead the court to pass a community sentence rather than a custodial one. Later, it transpires that the offer to pay compensation was unrealistic, and the Court of Appeal, on an appeal by the offender, is then asked to quash the order. An example of such a case is *Roberts* (1987) 9 Cr App R (S) 275. If it is clear that the offender has misled his legal advisers about the availability of funds to pay the compensation, the Court of Appeal has declined to quash the orders imposed (e.g. *Dando* [1996] 1 Cr App R (S) 155).

It is the responsibility of the offender to inform the court of his resources, and not for the sentencer to initiate inquiries into the matter (*Bolden* (1987) 9 Cr App R (S) 83). Nor is it the duty of the prosecutor to establish the offender's means (*Johnstone* (1982) 4 Cr App R (S) 141), but where the offender's lawyer advances mitigation on the basis that the offender will pay substantial compensation, the defence is under an obligation to ensure that the necessary means do in fact exist (*Coughlin* (1984) 6 Cr App R (S) 102). It may be thought that to place defence counsel under a duty to check that the offer of compensation is genuine is inconsistent with the commonly accepted view that counsel, subject to not deliberately misleading the court, acts on the client's instructions whether they seem credible to counsel or not.

It is generally wrong to make a compensation order which will require the sale of the offender's home (*Harrison* (1980) 2 Cr App R (S) 313). On the other hand, it is not unreasonable to expect the offender to sell items of personal property to pay the compensation (*Workman* (1979) 1 Cr App R (S) 335); in such a case the court should ascertain a realistic value for the asset (*Chambers* (1981) 3 Cr App R (S) 318). An order should not be made on the basis of sale of an asset unless it is quite clear that the offender will be able to dispose of that asset (*Hackett* (1988) 10 Cr App R (S) 388, where the relevant asset was the family home, which was in joint ownership). Nor should one be made on the basis of an uncertain promise of work or on the prospect of seasonal work which may not materialise (*Coughlin* (1984) 6 Cr App R (S) 102).

It follows from the above principles that co-defendants may be required to pay different sums by way of compensation if their capacity to pay is different. A good example is *Beddow* (1987) 9 Cr App R (S) 235, where the offender was one of two defendants who pleaded guilty to being carried in a vehicle taken without consent by a third defendant, who had fallen asleep at the wheel, causing the van to crash. The offender was conditionally discharged and ordered to pay £300 in compensation. The other two defendants received a suspended sentence and a conditional discharge respectively, but neither was required to pay compensation. The Court of Appeal approved the sentences on the basis that the offender was the only one of the defendants who was in work and could afford to pay. See also *Stapleton and Lawrie* [1977] Crim LR 366. A compensation order should not be imposed on the assumption that persons other than the offender will pay, or will contribute to, the order (*Hunt* [1983] Crim LR 270).

8.1.6 Compensation order should be complied with within a reasonable time

The court may allow the offender time to pay the sum due under the compensation order, or direct payment of the sum by instalments of such amounts and on such dates as the court may specify (PCC(S)A 2000, s. 141 and MCA 1980, s. 75(1)), but a compensation order should not be made which involves payments by instalment over an unreasonable length of time. In *Bradburn* (1973) 57 Cr App R 948, Lord Widgery CJ said that, in general, compensation orders 'should be sharp in their effect rather than protracted' and that an order which would take four years to complete was 'unreasonably long'. A batch of decisions including *Bradburn* and *Makin* (1982) 4 Cr App R (S) 180 have indicated that payment should not normally extend over a period longer than 12 months, but in *Olliver* (1989) 11 Cr App R (S) 10 the Court of Appeal said that a fine (or compensation order) might properly be repaid over a period of up to as long as three years. Lord Lane CJ in that case said that: 'Certainly it seems to us that a two-year period will seldom be too long, and in an appropriate case three years will be unassailable.' The Magistrates' Association Guidelines

(2000) state that an order for compensation should 'normally be payable within 12 months'. The court should also consider whether a protracted order is in the interests of the victim.

8.1.7 Compensation orders to be made only in clear cases

Compensation orders should be made only in clear, straightforward cases. The criminal court should not embark on complex issues of quantum of damages which are suitable only for a civil court. The importance of this point is clear when it is remembered that the vast majority of compensation orders are ordered by lay magistrates, who are inexperienced in such matters.

In *Donovan* (1981) 3 Cr App R (S) 192 the offender pleaded guilty to taking a conveyance, having hired a car for two days and failed to return it. The car had suffered no damage. He was fined £250 with £100 costs and £1,388 compensation, on the basis of the hire company's loss of use of the car. On appeal, Eveleigh LJ said that 'A compensation order is designed for the simple, straightforward case where the amount of the compensation can be readily and easily ascertained'. Since the amount of damages in a civil case of loss of use 'is notoriously open to argument', the compensation order was quashed and the hire company was left to pursue its civil remedy if it wished to do so. See also *Hyde* v *Emery* (1984) 6 Cr App R (S) 206, where the offender pleaded guilty to three charges of obtaining unemployment benefit by false representation. There was a dispute over whether the sum claimed in compensation by the DHSS should be reduced by the amount of supplementary benefit which he could legitimately have claimed. Watkins LJ said in the Divisional Court that the magistrates should have declined to deal with the matter. Another example is *White* [1996] 2 Cr App R (S) 58, where the offender made an insurance claim in respect of a burglary at his home but the claim was found, in part, to have been fraudulent. The insurance company applied for a compensation order for the amount which they had paid under the claim but were awarded a lesser sum equivalent to the value of property which the police had found hidden at the offender's house. Owen J said that the order should not have been made, it having been established in 'countless cases' that compensation orders should not be made when there were complex issues as to liability.

8.1.8 Combining compensation orders with other sentences or orders

Compensation orders may be imposed 'instead of or in addition to dealing with the offender in any other way' (PCC(S)A 2000, s. 130(1)). For the avoidance of doubt, it is expressly provided that a compensation order may be combined with an absolute or conditional discharge (s. 12(7)).

While a compensation order may be combined with a sentence of immediate custody where the offender is clearly able to pay the compensation or has excellent prospects of employment on his release from custody (*Love* [1999] 1 Cr App R (S) 484), it is often inappropriate to impose a compensation order as well as a custodial sentence. It may well be undesirable for a compensation order to be hanging over the offender's head after release, and the order may be 'counterproductive, and force him back into crime to find the money' (*Inwood* (1974) 60 Cr App R 70). While it is not wrong to combine a compensation order with a suspended sentence and, indeed, that combination is positively encouraged by s. 118(5), regard should be had to the fact that if the offender is in breach of the suspended sentence its activation may bring to an end any prospect of the payment of compensation (*McGee* [1978] Crim LR 370). It would appear to be contrary to principle to suspend a custodial sentence merely because of the offender's ability to pay compensation (see **8.1.4**).

Where it would be appropriate both to impose a fine and to make a compensation order, but the offender has insufficient means to pay both, the court must give preference to compensation, though it may impose a fine as well (s. 130(12)). This entails that the fine should be reduced or, if necessary, dispensed with altogether so as to enable the compensation to be paid. A compensation order may, thus, stand alone on sentence. It looks strange, perhaps, that a criminal court may dispose of a case purely by way of compensation. Although interesting in theory, there are relatively few cases so dealt with in the courts. In 1999 around 100 offenders were dealt with by way of compensation as the 'sole or main penalty' in the Crown Court, out of a total of over 5,500 offenders who were given compensation orders ancillary to their main sentence. In magistrates' courts in 1999, the equivalent figures were 6,700 cases out of 98,600. For both courts these figures exclude summary motoring offences. Where the court proposes to make a compensation order and a confiscation order under the CJA 1988 (see **9.2**), and the offender has insufficient means to pay both, the court must, by virtue of s. 72(7) of the CJA 1988, order that the compensation order shall be paid from sums recovered under the confiscation order.

8.1.9 Compensation: guidelines

Suggested starting points for the award of compensation are provided in the Magistrates' Association Guidelines (2000):

Type of Injury		*Suggested Award*
Graze	Depending on size	Up to £75
Bruise	Depending on size	Up to £100
Black eye		£125
Cut (no permanent scarring)	Depending on size and whether stitched	£100–500
Sprain	Depending on loss of mobility	£100–1,000
Loss of a non-front tooth	Depending on cosmetic effect	£500–1,000
Loss of front tooth	—	£1,500
Facial scar	However small (resulting in permanent disfigurement)	£1,500
Nasal	Undisplaced fracture of the nasal bone	£1,000
Nasal	Displaced fracture of bone requiring manipulation	£1,500
Nasal	Not causing fracture but displaced septum requiring sub-mucous resection	£2,000
Wrist	Simple fracture with recovery within month	£3,000
Wrist	Displaced fracture (limb in plaster; recovery 6 months)	£3,500

Type of Injury		Suggested Award
Finger	Fractured little finger; recovery within month	£1,000
Leg or arm	Simple fracture of tibia, fibula, ulna or radius with recovery within month	£3,500
Laparotomy	Stomach scar 6–8 inches long (resulting from operation)	£3,500

The Guidelines state that these are 'general guidance on appropriate starting points for general damages'. There may be factors which could cause any of the awards to be substantially increased (such as the effect of an assault upon an elderly or disabled person). It is for the criminal courts to decide what use should be made of the information, but a sentencer certainly cannot be criticised for having had recourse to it (*Broughton* (1986) 8 Cr App R (S) 379).

8.2 RESTITUTION ORDERS

8.2.1 Power to make restitution order

The Crown Court, an adult magistrates' court or a youth court may make a restitution order. The relevant law is contained in PCC(S)A 2000, s. 148. A restitution order is an order which is imposed by the court as ancillary to the sentence for the offence, and may be made in combination with any other sentence passed, including a deferment of sentence (s. 148(1) and (2)). Its basic object is simple compensation: to return stolen property from the offender to the victim from whom it was taken. The legal provisions are, however, rather complex since they must allow for the possibility that the offender has disposed of the goods in the meantime. Restitution orders have declined in importance since the introduction of compensation orders (see **8.1**), which in general are a much more flexible remedy, but restitution orders are still a potentially useful means of providing redress for the victim of property crime.

Power to make a restitution order arises where goods have been 'stolen'. This term is construed widely, to include not just theft and offences where theft is a constituent element, such as robbery and burglary, but also offences where the goods were obtained by blackmail or deception (Theft Act 1968, s. 24(4)). A restitution order can be made where goods have been stolen and the offender has been convicted of an offence 'with reference to the theft', or where such an offence has been taken into consideration when sentencing the offender for a different offence. An offence 'with reference to' the theft of stolen goods includes handling them, and would probably extend to conspiring to steal them or to assisting the thief to avoid arrest under CLA 1967, s. 4(1). Provided that it is sufficiently established that the goods were stolen, a restitution order may be made even though nobody has been convicted of the theft itself.

When the court is entitled to make a restitution order, it can order the offender (or anyone else who is in possession of the goods or has control over them) to restore them to any person who is entitled to them (s. 148(2)(a)). It may well be that the police will have taken possession of the stolen goods on arresting the offender, so the enforcement of the order will create no practical problems. Where the offender no longer has the stolen goods, but is in possesssion of goods which directly or indirectly represent them, he may be ordered to transfer to any person entitled to them the goods representing those which have been stolen (s. 148(2)(b)). Thus, if an offender steals a television set, sells it and buys a video recorder with the proceeds, the victim of the theft may apply to the court for an order that the video recorder be transferred to him. This form of order may be made only where the proposed beneficiary makes an application. Lastly, the court may order that, out of any money taken from the offender at the time of his apprehension, a sum not exceeding the value of the stolen goods should be paid to any person who would have been entitled to them if they had still been in the offender's possession (s. 148(2)(c)).

An order may be made of the court's own motion under s. 148(2)(a) without an application being made. If an order is made under s. 148(2)(a), it will be inappropriate to order restitution under s. 148(2)(b) or (c) in addition, since the person will thereby recover more than the value of the goods (*Parsons* (1976) CSP J3.2F01). For an order under s. 148(2)(a), the person in 'possession or control' need not be the offender, and might be an innocent purchaser. Where a person has, in good faith, bought the relevant goods from the person convicted, or has, in good faith, lent money to the convicted person on the security of the goods, the court may order payment of compensation to that person out of money taken from the offender under s. 148(2)(c) (s. 148(4)). Under s. 148(2)(b), an application must be made by the person claiming, and may not relate to goods held by a third party. Where the offender is no longer in possession of the goods, orders may be made under both s. 148(2)(b) and (c), with reference to the same goods, providing that the person does not thereby recover more than the value of the goods (s. 148(3)). An order may be made under s. 148(2)(c) with or without an application being made by the victim. The phrase 'taken out of his possession on his apprehension' in s. 148(2)(c) has been generously construed to extend to money seized from the offender after he has been arrested. In *Ferguson* [1970] 1 WLR 1246, the sum of £2,000, which was taken from the offender's safe deposit box 11 days after his arrest, was held to have been in his possession at the time of his apprehension. On the other hand, money seized prior to the offender's apprehension may not be the subject of an order (*Hinde* (1977) 64 Cr App R 213, a case decided in relation to forfeiture orders but applicable by analogy here). There is no need to show that the money is the proceeds of the relevant offence; all that is necessary is that it be shown that it is money belonging to the offender (*Lewis* [1975] Crim LR 353). It was also established in *Lewis*, where the offenders split the proceeds of a robbery between them, that a restitution order under s. 148(2)(c) may be made against one offender for a greater sum than he actually received as a result of the offence, provided that this is not for a greater amount than the total loss. This is in contrast to *Grundy* [1974] 1 WLR 139, a case which establishes that joint and several liability should not apply in the closely related context of compensation orders.

8.2.2 Procedure

The factual basis for making a restitution order may be established from evidence given at the offender's trial, from witness statements before the court in a case where he pleads guilty or from admissions made by the offender or by anyone else who would be adversely affected by the making of the order. Orders should, however, be made only in cases where the evidence is clear and has been given before sentence is imposed (s. 148(5) and (6) and *Church* (1970) 55 Cr App R 65). In particular, a restitution order should not be made where the question of title to the goods is unclear. According to Woolf J in *Calcutt* (1985) 7 Cr App R (S) 385 at p. 390:

. . . the criminal courts are not the appropriate forum in which to satisfactorily ventilate complex issues as to the ownership of such money or goods. In cases of doubt it is better to leave the victim to pursue his civil remedies or, alternatively, to apply to the magistrates' court under the Police (Property) Act 1897.

This point has been made in several cases, and is well established. Under the Police (Property) Act 1897, the police or any person claiming property at the end of criminal proceedings may invoke that Act and a magistrates' court can then make an order for the delivery of the property to the person who appears to the court to be the owner. If the owner cannot be ascertained the court may make such order in relation to the property as it thinks fit (s. 1(1)). This includes its sale or destruction in a case where no owner has been ascertained.

If a magistrates' court commits the offender for sentence to the Crown Court, the power to make a restitution order passes to the Crown Court, and should not be exercised by the magistrates. An offender may appeal against the making of a restitution order, as against any other sentence (MCA 1980, s. 108 and CAA 1968, s. 50(1)). Such an order is, however, subject to a unique proviso. Where the order is passed on conviction on indictment, it is made subject to an automatic suspension for 28 days from the date of conviction (unless the trial judge specifically directs to the contrary on the ground that 'the title to the property is not in dispute': CAA 1968, s. 30(1)) or, further, until the determination of any appeal. If the restitution order is made by a magistrates' court, it is subject to an automatic suspension for 21 days from the date of conviction (unless the court directs to the contrary as above: s. 149(4)) or, further, until the determination of any appeal.

8.2.3 Combining restitution orders with other sentences or orders

Since a restitution order is an ancillary order it is clear that it may be combined with any other sentence. A restitution order and a compensation order might be made at the same time, such as where the goods which are the subject of the restitution order are returned but have been damaged.

9   Confiscation

Confiscation orders may be made under the Drug Trafficking Act 1994 (DTA 1994), which consolidates earlier provisions, under the CJA 1988, and under the prevention of terrorism legislation. The legislation is designed principally to allow the courts to confiscate the profits of lucrative offending such as drug trafficking.

The drug trafficking legislation was passed to remedy defects in the law disclosed by the decision in *Cuthbertson* [1981] AC 470. That case revealed a startling inability of the criminal courts to use their existing powers of fine and forfeiture (see Chapter 6) to deprive an offender of the profits of his crime and, as a result, the House of Lords had, with 'considerable regret', to quash an order for forfeiture made under the Misuse of Drugs Act 1971 (MDA 1971), s. 27 (see **6.7.1**) under which the sentencer had sought to confiscate assets of the offenders to the value of £750,000, which included cash, cars, paintings and deposits of money and securities in bank accounts abroad. It was held that s. 27 could not extend to such assets. In consequence of that decision, Parliament introduced important new powers for the courts to order confiscation of assets, initially in drug trafficking cases, and subsequently in respect of other kinds of lucrative offending.

Crown Court powers in the DTA 1994 are complex in form and draconian in effect. Many feel that the seriousness of this kind of offending, and the desirability of confiscation of profits derived from it, are such that massive powers are appropriate. They have so far survived challenge as being incompatible with the ECHR (*Benjafield* [2001] 2 Cr App R (S) 221). It may be, however, that notwithstanding the laudable goals of the Act, its draconian provisions do damage to the sentencing system as a whole. The provisions are anomalous in requiring the prosecuting authorities to take the initiative in investigation and enforcement (a role at odds with the prosecution's traditional and much vaunted neutrality at the sentencing stage) and the applicable standard of proof is the civil one of balance of probability, rather than proof beyond reasonable doubt.

Part VI of the CJA 1988 provides the courts with power to order the confiscation of the proceeds of an offender's wrongdoing. The powers are available to the Crown Court for any indictable offence and, in a limited range of circumstances, to magistrates' courts. The order is designed to remove the profit from lucrative offending. It does not apply where the defendant has benefited from drug trafficking, since the more particular scheme under the DTA 1994 is then used. The CJA 1993 and the Proceeds of Crime Act 1995 (PCA 1995) have amended and further strengthened the relevant provisions of the CJA 1988.

In 1999, 1,009 confiscation orders were made under the DTA 1994, from a total number of 6,577 eligible cases, producing a total of £16.1 million. The percentage of drug trafficking cases in which orders have been made has been declining in recent years from 26% in 1994 to 15% in 1999, and most of the orders have been for relatively small sums. In 1999, 829 of the orders were for less than £3,000 but there were two cases in which an order for more than £1 million was made. There is less evidence about sums actually recovered as a result of these orders. There appear to be no published statistics on the courts' use of confiscation powers under the CJA 1988.

There is much in common in the ways in which the confiscation order provisions in the DTA 1994 and the CJA 1988 are drafted, but there are also some significant differences. Since they are mutually exclusive orders, it is necessary to deal with the two types of confiscation orders separately in this chapter, although this approach does involve a degree of repetition.

9.1 CONFISCATION ORDERS: DRUG TRAFFICKING

9.1.1 Outline of powers

According to Lord Lane CJ in *Dickens* (1990) 12 Cr App R (S) 191 at p.194, the Crown Court's powers to order confiscation of the assets of those convicted of drug trafficking offences are 'intentionally draconian'. The provisions are certainly also complex. The Crown Court must follow a set procedure, and the mandatory nature of these requirements was stressed in *Stuart* (1989) 11 Cr App R (S) 89. Normally the prosecutor will be asking the court to proceed in this way, but the court may do so without the prosecutor's invitation.

(a)   Under the DTA 1994, s. 2, where a defendant has been convicted before the Crown Court of a 'drug trafficking offence', or where he has been committed by the magistrates for sentence under the PCC(S)A 2000, s. 3 in relation to such an offence, the Crown Court may determine whether or not the defendant has benefited from drug trafficking. The court *must* proceed to do this if the prosecutor so requests, or the court may itself decide to do so (s. 2(1)(a) and (b)). By s. 2(3), the test of whether the defendant has so benefited is whether the defendant has 'at any time . . . received payment or other reward in connection with drug trafficking carried on by him or another person'. In making this determination the court may make certain 'required assumptions' set out in s. 4(3). These assumptions *must* be made unless they are shown to be incorrect in the defendant's case, or if serious injustice would be caused by so doing.

(b)   The prosecutor is required by s. 11 of the DTA 1994, in every case in which the prosecutor has asked the court to proceed under the Act, or in any other case in which the court asks the prosecutor to do so, to tender a 'prosecutor's statement' of any matters which are relevant to the determination of whether the defendant has benefited from drug trafficking. Any admission by the defendant of an allegation in the prosecutor's statement may be treated by the court as 'conclusive'. If the defendant does not admit any allegation, the court may require him to provide any information which he wishes to rely on, within a specified period. If he fails to do so, the court can treat such failure as an acceptance of the relevant allegation.

(c)   If, having heard the evidence and considered the statements, the court determines that the defendant has benefited from drug trafficking, it must then determine 'the amount to be recovered' in accordance with the terms of s. 5 of the DTA 1994, as elaborated in ss. 6 to 8. The court must determine the value of the defendant's proceeds of drug trafficking, and that sum is prima facie the amount to be recovered under the order. When the court has determined the value of the defendant's proceeds it should make a confiscation order in that sum, unless the court is satisfied that 'the amount that may be realised' from the defendant is a lesser sum. In determining the amount that may be realised the court must comply with the provisions of s. 6 of the DTA 1994, which defines the amount that may be realised as the total value of all realisable property held by the defendant at the time of the confiscation order, together with the total value of all 'gifts' made by him which are caught by the Act, less the total value of any obligations which have priority at that time.

(d)   A confiscation order in the appropriate sum can then be made. Determination of the sum to be paid should normally be done *before* sentencing the defendant for the drug trafficking offence. The confiscation order should be taken into account before fixing any fine or other sentence involving forfeiture or deprivation of property, but otherwise the court should leave the confiscation order out of account when determining the sentence (s. 2(5)).

'Drug trafficking offences' are defined in s. 1(3) of the DTA 1994 to mean offences under MDA 1971, ss. 4(2) and (3), 5(3) and 20 (production, supply and possession for supply of controlled drugs), the Customs and Excise Management Act 1979, ss. 50(2) and (3), 68(2) and 170 (improper importation, exportation, fraudulent evasion of prohibition on importation or exportation of controlled drug), the Criminal Justice (International Cooperation) Act 1990, ss. 12, 14 and 19, and ss. 49 to 51 of the DTA 1994 (concealing or transferring proceeds of drug trafficking etc. — 'laundering') together with conspiracy, attempt, incitement and participation in relation to those offences.

The object of the legislation is to ensure that the convicted drug trafficker is parted from the proceeds of his offending. The court should proceed in any case where the defendant might have so benefited, whether or not the benefit relates directly to the drug trafficking offence with which he has just been convicted. Where the prosecutor asks the court to proceed, the provisions of the DTA 1994 are mandatory and all must be fully complied with. The only exception is where the prosecutor does not ask the court to proceed, in which case the court still has a discretion whether to do so, the judge making a preliminary assessment of whether or not it is a 'benefit' case. The evidence from the trial, or the facts which emerge from the trial papers if there has been a guilty plea, should be enough to allow the judge to form this preliminary assessment. Sometimes the judge will hear evidence from prosecution witnesses (such as Customs and Excise officials) on the matter. The court's powers to fine, to make a compensation order or an order for costs or to make a deprivation order under PCC(S)A 2000, s. 143 or MDA 1971, s. 27 are unaffected by these powers of confiscation, but s. 2(5) makes it clear that the issue of confiscation has priority, and must be resolved first. This means that where the bulk of the defendant's assets are required to meet the confiscation order, there may well be insufficient funds to meet any other financial order. Further, s. 2(6) provides that no statutory provision restricting the court from combining sentences or orders shall prevent the Crown Court from dealing with the offender 'in any way the court considers appropriate in respect of a drug trafficking offence'. This means that the imposition of a confiscation order does not entail that the penalty for the offence, such as a custodial sentence, should thereby be reduced. The confiscation order is ancillary to sentence. The DTA 1994, by s. 3, provides for the possibility of a 'postponed determination', whereby the Crown Court may decide that it needs further information before determining whether the defendant has benefited from drug trafficking, or to what extent. It may then postpone making that determination for up to six months (s. 3(3)). In such a case the court may pass sentence immediately but must not impose a fine or make a forfeiture order (s. 3(7) and (9)).

These powers are available where the offender has been dealt with on indictment or on committal for sentence under PCC(S)A 2000, s. 3. Section 2(7) provides that they shall not be available where the offender is committed to the Crown Court for sentence under PCC(S)A 2000, s. 6 or where the court's powers are limited to dealing with the defendant in any way in which a magistrates' court might have dealt with him, such as on an appeal by the defendant to the Crown Court against conviction or sentence.

9.1.2 Determining whether the defendant has benefited from drug trafficking

By s. 4 of the DTA 1994, any 'payments or other rewards' received by a person at any time in connection with drug trafficking carried on by him or another person are his proceeds of drug trafficking, and the value of his proceeds of drug trafficking is the aggregate of the values of his payments or other rewards. Where there is more than one defendant before the court, a separate assessment of the proceeds of each defendant must be made but, in the absence of evidence to the contrary, the sentencer may assume that the proceeds were equally shared. A confiscation order cannot be imposed on two defendants jointly and severally (*Porter* (1990) 12 Cr App R (S) 377). In assessing the value of the defendant's interest in property which is jointly owned (such as a house), the sentencer should determine the extent of the defendant's own interest (*Buckman* [1997] 1 Cr App S 325). The meaning of 'payment or other reward' has been considered in a number of cases. In *Osei* (1988) 10 Cr App R (S) 289 the Court of Appeal rejected an argument that the phrase was limited to payment by way of reward, and held that it simply meant any payment or, as it was put in *Smith* (1989) 11 Cr App R (S) 55, 'any payment in money or kind'. A defendant's expenses must not be deducted from his proceeds when making an assessment of the value of the 'payments or other rewards': the court should take account of gross profits rather than actual or net gains. These cases were all decided on the legislation as it stood before consolidation into the DTA 1994, but the Court of Appeal in *Banks* [1997] 2 Cr App R (S) 110 confirmed that they have continuing effect.

In order to ease the problems of proof in such cases for the prosecution, s. 4(2) provides that certain 'required assumptions', set out in s. 4(3), must be made by the court regarding the defendant, except where these can be shown to be incorrect in the defendant's case or there would be a serious risk of injustice if such an assumption were to be made (s. 4(4)). The court should, for the purpose of determining whether the defendant has benefited from drug trafficking and, if he has, of assessing the value of his proceeds of drug trafficking, assume (s. 4(3)):

(a)   that any property appearing to the court —
    (i)   to have been held by the defendant at any time since his conviction; or
    (ii)   to have been transferred to him at any time since the beginning of the period of six years ending when the proceedings were instituted against him,
was received by him, at the earliest time at which he appears to the court to have held it, as a payment or reward in connection with drug trafficking carried on by him;

(b)   that any expenditure of his since the beginning of that period was met out of payments received by him in connection with drug trafficking carried on by him; and

(c)   that, for the purpose of valuing any property received or assumed to have been received by him at any time as such a reward, he received the property free of other interests in it.

For these purposes 'money' includes money and all other property, real or personal, heritable or movable, including things in action and other intangible or incorporeal property.

Property may be taken into account whether it is situated in England and Wales or elsewhere. Property is 'held' by a person if he holds any interest in it. For the purpose of assessing the value of the defendant's proceeds of drug trafficking in a case where a confiscation order has previously been made against him, the court must leave out of account any of the proceeds of drug trafficking that are shown to the court to have been taken into account in determining the amount to be recovered under the earlier order (s. 4(6)).

Section 4(2) is couched in mandatory terms, but no particular assumption should be made if it can be shown to be unfounded in the particular case. Thus in *Johnson* (1990) 12 Cr App R (S) 182, the sentencer was entitled to make the prima facie assumption that a particular car was a part of the proceeds of drug trafficking, but was not entitled to make the assumption under (a) above, since the defendant could demonstrate a legitimate source for the funds used to purchase the car. If the court does not apply one or more of the required assumptions, it must give reasons for not doing so (s. 4(4)). Where the prosecution seeks to rely upon the assumptions under s. 2 and if the defendant disputes the assumption which is being made, a prima facie case must be established by the prosecution to support the facts on the basis of which the assumptions are made (*Dickens* (1990) 12 Cr App R (S) 191 and *Comiskey* (1991) 13 Cr App R (S) 227). Once this has been done the defence is then required to rebut any of the assumptions, by showing on a balance of probabilities that the assumption is not justified in respect of that particular item.

9.1.3 Statements relating to drug trafficking

Sections 11 and 12 of the DTA 1994 are concerned with proof of the matters indicated in s. 4. Section 11 provides that, where there is tendered to the Crown Court a statement by the prosecutor as to any matters relevant to the determination of whether the defendant has benefited from drug trafficking, or to the assessment of the value of his proceeds from drug trafficking, and the defendant accepts to any extent any allegation in the statement, the court may, for the purpose of that determination and assessment, treat his acceptance as conclusive of the matters to which it relates (s. 11(7)). Where a statement has been tendered and the court is satisfied that a copy of that statement has been served on the defendant, the court may require the defendant to indicate to what extent he accepts each allegation in the statement and, so far as he does not accept any such allegation, to indicate any matters he proposes to rely on. If the defendant fails in any respect to comply with such a requirement the court may draw such inference from that failure as it considers appropriate (s. 11(8)), and he may be treated for these purposes as accepting the allegations made in the statement.

Where there is tendered to the Crown Court by the defendant a statement as to any matters relevant to determining the amount that might be realised at the time the confiscation order is made, and the prosecutor accepts to any extent any allegation in that statement, the court may, for the purposes of that determination, treat the acceptance by the prosecution as conclusive of the matters to which it relates (s. 11(9)). By s. 12, the court may order the defendant where appropriate to provide such information. In *Emmett* [1998] AC 773 the House of Lords considered the meaning of the phrase 'treat his acceptance as conclusive of the matters to which it relates', as used in these sections. It was held that they were procedural provisions designed to facilitate proof, and that the particular phrase should not be construed as ousting the jurisdiction of the Court of Appeal in a case where the defendant had made a fundamental mistake in accepting an allegation in the prosecutor's statement. 'Conclusive' did not deprive the defendant of a right of appeal where that had happened.

9.1.4 The amount to be realised

The amount to be recovered under a confiscation order is the amount the Crown Court assesses to be the value of the defendant's proceeds of drug trafficking (s. 5(1)).

The amount that might be realised under a confiscation order is the total of the values at that time of all the realisable property held by the defendant (less, where there are obligations having priority at that time, the total payments payable in pursuance of such obligations), together with the total of the values at that time of all gifts caught by the DTA 1994 (s. 6(1)).

If the court is satisfied that the amount that might be realised at the time of the confiscation order is made is less than the amount the court assesses to be the value of the defendant's proceeds of drug trafficking, then the order shall be of the amount appearing to the court to be the amount that might be so realised, or a nominal amount if the court concludes that nothing can be recovered (s. 5(3)). It seems that the burden is proof is on the defendant (on a balance of probabilities) to show that the amount which might be realised is less than the value of the proceeds of the drug offending (*Ilsemann* (1990) 12 Cr App R (S) 398 and *Carroll* (1992) 13 Cr App R (S) 99). The determination of the amount to be realised is always a matter, ultimately, for the sentencer. It is, therefore, open to the judge under s. 4(3) to mitigate the severity of the confiscation order if the amount of money available is less than the amount which the court decides was the value of the proceeds of the drug trafficking (*Smith* [1989] 2 All ER 948) or, where appropriate on the evidence received by the court, a sum in excess of that which was originally indicated by the prosecution may be ordered (*Atkinson* (1993) 14 Cr App R (S) 182; *Finch* (1993) 14 Cr App R (S) 226).

9.1.5 Effect of order upon sentence

The seriousness of drug trafficking offences renders it very likely that an immediate custodial sentence will be imposed upon the offender. While the court is obliged to have regard to the general picture of the offender's assets when determining the confiscation order, the sentencer should be careful to relate the length of the custodial sentence only to those offences of which the offender has been convicted (*Bragason* (1988) 10 Cr App R (S) 258). While the offender must not receive a heavier sentence on the basis of what the sentencer has learned during the course of investigation into the offender's involvement in drug trafficking, information received in this way may properly form the basis for rejection of mitigation, such as the offender's claim that he was involved in a 'one-off' transaction (*Harper* (1989) 11 Cr App R (S) 240; approved in *Thompson* [1997] 1 Cr App R (S) 289). It seems that in a case where the offender has failed to cooperate fully with the process of investigation of his assets for the purpose of making a confiscation order, this should not have the effect of reducing his discount for pleading guilty, since the confiscation and sentencing procedures are distinct (*Nicholson* (1990) 12 Cr App R (S) 58).

In *Hedley* (1989) 11 Cr App R (S) 298, the Court of Appeal disapproved the imposition of a fine of £5,000 on an offender, in respect of whom the court had made a confiscation order as well as passing a custodial sentence. The fine was 'not punishment, because that had already been meted out by means of the two years' imprisonment. It was not the removal of ill-gotten gains, because those ill-gotten gains had already been removed by reason of the proceedings under the . . . Act.' In *Hopes* (1988) 11 Cr App R (S) 38, the Court of Appeal said that it was inappropriate to order the offender (who was made subject to a £12,000 confiscation order and a sentence of 16 years' imprisonment) also to pay prosecution costs of £5,000, unless there was evidence that the offender had means to pay those costs over and above the means required to meet the confiscation order.

9.1.6   Variation of order

If, on application by the defendant or a receiver appointed by the court in respect of a confiscation order, the High Court is satisfied that the realisable property is inadequate for the payment of any amount remaining to be recovered under the order, the court must issue a certificate to that effect, giving its reasons (s. 17(1)). Where such a certificate has been issued, the offender or the receiver must then apply to the Crown Court for the sum specified in the confiscation order to be reduced accordingly (s. 17(3)). The Crown Court must substitute such lesser sum as it thinks just in all the circumstances of the case, and substitute for the term of imprisonment or detention to be served by the offender in default of payment a shorter default term to reflect the lesser sum (s. 17(4)). If the converse situation arises, and it turns out that the amount that might be realised is greater than the amount taken into account in the confiscation order, application may be made to the High Court, by the prosecutor or by the receiver, for the order to be increased, and to the Crown Court for the default term to be increased (s. 16).

9.1.7   Enforcement

Under the current provisions there are two distinct methods of enforcement: through default provisions akin to fine enforcement and through receivership. The former is the province of the Crown Court. The latter must be arranged by application to the High Court, which is given powers to make restraint and charging orders for the better enforcement of confiscation; these are not further dealt with in this work.

Where the Crown Court orders the offender to pay any amount under a confiscation order, the provisions of the PCC(S)A 2000 relating to the powers of the Crown Court in relation to fines, and enforcement of Crown Court fines, have effect as if that amount were a fine imposed on the offender by the Crown Court (DTA 1994, s. 9(1)). For fine enforcement, see **6.5**. Maximum default terms are set out at **6.1.2**. The court may allow time for payment and make arrangements for payment by instalments. If any sum required to be paid is not paid in due time (either forthwith or under any arrangements made for payment), the offender becomes liable to pay interest on the sum for the period for which it remains unpaid (DTA 1994, s. 10(1)). The Crown Court must fix a term in default (*Popple* (1992) 14 Cr App R (S) 60), although it was held in *Ellis* [1996] 2 Cr App R (S) 403 that failure to do so does not invalidate the order itself. If the offender is required to serve the term in default, that term must be served consecutively to any term of imprisonment which was imposed for the offence or offences of which the offender was convicted (DTA 1994, s. 9(2)). In contrast to the legal position in relation to fine default, s. 9(5) provides that the serving of the default term does not expunge the confiscation order.

9.2   CONFISCATION ORDERS: CJA 1988

9.2.1   Outline of powers

Sections 71 to 102 of the CJA 1988 provide the criminal courts with a broad power (and in some cases a duty) to investigate the extent to which an offender has benefited from his offence and/or order confiscation of the proceeds of crime. The arrangements for making confiscation orders under the 1988 Act have been modifed by the CJA 1993 and the PCA 1995, so that they are now broadly parallel to those in relation to drug trafficking contained in the DTA 1994. The 1988 Act scheme, which is described below, applies only where all the offences of which the offender has been convicted were committed on or after 1 November 1995. If any of the offences were committed before that date earlier versions of the scheme are applicable, but those earlier versions are not considered here. Formerly, a confiscation order under the CJA 1988 could not be made in a sum less than £10,000. This lower limit was anomalous (there has never been an equivalent rule under the DTA 1994) and it has now been removed. There is no maximum sum which may be seized.

Section 71(1) states that the courts have power (and in some cases a duty) to investigate the extent to which an offender has benefited from his offence (where that is 'an offence of a relevant description'), or more generally from his offending (see 'relevant criminal conduct', explained below). By section 71(1E) an 'offence of a relevant description' means, for the Crown Court, *all* indictable offences. Clearly this is a very broad provision, and may involve the Crown Court in confiscation order proceedings in any case where it appears that the offender has been involved in lucrative offending — perhaps theft, fraud, burglary, blackmail or handling stolen goods. It should be noted, however, that 'offence of a relevant description' does not include drug trafficking offences, where the confiscation order provisions under the DTA 1994 must be used instead. In the magistrates' courts the powers are limited to a group of summary offences listed in sch. 4 to the Act, relating to unlawful supply of videos, use of certain unlicensed premises, copyright offences and certain offences relating to social security. Magistrates cannot use a confiscation order in respect of an either-way offence which was tried summarily.

The court must proceed under s. 71 if the prosecutor has requested the court to proceed, or it may decide itself to do so (s. 71(1)). In either case the court must first decide whether the offender has 'benefited from any relevant criminal conduct' (s. 71(1A)). This term means the offence or offences with which he has been convicted taken together with any offences which the court has taken into consideration (for these, see **3.8**). Section 71 states that a person 'benefits from an offence' if he obtains property or a pecuniary (financial) advantage as a result of that offence. If so, his benefit is the value of the property or pecuniary advantage obtained. Where the court decides that the offender has benefited from any relevant criminal conduct it must assess the extent of that benefit and make a confiscation order requiring the offender to pay that amount (s. 71(1B)), or a lesser sum if it appears to the court that the full benefit cannot be recovered from the offender (s. 71(6)).

The rather oddly named s. 72AA of the CJA 1988 extends confiscation powers to a further group of cases not catered for by s. 71. As has been explained the courts may, under s. 71, make a confiscation order which relates to an offence with which the offender has been convicted or an offence which has been taken into consideration. Section 72AA goes further, and allows the court to confiscate property held by the defendant which is shown (in accordance with the civil standard of proof) to have been the proceeds of other offending. The section can operate only where the prosecutor has so requested and where the offender is convicted on the present occasion of two 'qualifying offences' or is now convicted of one qualifying offence and has a previous conviction for another within a six-year period. A 'qualifying offence' is an offence of a relevant description (see above) committed after 1 November 1995 and in respect of which the court is satisfied that the offender has benefited. One purpose of s. 72AA is, in a case where the prosecution has proceeded against the defendant at trial on the basis that the offences charged represent 'sample counts' (see **3.9**), a confiscation order can be made with respect to all of the alleged offending, not just the offences formally proved or taken into consideration. If these various conditions are made out, the court may make the same assumptions as can be made under the DTA 1994 and which were listed in **9.1.2**, unless the assumption is shown to be incorrect in the defendant's case or there would be a serious risk of injustice to the defendant if the assumption were made.

9.2.2 Making the order

The court must make the confiscation order, and take account of its likely effect upon the offender, before imposing a fine or other financial order, or before making a forfeiture order under the MDA 1971 (see **6.8.1**) or a deprivation order under PCC(S)A 2000, s. 143 (see **6.7**). This means that the confiscation order has priority and may well mean, in a case where the confiscation order removes a substantial proportion of the offender's assets, that another financial order cannot be imposed in addition, having regard to the offender's ability to pay. It should be noted, however, that in contrast to the position in respect of confiscation orders under the DTA 1994, a compensation order has priority over a confiscation order made under the CJA 1988. Thus, if the court makes both a compensation order and a confiscation order against the offender, and it appears to the court that the offender will not have sufficient means to pay both the orders in full, it must direct that so much of the compensation as will not be recoverable because of the offender's insufficiency of means shall be paid out of any sums recovered under the confiscation order (CJA 1988, s. 72(7)). The making of a confiscation order should not otherwise affect the sentence passed (e.g. whether a custodial sentence is imposed or the length of any such sentence) (s. 72(5)).

Section 72A provides for the possibility of a 'postponed determination', whereby the court may decide that it needs further information before determining whether the defendant has benefited from the offending. It may postpone making such a determination for up to six months (s. 72A(3)). In such a case the court may pass sentence immediately but not impose a fine (s. 72A(9)).

9.2.3 Statements relating to orders

The prosecutor, in any case where he has asked the court to proceed, or where the court requests him to do so, must provide a statement of any matters relevant to determining whether, and to what extent, the offender has benefited from the offence. Where the offender accepts to any extent any allegation in the statement, the court may, for the purpose of that determination and assessment, treat his acceptance as conclusive of the matters to which it relates (s. 73(1)). On the meaning of 'conclusive' see *Emmett* [1998] AC 773 discussed at **9.1.3**. Where a statement has been so tendered and the court is satisfied that a copy of that statement has been served on the offender, the court may require the offender to indicate to what extent he accepts each allegation in the statement and, so far as he does not accept any such allegation, to indicate any matters he proposes to rely on (s. 73(2)). If the offender fails in any respect to comply with such a requirement, he may be treated as accepting the allegations in the statement. Such failure cannot, however, be treated as an acceptance of a direct allegation that the offender has benefited from the offence or that any property was obtained by him as a result of, or in connection with, the commission of an offence (s. 73(3)).

Section 73A deals with information provided by the offender. Where the prosecutor has asked the court to proceed or where the court requests him to do so, the court may order the defendant to provide it with relevant information. Appropriate inferences may be drawn from a failure to provide the information (s. 73A(5)). Where the prosecutor accepts to any extent any information given in the statement by the defendant, the court may treat that acceptance as conclusive (s. 73A(6)).

If the court is satisfied as to any matter relevant for determining the amount that might be realised at the time the confiscation order is made, whether by an acceptance (under s. 73) or otherwise, the court may issue a certificate giving its opinion as to the matters concerned and the court must do so if it is satisfied that the amount that might be realised at the time the confiscation order is made is less than the amount the court assesses to be the value of the offender's benefit from any relevant criminal conduct (s. 73(6)).

9.2.4 Variation of order

Section 74A allows for later review and revision of a case in which a decision was made by the court not to proceed under these confiscation powers and where the prosecutor now has evidence that such a determination should have been made. Section 74B allows the court to revise its original assessment that the offender had not benefited from the offending but where the prosecutor now has fresh evidence to the contrary. Section 74C allows for an increase to be made in the amount to be recovered from the offender, in the light of fresh information. In each case the further information must come to light not later than six years after the original disposal of the case.

9.2.5 Enforcement

Confiscation orders under the CJA 1988 are enforced by a magistrates' court in the same way as if they were fines. Alternatively the prosecutor may apply to the High Court for a receiver to be appointed. The principal powers of the receiver provided by the Act are restraint and charging orders, but these are not further considered in this work.

Where the Crown Court orders the offender to pay an amount under a confiscation order, the provisions of the PCC(S)A 2000 relating to the powers of the Crown Court in relation to fines and enforcement of Crown Court fines have effect as if that amount were a fine imposed on him by the Crown Court (s. 75(1)). For fine enforcement, see **6.5**. The court may allow time for payment, and make arrangements for payment by instalments. If the offender is required to serve the term in default, that term must be served consecutively to any term of imprisonment which was imposed for the offence or offences with which the offender was convicted (s. 75(3)). The serving of the term of imprisonment in default of payment of the confiscation order does not have the effect of expunging the order (s. 75(5A)).

10 Disqualification and Exclusion

10.1 DISQUALIFICATION FROM DRIVING AND DRIVING LICENCE ENDORSEMENT

Most motorists who are convicted of road traffic offences are dealt with by way of a fine; 89 per cent of summary traffic offences were dealt with by way of fine in 1999. This high rate of use of the fine also applies to the more serious indictable traffic offences, such as dangerous driving, which in 1999 was dealt with in 56 per cent of cases by the imposition of a fine. Many motoring offenders are less concerned about the financial penalty to be incurred than about endorsement of their driving licence (penalty points) and possible disqualification from driving.

Most road traffic offences are 'endorsable'. This means that particulars of the offence are stamped on the offender's driving licence together with the number of 'penalty points' awarded by the court for the offence. The purpose of the penalty points system is to punish repeated offences, none of which are in themselves sufficiently serious to warrant disqualification, but which taken together indicate a pattern of bad driving or disregard for the law. Sentencing in road traffic cases has traditionally emphasised rather different penal aims than sentencing for what is sometimes misleadingly referred to as 'real crime'. The main emphasis has been on deterrence (e.g. through the progressive warning and threat inherent in the accumulation of penalty points) and prevention and public protection (through disqualification, sometimes with a requirement that the offender retake the driving test). In recent years, however, the courts have more frequently used the language of punishment in relation to penalty points, making it clear that the number of points awarded should reflect the seriousness of the offence committed. The question of the appropriate length of disqualification, however, seems to be a mix between reductivist and desert considerations (see **1.3** for discussion of these approaches). Lengthy bans following very serious offences have often been reduced on appeal, on the basis that such bans offer no hope to offenders and are counterproductive in tempting them to drive while disqualified.

If an offence is endorsable, it also carries with it discretionary or obligatory disqualification from driving. Where an offender is convicted of an offence which carries obligatory disqualification, he will almost certainly be disqualified for at least 12 months under the provisions of RTOA 1988, s. 34. If he is convicted of an offence for which disqualification is discretionary, he is unlikely to lose his licence unless the conviction also results in his total penalty points reaching or exceeding 12, these having been accumulated within a three-year period. In such a case he must normally be disqualified for at least six months, under RTOA 1988, s. 35.

Disqualification from driving debars the offender forthwith from holding or obtaining a driving licence to drive any sort of motor vehicle during the period of the disqualification. Periods of disqualification are not subject to statutory maxima, whether imposed in the Crown Court or by magistrates. Disqualification from driving may occur through four different routes:

(a)   in a magistrates' court or the Crown Court under the provisions of RTOA 1988, s. 34, following conviction for an offence carrying obligatory or discretionary disqualification;

(b)   in a magistrates' court or the Crown Court following the accumulation of 12 penalty points under RTOA 1988, s. 35;

(c)   by order of the Crown Court under PCC(S)A 2000, s. 147; or

(d)   in a magistrates' court or the Crown Court under PCC(S)A 2000, s. 146.

10.1.1   Obligatory and discretionary disqualification under RTOA 1988, s. 34

By RTOA 1988, s. 34(1), where a person is convicted of an offence involving *obligatory* disqualification (or an offence committed by aiding, abetting, counselling or procuring, or inciting the commission of an offence involving *obligatory* disqualification), the court *must* order the offender to be disqualified for such period not less than 12 months as the court thinks fit, unless the court for 'special reasons' thinks fit to order him to be disqualified for a shorter period, or not to order him to be disqualified at all. It will be seen that the word 'obligatory' is, in this context, somewhat misleading. It means 'obligatory in the absence of special reasons'. For some offences (listed below) the minimum period of obligatory disqualification is two years, or three years, rather than 12 months, again in the absence of special reasons. If, however, a person is convicted of an offence involving *discretionary* disqualification, the court *may* order him to be disqualified for such period as the court thinks fit.

Schedule 2 to the RTOA 1988 shows which offences carry obligatory or discretionary disqualification:

(a)   *Offences which carry obligatory disqualification.* These are:

(i)   causing death by dangerous driving,

(ii)   dangerous driving,

(iii)   causing death by careless driving while under the influence of drink or drugs,

(iv)   driving or attempting to drive when unfit through drink or drugs,

(v)   driving or attempting to drive with excess alcohol in blood, breath or urine,

(vi)   failing to provide a specimen (but see further **12.9.4**),

(vii)   motor racing or speed trials on public ways,

(viii) manslaughter, and

(ix)   aggravated vehicle-taking.

In any case where the offender establishes 'special reasons' (see **10.1.2**), the court is no longer obliged to disqualify but retains a discretion whether or not to disqualify.

By RTOA 1988, s. 34(4), if the offender is convicted of manslaughter, causing death by dangerous driving or causing death by careless driving while under the influence of drink or drugs, the minimum mandatory period of disqualification is *two* years. Further, if the offender has been twice disqualified for 56 days or more in the three years before the commission of the present offence, the minimum period of disqualification is *two* years. By s. 34(3), where a person has been convicted of causing death by careless driving when under the influence of drink or drugs, driving or attempting to drive while unfit, driving or attempting to drive with excess alcohol, or failing to provide a specimen (in circumstances where that is an offence involving obligatory disqualification), and has a previous conviction within the last ten years for any of these offences, the minimum period of disqualification is *three* years.

(b)   *Offences which carry discretionary disqualification*. There are many such offences, but the most important are:

(i)   all offences involving obligatory *endorsement* (see **10.1.3**),
(ii)   theft or attempted theft of a motor vehicle,
(iii)   taking a motor vehicle without consent, and
(iv)   going equipped to steal a motor vehicle,
(v)   speeding,
(vi)   careless driving,
(vii)   being in charge of a motor vehicle with excess alcohol in blood, breath or urine,
(viii) driving while disqualified,
(ix)   driving without insurance,
(x)   failing to stop after an accident.

10.1.2   'Special reasons' under RTOA 1988, s. 34

The effect of a finding by a court that there are special reasons for not applying the provisions as to obligatory disqualification is to allow the court a discretion whether or not it disqualifies under RTOA 1988, s. 34(1). In *Whittal* v *Kirby* [1947] KB 194, Lord Goddard CJ stated that:

A special reason within the exception is one which is special to the facts of the particular case, that is, special to the facts which constitute the offence. It is, in other words, a mitigating or extenuating circumstance, not amounting in law to a defence to the charge, yet directly connected with the commission of the offence, and one which the court ought properly to take into consideration when imposing punishment. A circumstance peculiar to the offender as distinguished from the offence is not a special reason within the exception.

The law relating to special reasons was reviewed in *Jackson* [1970] 1 QB 647, where the above principles were confirmed.

Even though special reasons have been established, the court retains a discretion and may still disqualify. In *Taylor* v *Rajan* [1974] QB 424 Lord Widgery CJ said that there 'is a very serious burden on the justices, even when a special reason has been disclosed, to decide whether in their discretion they should decline to disqualify in a particular case'. If the court exercises its discretion not to disqualify, or to disqualify for a shorter period, it should state the grounds for doing so in open court and, if it is a magistrates' court, enter the reasons in the register (RTOA 1988, s. 47(1)). Failure to comply with this requirement does not, however, provide a ground of appeal (*Brown* v *Dyerson* [1969] 1 QB 45). The facts relied upon as constituting 'special reasons' must be established by the defence by evidence on a balance of probabilities, unless the prosecution admits them (*Pugsley* v *Hunter* [1973] 1 WLR 578). Where there has been a trial and the defendant has been convicted of the offence, the defendant may give further evidence to establish whether there are 'special reasons' (*Director of Public Prosecutions* v *Kinnersley* [1993] RTR 105). The court should not find that 'special reasons' exist without allowing counsel to address the court on that matter (*Barnes* v *Gervaux* (1980) 2 Cr App R (S) 258). For sentencing principles applicable to the discretion to disqualify under s. 34, see **10.1.5**.

Examples of matters which have been held *not* to amount to special reasons are listed below; many of the reported cases are concerned specifically with excess alcohol offences (see (h) to (o) below):

(a) that the offender was a doctor who needed his car to answer calls (*Holroyd* v *Berry* [1973] RTR 145);

(b) that the offender was disabled and was reliant upon his transport (*Jackson* [1970] 1 QB 647);

(c) that the offender was a driver in the Army (*Gordon* v *Smith* [1971] RTR 52);

(d) that the offender had been a professional driver for 29 years with a clean driving record (*Steel* (1968) 52 Cr App R 510);

(e) that the motorist did not know that a system of street lighting indicated a 30 mph speed limit (*Walker* v *Rawlinson* [1976] RTR 94);

(f) that the disqualification is a severe penalty in the circumstances (*Williamson* v *Wilson* [1947] 1 All ER 306);

(g) that the offence was comparatively trivial (*Marks* v *West Midlands Police* [1981] RTR 471);

(h) the fact that the offender's blood/alcohol level is only just in excess of the permitted level (*Delaroy-Hall* v *Tadman* [1969] 2 QB 208);

(i) that the alcohol did not apparently affect the offender's driving ability and the accident was not his fault (*Taylor* v *Austin* [1969] 1 WLR 264);

(j) that the offender's metabolism is such that alcohol is retained in the blood for a longer than average period (*Jackson* [1970] 1 QB 647);

(k) the fact that no other road user was endangered by the offender's driving (*Milliner* v *Thorne* [1972] RTR 279);

(l) the fact that the motorist stopped his car as soon as he realised he felt incapacitated through drink (*Duke* v *Peacock* [1949] 1 All ER 318);

(m) the fact that the offender had been drinking in the evening and was found to have an excess alcohol level the following morning (*Director of Public Prosecutions* v *O'Meara* (1988) 10 Cr App R (S) 56);

(n) the offender's ignorance that a combination of sleeping tablets and drink would produce a greater impairment to driving ability than drink alone (*Scott* [1970] 1 QB 661);

(o) the offender's inability to distinguish the respective alcoholic strengths of different drinks (*Beauchamp-Thompson* v *Director of Public Prosecutions* [1988] RTR 54).

Examples of matters which *have* been accepted as constituting a special reason are listed below; again most of the cases relate to drink-driving offences.

(a) The motorist was anxious about his passenger's health and this caused him to overlook a slight degree of excess speed (*Marks* v *West Midlands Police* [1981] RTR 471).

(b)   The motorist thought he was within a 40 mph limit because nothing other than the street lighting system indicated a change to a 30 mph limit (*Burgess* v *West* [1982] RTR 269).

(c)   In *James* v *Hall* [1972] 2 All ER 59 it was held that the fact that the offender was only trying to drive a few yards from the highway outside a house into the driveway could amount to a special reason, but the authority has been restrictively interpreted in later cases, such as *Haime* v *Walklett* (1983) 5 Cr App R (S) 165. In *Director of Public Prosecutions* v *Humphries* [2000] RTR 52 the Divisional Court listed seven matters to be taken into account in a case of this sort: how far the vehicle was driven, the manner in which it was driven, the state of the vehicle, whether the driver intended to drive any further, the prevailing road and traffic conditions, whether there was any possibility of danger by contact with road users and the reason for the vehicle being driven at all. See also *Director of Public Prosecutions* v *Corcoran* [1991] RTR 329.

(d)   It is open to a court to find special reasons where the offender has consumed laced drinks. In such a case, however, the offender must show that he was misled by a third party, rather than simply failing to inquire about the strength of the drinks and that the added alcohol was responsible for the offence in that, without it, he would have been below the limit (*Director of Public Prosecutions* v *O'Connor* [1992] RTR 66).

(e)   Where an offender had consumed drink not intending to drive, and then drove because of an emergency, this may amount to special reasons only in clear and compelling circumstances (*Director of Public Prosecutions* v *Upchurch* [1994] RTR 366; *Director of Public Prosecutions* v *Whittle* [1996] RTR 154).

10.1.3   Disqualification following endorsement (penalty points): RTOA 1988, s. 35

When a person who is the holder of a licence is convicted of an offence which carries obligatory or discretionary disqualification or endorsement, his licence must be produced to the court (RTOA 1988, s. 27). Failure to produce the licence on request is punishable by a fine up to level 3 on the standard scale, although there is a defence if the offender has recently applied for a new licence which has not yet arrived. The court orders the licence to be endorsed with particulars of the offence and the appropriate penalty points. All endorsable offences involve penalty points and they are always obligatory, but, as with obligatory disqualification, the court is permitted to find special circumstances for not endorsing. The endorsement remains on the licence for four years after the conviction (if disqualification was ordered) or four years after the offence (if no disqualification was ordered) or for 11 years after the conviction (if the offence was for driving under the influence of drink or drugs or driving with an excess blood/alcohol level). A driver who wants to have a 'clean' licence, with no lapsed endorsements on it, must apply to the DVLA and pay for a replacement licence.

The number of penalty points to be attributed to an offence is to be derived from sch. 2 to the RTOA 1988. The court must determine the number of penalty points which are to be attributed to the offence (s. 28(1)). For some offences a range of points is available. The court should determine the appropriate number of points, given the relative degree of seriousness of the offence. Examples of offences carrying penalty points are:

(a)   causing death by dangerous driving (3–11);

(b)   dangerous driving (3–11);

(c)   causing death by careless driving while under the influence of drink or drugs (3–11);

(d) driving or attempting to drive when unfit through drink or drugs (3–11);
(e) driving or attempting to drive with excess alcohol in breath, blood or urine (3–11);
(f) motor racing or speed trials on public ways (3–11);
(g) manslaughter (3–11);
(h) aggravated vehicle-taking (3–11);
(i) careless driving (3–9);
(j) speeding (3–6);
(k) being in charge of motor vehicle with excess alcohol in blood, breath or urine (10);
(l) driving while disqualified (6);
(m) failing to provide breath specimen (4);
(n) driving without insurance (6–8);
(o) failing to stop and report an accident (5–10).

In a case involving aiding, abetting, counselling or procuring or inciting the commission of any offence involving obligatory disqualification, the number of penalty points is 10 (s. 28(2)). Where offences are committed on separate occasions but within three years of each other, the number of penalty points applicable to each offence in the period are added together (RTOA 1988, ss. 29 and 35). If a person is convicted of two or more endorsable offences committed on the same occasion then the court has a discretion to aggregate the penalty points imposed (s. 28(4) and (5)). This would probably be done where none of the offences standing alone merited disqualification but where it is seen as justified by the persistence of the offending. 'Same occasion' is not defined in the Act, but it seems that there must be some close physical or temporal link between the offences. In *Johnson v Finbow* [1983] 1 WLR 879 the offender was convicted of failing to stop after an accident and of failing to report that same accident to the police. The offences were attributed to the same occasion, Goff LJ stating that 'the lapse of time, although significant, is not sufficiently great to be able to say, as a matter of common sense, that those offences were committed on different occasions'. In *Johnstone v Over* (1984) 6 Cr App R (S) 420 it was said that where an offender commits two offences at the same time out of the use of different vehicles, it is a question of fact whether the offences are committed on the same occasion. The offender had parked two vehicles outside his home and had been charged with two offences of using a vehicle without insurance. It was held that the offences were committed on the same occasion.

By RTOA 1988, s. 29, where a person is convicted on one occasion of an offence involving obligatory or discretionary disqualification, the penalty points to be taken into account on that occasion are any that are to be attributed to the offence(s) of which he is convicted, and any ordered on a previous occasion against the offender, unless since such occasion the offender has been disqualified under s. 34 or 35, but if any of the offences was committed more than 3 years before another, the points in respect of that offence are not to be added to those in respect of the other. Where the disqualification is under s. 34, the licence is not wiped clean, and any penalty points which were on the licence at the time of conviction for the offence which resulted in disqualification under s. 34 remain there.

For most offences, the number of penalty points to be awarded is fixed. For some, however, there is a range available. Where the number of penalty points is variable, it seems that the number of points awarded should reflect the seriousness of the offence and, if so, it would seem to be wrong to have regard to the endorsements on the offender's licence before fixing the number of points for the new offence. On the other hand, it can be said that the perceived gravity of the new offence may be affected by the presence or absence of like offences on the offender's record, and thus it is appropriate to consider his record before fixing the number of points.

According to RTOA 1988, s. 35, where a person is convicted of an offence involving obligatory or discretionary disqualification and the penalty points to be taken into account on that occasion number 12 or more, the court *must* order him to be disqualified for not less than the minimum period, unless the court is satisfied, having regard to all the circumstances, that there are *grounds for mitigating* the normal consequences of the conviction, and thinks fit to order him to be disqualified for a shorter period or not to order him to be disqualified. The minimum period is:

(a)   six months if the offender has had no previous disqualification imposed upon him under RTOA 1988, s. 34 or 35 within the last three years; and

(b)   one year if one, and two years if more than one, such disqualification within the last three years is to be taken into account.

Section 35(3) states that, where an offender is convicted on the same occasion of more than one offence involving obligatory or discretionary disqualification, only one disqualification may be imposed, but the court should take into account all the offences when determining the period of the disqualification.

10.1.4   'Mitigating grounds' under RTOA 1988, s. 35

Section 35 speaks of the court being satisfied, 'having regard to all the circumstances, that there are grounds for mitigating the normal consequences of conviction'. Section 35(4) specifically excludes from such consideration any circumstances which are alleged to make the offence or any of the offences not serious, hardship (other than exceptional hardship) or any circumstances which, within the previous three years, have already been taken into account in ordering the offender to be disqualified for a shorter period or not ordering him to be disqualified. Apart from this, it seems that the court may have regard to circumstances relating to the offence, to the offender, or to both. This may be contrasted with the relevant considerations for establishing 'special reasons' for not disqualifying (see **10.1.2**).

It is for the offender to establish, on the balance of probability, the grounds which are relied upon, and it is for him to show that they are different from those put forward on an earlier occasion (*Sandbach Justices, ex parte Pescud* (1983) 5 Cr App R (S) 177). In *Thomas* (1983) 5 Cr App R (S) 354 it was held that the fact that the offender is sentenced to imprisonment may be a mitigating ground for these purposes.

In these cases 'exceptional hardship' is the factor which is most often advanced. The court may take into account hardship caused to the public as well as to the offender (*Cornwall* v *Coke* [1976] Crim LR 519). Exceptional hardship may be advanced in relation to the offender's employment, in which case the court should consider whether a licence to drive is essential to that employment. In *Owen* v *Jones* (1987) 9 Cr App R (S) 34 the Divisional Court said that in most cases the magistrates would need evidence of exceptional hardship but, on the facts of the particular case, where a police officer had acquired a total of 13 points and disqualification would have forced him to resign, thereby losing his job and his home, the magistrates could properly find that this would amount to exceptional hardship without putting the offender to proof.

10.1.5   Disqualification from driving: general principles

Any period of disqualification from driving begins to run from the day on which it is imposed, unless it is suspended by the court pending an appeal. On suspension see **10.1.8**. Consecutive periods of disqualification cannot be ordered (*Johnston* (1972) 56 Cr App R 859), nor may disqualification be ordered to commence at the expiry of a custodial term (*Meese* [1973] 1 WLR 675). Any disqualification must be for a certain period (*Fowler* [1937] 2 All ER 380). Disqualification for life has been held to be disqualification for a certain period, and may thus lawfully be imposed (*Tunde-Olarinde* [1967] 1 WLR 911), but it should be imposed only in very unusual circumstances. Disqualification for life was appropriate in *Buckley* (1994) 15 Cr App R (S) 695, where the offender had an appalling record, including six convictions for dangerous driving, and constituted a real threat to the public. In a case of obligatory disqualification, the stated statutory period is the minimum that must be imposed and is not the normal period (*Mills* [1974] RTR 215).

In any case where disqualification is discretionary, a sentencer in the Crown Court should not impose disqualification without warning counsel and allowing him to address the court on that matter (*Ireland* (1988) 10 Cr App R (S) 474). In a magistrates' court, by MCA 1980, s. 11(4), whenever the magistrates have disqualification of the offender in mind and the offender is not present in court, they should adjourn in order to give notice of this to the offender.

The policy of the courts has been that very long periods of disqualification should be avoided so far as possible, particularly where the offender does not have a bad driving record (*Dawtrey* [1975] RTR 101), or in cases where a custodial sentence is being imposed for the latest offence. When imposing a disqualification, a sentencer should have regard to the offender's employment prospects (*Weston* (1982) 4 Cr App R (S) 51). For that category of persistent offenders who seem to be incapable of leaving motor vehicles alone, the imposition of a long disqualification, or one which will extend long after the offender's release from custody, may in effect invite the offender to commit further offences and be counterproductive (*Matthews* (1987) 9 Cr App R (S) 1; *Callum* [1995] RTR 248), or handicap the offender in trying to rehabilitate himself (*West* (1986) 8 Cr App R (S) 266). Exceptionally, however, a long disqualification has been upheld as essential to protect the public, and to allow the offender time to mature in the interim (*Gibbons* (1987) 9 Cr App R (S) 21).

In determining the length of the period of disqualification, the court should not have regard to the provisions of RTOA 1988, s. 42, which enable the offender to apply for restoration of his licence before the end of the period of disqualification (*Lobley* (1974) 59 Cr App R 63 and *Lark* (1993) 14 Cr App R (S) 196: see **10.1.8**). Due credit should be given for a timely guilty plea. Indeed in *Harrington-Griffin* [1989] RTR 138 the Court of Appeal declared that 'in no class of case is a plea of guilty of more significance than in the present type, for acknowledgement of blame in driving gives some assurance that the driver will remember what has happened, and will take heed of that lesson'.

10.1.6   Disqualification pending passing of driving test and reduced disqualification for driver retraining

The RTOA 1988, s. 36 provides that where a person has been disqualified under s. 34 as a result of having been convicted of manslaughter (by the driving of a motor vehicle), causing death by dangerous driving or dangerous driving, the court *must* disqualify him until he passes the appropriate driving test (s. 36(1)). In the case of conviction for any other offence which carries obligatory endorsement, the court *may* order him to be disqualified until he passes the appropriate driving test (s. 36(4)). In any case where the court has a discretion to order disqualification until the test is passed, the court should have regard to the safety of road users (s. 36(6)). An 'appropriate driving test' means an extended driving test, which is more detailed and thorough than a normal test of competence to drive. Once the test has been passed by the offender the period of disqualification comes to an end upon production of evidence that the offender has passed the test. Such evidence must be produced in appropriate form to the Secretary of State (s. 36(8)). The power extends to those who are disqualified under s. 34 or s. 35 (as the Secretary of State may by order prescribe) but there is no power to order an extended driving test where a person is disqualified under other powers of the court (*Patel* (1995) 16 Cr App R (S) 756).

It is well established that this power should not be used punitively. According to Brooke J in *Buckley* (1988) 10 Cr App R (S) 477:

> There is a long line of authorities, which starts with the case of *Donnelly* [1975] 1 WLR 390 which makes it clear that this power of the court is not to be exercised as an additional punishment. It is only appropriate where there is some reason to think that the driver concerned might have difficulty in passing a driving test because of some inability to drive properly. In the case of *Lazzari* (1984) 6 Cr App R (S) 83 the court made it clear that the exercise of this power should only be used where it comes to the court's attention that because of his age or infirmity or the circumstances of the offence a person may not be a competent driver.

In addition to the cases cited by Buckley J, to the same effect is *Peat* (1984) 6 Cr App R (S) 311. In *Hughes* v *Challes* (1983) 5 Cr App R (S) 374 it was held to be inappropriate to make such an order where the offence arose from a temporary, though possibly recurrent, condition of mind due to illness; it was only proper where the offender was 'generally speaking lacking in competence to drive'. Section 36(6) requires the court to have regard to the safety of other road users, and this is an important consideration when deciding whether to make an order under s. 36. An order was upheld in *Miller* (1994) 15 Cr App R (S) 505, where the 23-year-old offender had never passed a driving test and had acquired numerous previous convictions, including 10 for driving while disqualified. See also *Bannister* [1991] RTR 1.

Sections 34A to 34C of the RTOA 1988 provide for driver retraining (on a course approved for that purpose by the Secretary of State) for offenders of or over the age of 17 who are convicted of certain offences. By s. 34A(1), these are:

(a) causing death by careless driving when under the influence of drink or drugs;
(b) driving or being in charge when under the influence of drink or drugs;
(c) driving or being in charge with excess alcohol; or
(d) failing to provide a specimen.

The provisions are also restricted to cases where the court makes an order under s. 34 disqualifying the offender for a period of at least 12 months. These provisions provide a strong incentive for drivers to attend such a course by allowing a reduction in the period of disqualification for those who do. The reduction must be for not less than three months nor for more than one quarter of the period of disqualification before its reduction. Before it makes such an order, the court must be satisfied that a place on the course specified is available for the offender, the effect of the order must be explained by the court to the offender in ordinary language and the offender must consent (s. 34A(4)). The offender must pay the appropriate fee for the course, before it starts. It may therefore be argued that this scheme discriminates against those who are unable to pay the fee. The retraining course must be completed, at the latest, two months before the period of disqualification comes to an end. If completed successfully, a certificate must be awarded, but the organiser of the retraining course has power not to give a certificate (s. 34B(4)). The order which has the effect of reducing the period of disqualification does not come into effect until the offender's certificate has been received by the clerk of the magistrates' court in the petty sessions area where the offender resides.

10.1.7 Combining orders for disqualification from driving with other sentences or orders

Disqualification from driving is an ancillary order and may be combined with any other sentence or order of the court. Notwithstanding PCC(S)A 2000, s. 14 (see **7.1.4**), a court which convicts a person of an offence involving obligatory or discretionary disqualification may make an order for absolute or conditional discharge as well as disqualifying him under s. 34 or 35 of the RTOA 1988 (RTOA 1988, s. 46). An order for disqualification under PCC(S)A 2000, s. 146 or s. 147 (see below) may also be combined with a discharge.

Although a driving disqualification may be combined with immediate custody, care should be taken that a driving ban which continues after the offender's release is not counterproductive since 'if a young man cannot drive a motor vehicle it is a grave handicap when he seeks employment' on leaving prison (*Weston* (1982) 4 Cr App R (S) 51). There is, however, no rule that the end of the period of disqualification should be set so as to coincide with the duration of the custody (*Hansel* (1982) 4 Cr App R (S) 368).

10.1.8 Appeal against, suspension and removal of disqualification

Section 38 of RTOA 1988 provides that a person disqualified by a magistrates' court under s. 34 or s. 35 may appeal against the order as against a conviction and, by CAA 1968, s. 9, a person disqualified by the Crown Court may appeal to the Court of Appeal.

Section 39 of RTOA 1988 states that a magistrates' court or the Crown Court may, if it thinks fit, suspend a disqualification pending an appeal against the order. Section 40 allows the Crown Court or the Court of Appeal to suspend a disqualification pending appeal to that court. Any period of suspension must be disregarded when determining the expiration of the period of disqualification (s. 43).

Section 42 provides for the situation where a person who has been disqualified applies to the court to have that disqualification removed prior to its normal expiry. The court, having regard to the character of the person disqualified and his conduct subsequent to the order, the nature of the offence and any other circumstances of the case, may remove the disqualification as from such date as may be specified in the order. No application can be made to the court under s. 42 before the expiration of the relevant period, namely:

(a) two years, if the disqualification is for less than four years;

(b) one half of the period of disqualification, if it is for less than ten years but not less than four years;

(c) five years in any other case.

If an application is refused, a further application may not be made within three months. A court dealing with an application should be somewhat less ready to remove an obligatory disqualification than a discretionary one (*Damer* v *Davison* [1976] RTR 45). Where a disqualification has been removed after such an application, the court has no power to add a requirement that the offender take a driving test (*Benham* (1981) 3 Cr App R (S) 229).

Sections 44 and 45 deal with the rules relating to endorsement of licences, and are not considered further in this book. Part III of the RTOA 1988 deals with fixed penalty notices, and these too are not considered further in this book.

10.1.9   Disqualification from driving under PCC(S)A 2000, s. 147

Where an offender has been convicted on indictment of an offence punishable with imprisonment for two years or more, or has been convicted summarily of such an offence and is committed to the Crown Court for sentence under PCC(S)A 2000, s. 3, the Crown Court may, under s. 147, of that Act disqualify him from driving if a motor vehicle was used to commit, or to facilitate the commission of, the offence. Power to disqualify under s. 147 extends to persons who have been convicted of an offence but discharged absolutely or conditionally (s. 12(7) and see **7.1.4**).

The power in s. 147 is widely drafted. It may be noted in particular that, providing the above conditions are satisfied, the offender may be disqualified from driving by the Crown Court even though the offence with which he has been convicted is non-endorsable. If robbers make their get-away from the scene of crime in a car, they are liable to disqualification under s. 147, notwithstanding that robbery is not an offence attracting mandatory or discretionary disqualification. The fact that the offender did not drive the motor vehicle in the course of the offence does not protect him from disqualification. It is sufficient that the vehicle was used in the circumstances specified in s. 147 (*Matthews* [1975] RTR 32). If one of several joint offenders used a vehicle for the purposes of the joint offence, any or all of the offenders may be disqualified. The phrase 'facilitating the commission of an offence' is defined by s. 147(6) as including 'the taking of any steps after [the offence] has been committed for the purpose of disposing of any property to which it relates or of avoiding apprehension or detection'.

No disqualification may be ordered under s. 147 unless the vehicle was actually used to commit the offence of which the offender has been convicted (*Parrington* (1985) 7 Cr App R (S) 18, though see now **10.1.10**). In *Riley* (1983) 5 Cr App R (S) 335, for example, a disqualification under s. 147 was quashed where the offender had been convicted of conspiracy to steal, but the agreement had been reached prior to his use of a motor vehicle to inspect a possible target. In *Patel* (1995) 16 Cr App R (S) 756, the offender had pursued another motorist who had executed a dangerous manoeuvre in front of his car. When both cars stopped at traffic lights the offender got out and seriously assaulted a passenger in the other vehicle. It was held that the use of the car had facilitated the assault, and an order under s. 147 was upheld. Section 147 does not empower the Crown Court to order endorsement of an offender's licence. If an offender is disqualified under s. 147 for a non-endorsable offence he simply surrenders his driving licence to the court and does not regain it until the end of the disqualification period, but particulars of the conviction and disqualification do not go on to the licence.

Where a sentencer is minded to impose a disqualification under s. 147, counsel should be permitted to address the court on that matter (*Powell and Carvell* (1984) 6 Cr App R (S) 354 and *Money* (1988) 10 Cr App R (S) 237).

10.1.10   Disqualification from driving under PCC(S)A 2000, s. 146

By s. 146 of the 2000 Act, a magistrates' court or the Crown Court may, in addition to dealing with an offender in any other way, order him to be disqualified for such period as the court thinks fit, from holding or obtaining a driving licence. It should be understood that this power is wider than that which exists under s. 147, in that it extends to *any* offence (apart from murder and where sentence falls to be imposed under, s. 109–111 of the 2000 Act), not just cases where a motor vehicle was used to commit or facilitate the commission of an offence. Disqualification may be ordered under s. 146 where no motor vehicle has been involved in the offence at all. On the face of it this power is so broad as to render redundant all the powers to disqualify from driving which have been discussed above, but presumably the courts will understand Parliament to have meant that s. 146 confers additional powers to disqualify where the other powers under the RTOA 1988 and s. 147 are not available. In contrast with the power under s. 147, disqualification under s. 146 is made available to magistrates' courts. In common with s. 147, however, s. 146 extends to persons who have been convicted of an offence but discharged absolutely or conditionally. As with s. 147, there is no power under s. 146 to order the offender to take an extended driving test under the RTOA 1988, s. 36.

By analogy with the power to disqualify under s. 147, it may be desirable for the court before disqualifying under s. 146 to give an opportunity to counsel to address that issue.

It is not clear whether an order under s. 146 affects totality of the sentence (by analogy with an order of deprivation of the offender's property under PCC(S)A 2000, s. 143 (see **6.7**), or whether it should be regarded as an ancillary order like the compensation order, imposition of which should not affect the punishment imposed for the offence. It is suggested that where disqualification is ordered under s. 146 it is imposed as a form of punishment, and so the former view is preferable.

10.2   DISQUALIFICATION OF COMPANY DIRECTORS

10.2.1   Power to make disqualification order

The Company Directors Disqualification Act 1986 specifies certain circumstances in which a court may (or in some cases, must) make an order disqualifying a person from acting as a director of a company. Some, but not all, of these circumstances relate to the commission of criminal offences by the person concerned. Only those provisions of the Act which deal with disqualification after conviction are considered here.

By s. 2(1), the Crown Court or a magistrates' court may make a disqualification order against an offender wherever he is convicted of an indictable offence in connection with the promotion, formation, management or liquidation of a company, or in connection with the receivership or management of a company's property. A disqualification order has the effect that the offender must not, for a specified period beginning with the date of the order, without the leave of the court:

(a) be a director of a company;
(b) be a liquidator or administrator of a company;
(c) be a receiver or manager of a company's property; or
(d) in any way, directly or indirectly, be concerned or take part in the promotion, formation or management of a company (s. 1(1)).

If a magistrates' court makes the order, the maximum period of duration of the order is five years. If the Crown Court makes it, the maximum is 15 years. In neither court is there a minimum period. In *Millard* (1994) 15 Cr App R (S) 445 the Court of Appeal identified an 'upper bracket' of disqualification for more than 10 years, which should be reserved for particularly serious cases (including those where the director has been disqualified before and a 'middle bracket' of six to 10 years.

It has been held that 'management' of a company is a term to be construed widely, and is not limited to the internal affairs of a company. It is sufficient that the offence has some relevant factual connection with the management of a company. In *Goodman* (1993) 14 Cr App R (S) 148 the offender, who was the chairman of a public company, pleaded guilty to insider dealing. Realising that the company was in trouble, and intending to submit his own resignation, he assigned shares which amounted to a very substantial part of the equity to a lady friend, with instructions for her to sell. He concealed the knowledge which he had about the true state of the company. The sentencer imposed a custodial sentence and disqualified Goodman from being a company director for ten years. This was upheld by the Court of Appeal. Disqualification orders have been upheld by the Court of Appeal in cases where offenders have been convicted of obtaining property by deception and similar offences committed in the course of their trading activities. Disqualification for 15 years was held to be appropriate in *Vanderwell* [1998] 2 Cr App R (S) 439 for a 'thoroughly dishonest fraudster' who was now being disqualified for the second time.

It is important to distinguish the criminal courts' powers under s. 2(1) with other powers to disqualify under the 1986 Act, particularly power under s. 6 (where disqualification is mandatory). Disqualification under s. 6 requires a finding that the person concerned has conducted himself in a manner which makes him unfit to be concerned in the management of a company. This limitation does not apply where disqualification is consequent upon conviction, since s. 2 provides the criminal courts with a 'completely general and unfettered power . . . to exercise its powers of disqualification in the very many and varied circumstances in which it may come to exercise those powers' (per Brooke J in *Young* (1990) 12 Cr App R (S) 262).

A disqualification order under the 1986 Act may be imposed in combination with any other sentence or order of the court, including an absolute or conditional discharge. It may well be inappropriate to disqualify an offender at the same time as imposing heavy financial orders upon him, where the disqualification will deprive him of the means to pay. Thus in *Holmes* (1992) 13 Cr App R (S) 29, where the offender pleaded guilty to fraudulent trading and was sentenced to nine months' imprisonment, suspended, together with a disqualification for 12 months, a compensation order for £25,000 and an order for costs of £2,400, the Court of Appeal quashed the compensation order.

10.2.2 Breach of disqualification order

A breach of a disqualification order is itself an offence, punishable with up to two years' imprisonment (1986 Act, s. 13). Where a disqualification order is made against a person who is already subject to such an order, the second period specified runs concurrently with the first (s. 1(3)).

10.3 RECOMMENDATION FOR DEPORTATION

Under the Immigration Act 1971 (IA 1971) the Secretary of State is empowered to order deportation from the UK of persons who are not British citizens. A court, on sentencing an offender aged 17 or over for an offence punishable with imprisonment, may make a recommendation that the offender be deported, by virtue of that Act and the British Nationality Act 1981. The final decision on deportation is taken by the Home Secretary, who is able to take account of a wider range of considerations than the court, such as the political situation in the country to which the offender will go (*Nazari* (1980) 2 Cr App R (S) 84). The fact that the offender has overstayed a limited permission to be in the UK is a matter for the Home Secretary, and is not a ground, in itself, for the court to make a recommendation for deportation (*Miller* v *Lenton* (1981) 3 Cr App R (S) 171). On the other hand, the fact that the offender has refugee status is not a ground, in itself, for not making an order (*Villa* (1992) 14 Cr App R (S) 34).

By IA 1971, s. 6(3), a recommendation may be made in respect of any person who is not a British citizen, who is aged 17 or over and who is convicted of an offence punishable with imprisonment as an adult. A 'British citizen' is, broadly, a person who has a right of abode in the UK. In addition a Commonwealth citizen or a citizen of the Irish Republic must not be recommended for deportation if that person was resident in the UK when the 1971 Act came into force (i.e. 1 January 1973) and has been ordinarily resident in the UK for at least the five years immediately prior to the date of conviction (s. 7(1)). Periods of six months or more spent in prison or detention do not count towards the period of five years mentioned in s. 7(1) (s. 7(3)). Whether continuity of residence has been broken by periods spent abroad is a matter for the sentencer to decide (*Hussain* (1971) 56 Cr App R 165) but temporary absence on holiday is not relevant (*Edgehill* [1963] 1 QB 593).

Whenever an offender's citizenship is questioned for these purposes, IA 1971, s. 3(8) places the onus on the offender to prove citizenship or entitlement to any exemption (see further s. 8 for exemptions in relation to crews of ships and aircraft, military personnel and persons subject to diplomatic immunity).

A recommendation for deportation may be made against a person protected by Article 48 of the Treaty of Rome (EC Treaty), if the conditions specified in Articles 3 and 9 of Directive 64/221 are satisfied. These were considered in *Bouchereau* [1978] QB 732 and the principles which emerged have been followed in subsequent cases, particularly *Escauriaza* (1987) 9 Cr App R (S) 542 and *Spura* (1988) 10 Cr App R (S) 376. The main requirement is that a recommendation should be made only if there exists a genuine and sufficiently serious threat to the requirements of public policy affecting one of the fundamental interests of society. The principles applicable here are the same as those which apply in respect of any other non-British subject who does not come within one of the exceptions in IA 1971. In *Escauriaza* it was accepted by the Court of Appeal that EC law 'simply mirrors the law and practice of this country'.

10.3.1 Procedural matters

The court should first determine the sentence which is appropriate for the offence committed and then consider the ancillary issue of deportation of the offender. If an order for deportation is then made, it is wrong to discount the punishment accordingly. It is also wrong to postpone passing sentence to see whether the Secretary of State will give effect to the court's recommendation (*Edgehill* [1963] 1 QB 593).

Section 6(2) of IA 1971 provides that a court shall not make a recommendation for deportation unless the offender has been given at least seven days' written notice of the court's intention. This may well require adjournment after conviction. If the court is considering making a recommendation for deportation, the defence should be given an opportunity to address the court on that matter (*Antypas* (1973) 57 Cr App R 207). No court should make a recommendation for deportation without a full enquiry into the circumstances. Reasons for its decision should always be given (*Nazari* (1980) 2 Cr App R (S) 84, *Compassi* (1987) 9 Cr App R (S) 270), although the Court of Appeal in *Bozat* [1997] 1 Cr App R (S) 270 said that a failure to give reasons might be remedied on appeal.

The Crown Court's common law power to bind over an offender to come up for judgment has on occasion been used as a means of requiring an offender to leave the country and not return (see **7.3**). This power is not restricted by the IA 1971. Bind over to come up for judgment might still be used in respect of British citizens, who are outside the scope of the IA 1971, but it is submitted that in other cases the statutory route should be used rather than common law powers.

10.3.2 Sentencing principles

In *Nazari* (1980) 2 Cr App R (S) 84 Lawton LJ said:

> The country has no use for criminals of other nationalities, particularly if they have committed serious crimes or have long criminal records. That is self-evident. The more serious the crime and the longer the record the more obvious it is that there should be an order recommending deportation. On the other hand a minor offence would not merit an order . . .

In that case Lawton LJ suggested that normally an offence of shoplifting would not justify a recommendation for deportation, but if the offender had been involved in a series of such offences or if he was a member of an organised shoplifting gang, it might be. A case in which the court found no evidence of community detriment is *Ariquat* (1981) 3 Cr App R (S) 83, a case of indecent assault, where the 19-year-old offender had sexual intercourse with a girl of 15, believing her to be over 16, and so was not guilty of unlawful sexual intercourse. The case of *Serry* (1980) 2 Cr App R (S) 336 decided that the fact that the offender is living on social security is not in itself to the community's detriment and, accordingly, is not a matter to be taken into account when considering whether to make a recommendation for deportation.

A recommendation for deportation should not be made purely on the basis of an offender's criminal record (*Secretary of State, ex parte Santillo* (1980) 2 Cr App R (S) 274), a principle described by Donaldson LJ as 'not only the law in accordance with Article 3 of the Council Directive [but] also only common sense and fairness'. A recommendation may be made, however, if the court considers that the offender's previous record, in the light of the current offence, renders it likely that he will offend again. In *Kraus* (1982) 4 Cr App R (S) 113 the offender, a West German citizen, pleaded guilty to two offences of theft of a total value of £2,000, in breach of trust. It was argued that a recommendation for deportation was inappropriate since the offender did not constitute a threat to the fundamental interests of society. The court heard, however, that the offender had committed the offences to pay off a blackmailer who had discovered the offender's membership of the Nazi party in Germany, an illegal organisation. Given the offender's membership of that group, together with a reasonable apprehension that he might be subject to further blackmail, the recommendation was upheld.

In *Nazari* Lawton LJ said:

The courts are not concerned with the political systems which exist in other countries . . . The court has no knowledge of those matters over and above common knowledge; and that may be wrong . . . It is for the Home Secretary to decide in each case whether an offender's return to his country of origin would have consequences which would make his compulsory return unduly harsh.

This principle had been applied in *Antypas* (1972) 57 Cr App R 207 and appears to represent the general rule. A different line was taken in *Thoseby and Krawczyk* (1979) 1 Cr App R (S) 280. In that case the court took account of information from Amnesty International that if the offenders were deported to Poland they would face severe custodial sentences. In the circumstances the Court of Appeal felt that the Home Secretary would have all the relevant information and the question of deportation should be left to his discretion without any recommendation from the court.

A related though distinct point is evidence of special hardship to the offender, or to the offender's family, if he is deported. In most of the decided cases the Court of Appeal has held that it is proper to weigh in the balance the consequences which the making of a recommendation for deportation would have upon third parties. In *Shittu* (1992) 14 Cr App R (S) 283 it was said that the court when considering whether to make a recommendation for deportation should always consider the effect of the recommendation on the offender's dependants, and balance that against the potential detriment to the country if he were to remain. The offender in that case was convicted of attempting to obtain property by deception (presentation of a stolen credit card) and handling stolen goods, and was sentenced to 12 months' imprisonment, which included the concurrent activation of a suspended sentence of nine months, and recommended for deportation. The offender was of Nigerian origin but had spent several years in the UK. He was married to a woman born in the UK and they had a child. The offender had been studying at university before receiving the custodial sentence. Since there was no evidence that the sentencer had given proper weight to the likely effect of deportation upon the family, the Court of Appeal quashed the recommendation.

10.3.3 Combining a recommendation for deportation with other sentences or orders

There is no statutory restriction upon combining a recommendation for deportation with any other sentence or order. It may be combined with a sentence of life imprisonment (IA 1971, s. 6(4)). A recommendation for deportation is most commonly combined with a fine or a custodial sentence. In *Akan* [1973] 1 QB 491 the Court of Appeal upheld a recommendation for deportation in conjunction with a conditional discharge. Although a conditional discharge is treated as a conviction for limited purposes only (see **7.1.4**), IA 1971, s. 6(3) states that for the purposes of a recommendation for deportation a person who has been found to have committed an offence 'shall be regarded as a person convicted of the offence'.

10.4 EXCLUSION FROM LICENSED PREMISES

10.4.1 Power to make exclusion order

By s. 1 of the Licensed Premises (Exclusion of Certain Persons) Act 1980, where a person is convicted of an offence committed on licensed premises and the court is satisfied that in committing that offence the offender resorted to violence, or offered or threatened to resort to violence, the court may make an exclusion order, which prohibits the offender from entering those premises, or any other specified premises, without the express consent of the licensee of the premises, or his servant or agent. The court should specify the relevant premises by name and address in the order (s. 4(1)), so that an order which purports to ban an offender from all licensed premises in Norfolk is unlawful (*Grady* (1990) 12 Cr App R (S) 152). An exclusion order takes effect for such period, being not less than three months nor more than two years, as is specified in the order. The expression 'licensed premises' means, in relation to England and Wales, premises in respect of which there is in force a justices' on-licence within the meaning of the Licensing Act 1964, s. 1. When the court makes an exclusion order it should ensure that a copy is sent to the licensee(s) of the establishment(s) listed in the order (s. 4(3)).

An exclusion order may be made in addition to any sentence which is imposed in respect of the offence of which the person is convicted. An exclusion order may be combined with an absolute or conditional discharge, notwithstanding the provisions of PCC(S)A 2000, s. 14 (see **7.1.4**). The order can be made either by the court on its own initiative, or prompted by an application made by the victim or an interested third party to the prosecutor (*Penn* [1996] 2 Cr App R (S) 214).

In *Grady* the offender pleaded guilty to assault occasioning actual bodily harm after she had been involved in an altercation in a public house, during which she had pushed or punched the landlady, causing bruising to her back. The exclusion order had been imposed in addition to a suspended prison sentence. The Court of Appeal said that exclusion orders were appropriate where people had been making a nuisance of themselves in public houses to the annoyance of other customers and so as to create a possible danger to the licensee. It was not suitable in this case, where the offender was a mature woman with a clean record.

10.4.2   Breach of exclusion order

Anyone who enters premises in breach of an exclusion order is guilty of an offence punishable on summary conviction with a fine not exceeding £200 or to imprisonment for one month, or to both (s. 2).

At the time of such conviction, the court must consider whether the exclusion order should continue in force, and it may terminate it, or vary it by deleting the name of any specified premises, if it thinks fit. There is, however, no power on breach to extend the period of the order. A copy of the order which terminates or varies the exclusion order must be sent by the court to the licensee(s) of the premises concerned (s. 4(3)).

10.5   FOOTBALL BANNING ORDERS

A series of legislative schemes have been created to try to deal effectively with those who commit offences in and around football matches, whether at domestic or international fixtures. Long-standing provisions in the Public Order Act 1986 have now been (almost entirely) repealed by the Football (Disorder) Act 2000. Other pre-existing powers contained in the Football Spectators Act 1989, designed to exclude offenders who have been convicted of 'a relevant offence' from attendance at football matches, have been substantially amended by the Football (Disorder) Act 2000, which came into effect on 28 August 2000 and applies to relevant offences committed after that date. Very few orders were in fact made by the courts under the earlier legislation, and it remains to be seen whether the new regime will be any more effective.

10.5.1 Power to make football banning order

The Football (Disorder) Act 2000 Act inserted new ss. 14 to 14J in the Football Spectators Act 1989, replacing ss. 14 to 17 (which it repealed). Accordingly there is now no s. 15, 16 or 17 of that Act. The 2000 Act has the effect of removing the distinction, found in earlier versions of these provisions, between 'domestic' and 'international' football banning orders.

By the FSA 1989, s. 14A, where the offender is convicted of a 'relevant offence' (see below) and the court is satisfied that there are reasonable grounds to believe that making a banning order would help to prevent violence or disorder at or in connection with any 'regulated football matches', it is required to make a banning order in respect of the offender (s. 14A(2)). If it is not so satisfied it must state that fact in open court and give its reasons (s. 14A(3)). On making a banning order, the court must explain the effect of that order to the offender in ordinary language (s. 14E(1)). The order requires the person to report initially at a specified police station within five days of the order being made (s. 14E(2)) and, unless there are exceptional circumstances, the order also requires that the offender (in connection with regulated football matches taking place outside the United Kingdom) surrender his passport (s. 14E(3)). If it appears to the court that there are exceptional circumstances, it must state in open court what they are (s. 14E(4)). There is power whereby the court may impose additional requirements on the person subject to the order in relation to any regulated football matches (s. 14G(1)). In particular, the court may make an order under the Public Order Act 1986, s. 35 (the only relevant section of the 1986 Act which remains in force), requiring the offender to attend at a police station within seven days of the making of the order to have his photograph taken (s. 35(1)). This particular requirement, however, can only be made by the court where it has been requested by the prosecutor (s. 35(3)).

A magistrates' court or the Crown Court has power to make a banning order. Such an order can only be made in addition to a sentence imposed in respect of the relevant offence, or in addition to a conditional discharge for that offence (s. 14A(4)). A banning order may be made in combination with a conditional discharge notwithstanding PCC(S)A 2000, s. 14 (see **7.1.4**). A banning order cannot be made where the offender has received an absolute discharge for the offence.

A banning order takes effect on the day when the order is made (FSA 1989, s. 14F(1)). If the order is made in addition to a sentence of immediate imprisonment (that term in this context 'includes any form of detention'), the maximum duration of the order is ten years and the minimum is six years (s. 14F(3)). Where any other sentence has been imposed for the offence, the maximum duration of the order is five years and the minimum is three years (s. 14F(4)).

The 'relevant offences' are listed in sch. 1 to the FSA 1989, as substituted by the 2000 Act. A wide range of offences is included, involving violence, possession of an offensive weapon, drunkenness, public disorder, damage to property and road traffic offences. These are 'relevant offences' if (but only if) they were committed at or in connection with a football match, or when travelling to or from a football match, whether or not that match was actually attended by the offender. Specified offences under the FSA 1989, offences under the Sporting Events (Control of Alcohol etc) Act 1985, any offence under the Football (Offences) Act 1991 and the ticket tout offence under the CJPOA 1994, s. 166 are also included. The offences listed extend to any attempt, conspiracy or incitement to commit such an offence, and to aiding, abetting, counselling or procuring the commission of such an offence. The racially aggravated offences in the CDA 1998, ss. 29 to 32 are not, however, listed.

In respect of a number of the offences listed in FSA 1989, sch. 1, before making a banning order the court is required to make a 'declaration that the offence related to a particular football match or matches' (formerly known as a 'declaration of relevance'), which ordinarily requires that the prosecutor must have given notice to the defendant, at least five days before the first day of the trial, that it was proposed to show that the offence charged did relate to a particular football match or matches. Exceptionally, however, the court may make such a declaration in a case where the required notice has not been given, but only if the defendant consents to waive the giving of full notice or the court is satisfied that the interests of justice do not require further notice to be given (s. 23).

The provisions as amended now relate to any 'regulated football match', which means 'an association football match (whether in England and Wales or elsewhere) which is a prescribed match or a match of a prescribed description' (FSA 1989, s. 14(2)). See also the Football Spectators (Designation of Football Matches in England and Wales) Order 1999 (SI 1999 No. 2461). A 'banning order' means an order made by the court which (in relation to regulated football matches in England and Wales) prohibits the person under the order from entering any premises for the purpose of attending such a match, and (in relation to regulated football matches outside England and Wales) requires that person to report at a police station (s. 14(4)).

If a banning order has been in force for at least two-thirds of the period of the order, the person subject to it may apply to the court by which it was made to terminate it early (s. 14H).

10.5.2   Breach of football banning order

A person subject to a banning order who fails to comply with any requirement imposed by the order is guilty of an offence punishable on summary conviction with imprisonment for a term not exceeding six months, or a fine not exceeding level 5, or both (s. 14J).

10.6   DISQUALIFICATION FROM WORKING WITH CHILDREN

By CJCSA 2000, ss. 26–31, the Crown Court has power to impose a disqualification order on a person who has been convicted of committing an offence against a child (for these purposes 'child' means a person under the aged of 18), and who has received a sentence which is a qualifying sentence'. The effect of the disqualification order will be to disqualify that person from working with children (again, defined as those under the age of 18) in the future.

For the purposes of these provisions, a person commits an offence against a child if he commits any of a very wide range of homicide offences, non-fatal offences against the person, or sexual offences specified in the CJCSA 2000, sch. 4, para. 1, or commits against a child any offence mentioned in sch. 2, para. 2 to that Act, or which falls within sch. 2, para. 3 (s. 26).

Where the person who has committed the qualifying offence is aged 18 or over and the Crown Court imposed a 'qualifying sentence' in respect of that offence, the court must order that the offender is to be disqualified from working with children unless the court is satisfied, having regard to all the circumstances, that it is unlikely that the offender will commit any further offence against a child. If the court so finds then it must state its reasons (s. 28). If the person who has committed the qualifying offence is aged under 18 and a qualifying sentence is imposed in respect of that offence, the Crown Court must order that the offender is to be disqualified from working with children if the court is satisfied, having regard to all the circumstances, that it is likely that the offender will commit a further offence against a child. If the court makes a disqualification order on an offender aged under 18, it must state its reasons for doing so (s. 29).

The qualifying sentences are imprisonment for 12 months or more, detention in a young offender institution for 12 months or more, detention at Her Majesty's pleasure, detention under PCC(S)A 2000, s. 91 for 12 months or more, a detention and training order for 12 months or more, and a hospital order or a guardianship order (s. 30).

Section 35 of the CJCSA 2000 explains the intended effect of the disqualification order. A person subject to such an order is guilty of an offence punishable with up to five years' imprisonment on indictment, or up to six months' imprisonment summarily if he knowingly applies for, offers to do, accepts or does any work in a regulated position. Regulated positions are defined under s. 36, and include positions where the duties include work on day care premises, positions involving caring for, training, supervising, or being in sole charge of children, and work in institutions which are mainly for the education of children, or for their treatment, care or detention.

10.7 OTHER DISQUALIFICATIONS AND EXCLUSIONS

These disqualifications should be distinguished from disqualifications which come into effect automatically upon conviction. See **13.5**. For the 'exclusion order' passed as a community sentence, see **5.8**.

10.7.1 Licensing and gaming

By the Licensing Act 1964, s. 100, where a person is convicted of an offence under ss. 161, 172, 175, 176 or 177 of the Act, or of an offence under s. 1 of the Betting, Gaming and Lotteries Act 1963, s. 1(1), the court may:

(a) disqualify that person for such period specified in the order, but not exceeding five years, from holding or obtaining a licence under Part IV of the Licensing Act 1964 (an on-licence) or under the Late Night Refreshment Houses Act 1969; and/or

(b) prohibit such licences from being held or granted within such a period to any person in respect of the premises at which the offence in question was committed.

Such an order may be exercised on conviction in addition to any other powers which the court is required to or does exercise on conviction.

A disqualification order under the Licensing Act 1964, s. 100 must not be made unless the person concerned has had an opportunity to be heard by the court (s. 101(2)). Such an order may be suspended pending an appeal (s. 101(1)).

By the Gaming Act 1968, s. 24, where a person is convicted of an offence under s. 23(1) or (2) of the Act (whether or not applied by s. 23(5)), the court may make a disqualification order prohibiting a licence under the Act being held in respect of those premises during such period as may be specified in the order but not exceeding five years.

10.7.2 Corruption

A person convicted of an offence under the Public Bodies Corrupt Practices Act 1889, s. 1, may, at the discretion of the court, be disqualified from any election or appointment to any public office for five years from the date of his conviction and to forfeit any such offence held by him at the time of his conviction (s. 2). If the offender was an officer, or was in the employment of, any public body, he shall be liable to forfeit his claim to any compensation or pension to which he would otherwise have been entitled. In the event of a second conviction for a like offence he shall be liable to be adjudged for ever incapable of holding any public office, and to be disqualified for five years as being registered as an elector and from voting at an election.

10.7.3   Animals

Owners can be disqualified from keeping an animal if they are convicted of cruelty to an animal (Protection of Animals Act 1911, s. 3; Protection of Animals (Amendment) Act 1954, s. 1). Disqualification can be for a specified period in the discretion of the court, or for life, and the disqualification may extend to animals of the species which were involved in the cruelty, or more generally.

11 Mentally Disordered Offenders

In the course of gathering material to inform the sentencing decision, if not before, it may have become apparent that the convicted offender is suffering from a degree of mental disorder. Suspicions may be raised by the nature and circumstances of the offence (such as certain forms of sexual offending, or the commission of arson), or information from the antecedents, the plea in mitigation, or the pre-sentence report. These documents may show that the offender has been suffering from severe depression when the offence was committed. It may become appropriate for the sentencer to adjourn to obtain a psychiatric report, if one has not already been prepared. Section 82 of the PCC(S)A 2000 states that in any case where the offender 'is or appears to be mentally disordered', a medical report should be obtained and considered. Where there is clear evidence of mental disorder, the sentence may well be selected with a view to addressing that problem in the offender, rather than simply punishing him for the offence. This preference will, however, always have to be balanced against the seriousness of the offence. Where the offender represents a risk to the public, the sentencer will have to choose between a hospital order (with or without additional restrictions) and a custodial sentence. Where the offence carries life as its maximum, and where the relevant criteria for the passing of a discretionary life sentence are made out, an indeterminate sentence can sometimes be preferable to a determinate sentence. Where, however, treatment can appropriately be provided in a non-secure setting, a community rehabilitation order or a supervision order which contains a requirement of treatment for the offender's condition may be the best option.

11.1 COMMUNITY REHABILITATION ORDERS WITH REQUIREMENT OF TREATMENT

Community rehabilitation orders (CROs) containing a treatment requirement are the most frequent form of psychiatric disposal in criminal cases, whether in the magistrates' court or the Crown Court. The relevant provision is sch. 2 to the PCC(S)A 2000. Paragraph 5 relates to the insertion by the court into a CRO of a condition of treatment for the offender's mental condition.

11.1.1 Power to make CRO with requirement of treatment

This power is available only in circumstances where the court would otherwise have power to make a CRO without such a requirement. It is therefore limited to cases where the offender is aged 16 or over and is convicted of an offence by or before a magistrates' court or the Crown Court. The duration of a CRO may not be for less than six months or more than three years. A CRO is a community order, and no community order can be imposed unless the court is satisfied that the offence (or offences) committed is (or are) serious enough to justify such an order. The court must then be satisfied that a CRO (with the relevant requirement) either standing alone or in combination with other sentences or orders of the court is the most suitable disposal for the offender and that the restrictions on the offender's liberty occasioned by the sentence are not disproportionate to the gravity of the offending behaviour (see **5.2.2**). A pre-sentence report is normally required before a CRO which contains a requirement of this kind can be made (PCC(S)A 2000, s. 36(4)).

Paragraph 5(1) provides that where the court is satisfied, on the evidence of a medical practitioner approved for the purposes of MHA 1983, s. 12 as being a person having special experience in the diagnosis and treatment of mental disorder, that the mental condition of an offender is such as requires and may be susceptible to treatment, but is not such as to warrant the making of a hospital order or a guardianship order under the MHA 1983, it may, if it makes a CRO, include in it a requirement that the offender shall submit, during the whole of the period of that order or during such part of that period as may be specified in the order, to treatment by or under the direction of a duly qualified medical practitioner or a chartered psychologist, with a view to the improvement of the offender's mental condition. For hospital orders see **11.3**, for guardianship orders see **11.3.4**, and for CROs generally see **5.2**. A CRO with a condition of psychiatric treatment may be made in a case where the offender is not suffering from one or other of the four forms of mental disorder which justify the making of a hospital order; for these see **11.3.1**. Before the condition of psychiatric treatment can be inserted into the order, the offender must express his willingness to comply with it (para. 5(4)).

11.1.2   Forms of treatment

The treatment required by a CRO must be specified in the order and must take one of the following forms (para. 5(3)):

(a)   treatment as a resident patient, which may be carried out in a mental hospital (within the meaning of the MHA 1983) or a mental nursing home, but not a high security special hospital;

(b)   treatment as a non-resident patient at such institution or place as may be specified; or

(c)   treatment by or under the direction of such duly qualified medical practitioner or chartered psychologist as may be specified.

No other forms of treatment may be specified.

As a precondition of the inclusion of a treatment requirement in a CRO, the court must be satisfied that the necessary arrangements have been made relating to the treatment intended to be specified in the order (including arrangements necessary for the reception of the offender) (para. 5(4)). While the offender is under treatment as a resident patient, the supervising officer must carry out his supervision of the offender 'only as may be necessary for the purpose of discharge or amendment of the order' (para. 5(5)).

Where a CRO with a condition of psychiatric treatment has been made, and the relevant medical practitioner or chartered psychologist takes the view that part of the treatment may more conveniently be given in or at an institution not specified in the original order (even where the institution is not one which could have been specified in that order: para. 5(7)), arrangements may be made, with the consent of the patient, for this to be done (para. 5(6)). Where such a change is made, the supervising officer must be notified in writing (para. 5(8)).

11.1.3 Breach etc. of CRO with requirement of mental treatment

If the offender fails to comply with any of the conditions specified in the order, including the requirement as to mental treatment and any breach of a condition inserted under para. 5(6) (provided para. 5(8) was complied with), he may be dealt with for breach of the CRO. A CRO is a community order within the meaning of the PCC(S)A 2000. For provisions relating to breach of community orders, see **5.6.1**.

If the offender commits a further offence within the currency of the CRO, he may be dealt with in respect of the original offence in the usual manner. For revocation of community orders, see **5.6.2**.

A CRO with a requirement of treatment for a mental condition may be amended on application to the court under the PCC(S)A 2000, sch. 3, para. 20. This paragraph permits the supervising officer, in response to a report in writing from the relevant medical practitioner, to apply to the court for a variation, or cancellation, of the mental treatment requirement.

11.1.4 Sentencing principle

In most cases the courts insert a requirement of treatment into a CRO where, without evidence of the offender's need for treatment, a CRO would have been an appropriate disposal in any event, being commensurate with the seriousness of the offence. An example might be the compulsive shoplifter whose underlying mental problems need attention. Here the court is simply tailoring the CRO to suit the particular needs of the offender. In the past, however, the Court of Appeal has indicated that a CRO with a requirement of treatment will sometimes be appropriate for an offender who has committed a serious offence, and represents some risk to the public. If there seems to the court to be a reasonable chance that such an order will have a beneficial effect upon the offender, the court may take the view that the risk to the public is thereby outweighed. An example is *Hoof* (1980) 2 Cr App R (S) 299, where the offender was convicted of arson with intent to endanger life, having set fire to two maisonettes (in one of which a woman was asleep at the time) and a motor car. The Court of Appeal varied a prison sentence of three years to a CRO with a treatment requirement. A requirement of residence at a hostel was also inserted into the order (see **5.2.4**). In *McDonald* (1983) 5 Cr App R (S) 419 the Court of Appeal, without any criticism of the trial judge, varied a sentence of two years' imprisonment on an offender who pleaded guilty to an indecent assault on a girl aged 11 to a CRO with a requirement of treatment, on hearing evidence that 'as much has been done as can practically be done to ensure that he will be properly supervised in the community, that he will have a proper place of residence, that the residence will be conveniently sited so that he may attend for treatment and, finally, that treatment will be available over an extended period of time'. A third example is *Jones* (1992) 13 Cr App R (S) 275, where the female offender pleaded guilty to seven counts of robbery, committed at building society branches, when she had pretended to have a gun and obtained £7,000. Sentence was varied from four years' imprisonment to a three-year CRO with a requirement of out-patient mental treatment by the Court of Appeal, which heard that Jones had been severely depressed as a result of family crises and financial problems. She was in need of long-term psychological help and her problems had been made worse by her experience of custody. The Court of Appeal said that the case was 'wholly exceptional'.

11.2 SUPERVISION ORDERS WITH REQUIREMENT OF TREATMENT

Power to insert a requirement of treatment for a mental condition into a supervision order may be found in PCC(S)A 2000, sch. 6, para. 6. The provisions are very similar to those relating to the insertion of a requirement of mental treatment into a CRO order (see **11.1**). For supervision orders generally see **5.11**.

This power is available only in circumstances where the court would otherwise have power to make a supervision order without such a requirement. It is therefore limited to cases where the offender is aged 10 to 17 inclusive and is convicted of an offence by or before a youth court or the Crown Court. The maximum duration of a supervision order is three years. A supervision order is a community order, and no community order can be imposed unless the court is satisfied that the offence (or the offence and one or more offences associated with it) is serious enough to justify such an order. The court must then be satisfied that a supervision order (with the relevant requirement), either standing alone or in combination with other sentences or orders of the court, is the most suitable disposal for the offender and that the restrictions on the offender's liberty occasioned by the sentence are not disproportionate to the gravity of the offending behaviour (see **5.2.2**).

By sch. 6, para. 6(1), where a court which proposes to make a supervision order is satisfied, on the evidence of a medical practitioner approved for the purposes of MHA 1983, s. 12, that the mental condition of a supervised person is such as requires and may be susceptible to treatment, but is not such as to warrant his detention under a hospital order, it may include in the supervision order a requirement that the supervised person shall, for a period specified in the order, submit to treatment of one of the following forms:

(a)   treatment as a resident patient in a hospital or mental nursing home, but not a high security hospital; or
(b)   treatment as a non-resident patient at a place specified in the order; or
(c)   treatment by or under the direction of a medical practitioner or chartered psychologist.

Such a requirement cannot be inserted into a supervision order unless the court is satisfied that arrangements have been made or can be made for the treatment to be carried out and, in the case of treatment as a resident patient, for the reception of the patient (para. 6(3)). A pre-sentence report is normally required before a supervision order which contains a requirement under para. 6 may be ordered (s. 36). Since a medical report will generally be required, in most cases the ordering of both reports would constitute good sentencing practice. The supervised person must express a willingness to comply with a requirement under para. 6(3), but if the supervised person is under the age of 14 there is an exception and no such expression of a willingness to comply is required. No such requirement shall continue in force after the supervised person has attained the age of 18.

11.3 HOSPITAL ORDERS

Criminal courts are given powers under MHA 1983 to make a hospital order on a person of any age convicted of an offence which is punishable with imprisonment in the case of an adult. The effect of a hospital order is that a social worker or other suitable person is authorised to take the offender to the mental hospital which is specified in the order. The hospital named in the order may be an ordinary NHS trust hospital, or the psychiatric ward of such a hospital, or it may be one of the secure special hospitals (Broadmoor, Rampton and Ashworth). The latter hospitals are high security institutions and are appropriate only where the patient is thought to represent a serious risk to the safety of the public, including other patients and hospital staff.

An admission to hospital by means of a hospital order has the same effect for most purposes as a compulsory civil commitment under MHA 1983, Part II, with the important exception that the patient's 'nearest relative' does not have the right to order the patient's discharge. The order in principle lapses after six months, but may be (and often is) renewed for a further six months and at yearly intervals thereafter, provided the responsible medical officer (RMO) considers further detention to be 'necessary for the protection of the public or in the interests of the patient's health or safety' (s. 20 and sch. 1). There is no limit to the number of renewals which might subsequently be made, so that a hospital order is in principle an indeterminate sentence, but the patient may be discharged from hospital by way of various powers exercised by the RMO, the hospital managers or a mental health review tribunal (MHRT). Clearly this sentence, while therapeutic in objective, involves a substantial restriction upon the liberty of the offender, or 'patient' as he should after disposal be called. Accordingly, in the case of an offender who is suffering from a degree of mental disorder, the sentencer must always consider whether compulsory hospital detention is appropriate. If not, a CRO with a condition of treatment for the mental condition may be a better alternative (*Birch* (1989) 11 Cr App R (S) 202 and see **11.1**).

Hospital orders are a relatively little-used form of sentence. In 1998 a grand total of 749 orders were made, 499 by the Crown Court (of which 55 also had a restriction order: see **11.5**) and 250 by magistrates' courts. These figures also include guardianship orders (as to which see **11.4**). In the Crown Court, the cases most likely to attract a hospital order on sentence were offences involving violence, followed by offences of criminal damage (including arson), robbery, burglary and sexual offences. It is well known that in a significant number of cases the offender's criminal conduct is clearly associated with his mental problems, but no hospital order is made by the court. Sometimes this is because the degree of restriction of liberty involved in a hospital order cannot be justified by the relative triviality of the offence, in which case a CRO with a requirement of treatment, or simply a lenient disposal, such as a conditional discharge or a bind over, will be used. Sometimes a hospital order is not made because the sentencer thinks that the offender was sufficiently responsible for his conduct to deserve to be punished for it by the passing of a custodial or community sentence in the ordinary way. Whenever the court is considering passing a custodial sentence on a person who is, or who appears to the court to be, mentally disordered, the court must first obtain a medical report (PCC(S)A 2000, s. 82(1)). Sometimes a different situation arises, where the court would like to make a hospital order, but the medical reports preclude it. Either the mental problem from which the offender suffers does not come within the categories mentioned in the MHA 1983 (see **11.3.1**) or, if he is suffering from psychopathic disorder or mental impairment, the further requirement of that Act, that the condition must be treatable, may not be satisfied in the offender's case. Sometimes no mental hospital has space to admit the offender, or the only hospital available is not a secure one and the judge is of the view that the offender represents a danger to the public and must be held in the secure environment of a special hospital. Should the secure mental hospitals be unable to admit the patient, the judge would be entitled to pass a determinate custodial sentence or, perhaps, a discretionary life sentence if the legal requirements for the passing of that sentence were made out (see **4.3.7**). It should be noted that, according to the Court of Appeal in *Newman* [2000] 2 Cr App R (S) 227, where the criteria for an automatic life sentence under PCC(S)A 2000, s. 109 are made out, the offender's acute mental illness does not constitute an 'exceptional circumstance' justifying the making of a hospital order instead of the life sentence. The undoubted effect of all this is that many offenders who are suffering from various degrees of mental disorder end up serving custodial sentences (where the availability of suitable psychiatric treatment is very limited), rather than receiving proper treatment for their condition in hospital.

It should be noted that the Home Secretary has power, upon receipt of appropriate medical advice, to direct the transfer of an offender who is serving a prison sentence, or a sentence of detention in a young offender institution, from that institution to a mental hospital (MHA 1983, s. 47). This 'transfer direction', as it is called, has the same effect upon the offender as the making of a hospital order in his case (s. 47(3)). A transfer direction lapses after 14 days unless it has been carried out within that time (s. 47(2)).

11.3.1 Power to make hospital order

If a person is convicted before the Crown Court or a magistrates' court of an offence punishable with imprisonment (other than murder or a case which falls to be sentenced under the PCC(S)A 2000, s. 109) and certain specified conditions are met, the court may make a hospital order under MHA 1983, s. 37. Only a youth court may make a hospital order or guardianship order on a juvenile (s. 8 of the 2000 Act). The specified conditions are as follows:

(a)   The court must be satisfied, on the written or oral evidence of two registered medical practitioners, that the offender is suffering from mental illness, psychopathic disorder, severe mental impairment or mental impairment. 'Mental illness' is not defined in the MHA 1983, but see *W v L* [1974] QB 711. 'Psychopathic disorder' means a persistent disorder or disability of the mind which results in abnormally aggressive or seriously irresponsible conduct by the person concerned. 'Severe mental impairment' means a state of arrested or incomplete development of the mind, including severe impairment of intelligence and social functioning, which is associated with the kind of conduct mentioned in the definition of psychopathic disorder. 'Mental impairment' is defined in almost the same way as severe mental impairment, save that in the phrase 'severe mental impairment', the word 'significant' is substituted for 'severe'. Thus, both mental impairment and severe mental impairment involve low intelligence, whereas a person suffering from a psychopathic disorder may be of normal, or high, intelligence. These definitions may be found in MHA 1983, s. 1(2).

(b)   In addition, the mental disorder from which the offender is suffering must be of a nature or degree which makes it appropriate for him to be detained in a hospital for medical treatment and, in the case of psychopathic disorder or mental impairment, such treatment must be likely to alleviate or prevent a deterioration of his condition (s. 37(2)(i)). There is no need to establish a causal link between the offender's mental disorder and the offence in respect of which the order is made (*McBride* (1972) CSP F2-2A01). In most cases this can safely be assumed.

(c)   One of the two medical practitioners must be approved for the purposes of MHA 1983, s. 12 as having special experience in the diagnosis or treatment of mental disorder (s. 54(1)). It may seem odd that only one of the doctors needs to be so qualified; this is explained by the fact that while one of the doctors needs to be a specialist the other will generally be the offender's own general practitioner. It is desirable in every case that oral evidence should be given by the doctor who will be in charge of the case if the order is made, or by a doctor who is fully informed of his views (*Blackwood* (1974) 59 Cr App R 170). Where the medical evidence is in written form, a copy of the medical report must be given to counsel or solicitor for the defence. If the offender is unrepresented, the gist of the report should be disclosed to him. In *Blackwood* the Court of Appeal said that a court should not normally make a hospital order if the offender was not legally represented. The defence may require the doctors to attend to give oral evidence, and other doctors may be called to give evidence in rebuttal (s. 54(3)). Whenever a hospital order is made the court must specify from which of the forms of mental disorder specified in s. 1(2) the offender is found by the court to be suffering (s. 37(7)). An order cannot be made unless the offender is described by each of the medical practitioners as suffering from the same form of mental disorder, whether or not the offender is also described by either of them as suffering from another of those forms (s. 37(7)).

(d)   A hospital order cannot be made unless the court is satisfied, on the written or oral evidence of the responsible medical officer (RMO), or of some other person representing the managers of the hospital, that arrangements have been made for the offender's admission to that hospital within 28 days of the date of the order (s. 37(4)). The health authorities are under no legal obligation to accept offenders from the courts, and the court is not empowered to order a hospital to accept an offender (*Parker*, 21 March 1975 (unreported)). Sometimes they are unable to do so, either because no bed is available, or through concern for the safety of staff in the case of a potentially violent or disruptive offender being received from the court. In *Harding* (1983) 5 Cr App R (S) 197, Lawton LJ commented that those who obstruct the court's wish to make such an order might be guilty of contempt of court, but this threat does not appear ever to have been carried out. Hospitals are, however, under a legal obligation to supply information to the court about the availability of beds in their region for the admission of a person under a hospital order (s. 39(1)). In an emergency or other special situation arising within the 28 days following the order, the Secretary of State may give directions for admission of the offender to a different hospital from that specified in the order (s. 37(5)). The court may, pending admission within the 28 days, order the offender's detention in some other 'place of safety' (s. 37(4)). Occasionally it may be appropriate to admit an offender to a hospital not situated locally, with a view to subsequent transfer (*Marsden* (1968) 52 Cr App R 301).

(e)   The court must be of the opinion, having regard to all the circumstances, including the nature of the offence and the character and antecedents of the offender, and to the other available methods of dealing with him, that a hospital order is the most suitable method of disposing of the case (s. 37(2)(b)). The matter is one for the sentencer, who may decide that, notwithstanding the offender's mental disorder, it is proper to pass a custodial sentence on the offender even though a place is available for him at a suitable mental hospital (*Gunnell* (1966) 50 Cr App R 242). Of course such a decision can only be taken after consideration of a medical report (CJA 1991, s. 4(1)).

11.3.2   Consequences of a hospital order

The making of a hospital order authorises the taking of the offender to the specified hospital and his detention there for an initial period of six months. He may be discharged even during that period, by either the RMO or the hospital managers, on the basis of an assessment of whether his continuing detention is 'necessary for the protection of the public or in the interests of the patient's health or safety' (MHA 1983, s. 20 and sch. 1). If he is not, the doctor examines him during the fifth or sixth month of his detention and prepares a report on him. If the report recommends that he should be further detained, that is sufficient authority for the hospital managers to hold him for a further six months. After that the same process may be repeated at yearly intervals (i.e. in the eleventh or twelfth month the doctor examines him and, if the resulting report so recommends, the hospital managers authorise detention for a further year). After the first six months the patient has a right to apply to the Mental Health Review Tribunal, once during each subsequent period of renewal of the order, for his case to be considered, and his nearest relative has a similar right. A MHRT consists of a legally qualified chairman, a psychiatrist and a lay person. In deciding whether to direct the patient's discharge they have regard to approximately the same considerations as did the RMO, although there are slight differences in the wording of the relevant sections of the MHA 1983.

Where these elaborate procedures fail to result in discharge, there is one very simple remedy which is open to the patient. He may simply abscond, and if he stays at liberty without coming to notice for more than 28 days he may not be taken into custody or returned to the hospital. There is no longer authority to detain him. This 'discharge by operation of law' as it is known is, on the face of it, rather surprising. It applies to patients who are in hospital as a result of a hospital order, unless a restriction order was added to the hospital order and is still in force (see **11.5**). The reason for a patient who avoids 'recapture' by a police officer or local authority social worker for 28 days no longer being liable to detention is that, by coming to no harm during that period, he has shown that he no longer needs to be in hospital.

11.3.3   Interim hospital order

Section 38 of MHA 1983, provides for the making an an 'interim hospital order'. The qualifying conditions are virtually the same as for the making of a hospital order under s. 37, but the interim order is available to the court 'before making a hospital order or dealing with him in some other way' and its purpose is to establish whether the offender is suitable to be the subject of a hospital order. One difference in the powers is that an interim order can be made only where one of the registered medical practitioners who gives evidence is employed at the hospital where the person is to be detained. An interim hospital order is thus not a final disposal of the case but, in a case where there is some doubt, it is an experiment to see if the case can be properly disposed of by way of a full order (*Birch* (1989) 11 Cr App R (S) 202). An interim hospital order can also be used to discover whether a person should be made subject to a hospital direction or a limitation direction under s. 45A of the MHA 1983 (see **11.6**).

An interim hospital order may last for up to 12 weeks, renewable for further periods of not more than 28 days at a time, but in no case to last for more than a total of 12 months (s. 38(5)). No minimum period is specified. At the end of the interim period the court must make a final disposal of the case, and the interim order comes to an end. In a case where a court renews an interim hospital order, or where it finally disposes of the case by making a hospital order under s. 37, the offender need not appear before the court, provided that he is legally represented and his representative has an opportunity of being heard (s. 38(2) and (6)).

The decision to make an interim hospital order does not commit the court to ultimately disposing of the case by means of a full hospital order. At the end of the interim order the court still has the full range of sentencing options at its disposal, although if it chooses to pass a sentence other than a hospital order the offender must, of course, be present for the hearing.

11.3.4 Combining a hospital order with other sentences or orders

By MHA 1983, s. 37(8), when a hospital order or a guardianship order (see **11.4**) is made the court must not pass a custodial sentence, impose a fine, make a CRO or supervision order in respect of the offence, make a referral order, or require a parent of a juvenile so dealt with to enter into a recognisance. The court may, however, 'make any other order which the court has power to make apart from this section'. This would permit the making of various ancillary orders, such as a compensation order, though this would always be subject to the offender's means.

11.4 GUARDIANSHIP ORDERS

Where the conditions for making a hospital order are satisfied, the court may, as an alternative, make a guardianship order (MHA 1983, s. 37(1)). The legal conditions for hospital orders and guardianship orders are identical, except that for a guardianship order:

(a) there is no requirement that the mental disorder from which the offender is suffering is of a nature or degree which requires detention in a hospital; and

(b) there is no requirement that the mental disorder must be treatable.

It must instead be shown that the mental disorder is of a nature or degree which warrants the offender's reception into guardianship.

The guardian, for the purposes of the order, will be the local authority social services department, or a particular person approved by that department. The order confers on the local authority, or the person who is named as guardian in the order, the same powers as a guardianship application made under MHA 1983, Part II (s. 40(2)). These powers, in outline, are to determine the patient's place of residence, to require the patient's attendance for treatment, occupation, education or training, and to require access to the patient in any place of residence for a doctor, social worker or other specified person (s. 8). A guardianship order cannot be made unless the relevant authority or person is willing to receive the offender into guardianship (s. 37(6)) and s. 39A empowers a court which is minded to make such an order to request the local social services authority to provide the court with information on how it would exercise its powers.

A guardianship order lasts for 12 months, but may be renewed.

11.5 RESTRICTION ORDERS

The Crown Court is given power by MHA 1983, s. 41, when it makes a hospital order under s. 37, to add to it a restriction order. A restriction order has no existence independent of the hospital order to which it relates, but it fundamentally affects the circumstances in which the patient is detained. In 1998 restriction orders were imposed on sentence in 55 cases. The Crown Court should make such an order only where it appears to the court that, given the nature of the offence, the antecedents of the offender and the risk of the offender's committing further offences if set at large, the making of a restriction order is necessary to protect the public from serious harm (s. 41(1) and *Courtney* (1987) 9 Cr App R (S) 404). This entails that the offender will probably require detention and treatment in one of the secure special hospitals rather than in a NHS hospital, and an order under s. 41 affects the arrangements for discharge (see below).

In this context, the protection of the public from 'serious harm' has been held not to be limited to personal injury, nor need it relate to the public in general. It is enough if a specific category of persons, or even one person, is adjudged to be at risk, although the category of persons at risk is taken to exclude the offender himself. The potential harm must be 'serious'. A high possibility of a recurrence of minor offences will not suffice (*Birch* (1989) 11 Cr App R (S) 202). Clearly medical evidence will be of great importance in making this assessment, but it is the court's decision and the court is not bound to accept the medical opinion it receives (*Birch*). In theory the court could reject unanimous medical advice but in practice is unlikely to do so. A sentencer should not add a restriction order to a hospital order simply to mark the gravity of the offence, nor as a means of punishment. It would be a mistake simply to equate the seriousness of the offence with the likelihood of a restriction order being made. It is only one factor, and the court would have to be very sure of its ground to pass a restriction order where the commission of a serious offence was coupled with a very low risk of reoffending. There is no requirement that a causal connection be established between the disorder and the offence (*Hatt* [1962] Crim LR 647, approved in *Birch*), although in most cases this can safely be assumed.

The main difference between an order under s. 37 and an order under s. 41 is that neither the RMO nor the hospital managers may discharge a restricted patient without the consent of the Secretary of State or a MHRT. Thus, in effect, the restriction order means that the criminal justice system retains a degree of control over the offender once he becomes a 'patient'. The Secretary of State or a MHRT may release a patient who is subject to a restriction order, either with or without the attachment of conditions to the release (s. 42(1) and (2)). If the patient is discharged from hospital conditionally, the restriction order remains in force and the patient may subsequently be recalled to hospital if he comes to notice. Unlike a hospital order under s. 37, a restriction order does not lapse in the ordinary way unless renewed, but continues for as long as the restriction order is in place. If the restriction order is for a fixed period, at the end of that period the restrictions no longer apply but the hospital order continues in effect (s. 41(5)). The restrictions which may thus be added to a hospital order may be declared by the court to be for a period of time which is specified in the order, or without limit of time. Virtually all restriction orders are, in fact, made without limit of time. The Court of Appeal has said that it would be 'imprudent' in any but the most exceptional circumstances to impose a restriction for a fixed rather than an unlimited period (*Haynes* (1981) 3 Cr App R (S) 330). A restriction order cannot be made unless at least one of the two doctors whose evidence is being taken into account by the court has given oral evidence in court (s. 41(2)).

The effect of a restriction order is that for its duration the offender can be discharged from hospital only on the direction of the Secretary of State or a MHRT. The offender may make an application every year to the MHRT for discharge and, if no application is made for three years, the Secretary of State is under a duty to refer the case to the MHRT for their consideration. The MHRT has power to order discharge against the wishes of the Home Secretary. As an alternative to unconditional discharge, the MHRT may direct that the offender shall be released subject to recall for treatment at the discretion of the Home Secretary. It has been held to be a breach of the ECHR, Article 5 to continue a restriction order if the patient's mental condition does not warrant it (*X* v *United Kingdom* (1981) 4 ECHR 181 and *Kynaston* v *Secretary of State* (1981) 73 Cr App R 281). Thus danger to the public alone cannot be sufficient grounds for the continued detention under a restriction order.

Only the Crown Court may make a restriction order, though magistrates may commit the offender to Crown Court, provided the offender is aged 14 or over, with a view to such a disposal being made (s. 43). The magistrates must commit the offender to Crown Court in custody unless there is a place available for him in a hospital, in which case they can direct that he be detained in the hospital.

If the criteria within s. 41 are established, the sentencer may, but is not obliged to, pass a restriction order. The likely alternative sentences are discretionary life imprisonment (see **4.3.7**) and custody for a fixed term. If an offender qualifies for a hospital order with restrictions, and a place is available in a suitable hospital, then the general rule is that a hospital order with restrictions should be made, and it is certainly wrong in principle for the sentencer to impose a life sentence in an attempt to prevent the patient's possible premature release by order of the MHRT (*Mitchell* [1997] 1 Cr App R (S) 90; *Hutchinson* [1997] 2 Cr App R (S) 60). If a sentencer considers that, notwithstanding the offender's mental disorder, there was an element of culpability in the offence which merited punishment, as where there was no connection between the disorder and the offence or where the offender's responsibility was diminished but not extinguished, the imposition of a prison sentence might be correct (*Birch* (1989) 11 Cr App R (S) 202). The cases make it clear that a discretionary life sentence is to be preferred to a fixed-term sentence where the offender is subject to a degree of mental instability which makes it probable that he will commit serious offences if not subject to indefinite detention (*Pither* (1979) 1 Cr App R (S) 209).

11.6 HOSPITAL AND LIMITATION DIRECTIONS

Sections 45A and 45B of the MHA 1983 are designed to apply in a case where the Crown Court has heard evidence from two registered medical practitioners, at least one of whom must have given oral evidence, that the offender is suffering from psychopathic disorder (for the definition of this condition see **11.3.1**), that his condition is of a nature and degree which makes it appropriate for him to be detained in hospital for treatment, and that such treatment is likely to alleviate his condition. The Crown Court may intend to pass a hospital order in that case rather than to impose a sentence of imprisonment, but may be anxious to ensure that when the offender's treatment is completed (or if it turns out that the offender is not, after all, capable of responding to treatment) he will be transferred to prison, rather than being released from hospital into the community. The court may make a 'hospital direction' under s. 45A to ensure that this will happen. Before making a hospital direction the court must be satisfied on the written or oral evidence of the RMO who would be in charge of the offender's treatment, or of some other person representing the managers of the relevant hospital, that arrangements have been made for the offender's admission to that hospital, and for his admission within 28 days of making the order. The court may also make a 'limitation direction', which ensures that the offender is made subject to the restrictions set out in MHA 1983, s. 41.

There is power in s. 45A(10) for the Secretary of State by order to provide that offenders suffering from other forms of mental disorder than psychopathic disorder may be made subject to hospital and limitation directions, but no such order has been made.

11.7 ORDERS CONSEQUENT UPON A FINDING OF INSANITY, UNFITNESS TO PLEAD, ETC.

The Criminal Procedure (Insanity) Act 1964, s. 5 (as substituted by the Criminal Procedure (Insanity and Unfitness to Plead) Act 1991) provides various powers of disposal after the Crown Court has either (a) returned a special verdict that the accused is not guilty by reason of insanity, or (b) recorded a finding that the defendant is under a disability (he is 'unfit to plead') and that he did the act or made the omission charged against him. In neither of these situations, of course, has the defendant been convicted of the offence charged, but provision is made for a range of disposals in such cases which are so closely similar to the sentencing options discussed elsewhere in this book that it is appropriate to consider them here.

The 1964 Act, by s. 5 and sch. 1, formerly stated that, on a finding that the defendant was not guilty by reason of insanity or was unfit to plead, the Crown Court judge was required to impose an order upon the defendant equivalent to an order under MHA 1983, s. 37 imposed upon a person convicted, together with a restriction order under MHA 1983, s. 41. Thus a person who was found not guilty by reason of insanity faced mandatory commitment to a mental hospital, with restrictions upon release. The 1991 Act broadened the options available to the Crown Court judge dealing with such cases so that the following options are available:

(a) To make an order for admission to hospital. By sch. 1 to the 1991 Act, such order shall be equivalent to a hospital order made under MHA 1983, s. 37, to which there *may* be added a restriction under MHA 1983, s. 41, with or without limit of time. A restriction order without limit of time is, however, mandatory in cases where the charge brought against the offender was murder.

(b) To make a guardianship order (see **11.4**).

(c) To make a supervision and treatment order. This order is very similar to a CRO with a requirement of treatment for a mental condition (see **11.1**) though there are minor differences. A supervision and treatment order may be made only on the evidence of two doctors (rather than one, in the case of a CRO) that the defendant's mental condition is such that it requires and may be susceptible to treatment but does not warrant the making of a hospital or guardianship order. The order requires the defendant to be under supervision for a period specified in the order of not more than two years (the maximum duration of a CRO is three years) and, during that period or a specific part of it, to submit to medical treatment. whether as a resident patient, a non-resident patient, or otherwise, with a view to the improvement of his mental condition. Such an order may also include residence requirements.

(d) To make an order for the defendant's absolute discharge (see **7.1.1**).

Section 37(3) of MHA 1983 gives power to magistrates' courts to make a hospital order (or guardianship order) in a case where such a court is satisfied that a person charged before it with an offence is suffering from mental illness or severe mental impairment and the court is satisfied that the person did the act or made the omission charged, without proceeding to conviction. This provision gives magistrates' courts a power which is rather similar to the Crown Court's powers to return a special verdict of not guilty by reason of insanity, or to make a finding that the accused is unfit to plead. Neither of these powers is available in the magistrates' courts, although it was confirmed in *Horseferry Road Magistrates' Court, ex parte K* [1997] QB 23 that a defence of insanity, leading to a clear acquittal rather than a special verdict, is available in the summary courts. The power in s. 37(3) should be very sparingly used (see *Lincoln (Kesteven) Justices, ex parte O'Connor* [1983] 1 WLR 335 and *Ramsgate Justices, ex parte Kazmarek* (1984) 80 Cr App R 366). If a magistrates' court makes such an order, the person so dealt with has the same right of appeal to the Crown Court as if he was appealing against conviction and sentence (MHA 1983, s. 45(1)).

12 Sentencing for a Range of Offences

'What sentence will I get if I am convicted of this offence?' asks the defendant before the trial. 'Is it worth appealing against this?' asks the offender after he has been sentenced. These commonly asked and very natural questions prompt a third: to what extent can the general principles of sentencing (discussed in Chapter 2 of this book) and Court of Appeal decisions be used to predict either the sentence which will be imposed on an offender or his chances of appealing successfully against whatever sentence has been imposed upon him?

The purpose of this chapter is to indicate the approach which has been approved by the Court of Appeal to sentencing in a wide variety of commonly encountered criminal offences. Where a guideline judgement has been issued in respect of a particular offence, prominence is given to that judgment. Whether or not there has been a guideline judgment, reference is then made to a sample of Court of Appeal decisions in relation to the particular offence. These decisions, taken together, often suggest a 'sentencing bracket', within which most examples of sentencing for a particular offence should fall, or suggest different brackets for different forms of that offence. The range within these sentencing brackets is not, and cannot be, a matter of precise formulation. Indeed the Court of Appeal will usually intervene and change a sentence on appeal only if it regards it as being wrong in principle, manifestly excessive or manifestly lenient. The normal upper and lower limits to the sentencing bracket can often, however, be gleaned from these decisions, as can important aggravating and mitigating factors which should be borne in mind by the sentencer when dealing with the offence.

When reading the material in this chapter, however, a number of very important considerations must be borne in mind:

(a) Until changes were made by the CJA 1988, the offender, but not the prosecution, had a right to appeal to the Court of Appeal against a sentence imposed by the Crown Court. A limited right of prosecution appeal was introduced in 1988 (see **13.8**). It remains the fact, however, that most appeals against sentence are brought by offenders, and that most Court of Appeal decisions involve offences at the very serious end of the spectrum of criminal offending. In consequence there is plenty of Court of Appeal guidance on sentencing for offences like importation of drugs, rape, and robbery, but hardly any guidance on the proper sentencing bracket for offences like the less serious assaults, property offences and criminal damage. Of course most of these offences are normally dealt with in magistrates' courts, where there is a right of appeal by the offender (but not the prosecution) to the Crown Court. Unfortunately appellate advice to magistrates from the Crown Court is rarely very detailed, is not reported in the law reports and so cannot be included in a book like this one. Important advice and guidance on sentencing matters is available to magistrates, however, in the form of the Magistrates' Association Guidelines, the latest version of which was published in 2000. Reference is made to these Guidelines where appropriate in what follows.

(b)   The coming into force of the CJA 1991 in October 1992 had a significant impact on the proper approach to sentencing for a number of the offences covered in this chapter. Any earlier decisions which are still referred to should, therefore, always be read in the light of the statutory sentencing structure and sentencing principles put in place by that Act (see further Chapter 2). In particular, it should be remembered that:

(i)   the imposition of a custodial sentence now requires justification in accordance with the terms of PCC(S)A 2000, s. 79, its length requires justification in terms of s. 80, and the imposition of any community order requires justification in terms of s. 35; and

(ii)   the length of custodial sentences in any pre-1992 cases, including the guideline judgments, will require adjustment in the light of the Lord Chief Justice's *Practice Statement (Crime: Sentencing)* [1992] 1 WLR 948 on early release and custodial sentence length (see **4.5**); and

(iii)   where sentence imposed by the Crown Court judge has been increased by the Court of Appeal following an Attorney-General's reference, it cannot be assumed that the sentence substituted by the appellate court is the sentence which it was right for the Crown Court judge to have passed, since the Court of Appeal reduces the new sentence by an (often unspecified) amount, to take into account the fact that the offender has had to suffer the anguish of being sentenced twice (see further **13.3**).

(c)   Since Court of Appeal guidance tends to relate mainly to the most serious offences, and often to rather untypical cases, reference is made throughout this chapter to material from the *Criminal Statistics for England and Wales* which, in their Supplementary Volumes, provide an overview of the actual sentencing practice of Crown Courts and magistrates' courts. It will be seen that the generality of sentencing is often at a more lenient level than that which is indicated by the Court of Appeal. This may be to some extent because the Court of Appeal is simply 'out of touch', but it should be remembered that the Court of Appeal will reduce a sentence only where it is regarded as manifestly excessive. This often leads to appellate approval of a broad sentencing bracket, with the upper end considerably above the level of sentence the average Crown Court judge is likely to impose.

12.1   SENTENCING FOR HOMICIDE AND RELATED OFFENCES

12.1.1   Murder

Murder carries a mandatory penalty of life imprisonment (Murder (Abolition of Death Penalty) Act 1965, s. 1(1)). If murder is committed by a person aged under 18, the mandatory sentence is detention during Her Majesty's Pleasure (PCC(S)A 2000, s. 90). In 1998 256 offenders were sentenced for murder, of whom 247 were men and 9 were women. Of this total, 225 received the mandatory life sentence, 21 received custody for life and 10 were dealt with under s. 90. The offence of attempted murder carries a discretionary life sentence; 64 people were sentenced for attempted murder in 1998, of whom 49 received immediate custody, nine received hospital orders, there were five CROs and one CPO.

For the procedures which determine the date of the release of an offender convicted of murder see **4.5.2**.

12.1.2 Manslaughter: diminished responsibility

By the OAPA 1861, the maximum penalty for manslaughter is life imprisonment (s. 5). The offence is triable only on indictment. The Crown Court sentenced 15 cases of manslaughter by diminished responsibility in 1998. Seven offenders received hospital orders (two with restrictions) and five received immediate custody. There were three CROs.

In *Chambers* (1983) 5 Cr App R (S) 190 Leonard J explained that in diminished responsibility cases there are various courses open to a judge. If the psychiatric reports recommend and justify it and there are no contrary indications, a hospital order may well be the right sentence. Where a hospital order is not recommended, or is not appropriate, and the defendant constitutes a danger to the public for an unpredictable period of time, the right sentence will, in all probability, be one of life imprisonment. In cases where the evidence indicates that the accused's responsibility for his acts was so grossly impaired that his degree of responsibility for them was minimal, then a lenient course will be open. Provided there is no danger of repetition of violence, it will usually be possible to make such an order as will give the accused his freedom, such as a probation order. There will however be cases where there is no proper basis for a hospital order, but in which the accused's degree of responsibility is not minimal. Then the judge should pass a determinate sentence of imprisonment, the length of which will depend on two factors: the degree of the accused's responsibility and the period of time, if any, for which the accused will continue to be a danger to the public.

An example of a case falling within the first category in *Chambers* is *Courtney* (1987) 9 Cr App R (S) 404. In that case the offender pleaded guilty to the manslaughter of his wife, whom he had strangled after a domestic argument. He immediately tried to revive her and to summon help. The offender had been undergoing treatment for depression and the medical witnesses agreed that the offender was suffering from depression to a degree which warranted his detention in hospital for treatment. The Court of Appeal, taking account of the medical advice that the offender did not represent a risk to other members of the public and that his depression could be cured within a year, varied a restriction order under s. 41 of the MHA 1983 to a hospital order under s. 37 of that Act. See further the decision in *Birch* (1989) 11 Cr App R (S) 202, where the criteria for deciding between a hospital order, a life sentence and a determinate custodial sentence were discussed. A life sentence was upheld in *Sanderson* (1994) 15 Cr App R (S) 263, where the offender was a man with a long history of drug addiction and violence towards women. He had battered his girlfriend to death. The period specified under s. 28 of the C(S)A 1997 was eight years (see **4.5.2**).

In the second category of case is *Sangha* [1997] 1 Cr App R (S) 262 where the offender had suffered physical and mental cruelty and abuse from her husband over a period of 22 years. She had made several attempts at suicide. Following discovery that the husband had been having an affair she took an overdose, but subsequently discharged herself from hospital and the following day stabbed her husband. He died four days later during which time the offender stabbed herself, causing minor injury. The medical evidence was that she was suffering from depressive illness and was subject to acute stress reaction. A sentence of 18 months' imprisonment was varied by the Court of Appeal to a probation order for three years, although by that time the offender had served five months of her sentence.

An example of the third type of case is *Leggett* [1996] 2 Cr App R (S) 77, where the appellant pleaded guilty to the manslaughter of her 14-month-old child. Psychiatric reports indicated that the offender had an immature personality disorder and that at the time of the killing she was in a state of emotional turmoil brought about by her separation from the child's father and her irrational fear that the child would be taken from her, together with the fact that the child would not stop crying. The medical advice was that the offender was unlikely to reoffend and that detention in a psychiatric institution might not alleviate her condition. The Court of Appeal regretted that a hospital order could not be made, but said that since the offender retained a degree of responsibility for the killing there had to be an element of retribution and deterrence. A prison sentence of four years was upheld. See also *Yeomans* (1988) 10 Cr App R (S) 63 (eight years' imprisonment reduced to five where a man drowned his 18-month-old daughter in the sea while suffering from acute reactive depression), *Michael* (1993) 15 Cr App R (S) 265 and *Bourne* (1994) 16 Cr App R (S) 237.

12.1.3 Manslaughter: provocation

The maximum penalty for manslaughter is life imprisonment (OAPA 1861, s. 5). The offence is triable only on indictment. The *Criminal Statistics* do not provide separate figures for sentences imposed for manslaughter under provocation. For manslaughter due to diminished responsibility see **12.1.2** and for other forms of manslaughter see **12.1.5**.

The usual sentencing bracket is three to seven years, but longer sentences are sometimes upheld. In *A-G's Reference (No. 33 of 1996)* [1997] 2 Cr App R (S) 10 the Court of Appeal said that when an offender went out armed with a weapon and used it to cause death, even where there had been provocation, seven years was too low. See also *A-G's Reference (No. 2 of 1997)* [1998] 1 Cr App R (S) 27 where seven years was increased to ten years. Much shorter sentences may be appropriate in exceptional cases (e.g. *Dimasi* (1981) 3 Cr App R (S) 146, where a man of exemplary character killed his daughter after intervening in a domestic argument and under severe provocation). What is the appropriate punishment in these cases seems to turn upon the amount of provocation present, any opportunity there was for 'cooling off' before the fatal injury was caused, the extent to which the offender was at fault in bringing about the situation in the first place and the means used to kill the victim. According to Shaw LJ in *Bancroft*:

> notwithstanding that a man's reason might be unseated on the basis that the reasonable man would have found himself out of control, there is still in every human being a residual capacity for self-control which the exigencies of a given situation may call for; that must be the justification for passing a sentence of imprisonment, to recognise that there is still some degree of culpability.

Lord Lane CJ commented in *Taylor* (1987) 9 Cr App R (S) 175 that sentencing in provocation cases was 'an almost impossible task' but that the sentencer should have two objects in view. These were 'to ensure that the criminal expiates his offence' (almost always requiring immediate custody) and to 'provide a lesson to other people that they should keep their tempers and not be provoked'. The task of the judge then is to determine what the least period is which will reflect those two matters.

A situation giving rise to particular difficulty in sentencing is that of so-called 'cumulative' provocation, where the offender has killed the victim after a prolonged period of violence or abuse. In *Gardner* (1993) 14 Cr App R (S) 364 the offender had lived together with the victim for five years, during which time the victim had subjected her to violence on many occasions. The offender had stabbed the deceased with a kitchen knife, after both of them had consumed a good deal of drink. There had been an argument and the deceased had assaulted her by banging her head on a door. Psychiatric evidence was received that the offender was in a 'cumulative state of exhaustion, hopelessness, helplessness and depression, these features being charactertic of what has been described as battered-woman syndrome'. In the light of this evidence, the Court of Appeal substituted a probation order for the original sentence of five years' imprisonment. By the time of the hearing of the appeal the offender had served the equivalent of 18 months in custody, and the case should not be taken as saying that a probation order would have been the correct original sentence for the offence. The case may be contrasted with *Harrison* (1992) 13 Cr App R (S) 40 where the offender and the victim had lived together for ten years, during which time the victim had 'taken control' of the offender's life, dictating how she should dress and not allowing her to leave the house on her own. She had been subjected to violent sexual acts, some of which were carried out in front of the children. The offender paid a man £15,000 to kill her husband and this was planned and carried out, with the offender present when the victim was strangled. The Court of Appeal upheld a sentence of seven years, stating that 'considerable though the provocation undoubtedly was . . . no-one, however desperate their plight, is entitled deliberately to plan the execution of another human being'.

12.1.4 Manslaughter: suicide pact

The maximum penalty for manslaughter is life imprisonment (OAPA 1861, s. 5). The offence is triable only on indictment.

The offender in *Sweeney* (1986) 8 Cr App R (S) 419 pleaded guilty to the manslaughter of his wife. He was prone to depression and had married the deceased when she was suffering from advanced muscular dystrophy. They decided to commit suicide together by taking tablets and then setting fire to their car when they were inside it. Once the fire started both tried to escape, but the wife was killed. The offender suffered serious burns. The Court of Appeal reduced a four-year prison term to one of two years, that being 'sufficient, in our judgment, to mark the seriousness of this matter'.

12.1.5 Involuntary manslaughter

The maximum penalty for manslaughter is life imprisonment (OAPA 1861, s. 5). The offence is triable only on indictment. The *Criminal Statistics* show that the Crown Court passed sentence in cases of manslaughter (other than manslaughter due to diminished responsibility) in 266 cases in 1998. Of those, 217 received immediate custodial sentences and there were eight suspended sentences. Twenty-nine hospital orders were imposed (20 with restrictions), and the remaining twelve cases were dealt with by CRO or supervision order.

These offences vary very widely in culpability and circumstances, since they cover the full range of homicide between murder and accidental death. Unless there are 'outstandingly serious features' a sentence in excess of ten years is rare (*Barrell* (1992) 13 Cr App R (S) 646). The main difficulty in sentencing for manslaughter is to gain an appropriate balance between a sentence which is properly reflective of the offender's culpability (which in some cases may be low) but which also marks the fact that a life has been taken. The Court of Appeal authorities are not consistent, but the general approach seems to be to assess the sentence which would have been appropriate if death had not occurred, and then to add on something to reflect the fact that a person was killed (see *Paget* (1982) 4 Cr App R (S) 399).

In manslaughter arising from fights, according to Cumming-Bruce LJ in *Stuart* (1979) 1 Cr App R (S) 228, 'English law has always regarded the causing of the death of a man as an offence of great gravity, although the circumstances in which death is caused are manifestly relevant to assessing the degree of criminal responsibility and wickedness.' A sentence of four years was reduced to two years in that case, where the offender, in the course of a fight, had pushed the victim down some steps where he had fallen and fractured his skull. In *Kime* [1999] 2 Cr App R (S) 3 the offender punched an elderly man in the head. The victim suffered a heart attack and died. Six years was upheld by the Court of Appeal. the men were of very different ages, and the victim had been minding his own business at the time of the assault. Some general indications of sentencing in this type of case, following a review of the earlier authorities, were given in *Coleman* (1991) 11 Cr App R (S) 159. Lord Lane CJ said that, in a case of involuntary manslaughter where the victim was felled by a blow, cracked his head on the floor or pavement, suffered a skull fracture and died, the starting point for sentence on a plea of guilty was 12 months. Relevant mitigating factors would be absence of premeditation, the fact that the injury resulted from a single blow of moderate force, remorse, and an immediate admission of guilt. Aggravating factors would include a history of violent behaviour, the fact that the assault was gratuitous or unprovoked, and the fact that more than one blow had been struck. Another example is *Bryant* (1993) 14 Cr App R (S) 621. Cases where there had been an accidental fall resulting in a fracture of the skull had to be distinguished from more serious cases where a victim on the ground had been kicked about the head or where a weapon had been used. An example is *Silver* (1994) 15 Cr App R (S) 836. In *Shelton* (1979) 1 Cr App R (S) 202, an exceptional case, the Court of Appeal said that a custodial sentence should not have been imposed where two brothers, both in their sixties had fought following a family quarrel. The offender had fallen on the victim, injuring him with his knee. The victim failed to take medical advice and died three days later.

In cases of manslaughter involving firearms, again much depends on the circumstances, particularly the degree of planning in the use of the firearm. In *O'Mahoney* (1980) 2 Cr App R (S) 57 a sentence of 15 years was upheld. The offender and two other men had set out to find a fourth man to give him a beating, having first obtained a pistol and some ammunition. Although they did not find the man they were looking for, the pistol was subsequently fired on two occasions on that same day and then a completely innocent man was shot in the chest at close range and killed after an argument at a club. Eveleigh J said that it was proper to take account of the whole day's events in fixing the sentence: 'This is not the case of a man who, having taken drink, is suddenly in possession of a firearm and then carelessly, because of drink, fires it.' This may be compared with *Wesson* (1989) 11 Cr App R (S) 161, a case of reckless manslaughter, where a sentence of seven years was reduced to two years. The offender had been cleaning his shotgun, waving it about but saying that it was unloaded, and it had gone off, killing his wife.

In cases where manslaughter is committed in the course of the commission of another offence, such as burglary, robbery or arson, the Court of Appeal has held that the sentence should not be the same as would have been imposed for the lesser offence and according to Russell LJ in *Daly* (1994) 16 Cr App R (S) 777, 'loss of life, however unintended, is a very serious aggravating feature of dangerous and unlawful behaviour'. Again, a great deal depends on the precise circumstances of the killing. In *Cook* (1982) 4 Cr App R (S) 237, where a manslaughter by stabbing in the course of a burglary was described as 'close to being accidental', six years was appropriate, while ten years was proper in *Brophy* (1995) 16 Cr App R (S) 652, where the victim, an elderly woman who lived alone, was pushed against a wall during the course of a burglary. She suffered a broken pelvis and died a few minutes later. In *Palma* (1986) 8 Cr App R (S) 148 the offender pleaded guilty to manslaughter, arson being reckless whether life was endangered and theft. He had been dismissed from his employment and sought revenge by pouring petrol through the letterbox of the person who had caused his dismissal and starting a fire. The son of his intended victim died in the fire. A sentence of 12 years was upheld, Lawton LJ saying that 'this was as bad a case of manslaughter as it is possible to have, short of murder'.

Manslaughter of a young child normally attracts a custodial sentence between two and eight years, depending upon the degree of culpability. A sentence at the top end of the range was upheld in *Ali* (1988) 10 Cr App R (S) 59, where the victim was a four-year-old child who had been maltreated over a lengthy period and died of a fractured skull; the child was found to have had a number of other fractures caused on various other occasions. In *Staynor* [1996] 1 Cr App R (S) 376, where the offender struck his baby daughter twice, fracturing her skull, three years' imprisonment was upheld.

There are few appellate cases dealing with reckless manslaughter, as opposed to manslaughter by unlawful act. One example is *Morgan* (1990) 12 Cr App R (S) 504. The offender, an engine driver, inexplicably ignored yellow and red track warning signals with the result that his train crashed into another. Five people were killed and 87 were injured. He pleaded guilty and was a person of good character, and there was no suggestion that he had been drinking. The Court of Appeal reduced a sentence of 18 months (with six months immediate and the balance suspended) to one of four months, saying that prison could achieve nothing in this case and that the crime would trouble the offender's conscience for the rest of his life. Another is *Kite* [1996] 2 Cr App R (S) 295, where two years' imprisonment was appropriate for the manager of a company which organised canoeing trips for young people. As a result of poor safety standards, four youngsters were drowned.

12.1.6 Child destruction, infanticide and abortion

The maximum penalty for child destruction, infanticide and procuring an illegal abortion is, in each case, life imprisonment (Infant Life (Preservation) Act 1929, s. 1, Infanticide Act 1938, s. 1 and OAPA 1861, s. 58). These offences are triable only on indictment.

The proper approach for sentencing in cases of infanticide was considered by the Court of Appeal in *Sainsbury* (1989) 11 Cr App R (S) 533. The offender had become pregnant at the age of 15. She did not tell anyone about this, and gave birth to the baby without medical assistance in the bathroom of her boyfriend's flat. The baby was then wrapped in a blanket, taken some distance away and drowned in a river. The sentencer accepted that the balance of the offender's mind was disturbed by the effect of giving birth and that she was very immature, but did not accept that her responsibility was removed altogether. He imposed a sentence of 12 months' detention in a young offender institution. The Court of Appeal, however, having regard to statistics which indicated that of 59 cases of infanticide dealt with between 1979 and 1988 there had been no custodial sentences (all offenders having been dealt with by way of probation, supervision or hospital orders), decided that although the offence was serious the mitigating factors were overwhelming, and varied the sentence to probation. See also *Lewis* (1989) 11 Cr App R (S) 457. The 1998 statistics show that two offenders were sentenced for infanticide in that year. One received a custodial sentence and the other was given a CRO.

12.1.7 Complicity in suicide

The maximum penalty for aiding suicide is 14 years' imprisonment (Suicide Act 1961, s. 2).

In *Hough* (1984) 6 Cr App R (S) 406 Lord Lane CJ commented that this crime could vary 'from the borders of cold-blooded murder down to the shadowy area of mercy killing or common humanity'. In that case a prison term of nine months was upheld on a 60-year-old woman of unblemished character who had been a regular visitor to an 84-year-old woman who was partly blind, partly deaf and suffered from arthritis. The old lady had persisted in various statements to the effect that she intended to take her own life and the offender eventually supplied her with tablets. When she became unconscious, the offender placed a plastic bag over her head. In *Wallis* (1983) 5 Cr App R (S) 342 a sentence of 12 months' imprisonment was described by the Court of Appeal as 'at the extreme of leniency' in a case where the offender pleaded guilty to aiding the suicide of a 17-year-old flatmate by buying her tablets and alcohol, sitting with her while she took the tablets and not calling an ambulance until she was dead. The case of *McGranaghan* (1987) 9 Cr App R (S) 447 was dealt with much more severely. The offender, who was serving a prison sentence and sharing a cell with another prisoner who suffered from physical disabilities, persuaded the other prisoner to attempt suicide. The offender made a noose from a sheet and helped the victim to climb onto a cupboard and jump with the noose round his neck. The victim survived. Despite a guilty plea, and evidence of remorse, a sentence of eight years was upheld for aiding and abetting attempted suicide. The Crown Court sentenced just one case of aiding suicide in 1998, for which a custodial sentence was imposed.

12.1.8   Causing death by dangerous driving

The maximum penalty for causing death by dangerous driving is ten years (RTA 1988, s. 1 and sch. 2). It carries a one-year minimum disqualification from driving (RTA 1988, s. 34 and sch. 2). It is triable only on indictment. In 1998, 203 offenders were sentenced for causing death by dangerous driving; of those, 169 received immediate custody, 17 were given community service, 19 were fined, there were four suspended sentences, three CPROs and one CRO.

The Guideline case for this offence is still *Boswell* (1984) 6 Cr App R (S) 257 (although at the time of that decision the offence was causing death by 'reckless driving' and the maximum penalty was only five years). According to Lord Lane CJ, the following matters, among others, may be regarded as aggravating features:

(a)   the consumption of alcohol or drugs, which may range from a couple of drinks to what was described by the Court of Appeal in *Wheatley* (1982) 4 Cr App R (S) 371 as a 'motorised pub crawl';

(b)   competitive driving against another vehicle on the public highway, and/or grossly excessive speed and/or showing off;

(c)   the driver having disregarded warnings from his passengers;

(d)   a prolonged, persistent and deliberate course of very bad driving;

(e)   committing other offences at the same time, including related offences, such as driving without ever having had any licence, driving while disqualified, driving whilst a learner driver without a supervising driver;

(f)   previous convictions for motoring offences, particularly offences which involve bad driving or offences involving the consumption of excessive alcohol before driving;

(g)   several people having been killed as a result of the particular incident of reckless driving;

(h)   aggravating behaviour at the time of the offence, for example, failing to stop or, even more reprehensible, trying to throw off the victim from the bonnet of the car by swerving in order to escape;

(i)   causing death in the course of reckless driving carried out in an attempt to avoid detection or apprehension.

According to *Boswell* the mitigating features may be numbered as follows:

(a)   where the piece of reckless driving might be described as a 'one-off', i.e. a momentary reckless error of judgment, such as briefly dozing off at the wheel or failing to notice a pedestrian on a crossing;

(b)   a good driving record;

(c)   good character;

(d)   a plea of guilty;

(e)   sometimes the effect on the offender, if he is genuinely remorseful and/or if he is genuinely shocked;

(f)   where the victim was either a close relative of the offender or a close friend and the consequent emotional shock is great.

If there are no aggravating features present, a non-custodial penalty may well be appropriate, but where any aggravating feature is present then a custodial sentence is generally necessary. Drivers who indulge in racing on the highway and/or drive with reckless disregard for the safety of others after taking alcohol, should, according to Lord Lane, lose their liberty for five years or more (the figure in the original case was 'two years or more', but this has since been adjusted because of the increase in the maximum penalty: see *A-G's Reference (Nos. 12 and 24 of 1993)* (1993) 15 Cr App R (S) 640). It will seldom be that a community sentence or a suspended sentence will be appropriate in a serious case. That type of driver should, according to Lord Lane, be removed from the road for a long period of disqualification. *Boswell* states that there is a distinction to be drawn, so far as disqualification is concerned, between cases of driving while disqualified and similar offences where there is no question of bad driving, and cases where the essence of the crime is the manner of the driving on the occasion in question. In the latter case, where the driver has shown himself to be a menace to others using the highway, he should be debarred from driving for a substantial length of time; in a bad case, seven to ten years will not be too long.

Examples where the offence was committed by a driver affected by alcohol are *A-G's Reference (No. 22 of 1994)* (1994) 16 Cr App R (S) 670 (where the custodial sentence was increased from 15 months to five years in a case where the amount of drink taken was very high and two people were killed), and *A-G's Reference (No. 48 of 1996)* [1997] 2 Cr App R (S) 46 (two years' imprisonment increased to four years where the offender drank seven pints of stout and was driving his car with five passengers when he struck another car killing one of the passengers; disqualification increased to four years). Examples where the offence was committed after the offender drove at excessive speed are *A-G's Reference (No. 67 of 1995)* [1996] 2 Cr Ap R (S) 373 (where the offender, on bail at the time for an offence of aggravated vehicle taking, stole a car from a car park and raced it on the highway, colliding with another car and killing the driver, five years was increased to seven years after a contested case) and *A-G's Reference (No. 6 of 1996)* [1997] 1 Cr App R (S) 79 (where the offender, who admitted driving at 45 m.p.h. in a built-up area in the early hours of the morning, had struck a woman on a crossing and killed her, a nine-month sentence was increased to 21 months; four-year disqualification unchanged). Other cases involve drivers who have fallen asleep at the wheel (*de Meersman* [1997] 1 Cr App R (S) 106: three years' imprisonment and four years' disqualification upheld) and offenders using vehicles which they know to be in a dangerous condition (*Kang* [1997] 1 Cr App R (S) 306: lorry with seriously defective brakes went out of control and killed a person sitting in a stationary car, where 30 months' imprisonment together with disqualification for four years was upheld). Finally, *Moore* [1997] 2 Cr App R (S) 239 was a case of momentary inattention by the driver, who was looking at a road map on the dashboard when he ran into the back of a stationary car, killing the driver. Six months' imprisonment was reduced to two months.

12.1.9 Threats to kill

The maximum penalty for making threats to kill is ten years (CLA 1977, sch. 12, replacing OAPA 1861, s. 16). The maximum penalty for solicitation of murder is life imprisonment (OAPA 1861, s. 4). The offences are triable only on indictment. The 1998 statistics indicate that 265 offenders were dealt with for making threats to kill or for conspiracy to murder in that year. Of that total, 163 received immediate custody, 12 received suspended sentences, 49 received probation orders, 11 received hospital orders and there were a number of other disposals, including six conditional discharges.

Sentences approved by the Court of Appeal for making threats to kill range downwards from the five years' imprisonment upheld in *Bowden* (1986) 8 Cr App R (S) 155, where the offender, who was receiving treatment for alcoholism, went to the home of a woman with whom he had formerly lived and threatened her with a sword. The woman barricaded herself in the bedroom and the police had to force their way into the house to arrest the offender. The court heard evidence that the offender had a large collection of weapons which he intended to use against a list of people, headed by his ex-girlfriend. In *Martin* (1993) 14 Cr App R (S) 645 four years' imprisonment was reduced to three years where the offender sent two anonymous notes stained with blood to the victim.

As far as solicitation of murder is concerned, in *Raw* (1983) 5 Cr App R (S) 229, where the offender attempted to contact someone who would murder his wife for a fee of £2,000, the Court of Appeal said that a prison sentence of seven years was 'the minimum sentence, regardless of the fact of the personality and circumstances of the appellant, that would constitute a proper deterrent'. This case was followed in *Peatfield* (1985) 7 Cr App R (S) 132, where a prison sentence of ten years was upheld on an offender who offered to pay a man £5,000 to murder his wife and ten-year-old daughter. Where a man solicited another to murder a political opponent, a 12-year term was held to be correct (*Gill* (1988) 10 Cr App R (S) 373).

12.2 SENTENCING FOR NON-FATAL OFFENCES AGAINST THE PERSON

12.2.1 Assault and battery

The maximum penalty for common assault and battery is six months' imprisonment, a fine not exceeding level 5 on the standard scale, or both (CJA 1988, s. 39). Assault and battery are triable only summarily. In 1998, 23,301 cases of common assault were sentenced by magistrates. Of those, 2,295 received custody. The most frequent disposals were the discharge (7,801) and the fine (4,986). Just over 900 cases were otherwise dealt with (mainly bind over, or compensation order alone).

The Magistrates' Association Guidelines (2000) state the following:

Aggravating Factors +
on hospital/medical premises, group action, offender in position of authority, premeditated, injury, weapon, victim particularly vulnerable, victim public servant, offence committed on bail, previous convictions and failures to respond to previous sentences, if relevant.

Mitigating Factors −
impulsive, minor injury, provocation, single blow.

The Guidelines state that magistrates should consider whether the offence is serious enough for a community penalty.

In *Fenton* (1994) 15 Cr App R (S) 682 the offender had pushed another motorist in the chest in the course of an altercation on the road. The Court of Appeal said that the appropriate sentence was 7 days' imprisonment. See also *Ross* (1994) 15 Cr App R (S) 384.

The maximum penalty for the racially aggravated form of common assault is two years, a fine or both on indictment; six months, a fine not exceeding the statutory maximum, or both, summarily (CDA 1998, s. 29). For guidance on sentencing for racially aggravated offences, see **12.2.3**.

12.2.2 Assault on a police officer

The maximum penalty for assault on a constable in the execution of his duty is six months' imprisonment, a fine not exceeding level 5, or both (Police Act 1996, s. 89). The offence is triable only summarily. In 1998, 11,127 cases of assault on a police officer were sentenced by magistrates. Of those, 1,320 received custody. The most frequent other disposals were fine (4,251), CPO (1,105) and CRO (1,121).

The Magistrates' Association Guidelines (2000) indicate the following:

Aggravating Factors +
any injuries caused, gross disregard for police authority, group action, premeditated, offence committed on bail, previous convictions and failures to respond to previous sentences, if relevant.

Mitigating Factors −
impulsive action, unaware that victim was PC.

The Guidelines state that magistrates should consider whether the offence is so serious that only custody is appropriate.

See also the sentencing considerations for assault occasioning actual bodily harm at **12.2.3**.

12.2.3 Assault occasioning actual bodily harm

The maximum penalty for assault occasioning actual bodily harm on indictment is five years' imprisonment (OAPA 1861, s. 47): on summary conviction, the maximum penalty is six months, a fine not exceeding level 5, or both.

The *Practice Note* (*Mode of Trial: Guidelines*) (1995) indicate that the following matters are relevant to determining mode of trial:

(1)   The use of weapon of a kind likely to cause serious injury.

(2)   A weapon is used and serious injury is caused.

(3)   More than minor injury is caused by kicking, head-butting or similar forms of assault.

(4)   Serious violence is caused to those whose work has to be done in contact with the public (e.g. police officers, bus drivers, taxi drivers, publicans and shopkeepers).

(5)   Violence to vulnerable people (e.g., the elderly and infirm).

The same considerations apply to cases of domestic violence.

The Magistrates' Association Guidelines (2000) indicate the following:

Aggravating Factors +

deliberate kicking or biting, extensive injuries (may be psychiatric), headbutting, group action, offender in position of authority, on hospital/medical premises, premeditated, victim particularly vulnerable, victim public servant, weapon, offence committed on bail, previous convictions and failures to respond to previous sentences, if relevant.

Mitigating Factors −

impulsive action, minor injury, provocation, single blow.

The Guidelines state that magistrates should consider whether the offence is so serious that only custody is appropriate.

Only a minority of sentences for assault occasioning actual bodily harm are custodial and, of those, most are for three months or less. Sentences of up to two or three years for this offence have, however, been upheld by the Court of Appeal where aggravating factors have been present or where the offence has been close to the borderline with the offence of wounding with intent. Heavier sentences will be imposed where the assault was committed against a police officer. In *McKenlay* (1979) 1 Cr App R (S) 161, when upholding a six-month prison term on the offender, a man of good character, who had punched and butted a police officer in the face in the course of an industrial dispute, Watkins J commented that a custodial sentence for 'an attack deliberately made upon a police officer inflicting upon him harm, no matter how slight it be, is never wrong in principle'. Two years' imprisonment was upheld in *Moore* (1993) 14 Cr App R (S) 273, where the offender misbehaved in a public house and, when two police officers arrived, one male and one female, he verbally abused and attacked them, causing numerous minor injuries by kicking and punching, and a custodial sentence of eight months was upheld in *Leather* (1993) 14 Cr App R (S) 736, where a 17-year-old woman had seized a police officer by the testicles, in order to prevent her boyfriend from being arrested. If it is not proved that the offender knew that the victim was a police officer, then the heavier sentence will not be appropriate (*Stosiek* (1982) 4 Cr App R (S) 205).

Other examples of cases where custodial sentences of more than three months may be proper are where a weapon is used by the offender and where the assault is committed upon a public servant (*Foster* (1982) 4 Cr App R (S) 101, where six months' detention was ordered for an assault by a youth on a bus conductor who had been cut on the head: see also *Tremlett* (1983) 5 Cr App R (S) 199). It will be an aggravating feature of the offence where the assault is committed at a football match, particularly against someone who was not involved in violence (*Birkin* (1988) 10 Cr App R (S) 303). In *Hassan* (1989) 11 Cr App R (S) 8 the Court of Appeal reduced a sentence of four months' imprisonment to two months on an offender who had punched another man after a dispute over who had priority to a car parking space. Lord Lane CJ said that normally such incidents could be dealt with by way of a fine, but that incidents involving drivers losing their tempers, getting out of their cars and striking other drivers or pedestrians were becoming too frequent. In *Arnold* [1996] 1 Cr App R (S) 115 it was said that an assault committed by one motorist on another was just as serious as an assault committed in other circumstances. Six months was proper in *McNally* [2000] 1 Cr App R (S) 535, where a relative of a hospital patient struck a doctor in the face and nine months was correct in *Byrne* [2000] 1 Cr App R (S) 282, where a school teacher was assaulted by an angry parent.

Examples of assaults committed in the course of competitive sporting matches are *Birkin* (1988) 10 Cr App R (S) 303, where the offender, after a late tackle by an opponent in a football match struck the victim and broke his jaw in two places (eight months' imprisonment reduced to six months on appeal) and *Davies* (1990) 12 Cr App R (S) 308 where the offender struck an opponent in the face and fractured his cheekbone, when tempers became frayed in a football match (six months' imprisonment upheld).

Assaults between spouses should not be treated more leniently than other assaults (*Nicholas* (1994) 15 Cr App R (S) 381). An offender convicted of assault committed by 'stalking' the victim over a four-year period received a custodial term of 21 months in *Smith* [1998] 1 Cr App R (S) 138.

Where the offence of assault occasioning actual bodily harm was racially motivated, the aggravated form of the offence should be charged. The maximum penalty for the racially aggravated form of the offence is seven years, a fine or both on indictment; six months, a fine not exceeding the statutory maximum or both, summarily (CDA 1998, s. 29).

Sentencing guidance can be found in *Saunders* [2000] 1 Cr App R 458 and in *Kelly and Donnelly* [2001] Crim LR 411. According to these authorities, in a case of racially aggravated actual bodily harm the sentencer should first determine what the sentence would have been for the 'basic' offence, without the element of racial aggravation. The sentencer should state what that sentence would have been, and then indicate the appropriate degree of enhancement to take account of the racial aggravation. The sentencer should have regard to the increased maximum sentence provided by Parliament for the racially aggravated form of the offence, and in some cases an offence which could have been dealt with by a community sentence in its basic form will require custody in its aggravated form. In *Saunders*, Lord Justice Rose indicated that when deciding the degree of enhancement to the sentence, relevant matters to take into account would be the form, duration and location of any demonstration of racial hostility. In *Kelly and Donnelly* his lordship further adopted a number of other relevant factors (as proposed by the Sentencing Advisory Panel), such as the offence being part of a pattern of racist behaviour by the offender, the offender's membership of a group promoting racist views, and the impact on the victim and the locality of the offence. Less serious examples would be those where the offence was not racially motivated as such, or where the expression of racial hostility was relatively minor or incidental.

12.2.4   Malicious wounding or inflicting grievous bodily harm

The maximum penalty for unlawfully and maliciously wounding or inflicting grievous bodily harm on indictment is five years (OAPA 1861, s. 20); on summary conviction, the maximum penalty is six months, a fine not exceeding level 5, or both.

The *Practice Note* (*Mode of Trial: Guidelines*) (1995) are the same for this offence as for assault occasioning actual bodily harm (see **12.2.3**). The Magistrates' Association Guidelines (2000) are also virtually identical.

Only a minority of sentences for malicious wounding are custodial but sentences of up to three years for this offence have been upheld by the Court of Appeal where aggravating factors have been present, or where the offence is close to the borderline with wounding with intent, or where it was committed against a police officer or other public servant, or a child.

The use of a weapon is an important aggravating feature. In *Lachtay* (1982) 4 Cr App R (S) 229 the offender grabbed the victim at a party, accused him of insulting the offender's girlfriend, and struck him on the forehead with a bottle, causing a one inch cut. In the Court of Appeal Michael Davies J described the six-month sentence imposed as 'lenient; some would say it was very lenient'. In other cases of 'glassing', where more severe injury has been caused, longer sentences have been imposed. In *Jones* (1984) 6 Cr App R (S) 55, where the victim was struck in the face with a beer glass which, when it broke, was pushed into the victim's face, causing grave injury including the probable loss of sight in one eye, a sentence of two years was upheld. See also *Marsden* (1993) 15 Cr App R (S) 177. In *Bayes* (1994) 16 Cr App R (S) 290, after a driving incident, the offender attacked the other driver, punching him and striking him on the back with a hammer. Fifteen months' imprisonment was reduced to nine months to take account of personal mitigation and remorse.

A sentence of three years' imprisonment was upheld in *Moore* (1991) 13 Cr App R (S) 130, where the offender, after a disagreement with another man over the use of a telephone box, struck the victim and then kicked him about the head and body as he lay on the ground. The victim suffered serious facial injuries and was detained in hospital for two weeks. In *Rogers* (1993) 15 Cr App R (S) 393 the offender head-butted an opposing player during an amateur soccer match, causing a displaced fracture of the cheekbone. Nine months' imprisonment was reduced to four months on appeal.

The maximum penalty for the racially aggravated form of malicious wounding is seven years, a fine or both on indictment; six months, a fine not exceeding the statutory maximum, summarily (CDA 1998, s. 29). For guidance on sentencing for racially aggravated offences, see **12.2.3**.

12.2.5 Wounding with intent to do grievous bodily harm

The maximum penalty for wounding or causing grievous bodily harm with intent to do grievous bodily harm is life imprisonment (OAPA 1861, s. 18). Closely related offences, all punishable with a maximum of life, are attempting to choke, suffocate or strangle with intent (OAPA 1861, s. 21) and throwing corrosive fluid (OAPA 1861, s. 29). All are triable only on indictment.

The normal sentencing bracket is three to eight years, although sentences over eight years have been upheld in particularly grave cases. A custodial sentence will almost inevitably be required (*A-G's Reference (No. 33 of 1997)* [1998] 1 Cr App R (S) 352). Relevant aggravating factors include extensive injuries, premeditation, use of a weapon and kicking or stamping on the victim. Relevant mitigating factors are a plea of guilty and previous good character of the offender, though these may be of little weight in very serious cases. Substantial provocation is also to be taken into account.

In a case involving stabbing, the Court of Appeal upheld a nine-year sentence in *Polley* [1997] 2 Cr App R (S) 356, where, after a disagreement over rent to be paid, the offender stabbed the victim several times with a kitchen knife, severing an artery in his arm. A term of seven-years was upheld on a 19-year-old in *Robinson* (1980) 2 Cr App R (S) 193, where the offender had accosted an older man and threatened him with a knife. When he refused to hand over any money, he was stabbed twice and could have died as a result of his injuries. In *Dunning* (1984) 6 Cr App R (S) 337, three years was upheld as 'the lowest sentence which could be passed' on an offender who called on his ex-wife and found her in the company of another man. He returned to the house later and stabbed the ex-wife in the stomach. The offender had a history of violence towards his ex-wife.

The use of other weapons will attract comparable sentences, depending upon the extent of the injuries, taken together with relevant mitigating and aggravating factors. In *Chesterman* (1984) 6 Cr App R (S) 151 a 12-year sentence was upheld on an offender who fired a shotgun twice at a police officer. The officer was permanently blinded and suffered other injuries. The offender was acquitted of attempted murder, but the case was described as 'at the very top of the scale for offences of causing grievous bodily harm with intent'. In *Craney* [1996] 2 Cr App R (S) 336 sentences of 11 years were proper for an unprovoked and racially motivated attack by two youths using a torch and iron bar, leaving the victim with severe head injuries and a badly broken leg. An axe was the weapon used in *Reilly* (1982) 4 Cr App R (S) 288. Six years was held to be proper in that case where a man, previously of good character, inflicted grave head injuries on his wife.

The Court of Appeal has considered cases of 'glassing' on several occasions. A sentence of five years was upheld in *James* (1981) 3 Cr App R (S) 223, where the offender attacked a shopkeeper with two broken milk bottles, pushing them into his face and cutting him very badly. The court described this as 'about as bad a case of . . . glassing as it is possible to imagine'. In *Harwood* (1979) 1 Cr App R (S) 354 Lord Lane CJ said that 'one cannot really recognise anything less than three years as being right for deliberate glassing', and exactly that sentence was upheld in the case of an 18-year-old who had been involved in a fight in a public house and had pushed a broken bottle into the victim's face. In *A-G's Reference (No. 23 of 1990)* (1990) 12 Cr App R (S) 575 the offender, who was at a New Year's Eve party at a public house, struck the victim on the back of the head with a bottle, and then pushed the broken bottle into his cheek and towards his neck. A sentence of 18 months' imprisonment was said by the Court of Appeal to be 'undoubtedly excessively lenient'. The minimum appropriate sentence on the facts was said to be four years, and the sentence was so increased, though Lord Lane CJ noted that something less than four years might have been proper if the offender had pleaded guilty.

It is clear that an offender who causes grievous bodily harm by kicking or stamping on the victim's head while the latter is on the ground should receive a substantial custodial term. In *Ivey* (1981) 3 Cr App R (S) 185 a man of previous good character became caught up in a fracas in a club, during the course of which he knocked a man to the ground and stamped on his head, inflicting grave injuries to his face and skull. A four-year sentence was upheld, Griffiths LJ commenting that 'The degree of injury likely to be caused by kicking a man when he is down is of a wholly different degree to that which is likely to be suffered in the course of a fist fight.' Those comments have been approved in several later cases, including *A-G's Reference (No. 59 of 1996)* [1997] 2 Cr App R (S) 250. In *Legge* (1988) 10 Cr App R (S) 208 the victim was stripped and subjected to various indignities, as well as being severely beaten and kicked: seven years upheld. Eighteen months' imprisonment was upheld in *Lloyd* (1989) 11 Cr App R (S) 36, where the deliberate kicking was inflicted by a rugby player on a member of the opposition during a match, the victim suffering a fractured cheekbone.

In cases where corrosive fluid is thrown, lengthy terms will be appropriate. In *Radford* (1986) 8 Cr App R (S) 61 five years was upheld where the offender squirted a corrosive substance into the victim's face, causing substantial loss of vision in one eye.

12.2.6   Administering poison

The maximum penalty for administering any poison or noxious thing with intent to injure etc. is five years (OAPA 1861, s. 24). Where the act is done with intent to endanger life or inflict grievous bodily harm, the maximum penalty is ten years (OAPA 1861, s. 23). These offences are triable only on indictment. In *Jones* (1990) 12 Cr App R (S) 233, the sentence bracket for the s. 24 offence was said to be the same as for malicious wounding (see **12.2.4**). Nine months was the correct sentence in *Hogan* (1994) 15 Cr App R (S) 834, where the offender gave to a woman a drink which contained a large quantity of a Class C drug. It caused her to fall into a deep sleep for a day.

12.2.7   False imprisonment and kidnapping

These are both common law offences and the penalties are at large. Both are triable only on indictment.

According to Lord Lane CJ in *Spence* (1983) 5 Cr App R (S) 413, such offences vary widely, from carefully planned abductions where the victim is used as a hostage or where ransom money is demanded (seldom less than eight years' imprisonment and more, perhaps much more, if violence or firearms are used) to incidents more akin to family tiffs or lovers' disputes (18 months or less, sometimes a great deal less). The Crown Court dealt with 351 cases of kidnapping in 1998, 261 of which were dealt with by custodial sentences. There were also 22 CROs and 20 CPOs.

Brown (1985) 7 Cr App R (S) 15 was a case of unpremeditated kidnapping and false imprisonment of a young woman by forcing her into her car and causing her minor injuries in an ensuing struggle. Sentences of five years concurrent imposed on the kidnapping and false imprisonment counts were upheld. In *Karunaratne* (1983) 5 Cr App R (S) 2, an 11-year-old child was abducted and ransom demands made. Sentences of 12 years and 10 years were imposed on the offenders for offences of kidnapping, false imprisonment and blackmail. Kidnapping was for a political motive in *Barak* (1985) 7 Cr App R (S) 404, where sentences varying between 10 and 14 years were imposed on the offenders involved.

12.3   SENTENCING FOR SEXUAL OFFENCES

12.3.1   Rape

The maximum penalty for rape is life imprisonment (SOA 1956, s. 37). The maximum penalty for attempted rape is also life (SOA 1985, sch. 2). Rape and attempted rape are triable only on indictment. In 1998 the Crown Court sentenced 674 cases of rape. Of those the overwhelming majority, 655, received immediate custody or detention under PCC(S)A 2000, s. 91; of the remaining 19 cases three were dealt with by suspended sentence, six by hospital order, six by CRO, two by supervision order, and two cases were otherwise dealt with.

The Guideline case for this offence is *Billam* (1986) 8 Cr App R (S) 48. The case states that 'rape is always a serious crime which calls for an immediate custodial sentence other than in wholly exceptional circumstances'. Lord Lane CJ went on to say:

> For rape committed by an adult without any aggravating or mitigating features, a figure of five years should be taken as the starting point in a contested case. Where a rape is committed by two or more men acting together, or by a man who has broken into or

otherwise gained access to a place where the victim is living, or by a person who is in a position of responsibility towards the victim, or by a person who abducts the victim and holds her captive, the starting point should be eight years.

At the top of the scale comes the defendant who has carried out what might be described as a campaign of rape, committing the crime upon a number of different women or girls. He represents a more than ordinary danger and a sentence of fifteen years or more may be appropriate.

Where the defendant's behaviour has manifested perverted or psychopathic tendencies or gross personality disorder, and where he is likely, if at large, to remain a danger to women for an indefinite time, a life sentence will not be inappropriate.

Lord Lane CJ then indicated that the crime should in any event be treated as aggravated by any of the following factors:

(a) violence is used over and above the force necessary to commit the rape;
(b) a weapon is used to frighten or wound the victim;
(c) the rape is repeated;
(d) the rape has been carefully planned;
(e) the defendant has previous convictions for rape or other serious offences of a violent or sexual kind;
(f) the woman is subjected to further sexual indignities or perversions;
(g) the victim is either very old or very young;
(h) the effect upon the victim, whether physical or mental, is of special seriousness.

Where 'any one or more' of these aggravating features are present, the sentence should be 'substantially higher' than the figure suggested as the starting point.

As far as mitigation is concerned, *Billam* indicates that the extra distress which giving evidence can cause to a rape victim means that a plea of guilty, perhaps more so than in other cases, should normally result in some reduction from what would otherwise be the appropriate sentence. The amount of such reduction will of course depend on all the circumstances, including the likelihood of a finding of not guilty had the matter been contested. The fact that the victim may be considered to have exposed herself to danger by acting imprudently (as for instance by accepting a lift in a car from a stranger) is *not* a mitigating factor, and the victim's previous sexual experience is equally irrelevant. But if the victim has behaved in a manner which was calculated to lead the defendant to believe that she would consent to sexual intercourse, then there should be some mitigation of sentence. Previous good character is of only minor relevance.

About one third of those convicted of rape are under the age of 21. In the ordinary case the appropriate sentence would be one of detention in a young offender institution, following the terms suggested as terms of imprisonment for an adult, but making some reduction to reflect the youth of the offender. In the case of a juvenile, the court will in most cases exercise the power to order detention under the PCC(S)A 2000, s. 91.

Life sentences for rape were approved in *Fox* (1995) 16 Cr App R (S) 688, where the offender, a man described as of 'dull intellect' but not mentally disordered, had committed several offences of rape on mentally deficient women resident in a hospital where the offender worked as a nursing assistant, and in *A-G's Reference (No. 6 of 1993)* (1994) 15 Cr App R (S) 375, where a 20-year-old offender with a previous conviction for rape was convicted of rape and robbery, the carefully planned offences having been committed within seven days of his release from prison. Psychiatric reports in the latter case indicated that the offender was suffering from a form of psychopathic disorder. In *Thomas* (1994) 16 Cr App R (S) 686, 15 years' imprisonment was upheld for the rape of a 78-year-old woman. The offender, who had numerous previous convictions for burglary and was on parole at the time of the offence, broke into the victim's home, assaulted her with his fists and with a piece of wood and then raped her. The Court of Appeal heard that the victim's life had been completely ruined by what had happened and that she was too frightened to return to her home where she had lived for many years. In *Farmer* (1993) 14 Cr App R (S) 664 the Court of Appeal upheld a 'severe' but 'warranted' sentence of 13 years in a case where the offender had lured a young woman into his car, assaulted her, tied her up and then raped her twice with considerable violence. The offender contested the case and the victim was required to give evidence and relive the circumstances of the offence in detail. A number of the aggravating features referred to in *Billam* were also present in *Malcolm* (1987) 9 Cr App R (S) 487. There the offender pleaded guilty to false imprisonment and rape. The victim was dragged to the offender's flat, threatened with a knife, forced to participate in oral sex and raped twice. The sentencer imposed a sentence of 12 years for the rape, with five years concurrent for the false imprisonment. He also stated that he regarded public awareness that a rape victim may contact AIDS as being a general aggravating feature in rape cases. The Court of Appeal reduced the sentence to ten years, taking 12 years from *Billam* as the starting point and reducing it by two years for the guilty plea. It was also said that fear of contacting AIDS would justify a heavier sentence if the victim had a valid reason for believing that she had contacted it from the offender, or where that had actually happened. In *A-G's Reference (No. 1 of 1991)* [1992] 3 WLR 432 the victim, a woman in her mid-sixties, worked as a bereavement counsellor and had invited the offender, who had posed as a distressed widower, to her home. He made sexual advances to her and, when these were resisted, he pushed her into the bedroom and raped her several times. The sentence of five years' imprisonment was said by the Court of Appeal to be 'inordinately low' in the light of the *Billam* guidelines. The aggravating features present, and the absence of mitigation to be derived from a guilty plea, required a minimum sentence of eight years.

A case without some of the aggravating features present in the preceding paragraph is *Harvey* (1987) 9 Cr App R (S) 124, where the victim had known the offender for about a year. She went to his home looking for her friend, the offender's cousin. When the victim rejected his sexual advances, the offender raped her. He had previous convictions for indecent assault on a young boy and for incest. Lord Lane CJ described the case as 'a typical *Billam* case' where five years was the appropriate starting point. The sentence of seven years was reduced to six, one year in addition to the baseline of five being sufficient to take account of the related previous convictions. In *A-G's Reference (No. 7 of 1989)* (1990) 12 Cr App R (S) 1 the offender was convicted of raping a woman with whom he had lived for about 18 months and with whom he had had regular sexual intercourse. The offence took place three months after the relationship had ended. The offender invited the complainant to visit his flat, which she did; he then pushed her across the room, removed her clothes and raped her. A sentence of two years was increased on appeal to four and a half years, Lord Lane CJ observing that previous cohabitation did not license a man to have sexual intercourse with the woman whenever he wished, but it was said that 'some weight' should be given to the previous relationship. The main reason for increasing the sentence in this case was that the defendant, in contesting the matter, had deprived himself of 'one of the most powerful points in mitigation which he has'.

The appropriate sentence for rape committed by a man upon his wife was considered in *Stephen W* (1993) 14 Cr App R (S) 256. The offender and his wife had been married and living together for three years. After an argument, the offender forced his wife to have sexual intercourse, threatening her with a knife. A sentence of five years was upheld. The Court of Appeal said it should not be thought that a lower scale of sentencing than that set out in *Billam* applied to rape by a husband. All would depend on the circumstances of the case. The existence of a previous consensual sexual relationship would be a mitigating factor in a case where the parties were cohabiting normally and the husband insisted on intercourse against the wife's will but without using violence or threats, but where there had been violence or threats the previous relationship was of little relevance. The instant case fell at the grave end of the scale and the offender had contested the case.

In *A-G's Reference (No. 12 of 1992)* (1993) 14 Cr App R (S) 233 the offender pleaded guilty to the rape of a prostitute, with whom he had previously had sexual relations. When the woman requested payment in advance, the offender threatened her with a knife and forced her to have oral sex and sexual intercourse. He also said that he would kill her if she reported the incident. The Court of Appeal said that the original sentence of two years' imprisonment was too lenient and that, bearing in mind that the offender had now been sentenced twice over, the 'least sentence that could properly be imposed' was three years. While the fact that the victim behaved in a manner calculated to lead the defendant to believe that she would consent to intercourse could be taken into consideration, according to *Billam*, in this case the basis upon which the woman was prepared to have intercourse was quite different from that on which the offender, armed with a knife, sought to have it. In *Masood* [1997] 2 Cr App R (S) 137, where the 16-year-old victim was held captive in the offender's car for four hours, was subjected to a series of violent attacks and was forced to have unprotected sexual intercourse, the Court of Appeal said that the fact that the victim was a prostitute was largely irrelevant to the sentence.

In *Taylor* (1983) 5 Cr App R (S) 241 a sentence of three years was varied to a probation order where the offender, who was mentally retarded, pleaded guilty to rape of a 19-year-old girl suffering from Down's syndrome who attended the same special school as the offender. The Court of Appeal justified the exceptional sentence on the ground of the nature of the sexual act itself (some degree of sexual penetration, but in the nature of sexual exploration with no real understanding), the mental deficiency of the offender (described as on the borderline between low intelligence and mental handicap) and the inability of the victim to communicate any effective protest at the conduct.

Following changes to the law on rape brought about by the CJPOA 1994, cases of non-consensual anal intercourse, whether committed on a woman or on a man, are now charged as rape rather than buggery. Although dating from before the statutory change, in *Mendez* (1992) 13 Cr App R (S) 9, a case where the offender had attacked the female victim while she was walking home, pushed her into an alleyway and twice committed buggery. Glidewell LJ referred to the *Billam* guidelines on rape and said that 'in our view forcible buggery of a woman is equivalent to rape but worse than normal vaginal rape'. A prison sentence of five years was upheld. This comment has been relied upon in later cases, including *A-G's Reference (No. 25 of 1994)* (1995) 16 Cr App R (S) 562.

The *Criminal Statistics* indicate that of the 675 cases of rape sentenced by the Crown Court in 1998, the victim was female in 632 cases and male in 43 cases.

12.3.2 Unlawful sexual intercourse

The maximum penalty for unlawful sexual intercourse with a girl aged under 13 is life imprisonment (SOA 1956, sch. 2). The maximum for attempted unlawful sexual intercourse with a girl under 13 is seven years (SOA 1956, sch. 2). The maximum for unlawful sexual intercourse with a girl under 16 is two years on indictment (SOA 1956, sch. 2); six months, a fine not exceeding the statutory maximum, or both, summarily.

Unlawful sexual intercourse with a girl under 13 is triable only on indictment. In 1998, 46 offenders were sentenced for this offence. Of these 28 received immediate custody, ten received CROs, four supervision orders, one hospital order, two CPOs and one combination order.

Unlawful sexual intercourse with a girl under 16 is triable either way. In 1998, 161 offenders were dealt with for this offence in the Crown Court. Of these 103 received immediate custody, five received suspended sentences, seven CPOs, 27 CROs, four supervision orders, five CPROs, two fines and eight disharges. In the magistrates' courts, 69 offenders were sentenced for this offence, of whom nine received a custodial sentence. Probation, fine and conditional discharge were the preferred disposals.

Where an offence of unlawful sexual intercourse is triable either way, *Practice Note (Mode of Trial: Guidelines)* (1995) indicate that the following matters are relevant to determining mode of trial:

(a) wide disparity of age;
(b) breach of position of trust;
(c) victim particularly vulnerable.

A number of cases illustrate the sentencing bracket for the offence of unlawful sexual intercourse with a girl aged under 13. In *Upfield* (1984) 6 Cr App R (S) 63 the offender pleaded guilty to one offence of unlawful sexual intercourse with a girl of 12. The offender had a long-standing relationship with the girl's mother and often acted as a baby-sitter for the daughter. The Court of Appeal said that the offence was 'a gross breach of trust' and a three-year sentence was upheld. Thirty months' imprisonment was appropriate in *Polley* [1997] 2 Cr App R (S) 144, where a 45-year-old man with no previous convictions pleaded guilty to having sexual intercourse with a girl of 12 who was described as 'alert, precocious and sexually experienced'. In *Luff* (1986) 8 Cr App R (S) 318 the offender committed a series of indecent assaults and unlawful sexual intercourse on his step daughter, starting when she was aged nine. The Court of Appeal said that there was no error in principle in a sentence of six years' imprisonment for the unlawful sexual intercourse and three years concurrent for the indecent assault, though it was a 'sentence at the top of the appropriate range, perhaps very near the top of it'. In *Robertson* (1988) 10 Cr App R (S) 183, however, a total of ten years' imprisonment was upheld on an offender who was convicted, after a trial, of four counts of indecent assault and one of unlawful sexual intercourse committed on his two stepdaughters, with whom the offender had sexual intercourse on several occasions over a period of years, threatening them with being taken into a home if they told their mother. Hazan J in the Court of Appeal, said that:

> This court approaches its task in this case only too conscious of the increase of sexual child abuse, especially within the home and the concern that is felt about that matter and the need to protect children not only from physical injury but from appalling psychological damage which may blight their lives as they grow from adolescence into adulthood.

In *A-G's Reference (No. 4 of 1991)* (1992) 13 Cr App R (S) 182 the Court of Appeal said that the most useful guide for sentencing in a case of unlawful sexual intercourse on a girl aged under 13 committed by her stepfather were the guidelines for cases of incest given in *A-G's Reference (No. 1 of 1989)* [1989] 1 WLR 1117 (see **12.3.5**).

The guideline case on sentencing for unlawful sexual intercourse with a girl aged under 16 is still the rather dated case of *Taylor* (1977) 64 Cr App R 183. According to Lawton LJ:

> At one end of [the] spectrum is the youth who stands in the dock, maybe 16, 17 or 18, who has had what started off as a virtuous friendship with a girl under the age of 16. That virtuous friendship has ended with them having sexual intercourse with one another. At the other end of the spectrum is the man in a supervisory capacity, a schoolmaster or social worker, who sets out deliberately to seduce a girl under the age of 16 who is in his charge. The penalties appropriate for the two types of case to which I have just referred are very different indeed.

In the former type of case, Lawton LJ said that there was no need to pass a punitive sentence. In the latter type, he said that a man in a supervisory capacity who abuses his position of trust for sexual gratification ought to get a sentence somewhere near the maximum of two years. He took the view that in between there come many degrees of guilt.

Court of Appeal decisions illustrate cases in the upper reaches of the tariff for this offence. In *Goy* (1986) 8 Cr App R (S) 40 the offender pleaded guilty to two counts of unlawful sexual intercourse and admitted having sexual intercourse with his stepdaughter on four occasions. A sentence of two years' imprisonment was upheld. A sentence of 15 months was upheld in *Dewar* (1986) 8 Cr App R (S) 311, where the victim was the 14-year-old stepsister of the offender's wife and was spending the night at the offender's house. The victim had been drinking during the evening, and the offender, aged 30, went to her room in the night and had sexual intercourse with her. In *Kalkan* (1992) 13 Cr App R (S) 547 the offender pleaded guilty to unlawful sexual intercourse with a girl aged 14, the daughter of the woman with whom he was living at the time. A sentence of 21 months' imprisonment was reduced to nine months by the Court of Appeal, on the basis that the girl was sexually experienced and was at the time of the offence acting as a prostitute. In *Carter* [1997] 1 Cr App R (S) 434 a 32-year-old man pleaded guilty to having sexual intercourse on one occasion with a 14-year-old girl, who was the daughter of a neighbour. She became pregnant and gave birth to a child. A sentence of six months' imprisonment was appropriate.

12.3.3   Indecent assault

The maximum penalty for indecent assault, whether committed on a male or on a female, is ten years on indictment; six months, a fine not exceeding the statutory maximum, or both, summarily (SOA 1956, sch. 2).

When dealt with summarily, the Magistrates' Association Guidelines (2000) indicate the following:

Aggravating Factors +
  vulnerable victim, breach of trust, age differential, injury (may be psychiatric), very young victim, prolonged assault, victim deliberately targeted, victim serving public, racial aggravation, offence committed on bail, previous convictions and failure to respond to previous sentences, if relevant.

Mitigating Factors −
  slight contact.

The Guidelines state that the magistrates should consider whether the offence is so serious that only custody is appropriate and consider whether magistrates' powers are appropriate.

In the Crown Court in 1998, there were 1,747 offenders sentenced for indecent assault on a female. Of those 1,200 received immediate custody and 70 received a suspended sentence. Of the remaining cases, 298 received CROs and 27 CPOs, 30 were discharged, 23 were fined, 40 received supervision orders and 22 CPROs; 102 were otherwise dealt with. By comparison, 381 cases of indecent assault on a male were sentenced, of which 263 received immediate custody and 91 received a probation or supervision order. In the magistrates' courts in 1998, 426 offenders were sentenced for indecent assault on a female. Of those 92 received immediate custody. The most frequently used disposals were CROs (131), discharge (73), fine (58), CPOs (26) and CPOs (20). For indecent assault on a man, magistrates dealt with 34 cases, of which four received custody. The most frequently used sentences were CROs or supervision orders (20) and conditional discharge (5).

For very serious cases of indecent assault, a sentence approaching the maximum will be approved. In *Sheen* (1987) 9 Cr App R (S) 164 the offender pleaded guilty to false imprisonment, indecent assault and assault occasioning actual bodily harm. The offender accosted a young woman, grabbed her by the hair and forced her into his car. He then indecently assaulted her in various ways, including ejaculating into her mouth. She eventually escaped. The offender had previous convictions for indecent assault. A sentence of eight years was upheld. Many of the worse cases concern indecent assaults committed on children by offenders who were in a position of authority, such offences often being repeated regularly over periods of time. In *A-G's Reference (No. 12 of 1994)* (1995) 16 Cr App R (S) 559 the offender was convicted of six offences of indecent assault, one of abduction of a girl and one of attempted rape. He persistently assaulted very young girls who were the daughters of his neighbours, or friends of his own children, at intervals over ten years. The Court of Appeal held that the original sentence of four and a half years was unduly lenient, and increased it to seven years.

Other examples of indecent assault which fall into a bracket somewhat below those cases are *Taylor* [1997] 1 Cr App R (S) 36, where the offender was a volunteer worker who indecently assaulted four disabled women while escorting them from one railway station to another — four years upheld; *Pike* [1996] 1 Cr App R (S) 4, where the offender pretended to be a hypnotherapist and conducted vaginal examinations on patients — four years upheld; *A-G's Reference (No. 25 of 1997)* [1998] 1 Cr App R (S) 310, where the offender sexually harassed a 15-year-old girl on work placement in his shop — a fine was increased to 12 months on appeal. In *Edwards* (1993) 14 Cr App R (S) 79 sentences of nine months for indecently assaulting two young women in the street by grabbing at their breasts, so that their clothes were torn and one of the women fell to the ground, were reduced to six months, on compassionate grounds and in the light of a psychiatric report prepared on the offender. In *Lennon* [1999] 1 Cr App R (S) 19 the offender had masturbated in the presence of his partner's nine-year-old daughter and had pulled off some of her clothes. Two years' imprisonment was upheld.

A case where a non-custodial sentence was approved was *Ariquat* (1981) 3 Cr App R (S) 83, where the offender had sexual intercourse with a 15-year-old girl with her consent. As he believed her to be over 16, he did not commit the offence of unlawful sexual intercourse. A conditional discharge was regarded as being the proper sentence. A custodial sentence was held to be 'wrong in principle' in *Neem* (1993) 14 Cr App R (S) 18, where the offender, who was convicted of indecent assault, had pressed against a young woman in an underground train in an indecent manner. Noting that 'cases of this kind are usually dealt with in the magistrates' courts', the Court of Appeal substituted a fine of £300, together with a compensation order for £250, and costs. In *Diallo* [2000] 1 Cr App R (S) 426, however, where the assault took place in similar circumstances but was planned and the amount was persisted in, a custodial sentence of three months was upheld.

12.3.4 Indecency with children

The maximum penalty for gross indecency with or towards a child aged under 14 (or inciting a child under 14 to commit an act of gross indecency) is ten years on indictment; six months, a fine not exceeding the statutory maximum, or both, summarily (Indecency with Children Act 1960, s. 1) The ten-year maximum applies to offences committed after 1997. Before then the maximum was two years. Related offences are those of possession of indecent photographs of children (CJA 1988, s. 160) the maximum penalty for which is increased by the CJCSA 2000 from six months (summary only) to five years on indictment, and taking or distributing indecent photographs of a child (Protection of Children Act 1978, s. 1), the maximum penalty for which is increased by the CJCSA 2000 from three years to ten years. For guidance on sentencing in a case involving downloading child pornography from the internet see *Toomer* [2001] Crim LR 149, but this guidance does not take account of the increase in the available maximum.

12.3.5 Incest

The maximum penalty for incest by a man with a girl aged under 13 is life imprisonment (SOA 1956, sch. 2). The maximum for incest by a man with a female over 13 is seven years (SOA 1956, sch. 2). The maximum for incest by a woman is seven years (SOA 1956, sch. 2). The maxima for attempts to commit the offence in these three circumstances are seven years, two years and two years, respectively. The maximum for incitement by a man of a girl under 16, whom he knows to be his granddaughter, daughter or sister to have sexual intercourse with him is two years on indictment; six months or a fine not exceeding the statutory maximum, or both, summarily (CLA 1977, s. 54). There were 47 incest cases sentenced in the Crown Court in 1998; 39 received immediate custody. There were five CROs, one supervision order and two discharges. In the magistrates' courts incest cases were all committed for trial to the Crown Court.

The guideline case is *A-G's Reference (No. 1 of 1989)* [1989] 1 WLR 1117. According to Lord Lane CJ, the gravity of incest varies greatly according to the age of the victim and the degree of coercion or corruption. At one end of the scale, he said, is incest committed by a father with a daughter in her later teens, or older, who is a willing participant and indeed may be the instigator. In such a case, little if any punishment is required. The most difficult area is that involving girls under the age of 13. As in the case of those between 13 and 16, sexual intercourse is an offence, quite apart from the parental relationship. For victims under the age of 13, however, a further factor comes into play. Although the girl may 'consent' to the act of intercourse in such a way as to render a charge of rape inappropriate, the girl is in a particularly vulnerable position, which the father is in a position to exploit. The following guide was suggested, on the assumption that there has been no plea of guilty:

(a) *Where the girl is over 16.* A range from three years down to a nominal penalty will be appropriate depending on whether force was used, the degree of harm, if any, to the girl, and the desirability, where appropriate, of keeping family disruption to a minimum. The lower the degree of corruption, the lower the penalty.

(b) *Where the girl is aged from 13 to 16.* Terms of custody of between about five years and three years will be appropriate. Much the same principles will apply as in (a), though the likelihood of corruption is greater here.

(c) *Where the girl is aged under 13.* It is here that the widest range of sentence is likely to be found. If one can properly describe any case of incest as the 'ordinary' type of case, it will be one where the sexual relationship between husband and wife has broken down, the father has probably resorted to excessive drinking and the eldest daughter is gradually, by way of familiarities, indecent acts and suggestions, made the object of the father's frustrated sexual inclinations. If the girl is not far short of her thirteenth birthday and there are no particularly adverse or unfavourable features on a not guilty plea, a term of about six years would seem to be appropriate. The younger the girl when the sexual approach is started, the more likely it will be that the girl's will was overborne and accordingly the more serious would be the crime.

Other aggravating factors, whatever the age of the girl may be, include the following:

(a)   If the girl has suffered physically or psychologically from the incest.

(b)   If the incest has continued at frequent intervals over a long period of time.

(c)   If the girl has been threatened or treated violently by, or was terrified of, the father.

(d)   If the incest has been accompanied by perversions abhorrent to the girl, e.g. buggery or fellatio.

(e)   If the girl has become pregnant by reason of the father failing to take contraceptive measures.

(f)   If the defendant has committed similar offences against more than one girl.

Possible mitigating features include the following:

(a)   A plea of guilty, which should be met by an appropriate discount, depending on how promptly the offender confessed, his degree of contrition etc.

(b)   If it seems that there was genuine affection on the offender's part, rather than the mere use of the girl as an outlet for his sexual inclinations.

(c)   Where the girl has had previous sexual experience.

(d)   Where the girl has made deliberate attempts at seduction.

(e)   Where, as very occasionally is the case, a shorter term of imprisonment for the father may be of benefit to the victim and the family.

12.3.6   Buggery

If the offender is aged 21 or over and the other person is under 16, the maximum is five years, but otherwise two years. Where buggery of a male or female victim is committed without consent, the offence committed is rape, not buggery (see **12.3.1**). The Crown Court sentenced 141 cases of buggery in 1998, 108 of which received custodial sentences. The maximum penalty for buggery committed with an animal is life imprisonment.

The Guideline case is still the rather old case of *Willis* (1974) 60 Cr App R 146, which deals with buggery committed between an adult and a male partner under the age of 16 at a time when the age of consent was 21. Lawton LJ said that in the absence of strong mitigating factors the offence should result in immediate custody. Should there be neither aggravating nor mitigating factors, the correct bracket is three to five years, with placement in the bracket depending on the age, intelligence and education of the offender.

Aggravating factors include:

(a) physical injury to the boy, whether by the penetration itself or by the use of force to overcome his resistance;

(b) emotional and psychological damage to the victim;

(c) moral corruption (e.g. use of gifts to corrupt boys);

(d) abuse of authority or trust.

Mitigating factors include the offender having been in a state of emotional stress or suffering from mental illness. Where the offender is suffering from a personality disorder which does not justify a hospital order, Lawton LJ advised that a CRO with a condition of psychiatric treatment might be appropriate, but if the offender represents a danger to boys if at liberty a lengthy custodial sentence will be necessary to protect other victims.

In *Malloy* [1997] 1 Cr App R (S) 189 the offender was convicted of buggery and indecent assault on a boy aged 15 at a time when the age of consent was 18. They both worked at a café and the offender took advantage of a relationship which had developed between them. The victim went in the offender's car to a car park where the offences took place. Five years' imprisonment was the appropriate sentence for the buggery, with three years concurrent for the indecent assault. In *A-G's Reference (No. 31 of 1996)* [1997] 1 Cr App R (S) 308 the offender, a man with no convictions, pleaded guilty to one count of buggery with a boy of 13, a count of rape not having been proceeded with. Payment of £10 was made. The Court of Appeal said that the sentence was unduly lenient and increased it from two years to three and a half years.

Where consenting parties to a homosexual act are both over the age of consent, but the act is still a criminal offence because of its taking place in a cubicle in a public lavatory, a custodial sentence is wrong in principle (*Tosland* (1981) 3 Cr App R (S) 265). The case was followed in *Bedborough* (1984) 6 Cr App R (S) 98. In these cases the Court of Appeal said that the proper sentence would have been a fine.

12.3.7 Gross indecency between men

The maximum penalty for gross indecency beween men, if by a man of or over the age of 21 with a man under the age of 16, is five years. Otherwise the maximum is two years, on indictment; six months, a fine not exceeding the statutory maximum, or both, summarily (SOA 1956, sch. 2). In the Crown Court there were seven such cases in 1998; immediate custody was given in three cases. In magistrates' courts 183 cases were sentenced; the great majority (131) were fined and 43 received conditional discharges.

The guideline case on the offence of gross indecency between men is *Morgan* (1978) CSP B4-9.2B, where the offenders, aged 61 and 39, had been seen committing an act of gross indecency in a public lavatory. Lawton LJ said that:

In general first offenders using public lavatories and behaving in this sort of way in them do not get sent to prison. They are generally fined. On occasions they may be put on probation or some other non-custodial order is made . . . Occasionally those who are convicted persist in this kind of behaviour and when they do, prison sentences may be appropriate.

See also *Clayton* (1981) 3 Cr App R (S) 67. In a case of importuning for an immoral purpose, *Gray* (1981) 3 Cr App R (S) 363, a fine was also held to be the appropriate sentence.

12.3.8   Offences related to prostitution

The maximum penalty for living on the earnings of prostitution is seven years on indictment; six months, a fine not exceeding the statutory maximum, or both, summarily (SOA 1956, sch. 2). The maximum for loitering or soliciting for the purposes of prostitution is (for an offence committed after conviction for a similar offence), a fine not exceeding level 3 on the standard scale; otherwise a fine not exceeding level 2 on the standard scale (Street Offences Act 1959, s. 1); this offence is triable only summarily. The maximum for 'kerb-crawling' is a fine not exceeding level 3 on the standard scale (SOA 1985, s. 1(2)); this offence is triable only summarily. Cases of prostitution and kerb crawling are dealt with in the magistrates' courts, and are usually dealt with by way of fine. Sentencing patterns for the offences in 1996 were as follows:

(a)   soliciting by a woman: 5,237 cases, of which 4,591 were fined, 539 discharged, and 47 placed on curfew orders;

(b)   soliciting by a man: 41 cases, of which 33 were fined, six discharged and two received CROs;

(c)   kerb crawling: 766 cases, of which 738 were fined and 27 discharged.

In the case of *Farrugia* (1979) 69 Cr App R 108, Lawton LJ said that the crucial factor in sentencing in cases of living on immoral earnings is whether there is any evidence of coercion, whether physical or mental, of the prostitutes involved or of corruption. A sentence exceeding two years should, he said, be reserved for cases where there is such coercion or corruption. In *Thomas* (1983) 5 Cr App R (S) 138 the Court of Appeal said that three years was proper, despite exceeding Lawton LJ's guidelines, since the offender had a history of similar offending. In *Kirk* (1995) 16 Cr App R (S) 895, where there were no relevant aggravating factors, a nine months' sentence was upheld.

Other cases concern the running of 'escort agencies' or 'massage parlours'. In *El-Gazzar* (1986) 8 Cr App R (S) 182, a sentence of 12 months for living on the earnings of prostitution was upheld on an offender who operated an escort agency.

Martin (1988) 10 Cr App R (S) 339 was a case where the offender was convicted of keeping a disorderly house where various sexual activities were offered for payment. No other prostitute was involved but the offender had previously been fined for a similar offence. Nine months was reduced to three months, to take account of the relatively small scale of the activites involved. By contrast, in *Malik* [1998] 1 Cr App R (S) 115, where the offender maintained premises for use by 40 prostitutes, a sentence of two years was upheld.

12.4   SENTENCING FOR THEFT AND RELATED OFFENCES

12.4.1   Theft

The maximum penalty for theft is seven years (Theft Act 1968, s. 1(7)) on indictment; six months or a fine not exceeding the statutory maximum, or both, summarily. Where triable either way, the *Practice Note* (*Mode of Trial: Guidelines*) (1995) state that theft should, in general, be tried summarily, unless the court considers that one or more of the following features is present in the case and that its sentencing powers are insufficient:

(a)   breach of trust by a person in a position of substantial authority, or in whom a high degree of trust is placed;

(b)   theft which has been committed or disguised in a sophisticated manner;

(c)   theft committed by an organised gang;

(d)   the victim is particularly vulnerable to theft (e.g. the elderly or infirm);

(e)   the unrecovered property is of high value (at least £10,000).

Theft is such a wide offence that there is little which can be said by way of general sentencing guidance. In *Upton* (1980) 2 Cr App R (S) 132, where the offender was convicted of theft of goods worth £5 from the supermarket of which he was deputy manager, Lord Lane CJ said:

This was petty theft and in ordinary circumstances it would, and should, not have attracted any immediate sentence of imprisonment . . . non-violent petty offenders should not be allowed to take up what has become valuable space in prison. If there really is no alternative . . . to an immediate prison sentence, then it should be as short as possible . . . a prison sentence, however short, is a very unpleasant experience indeed for the inmates.

When dealt with summarily, the Magistrates' Association Guidelines (2000) indicate the following guideline for theft:

Aggravating Factors +
   high value, planned, sophisticated, racial aggravation; adult involving children; organised team, related damage, vulnerable victim, offence committed on bail, previous convictions and failures to respond to previous sentences, if relevant.

Mitigating Factors −
   impulsive action, low value.

The Guidelines indicate that magistrates should consider whether serious enough for a community penalty.

For practical sentencing purposes the offence of theft is subdivided into several specific forms of the offence:

(a)   theft from shops;

(b)   theft from vehicles;

(c)   theft from the person;

(d)   theft in breach of trust.

(a)   *Theft from shops.*   In 1998, the Crown Court sentenced 2,125 offenders for shoplifting; of these 1,043 received custodial sentences (almost 50 per cent) and 53 suspended sentences. The most frequently used other disposals were CRO (411), conditional discharge (154), fine (110) and CPO (235). In the magistrates' courts in 1998, 64,321 offenders were sentenced for shoplifting; 8,519 received immediate custody. Overwhelmingly the most frequent disposals were the fine (19,759) and the discharge (19,136). CROs accounted for 9,461, and CPOs 2,733.

Court of Appeal decisions indicate that shoplifting should not attract a custodial sentence, unless the offender has a record of similar offending, the shoplifting was carefully planned and executed or there were other aggravating features. In *Ball* (1981) 3 Cr App R (S) 283, an old case but still a helpful authority, a suspended sentence for shoplifting a small quantity of children's clothes was quashed. The offender was a single woman aged 18 with one child, lived on social security benefit and was in breach of a conditional discharge imposed for handling stolen goods. That was her only previous conviction. Holding that 'this was not the sort of case which merited imprisonment at all, whether immediate or suspended', and accepting advice from the social enquiry report that the offender was not in need of supervision, the Court of Appeal substituted a small fine with six months in which to pay as being 'the least wrong course which is open to us'.

Where a custodial sentence is imposed for shoplifting, it will generally be very short. In *Roth* (1980) 2 Cr App R (S) 65 a one-month prison sentence was regarded as being a proper disposal for a man aged 58 who, together with his wife, committed a carefully planned theft from a shop involving goods to the value of £91; see also *MacLeod* (1981) 3 Cr App R (S) 247 (planned shoplifting of £100 worth of drink from supermarket; six weeks' imprisonment upheld). Much longer custodial sentences will be upheld in shoplifting cases where the offender has a serious record of similar offending (e.g. *Reeves* (1980) 2 Cr App R (S) 36: three-year sentence on offender sentenced for 40 shoplifting offences with 20 previous convictions for similar offences) or where 'professional' shoplifters are at work (e.g. *Jones* (1979) 1 Cr App R (S) 136: four years upheld on offenders with 'lamentable' criminal histories who stole £300 worth of records by use of a specially made box for concealing them). Taking young children along when shoplifting is regarded by the courts as a serious aggravating feature (*Moss* (1986) 8 Cr App R (S) 276).

(b) *Theft from vehicles.* In 1998 the Crown Court sentenced 100 offenders for theft from vehicles; of these 52 received custodial sentences. In magistrates' courts in 1998, 4,214 offenders were sentenced for theft from vehicles; only 658 received immediate custody (16 per cent). The most frequent disposals were the fine (1,011) and the discharge (842).

(c) *Theft from the person.* This category covers the taking of articles from handbags, shopping bags and the activities of pickpockets. In 1998 the Crown Court sentenced 2,437 offenders for theft from the person; of these 1,394 received custodial sentences (around 57 per cent). The most frequently used other disposals were CPOs (285), CROs (290), fine (96), and conditional discharge (134). In magistrates' courts in 1998, 3,614 offenders were sentenced for theft from the person; 722 received immediate custody (20 per cent). The most frequent disposals were the fine (748) and the discharge (853).

While recognising that the majority of cases involving theft from the person are dealt with by non-custodial sentences, custodial sentences have sometimes been upheld by the Court of Appeal, particularly in cases where the offender has a record of similar offending. One example is *Benon* (1982) 4 Cr App R (S) 45, where two years' imprisonment was upheld on an offender who had been 'at the pickpocketing game' since 1975. Another, said to be a case of 'professional' pickpocketing, is *Wilson* (1979) 1 Cr App R (S) 102, where three years' imprisonment was upheld on offenders who worked as a team, one distracting the victims while the other stole from the victim's bag; they had numerous previous convictions for similar offences. In *Masagh* (1990) 12 Cr App R (S) 568 Lloyd LJ stressed that while heavy custodial sentences were appropriate for systematic pickpocketing they were quite wrong for isolated offences committed by an individual.

(d) *Theft in breach of trust.* While this category of theft is well recognised in the case-law, it does not appear separately in the criminal statistics. The figures given below are derived by adding together the categories of 'theft by employee' and 'theft or unauthorised taking from mail' from the 1998 statistics. It is thought that this will give a good impresssion of the sentencing range used by the courts. In 1998, the Crown Court sentenced 488 offenders for theft in breach of trust; of these 251 received custodial sentences (51 per cent) and there were 38 suspended sentences. The other disposal most frequently used was the CPO (111). In magistrates' courts in 1998, 2,415 offenders were sentenced for theft in breach of trust; only 248 received immediate custody (10 per cent). The most frequent disposals were the CPO (755), the fine (440) and the discharge (415).

When this category of offence is dealt with summarily, the Magistrates' Association Guidelines (2000) note the following:

Aggravating Factors +
casting suspicion on others, racial aggravation, committed over a period, large amount, high value, organised team, planned, senior employee, sophisticated, vulnerable victim, offence committed on bail, previous convictions and failures to respond to previous sentences, if relevant.

Mitigating Factors −
impulsive action, low value, previous inconsistent attitude by employer, single item, unsupported junior.

The Guidelines indicate that magistrates should consider whether the offence is so serious that only custody is appropriate, and consider whether summary powers are appropriate.

The Guideline case of *Barrick* (1985) 7 Cr App R (S) 142 is concerned with cases towards the top end of the range of this offending normally dealt with in the Crown Court, where:

a person in a position of trust, for example, an accountant, solicitor, bank employee or postman, has used that privileged and trusted position to defraud his partners or clients or employers or the general public of sizeable sums of money. He will usually, as in this case, be a person of impeccable character. It is practically certain, again as in this case, that he will never offend again and, in the nature of things, he will never again in his life be able to secure similar employment with all that that means in the shape of disgrace for himself and hardship for himself and his family.

The *Barrick* guidelines indicate that such a case will attract immediate custody, save in very exceptional circumstances, or where the sum involved is small. Where the sum is less than £17,500, sentences ranging from the very short up to 21 months are appropriate. Where the sum is between, £17,500 and £100,000 the appropriate range is two to three years. For thefts totalling between £100,000 and £250,000 the range is three to four years, where the theft is between £250,000 and £1 million the range is five to nine years, and in cases where the theft is over £1 million the custodial sentence length will be 10 years or more. It should be noted that these figures are taken not from *Barrick* itself, but from the case of *Clark* [1998] 2 Cr App R (S) 137, which updated the sentencing brackets accordingly to take account of the effect of inflation, the reduction in the maximum penalty for theft from 10 years to seven years by the CJA 1991 and the effect of the *Practice Statement (Crime: Sentencing)* [1992] 1 WLR 948 (see **4.5**). These figures assume that the case is contested; in the event of a guilty plea, an appropriate discount should be given. Other matters to be taken into account by the court, apart from the size of the sum involved, are:

(a)   the quality and degree of trust reposed in the offender;
(b)   the period over which the thefts were committed;
(c)   the use to which the money was put;
(d)   the effect upon the victim;
(e)   the impact on the public and public confidence;
(f)   the effect upon fellow employees or partners;
(g)   the effect on the offender;
(h)   the offender's own history;
(i)   matters of mitigation special to the offender; and
(j)   any help given by the offender to the police.

The offender in *Clark* was employed as a bursar of the Royal Academy and he also acted as treasurer of his local church. The prosecution case was that in respect of both of these he had abused his position of trust in order to steal just under £400,000 from his employers and £29,000 from the church. It was significant for the purposes of sentence that the offender had been dishonest in two different directions and this would have entitled the trial judge to have passed consecutive sentences on the two counts. The offences were aggravated by the degree of trust reposed in the offender, the period of four years over which the offences took place and the fact that the money was spent on personal expenditure which was partly of an extravagant kind. The offender's good character, his frankness and co-operation, and pleas of guilty at the first available opportunity were among the factors mitigating the sentence in this case. It was also significant that he had repaid some £120,000. The total sentence of five years imposed by the trial judge was excessive, and the court quashed that and substituted a sentence of three years' imprisonment on count 1 and one year's imprisonment on count 2, the sentences to run consecutively.

12.4.2   Handling stolen goods

The maximum penalty for handling is 14 years (Theft Act 1968, s. 22(2)) on indictment; six months or a fine not exceeding the statutory maximum, or both, summarily. The *Practice Note (Mode of Trial: Guidelines)* (1995) state that handling stolen goods should, in general, be tried summarily unless the court considers that one or more of the following features is present in the case and that its sentencing powers are insufficient:

(a)   dishonest handling of stolen property by a receiver who has commissioned the theft;
(b)   the offence has professional hallmarks;
(c)   the property is of high value (at least £10,000).

When tried summarily, the Magistrates' Association Guidelines (2000) indicate the following:

Aggravating Factors +
    adult involving children, high value, organiser or distributor, offence committed on bail, previous convictions and failures to respond to previous sentences, if relevant.

Mitigating Factors −
    for personal use, impulsive action, low value, no financial gain, not part of a sophisticated operation, single item.

The Guidelines indicate that magistrates should consider whether the offence is serious enough for a community penalty.

In 1998 the Crown Court sentenced 3,902 offenders for handling stolen goods. Those receiving immediate custody totalled 1,762, and there were 105 suspended sentences. The most frequently used other disposals were CPO (694), CRO (645), conditional discharge (199), CRO (245) and fine (191). In magistrates' courts in 1998, 14,200 offenders were sentenced for handling stolen goods. Only 1,854 received custodial sentences. The most frequent disposals were the fine (3,200), the conditional discharge (3,144), CRO (2,332), CPO (1,861) and CPRO (629).

The maximum penalty available for handling stolen goods is significantly higher than that available for theft, reflecting the view that some cases of handling may be more serious than any case of theft. Long custodial sentences are, however, rare, being reserved for cases where the handler was closely involved in a large-scale criminal enterprise. In *Patel* (1984) 6 Cr App R (S) 191 a sentence of four years was upheld on a man who received 660 cartons of cigarettes, worth £160,000, part of a larger consignment worth £1 million which had been stolen from a manufacturer's depot. The offender had previously served a six-year term for importing drugs. Lord Lane CJ said that:

> Proper penalties for cases of handling will vary enormously according to the circumstances. At the top end of the scale come the cases where the handler provides an outlet for the proceeds of very substantial thefts or robberies, where the advantages to the thief of having such an outlet are very great and where accordingly the receiver or handler is indirectly encouraging the thefts to take place, and where also the profits to the handler are likewise very great, as plainly they were going to be here . . .

See also *Hutchings* (1994) 15 Cr App R (S) 498. Where a 'fence' deals directly with thieves or burglars, and provides a regular outlet for whatever property they may steal, sentences in a bracket of two to four years will be appropriate. In *Byrne* (1994) 15 Cr App R (S) 34 a sentence of 15 months was upheld for handling stolen computers worth £48,000 and in *Amlani* (1995) 16 Cr App R (S) 339 the appropriate sentence for handling a large number of stolen mobile phones was 21 months. Most handlers receive non-custodial sentences. For the 'one-off', opportunistic offence, the Court of Appeal has indicated that a fine will often be the correct penalty. In *Webbe and Others* (2 May 2001, unreported) the Court of Appeal issued sentencing guidelines for this offence, closely based upon a proposal submitted to it by the Sentencing Advisory Panel.

12.4.3 Robbery

The maximum penalty for robbery is life imprisonment (Theft Act 1968, s. 8(2)). This offence is triable only on indictment. In 1998 the Crown Court sentenced 4,325 offenders for robbery. Those receiving immediate custody, including detention under PCC(S)A 2000 s. 91, totalled 3,734 (over 86 per cent) and there were 16 suspended sentences. The other disposals used were mainly CRO and supervision orders (243), CPO (89), CPRO (134) and hospital order (42).

The combination of violence and theft makes robbery the most serious of the common offences of dishonesty. The great majority of offenders convicted of robbery receive custodial sentences. In *Turner* (1975) 61 Cr App R 67, still the guideline case, there were 19 appellants, members of a gang which over a period of four years had carried out 20 armed robberies on banks and security vans, netting over £1 million at 1975 values. Firearms and ammonia were carried, but used only to frighten, and injuries inflicted were slight. Lawton LJ said that the normal starting point for sentence for anyone taking part in a bank robbery, or in the hold-up of a security vehicle or a Post Office van, should be 15 years, if firearms were carried and no serious injury done. The lack of a previous criminal record is not, he said, to be regarded as a powerful mitigating matter. In *Daly* (1981) 3 Cr App R (S) 340 Lord Lane CJ indicated that in a bank robbery type of case the most serious features calling for heavy sentences:

> are detailed planning, use of loaded firearms or ammonia, where a number of men execute a planned attack on a bank or similar target in the hope of stealing substantial sums of money, where the participants are masked and armed either with guns, handguns or sawn-off shotguns, or sometimes with ammonia, and squirt ammonia into the faces of clients or staff of the bank in order to overpower resistance. In such cases, as Lawton LJ in *Turner* . . . has rightly said, a starting point of 15 years is correct. It may be, and no doubt will in nearly every case where there has been a plea of guilty, possible to reduce that term in the light of the plea and in the light of assistance given to the police and other mitigating factors. It may be necessary on the other hand in some cases to increase the starting number of years because of the number of offences which the particular defendant has committed during the course of his depredation.

In *Gould* (1983) 5 Cr App R (S) 72 Lord Lane CJ confirmed that the *Turner* guidelines remained the basis for sentencing in armed robbery offences. He also added that some of the features likely to mitigate an offence are:

(a)   a plea of guilty;
(b)   the youth of the offender;
(c)   a previously clean record;
(d)   the fact that the defendant had no companion when committing the offence; and
(e)   the fact that no one was injured.

Against these matters must be weighed, amongst other things:

(a)   that a real, rather than an imitation, weapon was used;
(b)   that the weapon was discharged;
(c)   that violence was used upon the victim;
(d)   that a number of men took part in the attack;
(e)   that careful reconaissance and planning were involved; and
(f)   that there was more than one offence committed by the offender.

For robberies in the so-called 'first division', which are the subject of the guideline cases described above, the normal starting point is 15 years. Sentences of 18 years and 17 years were imposed in *Knight* (1981) 3 Cr App R (S) 211 and *Reed* (1988) 10 Cr App R (S) 243 respectively. Wholly abnormal crimes, such as the Great Train Robbery, will attract sentences in excess of 18 years (*Wilson* (1964) 48 Cr App R 329). The 'irreducible minimum' in such cases is said to be 11 years (*Davis* (1980) 2 Cr App R (S) 168).

Robberies at sub-post offices, shops and similar premises will also attract substantial custodial sentences, though generally in a bracket below the 'first division' for the offence.

The relevant aggravating and mitigating factors appear to be very similar to those cited in that context. In *Stanford* (1988) 10 Cr App R (S) 222 the offenders, aged between 20 and 22, pleaded guilty to two counts of robbery, two of attempted robbery and two of taking a conveyance. In the robberies, they had entered post offices, threatened the owners with an imitation firearm and demanded money. A sentence of seven years was upheld on the offender who 'was the front man with the gun'. Sentences on the others were reduced to five years to take account of the fact that no actual violence was used and that the offenders gave up their attempts very easily when meeting any resistance, their guilty pleas, previous good character and ages. In *A-G's Reference (Nos. 26 and 27 of 1996)* [1997] 1 Cr App R (S) 243 sentences of four and a half years' detention in a young offender institution for robberies at building society branches in which imitation firearms were brandished were increased to seven and a half years. In *A-G's Reference (No. 3 of 1990)* (1991) 92 Cr App R 166 the Court of Appeal dealt with four separate references and increased custodial sentences on seven offenders involved in robberies of small shops, off-licences and similar premises; in each case the sentences were increased to ranges between three and a half and six years.

A third category of robbery is street robbery or 'mugging'. The Court of Appeal's approved tariff seems to be in a bracket of two to five years, although six years was upheld in *Buck* [2000] 1 Cr App R (S) 42 where two elderly ladies were robbed after collecting their pensions. Custodial terms of five years were reduced to three years in *Brennan* (1980) 2 Cr App R (S) 250, 'a typical case of mugging', where the offenders, both with substantial records, had jostled and punched a man in a public lavatory and stolen his wallet containing £63. The victim did not require medical attention. In *A-G's Reference (No. 6 of 1994)* (1994) 16 Cr App R (S) 343 a community service order was held to be an unduly lenient sentence on an offender who accosted an 18-year-old victim and made him hand over his pay packet. A female mugger received 30 months in *Williams* (1982) 4 Cr App R (S) 156. A case at the lower end of seriousness is *Golding* (1992) 13 Cr App R (S) 142, where a sentence of six months' detention in a young offender institution was upheld on an 18-year-old youth who had accosted a 16-year-old and threatened to beat him up if he did not hand over his bicycle. Despite a guilty plea and the offender's good record, it was held that the offence was so serious that a non-custodial sentence could not be justified. See also *Pretty* (1992) 13 Cr App R (S) 280.

Finally, where victims are attacked in their own homes, sentence varies according to the degree of violence used and the value of the property taken. In *Clark* (1994) 16 Cr App R (S) 546 the offender, together with two others, attacked a 69-year-old woman and beat her about the head, fracturing her cheekbone. A sentence of 11 years' imprisonment was correct. In *Skilton* (1982) 4 Cr App R (S) 339 a sentence of three and a half years was held to be proper where the offenders tricked their way into the home of a blind man, tied him up and then made off with his £28 social security payment.

12.4.4 Blackmail

The maximum penalty for blackmail is 14 years (Theft Act 1968, s. 21(3)). It is triable only on indictment. In 1998 the Crown Court sentenced 179 offenders for blackmail; of those 136 received immediate custody and 9 suspended sentences. Other disposals included CRO (10), CPO (14) and CPRO (5).

Sentences of six years and five years were reduced to four years and three years in *Cox* (1979) 1 Cr App R (S) 190, where the offenders removed valuable computer discs and tapes from their employer and demanded £275,000 as the price for returning them. In *Read* [1996] 2 Cr App R (S) 240 the offender wrote to a clergyman and threatened to make fake allegations of homosexual behaviour unless £7,000 was paid. The proper sentence was 21 months' imprisonment. *Riolfo* [1997] 1 Cr App R (S) 57 is a case where the offender telephoned a supermarket to say that food on the shelves had been contaminated with the AIDS virus. He demanded £250,000 and received £7,500. Eight years' imprisonment was reduced to six on appeal. In a 'wholly exceptional' case, where the claim which was made was on the face of it warranted, but improper means were used to enforce the claim (threat to publish nude photographs of the victim) a sentence of six months' imprisonment, suspended for two years was imposed (*Helal* (1980) 2 Cr App R (S) 383). See also *West* (1985) 7 Cr App R (S) 46, where the offender kidnapped the victim's dog and demanded money for its safe return.

12.4.5 Burglary

When sentencing for this offence, a distinction is drawn between burglaries from dwellings and burglaries from buildings other than dwellings, such as shops, offices, commercial premises and schools.

(a) *Burglary from a dwelling.* The maximum penalty for burglary, when committed in a dwelling is 14 years on indictment; six months or a fine not exceeding the statutory maximum, or both, summarily (Theft Act 1968, s. 9(4)). The offence is triable either way. The *Practice Note* (*Mode of Trial: Guidelines*) (1995) indicate that, in general, cases of burglary committed in a dwelling should be tried summarily unless the magistrates' court considers that one or more of the following features is present and that its sentencing powers are insufficient:

(a) entry in the daytime when the occupier or another person is present;
(b) entry at night of a house which is normally occupied, whether or not occupied at that time;
(c) the offence is alleged to be one of a series of similar offences;
(d) soiling, damage or vandalism has occurred;
(e) the offence has professional hallmarks;
(f) the unrecovered property is of high value (at least £10,000).

If the offence is dealt with summarily, the Magistrates' Association Guidelines (2000) indicate the following:

Aggravating Factors +
    racial motivation, group offence, people in house, occupants frightened, professional operation, forcible entry, repeat victimisation, soiling, ransacking, damage, offence committed on bail, previous convictions and failures to respond to previous sentences, if relevant.

Mitigating Factors −
    low value, nobody frightened, no damage or disturbance, no forcible entry, opportunist.

The Guidelines suggest that magistrates should consider whether the offence is so serious that only custody can be justified and to consider whether summary powers are appropriate.

In 1998 the Crown Court sentenced 11,326 offenders for burglary in a dwelling (excluding aggravated burglary). Those receiving immediate custody totalled 8,435, and there were 103 suspended sentences. The most frequently used other disposals were CRO (1,083) CPO (558), CPRO (643), supervision order (558), discharge (73), hospital order (29), and fine (24). In magistrates' courts in 1998, 6,247 offenders were sentenced for burglary in a dwelling. Of those, 1,493 received custodial sentences. The most frequent other disposals were the supervision order (829), CRO (1,771), CPO (1,413), the discharge (1,646), CPRO (811), attendance centre order (580) and fine (953).

In respect of burglaries from dwellings, in *Brewster* [1998] 1 Cr App R (S) 181 Lord Bingham of Cornhill CJ issued the following sentencing guidance.

Domestic burglary is, and always has been, regarded as a very serious offence. It may involve considerable loss to the victim. Even where it does not, the victim may lose possessions of particular value to him or her. To those who are insured, the receipt of financial compensation does not replace what is lost. But many victims are uninsured: because they may have fewer possessions, they are the more seriously injured by the loss of those they do have.

The loss of material possessions is, however, only part (and often a minor part) of the reason why domestic burglary is a serious offence. Most people, perfectly legitimately, attach importance to the privacy and security of their own homes. That an intruder should break in or enter, for his own dishonest purposes, leaves the victim with a sense of violation and insecurity. Even where the victim is unaware, at the time, that a burglar is in the house, it can be a frightening experience to learn that a burglary has taken place; and it is all the more frightening if the victim confronts or hears the burglar. Generally speaking it is more frightening if the victim is in the house when the burglary takes place, and if the intrusion takes place at night; but that does not mean that the offence is not serious if the victim returns to an empty house during the daytime to find that it has been burgled.

The seriousness of the offence can vary almost infinitely from case to case. It may involve an impulsive act involving an object of little value (reaching through a window to take a bottle of milk, or stealing a can of petrol from an outhouse). At the other end of the spectrum it may involve a professional, planned organisation, directed at objects of high value. Or the offence may be deliberately directed at the elderly, the disabled or the sick, and it may involve repeated burglaries of the same premises. It may sometimes be accompanied by acts of wanton vandalism.

The record of the offender is of more significance in the case of domestic burglary than in the case of some other crimes. There are some professional burglars whose records show that from an early age they have behaved as predators preying on their fellow citizens, returning to their trade almost as soon as each prison sentence has been served. Such defendants must continue to receive substantial terms of imprisonment. There are, however, other domestic burglars whose activities are of a different character, and whose careers may lack any element of persistence or deliberation. They are entitled to more lenient treatment.

It is common knowledge that many domestic burglars are drug addicts who burgle and steal in order to raise money to satisfy their craving for drugs. This is often an expensive craving, and it is not uncommon to learn that addicts commit a burglary, or even several burglaries, each day, often preying on houses in less affluent areas of the country. But to the victim of burglary the motivation of the burglar may well be of secondary interest.

Self-induced addiction cannot be relied on as mitigation. The courts will not be readily persuaded that an addicted offender is genuinely determined and able to conquer his addiction.

Generally speaking, domestic burglaries are the more serious if they are of occupied houses at night; if they are the result of professional planning, organisation or execution; if they are targeted at the elderly, the disabled and the sick; if there are repeated visits to the same premises; if they are committed by persistent offenders; if they are accompanied by vandalism or any wanton injury to the victim; if they are shown to have a seriously traumatic effect on the victim; if the offender operates as one of a group; if goods of high value (whether actual or sentimental) are targeted or taken; if force is used or threatened; if there is a pattern of repeat offending. It mitigates the seriousness of an offence if the offender pleads guilty, particularly if the plea is indicated at an early stage and there is hard evidence of genuine regret and remorse.

Lord Bingham CJ stated that, overall, the cases showed that:

(a)   burglary of a dwelling house, occupied or unoccupied, is not necessarily and in all cases an offence of such seriousness that a non-custodial sentence cannot be justified;

(b)   the decision whether a custodial sentence is required, and if so the length of such sentence, is heavily dependent on the aggravating and mitigating features mentioned above and, usually to a lesser extent, the personal circumstances of the offender;

(c)   the courts, particularly the higher courts, have generally reflected in their sentences the abhorrence with which the public regard those who burgle the houses of others.

This guidance supersedes that which had earlier been provided by the Court of Appeal in *Mussell* [1991] 1 WLR 187 and in *Edwards* (1996) *The Times*, 1 July 1996. In respect of the latter case, Lord Bingham CJ commented that the decision had sought to establish clear sentencing brackets for the offence where it was not possible or desirable to do so, and that it had placed too much emphasis upon a distinction between burglary of occupied and unoccupied houses.

(b)   *Burglary from buildings other than dwellings.*   When committed elsewhere than a dwelling the maximum penalty for burglary is ten years (Theft Act 1968, s. 9(4)). Burglary is triable either way and, when dealt with summarily, the maximum penalty is six months or a fine not exceeding the statutory maximum, or both, summarily. The *Practice Note (Mode of Trial: Guidelines)* (1995) indicate that, in general, cases of burglary committed in premises other than a dwelling should be tried summarily unless the magistrates' court considers that one or more of the following features is present and that its sentencing powers are insufficient:

(a)   entry of a pharmacy or doctor's surgery;

(b)   fear is caused or violence is done to anyone lawfully on the premises, such as a nightwatchman or a security guard;

(c)   the offence has professional hallmarks;

(d)   there has been vandalism on a substantial scale;

(e)   the unrecovered property is of high value (at least £10,000).

If the offence is dealt with summarily, the Magistrates' Association Guidelines (2000) indicate the following:

Aggravating Factors +

racial motivation, occupants frightened, group offence, professional operation, forceable entry, soiling, repeat victimisation, school premises, ransacking, damage, serious harm to business, offence committed on bail, previous convictions and failures to respond to previous sentences, if relevant.

Mitigating Factors −

low value, nobody frightened, no damage or disturbance, no forcible entry.

The Guidelines indicate that magistrates should consider whether the offence is serious enough for a community penalty.

In 1998 the Crown Court sentenced 2,446 offenders for burglary not in a dwelling (excluding aggravated burglary). Those receiving immediate custody totalled 1,795, and there were 27 suspended sentences. The most frequently used other disposals were CRO (265), CRO (162), CPRO (133), discharge (28) and fine (9). In magistrates' courts in 1998, 10,819 offenders were sentenced for burglary not in a dwelling. Of those, 2,610 received custodial sentences. The most frequent other disposals were CRO (1,771), discharge (1,646), CPO (1,413), CPRO (811), supervision order (828), attendance centre order (580) and fine (953).

Burglary from commercial premises, such as factories and offices, has always been considered as somewhat less serious than burglary of someone's home. Ordinarily, the victim will be in a better position to recover from the loss, and commercial burglary does not usually involve the same kind of emotional impact as burglary of the home. Otherwise, the appropriate sentence will reflect the value of the property taken, the level of associated damage and the degree of planning involved in the offence, as well as matters relating to the offender, such as degree of involvement in the offence, previous record and mitigating matters. In *Dorries* (1993) 14 Cr App R (S) 609 the offenders pleaded guilty to burglary of a shop. They had been seen in the vicinity of the shop and, when the police arrived, they drove away. Entry had been effected by removing bricks from a wall, and property worth £600 had been taken. A hammer, crowbar and radio scanner were found in their car. The Court of Appeal agreed with the trial judge that the offence was so serious that only custody could be justified, but reduced the sentence from 10 months to six months. In contrast, the Court of Appeal held in *Tetteh* (1994) 15 Cr App R (S) 46 that the offence did not pass the custody threshold. The offender had forced open the spirits store at a YMCA club and the drayman's entry cover had been opened to give access to the street. Nothing had been taken, however, and it had been an opportunistic rather than a planned offence.

Some other specific types of non-domestic burglary have been the subject of comment by the Court of Appeal. In *Larcher* (1979) 1 Cr App R (S) 137 the offender admitted a series of burglaries of doctors' premises and chemists' shops in order to obtain drugs. Although he had not served a custodial sentence before, five years was imposed by the Court of Appeal. In *Percy* (1992) 14 Cr App R (S) 10 a sentence of five years' imprisonment was upheld on 25-year-old offenders for a 'ram-raid' on a shop carried out by a group of men using stolen cars to break through a security fence and a window. They stole £2,000 worth of clothing from the shop, and did £,6000 worth of damage to the premises and the vehicles.

Sentences of five years were approved in two cases of burglary with intent to rape. In *Bolland* (1988) 10 Cr App R (S) 129 the offender entered at night the house of a woman known to him, assaulted her and threatened her with a knife. In *Palmer* (1990) 12 Cr App R (S) 550 the offender broke into a woman's home at night and made sexual advances to her. Concurrent sentences for indecent assault were approved in both cases.

12.4.6 Aggravated burglary

The maximum penalty for aggravated burglary, whether committed in a dwelling or not, is life imprisonment (Theft Act 1968, s. 10(2)). In 1998, the Crown Court sentenced 221 offenders for aggravated burglary in a dwelling; of those 196 received immediate custody (89 per cent) and 5 received suspended sentences. Other disposals were CRO (4), CPO (2), supervision order (3), CPRO (5) and hospital order (2). The Crown Court also sentenced 21 offenders for aggravated burglary not in a dwelling; 18 received immediate custody.

In *A-G's Reference (No. 16 of 1994)* (1995) 16 Cr App R (S) 629 the offender, a man with a record of violent offences, went to the flat of a man he knew, armed with a baseball bat. He used the bat to smash property in the flat, thereby frightening the occupant. A sentence of 18 months' imprisonment was increased to three years. In *Funnell* (1986) 8 Cr App R (S) 143 nine years' imprisonment was reduced to six on two men who burgled the home of a man aged 84, armed with an imitation firearm, and then tied up the victim. Towards the top of the scale of seriousness is *O'Driscoll* (1986) 8 Cr App R (S) 121, where the offender gained access to the home of an elderly man and struck him a number of blows with a hammer. The victim was also threatened with a lighted gas poker, tied up with wire and gagged. A sentence of 15 years was upheld. Subsequent decisions which treat *O'Driscoll* as a guideline case include *A-G's Reference (Nos. 32 and 33 of 1995)* [1996] 2 Cr App R (S) 345 and *Eastap* [1997] 2 Cr App R (S) 55.

12.4.7 Abstracting electricity

The maximum penalty is five years (Theft Act 1968, s. 13) on indictment; six months or a fine not exceeding the statutory maximum, or both, summarily. In 1998, 25 cases of abstracting electricity were sentenced at Crown Court; three received immediate custody and there were two suspended sentences. In magistrates' courts in 1998, 743 offenders were sentenced for this offence; only 41 received immediate custody. Other disposals were fine (312), conditional discharge (240), CRO (66) and CPO (40); 24 offenders were otherwise dealt with.

In *Hodkinson* (1980) 2 Cr App R (S) 331 the offender pleaded guilty to abstracting electricity, in that he had fitted a device to the electricity meter at his home, which caused the meter to give a false reading. Bristow J commented that: 'In the judgment of this Court deliberately stealing electricity in this way is an offence which calls for deterrent treatment when caught. In the circumstances of this case the Court has come to the view that the necessary deterrent element would be sufficiently dealt with by a sentence of one month's imprisonment, accompanied by a fine of £750.' See also *Western* (1987) 9 Cr App R (S) 6.

12.4.8 Obtaining property by deception

The maximum penalty for obtaining property by deception is ten years (Theft Act 1968, s. 15(1)) on indictment; six months, or a fine not exceeding the statutory maximum, or both, summarily. The maximum penalty looks somewhat anomalous, given the very substantial overlap between theft and deception offences (see *Gomez* [1993] AC 442) and the reduction in the maximum sentence for the former offence to seven years by the CJA 1991.

The *Practice Note* (*Mode of Trial: Guidelines*) (1995) indicate that, in general, cases of fraud should be tried summarily unless the court considers that one or more of the following features is present and that its sentencing powers are insufficient:

(a)   breach of trust by a person in a position of substantial authority, or in whom a high degree of trust has been placed;
(b)   fraud which has been committed or disguised in a sophisticated manner;
(c)   fraud committed by an organised gang;
(d)   the victim is particularly vulnerable to fraud (e.g. the elderly or infirm);
(e)   the unrecovered property is of high value (at least £10,000).

If the offence is dealt with summarily, the Magistrates' Association Guidelines (2000) indicate the following:

Aggravating Factors +
   committed over lengthy period, large sums or valuable goods, two or more involved, victim particularly vulnerable, offence committed on bail, previous convictions and failures to respond to previous sentences, if relevant.

Mitigating Factors −
   impulsive action, short period, small sum.

The Guidelines indicate that magistrates should consider whether the offence is serious enough for a community penalty.

In 1998, the Crown Court sentenced 2,865 offenders for the offence category 'other fraud', which includes the offence of obtaining property by deception. Of those sentenced, 1,543 received custodial sentences (54 per cent) and there were 163 suspended sentences. The main other disposals were CPO (475), CRO (284), CPRO (165), discharge (104) and fine (104). In the magistrates' courts in 1998, 12,423 offenders were sentenced for 'other fraud', of whom 1,545 received custodial sentences. The main other disposals were discharge (2,950), fine (2,627), CRO (2,246), CPO (1,785) and CPRO (729). A further 228 cases were otherwise dealt with, presumably by way of compensation order.

The sentencing pattern for this and related offences of deception overlaps substantially with that for theft (see **12.4.1**). Since the offence varies so widely, there is no guideline judgment. The appropriate sentencing bracket for frauds committed by professional persons was reconsidered in *Barrick* (1985) 7 Cr App R (S) 142, which was discussed at **12.4.1**.

Large-scale commercial frauds will attract lengthy custodial sentences. In *Copeland* (1982) 4 Cr App R (S) 110 the offender was involved in a well organised scheme by which cheque books and cheque cards were stolen in Britain, passports were obtained in the names of the losers, and teams of two went to the continent, using the passports, and obtained money by means of the stolen cheque books and cards. Each trip netted about £15,000 and the scheme had been operational for a considerable time. The offender had several previous convictions for dishonesty resulting in prison terms of up to three years. The Court of Appeal reduced the sentence from six years to four and a half years. In *Griffiths* (1989) 11 Cr App R (S) 216 the offender, an 'intelligent and resourceful man', pleaded guilty to 23 counts of deception relating to a total of 93 multiple applications for shares. He made a profit of £5,000, but if all the applications had been successful he would have made £64,000. The Court of Appeal said that an immediate custodial sentence was appropriate, varying the original sentence of 12 months, with six to serve and six suspended, to an immediate term of six months. In one of a series of recent decisions on sentencing for 'mortgage frauds', the Court of Appeal upheld a custodial term of three and a half years together with a confiscation order of £142,000 in *Judge* (1992) 13 Cr App R (S) 685, where a total of £1 million had been procured by separate mortgage advances on 12 properties. See also *Stevens* (1993) 14 Cr App R (S) 372, where the Court of Appeal said that relevant matters in this type of case are the degree of involvement of the offender, the scale and duration of the fraud, the personal benefit derived and whether the offender is a professional person.

In contrast to the large-scale frauds are what may be described as the activities of 'con men'. Non-custodial sentences will often be appropriate but, once again, much turns on the sum involved. Also relevant is the method of deception (callous deception of the elderly, for example, will attract a more severe sentence) and the previous record of the offender. In *Pashby* (1982) 4 Cr App R (S) 382 the offender pleaded guilty to five counts of obtaining property by deception, by calling at the homes of elderly people, telling them that their roofs required repair and obtaining various sums by pretending that he would do, or had done, the necessary work. A sentence of five years was reduced to three years. In *Williams* (1983) 5 Cr App R (S) 244 the offender, 'a confidence trickster, especially of gullible women', who had a record of dishonesty over 15 years, had obtained £300 and £175 from different women by telling false hard-luck stories. A sentence of 15 months was reduced to nine months.

12.4.9   Social security and benefit fraud

Serious offending involving large-scale benefit fraud will usually be dealt with as an obtaining of property by deception (see **12.4.8**). A large number of social security and other benefit frauds have reached the Court of Appeal. In *Livingstone Stewart* (1987) 9 Cr App R (S) 135 Lord Lane CJ provided the following guidance for sentencers:

> only a small proportion of offences of this nature . . . are dealt with in the Crown Court. It will only be the apparently more serious cases which will come before the Crown Court. These offences involve the dishonest abstraction of honest taxpayers' money and are not to be treated lightly. They are easy to commit and difficult and expensive to track down. However it must be remembered that they are non-violent, non-sexual and non-frightening crimes.

Lord Lane CJ indicated that immediate custody was required at the top of the range of offenders, where there had been carefully organised frauds on a large scale. As to the remainder, who form the great majority, it may well be advisable for the court to enquire what steps the DSS proposes to take to recover their loss from the offender. Other considerations which may affect the sentence are:

(a)   a guilty plea;

(b)   the amount involved and the length of time over which the defalcations were persisted in (bearing in mind that a large total may in fact represent a very small amount weekly);

(c)   the circumstances in which the offence began (e.g. there is a plain difference between a legitimate claim which becomes false owing to a change of situation and on the other hand a claim which is false from the very beginning);

(d)   the use to which the money is put (the provision of household necessities is more venial than spending the money on unnecessary luxury);

(e)   previous character of the offender;

(f)   matters special to the offender, such as illness, disability, family difficulties, etc;

(g)   any voluntary repayment of the amounts overpaid.

If immediate custody is necessary, Lord Lane suggested that a term of up to about nine or 12 months will usually be sufficient in a contested case where the overpayment is less than £10,000. If no immediate custodial sentence is imposed, and the amount of overpayment is below £1,000, a compensation order is often of value. This will usually only be the case where the defendant is in work. Lord Lane concluded by saying that '... we do not think that the element of deterrence should play a large part in the sentencing of this sort of case'.

The guidelines in *Livingstone Stewart* have been applied in numerous later cases. Examples are *Breeze* (1993) 15 Cr App R (S) 94, where the offender, a 'foot soldier' in a larger fraudulent enterprise who obtained £264 by deception, should not have received a custodial sentence despite having relevant previous convictions; *Tucker* (1993) 15 Cr App R (S) 349, where a sentence of six months' imprisonment for an offender who had been claiming supplementary benefit to which he was not entitled for about 18 months, obtaining £8,500, was upheld in light of considerable personal mitigation; and *Adewuyi* [1997] 1 Cr App R (S) 254, a case of 'exceptional seriousness', where more than £100,000 had been obtained over four years, and four years' imprisonment was upheld on appeal.

As indicated above, the great majority of social security benefit frauds are dealt with in magistrates' courts, and most are prosecuted by use of the summary offence in the Social Security Administration Act 1992, s. 112. The maximum penalty available for this offence is three months' imprisonment, a fine not exceeding £5,000, or both (s. 112(2)).

In the magistrates' courts in 1998, 5,891 offenders were sentenced for this offence. Most offenders were fined (1,716) or discharged (2,141). There were 1,296 CPOs and 90 custodial sentences (1.5 per cent).

12.4.10 Other deception offences

The maximum penalty for the offences of obtaining a pecuniary advantage by deception, for obtaining services by deception, and for evasion of liability by deception is, on conviction or indictment, five years (Theft Act 1978, s. 4(2)(a) and Theft Act 1968, s. 16(1)) and on summary conviction, six months, a fine not exceeding the statutory maximum, or both. The maximum for false accounting is seven years (Theft Act 1968, s. 17(1)) on indictment; six months, a fine not exceeding the statutory maximum, or both, summarily. The maximum for making off without payment is two years (Theft Act 1978, s. 4(2)(b)) on indictment; six months, a fine not exceeding the statutory maximum, or both, summarily.

12.5 SENTENCING FOR CRIMINAL DAMAGE AND ARSON

12.5.1 Criminal damage

The maximum penalty for criminal damage, committed with intent to endanger life or with recklessness whether life is endangered, is life imprisonment (Criminal Damage Act 1971, s. 4(1)). This offence is triable only on indictment. The maximum penalty for any other form of criminal damage is ten years (Criminal Damage Act 1971, s. 4(2)) on indictment; six months or a fine not exceeding the statutory maximum, or both, summarily. If, however, the damage is quantified at not more than £5,000 (unless it was caused by fire and thus constitutes arson: see **12.5.2**), criminal damage is treated as summary only: the maximum penalty is then three months, a fine not exceeding level 4 on the standard scale, or both. The maximum penalty for the racially aggravated form of criminal damage is 14 years on indictment or six months, a fine not exceeding the statutory maximum or both, summarily (CDA 1998, s. 30(2)). This applies whether or not the damage exceeds £5,000. For guidance on sentencing for racially aggravated offences, see **12.2.3**.

Even if the value involved is more than £5,000 the offence should, in general, be tried summarily unless the court considers that one or more of the following features is present and that its sentencing powers are insufficient:

(a)   deliberate fire-raising;
(b)   committed by a group;
(c)   damage of a high value (at least £10,000);
(d)   the offence has a clear racial motivation.

Where tried summarily, the Magistrates' Association Guidelines (2000) indicate the following:

Aggravating Factors +

deliberate, group offence, serious damage, offence committed on bail, previous convictions and failures to respond to previous sentences, if relevant.

Mitigating Factors −

impulsive action, minor damage, provocation.

The Guidelines indicate that magistrates should consider whether discharge or a fine is appropriate.

In 1998, the Crown Court sentenced 63 cases of criminal damage endangering life; of which 43 offenders received immediate custody, nine were given CROs, two were given CPOs and there were two hospital orders.

In *Dodd* [1997] 1 Cr App R (S) 127, a case of criminal damage being reckless as to whether life was endangered, the offender drove his car at 40 m.p.h. through the glass-fronted doors of Plymouth magistrates' court, causing £34,000 worth of damage. Four years' imprisonment was upheld by the Court of Appeal. See also *McCann* [2000] 1 Cr App R (S) 995.

For 'ordinary' criminal damage, the Crown Court sentenced 876 offenders in 1998. The disposals were CRO (250), immediate custody (182), CPO (111), discharge (98), fine (63), hospital order (20), 52 cases were otherwise dealt with. In 1998, magistrates' courts sentenced 8,054 such cases. Disposals were fine (1,808), discharge (2,619), CRO (1,081), CPO (559), immediate custody (406, which is 5 per cent of the total), attendance centre order (221), supervision order (433), combination order (355); 517 cases were otherwise dealt with.

As can be seen from these statistics, most cases of minor criminal damage are dealt with by non-custodial means, particularly fines and discharges. Compensation should be ordered wherever possible. In *Fenton* (1988) 10 Cr App R (S) 250 and *Ferreira* (1988) 10 Cr App R (S) 343, community service was regarded as an appropriate penalty for criminal damage.

There are few Court of Appeal decisions relating to simple criminal damage. In *Bowles* (1988) 10 Cr App R (S) 146, a sentence of 14 days' imprisonment was upheld in a case where the offender daubed paint over the door and surrounding walls of South Africa House, as a political protest. In *Toomey* (1993) 14 Cr App R (S) 42 the offenders smashed the windows and door of a restaurant after an argument with the owner, causing £2,000 worth of damage. Eighteen months' imprisonment was reduced to 12 months on appeal.

12.5.2 Arson

The maximum penalty for arson (i.e. where any form of criminal damage dealt with at **12.5.1** is committed by fire) is life imprisonment (Criminal Damage Act 1971, s. 4(1)) on indictment. If the criminal damage has been caused by fire but it does not amount to criminal damage with intent or recklessness whether life is endangered, the arson is triable either way and, on summary conviction, is punishable with six months or a fine not exceeding the statutory maximum, or both. The £5,000 rule (see **12.5.1**) does not apply where criminal damage amounts to arson. PCC(S)A 2000, s. 161 states that any offence which is required to be charged as arson is included within the meaning of 'violent offence' (see **4.2.7**), whether or not it would fall within the definition.

In 1998, the Crown Court sentenced 794 cases of arson. Fifty three per cent of these offenders received immediate custody (422), and a further 25 received suspended sentences. The main other disposals were CRO (153), supervision order (50), hospital order (54), CPO (40) and CPRO (34). In 1998, magistrates' courts sentenced 544 cases of arson. The main sentence disposals were discharge (126), supervision order (113), custody (5) and CRO (71).

According to Donaldson LJ in *Priest* (1980) 2 Cr App R (S) 68, '(a)rson is a very odd offence in the sense that it covers a very wide range of circumstances. There can be very simple arson cases — simple in terms of sentencing — and there can be very difficult ones.' The Court of Appeal cases taken together indicate that there should be a psychiatric report available on the offender in cases of arson, and that, where there is appropriate psychiatric evidence, a medical disposal, such as a probation order with a condition of psychiatric treatment or a hospital order, may be passed. Minor cases can be dealt with by non-custodial sentences. Otherwise, in the absence of mitigation, a custodial sentence will generally be appropriate. Longer custodial sentences are appropriate where substantial damage has been caused or where death or serious injury has been risked by the offender. In *Hartley* (1993) 14 Cr App R (S) 198 Roch J, upholding sentences of three years custody imposed on offenders who pleaded guilty to setting fire to their employer's factory, causing losses of £690,000, said that:

> Arson cases are difficult. Sentences passed must reflect the grave consequences which can flow, and in this case did flow, from the fire. It has to be remembered that firemen called to large fires are always in danger, and that commercial companies whose premises are damaged by fire can also face serious consequences. Sentences passed on arsonists must contain an element of deterrence . . .

In *A-G's Reference (No. 66 of 1997)* [2000] 1 Cr App R (S) 149, a case of arson with intent to endanger life, it was said that a sentence in the range of 8–10 years would have been proper in a contested case where the offender set fires in a bungalow where people were asleep. In *Smith* (1993) 15 Cr App R (S) 594 the offender was an animal rights activist, who placed incendiary devices under a number of tractor units at the victim's farm. They were removed before any damage was done, but it was estimated that loss to the value of £200,000 would have been incurred if they had gone off. The offender had served a previous custodial sentence for a similar offence, and six years' imprisonment was upheld on this occasion as a deterrent sentence to the offender and to others. In *A-G's Reference (No. 35 of 1996)* [1997] 1 Cr App R (S) 350 the offender pleaded guilty to arson being reckless whether life was endangered. In arrears with his rent and following a number of letters from the landlord, the offender started a fire in his own flat. It was quickly discovered, but £2,000 worth of damage was done. The Court of Appeal held that the combination order imposed by the trial judge had been unduly lenient, and substituted a custodial sentence of 18 months.

12.6 SENTENCING FOR OFFENCES RELATED TO PUBLIC ORDER

12.6.1 Firearms offences

The maximum penalty for possessing a firearm, shotgun or ammunition without a certificate is five years' imprisonment, a fine, or both, on indictment; six months, a fine not exceeding the statutory maximum, or both, summarily. Where the firearm is a shortened shotgun, the maximum penalty on indictment is seven years, a fine, or both. The maximum penalty for shortening a shotgun is seven years, a fine, or both, on indictment; six months, a fine not exceeding the statutory maximum, or both, summarily.

The maximum penalty for each of the following offences is life imprisonment: possession of a firearm with intent to endanger life or damage property, the use of a firearm to resist arrest, possessing a firearm while committing an offence specified in the Firearms Act 1968, sch. 1 (currently offences under Criminal Damage Act 1971, s. 1; OAPA 1861, ss. 20, 21, 22, 30, 32, 38 and 47; Child Abduction Act 1984, Part I; Police Act 1996, s. 89; SOA 1956, ss. 1, 17, 18 and 20; theft, burglary, blackmail and any offence under s. 12(1) of the Theft Act 1968), or for carrying a firearm or an imitation firearm with intent to commit an indictable offence.

The maximum penalty for carrying a loaded firearm in a public place is seven years' imprisonment, a fine, or both, on indictment; six months, a fine not exceeding the statutory maximum, or both, summarily. The maximum penalty for the summary offence of a person aged under 17 acquiring a firearm is six months, a fine not exceeding level 5 on the standard scale, or both.

All the above penalties are listed in Firearms Act 1968, sch. 6 and many of them were increased by the CJPOA 1994.

The Crown Court sentenced 537 offenders for offences under the Firearms Act 1968 during 1998. Of these, 288 received immediate custody (54 per cent) and there were 28 suspended sentences. The other disposals were fine (41), discharge (44), CPO (59), CRO (52), CPRO (16), hospital order (3). Five cases were otherwise dealt with. In the magistrates' courts in 1998, 1,316 Firearms Act 1968 cases were sentenced. Of those, 80 received immediate custody (6 per cent). Other significant disposals were fine (597), discharge (348), CPO (150) and CRO (81).

Following revision in recent years of the maximum penalties for firearms offences, the Court of Appeal has indicated that the appropriate level of sentencing, particularly for serious offences, has been revised upwards. In *Clarke* [1997] 1 Cr App R (S) 323 the Court of Appeal confirmed that it was no longer appropriate to follow the sentencing levels prescribed in cases before the 1994 Act. In *Avis* [1998] 1 Cr App R 420, Lord Bingham CJ said that the criminal statistics indicated that there had been a sharp increase in the number of certain firearms offences coming before the courts, a fact which had confirmed the subjective impression of the judges. The unlawful possession and use of firearms was generally regarded as a grave source of danger to society. Firearms could be used to take life, to cause serious injury, or to further the commission of other serious crime. Often the victims would be those charged with the enforcement of the law or the protection of persons or property. In the conflicts which arose between competing criminal gangs, often related to the supply of drugs, the use and possession of firearms provoked an escalating spiral of violence. Where imitation firearms were used, the risk to life and limb was absent but such weapons could be and often were used to frighten victims in order to enforce unlawful demands, and such weapons were often difficult to distinguish from the real thing. His lordship commented that, although the Court of Appeal would not lay down precise guidelines for firearms offences, sentencers dealing with such cases should ask themselves:

(a) What sort of weapon was involved? Genuine weapons were more dangerous than imitation ones, loaded than unloaded, unloaded for which ammunition was available than where it was not. Possession of a firearm which had no lawful use, such as a sawn-off shotgun, would be viewed even more seriously than possession of a firearm which could have a legitimate use.

(b) What use had been made of the weapon? The more prolonged and violent the use of the weapon the more serious the offence was likely to be.

(c) With what intention was the weapon possessed or used? Generally the most serious offences under the Act were those requiring proof of an intention to endanger life, cause fear of violence, resist arrest etc. The more serious the act intended, the more serious the offence.

(d) What was the defendant's record? Inevitably the offence was worse if the offender had a record of firearms offences or crimes of violence.

His lordship stated that some of the sentences passed for firearms offences in the past had failed to reflect their true degree of seriousness and the justifiable public concern which they aroused. Save for minor infringements which could properly be dealt with by magistrates, offences against these provisions would almost invariably merit terms of custody, even on a plea of guilty and where the offender had no previous record.

12.6.2 Offensive weapons

The maximum penalty for carrying an offensive weapon without lawful authority or reasonable excuse is four years, a fine, or both, on indictment (Prevention of Crime Act 1953, s. 1); six months, a fine not exceeding the statutory maximum, or both, summarily. The maximum penalty was increased from two years in 1996.

When dealt with summarily the Magistrates' Association Guidelines (2000) indicate:

Aggravating Factors +
location of offence, group action or joint possession, racial aggravation, people put in fear/weapon brandished, planned use, very dangerous weapon, offence committed on bail, previous convictions and failures to respond to previous sentences, if relevant

Mitigating Factors −
acting out of genuine fear, not premeditated

The Guidelines indicate that magistrates should consider whether the offence is so serious that only custody can be justified.

No separate sentencing statistics are provided for this offence in the *Criminal Statistics*, but according to the Sentencing Advisory Panel's advice to the Court of Appeal for the offence, in 1998 90 per cent of such cases were dealt with in the magistrates' courts. Of those sentenced, about 25 per cent were discharged, 25 per cent fined and 25 per cent received a community sentence. One eighth of offenders receive a custodial sentence.

The Court of Appeal has considered the appropriate sentencing bracket for the offence of possessing an offensive weapon in a number of reported cases. In *Webster* (1985) 7 Cr App R (S) 359 the offender, aged 27, after having been arrested for urinating against a wall, was found to be in possession of a Stanley knife, which he claimed to carry in case he was attacked. He had 11 previous convictions for violence and one previous conviction, two years earlier, for possession of an offensive weapon for which he had received three months' imprisonment. The Court of Appeal noted that a Stanley knife was capable of inflicting a very serious injury, and in light of the fact that the offender had contested the case and had a poor record, no mitigation was available from either of those sources; 12 months' imprisonment was upheld. In *Shorter* (1988) 10 Cr App R (S) 4, where the offender had two similar previous convictions, six months' imprisonment was upheld on an offender found in possession of a vegetable knife. Nine months was appropriate in *Simpson* (1992) 13 Cr App R (S) 665, where the offender had a flick knife, and in *Norman* (1995) 16 Cr App R (S) 848, 15 months was upheld for an offender with a previous conviction for the offence who was found in possession of a broken pool cue and a nasal spray containing ammonia.

The Sentencing Advisory Panel has proposed to the Court of Appeal that it should issue a sentencing guideline for this offence. For the Panel's advice see www.sentencing-advisory-panel.gov.uk.

12.6.3 Riot

The maximum penalty for riot is ten years (Public Order Act 1986, s. 1(6)). The offence is triable on indictment only. In 1998 there were 12 cases of riot tried by the Crown Court. Oddly enough, all the defendants were acquitted, so there are no sentencing figures to report!

Some general guidance on the gravity of public order offences, including riot, is to be found in *Caird* (1970) 54 Cr App R 499, although that case was decided in respect of common law offences of public order which were replaced by the statutory scheme in 1986. Sachs LJ said that where there had been 'wanton and vicious violence of gross degree' the court is not concerned with whether it originates from gang rivalry or from political motives. It is the degree of mob violence which matters and the extent to which the public peace is being broken. He also said that it was wrong to deal leniently with those who had been caught because others had not been. Individual acts of the perpetrators should not be seen in isolation, since they were not committed in isolation and it is that very fact that constitutes the gravity of the offence.

In *Pilgrim* (1983) 5 Cr App R (S) 140 three offenders had been involved in a riot in which 100 youths, equipped with various weapons, had attacked a public house frequented by members of an opposing group, and subsequently attacked a number of people who were unconnected with the event, one of whom was killed. The first offender was convicted of manslaughter in respect of that, and received sentences totalling eight years. The other two received sentences of five years and three years respectively. The Court of Appeal upheld the sentences, Lord Lane CJ noting that factors of particular importance in fixing sentence in such cases are:

(a)   the level of violence used;
(b)   the scale of the riot or affray, as described by the witnesses;
(c)   the extent to which it is premeditated, or arises spontaneously; and
(d)   the number of people involved.

The case of *Sallis* (1994) 15 Cr App R (S) 281, concerning prisoners who took part in a riot at a remand centre, confirms the continuing relevance of the above principles. Sentences of four and a half and five years were imposed on two of those involved.

12.6.4   Violent disorder

The maximum penalty for violent disorder is five years, a fine, or both, on indictment (Public Order Act 1986, s. 2(5)); six months, a fine not exceeding the statutory maximum, or both, summarily.

The *Practice Note (Mode of Trial: Guidelines)* (1995) indicate that cases of violent disorder should generally be committed for trial. When dealt with summarily, the Magistrates' Association Guidelines (2000) indicate that:

Aggravating Factors +
racial aggravation, busy public place, large group, fighting between rival groups, large group, people put in fear, planned, vulnerable victims, weapon, offence committed on bail, previous convictions and failures to respond to previous sentences, if relevant.

Mitigating Factors −
impulsive, nobody actually afraid, provocation.

The Guidelines indicate that magistrates should consider whether the offence is so serious that only custody can be justified and consider whether summary powers are appropriate.

In 1998 the Crown Court sentenced 700 offenders for violent disorder. Of those, 458 received a custodial sentence (65 per cent). Other significant disposals were CPOs (127), CPROs (43) and CROs (12). In the magistrates' courts in 1998, 188 cases of violent disorder were sentenced. Of those, 40 received immediate custody. Other sentences included CPOs (41), supervision order (19), fine (22) and attendance centre order (21).

There are a few examples of Court of Appeal decisions in relation to sentencing for violent disorder. In *Vanes* (1989) 11 Cr App R (S) 147 the offenders pleaded guilty to violent disorder. They took part in a fight between members of two families. Between 15 and 20 people were involved. Various implements were used as weapons and there was £800 worth of damage done to a public house. Although no serious injury resulted the disorder was premeditated. Sentences of two years' and 12 months' imprisonment were upheld, the offenders being distinguished on grounds of the degree of their involvement and their records. Another example is *Alderson* (1989) 11 Cr App R (S) 301, where the offender and others created a disturbance in a restaurant which was directed at a party of Jordanian students. The victims were kicked, punched and hit with furniture and £500 worth of damage was done to the restaurant. A sentence of 30 months' imprisonment was upheld, the court taking account of the aggravating racial element in the offence. A third is *Coote* (1992) 14 Cr App R (S) 40, where the offender and a number of friends were celebrating his birthday in a nightclub. A fight broke out after a doorman warned one of the group about his behaviour. A police officer who tried to restrain one of the group was held by the offender in an attempt to prevent arrest. A sentence of 12 months' imprisonment was upheld. Finally, in *Green* [1997] 2 Cr App R (S) 191 four years' imprisonment was upheld in a case where the offender took part in a violent revenge attack on the home of a man believed to have assaulted a relative of one of the offenders. Two people in the house were attacked and baseball bats were used to smash windows. The court noted that all the offenders had records and had armed themselves in advance.

12.6.5 Affray

The maximum penalty for affray is three years, a fine, or both, on indictment (Public Order Act 1986, s. 3(7)); six months, a fine not exceeding the statutory maximum, or both, summarily.

The *Practice Note (Mode of Trial: Guidelines)* (1995) indicate that cases of affray should be tried summarily unless the court considers that one or more of the following features is present in the case and that its sentencing powers are insufficient:

(a) organised violence or use of weapons;
(b) significant injury or substantial damage;
(c) the attack has clear racial motivation;
(d) an attack upon police officers, ambulancemen, firemen etc.

When dealt with summarily, the Magistrates' Association Guidelines (2000) indicate that:

Aggravating Factors +
  racial aggravation, busy public place, group action, large group, people put in fear, vulnerable victims, offence committed on bail, previous convictions and failures to respond to previous sentences, if relevant.

Mitigating Factors −
  offender acting alone, provocation, did not start the trouble, stopped as soon as police arrived.

The Guidelines indicate that magistrates should consider whether the offence is so serious that only custody can be justified, and consider whether summary powers are appropriate.

Another example is *Williams* [1997] 2 Cr App R (S) 67, where the offender was one of about 35 men involved in a racially motivated incident in which bottles were thrown in the vicinity of a corner shop in the early hours of the morning. A sentence of 21 months' imprisonment was reduced to 12 months on appeal.

12.6.6 Minor public order offences

The maximum penalty for the offence of causing fear or provoking violence is six months, a fine not exceeding level 5 on the standard scale, or both (Public Order Act 1986, s. 4(4)). For the offence of *intentionally* causing harassment, alarm or distress the maximum penalty is six months, a fine not exceeding level 5 on the standard scale, or both (Public Order Act 1986, s. 4A). The maximum penalty for causing harassment, alarm or distress is a fine not exceeding level 3 on the standard scale (Public Order Act 1986, s. 5(6)). All these offences are triable only summarily. The maximum for the racially aggravated form of the s. 4 offence and the s. 4A offence is, however, two years, a fine or both on indictment; six months, a fine not exceeding the statutory maximum or both summary (CDA 1998, s. 31). The maximum for the racially aggravated form of the s. 5 offence is a fine not exceeding level 4.

There were 30,197 summary offences under the 1986 Act sentenced in 1998. The disposals used most were fine (16,957) and discharge (9,224) but 876 offenders received immediate custody.

12.6.7 Bomb hoaxes

The maximum penalty is seven years on indictment (CLA 1977, s. 51(4)); six months, a fine not exceeding the statutory maximum, or both, summarily.

In *Browne* (1984) 6 Cr App R (S) 5 a codefendant had made two hoax telephone calls to a bank saying that he and the offender were members of the IRA and that there was a bomb in the building which would explode in 40 minutes. Both were sentenced to two years' imprisonment. The Court of Appeal varied the sentence on the offender to bring about his immediate release (he had already served just over 12 months) in the light of his lesser participation in the offence and personal mitigation, but said that this should not encourage the codefendant to appeal. In *Dunbar* (1987) 9 Cr App R (S) 393 the offenders pleaded guilty to communicating a bomb hoax. They telephoned the police to say that incendiary devices had been placed in various stores, apparently in order to cause financial loss to the stores. Sentences of 12 months' imprisonment were upheld by the Court of Appeal, Leggatt J commenting that: '[a] bomb hoax of this kind, as this Court has had occasion to say in the past, is a public nuisance, and it is important not to underrate the anxiety and apprehension that this kind of offence engenders. The public rightly expects judges to pass severe sentences as a mark of public disapprobation'. Imprisonment for 12 months was also upheld in *Rung-Ruangap* (1993) 15 Cr App R (S) 326, where the offender made a call to the police to say that there was a bomb outside a Wimpy bar. The offender later admitted she had rung up for a 'dare'.

12.6.8 Official secrets

The maximum penalty for spying, contrary to the Official Secrets Act 1911, s. 1, is 14 years (Official Secrets Act 1920, s. 8(1)). The maximum for wrongful communication of information, contrary to the Official Secrets Act 1989, s. 1, is two years on indictment (Official Secrets Act 1920, s. 8(2)); three months, a fine not exceeding the statutory maximum, or both, summarily.

Offences committed under the Official Secrets Act 1911, s. 1 (spying) will inevitably attract a lengthy custodial sentence. In *Prime* (1983) 5 Cr App R (S) 127 the offender pleaded guilty to two indictments. On the first, he admitted seven offences against the Official Secrets Acts. The offender had been employed for nine years in the Government Communications Service, where he had access to highly sensitive intelligence information of importance to national security. During that period he passed on information to the Soviet Union. On the second indictment, he pleaded guilty to counts of indecent assault against young girls. For the espionage offences, he received consecutive terms of 14, 14 and seven years' imprisonment. For the indecent assault offences he received a further three years, consecutive, a total of 38 years. These sentences were upheld on appeal. In *Schulze* (1986) 8 Cr App R (S) 463 the offenders' home was found to contain spying equipment, forged documents and radio-receiving equipment. They were convicted of doing acts preparatory to the commission of an offence under s. 1 of the 1911 Act. Sentences of 10 years were upheld in each case.

Where the offence is committed under the Official Secrets Act 1989, much will depend upon the precise nature of the offence. Few appellate decisions are reported and all precede the 1989 Act. In *Tisdall* (1984) 6 Cr App R (S) 155 the offender was a civil servant who made additional copies of Foreign Office documents and sent them anonymously to a national newspaper. She was sentenced to six months' imprisonment, which was upheld on appeal, Lord Lane CJ commenting that because:

an individual disapproves of the law, or thinks that it is unreasonable for him or her to have to obey it in any particular circumstance, does not mean that that individual will escape prosecution or, if convicted, will escape punishment . . . in the circumstances of this case an immediate custodial sentence was unavoidable.

Twelve months' immediate custody was upheld in *Jackson* (1987) 9 Cr App R (S) 315 where an ex-soldier had retained confidential documents after leaving the army.

12.6.9   Racial hatred

The maximum penalty for using words or behaviour or displaying written material intended to stir up racial hatred, contrary to the Public Order Act 1986, s. 18, is two years, a fine, or both, on indictment (Public Order Act 1986, s. 27(3)); six months, a fine not exceeding the statutory maximum, or both, summarily.

In *Relf* (1979) 1 Cr App R (S) 111 the offenders were convicted of publishing leaflets containing derogatory remarks about West Indians, the leaflets being displayed in public places. The conduct did not lead to disorder. The Court of Appeal agreed with the trial judge that an immediate custodial penalty was necessary for Relf, but reduced the sentence from 15 months to nine. Cole, more peripherally involved in the offence, received a nine-month prison sentence, suspended, together with a fine of £250. In *Edwards* (1983) 5 Cr App R (S) 145, where the offender had drawn up a comic strip to be published in a magazine intended to stir up racial hatred, he received a 12-month sentence. Lawton LJ, in the Court of Appeal, said that the sentence 'was not a day too long', since the offender's conduct had been 'intended to prejudice children against Jews, Asians and people of coloured blood'.

12.7   SENTENCING FOR OFFENCES AGAINST THE ADMINISTRATION OF JUSTICE

12.7.1   Perjury

The maximum penalty for perjury in judicial proceedings is seven years (Perjury Act 1911, s. 1). The offence is triable only on indictment. In the Crown Court in 1998, 96 offenders were sentenced for perjury. Immediate custody was imposed in 55 cases (57 per cent) and there were 11 suspended sentences. Other disposals for perjury were fine (4), conditional discharge (4), CRO (5) and CPO (15).

There are several Court of Appeal decisions dealing with sentencing for this offence. They stress that a custodial sentence is almost always necessary where perjury has been committed in judicial proceedings. This may not appear to be borne out by the statistics given above, but those figures contain an (unknown) number of cases where perjury was committed in other, perhaps less serious, circumstances (e.g. making a false statement to a registrar of births, marriages or deaths).

The reason for insistence upon custody is, according to Roskill LJ in *Davies* (1974) 59 Cr App R 311 that:

there is too much perjury committed in courts . . . But it is one thing to suspect that perjury has been committed and another thing to prove it. Perjury is not always easy to prove. Perjurers are not easily brought to justice. When they are they must be punished.

In *Rothwell* (1980) 2 Cr App R (S) 338 the offender was a passenger in a car of which he was the owner when it was involved in a collision. He gave false evidence to the effect that he had been the driver. The perjury was believed in the magistrates' court but the other driver's conviction was overturned when the perjury came to light. A sentence of three years was reduced to a 'richly deserved' 18 months on appeal. In *Hall* (1982) 4 Cr App R (S) 153 Talbot J said that 'it is almost inconceivable that a sentence of less than three months would be given for a deliberate perjury in the face of the court', since 'such false evidence strikes at the whole basis of the administration of the law'. In that case a three-month sentence was upheld on a 62-year-old woman who had given false alibi evidence at a magistrates' court in respect of a man charged with assault occasioning actual bodily harm. Exceptionally, in *Stanley* (1981) 3 Cr App R (S) 373, where the offenders pleaded guilty to perjury in the course of summary proceedings against the first offender for driving a car while unfit through drink, custodial sentences of three months were reduced to conditional discharges, to take account of mitigating factors, in particular their impending discharge from the Army should their custodial sentences stand.

In *Lewins* (1979) 1 Cr App R (S) 246 the offender, a police officer, was sentenced to four years for perjury and subornation. He had persuaded witnesses to testify that he had taken drink between the time of a road accident he had been involved in and the administration of a breath test. The sentence was reduced to two years to take account of personal mitigation including loss of his employment, the fact that the perjury was not committed in his capacity as a police officer and the fact that a custodial sentence 'for an ex-police officer is a great deal more unpleasant than it is for other members of the community'. It seems that where the original charge in relation to which the perjury was committed was one of very serious crime, the penalty for the perjury should be proportionally higher. Six months' imprisonment was upheld in *Healey* (1990) 12 Cr App R (S) 297, where the offender committed perjury in the course of a means inquiry in a magistrates' court.

12.7.2 Perverting the course of justice

This is a common law offence, so the penalty is at large. It is triable only on indictment. The Crown Court sentenced 1,938 offenders for this offence in 1998. Immediate custody was imposed in 1,008 cases (52 per cent) and there were 99 suspended sentences. Other disposals were CPO (340), CRO (260), discharge (51), fine (63), and CPRO (98).

A number of Court of Appeal authorities give guidance on the appropriate sentencing bracket for this offence. In *Hill* (1980) 2 Cr App R (S) 110 a sentence of 18 months' imprisonment was upheld where the offender, awaiting trial on a charge of attempted theft of a battery, threatened to kill an intending prosecution witness. The attempt to pervert the course of justice was committed on the spur of the moment. If, according to the Court of Appeal, there had been an element of premeditation the sentence would have been longer. The relative triviality of the attempted theft charge was, apparently, irrelevant. See also *McFarlane* (1984) 6 Cr App R (S) 49, where 18 months was upheld on an offender who threatened a potential witness with violence if he did not change his statement. In *Bilby* (1987) 9 Cr App R (S) 185 a young woman aged 17, of previous good character, pleaded guilty to doing an act tending to pervert the course of justice. Her father and brother were due to appear for trial at a magistrates' court and the offender approached an intending prosecution witness and threatened to kill her if she gave evidence. A sentence of three months' youth custody was upheld, Ian Kennedy J saying that: 'In very few cases will threats to witnesses not be followed by immediate sentences of custody. A feeling of family loyalty will be of no avail. This is not one of the exceptional cases. The sentence passed by the learned judge was correct in principle and its length was not excessive.' See also *Kelly* (1993) 14 Cr App R (S) 170.

Comparable sentences would appear to be appropriate where the offence takes the form of a false allegation of crime. In *Goodwin* (1989) 11 Cr App R (S) 194 a 20-year-old woman made a false complaint of rape, naming a particular man. The man was arrested and held in custody for 14 days, but released subsequently when the woman admitted what she had done. A sentence of three years' detention in a young offender institution was reduced on appeal to 18 months. Lord Lane CJ said that: 'It is necessary to make people understand that this sort of lie will be met by severe punishment. But we have to balance against that the age of this young woman and the circumstances in which she saw fit to tell these lies'. A comparable case is *Gregson* (1993) 14 Cr App R (S) 85, where the false allegation was withdrawn after the man had been in custody for 20 hours. A sentence of four months was appropriate. Another example is *Nutbrown* (1994) 15 Cr App R (S) 269, where the offender, who was stopped by the police when driving while disqualified gave the name of another man. The other man was subsequently arrested before the deception was discovered. A sentence of 12 months for perverting the course of justice was reduced to six months on appeal.

12.8 SENTENCING FOR OFFENCES INVOLVING DANGEROUS DRUGS

In the Crown Court in 1998, 11,831 offenders were sentenced for drug-related offences. For sentencing purposes it is necessary to draw a distinction between three different types of drugs:

(a) Class A Drugs (such as heroin, morphine, cocaine, LSD, Ecstasy, opium and mescaline);
(b) Class B Drugs (such as amphetamine, cannabis, cannabis resin and codeine); and
(c) Class C Drugs (such as benzphetamine and permoline).

For powers to confiscate drugs and drug-related equipment from offenders see **6.7.1** and for powers to deprive drug traffickers of the proceeds of their offending under the DTA 1994, see **9.1**. It is important to note that a normal minimum sentence of seven years applies to the third Class A drug trafficking offence committed by an offender. See further **4.3.2**.

12.8.1 Class A drug offences

The maximum penalty for producing heroin or another Class A drug, supplying such a drug, or possessing such a drug with intent to supply is life imprisonment (MDA 1971, sch. 4) on indictment; six months, a fine not exceeding £5,000, or both, summarily. The maximum for possessing such a drug is seven years (MDA 1971, sch. 4) on indictment; six months, a fine not exceeding £5,000, or both, summarily. The maximum, for being concerned in the management of premises etc. is 14 years (MDA 1971, sch. 4) on indictment; six months, a fine not exceeding £5,000, or both, summarily, and the maximum for fraudulently evading prohibition on importation or exportation of a Class A drug is life (Customs and Excise Management Act 1979, s. 170) on indictment; six months, a fine not exceeding £5,000, or both, summarily.

In the Crown Court in 1998, 582 offenders were sentenced for unlawful importation of Class A drugs. Of those 568 received immediate custody, 98% of offenders dealt with. There were 359 imports of Class B drugs, of whom 96 per cent received custody, and just four importers of Class C drugs, all of whom received custody. In the Crown Court in 1998, there were 3,328 offenders sentenced for production, supply, or possession with intent to supply a Class A drug. Of those, 2,768 received immediate custodial sentences, 83 per cent of offenders dealt with. There were 1,004 offenders sentenced for possession of a Class A drug, 392 of whom received custody. Other significant disposals for possession were fine (89), CRO (244) and CPO (106).

The starting point for sentencing for these offences is the guideline case of *Aramah* (1982) 4 Cr App R (S) 407, modified in later cases to take account of the alteration in maximum penalties for these offences and other matters. The following guidelines from *Aramah* (Lord Lane CJ at pp. 408–9) have, therefore, been amended to incorporate those changes:

Class A Drugs and particularly heroin and morphine: It is common knowledge that these are the most dangerous of all the addictive drugs . . .

I turn to the importation of heroin, morphine and so on: Large scale importation, that is where [the weight of the drugs at 100 per cent purity is of the order of 500 g] or more, sentences of [ten years] and upwards are appropriate. There will be cases where the [weight at 100 per cent purity is of the order of 5 kg] or more, in which case the offence should be visited by sentences of [14 years] and upwards. It will be seldom that an importer of any appreciable amount of the drug will deserve less than four years. This, however, is one area in which it is particularly important that offenders should be encouraged to give information to the police, and a confession of guilt, coupled with considerable assistance to the police can properly be marked by a substantial reduction in what would otherwise be the proper sentence.

Next, supplying heroin, morphine and so on: It goes without saying that the sentence will largely depend on the degree of involvement, the amount of trafficking and the value of the drug handled. It is seldom that a sentence of less than [five] years will be justified and the nearer the source of supply the defendant is shown to be, the heavier will be the sentence. There may well be cases where sentences similar to those appropriate to large scale importers may be necessary. It is however unhappily all too seldom that those big fish amongst the suppliers get caught.

Possession of heroin, morphine etc. (simple possession): It is at this level that the circumstances of the individual offender become of much greater importance. Indeed the possible variety of considerations is so wide, including often those of a medical nature, that we feel it impossible to lay down any practical guidelines. On the other hand the maximum penalty for simple possession of Class A drugs is seven years' imprisonment and/or a fine, and there will be very many cases where deprivation of liberty is both proper and expedient.

In *Martinez* (1984) 6 Cr App R (S) 364, Lord Lane CJ confirmed that the *Aramah* guidelines were not confined to heroin, but applied equally to other Class A drugs such as cocaine and LSD, and in *Allery* (1993) 14 Cr App R (S) 699 the Court of Appeal said that there was no basis for treating Ecstasy as a less dangerous Class A drug. In *Morris* [2001] 1 Cr App R (S) 297 the Court of Appeal said that the amount of a Class A drug with which the offender was involved was often a vital factor. The amount should be based on weight of the drug at 100 per cent purity and not, in general, on street value. Street value might however, sometimes be useful as a cross-check. In *Hurley* [1998] 1 Cr App R (S) 299, the Court of Appeal issued guidance on sentencing levels for importation of LSD. In the case of 25,000 or more quarter-inch squares or dosage units the sentence should in the ordinary case be 10 years plus. For 250,000 or more dosage units the sentence should ordinarily be 14 years plus. In each case their lordships were assuming that the dosage unit was of approximately 50 micrograms content pure LSD. Adjustment might be needed when it was shown to vary significantly from that figure. Where the seizure was of tablets or of crystals in a form which enabled a precise weight to be ascertained readily there should be no problem in calculating the number of 50 microgram doses. The Court of Appeal appreciated that cases might arise where, to do justice in individual cases, the sentence level could vary from the guidelines indicated.

The Court of Appeal has also rejected arguments that Ecstasy is to be treated as a drug less dangerous than other Class A drugs such as heroin or cocaine. In *Warren* [1996] 1 Cr App R (S) 233 the Court of Appeal tied this drug into the *Aramah* guideline framework by stating that in cases involving importation of 5,000 or more Ecstasy tablets the appropriate sentence would be in the order of 10 years and upwards, while for 50,000 or more tablets it would be 14 years and upwards. These figures were based on the assumption that the tablets were of average, or near average, quality. If analysis showed a substantially different content, the weight of the constituent would be the determinative factor. The Court again stressed that other matters were also of importance, such as the role of the offender in the offence, his plea, and whether he had provided assistance to the authorities. In *Mashaollahi* [2001] 1 Cr App R (S) 330 the Court of Appeal issued guidelines, following a referral from the Sentencing Advisory Panel, on the importation of opium and possession of that drug with intent to supply. The sentence in a contested case for possession with intent to supply 40 kilos or more of opium was 14 years and upwards and for 4 kilos or more the sentence was ten years and upwards.

The *Aramah* guidelines show that most offences relating to Class A drugs are not suitable for summary trial. The only exceptions seem to be cases of simple possession of a small amount of Class A drugs. In such cases, the Magistrates' Association Guidelines (2000) indicate the following:

Aggravating Factors +
an amount other than a very small quantity, offence committed on bail, previous convictions and failures to respond to previous sentences, if relevant.

Mitigating Factors −
very small quantity.

The Guidelines indicate that magistrates should consider whether the offence is serious enough for a community penalty. Forfeiture of all drugs and equipment should be considered in every case.

Magistrates sentenced 7,103 such cases in 1998, of which 424 were dealt with by immediate custody. Most offenders were fined (3,407), discharged (1,214) or received a CRO (136).

There are many Court of Appeal decisions which apply the *Aramah* guidelines to Class A drug offences. The first group is concerned with importation. An example is *Latif* [1995] 1 Cr App R (S) 270, where 20 kg of heroin had been imported by a 'principal organiser'. A sentence of 20 years' imprisonment was upheld on appeal. In *Bayley* (1995) 16 Cr App R (S) 605, 15 years was upheld for the importation of 58 kg of Ecstasy. In *Bilinski* (1987) 9 Cr App R (S) 360 the offender pleaded guilty to importing over 3 kg of heroin. The Court of Appeal said that a sentence of eight years was appropriate, bearing in mind the guilty plea and the offender's assistance given to the authorities. The case also establishes that an offender's belief that the drugs were in fact Class B and not Class A drugs is relevant to sentence (see, to the same effect, *Ghandi* (1986) 8 Cr App R (S) 391). If this matter is in dispute, a *Newton* hearing may be appropriate to determine it (see **3.3.2**). In *Bilinski*, it seems, a cursory enquiry would have revealed the true nature of the drug and, accordingly, the appropriate reduction was small. Other cases are *Daniel* (1995) 16 Cr App R (S) 892 (offender stopped at Gatwick Airport and found to be in possession of 1.43 kg of heroin of 45 per cent purity; nine years' imprisonment upheld) and *Mouzulukwe* [1996] 2 Cr App R (S) 48 (offender concealed within his body 31 packets containing 231 g of powder, including 38 g of pure heroin; six years' imprisonment upheld). A sentence of eight years was upheld in *Gerami* (1980) 2 Cr App R (S) 291, where the offender and his codefendant had been involved in the importation of 8.87 kg of prepared opium. The sentence on the codefendant was reduced to six years to reflect his lesser role in the offence.

As far as distribution of Class A drugs is concerned, in *Djahit* [1999] 2 Cr App R (S) 142 the Court of Appeal said that the appropriate level of sentence for 'a typical low-level retailer' of heroin or other Class A drug, with no relevant previous convictions, selling to other addicts in order to be able to sustain his own habit and earn enough to live modestly was six years imprisonment. See also *Twisse* [2001] 2 Cr App R (S) 37. Four years' detention in a young offender institution was held to be correct in *Thompson* [1997] 2 Cr App R (S) 223, where a 20-year-old offender with one previous conviction for possession of drugs, pleaded guilty to supplying Ecstasy tablets at a nightclub.

As far as sentencing for possession of Class A drugs is concerned, the *Aramah* guidelines indicate that sentence may differ widely according to the circumstances, but that 'there will be very many cases where deprivation of liberty is both proper and expedient'. In *Layton* (1988) 10 Cr App R (S) 109 the offender, who had a bad criminal record but no previous drug-related convictions, pleaded guilty to possession of 5.6 gm of cocaine. A sentence of three months' imprisonment was substituted for the 30 months imposed by the sentencer. Three-month sentences were also appropriate in *Long* (1984) 6 Cr App R (S) 115, where the offenders pleaded guilty to possession of heroin for personal use and each had a previous conviction for possession of cannabis and in *Cox* (1994) 15 Cr App R (S) 216, where the offender was in possession of 16 Ecstacy tablets and 1.5 g of crack cocaine.

12.8.2   Class B drug offences

The maximum penalty for producing cannabis or another Class B drug, supplying such a drug, or possession of such a drug with intent to supply, is 14 years' on indictment (MDA 1971, sch. 4); six months, a fine not exceeding £5,000, or both, summarily. The maximum for possession of such a drug is five years on indictment (MDA 1971, sch. 4); three months, a fine not exceeding £5,000, or both, summarily. The maximum penalty for being concerned in the management of premises etc. is 14 years on indictment (MDA 1971, sch. 4); six months, a fine not exceeding £5,000 or both, summarily. The maximum for fraudulently evading prohibition on importation or exportation of such a drug is 14 years on indictment (Customs and Excise Management Act 1979, s. 170); six months, a fine not exceeding £5,000, or both, summarily. The maximum for cultivation of cannabis plants is 14 years on indictment (MDA 1971, sch. 4); six months, a fine not exceeding £5,000, or both, summarily.

In the Crown Court in 1998, there were 4,954 offenders sentenced for production, supply, or possession with intent to supply a Class B drug, of whom 2,976 received immediate custody, 60 per cent of offenders dealt with. There were 1,448 offenders sentenced for possession of a Class B drug, 293 of whom received immediate custody. Other significant disposals were fine (338), CRO (212) and CPO (179).

The Court of Appeal guideline case for these offences is, again, *Aramah* (1982) 4 Cr App R (S) 407, where Lord Lane CJ distinguished importation, supply and possession of cannabis. The passage is set out as amended by later decisions, including *Ronchetti* [1998] 2 Cr App R (S) 100.

Class B Drugs, particularly cannabis:

Importation of cannabis: Importation of very small amounts for personal use can be dealt with as if it were simple possession, with which we will deal later. Otherwise importations of amounts up to about 20 kg of [cannabis resin and cannabis, or the equivalent in cannabis oil] will, save in the most exceptional circumstances, attract sentences of between 18 months and three years, with the lowest ranges reserved for pleas of guilty where there has been small profit to the offender. The good character of the courier (as he usually is) is of less importance than the good character of the defendant in other cases. The reason for this is, it is well known that the large scale operator looks for couriers of good character and for people of a sort which are likely to exercise the sympathy of the court if they are detected and arrested. Consequently one will frequently find that students and sick and elderly people are used as couriers for two reasons: first of all they are vulnerable to suggestion and vulnerable to the offer of quick profit, and secondly it is felt that the courts may be moved to misplaced sympathy in their case. There are few, if any, occasions when anything other than an immediate custodial sentence is proper in this type of importation. Medium quantities, over 20 kg, will attract sentences of three to six years' imprisonment, depending upon the amount involved, and all the other circumstances of the case. [Importation of 100 kg by persons playing more than a subordinate role should attract a sentence of seven to eight years.] Large scale or wholesale importation [500 kg or more] will justify sentences in the region of 10 years' imprisonment for those playing other than a subordinate role. [Larger importations would attract a higher starting point, which should rise according to the roles played, the weight involved and all the other circumstances of the case, up to the statutory maximum of 14 years provided by Parliament.]

Supply of cannabis: Here again the supply of massive quantities will justify sentences in the region of 10 years for those playing anything more than a subordinate role. Otherwise the bracket should be between one to four years' imprisonment, depending on the scale of the operation. Supplying a number of small sellers — wholesaling if you like — comes at the top of the bracket. At the lower end will be the retailer of a small amount to a consumer. Where there is no commercial motive (for example, where cannabis is supplied at a party), the offence may well be serious enough to justify a custodial sentence.

Possession of cannabis: When only small amounts are involved being for personal use, the offence can often be met by a fine. If the history shows however a persistent flouting of the law, imprisonment may become necessary.

In *Wijs* [1998] 2 Cr App R (S) 436 sentencing guidelines were issued by the Court of Appeal for unlawful importation of amphetamine and possession of that drug with intent to supply. Lord Bingham CJ said that no distinctions should be drawn between different drugs within Class B but that, weight for weight, amphetamine was much more valuable than cannabis. Sentencing should depend not on market value but on the quantity of amphetamine calculated on the basis of 100 per cent purity. On that basis, between 10 and 15 kg of the drug should attract 7–10 years, and more than 15 kg upwards of ten years to the maximum of 14 years.

As far as supply, and possession with intent to supply, a Class B drug is concerned, when tried summarily, the Magistrates' Association Guidelines (2000) indicate the following:

Aggravating Factors +
commercial production, large amount, venue (e.g., prisons, educational establishments), deliberate adulteration, offence committed on bail, previous convictions and failures to respond to previous sentences, if relevant.

Mitigating Factors −
not commercial, small amount.

The Guidelines suggest that magistrates should consider whether the offence is so serious that only custody can be justified. Other cases should be committed for trial. In all cases forfeiture of drugs and equipment should be considered.

When cases of simple possession of Class B drugs are dealt with summarily the Magistrates' Association Guidelines (2000) indicate the following:

Aggravating Factors +
for example large amount, offence committed on bail, previous convictions and failures to respond to previous sentences, if relevant.

Mitigating Factors −
for example small amount.

Guideline level of sentence is a fine. In all cases forfeiture of all drugs and equipment should be considered.

The Association Guidelines relating to cultivation of cannabis are similar. Specific factors indicating a lesser degree of seriousness are where the cultivation was for personal use rather than commercial, and where the offender was not responsible for the planting.

In 1998 magistrates' courts sentenced 2,702 cases of possession of Class B drugs with intent to supply. Of those, 24 received custodial sentences. More frequent disposals were fine (1,044), discharge (376), CPO (462) and CRO (281). There were 25,868 cases of simple possession of Class B drugs. The great majority (17,868) were fined. Other disposals included discharge (5,135), CRO (1,149) and custody (331).

There are several Court of Appeal decisions following and applying the guidelines in *Aramah* and dealing with the appropriate sentences for offences in connection with Class B drug offences, mainly cannabis. The first group is concerned with importation. At the top end of the scale, the offenders in *Fishleigh* [1996] 2 Cr App R (S) 283 imported four tonnes of cannabis, worth £13 million, in a fishing boat. Sentences of $12\frac{1}{2}$ years were reduced to nine years on appeal. In *Klitkze* (1994) 16 Cr App R (S) 445 the offender imported over 15 kg of herbal cannabis concealed in a crate containing machinery. A prison sentence of four years was reduced to three years on appeal. Towards the lower end of the importation scale, in *Watson* (1988) 10 Cr App R (S) 256 the offender and another woman imported 12 kg of cannabis, the offender's suitcase containing 7.4 kg. She was convicted after a trial and sentenced to four years. This was reduced to two years, in line with the *Aramah* guidelines. In *Harris* (1989) 11 Cr App R (S) 169, where the amount involved was just over 6 kg and the offender pleaded guilty, a three-year sentence was reduced to 18 months.

In *Morgan* (1985) 7 Cr App R (S) 443 sentences of six years, seven years and eight years were upheld on offenders convicted after a trial of conspiring to manufacture amphetamine sulphate and who had already successfully marketed 2.5 kg of the drug with a street value of £40,000 to £50,000. See also *Shaw* (1986) 8 Cr App R (S) 16, where a sentence of ten years was upheld in respect of a carefully planned operation to produce amphetamine, albeit that 'some of the arrangements were ill-concealed, and even inept'.

The second group of cases involves distribution of Class B drugs, mainly cannabis. Again, a scale of sentences may be ascertained, following the *Aramah* guidelines. Distribution on a large scale was involved in *Netts* [1997] 2 Cr App R (S) 117, where the offender was stopped while driving his car and found to be in possession of 90 kg of cannabis resin in 24 packages. It was accepted that he was acting as a courier for the drugs. Taking account of the fact that the offender had no previous convictions, a sentence of seven years was reduced to five years on appeal. In *Chatfield* (1983) 5 Cr App R (S) 289 the offenders pleaded guilty to possession of 2 kg of cannabis with intent to supply. Sentences of 30 months were upheld by the Court of Appeal, Watkins LJ commenting that: 'They came somewhere between about half-way towards and the end of the bracket, allowance being made for the fact that they pleaded guilty and for their characters.' In *Hill* (1988) 10 Cr App R (S) 150 the offender had been dealing in cannabis from his home on a regular basis for some time, earning £100 per week from this activity. A 30-month sentence, described by the Court of Appeal as 'near the top end of the bracket for offences of this sort' was reduced to 21 months, since 'although the supply was on a regular basis to a large number of people, the amounts involved were comparatively small' and greater recognition should have been given to the offender's guilty plea. Thirty months was reduced to 15 months in *Barton* [1997] 1 Cr App R (S) 140, where the amount of the drug was relatively small (7.2 kg) but the offence was aggravated by the fact that the offender had supplied a serving prisoner.

For cases of simple possession of small amounts of cannabis for personal use, the guidelines in *Aramah* indicate that a fine will often be an appropriate penalty, unless there is repetition involving 'flouting of the law'. In *Jones* (1981) 3 Cr App R (S) 51 the offender was convicted of possession of 3.2 g of cannabis. Five years earlier he had been convicted of cultivating and possessing cannabis and fined £30. This time he was sentenced to three months' imprisonment, suspended, plus a £50 fine. The Court of Appeal said that the prison sentence was inappropriate, and quashed it, leaving the fine in place. See also *Aldred* (1983) 5 Cr App R (S) 393.

In cases involving the cultivation of cannabis, a crucial matter is whether the cannabis was for personal use or for supply. In *Stearn* (1982) 4 Cr App R (S) 195 the Court of Appeal said that an immediate custodial sentence was necessary where the offender grew 44 cannabis plants and admitted selling cannabis at about £20 an ounce, earning £1,500 from a crop of plants. A sentence of three and a half years was reduced to two years, taking account of the offender's previous good character, cooperation with the police and guilty plea. Other cases involving commercial cultivation of plants are *Challis* [1997] 1 Cr App R (S) 425 and *Mineham* [1997] 1 Cr App R (S) 268. Custodial sentences of two years and three years respectively were correct. Few cases are reported on the appropriate sentencing pattern for the offence of permitting premises to be used for smoking cannabis. In *Morrison* [1996] 1 Cr App R (S) 263 the offender allowed young people aged 14 or 15 to visit his home and smoke cannabis, but he did not supply them with the drug. Twelve months' imprisonment was upheld. In *Pusser* (1983) 5 Cr App R (S) 225, however, the offender was the licensee of a public house at which cannabis was smoked, though there was no evidence that he used cannabis himself. After a warning, the police searched the premises and found cannabis in several forms. The Court of Appeal described this as 'a bad case' and upheld the sentence of six months' imprisonment.

12.8.3 Class C drug offences

The maximum penalty for producing, supplying, or possession with intent to supply a Class C drug is five years on indictment (MDA 1971, sch. 4); three months, a fine not exceeding £2,500, or both, summarily. The maximum penalty for possession of a Class C drug is two years on indictment (MDA 1971, sch. 4); three months, a fine not exceeding £1,000, or both, summarily.

In the Crown Court in 1998, there were 58 offenders sentenced for production, supply, or possession with intent to supply a Class C drug, of whom 27 received immediate custody. There were 14 offenders sentenced for possession of a Class C drug, five of whom received custody. In the magistrates' courts in 1998, 50 offenders were sentenced for production, supply, or possession with intent to supply a Class C drug, of whom 11 received immediate custody. There were 174 offenders sentenced for possession of a Class C drug, seven of whom received custody.

12.9 SENTENCING FOR ROAD TRAFFIC OFFENCES

It should be noted that where the power to endorse is specified in relation to the offences below, the court must endorse, unless special reasons are established. The court has discretion to disqualify in every case where it endorses a licence. Where mandatory disqualification is indicated, the court must disqualify for at least 12 months, unless special reasons are established (see **10.1**). The power to order disqualification until the offender passes the driving test is considered at **10.1.7**. For causing death by dangerous driving, see **12.1.8**.

12.9.1 Dangerous driving

The maximum penalty for dangerous driving is two years on indictment; six months, a fine not exceeding £5,000, or both, summarily (RTA 1988, s. 2). The court must disqualify for at least 12 months. It must endorse the licence (3–11 points) if not disqualified. An extended re-test must be ordered.

When tried summarily, the Magistrates' Association Guidelines (2000) indicate the following:

Aggravating Factors +
avoiding detection or apprehension; competitive driving; racing, showing off; disregard of warnings e.g. from passengers or others in vicinity; evidence of alcohol or drugs; excessive speed; prolonged, persistent, deliberate, bad driving; serious risk, using a hand-held mobile phone, offence committed on bail, previous convictions and failures to respond to previous sentences, if relevant.

Mitigating Factors −
emergency; single incident; speed not excessive.

The Guidelines advise that magistrates should consider whether the offence is so serious that only custody can be justified; the offender's licence must be endorsed and he should be disqualified for at least the compulsory minimum and required to re-test.

In the Crown Court in 1998, there were 1,623 offenders for dangerous driving, of whom 971 received immediate custody, 60 per cent of offenders dealt with. Other significant disposals were CRO (216) and fine (116). In the magistrates' courts, there were 2,853 offenders sentenced for the offence, of whom 568 received immediate custody, 20 per cent of offenders dealt with. Other significant disposals were fine (947) and CPO (578).

There is no guideline judgment on the offence of dangerous driving, though some of the observations of the Court of Appeal in the guideline case of *Boswell* (1984) 6 Cr App R (S) 257, which relates to the offence of causing death by dangerous driving, are relevant (see **12.2.8**). There are several helpful Court of Appeal decisions dealing with sentencing for the most serious instances of dangerous driving. In *Steel* (1993) 14 Cr App R (S) 218 Tudor Evans J said 'when sentencing in cases of [dangerous] driving where personal injury has been caused the judge must consider and give full weight to all the facts and circumstances, including the gravity of the consequences of the driving to members of the public. It seems to us that if a driver drives recklessly he takes his chance as to the consequences of his driving.' In that case the offender, who had a blood alcohol level of 146 mg per 100 ml of blood (the legal limit is 80 mg) was driving at an excessive speed and executed a dangerous overtaking manoevre on a dual carriageway. His car hit the central verge and landed in the other carriageway, where it collided with a motor-cyclist. The motor-cyclist was severely injured, part of his leg being severed in the impact. The Court of Appeal reduced a sentence of 15 months' imprisonment to 12 months, having regard to the fact that the maximum sentence was two years and giving proper weight to mitigation in 'what was a bad case of reckless driving but not at the top of the scale'. Disqualification for five years was upheld. The weight given in this case to the results of the bad driving may be contrasted with the approach taken in *Krawec* (1984) 6 Cr App R (S) 367 (see **12.9.2**).

In *Moore* (1995) 16 Cr App R (S) 536, a sentence of nine months' imprisonment was upheld. The offender had driven a heavy goods vehicle in foggy conditions and had collided with a van at some road works. The van driver was injured. Disqualification was, on appeal, reduced for five years to three years. In *Garraway* (1988) 10 Cr App R (S) 316 the offender had been seen by police officers driving at an excessive speed in a restricted area. When they pursued him, he drove past a second police car which attempted to stop him, mounting the pavement to do so, and drove away with no lights at high speed, crossing traffic lights at red in a 'deliberate and determined attempt to avoid the police'. Three months' imprisonment was upheld. In *Offer* [1996] 1 Cr App R (S) 143 the offender was seen driving on the motorway at speeds in excess of 100 m.p.h. while using a mobile telephone and with a map draped over the steering wheel. While driving at this speed he narrowly missed a workman who was putting out cones and who was forced to jump out of the way. The offender had an exemplary character and clean record. A prison sentence of three months was reduced to 28 days, and disqualification for 18 months was upheld. In *Bull* [1997] 2 Cr App R (S) 178 the offender drove very close behind another car with his lights full on, and twice overtook the car and slowed down in front of it. The Court of Appeal accepted that this was 'a dreadful exhibition of a course of driving which was intended to terrify' the other driver, who eventually got out and hid in a garden. A sentence of six months' imprisonment was upheld but the term of disqualification was reduced from three years to two.

12.9.2 Careless driving

The maximum penalty for careless driving is a fine not exceeding level 4. The court must endorse (3–9 penalty points) or may disqualify (RTA 1988, s. 3). The offence is triable only summarily.

The Magistrates' Association Guidelines (2000) indicate that:

Aggravating Factors +
excessive speed, serious risk, high degree of carelessness, using a hand-held mobile phone, offence committed on bail, previous convictions and failures to respond to previous sentences, if relevant.

Mitigating Factors −
sudden change in weather conditions, minor risk, momentary lapse, negligible/parking damage.

The Guidelines indicate that magistrates should consider whether discharge or a fine is appropriate.

In straightforward cases of careless driving, the appropriate penalty is almost invariably a fine, together with the imposition of penalty points, with the possibility of disqualification in a very bad case. Where the careless driving results in unforeseen and tragic results, a difficult sentencing problem arises. Since the offence is summary only, few opportunities arise for Court of Appeal guidance. In *Krawec* (1984) 6 Cr App R (S) 367, however, the offender had been convicted of careless driving on an indictment for causing death by reckless driving. While riding his motor-cycle he had collided with an elderly pedestrian, who was killed. The offender said that at the time of the collision he had been concentrating on a car in front of him which was turning right at traffic lights and he failed to see the pedestrian until it was too late. The offender was fined £350 and his licence was endorsed with five penalty points. According to Lord Lane CJ, on appeal, 'In our judgment the unforeseen and unexpected results of the carelessness are not in themselves relevant to penalty. The primary considerations are the quality of the driving, the extent to which the appellant on the particular occasion fell below the standard of the reasonably competent driver; in other words, the degree of carelessness and culpability. The unforeseen circumstances may sometimes be relevant to those considerations. In the present case the fact that the appellant failed to see the pedestrian until it was too late and therefore collided with him was plainly a relevant factor. We do not think that the fact that the unfortunate man died was relevant to this charge.' The fine was reduced to £250. *Krawec* was followed in subsequent cases, including *Soutar* (1993) 15 Cr App R (S) 432, but in *Simmonds* [1999] 2 Cr App R (S) 18 it was said that the sentences must bear in mind the fact that a life has been lost when sentencing in such cases. There is now some doubt as to the correct approach to be adopted.

In *Sanders* (1987) 9 Cr App R (S) 312 the offender, aged 44, pleaded guilty to careless driving on an indictment for reckless driving. He had driven at an excessive speed, lost control of his car on a bridge and collided with a car coming in the opposite direction, severely injuring the other driver. The offender was fined £750 and disqualified for 12 months. The Court of Appeal noted the mitigating factors of the offender's guilty plea and his completely clean record. The fine was approved, but the period of disqualification was reduced to six months. Another example is *Soutar* (1993) 15 Cr App R (S) 432, where the offender was driving at 50 mph in a 40 mph limit late at night and failed to see a pedestrian who was crossing the road. The pedestrian was gravely injured. The Court of Appeal adjusted the penalty to a fine of £750 and disqualification for 18 months. In *Downing* [1996] 1 Cr App R (S) 419 the offender, driving a car with four passengers, crossed to the opposite carriageway at a bend, swerved to avoid an oncoming car and collided with a pub sign. Three of the passengers were killed. There was no suggestion that the offender had been drinking. The penalty was a £500 fine together with disqualification for six months.

12.9.3 Drunken driving

The maximum penalty for drunken driving or driving with excess alcohol is six months, a fine not exceeding £5,000, or both. Disqualification (at least 12 months) and endorsement (3–11 penalty points) are obligatory. The offence is triable only summarily.

The level of penalty is closely related to the extent by which the offender exceeds the legal limit. The legal limits are:

(a) breath: 35 mcg per 100 ml;
(b) blood: 80 mg per 100 ml;
(c) urine: 107 mg per 100 ml.

The Magistrates' Association Guidelines (2000) indicate:

Aggravating Factors +
police chase, caused injury/fear/damage, type of vehicle e.g. carrying passengers for reward/large goods vehicle, evidence of nature of the driving, high reading (and in combination with above) ability to drive seriously impaired.

Mitigating Factors −
spiked drinks, moving a vehicle a very short distance, emergency.

The following table indicates the suggested level of sentence:

Breath	Blood	Urine	Disqualify	Guideline
36–55	80–125	107–170	12 months	Fine of net income for 1 week
56–70	126–160	171–214	18 months	Fine of $1\frac{1}{2}$ times net income for 1 week
71–85	161–195	215–260	24 months	Fine of $1\frac{1}{2}$ times net income for 1 week
86–100	196–229	261–308	24 months	Consider community penalty
101–115	230–264	309–354	30 months	
116–130	265–300	355–400	30 months	Consider custody
131 +	301 +	401 +	36 months	

In *Tupa* (1973) 58 Cr App R 234 Roskill LJ commented in respect of an offender who was found to have 289 mg of alcohol per 100 ml of blood (equivalent to 125 mcg of alcohol in breath) that 'this court wishes to make it as clear as it can that, in many cases of this kind where the amount of alcohol imbibed and found in a person's blood after he had been breathalysed is anything like the quantity in the present case, a custodial sentence is entirely proper and ought not to be interfered with on appeal'. In *Shoult* [1996] 2 Cr App R (S) 234 Lord Taylor of Gosforth CJ said that 'We consider that the guidelines as to penalties set out by the Magistrates' Association are sound and appropriate although, of course, each case has to be considered individually on its own merits.'

12.9.4 Refusal to provide a specimen

The maximum penalty for refusing to provide an evidential specimen after driving is six months, a fine not exceeding £5,000, or both. Disqualification (at least 12 months) and endorsement (3–11 penalty points) are obligatory. The offence is triable only summarily. The Magistrates' Association Guidelines (2000) suggest a fine of $1\frac{1}{2}$ times net income for 1 week and disqualification for 18 months.

The maximum penalty for being drunk in charge of a vehicle or refusing to provide an evidential specimen is three months, a fine not exceeding level 4, or both. Endorsement (10 penalty points) is obligatory. The offence is triable only summarily. The Magistrates' Association Guidelines (2000) suggest a fine of net income for 1 week.

The maximum penalty for refusing a roadside breath test is a fine not exceeding level 3. Endorsement (4 penalty points) is obligatory; disqualification is discretionary. The offence is triable only summarily. The Magistrates' Association Guidelines (2000) suggest a fine of one half of net income for 1 week.

12.9.5 Failing to stop

The maximum penalty for failing to stop after an accident (or failing to report it) is six months' imprisonment, or a fine not exceeding level 5, or both. Endorsement (5–10 penalty points) is obligatory; disqualification is discretionary. The offence is triable only summarily. The Magistrates' Association Guidelines (2000) suggest a fine of net income for 1 week for either of these offence, and disqualification in serious cases.

12.9.6 Exceeding speed limit

The maximum penalty for exceeding the speed limit is a fine not exceeding level 3 (or level 4 if on the motorway). Endorsement (3–6 penalty points) is obligatory; disqualification is discretionary. The offence is triable only summarily. The Magistrates' Association Guidelines (2000) suggest the following table of penalties for speeding:

Guideline penalty points	Legal speed limits	Excess speed	Guideline fines
3	20–30 m.p.h. 40–50 m.p.h. 60–70 m.p.h.	Up to 10 m.p.h. Up to 15 m.p.h. Up to 20 m.p.h.	$\frac{1}{2}$ of net income for one week
4 or 5 or disqualify up to 42 days	20–30 m.p.h. 40–50 m.p.h. 60–70 m.p.h.	From 11–20 From 16–25 From 21–30	Net income for one week
6 or disqualify up to 56 days	20–30 m.p.h. 40–50 m.p.h. 60–70 m.p.h.	From 21–30 From 26–35 From 31–40	Net income for one week

Relevant aggravating features of the offence are where the vehicle was an LGV, HGV, PCV, or minicab, depending on the location, time of day, and whether the vehicle was drawing a caravan. Relevant mitigating factors are where there was a genuine emergency or where there was a sudden charge of speed limit (e.g., from 40 m.p.h. to 30 m.p.h.).

12.9.7 Driving while disqualified

The maximum penalty for driving while disqualified is six months, a fine not exceeding £5,000, or both (RTA 1988, s. 103). Endorsement (6 penalty points) is obligatory; disqualification is discretionary. The offence is triable only summarily.

The Magistrates' Association Guidelines (2000) indicate that:

Aggravating Factors +

efforts to avoid detection; long distance driven; planned, long term evasion; recent disqualification, offence committed on bail, previous convictions and failures to respond to previous sentences, if relevant.

Mitigating Factors −

emergency established; short distance driven, full period expired but test not re-taken.

The Guidelines suggest that magistrates should consider whether the offence is so serious that only custody can be justified.

12.9.8 Taking vehicle without consent

The maximum penalty for taking a conveyance, usually a motor vehicle, without the owner's consent (known colloquially as TWOC) is six months, a fine not exceeding £5,000, or both (Theft Act 1968, s. 12). The court may disqualify. The offence is triable only summarily.

Magistrates' courts sentenced 6,721 cases of TWOC in 1998, and imposed custodial sentences in 1,443 of those cases (21 per cent). The most frequent disposals were discharge (1,333), fine (1,046), CPO (720), CRO (629), attendance centre (538), supervision (546) and CPRO (345). The Crown Court also sentenced 196 offenders for this offence where the matter was committed there. Custody was imposed in 108 of those cases (55 per cent).

The Magistrates' Association Guidelines (2000) indicate:

Aggravating Factors +

group action, premeditated, related damage, professional hallmarks, vulnerable victim, offence committed on bail, previous convictions and failures to respond to previous sentences, if relevant.

Mitigating Factors −

misunderstanding with owner, soon returned, vehicle belonged to family or friend.

The Guidelines indicate that magistrates should consider whether the offence is serious enough for a community penalty.

This offence was formerly triable either way. Hence there is some Court of Appeal guidance as to the more serious examples of this offence, though such cases might now be charged as aggravated vehicle-taking (see **12.9.9**). In *Bushell* (1987) 9 Cr App R (S) 537 the offender, aged 17 and with no previous convictions, took a friend's car without permission and subsequently crashed it, damaging it beyond repair. A sentence of 180 hours' community service, together with a disqualification for one year, was upheld by the Court of Appeal. Where the offence is combined with other offences arising out of the same circumstances, an immediate custodial sentence may be appropriate. Thus in *Jeary* (1986) 8 Cr App R (S) 491 the offender, who was aged 18 and had one previous finding of guilt for assault occasioning actual bodily harm, pleaded guilty to two counts of taking a conveyance, two counts of theft and asked for two other offences to be taken into consideration. He was involved with others in taking several cars in the course of an evening and driving them at high speed in a city centre 'just as a bit of fun'. Three cars were damaged, one beyond repair. The offender also admitted taking property from the cars, though most of that was recovered. The Court of Appeal agreed with the sentencer's view that the offences were so serious that a non-custodial sentence could not be justified because, in addition to the unlawful taking, the cars had been deliberately damaged. Four months' detention was upheld.

12.9.9 Aggravated vehicle-taking

The maximum penalty for this offence is two years on indictment (or five years where it is proved that the accident caused the death of the person concerned); six months, a fine not exceeding £5,000 or both, summarily (Theft Act 1968, s. 12A). Disqualification and endorsement (3–11 penalty points) are obligatory.

Magistrates' courts sentenced 1,345 cases of summary aggravated vehicle-taking in 1998, and imposed custodial sentences in 314 of those cases (23 per cent). The Crown Court sentenced 1,388 offenders for aggravated vehicle-taking in 1998, imposing custody in 1,064 cases (77 per cent).

When dealt with summarily, the Magistrates' Association Guidelines (2000) indicate:

Aggravating Factors +
trying to avoid detection or apprehension, competitive driving, racing, showing off, disregard of warnings, e.g. from passengers or others in vicinity, group action, police chase, pre-meditated, serious injury/damage, serious risk, offence committed on bail, previous convictions and failures to respond to previous sentences, if relevant.

Mitigating Factors −
impulsive, no competitiveness/racing, passenger only, single incident of bad driving, speed not excessive, very minor injury/damage.

The Guidelines suggest that magistrates should consider whether the offence is so serious that only custody can be justified.

In *Bird* (1993) 14 Cr App R (S) 343 the Court of Appeal said that when sentencing for this offence, relevant aggravating features would be related to the overall culpability of the driver: how bad the driving was and for how long it had lasted and, to a lesser extent, how much injury or damage had been caused. Drink would affect the assessment of culpability, but where drink was a major factor in the case it would be the subject of a separate charge. Mitigation might be found in a guilty plea showing contrition, but the youth of the offender would be of less significance in this type of case than in others, since the offence was committed primarily by young offenders. Subsequent cases include *Evans* (1993) 15 Cr App R (S) 13, where the offender, after spending the afternoon drinking, so that he had a blood alcohol level of 142 mg per 100 ml of blood, took a car which had the keys left in it. He drove for a mile or so and then hit a tree, killing one of the passengers. Nine months' detention in a young offender institution was upheld. Another example is *Robinson* (1993) 15 Cr App R (S) 342, where the offender and an accomplice took the car, used it in connection with a burglary and then drove it at over 100 mph until colliding with another car and injuring its occupants. Twenty-one months' detention in a young offender institution was appropriate for the offender who drove the car, and 18 months for his accomplice passenger. In *Sealey* (1993) 15 Cr App R (S) 189 the offender was a passenger in a car which had been taken unlawfully and then driven at excessive speed and dangerously when chased by the police. Nine months' imprisonment plus disqualification for two years was upheld.

12.9.10 Interference with motor vehicles

The maximum penalty is three months' imprisonment, a fine not exceeding level 4 on the standard scale, or both (Criminal Attempts Act 1981, s. 9). The offence is triable only summarily. In 1998 magistrates sentenced 2,652 offenders for this offence. The main disposals were discharge (698), fine (607), custody (371) and CPO (280).

13 Appeals, Rehabilitation and Pardon

The courts which hear appeals against sentence have, it is suggested, two vital tasks to perform in addition to the obvious one of ensuring that any injustice done to an individual appellant when sentenced at first instance is corrected. The first of these tasks is to establish, explain and develop a coherent body of sentencing principles which can be applied by all sentencers. The second is to encourage consistency in sentencing practice, within the appropriate statutory framework and sentencing guideline cases, so that there are not wild fluctuations from one court to another in the way in which similar cases are dealt with. This chapter considers the arrangements for appeal against sentences passed by magistrates' courts and by the Crown Court.

13.1 APPEAL AGAINST SENTENCE PASSED BY A MAGISTRATES' COURT

Most appeals against sentence passed by a magistrates' court are heard by the Crown Court. A small minority are heard by a Divisional Court of the Queen's Bench Division. These methods of appeal are the same whether the sentence was passed for a summary offence or for an offence triable either way, and irrespective of whether the sentence was passed in the youth court or in the adult magistrates' court.

13.1.1 Appeals to the Crown Court

Only the offender may appeal (and of course he may be appealing solely against sentence or, if he pleaded not guilty at his trial, he may appeal against conviction and sentence). There is no right of prosecution appeal against a sentence which is considered to be too lenient (in contrast to the position on appeal from some sentences passed in the Crown Court). The offender's right of appeal is automatic, and lies without any requirement of leave (MCA 1980, s. 108). Notice merely has to be given to the clerk of the magistrates' court which passed the sentence, within 21 days of being sentenced, that the offender intends to appeal. The appellant can appeal against any sentence or order made by the magistrates, apart from:

(a) an order to pay prosecution costs; or

(b) an order under the Protection of Animals Act 1911, s. 2, ordering the destruction of an animal; or

(c) an order connected with the contribution which he should make to his own legal aid costs (*Hayden* [1975] 1 WLR 852).

For avoidance of any doubt, appeal does lie against a magistrates' court's decision to pass an absolute or conditional discharge upon an offender (MCA 1980, s. 108(1A)), though it is unlikely that an offender would wish to appeal against such a sentence. Appeal does lie against an order disqualifying the offender from driving, ordering his deportation, making a hospital order or a compensation order against him or binding him over to keep the peace. On this last, see Magistrates' Courts (Appeals from Binding Over Orders) Act 1956, s. 1(1).

A further possibility, in the event of an unsuccessful appeal having already been made, is that the Criminal Cases Review Commission (established by the CAA 1995) may choose to refer the case to the Crown Court if, according to the test in s. 13 of the CAA 1995, there is a real possibility that the [conviction or] sentence will not be upheld if the reference is made. A reference by the Commission is treated for all purposes as an appeal under MCA 1980, s. 108, except that in these circumstances the Crown Court cannot increase the sentence (CAA 1995, s. 11(6)).

The appeal is heard by a Crown Court judge, probably a circuit judge or a recorder, who sits for this purpose with at least two lay justices. The involvement of lay justices in the appeal process is to ensure that the judge is fully aware of magistrates' sentencing practice. The appeal takes the form of a rehearing of the stage between conviction and sentence. There may be additional material before the court, such as an updated pre-sentence report. Whenever a Crown Court judge sits with lay justices, the latter should take a full part in the proceedings. In the event of disagreement, the majority view prevails. Thus, at least in theory, the magistrates can outvote the judge. The justices must, however, accept any directions from the judge on any point of law relevant to the appeal (*Orpin* [1975] QB 283). The Crown Court may confirm the sentence which was passed by the magistrates and dismiss the appeal, it may reduce the sentence or it may *increase* it up to the maximum which the magistrates could have imposed. Thus, unlike the Court of Appeal (see **13.2**), the Crown Court does have a limited power to increase sentence on appeal. In fact it is unusual for the Crown Court to increase sentence but, bearing in mind that leave is not required for appeal to the Crown Court, the possibility of increasing sentence may act as a deterrent against unmeritorious appeals. Further, whenever an appeal fails, the appellant may be ordered to pay the prosecution costs (POA 1985, s. 18(1)(b)). The Crown Court can increase any part of the original sentence, even if the appellant is not appealing against that part (SCA 1981, s. 48(2)).

In announcing its decision on an appeal from a magistrates' court, the Crown Court will give only brief oral reasons, which are not reported. Thus, appeal to the Crown Court provides a quick and convenient way of correcting sentencing errors made by the magistrates in individual cases, but this procedure has not developed into a means for Crown Court judges to provide general sentencing guidance for magistrates. A note of the Crown Court's decision, and a short summary of reasons, is sent from the Crown Court to the clerk of the magistrates' court concerned. The clerk may wish to show this to the magistrates who made the original decision.

A decision of the Crown Court on an appeal from a magistrates' court may be appealed by way of case stated (see **13.1.2**) in the same circumstances as a decision by magistrates may be appealed (SCA 1981, s. 28). Judicial review may also be available (SCA 1981, s. 29).

13.1.2 Appeal to the Divisional Court: case stated

Either the offender or the prosecution may appeal to the Divisional Court against a sentencing decision made by a magistrates' court. The appeal must either be on the grounds that the sentence was wrong in law or that the sentence was in excess of jurisdiction (MCA 1980, s. 111). Appeals to the Divisional Court are relatively rare because, whilst many offenders might claim that they were sentenced by magistrates more severely than they should have been, only a handful can claim that the magistrates demonstrably approached their sentencing task on the wrong legal basis or passed a sentence which was beyond their powers. If the offender's complaint is simply that he was sentenced too severely, his recourse must (subject to one exception considered below) be to the Crown Court. Indeed, if an appellant chooses to appeal to the Divisional Court, he loses his right of appeal to the Crown Court (MCA 1980, s. 111(4)). An offender will succeed in such an application only where the sentence imposed by the magistrates was 'truly astonishing' (*Tucker* v *Director of Public Prosecutions* [1992] 4 All ER 901). The imposition of such a sentence shows that the magistrates must have made an error of law.

This method of appeal is known as appeal by case stated. The magistrates, on application by the appellant made within 21 days, are required to draw up a document listing the facts which they found proved, the question of law or jurisdiction upon which the view of the Divisional Court is sought and their own ruling on the matter. The 21-day period is strict, and cannot be varied, even by the High Court (MCA 1980, s. 111(2); *Michael* v *Gowland* [1977] 1 WLR 296). The hearing in the Divisional Court generally takes the form of legal argument based on the facts set out in the case which the magistrates have stated (rather than being a rehearing). The Divisional Court must consist of at least two High Court judges (SCA 1981, s. 66(3)). Often three judges sit, including the Lord Chief Justice and, at his request, Lords Justices of Appeal may also sit. Thus, there is a considerable overlap of personnel between the Divisional Court and the Court of Appeal. Full, reasoned judgments are given, which are reported in the same way as judgments of the Court of Appeal. If a two-judge court is evenly divided, the appeal fails (*Flannagan* v *Shaw* [1920] 3 KB 96). Section 111 of the MCA 1980 states that, in addition to the offender and the prosecution, 'Any person who . . . is aggrieved by the conviction, order, determination, or other proceeding of the court' may state a case for the Divisional Court. It is thus possible that, say, the victim of an offence who feels aggrieved by the failure of the magistrates to make a compensation order in a clear case or, perhaps, by the imposition upon the offender of what the victim regards as an unduly lenient sentence, might take the complaint to the Divisional Court in this way.

In disposing of an appeal, the Divisional Court may 'reverse, affirm or amend' the magistrates' decision, remit the matter to them with their opinion thereon or make any other order it thinks fit (SCA 1981, s. 28A). Thus, to take an example encountered frequently in practice, if the prosecution appeals against the magistrates' refusal to disqualify for an offence carrying obligatory disqualification, the Divisional Court could send the case back to the magistrates with its opinion that the facts relied on by the motorist concerned were not capable in law of amounting to special reasons. The magistrates would then have to disqualify for at least 12 months. In other cases, where it is plain what the proper sentence should be, the Divisional Court may simply substitute the correct sentence for the original one.

A decision of the Crown Court on an appeal from a magistrates' court may be appealed by way of case stated in the same circumstances as a decision by the magistrates may be appealed (SCA 1981, s. 28). An application for judicial review might also be made (SCA 1981, s. 29).

13.1.3 Application to the Divisional Court: judicial review

One of the High Court's tasks is to supervise the work of inferior tribunals. In doing so, the High Court exercises its powers of judicial review (principally the issuing of prerogative orders) to control the way in which a wide variety of courts and tribunals, and other persons who are under a duty to act judicially, exercise their powers. Judicial review is available in respect of all decisions taken by magistrates, including sentencing decisions. It is also available with respect to decisions of the Crown Court, when that court is not exercising its jurisdiction in matters relating to trial on indictment. As an alternative to appealing by case stated, a person having 'sufficient interest' in the matter (which certainly includes the offender and the prosecution) who considers that a sentence passed (whether by a magistrates' court, or by the Crown Court on appeal from magistrates) was outside the scope of the court's powers, that person may apply for judicial review of the decision which was made. While the offender and the prosecution clearly have 'sufficient interest' to make an application, it seems clear that other persons, such as the victim of an offence, might have such an interest. The application is to the Divisional Court, which may quash the sentence by means of an order of *certiorari* and replace it with whatever sentence it considers best (SCA 1981, ss. 31(5) and 43). As with case stated, the normal appeal process should have been exhausted before such an application is made.

On the face of it, the case stated and judicial review procedures are available in very similar circumstances and are likely to produce the same result. It was held in *St Albans Crown Court, ex parte Cinnamond* [1981] QB 480 that if magistrates pass a sentence which is far above the normal level of sentence for the offence in question, so that it may fairly be described as 'harsh and oppressive', they thereby err in law or act in excess of jurisdiction, and consequently the Divisional Court has power to reduce that sentence, even though the sentence passed was within the magistrates' statutory powers. The Divisional Court stated in *Universal Salvage* v *Boothby* (1983) 5 Cr App R (S) 428, that the Court is entitled to assume, either on a case stated or on an application for judicial review, that magistrates must have erred in law in a case where they have passed a sentence grossly out of line with good sentencing practice.

It seems that, where both case stated and judicial review might be available to an applicant, the former is the preferable course to choose because it enables the facts found by the magistrates, or by the Crown Court, to be placed more clearly before the Divisional Court. See further *Morpeth Justices, ex parte Ward* (1992) 95 Cr App R 215.

13.2   APPEAL BY OFFENDER AGAINST SENTENCE PASSED BY THE CROWN COURT

Appeals against sentences passed by the Crown Court are heard by the Court of Appeal (Criminal Division). This is so whether the sentence was passed following the offender's conviction on indictment or following his summary conviction and committal for sentence. This has been the case since 1907, when the Court of Criminal Appeal (as it was then called) was created.

All the Lords Justices of Appeal are members of the Court of Appeal (Criminal Division) (SCA 1981, s. 2(2)). In addition, the Division has certain ex officio members, notably the Lord Chief Justice, who is its president (SCA 1981, s. 3(2)). Although all the Lords Justices are entitled to sit in the Criminal Division, in practice only a minority do so, chiefly those who have had experience of the criminal courts either at the Bar or as a judge at first instance. The Lords Justices are assisted by High Court judges who may be requested (in effect, required) by the Lord Chief Justice to act as judges of the Criminal Division (s. 9(1)). Much of the Division's work is, in fact, carried out by High Court judges although, as one would expect, a judge is not allowed to be involved in any way in the disposal of an appeal against sentence which he imposed when sitting as a Crown Court judge (s. 56(2)). Any number of courts of the Criminal Divison may sit at any one time (s. 3(5)). For the purposes of determining an appeal against sentence, or granting or refusing any application connected with an appeal against sentence, a court is validly constituted if it comprises at least two judges qualified to sit in that Division (s. 55(4)). Decisions may be taken by a majority, but if a two-judge court is divided the case must be reassigned and re-argued before three judges (s. 55(5)). Only one judgment is given, that being pronounced either by the senior judge or such other member of the court as he directs to pronounce it (s. 59). Typically, a court hearing appeals against sentence might consist of the Lord Chief Justice plus two High Court judges or a Lord Justice plus one or two High Court judges, or even just two High Court judges. It should be noted that many ancillary decisions connected with an appeal (e.g. granting leave to appeal) do not have to go before a court but may be taken by a single judge, either a Lord Justice or a High Court judge requested by the Lord Chief Justice to act as a judge of the Criminal Division (see CAA 1968, s. 31). It should also be noted that the administration of the Division's work is in the hands of an official, the Registrar of Criminal Appeals, and his staff. In addition, the Registrar has certain quasi-judicial powers (e.g. in respect of granting legal aid).

As a result of the broad definition of 'sentence' contained in CAA 1968, s. 50(1), almost any order made by a Crown Court judge in respect of a convicted offender is capable of being the subject of an appeal to the Crown Court against sentence. This is so whether the order is a punishment or an ancillary order. The exceptional orders against which there is no possibility of an appeal are:

(a) the mandatory sentence of life imprisonment, custody for life, or detention at Her Majesty's pleasure which, depending on the offender's age, must be passed on an offender convicted of murder;

(b) a recommendation that an offender sentenced to life for murder should serve a minimum term in prison before being considered for early release on licence (*Aitken* [1966] 1 WLR 1076);

(c) an order concerning the contribution which the offender should make to his own legal aid costs, since even an acquitted defendant may be ordered to make such a contribution (*Raeburn* (1982) 74 Cr App R 21).

Subject to obtaining the Court of Appeal's leave, an offender convicted on indictment may appeal to the Court of Appeal against any sentence passed on him for the offence (CAA 1968, s. 9). Again, subject to obtaining leave, an offender summarily convicted and then committed by the magistrates to the Crown Court to be sentenced may appeal to the Court of Appeal against the Crown Court's sentence, but only if:

(a) it was one of custody for six months or more;

(b) a suspended sentence was brought into effect;

(c) the offender was disqualified from driving, or an order was made for his deportation; or

(d) the sentence is one which the convicting court had no power to pass (CAA 1968, s. 10).

Where the Crown Court has passed two or more sentences on the offender, an application for leave to appeal against any one of the sentences is treated as an application in respect of all of them (s. 11(2)).

A further possibility in the event of an unsuccessful appeal having been made or leave to appeal having been refused, is that the Criminal Cases Review Commission (established by the CAA 1995) may choose to refer a case decided in the Crown Court to the Court of Appeal if, according to the test in s. 13 of the CAA 1995, there is a real possibility that the conviction or sentence will not be upheld if the reference is made. A reference by the Commission is treated for all purposes as an appeal under the CAA 1968.

Appeals to the Court of Appeal against sentence normally lie only with leave of the court itself (CAA 1968, s. 11). It seems that leave is needed even where the trial court did not have power to pass the sentence it did (*Briggs* (1909) 1 Cr App R 192). The only exception is where the Crown Court judge who has just passed the sentence then grants a certificate that the case is fit for an appeal against sentence without the leave of the Court of Appeal (s. 11(1) and (1A)). This occurs very infrequently (an exceptional case is *Grant* (1990) 12 Cr App R (S) 441). So, for all practical purposes, leave of the Court of Appeal is always required. The granting of leave to appeal is customarily considered by a single judge. In summary, the procedure is that the appellant's solicitors serve on the Registrar of Criminal Appeals a Notice of Appeal and Grounds of Appeal. Notice should be served within 28 days of the date on which sentence was passed or order made (s. 18). If sentence was subsequently varied under SCA 1981, s. 47, then notice should be served within 28 days of that variation (SCA 1981, s. 47(5)). The Court of Appeal has power to extend the time-limit for giving notice (CAA 1968, s. 18(3)), but an application for an extension of time should be accompanied with an explanation for the delay (*Cullum* (1942) 28 Cr App R 150). The grounds are usually settled by counsel, and must identify with reasonable detail the matters relied on by the appellant to justify a reduction in sentence.

The Registrar of Criminal Appeals then obtains all the relevant documents, such as a transcript of the proceedings in the Crown Court at the sentencing stage, together with copies of any reports which were put before the Crown Court judge. These documents, plus the Notice and Grounds of Appeal, are handed to the single judge who considers them privately and without hearing legal argument (CAA 1968, s. 31(1)). If the judge thinks that there is a reasonable possibility that an appeal might succeed, leave to appeal is granted; otherwise it is refused. In the latter event the would-be appellant may renew the application for leave to a full court of the Criminal Division, provided that the Registrar is served with notice within 14 days from the date of refusal. There are a number of variations on the above procedure. In particular, it is always open to an appellant to settle his own Grounds of Appeal. Also, to save time, an application for leave to appeal is occasionally referred at once to a court of the Criminal Division (rather than going to a single judge first) and that court may then treat the application for leave as the hearing of the appeal and reduce the appellant's sentence forthwith.

At the hearing of the appeal, the Court of Appeal will have before it the documents considered by the single judge, plus possible additional documents, such as an up-to-date pre-sentence report or, if the offender was given a custodial sentence, a report on his progress at the institution at which he has been detained. Counsel for the appellant will then present the arguments in favour of reducing the sentence. The prosecution are unlikely to be represented, this being in keeping with their generally neutral attitude to sentence.

In disposing of an appeal their lordships may quash the sentence or order appealed against and replace it with whatever they consider appropriate, provided that:

(a)   the replacement sentence or order is one which the Crown Court had power to make when dealing with the appellant; and

(b) the appellant, taking the case as a whole, is not dealt with more severely on appeal than he was at the Crown Court (CAA 1968, s. 11(3)).

In other words the Court of Appeal may reduce but not increase sentence on an appeal by the offender against sentence. This may be contrasted with the powers of the Crown Court when dealing with an appeal against sentence imposed by magistrates (see **13.1.1**). The Court of Appeal formerly had power to increase sentence on appeal, but this power was removed in 1966. However, provided that the total effect of what the Court of Appeal does is not to increase the aggregate sentence, their lordships may make the sentence for one of several offences for which the appellant was dealt with at Crown Court more severe. Or, where two orders were imposed on sentence for a single offence, they can both be adjusted so as to achieve no more severe a result (*McLaren* (1983) 5 Cr App R (S) 332, where the offender's fine was increased but his driving disqualification reduced). There are several cases which have considered what does or does not amount to being 'more severely dealt with on appeal'. In *Socratous* (1984) 6 Cr App R (S) 33 the offender was put on probation for shoplifting and imprisoned for three months for contempt of court which consisted of intimidating a witness. The Court of Appeal held that it was wrong in principle to make a probation order at the same time as passing an immediate custodial sentence, and so the Court varied the probation order to three months' imprisonment, to be served concurrently with the three months for contempt. Although the sentence for shoplifting was clearly more severe, the Court was acting within its powers because the sentence's overall effect was to the appellant's advantage in that he would not serve any longer in prison and, when he was released, he would not be subject to probation supervision. It was held in *Whittaker* [1967] Crim LR 431 that a sentence of imprisonment for a fixed term of years could not be varied to a life sentence on appeal, and this is still true today, since the PCC(S)A 2000, s. 80(4) states that a life sentence is to be regarded as a custodial sentence 'for a term longer than any actual term'. An immediate term of imprisonment is more severe than a suspended sentence, even where the immediate term is much shorter than the suspended term (*Thompson* (1977) 66 Cr App R 130).

It may appear that the lack of any general power in the Court of Appeal to increase sentence on appeal means that there is no bar to unmeritorious appeals. There is one way, however, in which the Court of Appeal may penalise an appellant for commencing such an appeal. That is to direct that some or all of the time the offender has spent in custody between the submission of the Grounds of Appeal and the dismissal of his application for leave to appeal shall not (as it normally would) count towards service of any custodial sentence imposed on him by the Crown Court (CAA 1968, s. 29). This is known as a direction for loss of time. Such a direction cannot, however, be made in a case where counsel (rather the appellant himself) settled the Grounds of Appeal, unless the appellant insists on renewing the application for leave to appeal after it has been turned down by the single judge (see *Practice Direction (Crime: Sentence: Loss of Time)* [1980] 1 WLR 270). This is because counsel is under a duty not to settle Grounds of Appeal unless they are reasonable and there is a genuine prospect of success. It would therefore be unfair to penalise an appellant who had merely pursued his appeal to the single judge stage in reliance on counsel's advice that there were reasonable grounds upon which an appeal could be based.

Where an appellant is appealing against a custodial sentence, the single judge has power to grant bail pending determination of the appeal (CAA 1968, ss. 19(1) and 13). If the single judge refuses bail, an application may be made to a court of the Criminal Division. Unless the sentence appealed against is very short, there is a marked reluctance to grant bail. In *Watton* (1979) 68 Cr App R 293 Geoffrey Lane LJ commented that the circumstances in which bail would be appropriate are 'exceptional'. Consequently the majority of appellants have spent several weeks, if not months, in custody before their appeals are heard. It quite often happens then that the Court of Appeal will reduce the term of the sentence appealed against to one which will permit the appellant's immediate release. Such cases are unreliable guides to the level of sentence the court considers appropriate for the type of case in question. It may be that their lordships really think the original sentence should not have been a custodial one at all, but prefer not to say so; they may genuinely consider that the time the appellant has already served in custody represents about the proper penalty; or they may even approve of what the Crown Court judge did but feel, perhaps in the light of a report from the custodial institution where he has been held thus far, that the offender has learned his lesson and should, as an act of clemency, be released.

At the outset of this chapter it was said that there were two vital tasks which the appellate system should perform in sentencing in addition to ensuring the correction of injustice done to an individual offender on sentence. These are to establish, explain and develop sentencing principles and to encourage sentencing consistency. How well does the body of Court of Appeal sentencing decisions measure up to these objectives? The Court of Criminal Appeal soon after its creation in 1907 accepted that these objectives were part of its remit, but took the line, which the Court of Appeal has adhered to ever since, that it should only alter a sentence where that sentence was 'wrong in principle' (*Gumbs* (1926) 19 Cr App R 74). The principle that the maximum sentence should be reserved for the most grave cases was developed early on; other principles have evolved gradually over the years, on a case-by-case basis. The principled development of a jurisprudence of sentencing was initially hampered by a number of factors, such as the lack of systematic reporting of appellate sentencing decisions, the failure to regard sentencing decisions as in any sense precedents and the prevailing orthodoxy of substantial sentencing discretion. The development of useful guidance for lower courts has also been hampered by the fact that the Court of Appeal sees an atypical selection of cases, generally appeals brought by offenders against long custodial sentences for very serious offences.

There have been a number of important developments in this area over the last 30 years:

(a)   The first change has been that reporting of sentencing decisions has become more widespread and systematic. This trend began with the reports and commentaries by Dr Thomas in the *Criminal Law Review* and has continued with the introduction in 1979 of a set of law reports, the *Criminal Appeal Reports (Sentencing)*, dedicated to Court of Appeal and Divisional Court sentencing decisions and, from 1982, the publication of a looseleaf sentencing encyclopaedia *Current Sentencing Practice*, which is also edited by Dr Thomas. While in the past there was a reluctance amongst judges to accept the citation to them by counsel of previous sentencing decisions, on the ground that sentencing decisions turned on their own particular facts, such citation is now the norm in sentencing appeals.

(b)   The second development has been the gradual appreciation amongst practitioners of the importance of more formal legal principles in sentencing. One of the most important areas has been the development of improved procedural arrangements at the sentencing stage, arising from a large number of cases clustered around the decision in *Newton* (1982) 4 Cr App R (S) 388. These cases were considered in Chapter 3. This has also been reflected in sentence selection. The importance of giving reasons for sentence is now well accepted and is formally required by statute in a range of situations. There has been considerable development in the shaping of sentence decision-making, partly through legislative change and partly through judicial development. Section 1(4A) of the CJA 1982 was a milestone in this area, requiring sentencers for the first time to articulate clearly their reason for imposing a custodial sentence on a young offender, and requiring them to select that reason from a limited statutory menu. That approach has led to the more general statutory framework of the CJA 1991 and the PCC(S)A 2000 (see Chapter 2).

(c) Thirdly, the Court of Appeal, under Lawton LJ and successive Lords Chief Justice have taken the opportunity, when dealing with a particular sentencing appeal or a batch of sentencing appeals gathered together to illustrate a particular point, to develop more general and principled sentencing guidance. The so-called 'guideline judgments' are of greater significance as precedents than other sentencing appeals, and they form the basis for the sentencing pattern for a particular type of offending. Some of the most important of the guideline judgments are *Aramah* (1982) 4 Cr App R (S) 407 on drug offences, *Barrick* (1985) 7 Cr App R (S) 143 on theft in breach of trust, *Billam* (1986) 8 Cr App R (S) 48 on rape, *A-G's Reference (No. 1 of 1989)* [1989] 1 WLR 1117 on incest, and *Brewster* [1998] 1 Cr App R (S) 181 on domestic burglary. The guideline judgments are set out, or referred to, where appropriate, in Chapter 12 of this book. Guideline judgments typically indicate a normal sentencing bracket for a particular offence, or sometimes several sentencing brackets for different forms of the offence. Then a series of significant aggravating and mitigating factors, which may often accompany such cases, are identified. It is rare for the Court of Appeal to go further and to attempt to quantify the relative weight of such factors, or to suggest how the sentencer should deal with a case in which several aggravating factors appear, or where there appear both aggravating and mitigating factors. These adjustments are left largely to the sentencer's discretion, though examples of comparable cases involving sentencing for the same offence might be considered at this point. The main function of the guideline judgment is to direct the sentencer towards the correct sentencing bracket or 'starting point', and to identify relevant aggravating and mitigating factors. Sometimes the Court of Appeal will also point out a factor which should not be taken into account, but which a sentencer might be misled into thinking is relevant (e.g. the victim's 'contributory negligence' in a rape case: *Billam*).

Despite these changes, the body of sentencing principles generated by the Court of Appeal is still of limited help to the lower courts. This is because it remains true that the majority of cases before the Court of Appeal lie at the top end of the range of seriousness. This means that, in general, those offences and those sentencing measures which are most frequently encountered in the courts are subject to the least amount of helpful guidance. While there are numerous Court of Appeal decisions on drug trafficking, rape and armed robbery, for example, there is relatively little guidance on some of the most commonly encountered offences, such as theft, deception, and handling stolen goods. The Crime and Disorder Act 1998, by s. 80, placed a statutory duty on the Court of Appeal to produce new sentencing guidelines for criminal offences, and to revise existing ones. Section 81 established the Sentencing Advisory Panel to act as an independent advisory body to the Court of Appeal in framing those guidelines.

The Panel began its work in 1999. By early 2001 it had sent its advice to the Court of Appeal (after consulting with a range of interested organisations and individuals) on a number of areas of sentencing, including possession of offensive weapons, handling stolen goods and racially aggravated offences. The Court has so far adopted the Panel's advice on racially aggravated offences in *Kelly and Donnelly* [2001] Crim LR 411; on the importation and possession of opium with intent to supply (a topic specifically referred to the Panel by the Court) in *Mashaollahi* [2001] 1 Cr App R (S) 330; and in handling stolen goods (*Webbe and Others* 2 May 2001, unreported). The Panel's Web site (at www.sentencing-advisory-panel.gov.uk) contains information on the membership of the Panel, full explanation of its terms of reference, and on its completed and current projects.

As we have seen, one of the principal limitations on the usefulness of Court of Appeal guidance has been the restricted class of cases which come before it. This, in turn, is because until 1988 it was only the offender who had the opportunity to bring an appeal against sentence and so, in practice, appeals were confined to cases where the sentence was thought to be much too severe. The procedure, introduced by the CJA 1988, allows the Attorney-General to refer a Crown Court sentence which is thought to be unduly lenient, to the Court of Appeal. This is considered next.

13.3   REFERENCE BY ATTORNEY-GENERAL IN RESPECT OF SENTENCE PASSED BY THE CROWN COURT

The effect of ss. 35 and 36 of the CJA 1988 is that where the Attorney-General considers that an offender's sentence was unduly lenient in proceedings in the Crown Court he may refer the matter to the Court of Appeal (Criminal Division) for a review of that sentence (s. 36(1)). This is subject to:

(a)   the Court of Appeal giving leave; and

(b)   the offence for which sentence was passed being either one which is triable only on indictment or one which is triable either way and specified in an order made by the Home Secretary by statutory instrument (CJA 1988, s. 35(3)).

The reference procedure has been extended by the Criminal Justice Act 1988 (Reviews of Sentencing) Order 1994 (SI 1994/19) to cover offences of indecent assault, threats to kill, cruelty to a person under 16 and attempting to commit or inciting the commission of those offences. It was further extended by the Criminal Justice Act 1988 (Reviews of Sentencing) Order 1995 (SI 1995/10) to include some cases of serious fraud.

In *A-G's Reference (Nos. 3, 4 and 5 of 1992)* (1993) 14 Cr App R (S) 191 the offenders had pleaded guilty to conspiracy to evade the prohibition on the importation of a Class A drug (LSD). They also pleaded guilty to certain offences triable either way, which were charged on a separate indictment. The Court of Appeal increased the sentence for conspiracy from two and a half years to five years in the case of two of the offenders and four years in the case of the other. It was accepted that the Court had no power to review the sentences for the offences triable either way, but the Court regarded the fact that the conspiracy had been committed while the offenders were on bail for those offences as an aggravating feature of the conspiracy, in part justifying the increase in sentence. For the purposes of a sentencing reference by the Attorney-General, 'sentence' has the same wide meaning as it has under CAA 1968, s. 50(1), except that it does not extend to an interim hospital order (CJA 1988, s. 35(6)). It extends to a decision by the Crown Court to grant a conditional discharge (*A-G's Reference (No. 57 of 1995)* [1996] 2 Cr App R (S) 159 and to a decision by the Crown Court to defer sentence (*A-G's Reference (No. 22 of 1992)* [1994] 1 All ER 105).

If the Court of Appeal does give leave for reference, in disposing of the appeal it will, in contrast to appeals against sentence brought by offenders, hear argument from both sides. Upon an Attorney-General's sentencing reference the Court of Appeal may quash the sentence passed by the Crown Court and replace it with the sentence which it thinks is appropriate. It is specifically provided in s. 36(2) that the Attorney-General may refer a sentence to the Court of Appeal if he considers that the judge has erred in law, but the powers of the Court of Appeal to review the sentence go much wider than that. In the majority of cases the judge has understood his powers correctly but has chosen, in his discretion, to pass a sentence that appears to the Attorney-General to be too lenient in all the circumstances of the case. The replacement sentence must be one which the Crown Court would have had power to pass on the offender (s. 36(1)). Of course, the judge whose sentence is under consideration cannot sit in the appeal (s. 36(4)).

In *A-G's Reference (No. 4. of 1989)* (1989) 11 Cr App R (S) 517 the Court of Appeal set out its approach to the disposition of references under s. 36. According to that case, two main considerations must be borne in mind in all such cases.

(a) The Court of Appeal should only increase a sentence which is clearly unduly lenient. It is not enough that the members of the Court of Appeal would themselves have imposed a more severe sentence. To be 'unduly lenient' a sentence must fall outside the range of sentences which the judge, applying his mind to all the relevant factors, could reasonably consider appropriate. In that connection regard must be had, of course, to reported cases and, in particular, to guideline judgments of the Court of Appeal. Nevertheless, it must be remembered that the trial judge is particularly well placed to assess the weight to be given to various competing considerations, and that leniency in sentencing is, in itself, not a vice. In *A-G's Reference (No. 5 of 1989)* (1990) 90 Cr App R 358 the Court of Appeal said that it would not intervene unless it had been shown that there was some error of principle in the judge's sentence, so that public confidence would be damaged if the sentence was not altered. This test has been mentioned in several subsequent cases. In *A-G's Reference (No. 16 of 1992)* (1993) 14 Cr App R (S) 319 a sentence of four years for a particular case of rape was 'as lenient as it possibly could be, without this Court interfering with it'.

(b) The second point was that, even where a sentence is considered to be unduly lenient, the Court of Appeal has a discretion whether to exercise its powers. It may be, for instance, that in the light of events which have occurred since the trial, the sentence now turns out to be an appropriate one, or that it would be unfair to the offender or detrimental to others to increase it. An example is *A-G's Reference (No. 8 of 1992)* (1993) 14 Cr App R (S) 130. A youth aged 17 was convicted of manslaughter on an indictment for murder. Following an argument in a park and a degree of provocation, he stabbed the unarmed deceased in the chest with a lock-knife which he had been carrying for his own protection. After the incident, the offender was attacked in his own home by friends of the deceased seeking revenge. The trial judge imposed a probation order for two years. The Court of Appeal was clear that the sentence was unduly lenient, but considered whether it should, in the exercise of its discretion, vary it. The Court gave weight to the fact that the jury at the trial had added a rider to the verdict saying that they had 'great sympathy' for the offender and asking the judge to pass a lenient sentence, that the offender was a young man of 'excellent reputation' who was training for a professional career, that since the trial the offender's family had moved to another area and that the offender 'has become as a result of this matter a religious young man'. The sentence was, nonetheless, increased to two years' detention in a young offender institution.

(c) The Court of Appeal has established where it does increase the sentence it will bear in mind that the offender has undergone the additional stess of having to be sentenced twice over. This may be especially the case where the Court of Appeal, in the event, varies a non-custodial sentence to a custodial one. Some discount from the properly justified sentence would, then, often be appropriate. In *A-G's Reference (No. 15 of 1992)* (1993) 14 Cr App R (S) 324, a case where a sentence of nine months' imprisonment suspended for 18 months for buggery committed by a man on his wife without her consent was increased to four years' immediate imprisonment, Lord Taylor CJ said that 'allowance should be made for the fact that the offender has to be sentenced on a second occasion, that he will have had a second period of suspense awaiting the decision of the court, and . . . that he is a man who, having been allowed his liberty after his trial, now finds himself called upon to serve a sentence of imprisonment'.

It will be appreciated that points (a) and (b) above, while designed to ensure fairness for the appellant, tend to rob the procedure of much of its potential usefulness as a source of guidance. They entail that a decision of the Court of Appeal not to interfere with a sentence does not mean that the original sentence is viewed by the Court as being correct; merely that it is not so far wrong as to justify correction. In *A-G's Reference (No. 16 of 1992)* (1993) 14 Cr App R (S) 319 Lord Taylor CJ said that it should not be thought that 'leaving this sentence of four years unaltered is to be regarded as a guideline . . . the level of sentencing which ought to be applied at first instance cannot be translated directly from the decision in this case'. While a similar principle against 'tinkering' with sentence also operates where the Court is dealing with offender appeals against sentence, there is even greater reluctance to vary a sentence to the offender's detriment unless the case for doing so is very clear indeed. Requirement (c), that the Court should have regard to 'double jeopardy' (that the offender has had to undergo the strain of being sentenced twice) also tends to dilute the guidance value of these cases. Typically, where the Court does increase the sentence, it states that it has made such an allowance but does not make it clear what discount has been allowed the offender. When no figure is given for the discount, the sentence selected by the Court of Appeal may well be a misleading guide. Thus in *A-G's Reference (No. 8 of 1992)* (see above) the Court of Appeal varied the sentence upwards to two years' detention, commenting that this was 'a much shorter sentence than would otherwise have been the case'. It would be helpful in all cases for the Court to indicate clearly what the proper sentence should have been, and then either to dismiss the appeal on the basis that the difference between that sentence and the one actually imposed is not sufficient to justify any variation, or to increase the sentence, making it clear what discount has been allowed the offender in all the circumstances.

13.4 APPEAL TO HOUSE OF LORDS AGAINST SENTENCE

Appeal lies to the House of Lords against the decisions of both the Court of Appeal (Criminal Division) and the Divisional Court (CAA 1968, s. 33 and Administration of Justice Act 1960, s. 1(1)(a), respectively). In the case of the Divisional Court, a direct appeal to the House of Lords is possible only if the decision in question was taken in a criminal cause or matter, but that obviously will be so where the decision relates to sentencing. The right of appeal to the House of Lords is not restricted to the offender. In particular, if the offender in the Crown Court successfully appealed to the Court of Appeal, the prosecution could in theory then appeal to the House of Lords to have the original Crown Court decision reinstated. An appeal to the House of Lords is restricted to cases where:

(a) the lower court certifies that there is a point of law of general public importance; and
(b) either the lower court or the House of Lords gives leave to appeal.

It is the first restriction which makes appeals to the House of Lords on sentencing matters so rare. Sentencing rarely raises points of law (as opposed to sentencing principle), let alone points of law of general public importance. Moreover the argument that an exceedingly harsh sentence necessarily raises a point of law was rejected in *Ashdown* [1974] 1 WLR 270. It was said in that case that, provided the sentence was within the sentencing court's powers, the propriety of the sentence could never raise a point of law of general public importance. The rarity value of sentencing appeals which reach the House of Lords is neatly illustrated by the remarks of Lord Diplock in *Courtie* [1984] AC 463, in which he said that the case came before the House in the guise of an appeal against sentence only, but in fact raised questions of substantive law. He then continued: 'I cannot myself recall any criminal appeal confined to sentence only having come before this House since I started to sit here in 1968.'

Where a sentencing matter has gone to the Court of Appeal on a reference by the Attorney-General (see **13.3**) and the Court of Appeal has concluded its review and either upheld an allegedly lenient sentence or varied it, the Attorney-General or the person to whose sentence the reference relates may refer a point of law involved in the sentence to the House of Lords for their opinion. The House of Lords may either deal with the matter themselves or remit the case to the Court of Appeal to be dealt with there (CJA 1988, s. 36(5)). Such a reference to the House of Lords can only be made with the leave of the House of Lords or the Court of Appeal, and leave requires that there is a point of law of general public importance involved in the case (s. 36(6)). No such cases have yet been reported.

Although not an appeal against sentence as such, a very important decision of the House of Lords which is closely related to sentencing is *Secretary of State for the Home Department, ex parte Venables* [1998] AC 407. This was a case involving judicial review of the powers of the Home Secretary with respect to the sentence of detention at Her Majesty's pleasure, the mandatory sentence for offenders convicted of murder who were aged under 18 at the time of the offence. The House of Lords held that the welfare of the child or young person was of great importance, and had to be balanced against the gravity of the crime committed when determining the date at which he should be considered for early release. Their lordships also held that it was wrong for the Home Secretary to take into account an orchestrated campaign by a popular newspaper when fixing the appropriate period to be served.

13.5 PETITIONING THE EUROPEAN COURT OF HUMAN RIGHTS

Over the years a number of important sentencing-related cases in English law have (eventually) found their way before the European Court of Human Rights in Strasbourg, on the basis of alleged infringement by English law of one or more of the articles of the ECHR. Several of these cases are referred to elsewhere in this work (see for example *Hashman and Harrup* v *UK* (2000) 30 EHRR 241, at **7.2.1** and *Ibbotson* v *UK* [1999] Crim LR 153, at **13.6**). Until 1998 complaints regarding breach of the Convention went initially to the Commission, which acted as a filter on applications to the Court. but the Commission has since been abolished and the Court itself determines questions of admissibility as well as establishing the facts, giving judgment and providing remedy. For a complaint to be admissible, the applicant must normally have already exhausted all appropriate domestic appeal remedies, although there is an exception in a case where there is a domestic legal authority of high standing which is against the applicant. The Venables and Thompson case, referred to in the last paragraph, was taken before the European Court of Human Rights in

2000, after having proceeded through the English appeal process, including the House of Lords. The case is reported as *V* v *UK* (2000) 30 EHRR 121. As was explained at **4.3.5**, the European Court found that although there had in that case been no breach of Article 3 (inhuman and degrading treatment or punishment), there had been two separate breaches of Article 6 (right to fair trial), one of which related to the inappropriateness of Crown Court proceedings where very young defendants were involved, and the second of which was the finding that fixing the 'tariff' on a child detained at Her Majesty's pleasure amounted to a sentencing exercise and that the Home Secretary was not an 'independent and impartial tribunal' as required by that Article. In light of this decision, legislation was passed (in the CJCSA 2000, s. 60) effectively transferring the tariff-setting functions for this sentence from the Home Secretary to the sentencing judge.

Since the implementation of the Human Rights Act 1998, on 2 October 2000, it is now of course possible for complaints of violation of the ECHR to be argued before any domestic criminal court. Any relevant Strasbourg jurisprudence must be taken into account. Section 3 of the Act requires the courts wherever possible to construe legislation in a manner which is compatible with Convention rights but, if this cannot be done, the higher courts may make a declaration of incompatibility, which will place great pressure on the legislature to amend or revoke the offending domestic law. Petitioning the European Court of Human Rights remains available to the individual as a remedy of last resort, but the Human Rights Act 1998 requires that the Convention points be fully argued before the domestic courts (to ensure that these remedies are exhausted) before that final step may be considered.

13.6   DISQUALIFICATIONS UPON CONVICTION

While detained in custody following conviction for any offence, an offender is legally incapable of voting at any parliamentary or local government election (Representation of the People Act 1983, s. 3(1)). Any person who has been convicted of an offence and had imposed upon them a custodial sentence of three months or more, whether suspended or not, is disqualified from being, or being elected, a member of a local authority for a period of five years from the date of the conviction (Local Government Act 1972, s. 80(1)(d)). A person convicted of an offence for which he has received a custodial sentence of three years or more is prohibited from possessing or acquiring any firearm or ammunition for life (Firearms Act 1968, s. 21). Where the sentence was for three months or more but for less than three years, the ban lasts for five years. An offender who has served at any time a custodial sentence of five years or more, or within the last ten years has served a custodial sentence of any length, or within the last ten years has had imposed on them a suspended prison sentence or a community service order, or within the last five years have been placed on probation, is disqualified from jury service (Juries Act 1974, sch I, Part II).

On conviction for treason (a rare event), a person is rendered incapable of holding any military or related office, being an MP or, indeed, voting (Forfeiture Act 1870, s. 2).

By the Sex Offenders Act 1997, where a person has been convicted of a sexual offence to which the Act applies, or where he has been found not guilty of a sexual offence by reason of insanity, or has been found to be under a disability (unfit to plead) and to have done the act charged against him, he is required to register his name, address and date of birth, and any subsequent changes, with the police. Following changes made by the CJCSA 2000, the offender may also be required to provide his fingerprints, to be photographed, and to provide notice of any intention to leave or return to the UK. All such requirements come into effect automatically upon conviction.

The requirements of the Act do not constitute an additional form of punishment, so should not be taken into account when sentence is passed (see *A-G's Reference (No. 50 of 1997)* [1998] 2 Cr App R (S) 155). It will normally be appropriate, however, for the sentencer to make a statement in open court as to the registration period that will be applicable to the offender under the Act (see s. 5). Registration under the 1997 Act is not a 'penalty' within the meaning of the ECHR, Article 7 (see *Ibbotson* v *UK* [1999] Crim LR 153, where it was held that the retrospective registration requirements in the 1997 Act did not breach convention rights).

The duration of the notification period varies with the sentence passed for the sexual offence. In the case of a custodial sentence for life, or for a fixed term of 30 months or more, or a hospital order with restrictions, the period is indefinite. If the custodial sentence was for more than six months but less than 30 months the period is 10 years, and for a custodial sentence for six months or less the period is seven years. If the offender received a hospital order without restrictions, the period is seven years, and for any other sentence the period is five years. For offenders aged under 18 the fixed periods are reduced by half. Offenders who have been formally cautioned after admitting the offence, as well as those convicted, are subject to the requirements of the Act (see the Sex Offenders (Certificate of Caution) Order 1997 (SI 1997/1921)). Failure to comply with the requirements listed above is an offence, punishable with a maximum of five years imprisonment on indictment.

The definition of 'sexual offence' for the purposes of the 1997 Act (listed in sch. 1) is slightly different from that in the PCC(S)A 2000, s. 161(2) (see **4.2.7**). In particular, the offence of burglary with intent to commit rape under the Theft Act 1968, s. 9 and the offence under MHA 1959, s. 128 are included in s. 161(2) but not in sch. 1 to the 1997 Act, and the offences under s. 160 of the CJA 1988 (possession of indecent photographs of a child) and s. 170 of the Customs and Excise Management Act 1979 (penalty for fraudulent evasion of duty on certain goods) are included in sch. 1 but are not listed in s. 31.

13.7 REHABILITATION OF OFFENDERS

Under the ROA 1974, after the passage of time convictions may become 'spent', and a convicted person may consider himself legally 'rehabilitated'. When a conviction is spent, the offender is treated for a range of purposes as if he had never been convicted of the offence concerned. While ROA 1974, s. 7(2) strictly excludes from its scope the operation of criminal proceedings, *Practice Direction (Crime: Spent Convictions)* [1975] 1 WLR 1065 none the less requires that spent convictions which appear on an offender's record should be marked as such, and that nobody should refer in open court to such spent convictions without the authority of judge. This matter was considered at **3.4.4**.

13.7.1 Main provisions of the ROA 1974

The protection of the ROA 1974 applies to all convictions, except those which result in an excluded sentence (see below). The term 'conviction' is given a broad meaning in the Act, but would not extend to cover the imposition of a bind over to keep the peace which is imposed at any time except at sentence (see **7.2**). It is unclear whether the Act applies to a recommendation for deportation. An offence for which an order for absolute or conditional discharge is made does not count as a conviction for a variety of purposes (see **7.1.4**), but s. 1(4) of the Act provides that discharges are sentences which may be the subject of rehabilitation. Certain sentences fall outside the scope of the Act and an offender who has received such a sentence can never become rehabilitated with respect to that conviction. Those excluded sentences are:

(a)   life imprisonment;

(b)   imprisonment or detention in a young offender institution (or youth custody) for a term exceeding 30 months;

(c)   detention at Her Majesty's pleasure;

(d)   detention under PCC(S)A 2000, s. 91 for a term exceeding 30 months; and

(e)   custody for life.

The commission of an offence resulting in one of these excluded sentences also acts so as to prevent any earlier unspent conviction from becoming spent.

Rehabilitation periods in respect of other sentences are set out in the table below. Some sentences mentioned in the table appear in square brackets; these have been abolished by statute and are no longer available to sentencers, but will still appear on criminal records. The relevant period runs from the date of conviction, even where sentence is deferred. Some of the rehabilitation periods are, as indicated, reduced where the offender was under 18 years of age at the date of conviction.

Sentence	*Rehabilitation period*
A sentence of imprisonment or detention in a young offender institution [or youth custody] for more than 6 months but not more than 30 months	10 years for an adult, 5 years for a juvenile
A sentence of imprisonment or detention in a young offender institution [or youth custody] of 6 months or less	7 years for an adult, $3\frac{1}{2}$ years for a juvenile
Detention and training order (offender 15 or over at date of conviction)	5 years if DTO exceeded 6 months; $3\frac{1}{2}$ years if 6 months or less
Detention and training order (offender under 15 at date of conviction)	One year after DTO expires
[A sentence of detention in a detention centre]	3 years
A fine	5 years for an adult, $2\frac{1}{2}$ years for a juvenile
A community service order or combination order	5 years for an adult, $2\frac{1}{2}$ years for a juvenile
Probation, (offender placed on probation before 3 February 1995) bind over to keep the peace or be of good behaviour, conditional discharge	The date the order or bind over ceases or 1 year, whichever is the longer

Sentence	*Rehabilitation period*
Probation (offender placed on probation on or after 3 February 1995)	5 years for an adult, $2\frac{1}{2}$ years for a juvenile
Supervision order [or care order]	The date the order ceases or 1 year, whichever is the longer
Attendance centre order	1 year after the order expires
[Secure training order]	One year after the order expires
Referral order	When the contract ceases to have effect
Hospital order	5 years from the date of conviction or 2 years after the order expires, whichever is the longer
Disqualification and other orders imposing disability, prohibition, or other penalty	The date the order ceases to have effect
Absolute discharge	6 months

Some sentences or orders do not appear in this table. For the purposes of the ROA 1974, a suspended sentence of imprisonment counts as a sentence of immediate imprisonment of the same length. The relevant length of a partly suspended sentence (a sentence now abolished) is the length of the served and suspended parts of the sentence added together. Two consecutive custodial sentences are aggregated for the purposes of the ROA 1974 (s. 5(9)(b)). Where an offender receives more than one sentence or order in respect of a single offence, the relevant rehabilitation period is the longest of those applicable (s. 6(2)).

A person who has been convicted can only become rehabilitated under the Act if that person is not reconvicted within the relevant rehabilitation period (s. 6(4)). If an offender is reconvicted of anything other than a summary offence (s. 6(6)), the rehabilitation period for the first offence continues to run until the expiry of the period for the second offence. This is a very important rule, and has the practical effect that persistent offenders are unlikely to have any spent convictions, even if the earliest of these may have been committed many years before. An exception to the subsequent offence rule is that periods arising from orders of disqualification, disability, prohibition or other penalty are to be disregarded (s. 6(5)), whether such disqualification etc. relates to the first or the second conviction. If an excluded sentence (see above) is passed for the second offence, then this excludes both convictions permanently from the possibility of rehabilitation.

13.7.2 Exceptions to the scope of the ROA 1974

The practical operation of the ROA 1974 is affected by the far-reaching exceptions which apply to it. The relevant law can be found in the Rehabilitation of Offenders Act 1974 (Exceptions) Order 1975, as amended.

The exceptions have the effect that none of the provisions of s. 4(2) of the Act apply (and hence details of spent convictions must be revealed) in relation to any questions asked by a person, in the course of their office or employment, in order to assess the suitability of a person for the following:

(a) *professions*: doctor, lawyer, accountant, dentist, vet, nurse, midwife, optician or pharmacist;

(b) *offices or employments*: judges, prosecutors, justices' clerks, police, prison staff, traffic wardens, probation officers, employees of local authorities who have access in their normal duties to vulnerable persons (including those over 65 years of age, persons suffering from serious illness or mental disorder, persons addicted to drink or drugs, persons who are blind, deaf or dumb and persons who are substantially and permanently handicapped by illness or injury), any employment concerned with the provision of health services where the person employed has access to persons in receipt of such services in the normal course of their duties, any employment concerned with the provision to persons under 18 of accommodation, care, leisure and recreational facilities, schooling, social services, supervision or training, where the person has access in the normal course of their duties to persons under 18;

(c) *regulated occupations*: firearms dealer, occupations requiring a betting or gaming licence, senior officials in insurance companies, management of any place approval of which is required by the Secretary of State under the Abortion Act 1967, or management of a nursing home requiring registration under statute, or any occupation involving the supervision of explosives under the Explosives Act 1875;

(d) *licences*: firearm certificate or shotgun certificate issued under the Firearms Act 1968, licence to keep explosives issued under the Explosives Act 1875.

The ROA 1974 does not affect the operation of any of the statutory provisions mentioned in **13.6** by which, in consequence of conviction, a person is subject to a disqualification or prohibition (s. 7(1)(d)).

13.8 PARDON AND RELEASE ON COMPASSIONATE GROUNDS

As an act of grace, the Sovereign may either grant a free (or conditional) pardon or remit the rest of an offender's sentence (the royal prerogative of mercy: CAA 1968, s. 49). In practice, of course, these powers are not exercised personally by the Sovereign, but are administered on her behalf by Home Office officials.

A pardon is normally granted only where it has been established that the original conviction was unjustified, such as where a miscarriage of justice is shown to have occurred. An example encountered not infrequently is where an offender has been convicted and fined for speeding, only for it to emerge later that the stretch of road concerned was not subject to a speed limit. Although it was once thought that the pardon 'wipes out not only the sentence for the offence but the conviction and all its consequences' (*Hay* v *Tower Division of London Justices* (1890) 24 QBD 561), it is now clear that the pardon 'does not in any sense eliminate the conviction', although it relieves the subject of the effect of any penalties as a result of conviction (*Foster* [1985] QB 115). In that case the Court of Appeal held that a person who had been pardoned in respect of an offence of rape, following later confession to that offence by another man, might properly still bring an appeal against conviction. See also *Bolton Justices, ex parte Scally* [1991] 1 QB 537. A pardon may have great symbolic importance to those concerned, so that pardons are sometimes sought by an offender's relatives long after the offender's death. See, for example, *Secretary of State for the Home*

Department, ex parte Bentley [1994] QB 439. In that case the court indicated that the prerogative was a 'flexible power', and that the grant of a conditional, rather than a free, pardon was appropriate where 'a mistake had been made' and the offender should not have been executed. There are about 200 pardons granted every year. A person pardoned may receive compensation under CJA 1988, s. 133. The Criminal Cases Review Commission, established under the CAA 1995, has power to conduct investigations and, where appropriate, requests the Court of Appeal cases where they consider that there is 'a real possibility' that the verdict or sentence will not be upheld in the light of new information not available at the trial.

In contrast to the grant of a pardon, remission of an offender's sentence by executive authorities certainly does not imply that the original conviction was unjustified: it means merely that the rest of the sentence need not be served. Remission is generally used for one of two reasons. The first is where a prisoner has given particular help to the authorities in the detection of other offences or the apprehension of other offenders. The second is in cases where the offender is discovered to be suffering from a terminal disease and has a short time left to live. Sentence is remitted so that the person need not die in custody (see **2.2.4(i)**). In an exceptional case two prisoners were released early after they rescued a prison officer being gored by a giant boar (news item, *The Times*, 19 June 2001). Sentence is remitted by executive authority under statutory provisions such as CJA 1991, s. 36, in about 150 cases each year. In such cases the matter may be drawn to the attention of the Home Office by a member of staff of the prison, the offender or the offender's family or by any other interested party. There is also the possibility of remission of other sentences. For the circumstances in which fines may be remitted see **6.5**.

Appendix

Referral Orders (not yet in force)

Under Part 3 of the PCC(S)A 2000 a youth court or, exceptionally, an adult magistrates' court, which is dealing with an offender under the age of 18 for whom this is his first conviction, is in certain circumstances required to deal with the young offender by ordering him to be referred to a youth offender panel. In other circumstances the court has a discretion to deal with the young offender in that way.

The court *must* so deal with the young offender where he has pleaded guilty, and where the court is not intending to pass a custodial sentence, a hospital order, or an absolute discharge. The court *may* make such an order where the young offender has pleaded guilty to one but not all of the offences for which he is to be sentenced and where the court is not intending to pass a custodial sentence, a hospital order, or an absolute discharge. If the court makes a referral order, such an order is clearly designed to stand alone, because it cannot be combined with any form of community order, a reparation order, a fine, a conditional discharge, a bind over or a parental bind over. A compensation order may, however, be imposed along with a referral order.

The youth offender panel will agree a 'contract' with the young offender and his family which will be aimed at tackling the offending behaviour and its underlying causes. The contract will set out requirements with which the young offender must comply. These may include requirements to apologise to, or carry out some reparation for, the victim, or to carry out some community work, or attend family counselling or drug rehabilitation meetings. These requirements are for the youth offender panel, and not the court, to fix. If the young offender fails to comply, he may be referred back to the court. The court may then evoke the referral order and deal with the young offender in any way in which they could have dealt with him when he was convicted.

Referral orders are not yet in force. They are currently being piloted and are expected to be brought fully into operation during 2002.

Index